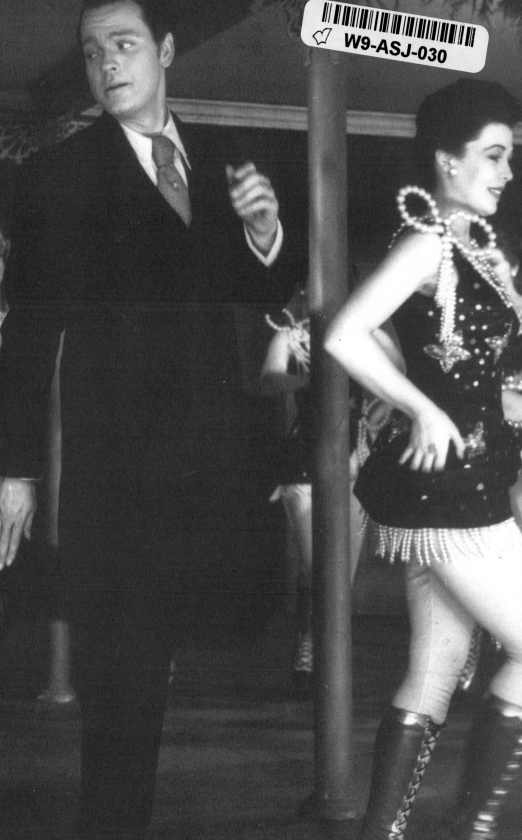

YOUNG ORSON

ALSO BY PATRICK MCGILLIGAN

Cagney: The Actor as Auteur

Robert Altman: Jumping Off the Cliff

George Cukor: A Double Life

Jack's Life: A Biography of Jack Nicholson

Fritz Lang: The Nature of the Beast

Clint: The Life and Legend

Alfred Hitchcock: A Life in Darkness and Light

Oscar Micheaux: The Great and Only

Nicholas Ray: The Glorious Failure of an American Director

EDITED BY PATRICK MCGILLIGAN

Tender Comrades: A Backstory of the Hollywood Blacklist (with Paul Buhle)

Six Screenplays by Robert Riskin

Film Crazy: Interviews with Hollywood Legends

Backstory: Interviews with Screenwriters of Hollywood's Golden Age

Backstory 2: Interviews with Screenwriters of the 1940s and 1950s

Backstory 3: Interviews with Screenwriters of the 1960s

Backstory 4: Interviews with Screenwriters of the 1970s and 1980s

Backstory 5: Interviews with Screenwriters of the 1990s

YOUNG ORSON

The Years of Luck and Genius
on the Path to *Citizen Kane*

Patrick McGilligan

HARPER

An Imprint of HarperCollins*Publishers*

HarperCollins books may be purchased for educational, business, or sales promotional use. For information, please e-mail the Special Markets Department at SPsales@harpercollins.com.

Endpapers: Courtesy of Jerry Ohlinger's Movie Material Store

Grateful acknowledgment is made to the following for permission to reprint photographs: Orson Welles Collection, Lilly Library, Indiana University; Federal Theatre Project Collection, George Mason University; Keeneland (Old Rosebud); Kenosha County Historical Society: Joseph McBride; Russell Merritt; Milwaukee Art Museum (Dudley Crafts Watson); Jerry Ohlinger's Movie Material Store; Ashton Stevens Collection, Newberry Library; Duane Paulsen (Hotel Sheffield); Sangamon Valley Room, Springfield Public Library; Todd Tarbox; Oja Kodar, Orson Welles, Richard Wilson and Chris Feder Welles Collections, Special Collections, University of Michigan Library; Charles Higham Collection, Archives of the Cinematic Arts, University of Southern California (Dick Welles group photo); *Los Angeles Times* Collection, Doheny Library, University of California at Los Angeles (Richard I. Welles photograph); Woodstock Public Library.

FIRST EDITION

Designed by Leah Carlson-Stanisic

Library of Congress Cataloging-in-Publication Data has been applied for.

ISBN: 978-0-06-211248-4

15 16 17 18 19 DIX/RRD 10 9 8 7 6 5 4 3 2 1

For Bertrand Tavernier

Everyone will always owe him everything.

—Jean-Luc Godard

Contents

IV. SEVENTY YEARS IN A MAN'S LIFE

V. AFTER THE END

I

BEFORE THE BEGINNING

CHAPTER 1

The Backstory to 1905

The deep backstory of the most celebrated film ever made begins in the winter of 1871 at a boardinghouse in the fictional town of New Salem, Colorado. As the handwritten line of an unpublished reminiscence drifts by onscreen, the camera reveals "the white of a great field of snow," according to the screenplay, and "in the same position as the last word" of the manuscript "appears the tiny figure of CHARLES FOSTER KANE, aged five." The scene was shot on Stage 4 at RKO in Hollywood, and the snow was actually a carpet of crushed cornflakes. The artificiality worried the filmmaker, who knew that audiences familiar with cold winters might expect to see puffs of vapor when the characters breathed. But the young boy's action diverts our attention. "He throws a snowball at the camera. It sails towards us and out of scene."

Smack in the middle of the evocative "Snow Picture" passage in Bernard Herrmann's score—a "lovely, very lyrical" musical phrase, in Peter Bogdanovich's words—the filmmaker cuts the music abruptly just as five-year-old Charlie Kane's snowball slams into the house.

"Typical radio device. We used to do that all the time," Orson Welles explained to Bogdanovich.

The winters in Wisconsin could be as frigid as those in Colorado. But the white carpet had melted in the southeastern part of the state by May 6, 1915. The customary spring storms that pounded Wisconsin's fifth-largest city had turned its streets into muddy rivers. It was a Thursday, and the rain had vanished for the weekend. Kenosha woke up to a morning cool, cloudy, and dry.

Anyone interested in the ongoing annihilation in the Dardanelles, the retreat in Hungary, or the ultimatums in Japan would have to turn to the inside pages of the *Kenosha News*. The front page was taken up with the boom in factory manpower; improvements on the north shore road; plans for the eightieth founders' festival, including a baseball match pitting a local team against the Chicago Cubs; and the grand opening of a downtown beauty parlor promising facials, manicures, and electrolysis.

The southernmost Wisconsin city on the shore of Lake Michigan, Kenosha was no longer a Podunk. With a swelling population of twenty-six thousand, the city looked toward a bright future. Its size and attractions could never compare with those of other cities hugging the same Great Lake shoreline: Chicago, sixty-five miles south; or Milwaukee, Wisconsin's largest city, forty miles north. But life was good in Kenosha. That spring, a forty-nine-pound sack of Gold Medal flour cost $1.95. A tailored woolen suit went for $16.50. A Ford roadster sold for $458, which included delivery and a $50 rebate.

The city theaters were booked for Mother's Day, which was coming up on Sunday. The respectable Rhode Opera House, the largest theater in Kenosha, seating nearly one thousand, advertised the Western *M'Liss* starring Barbara Tennant. The New Majestic would show Thomas H. Ince's version of Ferenc Molnár's *The Devil*, a satire about a charming, debonair Devil who delights in fostering infidelity. This five-reeler was just the kind of sordid entertainment the *Kenosha News* complained about in its May 6 editorial, deriding moving pictures as "the people's book" for impressionable youth who were abandoning healthful reading in favor of screen fare that glamorized sinful behavior.

The city's only female public official, a member of the Kenosha School Board, led the ongoing civic crusade against these sordid moving pictures. In the early hours of May 6, she could be found in her home on the second floor of the two-story wood-frame house at 463½ Park Avenue in Library Park, a fashionable downtown area known for its massive churches, imposing brick mansions, and public commons, crowned by the Gilbert M. Simmons Memorial Library.

That wood-frame house on Park Avenue was neither architecturally distinguished nor luxurious, however, and, as the "½" in her address suggested, the school board official and her family were merely leasing the home's upper floor. Although she and her husband were among Kenosha's most prominent and admired citizens—appearing regularly in the newspaper's society items—the couple prided themselves on their ties to ordinary people. The first female voted into a citywide office in Kenosha, she was not only a community activist and passionate suffragist, but an accomplished pianist and recitalist too. Her equally civic-minded husband, a founder of one of the city's large metal and brass factories, was also an inventor who held a dozen patents.

Although the husband traveled frequently, he was at home on May 6, waiting with a cigar to celebrate the birth of the couple's second child. The first child, a son born ten years earlier, was sequestered in his room under the eye of the family's Irish live-in servant. The expectant mother's attending physician, like many of Kenosha's doctors, had earned his medical degree in Chicago from the homeopathic Hahnemann Medical College.

Another doctor in this unfolding saga, a family friend, was not in the house at the time of the baby's delivery. Dr. Maurice A. Bernstein was an orthopedic surgeon, not an obstetrician, but in later years—after he outlived the school board official and her businessman-inventor husband—he would emerge as the chief chronicler of the boy's birth, and other milestones of his early life.

Over the years Orson Welles took a lot of ribbing about having been born in Kenosha. He had to spell the humble city's name for interviewers in the great metropolises of the world: New York, Los Angeles, Dublin, Paris, London, Rome, Madrid. At times he mocked and disparaged Kenosha, and he had his reasons. But he was also shaped by his roots, and no matter where he roamed he insisted in interviews that he was a proud "Middle Westerner."

"I am almost belligerently Midwestern," he wrote on one occasion, "and always a confirmed 'badger.'" The badger was Wisconsin's state animal and mascot.

According to Dr. Bernstein, when the baby was born, his mother noticed that his first cries mingled with the sound of factory whistles. The baby's birth certificate notes the time as 7 A.M., when local workers began their typical ten-hour shifts—so this, at least, is plausible. "The sounds of factory whistles are significant," Bernstein quoted Mrs. Welles as saying. "They herald my baby into the world." Her husband's company employed hundreds of laborers, and Mrs. Welles sympathized with the workers.

Dr. Bernstein said later that the newborn entered the world with "a considerable growth of black hair on its head" and peculiarly slanted eyes that made him look Eskimo or Chinese. Since Bernstein lived in the neighborhood, he well may have seen the infant within hours or days of the birth. Bernstein said he noticed "a strange soberness in its countenance . . . when it looked into your face you felt uneasy as it if looked right through your soul." Jotting notes years later for a book that he would never finish, Bernstein wrote that the child "looked as if it wakened from the sleep of a former existence."

Perhaps more than anyone else, Dr. Bernstein was responsible for the idea that the boy was a wonder, special from birth. But even Orson Welles felt the doctor "gilded the lily rather thickly" in his myth-making. Bernstein himself realized he was prone to exaggerate, and he could be very amusing on the subject. Writing to an RKO studio publicist in 1940, Bernstein claimed that within a day after his birth the baby "spoke his first words, and unlike other children who say the commonplace things like 'Papa' and 'Mamma' he said, 'I am a genius.' On May 8th, 9th, and 10th, 1915, little was heard about him in the press," the doctor continued, "but on May 15th he seduced his first woman."

Still, the baby *was* special from birth. Not every newborn in Kenosha was welcomed to the world on the front page of the local newspaper. But there it was, in the very next edition after his birth: hearty congratulations to the parents and the proclamation of his name, George Orson Welles.

The child wonder. The boy genius. The maker of *Citizen Kane.*

The words "genius" and "gene" share an etymology. In ancient Rome, the *genius* was the guiding deity of the family, or *gens.* The words derived from the Latin verb *generare,* to create. When individuals exhibited extraordinary traits that indicated the presence of the family's guiding spirit, the word "genius" came to mean someone who was *inspired* or *talented*—suggesting that the creativity of a genius began with the qualities of his or her family. By that light, the lasting depth, complexity, and power of *Citizen Kane* might be traced to the filmmaker's family. They launched a singular life story, one with the richness, layers, and texture of a novel.

The father of George Orson Welles was forty-two-year-old Richard Head Welles, known to all as Dick Welles. The boy's mother was thirty-five-year-old Beatrice Ives Welles. Together Mr. and Mrs. Welles would carve the destiny of their second son, pointing him toward greatness from the cradle.

Beatrice Ives Welles had inherited a family legacy of artistry, spirituality, self-fulfillment, and civic-mindedness. The story of her Ives ancestors—dating back to seventeenth-century New England—reflected, and in some ways personified, the first years of American history.

In the early nineteenth century, one branch of the Ives family made its way to Oswego, New York, where J. C. Ives established himself as a builder of town walls, settlers' stone residences, and lighthouses on Lake Ontario. His son John G. Ives traveled from Oswego south to Auburn, New York, to learn the jewelry trade, and then at age twenty-one he headed west to Springfield, Illinois. The year was 1839, and Springfield, settled as a trapping and trading outpost, had just been named the state capital. Ives and a fellow New Yorker, Isaac Curran, opened a watch, jewelry, and silverware store called Ives and Curran, on the west side of the Springfield public square.

In Springfield, Ives met Abigail Watson, whose English ancestors had traveled from New Jersey to Tennessee and Missouri before landing in Illinois. Abigail's father, William Weldon Watson, lugged a soda fountain in a prairie schooner from Philadelphia to Nashville, using money from sales of the soda water ("to counteract the local whisky demon," as his Nobel Prize–winning descendant James Watson put it) to build a church, establishing the first Baptist ministry west of the Appalachians. After his spouse died, Watson and his five children moved first to Saint Louis, then Springfield, where he remarried and opened a confectionery store. His oldest girl, Abigail, was twenty years of age when she married John G. Ives in Springfield in 1843.

Springfield was also home to a prairie lawyer named Abraham Lincoln, and the place was growing into a stronghold of liberal opinion about slavery, the gold standard, and high tariffs. The Ives and Watson families were both friendly with the Lincolns and shared their political views. Lincoln is said to have enjoyed the macaroon pyramids baked in the Watson sweet shop. The oldest Watson son, Ben, was an early booster of Lincoln, and a neighbor who helped renovate the one-story cottage on Jackson and Eighth into the iconic Lincoln family residence: a two-story house with a kitchen, two parlors, and a dining room. The Ives family also lived nearby, about one block away from the Lincoln home on the north side of Market (later Capitol) Street. The rooms and space above Ives and Curran, which included the residential quarters of Isaac Curran, served as a political watering hole for Republicans, hosting community socials whose attendees included Mary Todd Lincoln.

When Lincoln won the presidential election of 1860, he was accompanied on his train trip east by Abigail's older brother Ben. Abigail handcrafted a U.S. flag with thirty-one stars, the last for California, that decorated the engine of the train. Abigail Ives treasured a rare photograph of the Great Emancipator from these days; eventually, like many Welles talismans, it would end up in the hands of Dr. Maurice Bernstein.

Abigail Ives served admirably on the board of the Springfield Soldiers Aid Society, assisting Civil War soldiers before and after the war. The Ives family saw itself as playing an active role in history, and she and John passed on the Lincolnesque tradition of good citizenship to their one daughter and three sons.

Orson's maternal great-grandfather led "a quiet tick-tock, tick-tock existence," in the words of Lincoln's biographer, the poet Carl Sandburg, "and looked like a clock of a man." John G. Ives's progress toward prosperity was also metronomic. Beyond his jewelry and silverware shop, Ives dabbled profitably in the coal and grain markets, and he became a leader of the Springfield branch of the Republican Party. Twice he served as treasurer of Sangamon County, "elected on the Republican ticket against a usual Democratic majority of several hundred," according to a local history, and twice he was voted onto the county board of supervisors.

The youngest of the Ives children, Benjamin, was born in 1850. He worked for his father as a notary and accountant, and in 1876, when he was still living under his parents' roof, married a woman ten years his junior. No older than seventeen when she married, Lucy Alma Walker was a Springfield native from a farming family; not until she bore her first child did the couple move into their own home on South Seventh

Street. Though accounts vary, the baby girl was most likely born on September 1, 1883. Her parents named her Beatrice Lucy, although as an adult Beatrice would rarely use her middle name.

The home where Beatrice Ives grew up was just a few blocks from the state capitol, hailed as one of the great buildings of the Midwest after its completion in 1889. One of her father's boyhood playmates was his cousin William Weldon Watson III, who went on to marry a banker's daughter named Augusta Crafts Tolman in an Illinois town called Kane in the county of Kane. Beatrice, too, would find many playmates amid her seemingly limitless Watson cousins.

Much of what we know about Beatrice's girlhood was handed down by Dr. Bernstein, who adored her and filled in the gaps in her story with embellishments. Bernstein insisted that Beatrice as a young woman "rode horseback like a man," and that she was a "splendid marksman" who engaged in regular target practice and country shooting, though "never at birds." (Orson sometimes parroted this received version of events in interviews.) In Beatrice's day and age people were raised close to the land, but such expertise was not as common among girls, and Beatrice's poise and physical appearance—she was a tall young woman, people remembered, ladylike but with a strong chin, always smartly dressed—were part of her mystique.

Beatrice also had an unusually husky voice; newspapers later praised its musical lilt, and her son, Orson, finding the mot juste, likened it to a "cello" in tone. Even as a teenager, Beatrice was recognized as something of a musical prodigy. Musicianship ran in the family: her mother, Lucy, played piano, as did her aunt Augusta, who had been a recitalist, and who encouraged her own progeny to dedicate themselves to artistic self-expression through art and music. Like her aunt, with whom she was close, Beatrice would favor classical over popular music; though she would oblige partygoers with a Sousa march, delivering the straightforward music with a smile and a flourish, she preferred to challenge herself with complex piano pieces.

One photograph of the beautiful and intelligent young Beatrice, seated at her piano, suggests a sweeter, more vulnerable side to her strong personality. By the time the photo was taken, her father, Benjamin Ives, had found a business foothold in Chicago, making regular trips there to promote his Illinois Fuel Company, with stock capitalized at $1.5 million—most of the stock his—and mines in Minnesota and in Sangamon County, where Springfield was located. Ives doted on his promising daughter, who soon set her sights on attending a fine arts academy in the city.

After Beatrice finished secondary school in Springfield—probably at the Academy of Our Lady of the Sacred Heart, the Catholic girls' school—she and her mother joined the head of the family in Chicago. The Iveses found a flat in the Hyde Park area. Beatrice enrolled in the Chicago Conservatory, the city's most reputable school of music and dramatic arts, located in the Chicago Symphony Orchestra's monumental Auditorium Building, touted as the tallest and largest building in America when it opened in 1889.

Beatrice took private tutoring from a Russian Lithuanian–born former child prodigy, Leopold Godowsky, then at his peak as a prolific composer of daunting virtuoso piano pieces. An eclectic teacher who inspired loyalty among his many students, Godowsky was a champion of Chopin, Bach, Haydn, and Mozart, and a performer of impeccable technique whose novel percussionist approach relied on weight release and relaxation rather than muscular impetus. Beatrice basked in his guidance, and under his eye her technical playing developed emotional expressiveness, alternating power with delicacy and feeling. She also studied music theory under the German-born Adolf Weidig, an authority on theories of composition and harmony, citing his influence in her publicity materials later in life.

Conservatory students were expected to immerse themselves in a rounded curriculum that included elocution, oratory, poetry reading, dramatics, and even fencing and pantomime. Beatrice studied the plays of Shakespeare, along with the fashionable Delsarte system of acting, which associated inner emotions with specific gestures and movements. The students were also expected to develop a working knowledge of French, Italian, German, and Spanish, which was crucial in familiarizing themselves with the work of contemporary foreign-language composers. And they were steered to the nearby Art Institute of Chicago where they could find inspiration in a wealth of masterpieces; Beatrice walked through the gallery halls for long hours, and returned there for years thereafter.

The conservatory was like a finishing school; even students like

Beatrice, who arrived with considerable social poise, received instruction on proper deportment in public situations: how to walk, bow courteously, shake hands. Many of the musicians aspired to be educators, and the curriculum included mandatory lessons in civic responsibility, rhetoric, and parliamentary procedure, so that graduates would "be able to organize a public meeting and direct its business," according to one brochure. The conservatory's ambitious goal was to nurture "a cultivated voice and a cultivated body, the harmonious development of which enables one to enter upon any vocation in life, either social or artistic, and to add to natural talents those rare advantages—ease and confidence."

The conservatory experience reinforced Beatrice's natural ease and confidence. She made friends without difficulty among her peers and just as easily among the society figures and benefactors who attended recitals in the school's magnificent main hall. Performing at local luncheons and club events also afforded young Beatrice a small income, increasingly vital by the end of the decade as her father's career began to suffer a series of setbacks.

Benjamin Ives poured all of his savings and inheritance into his business plans, but one by one his investments turned out to be no more than pipe dreams. As early as 1893, impatient creditors filed mismanagement claims against his fledgling Illinois Fuel Company. Ives fought the claims in Chicago courts, fending off lawsuits for the better part of a decade, but oil discoveries in Texas and Alaska depressed fuel prices throughout the 1890s, and Ives's enterprise never gained traction. By 1900 Ives was forced to declare bankruptcy with liabilities of $44,000 and assets of only $700. Beatrice's father never recovered his health or his optimism, and the family's ordeal left a deep impression on the girl; her example of stoicism bordering on fearlessness was not lost on her son during his own reversals of fortune.

Her father's woes forced Beatrice, in her late teens, to make certain adjustments. She may briefly have taken work as a "typewriter," as stenographers were known in that era, as Welles claimed in later interviews. At the Chicago Conservatory she shifted from Godowsky—who charged $140 for two thirty-minute lessons a week—to Julia Lois Caruthers, who offered two *hour*-long lessons for $120.

But there were consolations. Whereas Godowsky was a brusque

instructor, Caruthers was a nurturer, beloved by her students. As a performer—she had made a spectacular debut in Chicago in 1887 playing the Schumann Quintet—Caruthers alternated strength with delicacy. As a teacher, she recommended deep study of each composer along with individualized expression, and she encouraged her students to explore the spiritual component of their art. One of her specialties was piano instruction for children; she was at work on a manual called *Piano Technic for Children.*

Though her father was reduced to working as an accountant, the forward-looking Beatrice never seemed to miss a step. Blossoming as a performer, she mingled effortlessly with the arts patrons of Chicago, the traveling players she met backstage at theatricals, and the earthy newspapermen who covered local concerts and shows. On weekends she traveled throughout northern Illinois and southern Wisconsin, and often spent summers in the North Shore towns of Lake County in Illinois or at rustic Lake Geneva in Wisconsin, where Aunt Augusta and her husband had run a showplace, the Whiting House hotel.

By the turn of the century, as she entered her twenties, Beatrice Ives had crossed paths with the man who became her husband: Richard Head Welles.

The Welles name arrived with the filmmaker's forebears on the *Mayflower.* Orson Welles's early American ancestors called themselves "Wells," sometimes "Welles," the spelling changing at the whim of individual family members and record keepers. Orson's father's ancestors were not especially artistic-minded; like the Ives family, though, they were patriotic and commercial-minded, while also scarred by misfortune and—a darker tendency—recklessness.

The Welleses had been landed gentry in England, and in the eighteenth century Richard Wells, a dry goods merchant in Burlington, New Jersey, became an officer of the Bank of North America. In time Richard's family moved to Delaware, where his son, William, born in 1769, joined his father's several thriving businesses and studied to become an attorney. William H. Wells married Rachel Dagworthy, the daughter of a Revolutionary War general. She stood to inherit timber and tannery holdings, and their union enhanced William's portfolio, but Rachel may have been an illegitimate daughter, and William had to forswear his Quaker faith to wed her in an Episcopalian church.

A liberal member of the Federalist Party—America's first political party, formed by Alexander Hamilton—William H. Wells opposed strong central government but looked kindly upon the Bank of North America, the first central bank, over which his father helped to preside. Elected to the Delaware State Assembly in 1795, William served several terms there and in the state senate before occupying a U.S. Senate seat from 1813 to 1817. After retiring from politics, he practiced law while amassing a small fortune from Pennsylvania oil and other interests. Wells and his wife raised five sons, all of whom would become lawyers—including Henry Hill Wells, who was born in 1797.

An officeholder like his father, Henry Hill Wells served as secretary of state for two governors of Delaware in the early 1820s. In his book *Orson Welles: The Rise and Fall of an American Genius*, biographer Charles Higham credited Henry Hill Wells with helping to free slaves via the Underground Railroad, but documentation of this abolitionist spirit in both the father and his sons is sparse. Henry Hill Wells never enjoyed fabulous wealth, Higham wrote, and the sons gained little from their father's estate, which had dwindled by the time of William's death in 1829.

Henry Hill Wells was not quite the political animal his father was, and in the mid-1830s he left government and Delaware for Wilkes-Barre, Pennsylvania, where he had a number of relatives, purchasing a vacant lot near St. Stephen's Church and hanging his shingle as a lawyer around 1835. He built a practice and a home for his wife and three children: Lucretia Wells, their only daughter, born in 1833; William Dagworthy Wells, born in 1837; and Richard Jones Wells (his middle name was probably his mother's maiden name), probably born in 1843.

Henry Hill Wells, Orson's paternal great-grandfather, died in 1856, shortly after moving to Skaneateles, New York. His eldest son, nineteen-year-old William, lit out for Quincy, Illinois, where he found work as a freight clerk on the Chicago, Burlington, and Quincy Railroad. Richard lingered behind long enough to complete his basic education and an apprenticeship, then trailed his brother to Quincy. By the time Richard was hired by American Express, a new mail delivery service, he could read and write and calculate. Richard showed a knack for mechanical engineering and draftsmanship, and he could ride horses surpassingly well.

Every train traveler heading west to Chicago or Saint Louis passed through Quincy, then Illinois's second-largest city, on the eastern shore of the Mississippi River. The Wells brothers shared a room at the handsome Quincy House, where the U.S. senator Stephen A. Douglas, Abraham Lincoln's opponent, maintained an office. The brothers were in Quincy when Lincoln defeated Douglas in late 1860.

The following April, the rebel attack on Fort Sumter launched the Civil War. Five feet eight and a half, trim and fair-complexioned, with sandy brown hair and blue eyes, Richard Jones Wells was not yet twenty on August 9, 1862, the day he enlisted, in Chicago, as a private and "express messenger" for M Company of the Illinois Volunteers, or First Regiment, Light Artillery. His brother William, meanwhile, stayed at his railroad job in Quincy, which was an important hub for wartime operations. With trains bringing vital supplies to the Union general S. A. Hurlburt's forces in northern Missouri, there was plenty of work.

Richard J. Wells would have a brief but noteworthy career as a soldier in the War Between the States. Stationed early in 1863 near Campbellsport, Kentucky, Richard was involved in the famous Battle of Tebbs Bend, with Illinois, Michigan, and Kentucky companies striving to hold a key bridge on the Green River. By now a sergeant, Richard commanded a field piece and caisson in the battle, riding hard and fast against the Confederate troops, but his weary horse stumbled and he was thrown violently onto the pommel of the saddle. Rejoining the pursuit, Richard felt "a colic or severe pain in my bowels." Later he discovered a sore spot and a lump on the right side of his abdomen, but at first he said nothing. The next morning, the company surgeon sent him to a military hospital in Nashville, where he was diagnosed with a right inguinal or groin hernia. Richard's initial failure to report his injury cast a permanent shadow over his claim; no eyewitness could attest to the horse-riding accident. Wells—who had been too embarrassed to tell any of his blue-uniformed comrades about the wound in his private parts—would later be investigated repeatedly with regard to pension and medical benefits.

But his injury was real, and Richard J. Wells spent two months convalescing in the hospital before being discharged with what was considered a permanent disability. (A groin hernia tends to enlarge over time, leading to swelling and inflammation in the scrotum.) Richard spent his convalescence sketching ideas for patents he had dreamed up in hopes of striking it rich. (The oft-repeated claim that one of Welles's forebears invented a military mess kit may have its fuzzy origins here.) Still recovering, Richard returned to Quincy in mid-1863, working for both the railroad and American Express.

When Richard's older brother William took a job with the Hannibal and St. Joseph Railroad in Saint Joseph, Missouri, about two hundred miles west on the Chicago, Burlington, and Quincy route, Richard joined him, hoping his new position as a station agent would help him find investors for his inventions. Like other Welles men Richard was a born salesman, handsome and charming, and he would make "hundreds of friends" working for the railroad, according to one local newspaper account. About 1868, probably in Chicago, where so many train lines—and human paths—converged after the Civil War, the twenty-six-year-old Richard J. Wells met and courted a young woman, a few years younger than himself, from Kenosha, Wisconsin.

This young woman, Mary Blanche Head, has been ill-served by film historians and biographers. Charles Higham claimed in his 1985 biography of Orson Welles that she was only fourteen and a half, a sullen, stocky runaway from a "harsh and terrifying father," when she encountered the dashing Wells in Saint Joseph and "entered immediately into an affair" with the older man. "Soon after," Higham wrote, "with great daring, [she] decided that they would get married." According to this biographer, Mary Head had a "fierce and ambitious disposition" and was "uncontrollable . . . ill-tempered and harsh when crossed." This colorful fiction was essential to Higham's portrait of the Heads as the family who introduced the gleam of fanaticism into Welles's genealogy. Although Higham's life of Welles has been discredited in many respects, this portrait of Mary Head and her family has persisted in subsequent accounts.

In truth, the Heads were sobersided Yankees living the American dream; their family roots ran as deep as those of the Iveses, the Watsons, and the Welleses. The Heads, too, had come over on the *Mayflower*.

Mary's father, Orson Sherman Head, was a former Oneida County, New York, farm boy with flaming red hair and a robust physique. He studied law in the office of a local attorney before pulling up roots and heading west. In 1841, at twenty-four, he landed in the Wisconsin village of Southport. Head's rise to wealth and local prestige was symbolized by the imposing two-story brick dwelling he built there, the home where his daughter Mary Head was raised, at the corner of Chicago and Prairie, in the burgeoning city soon to be renamed Kenosha. Many relatives from New York followed Orson S. Head to Southport, opening the first foundries, lumberyards, and wagon works.

After being admitted to the Wisconsin bar, Orson Welles's maternal great-grandfather and namesake was elected district attorney of Kenosha several times. "A desirable ally and a dangerous enemy in the courts," according to one obituary, Head was known for his dedication to clients ("it mattered not how poor and humble") and for cross-examinations that could be brutal and intimidating. "There was no more chance for falsehood to survive one of his examinations than for a kernel of wheat to pass unbroken between the upper and nether millstones."

Another politician in the Welles family tree, Head served a short stint in the Wisconsin State Senate in 1851, making a name for himself in the capital, Madison, as an enemy of fraud and corruption. "Outspoken" and "brusque," according to local opinion, Head was seen as a "hard-hearted" fellow by some, by others as a good man with "a peculiar vein of tenderness" that tempered his toughness, a product of struggle and rectitude. He doted on his horses and—like the Iveses—revered Abraham Lincoln, more than once breaking into tears as he recited the Gettysburg Address. Above all, his obituaries noted, Head was a kindly father and a providing one. After his death, the fortune he had made in agriculture, land, and speculation was divided equally among his six children. According to most documents, Mary, his oldest child, was born in Kenosha in 1845; she was neither fourteen nor a runaway when she met and was beguiled by Richard J. Wells—a man not much older than she.

Nor was she unattractive. In her early twenties, Mary Blanche Head was pretty and cultivated, probably classically tutored at home, and she was interested in art, music, and literature. Her father had business interests in Chicago, where the Head family traveled for recitals, entertainment, and shopping. She met Wells when he visited Chicago, searching for investors in the biggest city in the Midwest, which was mushrooming with newcomers and trade since the Civil War.

Richard J. Wells's first visit to Kenosha, however, was undoubtedly for his wedding to Mary Head on October 29, 1868. The minister was Episcopalian, as were (since birth) the bride and groom. The new Mrs. Wells moved to Saint Joseph, going to work as a cashier for the Pacific House, the residential hotel where her husband lived. Her husband's first patent, registered from the address of the Pacific House in August 1869, was for "certain new and useful Improvements in Car-Couplings" for trains. His next patent, for an improvement in umbrella holders, showed his versatility, and in more ways than one: For the first time he added an "e" to his surname, transforming himself into "Richard J. Welles." Perhaps the change was an affectation, perhaps a subtle flourishing of a new pride and identity.

According to Higham's research, the couple moved from elegant hotels to expensive houses to failed land developments and finally to bare lodgings, all within a few years. On November 13, 1872, still living in Saint Joseph, Mary gave birth to a son. The couple gave the boy a name that knitted the two family histories together: Richard Head Welles. Yet trouble was already in the air: "within a month Richard had been fired," Higham notes, and their marriage was doomed.

Mary Head Welles wanted children and a stable family life, but her husband was fixated on patents and get-rich schemes. At first their marriage was convenient for Richard, who relied on his father-in-law for investment and for other opportunities. One of Welles's inventions was for "certain improvements in harness-trimmings," and Mary's sister Harriet was married to the son of the superintendent of Kenosha's Bain Wagon Works, in which the Head family had invested. Bain was the largest manufacturer and supplier of wagons in the United States and perhaps the world, at a time when wagons were the principal means of transportation.

Upon marrying Orson S. Head's daughter, Richard J. Welles borrowed $7,000 from his father-in-law, a goodly sum at the time; when Head died in 1875, Welles was able to dodge the debt. Welles was also accused of embezzling another $20,000 from the Hannibal and

St. Joseph Railroad; this was the charge that got him fired soon after his son's birth. But a jury believed his version of events, and crowds cheered the popular ex–station agent as he departed by train for Chicago in July 1876. After intermediate stops in Kenosha and elsewhere, Welles took up residence in Chicago with Mary and their four-year-old son, Richard.

Although Richard J. Welles never attained a law degree like his father, his life would give him plenty of exposure to statutes and courtrooms. In Chicago, Welles and some shadowy partners launched a company that was meant to manufacture new harness and bridle wares based on his patents. He had expected to sell his wares to big national distributors like Bain Wagon Works, but Orson S. Head's death, coupled with Richard's growing estrangement from his wife, Mary, scotched that connection to relatives. Welles turned to new brainstorms; like other Welleses who never found a true, permanent home, he talked vaguely of opening a hotel for businessmen. But the money he took from investors disappeared like rabbits in a hat.

By 1878, Welles's illusory saddlery empire had evaporated. When he wasn't in court defending himself from aggrieved patent investors, he was heading off on vague trips to other cities drumming up more believers. His indifference to his wife lapsed into hostility, and when young Richard was six, Mary finally took the boy and fled to Kenosha. For a few months Welles sent child support, but it was scanty, and soon it dwindled to nothing.

At first, Mary Head Welles lacked for little except a husband's attentions. She had inherited nearly $20,000 from her father's estate in addition to land and possessions, with a nearly equal sum placed in trust for her son Richard, the eldest Head grandchild. Her trust was doled out in increments by one of the extended Head family, banker Daniel Head, who also came originally from Oneida County, and Mary used the money to invest in oil and grains. By degrees rejoining Kenosha society, she attended soirees and dance parties and vacationed with her little boy, nicknamed Dickey, in Lake Geneva, a favorite getaway for Kenoshans as well as Chicagoans.

After a year, Mary Head Welles finally filed for divorce. She may have been ignorant of her wayward husband's mounting crises, because her divorce documents describe Richard not as a scam artist but as a man with superior business acumen climbing the ladder to success. Though Richard was served with divorce papers in Chicago in 1881, he refused to appear at proceedings and made no child custody claims.

Court records depict him as outwardly in "good health," although his constitution was already failing. Four years after the divorce filing, living temporarily in Athens, Pennsylvania, he filed for what amounted to a disability pension owing to his aggravated hernia. Examined by a doctor, the Civil War veteran, now in his forties, was found to have a rupture on his right side "larger than a goose egg," which the medical examiner felt might be controlled by a "suitable truss." Granted his pension, Welles moved to New York City; he stayed there for the next fifteen years, registering minor patents ("Improvements in Bed Couches" and "Improvements in Bed-Chairs") and announcing Welles Manufacturing Company products that never saw fruition. He too made ends meet as a bookkeeper.

In 1904, time finally ran out on him. That October, Welles suffered an abdominal aortic aneurysm, a catastrophic breach triggered by the hernia. He was registered as a pensioner—$12 a month—at the National Soldiers Home in Hampton, Virginia. Doctors diagnosed a hernia, vertigo, eye disease, severe rheumatism, heart disease, and general feebleness. In his early sixties, Orson Welles's paternal grandfather was a tremulous old man: his hair all white, his muscles flabby. (The doctors took care, however, to attribute Richard's feeble condition to his hernia, "not to vicious habits.")

Discharged in February 1905, Richard Jones Welles died in Washington, D.C., in May of the following year, at the age of sixty-two or -three. Asked repeatedly by government officials whether he had been married or fathered any children, he repeatedly answered no. As his next of kin he named his sister, Lucretia, married to another railroad agent in Madison, Wisconsin. At the end of his life, he reverted to spelling his name "Wells."

The son he left behind, Richard Head Welles, certainly never forgot his father—among other things, he would follow in his footsteps as a resourceful inventor—but after the age of seven the boy probably never saw him again. His father became a taboo subject in the family. His own son would make a film about a fictional boy named Kane who never really knew his father either—neither the man called Kane Sr. in the motion picture, nor the man (possibly Kane's father) described only as a "defaulting boarder" whose last testament sets Rosebud in motion. Richard Head Welles would not be the last Welles to grow up with an unseen father, or to become a flawed parent himself.

Richard Head Welles was known as Dickey, never Junior, and finally he was Dick, rarely Richard. Strictly speaking, he didn't remain fatherless for long. Four years after his mother's divorce, at Christmas 1885, Mary Head Welles married Frederick J. Gottfredsen, the eldest son of a Danish-born Kenosha pioneer who had built a successful business manufacturing and selling cigars, bricks, wood, flour, vinegar, and spirits. Frederick was a partner in the Gottfredsen Brewery; another Gottfredsen ran Kenosha's oldest jewelry store.

Mary Head Welles Gottfredsen, as she now called herself, gave birth to a second son, Jacob Rudolph Gottfredsen, in 1887. She and her second husband built a picturesque two-and-a-half-story stone-and-shingle house in downtown Kenosha and dubbed it Rudolphsheim. (According to a local pamphlet, the house, which still exists and is featured on local historic tours, "includes pieces of beer bottles, reportedly from the Gottfredsen Brewery, embedded in the stucco" of the gable.)

But young Dick Welles would not grow up in Rudolphsheim. His new stepfather never adopted him, and Dick never developed a close relationship with his half brother Jacob Rudolph, partly owing to the fifteen-year difference in their ages. By the time the new house was finished, Dick was fifteen years old and spending much of the year at the Racine College Grammar School, an exclusive boarding school on a bluff overlooking Lake Michigan at the southern limit of Racine, a small city about ten miles north of Kenosha.

Racine College was an Episcopalian institution, organized according to a military system that had been modified to eliminate undesirable features, and it specialized in scientific and business training. The school also prided itself on a progressive curriculum that blended a classical education (including mandatory Greek and Latin) with a full range of arts programs.

In his prep school days, Dick Welles was regarded as "impetuous

and talented," according to Victoria Price, the daughter of future
Mercury Theatre actor Vincent Price, whose father, Vincent Leonard
Price, was Dick's classmate at Racine College. Dick and the elder Price
were active in school theatricals, and they teamed up to stage an "ex-
travagant magic show" for the whole school, according to *Vincent Price:
A Daughter's Biography.*

Racine College Grammar School offered the equivalent of a high
school diploma, but after graduating Dick Welles may briefly have
attended one of several university-type academies in Kenosha or Milwaukee. "He studied law but did not complete the courses," Dr. Bernstein wrote of Orson's father. "He was a well read man who took an
interest in many things." Along with skills in reading, writing, and
mathematics, Dick also showed an interest in mechanical engineering,
much like his derelict father. A hunter and sportsman, he took up cycling when it was still a novelty, sailed on Lake Michigan, and golfed
on the makeshift greens of Kenosha.

But the most astonishing thing young Dick Welles did, at the tender
age of sixteen, was to file suit against the banker in charge of his trust
fund—his own close relative and one of Kenosha's pillars of commerce. Working through his fiduciary guardian, a prominent Kenosha
attorney, Dick accused Daniel Head, executor of his grandfather's will,
of furnishing no reliable account of expenditures from the trust fund
for ten years following the death of Orson S. Head.

It was a play for independence on the young man's part, but it
had other consequences, intentional or not—including exposing his
mother's growing fear of debt before her second marriage and her pattern of unsuccessful investment in Chicago stocks. The suit divided
the numerous Head siblings, with each weighing in with his or her version of the facts. Partly to defend her own financial decisions, Dick's
mother was compelled to join the attack on Daniel, the nominal elder
statesman of the extended Head family; she even tried (unsuccessfully)
to claim a share of the trust fund for Jacob Rudolph, unborn at the
time of her father's death.

The case droned on for years, like *Jarndyce v. Jarndyce,* but the final
ruling after appeals in 1895 made headlines throughout the state
of Wisconsin. The bank was unable to furnish sufficient paperwork
to back up its claims, and the case was settled in favor of Richard

H. Welles, as he was now known formally after attaining his majority. Young Welles received $6,972 as the residue of his share of the Head trust fund, originally calculated at $15,054.81, the balance of which had been paid out for his support and education since his grandfather's death twenty years earlier. (The settlement—the equivalent of nearly $200,000 today—was a fair bundle at the time.)

The next five years went by in a blur. With bicycling all the rage, the first thing Dick Welles did with his windfall inheritance was sail from New York to Liverpool to embark on a five-week biking tour of England and France with a gang of well-heeled Kenosha friends. Welles organized a group called the Kenosha Wheelmen to participate in the earliest statewide long-distance races, and he traveled to several midwestern cities for conventions. He could have put a little time and money into the six-day track cycling races that started in Madison Square Garden before sweeping the Midwest, as his son the filmmaker later claimed.

Dick Welles may also have done a brief stint in the Yukon searching for gold in the late 1890s, palling around with the free-spirited budding playwright Wilson Mizner and Sid Grauman, later of Grauman's Chinese Theatre. At least his son Orson claimed as much in interviews, and while no proof of those travels has surfaced, Alaska records are incomplete, and the facts, timing, and spirit of the story all jibe with what's known of his father's character.

Even before the court ruling gave him financial security, Orson's father loved to travel. Though he often went by boat or train, Dick Welles also went in with friends on a pleasure yacht they kept docked in Kenosha. He made frequent excursions to Chicago and New York, headed south in the spring to roam Civil War battlefields, and regularly made it to the West Indies.

Chicago got to know Orson's father particularly well. He mingled there widely and democratically. At the racetrack, boxing matches, and vaudeville shows, Dick Welles befriended the city's best-known newsmen, including the racetrack humorist Drury Underwood of the *Chicago Chronicle*; the cartoonist and illustrator John T. McCutcheon of the *Chicago Record-Herald*; and the columnist George Ade, McCutcheon's *Record* colleague collaborator, and Sigma Chi brother at Purdue University.

Orson's father increasingly mixed pleasure with business in Chicago. Bain Wagon Works had gone into bicycle manufacturing in the 1890s, and toward the end of his five years of wanderlust Dick Welles was hired by the Yules as a road representative for Bain. George Yule, born in Scotland, had been Edward Bain's longtime right-hand man at Bain before taking over as boss. His son, George A. Yule, had risen up under his father to superintendent at Bain. George A. Yule was fourteen years older than his wife's sister's son, but he and Dick had a strong bond.

Dick Welles proved a tremendous man on the road for Bain. Dapper and friendly, he was a hail-fellow-well-met, a man people remembered and looked forward to seeing again. Visiting Chicago, he formed friendships with such forward-thinking businessmen as Thomas B. Jeffery, the inventor and manufacturer of the Rambler bicycle; and Charles N. and Walter J. Frost, a father and son who ran a brass, bronze, and aluminum casting business. Welles hoped to intrigue them with his vision for a new Kenosha company, anchored by his relationship with George A. Yule and their family ties to the Bain Wagon Works network, which would combine the exploding market for crucial bicycle parts with the coming boom in horseless carriages.

Film scholars have pointed out that Dick Welles resembles the character Eugene Morgan in Booth Tarkington's *The Magnificent Ambersons*, played in Orson Welles's screen adaptation by Joseph Cotten. Morgan is not an Amberson but an outsider enamored of the ill-fated Isabel Amberson, and not an inventor but a horseless-carriage pioneer and entrepreneur. In the backstory of the novel, as a young man, Morgan loses favor with Isabel after causing a drunken scene on the lawn of the Amberson mansion, serenading her and stepping through a bass viol before being led away. Isabel then marries the persistent Wilbur Minafer, "a steady young businessman and a good churchgoer." After the death of his first wife, Morgan returns to town with plans to build an automobile factory, having left behind his wildness. To Isabel's spoiled son George, the central figure of the story, Morgan is a despised rival for his mother's affections and a symbol of the vulgar parvenu. Yet ultimately it is Morgan who proves the sensible one in the story: when George's uncle and aunt consider investing in early automobile lamplights, Morgan advises them to "go slow"—but the Ambersons ignore his advice and lose the remainder of their fortune investing in poorly designed headlights.

Years later, the filmmaker would claim that his father, a headlight inventor, had been a model for Tarkington's character Morgan—a claim that was scoffed at by some interviewers. But Dick Welles did get to know Tarkington, who was a kind of third musketeer from Purdue and Indiana along with McCutcheon and Ade. Then a budding author flitting through Chicago, Tarkington was struck by Welles, seeing him as typically midwestern, with depth charges beneath the surface impression. Like Eugene Morgan, Welles once had been "a fairly wild young fellow," in the novel's words. But the wild young Welles had grown into a savvy, prudent businessman. When he told Jeffery and Frost that he was going to invest his personal savings in the new headlight company, they were won over.

Dick Welles sought out a bicycle lamp inventor, E. L. Williams, in England. Williams had just patented the Solar lamp, named for its purported brightness; it consisted of a small petroleum lamp "inside a casing with a wick that could be lit before a reflecting parabolic mirror," in the words of John F. Kreidl, author of an unpublished study emphasizing Dick Welles's importance to the bicycle and car lamp industry. According to Kreidl, the Solar was "a Rube Goldberg invention at best," and Williams's tireless tinkering and minor improvements could not change the fact that it was dirty and foul-smelling in operation. But the inventor's timing was good: the Solar emerged at the height of the bicycle craze, just as riders were discovering the dangers of biking at night.

Williams intended his invention purely for bicycles and never foresaw a potential application to automobiles. It was Dick Welles who had the brainstorm and the idea of forging links between Williams and midwestern businessmen who were interested in opening up the market for headlights for mechanical and motorized vehicles. By late 1897, Welles had the English inventor on board as a partner in the new Kenosha venture, and he was ready, with George A. Yule, to announce the formation of the Badger Brass Company, with an exclusive world license to manufacture and sell Solar lamps.

E. L. Williams, Charles N. Frost, George A. Yule, and Dick Welles were the original Badger Brass partners. Williams remained in England, banking his share of profits; there is no record that he ever even visited Kenosha. The Frosts soon went their own way, establishing Frost Manufacturing in Kenosha to stamp out parts for industrial, household, and automotive use. Yule and Welles remained at the helm from the beginning to the end.

Under the elder George Yule's management, Bain Wagon Works would stay independent of Badger Brass, but the established company's gradual changeover from wagons to modern vehicles was closely intertwined with the new lamp-making concern. By virtue of age, experience, and money, George A. Yule was the senior partner. Dick Welles was the next-largest investor, however, sinking a good deal of his remaining inheritance into Badger Brass. Together the two men owned three-fifths of the new company, initially capitalized at a reported $25,000.

In the coming years Orson Welles's father was listed variously as the secretary or treasurer of Badger Brass, but from the first he was a key member of the operation and did a little of everything. When he wasn't traveling to promote the product and firm up contracts, Dick Welles worked daily at the first plant on the corner of Elizabeth and Pleasant. The business ignited like a firecracker, and within two years of its founding Badger Brass boasted ninety employees and had sold more than 200,000 exclusive Solar lamps around the globe.

The wild years of youth were over for Dick Welles, now ensconced with his mother and her husband at Rudolphsheim. He was not yet thirty years of age. Though his son later described him from memory as "a little small-boned man," Dick was about five feet ten and of medium build, with thin brown hair, dark amber eyes, and a winning smile that lit up his round face like a pumpkin. The young adventurer and *bon viveur* (one of Orson's pet descriptions of him) had transformed himself into a well-respected businessman who seemed to represent Kenosha's shining future. Welles was an early proponent of better roads for bicycles and automobiles, and joined fund-raising campaigns for hospitals, city parks, and the city's crown jewel: its library. He was among the organizers of the Kenosha Country Club. Like Eugene Morgan in *The Magnificent Ambersons*, Welles was a dedicated cigar smoker who favored an inexpensive brand made exclusively for him by a Chicago company. (Amused friends dubbed the budget brand the "Dick Wells.") On special occasions, however—including the day Badger Brass was incorporated, and the day of George Orson Welles's birth in 1915—he was known to light up a Havana.

His youth—and flair—set Dick Welles apart from other city leaders. When the very first automobile appeared on Kenosha's streets in 1899, Welles was behind the wheel. Perhaps unsurprisingly, the car was one of Thomas B. Jeffery's new Ramblers, and the stunt publicized Jeffery's sale of his bicycle firm in Chicago. Welles had persuaded Jeffery to shift from bicycles to automobiles and move his operations to Kenosha, manufacturing his Ramblers on a national scale—and contracting to buy all its headlights from Badger Brass.

As he turned thirty in 1902, Dick Welles was being whispered about as the consensus candidate for mayor among local Republicans, still the liberal party of Lincoln.

Rudolphsheim was the center of a social whirl that included the Gottfredsens and other well-known Kenosha settler families, many of whom were related through marriage. The larger Pabst Brewing Company of Milwaukee had absorbed the Gottfredsen Brewery, and Frederick Gottfredsen now managed the Kenosha branch of Pabst. Mary Gottfredsen hosted the Dickens Club and artistic discussion groups and musical afternoons at Rudolphsheim. She led theater parties to Racine, Milwaukee, and Chicago. Orson Welles's maternal grandmother had transferred her religious allegiance from the Episcopalians to the Unitarians, the most open-minded church in Kenosha.

It must have been sometime in early 1902 that Dick Welles met Beatrice Ives. The pianist was living with her parents in an apartment house on Madison Avenue in Chicago. Chicago was Dick Welles's second home now, as it would be for his son Orson. Dick Welles was all but famous in Chicago by late 1902, in part for the meteoric exploits of a horse that raced under his name.

A close friend, Kenosha boxing promoter John E. Keating, had purchased the horse and named it "Dick Welles."* After being sold to a stablemaster named Rome Respess, the horse was running his first

---

* As often as not the horse's name was spelled "Dick Wells."

thrilling races at Washington Park racetrack in Chicago by the end of 1902. Soon the horse was racing nationally, celebrated as "the fastest horse in the world" in the six furlongs and one mile. The businessman from Kenosha could go to the Chicago racetrack and enjoy the rare privilege of betting on a champion named after himself. (A few years later, Orson's father also could bet on the winner of the 1909 Kentucky Derby, a horse named Wintergreen sired by stallion Dick Welles.)

Orson Welles often told interviewers that he didn't think his mother and father had very much in common—that he couldn't imagine where they could possibly have met. But Dick Welles and Beatrice Ives had a good deal in common, including their mutual friends the Chicago newspapermen Drury Underwood, John McCutcheon, and George Ade. They could have met at newspaper offices, which they both frequented, or been introduced by Underwood at the racetrack.

The standard comment about Dick Welles is that he preferred low nightlife. True, he could be spotted at vaudeville performances, musicals with pretty chorines, touring magic shows, or the revues put on by black song-and-dance men Williams and Walker at the Great Northern on Chicago's South Side. He frequented boxing matches as well as racetracks. But Orson's father was at ease everywhere. He was just as likely to spend a night at the opera, or the symphony, or a Shakespeare production, or to stroll through the galleries of the museum. He could have met his future wife at a recital or stage play or high-society occasion. The two could have locked eyes first in Lake Geneva, where they were both spending long weekends as guests of a friend in 1902.

Yet it was a stealth romance. Dick Welles kept the seriousness of his intentions secret from even his closest friends until the front-page announcement in the *Kenosha News* on February 9, 1903, that "one of the best known young men of the city" was engaged to "one of the most beautiful and accomplished women in Chicago society," a lucky lady who was all but a mystery to Kenosha. As with the engagement of Charles Foster Kane and Emily Monroe Norton in *Citizen Kane*, the news came out of nowhere. And the air of mystery extended to the wedding itself: When the lovers exchanged vows on Saturday afternoon, November 21, 1903, in the Chicago apartment near Lincoln Park where Mr. and Mrs. Benjamin Ives lived, the local press was agog. "Ceremony Surprises Friends," was the headline on the front page of the *Kenosha News.* "The engagement of the well known young people was announced last summer," the story read, "but none of their friends and not even the relatives were advised of the date set for the wedding." Beatrice had shrugged off her early Catholic influences, and an Episcopalian minister performed the ceremony. "Only a few relatives of the contracting parties were present," noted the *Kenosha News,* among them Mr. and Mrs. Gottfredsen and teenager Jacob Rudolph.

After a luncheon, the newlyweds departed for a monthlong honeymoon that would begin in New York and continue on to the West Indies. They arrived back in Kenosha after the New Year, accepting the congratulations of well-wishers at a party held in their honor at Rudolphseim, before moving into temporary quarters downtown.

Chicago was a vertical jungle of steel and stone, choking with people and problems of growth. "First in violence" is how muckraking reporter Lincoln Steffens described the city in 1903, "deepest in dirt, loud, lawless, unlovely, ill-smelling, irreverent, new, an overgrown gawk of a village."

Many people saw Kenosha as a "little Chicago," because it was close enough to and faintly reminiscent of the larger city, though it was tiny by comparison and Kenoshans lived closer to the land and sky. Carl Sandburg, who had lived in both Chicago and Kenosha, evoked the cities' shared midwestern melancholy in his poem "Sunset from Omaha Hotel Window":

Here in Omaha
The gloaming is bitter
As in Chicago
Or Kenosha.

Beatrice and Dick Welles would never leave Chicago altogether; they would often travel there by train for events and shows and business and shopping, and for seeing friends and Beatrice's parents. For now, however, humble Kenosha suited them both.

Dick Welles kept busy, traveling often not only to Chicago but to Detroit, Syracuse, and New York City for sales meetings and auto shows, and logging daily hours at the Badger Brass plant when he was home. Beyond maintaining the company books, he acted as a point man with the workers and as an industry spokesman to the newspapers.

He was also starting to register patents for enhancements in his field. The first year of his marriage was the year Orson Welles's father unveiled his first invention: an "acetylene-generator" for use in headlights "for vehicles, such as automobiles." Grasping the usefulness of the bicycle lamp to the car industry—at a point when the car industry barely existed—Dick Welles had improved E. L. Williams's acetylene gas lamp for effective application to automobiles. "[Welles] reasoned that the acetylene generator and the lamp could be in two different places on a car," wrote John F. Kreidl. "Combining them in one spot was not so important as insuring a steady, smooth and continual gas flow of long duration." Welles's patent application included his sketch of a portable acetylene generator that could be fitted onto the rear of an auto, keeping it supplied with gas for weeks. "Credit here must be given to the man who straddled inventing *and* marketing," observed Kreidl.

Over the next fifteen years, more than a dozen patents would be filed under the name of Richard H. Welles, each meticulously drawn with accompanying technical specifications. Most were for tweaks in standard headlight design, but Welles also devised a new type of searchlight, an improved automobile jack, and a chart for cataloging mechanical devices with numerous intricate small pieces. Some books about Orson Welles have trivialized his father's inventions, but even when they were adjustments to existing designs, the inventions were of material value to Badger Brass, and they added to his income. (One Kenosha car parts company, for instance, snapped up Welles's automobile jack exclusively for its vehicles.) Such innovations were also important for publicity. As companies with copycat brands of vehicle lights sprang up to compete with Badger Brass, Welles's steady stream of new patents attracted attention from the local press and national industry.

The factories slowed down during the summer, as did much of Kenosha. After vacationing at nearby Lake Powers, the Welleses moved into their first real home, at 210 Deming Street, less than a block away from Rudolphsheim. But Dick Welles would always lease his homes, never purchase them outright—a cautious streak that also distinguished the young power couple from the more confident wealth of the town's early settler and ownership class. Though sixteenth in population, Kenosha was the state's third-wealthiest city in 1905, with more than a dozen individuals worth at least $300,000: one Head, one Bain, one Simmons, several Yules, and Thomas B. Jeffrey, but no Welles.

The couple often traveled to Chicago or Milwaukee to attend the theater, but just as visits from Edwin Booth and Helena Modjeska brightened life in the small town of *The Magnificent Ambersons*, many shows came to the Rhode Opera House, a short walk from the Welles home. The prestigious Rhode showcased everything from Shakespeare productions featuring John Griffith (who began his career with Edwin Booth) to popular spectacles such as "The World's Greatest Seeress," Madame Gertrude, a blindfolded mind-reader who divined messages in slips of paper passed to her onstage. Dick Welles's friends Drury Underwood, John McCutcheon, and George Ade all moonlighted as playwrights, and Ade's stage comedies, set in a bucolic Midwest, were especially popular at the Rhode. The Welleses entertained the newspapermen and other Chicago friends whenever they visited Kenosha.

On Labor Day weekend 1904, the Welleses attended a production of Richard Carle's Texas comic opera *Tenderfoot*, typical of the light-hearted entertainments that dominated the Rhode's calendar. When the electric lights burned out during the second act, Carle, an all-around entertainer in the mode of George M. Cohan, improvised with jokes and songs until they were repaired. Dick and Beatrice Welles enjoyed making their way backstage, often greeting the performers once in Chicago and then again when their tours stopped in Kenosha. The Welleses befriended Carle, hosted him for dinner, and saw him frequently on their trips to New York. (Though it was dropped from the final cut, their friendship was referred to in the *Citizen Kane* script: when Kane makes Jed Leland the *Inquirer's* new drama critic, his first assignment is reviewing *Spring Chicken*, an actual 1906 Broadway play starring Carle.)

In September 1904, the Welleses spent a week at the Saint Louis Exposition, subtly advertising their politics by telling the Kenosha newspaper that they had lingered at Wisconsin's impressive public education exhibit, organized by former Kenosha High teacher Mary D. Bradford, now on the staff of the Normal School at Stevens Point. In the November elections, Welles voted for the most progressive candidates: Theodore Roosevelt for president and Robert M. La Follette for governor of Wisconsin. Kenosha County went heavily for Roosevelt and La Follette, and each won his race. The Welleses lived in the Second Ward, along the edge of the Third, the county's most liberal district. The statutes permitted women to vote only for school board representatives, but the Kenosha newspaper reported a scant turnout among the eligible female electorate, claiming that they "show little interest in voting." Not true of Beatrice, who voted in the school board race and declared that one day she intended to vote for president too.

At Christmastime the couple enjoyed the performance of ex-pugilist James J. Corbett touring in the melodrama *Pals* and celebrated Christmas Eve at the Unitarian Church, where Beatrice had taken charge of the choir and music for increasingly thronged religious services.

Their first full year in Kenosha was a decidedly happy one, and by early March 1905 Dick Welles was telling relatives that his wife was pregnant. On March 20 the couple headed to Chicago for the opening night of the Metropolitan Grand Opera season, with Enrico Caruso making his debut in the city as Edgardo in Donizetti's *Lucia di Lammermoor* at the Auditorium. After the performance they attended a party for Caruso and initiated a friendship with the celebrated tenor. Caruso, a notorious masher, was not immune to Beatrice's beauty, and in time he would hear her play the piano, admiring her musicianship. Caruso never sang in Kenosha, but whenever he appeared in Milwaukee or Chicago, or if Beatrice happened to be in New York when he was performing, she was in the audience. Later, when Orson's mother returned to living in Chicago, Caruso faithfully attended her soirees when he was in the city.

"[Caruso] used to be in the house a lot before I was born and when I was a baby," her son Orson Welles remembered decades later. "There's a cartoon he made of my mother at the piano. He was a very good cartoonist."

Business was good at Badger Brass. Solar brand acetylene lamps were selling widely now in England and Europe, and before long sales of Welles's automobile variant overtook the original bicycle lamp. By late 1904, Badger Brass, with more than one hundred workers, had the seventh-largest payroll in Kenosha. In early 1905 the company moved into a new, larger plant on Lyman Avenue, touted in advertising and publicity as the "largest lamp making plant in the United States." Dick Welles rushed to New York to organize an East Coast branch with a long-term lease on two floors of the Iron Age Building, at the corner of Twenty-Fifth Street and Eleventh Avenue.

After another protracted business trip east that fall, Welles had only just returned to Kenosha when, on October 7, 1905, Beatrice gave birth to a boy. The baby was christened Richard Ives Welles, his first and middle names a nod to his father and mother.

CHAPTER 2

1905–1915

"Mythically Wonderful" Parents

Though some books have portrayed her as a sophisticate trapped in a suffocating hamlet, Beatrice Welles, not quite twenty-one when she married Dick Welles, thrived in Kenosha, at least at first. Although she arrived as an outsider, she did not lack confidence or charm, and she swiftly found her foothold in the community. In particular, she found a home at the Unitarian Church, where her mother-in-law, Mary Gottfredsen, sat on the board; and at the Woman's Club—two organizations that were every bit as important to Kenosha as Badger Brass.

The Unitarians were one of the first churches to ordain women, and their congregation in Kenosha was presided over by the young and charismatic Reverend Florence Buck. A highly intelligent and cultured speaker, Florence Buck gave public lectures on artistic and scientific topics, and was an outspoken activist for causes that included public education and feminism. Beatrice stepped up her involvement with the Unitarian Church in the year after her first son's birth, growing close to Buck and Buck's associate, Reverend Marion Murdoch. The two Unitarian ministers were so deeply attached in public and private that they were widely presumed to be lesbian lovers.

By Christmas 1906, with little Richard now a year old, Beatrice was ready to make her theatrical debut in Kenosha. The Unitarians were leaving their house of worship—the church building in Kenosha, dedicated in 1867—for a new structure that was in the early stages of construction, and Florence Buck was planning a benefit to raise money for the furnishings. The benefit would feature a dramatic recital of Charles Kingsley's historical novel *Hypatia; or, New Foes with an Old Face*, set in Roman Egypt, and Beatrice Welles would direct the church and clubwomen in a series of tableaux corresponding to Buck's recitation—a style of dramatic presentation that was in vogue at the turn of the twentieth century, based on the techniques, developed by François Delsarte, that Beatrice had studied at the Chicago Conservatory. Mrs. Z. G. Simmons, wife of the head of Simmons Manufacturing and president of the Woman's Club, agreed to portray Hypatia, the fifth-century astronomer, mathematician, and philosopher. Besides directing, Beatrice would play Pelagia, a beautiful woman who lives as a hermit to atone for her sins.

The Kenosha wellborn packed the large Guild Hall auditorium, paying fifty cents a ticket to hear Florence Buck narrate as Beatrice Welles and other costumed society women assumed dignified poses "illustrating the most dramatic points of the story," reported the *Kenosha News*. The resulting spectacle was "one of the most novel and artistic ever enjoyed" in the city.

Over at Badger Brass, however, clouds darkened the horizon. Almost as soon as it was founded, the company ran into friction from labor activists. After some early skirmishes with workers who wanted improved wages and conditions, the management, under Welles's enlightened leadership, shrewdly recognized a union shop affiliated with the International Metal Workers Union.

The early twentieth century was a period of tremendous growth and transformation in Kenosha. The city's earliest settlers had come mainly from New England and New York. When the population exploded, immigrants from Ireland, Germany, and Scandinavia took the skilled positions in city industry, and a later wave, primarily from Italy or eastern Europe, claimed the remaining jobs, largely unskilled. At Badger Brass the skilled metal polishers, buffers, and molders drew better pay and had better working conditions than the less skilled solderers, screw machine hands, press room riveters, and drillers—and this disparity became a sore point for the union.

Like many American cities, Kenosha proved a hotbed of labor agitation in the early years of the century. Unrest dogged all the major factories: Simmons Manufacturing (bedroom furniture), Chicago-Kenosha Hosiery (stockings), and N. R. Allen's Sons (leather goods). But the city's brass- and metalworkers were the most comprehensively organized, with thousands of members employed by the Jeffery Company, Chicago Brass, Bain Wagon, and Badger Brass. Thanks to its progressive history with the union, Badger Brass stood out as a bellwether for potential union action, and flare-ups there spread fast to the other brass and metal workshops.

As the company grew, with record earnings again reported in 1906, the union became balky. The less skilled laborers, who worked ten hours but were paid for nine (their wages averaged $2.10 a day), were always the most militant faction and perhaps the largest, but they were constantly outflanked in negotiations by buffers, lamp makers, and other groups that regularly exacted concessions from the company. When Badger Brass union officials reached out to the international organization, the leadership dispatched operatives from Cincinnati and Chicago to rally union solidarity and stage a walkout for uniform higher pay and shorter hours. The advances they sought would set a new national standard for the brass and metal industry.

The trouble came to a head in February 1907. The militant unskilled workers walked out in a job action, sympathetic lamp makers and buffers joined the incipient strike, and soon the Badger Brass factory found itself at a standstill. Dick Welles spoke publicly on behalf of management and represented the company in round-the-clock talks with the strike committee at the downtown Hotel Eichelman. George A. Yule was never very far away from the action, but despite his otherwise liberal politics, he did not care for ultimatums—or unions, for that matter.

Sitting across from Dick Welles and other Badger Brass executives, the brass and metal unionists demanded ten hours' compensation for a nine-hour day, for all employees. Welles stood his ground, insisting that Badger Brass would not tamper with a contract that was still in force until the fall, but offered a temporary and voluntary nine-hour day for nine hours' wages, covering most but not all workers. (Some would still be obliged to work ten hours, while earning only nine hours' pay.) That winter, as it turned out, the union had no appetite for a long work stoppage; within a week the union rescinded the walkout, and the strikers were all hired back.

Still, resentment simmered until the union contract came up for its annual renewal in the fall of 1907. The international had spent the intervening months quietly importing hardened partisans to Kenosha and slipping them onto the Badger Brass rolls. The company suspected as much and anticipated a showdown. Presented with fresh union demands for reduced hours with higher pay, the company again refused to budge, and this time management announced that the weak economy was forcing the company to revert to the ten-hour workday for nine hours' pay in most departments and job classifications. All but sixty of the three hundred Badger Brass workers marched out of the factory in September, with the rest following soon thereafter.

This time, Badger Brass showed an iron fist. The company denounced the outside "agitators and disturbers" who had flooded into Kenosha to stir up discontent. Badger Brass was the largest unionized lamp factory in the United States, the company insisted in press statements, and it offered higher salaries and better working conditions than any other similar-size firm. Decent-minded Kenosha laborers were being led astray by outside ideological "fanatics."

With another Yule—George's younger brother William—stepping in as the obdurate public spokesman for the company, management drew the line, declaring Badger Brass an open shop from then on. Strikers and picketers who were found missing from their jobs would be discharged and not hired back. Moreover, if the strike persisted, the Yules threatened grimly, the Kenosha factory would be shut down and all manufacturing moved to the New York branch.

Thousands of workers from every factory in Kenosha attended mass rallies for the Badger Brass union, held at the same Rhode Opera House where the Welleses had spent so many evenings of carefree entertainment. National union executives and state labor officials visited Kenosha, trying to mediate a compromise acceptable to both sides, but Badger Brass refused to yield. The strike dragged on for two months, and the city's other factory owners sided with Badger Brass, slashing payrolls and cutting hours across Kenosha.

In mid-November, the metal and brass union began to knuckle

under. Owing to the "unsettled conditions of business," union leaders announced, the membership was willing to return under the same wages and conditions that had prevailed before the strike. Company officials flatly rejected this peace offer, announcing that Badger Brass had already transferred all its automobile lamp manufacture to New York. Going forward, only the increasingly secondary bicycle lamps would be made in Kenosha—"by machines and girls," as William Yule declared contemptuously.

A few dozen men quickly accepted individual contracts proffered by the company and returned to work at the embattled factory, inflaming the strikers who were still picketing. A judge issued an injunction against known militants, who tossed the court papers into the trash in front of reporters.

The union radicals were persistently harassed by police and company operatives, and violence flared on both sides. There were many scuffles on the picket lines, and on at least one occasion paid company detectives from Milwaukee were swarmed by an angry unionist mob, beaten into submission, and shoved aboard a train heading north to home.

Dick Welles joined the company's effort to intimidate militants. One night, the week before Thanksgiving, he and a group of friends and business partners forcibly entered the home of a hard-line unionist named Louis Kekst and dragged him off to the county jail. Kekst later filed a court complaint asserting that he'd been subjected to "physical and mental ills" throughout that night, before being charged with assaulting a deputy sheriff on the picket line. Welles's fellow vigilantes were William Yule; Charles Hall, Welles's best friend among the Badger Brass executives; Thomas B. Jeffery, recently named president of the newly organized Kenosha Manufacturers Association; and finally, Charles Pfenning, the sheriff of Kenosha. Kekst sued the five for assault and false imprisonment, claiming that they offered him "immunity and large sums of money" to fabricate testimony impugning fellow strikers.

Although industrialists often issued spurious warnings about "outside agitators," Kekst appears to have been just that. He belonged to a small band of out-of-town anarchists who had rushed to the city at the start of the Badger Brass strike, setting several small fires near the factory while hatching plans to blow up the main plant. They left evidence behind—drawings of "infernal machines" they intended to wedge into ventilator spaces in the plant. Company detectives infiltrated the anarchist conspiracy and broke it up, and Kekst's lawsuit fizzled when the troublemaker skipped town. By Christmas 1907, the war was all but over.

That Christmas was "one of the quietest holidays ever known," but also one of the unhappiest, in the deeply divided city, according to the *Kenosha News*. Negotiations at the Hotel Eichelman failed to click, and by February Badger Brass had "practically gone out of business" in Kenosha. Not until mid-March did the union men throw in the towel, saying that the remaining strikers would return to their jobs, if and when they were offered individual contracts under the new open shop agreement. But local strike leaders and known radicals were passed over in the slow rehiring process, while others returned to jobs that now paid 10 to 12 percent less than they had before the strike. The union had been destroyed.

Dick Welles had fought as hard on behalf of the company as radicals had for the union, and he became a hero to the industrialists of Kenosha and other factory owners trying to hold the line across America. The company brought its auto lamp business back from New York—it had been bluffing after all—and Badger Brass profits surged anew.

Yet Orson's father was also a leader behind the scenes as Badger Brass took steps to effect a lasting reconciliation. The company instituted unusual employee perquisites, including on-site night school for its workers and annual employee picnics and parties on holidays. And despite the ugly events of 1907, Badger Brass managed to preserve its reputation as a good place to work—one of the best in Kenosha—when it came to pay, conditions, and fringe benefits.

The public persona Beatrice Welles presented during these dramatic times was as complex as her husband's. She maintained a discreet profile as labor tensions simmered at Badger Brass through the first half of 1907, joining the Whist Club circuit and taking an increasing role in the Shubert Club. Among other speakers at the fortnightly afternoon meetings of the Woman's Club, held at the spacious Simmons Memorial Library, Beatrice attended Reverend Florence Buck's lectures on novelists Edith Wharton and Henry James and playwright George Bernard Shaw. In the winter, she and little Richard stole away for a month to Biloxi, Mississippi, on the Gulf of Mexico, and during the summer she embarked with her husband and friends on a special train from Kenosha to Highland Park, in northern Illinois, for an outdoor park presentation of one of her favorite Shakespeare plays, *A Midsummer Night's Dream*, presented by the Ben Greet Players with music by the New York Symphony. And before the worst violence of that fall at Badger Brass, the Welles family spent two weeks mingling with other Kenosha businessmen and their families at the Quarles Camp near the northern town of Mercer. The Quarleses were an influential Kenosha family, with many lawyers and politicians among their number, and the Quarles Camp was probably where the Kenosha factory owners hatched and consolidated their union-busting plans.

That fall, the Woman's Club announced its annual schedule of programs extending throughout the rest of the year and into the spring of 1908—including, for the first time, piano recitals by Beatrice Welles.

Until now, nearly four years after her arrival, Beatrice had never played the piano publicly in Kenosha. She was known to be a talented pianist, performing at dinner parties for friends, but it took the clubwomen by surprise when her first public performance in November— held in a temporary space, the Masonic Temple—filled the parlor to capacity, setting an attendance record. That afternoon, as strikers clashed with scabs and police on the picket lines just blocks away, the ladies heard Beatrice give a charming interpretation of "Six Poems After Heine" by Edward MacDowell, a contemporary American Romantic whose work she favored.

Beatrice began to assume supervision of the club's programs, arranging a diverse array of entertainment and fund-raising events. One Woman's Club benefit she booked was an appearance at Rhode Opera House by John T. McCutcheon, the Chicago newspaper artist, who was a friend of hers and her husband's. McCutcheon was feted in the Welles home. Later in one of his serials McCutcheon would create a character named "Richard Wellborne, alias Dick Wells," whose disguise as a slovenly chauffeur with mechanical expertise concealed his affluent breeding.

Beatrice was keenly aware of her husband's complicity in crushing the Badger Brass labor union, and in 1908 she began to expand her activities into the broader community. At first her outreach to local immigrants and workers had an air of noblesse oblige, as she sought to "uplift" the less fortunate through the arts, public education, and material aid. She arranged musical guests for occasions at the Unitarian Church; one such guest was the celebrated organist Wilhelm Middelschulte, whom she knew from the Chicago Conservatory. After performing for the congregation one Sunday, the organist returned for a church benefit, alternating with Beatrice on her concert grand piano. Beatrice saw to it that tickets were rationed for visitors from Chicago and Kenosha Woman's Club members who were not Unitarians.

The Chicago organist may have been the headliner, but "the greatest interest of the evening," reported the *Kenosha News*, "centered on the piano solos by Mrs. Welles, which for brilliance of execution, perfection of memorizing and distinction of interpretation, could not have been surpassed." Beatrice played a gigue by Bach, nocturnes by Chopin, a polonaise, and the *Bal d'Enfants* after thunderous applause demanded an encore. A few days later, she reprised her program, this time free of charge, for anyone who wished to attend, regardless of religious affiliation or social standing. Taking place at the same time as the looming defeat of the Badger Brass union, it was a distinctly public-spirited gesture.

Also early in 1908, Beatrice helped to found a church activist group called the Woman's Alliance to extend aid to the city's poor. Its first goal was establishing a Progressive Club, offering beneficial training in domestic skills—sewing, cooking, millinery, and physical culture—for young "working girls" mired in factory jobs. "There will be no consideration of nationality or religious affiliation in carrying out the club work," the Woman's Alliance declared, marking a departure from the exclusive nature of the older, more staid Woman's Club.

In contrast to the elite Woman's Club, the Unitarian Church, with Florence Buck and Marion Murdoch as its ministers and Beatrice

Welles as their chief lieutenant, extended its welcome to all Kenosha citizens regardless of sex, race, ethnicity, or class. The church launched regular rummage sales to benefit the city's impoverished, and congregants hosted Friday night fish suppers for financially struggling parents and children. These suppers often included entertainment, with Beatrice in charge of the programs, frequently highlighted by her own piano recitals.

The membership of the Woman's Club and the Unitarian Church overlapped. Yet owing in large part to Beatrice Welles's growing activism, increasingly sharp distinctions began to divide the two groups of women, along ideological as well as generational lines.

The Woman's Club, led by the early settler families of Kenosha, the wives of the ruling class, prided itself on lofty lectures and artistic presentations. So did the Unitarian Church, which hosted similar recitals, travel lectures, and talks on art and poetry and music. Under Reverend Florence Buck, however, the Kenosha Unitarians increasingly adopted the view that poverty was immoral; that child labor and abuse, tuberculosis, and consumption were among the social ills disproportionately suffered by the underprivileged in society. From the pulpit, Florence Buck was quite capable of linking the teachings of the Bible to a stern critique of U.S. militarism abroad, and of adding her own reflections to the ideas of urban muckraker Jacob Riis; after Riis spoke in Kenosha, for example, she gave a Sunday sermon on "The Struggle of a Working Girl." For many Kenosha Unitarians, their religious credo of joining their faith to action evolved naturally into a progressive political philosophy.

Although the Woman's Club was more conservative-minded, its members did align with the Unitarian Church on many community issues touching on children, family, or education. When Beatrice Welles and the Woman's Alliance launched a drive to raise money for new playgrounds for the city's less prosperous neighborhoods, for instance, the older clubwomen took up the cause alongside younger Unitarians. Together the two women's groups pursued initiatives to stamp out child neglect, upgrade school buildings, and improve city beaches. The Club and the Alliance cohosted the opening-day ceremony for a new bathhouse at Washington Island, ferrying hundreds of children to the island, with peanuts and candy for every child.

The older clubwomen and younger Unitarians also found a common adversary in longtime Kenosha mayor Matthias J. Scholey, a Democrat who stubbornly opposed additional government funding for public education. Mayor Scholey vowed to veto any legislation that authorized financing for new school buildings, the rebuilding of old ones, or the repairing of rural schools—often the most inadequate, with pupils of all ages herded together in small rooms. Scholey also opposed adding nurses to school staffs, decrying the extra costs, and he regarded the notion of sending four-year-olds to kindergarten as experimental foolery wafted in from Chicago like the stench of sewage. (At the time, public school was not required for city children under seven.)

Scholey also scorned the idea of open-air schools, another of Beatrice's pet causes. An avid hiker, swimmer, and physical culture enthusiast, Orson's mother was in the forefront of the local open-air campaign, which had roots in England but was spreading fast across the United States. Open-air enthusiasts believed that physically weak or sickly children from the poorest families would benefit from special public schools with open windows and outdoor classes. The daily schedule would incorporate fresh air and sunshine, periods of physical activity and rest, and a nutritious diet. Beatrice coaxed many Unitarians and some Woman's Club members into signing petitions and holding fund-raisers for open-air education.

Mayor Scholey's intransigence on public education gave a special urgency to the city's biennial school board elections, which were always heavily contested. Women still did not enjoy full suffrage in Wisconsin, but as mothers they were granted the right to vote for school board commissioners in Kenosha and elsewhere. In 1909, a new state law was adopted, for the first time also allowing women to run for office as members of local school boards. Beatrice Welles and her friends in both the Unitarian Church and the Woman's Club, young and older mothers alike, set their sights on electing one of their own to the Kenosha school board.

Five years before the birth of Orson Welles, a number of leading characters in his parents' early Kenosha years exited the stage, supplanted by new dramatis personae who would play important roles in the years ahead.

To general dismay, Reverend Florence Buck announced that she was taking a yearlong leave of absence, relocating to southern California to help care for her partner, Reverend Marion Murdoch, who was seriously ill. Florence Buck's last public lecture addressed the subject of Halley's comet, which was soon to reappear, as it does about once every seventy-five years. As usual, during the lecture, she employed a stereopticon—or "magic lantern"—to project photographic slides. Beatrice outdid herself rehearsing the choir for Florence Buck's final church service, a performance of the cantata *Faith and Praise* by Chicago composer John A. West. Beatrice conducted the choir, with fourteen interweaving voices accompanied by an organist and by herself at the piano, for an audience of hundreds of parishioners and out-of-town guests.

Florence Buck would return to Kenosha now and then, but always fleetingly, and she never resumed her ministry there. Yet Beatrice and others in the congregation never forgot her—and Buck and Marion Murdoch never forgot their favorite parishioner. They kept in touch, and Murdoch dedicated a poem to "B.I.W." in her slender volume of published poetry, *The Hermit Thrush.* "White Butterflies" recalled how Beatrice's music transported hearts to a higher dimension:

O art, that in her touch o'erwhelms,
What witchery can be,
To lend release from lower realms,
And set the spirit free

Florence Buck was replaced by the renowned Reverend Rowena Morse, a graduate of the University of Chicago Divinity School. Rowena Morse was every bit the activist that her predecessor was, and during her tenure the meetings of the Woman's Alliance featured presentations on the persecution of Jews in Russia and on the socialist ideas of the German philosopher Ferdinand Lassalle. But Morse left Kenosha after a year, and though the local Unitarians scrambled for another pastor, the position stayed vacant for months on end.

In the same month that Florence Buck departed, Mary D. Bradford arrived to lead the Kenosha public schools. Many of the older women knew Mary Bradford from their youth—she was a graduate of Kenosha High School, and later taught there—and she had since earned a national reputation as an educator. When the position of school superintendent opened up in Kenosha, she announced that she was willing to leave her job as a state kindergarten specialist for Wisconsin's normal schools if the school board would make her the city's first female head of public education, following a precedent recently set in Chicago.

The Kenosha school board decided unanimously to offer Bradford a three-year contract, doing away with the customary one-year term. She took a house on Park Avenue in the Library Park district, on the same street and block where the Welles family would move a year or two later. For Beatrice Welles, the void left by Florence Buck's departure would be filled by Mary Bradford's friendship, while the flux within the church would consolidate her own role as the leader of the Woman's Alliance.

As summers usually did in Kenosha, the summer of 1910 brought heavy storms. The high winds and torrential rains caused widespread crop damage and flattened fences and trees. When nature cooperated, Dick and Beatrice Welles took the steamboat to Milwaukee, rode special trains to the pastoral lakes in the countryside surrounding Kenosha, and visited Chicago to see Beatrice's parents and enjoy the shows. They were among the thousands of Kenoshans drawn to the annual Old Settlers' Picnic at Paddock Lake, with lectures, games, music, and basket dinners at noon. Each year, sadly, the number of actual old settlers decreased.

The highlight of that summer was the four-day Home Talent Spectacle, an elaborate benefit for the Kenosha YMCA that Beatrice Welles staged at the Rhode Opera House in the last week of June. The show involved hundreds of local singers, dancers, and musicians performing their specialties against a series of posed and pantomimed tableaux. Besides helping to organize and stage the extravaganza, Orson's mother played pieces on the piano and even sang "You're Just the Girl I'm Looking For," the hit of the 1906 Shubert light opera *The Social Whirl*. While her personal tastes were more sophisticated, Beatrice showed a good-humored willingness to try anything to entertain people, laughing at herself if she stumbled. In the final patriotic offering, "Pageant of the Nations," she even posed as the Goddess of Liberty.

July Fourth was always busy. In the morning the Welles family motored to Racine for the annual parade by veterans of the Spanish-American War. Part of the afternoon was spent at the races for trotters and pacers at the Bain racetrack. The family stopped by the Caledonian Society cricket matches, where the Yules figured prominently, and, like many Library Park families, they ended Independence Day with dinner and dancing at the Kenosha Country Club.

On Labor Day, Kenosha held a downtown parade with floats and a thousand marchers, the streets lined with cheering citizens. The city's brass workers were always the highlight of the procession, garbed in white duck suits and carrying brass canes, with the female lacquerers wearing white dresses. The following weekend, Badger Brass sponsored a separate field day for its employees, one of the company's gestures after the strike. Workers and their families rode by rail to Silver Lake for the all-day company picnic, with games, prizes, music, dinner, and moonlight dancing. By now Badger Brass employed six hundred workers, Solar lamp orders continued to rise, and Dick Welles helped tally the profits.

At the last important meeting of the summer, Beatrice Welles ascended to the office of vice president of the Woman's Club. And, when its fall-winter schedule for 1910–1911 was unveiled, the new vice president dominated the programming, contributing not just her piano performances to the listed events but the first fully staged play the club had attempted.

Ambitiously slated for the Rhode Opera House, *Seven-Twenty-Eight; or, Casting the Boomerang* was Augustin Daly's adaptation of a German sex farce, first successfully produced in New York in 1883. The original stage show had featured Mrs. G. H. Gilbert, a specialist in playing grandes dames, in the role of Mrs. Bargiss, who entertains grandiose ambitions for her husband, an unproductive poet. Now, showing a surprising taste for age makeup and ribald comedy, the much-younger Beatrice Welles undertook the Mrs. Gilbert role in the club's ambitious production.

Although the play was nominally staged by a local schoolteacher, *Seven-Twenty-Eight* was entirely the brainchild of Beatrice Welles, and she was its driving force. And the show proved a triumph with audiences, although some clubwomen found it frivolous and risqué. Afterward Beatrice announced that *Seven-Twenty-Eight* was merely the first theatrical offering of a new Kenosha dramatics organization that would be permanently supported by the Woman's Club.

That year, the Welles family had an early Christmas Eve dinner at home. Later, Dick and Beatrice went to Guild Hall for a high-society party with refreshments and musicians imported from Chicago. After midnight services at the Unitarian Church, the couple returned home to little Richard, each opening one Christmas present before bed. On New Year's Day the family departed for a much-needed getaway, motoring first to the annual automobile show in New York City, then going south for a sightseeing trip that included a foray to the West Indies.

The Welleses had not yet returned to Kenosha by the day, in early 1911, when another important new character in the backstory arrived in the city.

This was Dr. Maurice Abraham Bernstein. Although his birth date varies in records, Bernstein was born, probably in 1883, in the town of Pereyaslav in Ukraine. The eldest of four, Bernstein emigrated with his parents to Chicago when he was a child. He was awarded high school equivalency credentials by the Lewis Institute, a junior college in Chicago; he was naturalized as a citizen in 1906; and two years later he graduated from Northwestern University medical school. In the three years after his graduation, the young physician worked for the Chicago department of health, the Cook County Institution for Nervous and Mental Diseases, and the Dunning Hospital for the Insane.

At twenty-eight, Dr. Bernstein was the same age as Beatrice Welles, and roughly the same height though wirier than her husband, Dick— in *Citizen Kane*, the character to whom the doctor lent his name is described as "an undersized Jew," in the words of the script, "spry, with remarkably intense eyes." Bernstein's gray eyes, framed by thin spectacles, were indeed penetrating. He had an oval face, a square chin, an imposing straight nose, and short brown hair combed straight back from his forehead. The doctor may have known Dick and Beatrice Welles before coming to Kenosha; they could have met at music recitals or cultural events in Chicago. A lover of the arts, Bernstein especially cherished opera and classical music, and was an amateur cellist.

Bernstein was a young, modern doctor, without affiliation to Hahnemann Hospital and with no homeopathic orientation. Kenosha struck him as a place of opportunity where Jewish people were welcome—the Jewish community had a local foothold downtown—and more doctors were needed. Since obtaining his medical degree Dr. Bernstein had occupied only lowly institutional offices, and despite his genuinely charitable impulses toward the arts, or perhaps because of them, he was not a prosperous man. Bernstein thought he could forge a better living with his own practice. Kenosha offered him that independence, within the context of a fast-growing population.

Bernstein found modest office space above a saloon at the corner of Main and Market. By May 1 his name was appearing in Kenosha newspapers—he was quite good at getting his name in the paper—as the city's newest doctor. He advertised a specialty in orthopedic surgery—"deformity cases"—and expertise in mental diseases. The new physician declared his politics as liberal Republican, and was reported to favor a health crusade to remove children's tonsils as a guard against rheumatic diseases—another sign of his affinity with Beatrice Welles.

No sooner had the doctor arrived, however, than he departed. After a mere two months in Kenosha, Bernstein was unexpectedly offered the job of senior physician of the Cook County infirmary in Oak Forest, Illinois, a complex that also housed the Dunning Hospital for the Insane. Dr. Bernstein left for Oak Forest at once, according to press accounts, pledging to check up on his new Kenosha patients on weekends.

And no sooner had he departed than he returned. According to the *Kenosha News* and several Chicago newspapers, Bernstein resigned from the Cook County infirmary after only two months, following a heated exchange of malpractice charges and countercharges, and a physical altercation with Peter Bartzen, nominally his boss, president of the Cook County board.

According to Bernstein, after arriving in Oak Forest he had discovered "gross incompetency" at the Cook County Infirmary in the form of an entrenched staff doctor whose improper administering of anesthesia had caused the death of at least one patient. Bernstein's accusation stirred up the medical establishment and prompted a coroner's inquiry, but the investigation exonerated the staff doctor. According to Bartzen, the real problem was Bernstein, who he claimed had "left a piece of sponge in a patient after an operation." Bernstein struck back by publicly calling the county board president a liar.

What happened next was one of the colorful and improbable incidents that seemed to dog Maurice Bernstein throughout his life. Bartzen was on his way to the Oak Forest clinic to fire Bernstein when they bumped into each other at the train depot. Bartzen, incensed at having been called a liar, according to his own account, marched up to Dr. Bernstein and struck him on the jaw, then followed up with a quick kick. "When I went to hit him again he jumped on the train which was moving out." Bernstein scoffed at this version of events, giving the local press a statement full of his characteristically flowery language. When "this vitriolic Czar of the Cook County Board descended upon me like a modern Mars with flaming nostrils and language that would have put a dock walloper to blush," demanding to know "why I had presumed to find fault with his friends," Bernstein said he was "obliged to administer to him a sound and much-deserved chastisement."

The unapologetic Bernstein claimed that he, not Bartzen, won the "Battle of the Train Depot." Furthermore, Bernstein insisted that he'd resigned his Cook County position "*before* our little one-sided combat and not *after*, as [Bartzen] would have the public believe."

Both men filed defamation lawsuits, and the brouhaha was settled and hushed up by lawyers. While the facts are indeterminate, the anecdote captures something about the man who became Orson Welles's guardian after the death of his parents. Some who knew him believed that the formidable doctor was fundamentally a man of probity; others saw Dr. Bernstein as a slippery human sphinx. He was a man of thought who could also be, for better and worse, a man of decisive action. He was a sophisticated man of ideas who could also be a bumbler and a buttinski. He was a Dickensian character of many odd and discrepant parts.

By August 2, restored to Kenosha, Dr. Bernstein was summoned by Beatrice Welles to tend to five-year-old Richard, who had broken his arm "while playing in the door yard of the Welles home on Pleasant Street," according to newspaper accounts. Beatrice was already worried that her little boy might be a tad accident-prone. And, from that summer day forward, Dr. Bernstein became an unofficial member of the Welles family, a close friend and deep admirer of Beatrice especially, but also friendly with her husband, Dick, and fatherly to their children. No one could have predicted how much the new Kenosha physician's first house call to the Welleses would bring him inside the family and call on his expertise in both surgery and mental illness.

Young female artists and activists dominated Beatrice Welles's circle of friends. Many were single working teachers—school board policy mandated that teachers be unmarried. Among her closest friends were the city's most dedicated suffragists, who wanted voting rights for women for all offices.

These young progressive women increasingly diverged from the older guard of the Woman's Club, who never warmed to the suffrage movement. Many of the older women felt threatened by their younger peers' community activism, and in some cases by their personalities.

Among other things, the old guard believed that the activists and suffragists—even those who sprang from settler bloodlines—could not be counted on to stay in Kenosha. Among Beatrice's friends was Harriet Bain, who was a niece of Bain Wagon Works' founder Edward Bain and also a staunch feminist. A talented artist, Harriet taught at the private Kemper School for Girls, and gave stereopticon lectures on the Italian Renaissance at the Woman's Club; she frequently mused aloud about one day leaving Kenosha for Europe to study painting.

Another of Beatrice's activist friends was Charlotte Hannahs Jordan, the daughter of the founder of Hannahs Manufacturing, a purveyor of furniture and wood products in Kenosha. Lottie Jordan was married to Edward S. Jordan, a Rambler executive who had plans to form his own car company. The Jordans had lived in Cleveland for a time, and they often talked about how much they missed the larger city. They had conducted an investigation of tenement and sweatshop conditions in Cleveland, and in Kenosha, Lottie led discussion groups exploring the pioneering 1904 book *Poverty* by the socialist Robert Hunter, who was involved in the settlement house movement.

A third associate of Beatrice Welles's was Ray Elizabeth Needham, who was born in Colorado but raised in Ripon, Wisconsin. Tall, blond, and soignée, Ray Elizabeth Needham plunged into every community issue, but above all she was a suffragist. She met her husband at the University of Wisconsin in Madison before she transferred to Smith College. Her husband, Maurice, was an ad man for the Jeffery and Nash motor companies in Kenosha, but he had his sights set on running his own ad agency in Chicago. Everyone knew that Harriet Bain, Lottie Jordan, and the Needhams would move away from Kenosha one day.

The Woman's Club stalwarts resisted engagement with the grittier realities in Kenosha, and friction between the factions led Beatrice Welles and her friends to mount a brazen challenge to the entrenched leadership in May 1911. Just after finishing her term as vice president—"in a very acceptable manner," said the *Kenosha News*—Beatrice confronted the club with an alternative slate of officers, challenging the ticket approved by the formal nominating committee.

"The insurgents," as Beatrice's slate was dubbed locally, offered candidates for all available offices—including Beatrice herself, running for president against a Kenosha dowager, Caroline Rowe. By narrow margins, however, the establishment regulars won all the club races. Beatrice hurried to proclaim her loyalty to the victors, but the older women had been deeply and permanently affronted. The division in the Woman's Club, which had festered quietly over the past few years, now became an open rift. The Woman's Club always went dark over the summer, but when the next season's programming was announced, Beatrice Welles's presence was pointedly diminished. She tried to maintain cordial relations with the older clubwomen, but they were wary of her now, regarding her as too self-righteous, radical, and avant-garde.

For her part, Orson's mother started shifting her time and energy to the burgeoning suffragist movement, taking a lead in forming a Kenosha branch of the National Political Equality League.

On October 6, 1911, Beatrice Welles's father, Benjamin Ives, died at his home in Chicago. He was sixty-one years old. After his years of financial troubles, and the months he had spent enduring "a complication of diseases," according to newspapers, his death was a mercy. After a Chicago funeral, his remains were interred in a family plot arranged by the Welleses in Kenosha's Green Ridge Cemetery, close to downtown. His widow, Lucy, then moved to Kenosha to live with her daughter's family. Beatrice employed a nanny, but now her mother would be on hand to help with six-year-old Richard, who was just entering school. Lucy Ives, who had visited Kenosha often, was befriended by members of the Woman's Club in her age bracket—helping to bridge the divide between young and old.

Another woman who bridged all the blocs in Kenosha was the school superintendent, Mary Bradford. Although she was a community activist and suffragist to rival any of the "insurgents," she was also matronly and a contemporary of the older clubwomen, and she had a diplomatic touch that served her causes well. Her foremost interest was in local education reform, a concern she shared with Beatrice Welles. Both were proponents of publicly funded kindergartens for children starting at age four. Both were in favor of open-air schools. Both called for more truant officers and for stricter enforcement of laws that stipulated compulsory education from ages seven to fourteen. Both advocated "special classes" for delinquent, handicapped, and foreign-born children. Both supported retirement funds for teachers, and annual examinations of children by qualified physicians. Both sought public and private moneys to ensure adequate food and clothing for schoolchildren.

Mary Bradford brought an air of respectability to the issues she embraced, and hers was one of the few voices that tended to unite the local women. Indeed, she seemed as popular with most Kenosha men as with the women, and larger Wisconsin cities repeatedly tried to lure her away with lucrative offers, which she invariably declined. In November 1911, Bradford was elected president of the Wisconsin State Teachers Association.

Mary Bradford, Beatrice Welles, and their circle of feminists looked ahead to the spring 1912 municipal elections. The two-term Democratic incumbent, Matthias J. Scholey, still a stubborn opponent of school improvements, was vulnerable, having served the past two years simultaneously as a state legislator. His liberal Republican challenger, lumberman Dan O. Head, embraced educational reform, improved public works, regular tax levies, and honest government, along with opposition to "bad houses, wine rooms, and evil dance halls." The well-liked Head was another relative of Dick Welles's: the nephew of the banker Welles had sued for the inheritance that helped seed the founding of Badger Brass.

Beatrice and Kenosha's nascent branch of the National Political Equality League handed out hundreds of flyers and posters crying, "Women, You Must Vote for the Sake of Your Children." On election night in April, Scholey's forces were annihilated as Head clinched the mayoralty by a huge margin. A cheering crowd formed downtown, and local women headed up a parade that marched through the streets, shooting off fireworks.

The other election results, however, were discouraging for the sisterhood. Only 169 of an estimated 1,000 eligible women bothered to vote, and the school board results—all the winners were men, the majority of them illiberal—reflected weak support for the feminist agenda. The largest number of women voters in any Kenosha neighborhood, forty, showed up in the Third Ward, near the Welles's home.

In the wake of the disappointing results, Beatrice, Mary Bradford, and Harriet Bain held many soul-searching conversations about how the movement should respond. The Kenosha Political Equality League announced a summer-long campaign to raise the political consciousness of local women and men, and to prepare for a suffrage referendum to coincide with the statewide fall 1912 election. A bitter debate was raging in the Wisconsin legislature over a proposed bill endorsing women's suffrage, and as a compromise a state referendum on female enfranchisement had been added to the ballot in the fall. Beatrice and her fellow suffragists fought hard to promote the referendum, donning yellow ribbons emblazoned with "Vote for Women" and giving speeches at county fairs and picnics. Reverend Florence Buck returned to the city to give an address on the subject, and national activists such as Inez Milholland from New York and Jane Addams from Chicago's Hull House headlined right-to-vote rallies.

Beatrice introduced Addams to a jammed fund-raiser at Rhode Opera House, where the pioneering settlement house worker and social activist described suffrage as the solution to "deplorable social conditions" in every dark corner of American society. "Those departments of city government which are most badly administered are nearest to the woman in the home," Addams told the Kenoshans, "and only by exercising the privilege of the ballot will she be able to exert influence necessary to take those departments out of the hands of politicians."

The Kenosha Political Equality League sponsored a full-page advertisement in the main city newspaper on the day before the referendum, invoking Abraham Lincoln and motherhood and explaining "The Reasons for Voting Yes on Women Suffrage." The advertisement included six hundred women's signatures, with the name Beatrice Welles conspicuously third on the list.

But many of the older Kenosha women were just as conspicuously absent from the petition, and the gulf between suffragists and anti-suffragists continued to widen. The battle over suffrage tore families apart, even separating some wives from their husbands. The older clubwomen urged Kenosha women to restrict themselves to family and education, warning that too much activism outside the home meant neglecting a woman's duties inside the home. An "Anti-Suffragette" letter signed by older members of the Woman's Club appeared on the front page of the *Kenosha News*, suggesting that the lack of significant progress on education issues—public playgrounds, early kindergarten, and clubhouses for the poor—could be blamed on the fact that activists had poured time, money, and energy into the all-consuming suffragist movement.

The 1912 election brought statewide defeat for the suffrage referendum. But while the referendum also lost by 1,809 to 1,338 in Kenosha proper, real progress had been made. The measure had received strong support in the Third Ward, for example, and the overall high number of votes cast in its favor throughout the city attested to the growing legitimacy of the movement. Mary Bradford, who worked hand in glove with the suffragists but escaped the opprobrium heaped on the younger generation, announced that the Kenosha Political Equality League would continue to agitate until women were fully enfranchised.

Not long thereafter, Beatrice Welles, officiating at a tea of seventy-five women at the Unitarian Church, was elected vice president, and Harriet Bain was named as president of the new permanent Kenosha County Political Equality League.

Ironically, while women could vote for the local school board, they could not vote on the suffrage referendum itself. It was crucial therefore that the Kenosha County Political Equality League attract male voters to its cause. Husbands did not always agree with the politics of their wives, and in some notable instances it was the men in Kenosha, not their wives, who waved the suffragist flag. On the day before the November 1912 election, an advertisement in the *Kenosha News* stirred controversy by listing, for the first time, thirty Kenosha men willing to declare they were in favor of suffrage. Richard H. Welles was prominently featured on the list—the only Badger Brass executive listed—along with five ministers and two doctors. Edward Jordan, husband of Lottie Jordan; F. C. Hannahs, Lottie's father; and H. B. Robinson, husband of suffragist Emma Robinson, were among the brave thirty who went public with their support.

Dick Welles kidded about the subject—he told the *Kenosha News* that his feminism predated his wife's—but he buttonholed his businessmen friends to sign petitions and contribute money to the cause. He appeared with his wife at public events promoting a wide array of progressive causes, nodding as Beatrice delivered her speeches. And when Dick Welles himself spoke up, as he occasionally did, people listened.

In 1911, Dick Welles had introduced the first jitney "auto buses" to Kenosha. To Welles this was a sideline investment but also a civic improvement, a much-needed supplement to the city's limited railway service, extending public transportation to its poor and rural areas. In his typical form, Welles promoted the jitneys by driving one of the buses around the streets of Kenosha himself.

The jitney buses quickly became unpopular among certain Library Park elements. Some complained that they whizzed around city streets unsafely, but there was another motive: The jitneys competed with the city's electric railway line. Moreover, many of the jitney drivers were socialists, opposed to railway monopolies. When the Kenosha city government proposed legislation to restrict and regulate the jitney operators, the drivers denounced the move as a step toward suppression of their profession, and hordes of angry jitney men flocked to a city council hearing to jostle with their well-heeled adversaries.

The crowd hushed when Dick Welles rose to speak at the city council hearing. Everyone knew Welles as a businessman with a heart—and as a man who had a financial interest in the jitneys, and friends among the jitneys' enemies. "He drove the jitney men from fervid cheering to groans by a really fair discussion," reported the *Kenosha News*. "He declared that the jitney bus had a right to exist and in the same breath he declared that it was the duty of the council to regulate them. He held that the jitney brought a new economic problem" to Kenosha, but "that it was helping to solve the problem of transportation in cities. He held right after this that reasonable regulation was necessary to have the jitney bus continue."

It wasn't the last time Dick Welles made himself heard at a public forum. At a mass meeting on child labor organized by his wife and Mary Bradford, Welles made a speech demanding that the federal government penalize any business that exploited underage workers in the manufacture of newly patented inventions and products. Welles, of course, was an inventor himself, and a man who was careful with money in his professional and personal life, and the crowd was impressed that his commitment to children's safety inspired him to take such a stand.

Most of the time, Dick Welles left the activism to his wife. He was preoccupied with Badger Brass, which was steadily expanding, adding employees, and logging impressive earnings. But Orson Welles's father was hardly apolitical, or reactionary, as some accounts—including Orson's own sketchy musings—have suggested. Dick Welles was especially a kindred spirit to his wife, Beatrice, in the years leading up to Orson's birth, and he was a complement to her in most ways, including her progressive political activism.

In 1914, the Kenosha activists waged another battle. Wisconsin Republicans had reintroduced the suffrage referendum for the election of November 1914, but the Republican governor, Frances E. McGovern, broke with the progressive La Follette wing of the party and vetoed a second statewide referendum on the issue. The Political Equality

League dispatched Beatrice Welles and other local feminists to the state capital, in an effort to overturn the governor's veto and reinstate the state suffrage referendum for the fall election. Beatrice whipped up a letter-writing campaign and made several trips to Madison to meet with lawmakers. She also reached out to playwright and author Zona Gale, living in the nearby town of Portage, who would become the first woman to win a Pulitzer Prize for drama, for her 1920 feminist play *Miss Lulu Bett.*

Beatrice deeply admired Gale, already a national figure in the suffrage movement, and enlisted her as, in a sense, a guardian angel of the Kenosha feminists. At the fall 1913 meeting of the Political Equality League, Beatrice gave a reading of Zona Gale's story "Extra Paper." This spoken-word recital, combining her politics with artistic expression, marked her debut as a diseuse. A short time later, Gale visited Kenosha and shared a podium with Beatrice, extolling the value of public playgrounds.

At the same time, Beatrice's pet Unitarian Church project, a Progressive Club for young working girls, came to fruition. In October, the Woman's Alliance took over a small house on Bond Street, offering the girls access to a kitchen (where they learned cooking and nutrition), living room, bathroom, and reading room with books and newspapers, as well as outdoor activities including tennis, volleyball, and hiking. Beatrice had cut back on her public music recitals in favor of social activism, but she often performed for the Girls' Progressive Club— including on Easter Sunday 1914.

The tensions between the conservative and activist factions in the Woman's Club had never really gone away, and early in 1914 they would spike. The club was preparing to send three delegates to the upcoming biennial convention of the National Federation of Women's Clubs in Chicago. Beatrice Welles and her allies asked that at least one suffragist represent their membership in Chicago, to bring the issue of enfranchisement in front of the national organization, which, like the Kenosha club, was reluctant to engage the topic. The suffragists put forth as their candidate Harriet Bain, the head of the Kenosha County Political Equality League, who had exhorted the Woman's Club to broaden its scope from art and literature to include social inequities. Harriet and Beatrice had annoyed the club's conservative members repeatedly by pointing to the Chicago Woman's Club as a model of social commitment.

When the delegates for Chicago were announced in late January, however, Beatrice and her friends were "astonished and indignant," according to newspaper accounts, to discover that all three were "dyed in the wool" anti-suffragists. When Harriet Bain's supporters demanded a roll call vote of the full membership, the president, Mrs. L. D. Grace, gaveled them down. The suffragists then called for the club, historically limited to one hundred women of standing, to open itself up to a broader, more "cosmopolitan" (i.e., egalitarian) membership, which would of course bolster their side. The chair tabled their motion. Mrs. Grace brought in a lawyer to block further appeals by the activists, and five wealthy older members resigned, signaling an irreparable breach between the "antis" and the suffragists.

Throughout Kenosha, the public standoff pitted family members and onetime friends against one another. Beatrice Welles's mother, Lucy Ives, and mother-in-law, Mary Gottfredsen, were close, and they sided reluctantly with their peers among the "antis." Other Gottfredsens, including Alice, a music teacher who helped Beatrice with the Unitarian choir and the Shubert Club, discreetly aligned themselves with the suffragists. Harriet Bain and Hazel Lance—the latter an "anti" who received an official invitation to the Chicago convention— had been chummy since their schoolgirl days at Kemper School. Although the former classmates lived within two blocks of each other in the Library Park district, they and many others in the feud would "detour to avoid meeting," as the *Chicago Tribune*, covering the ruckus, reported. Beatrice had a long amicable relationship with her downstairs neighbor, Mrs. Levi C. Graves, a former Woman's Club president, but Mrs. Graves was anti-suffrage, and their friendship too was now suspended.

The spring 1914 municipal elections became a matter of do or die for the Kenosha County Political Equality League. The activists had to gain a school board seat finally, or all their efforts would look like a fool's errand. There was only one problem: no woman would offer herself up for the public ordeal of electioneering.

Finally, Harriet Bain and Mary Bradford approached Beatrice Welles. Beatrice was reluctant: she considered herself more an artist and a charitable reformer than a political zealot, and above all she feared that running for office would limit her artistic opportunities.

Mary Bradford, who was old enough to be Beatrice's mother—but was far more of a progressive social crusader—reminded her that running for office would mean safeguarding the future for children like her own son, now eight years old. This argument touched a nerve. Beatrice and her husband worried about little Richard. He was a bright boy who enjoyed reading and music and magic tricks, but he stuttered, and he hadn't taken to school or made friends easily. Richard needed special attention—the very kind of individual treatment that was a constant issue for the school board. Beatrice was sold.

The news that Beatrice Welles had decided to throw her hat into the ring—coming just days after the Woman's Club showdown, in which her friends and supporters had been steamrollered—electrified Kenosha. The "antis" had been thrown a gauntlet, and young and old voters, female and male, poured out across the city. And the results gave Kenosha activists the victory they'd long been seeking: Beatrice Welles defeated her opponent, John I. Chester, vice president of the N. R. Allen and Sons tannery, by a vote of 293 to 189.

Though the results were tempered by a disappointment at the top of the ticket—where liberal Republican Dan O. Head had declined to run for a second term as mayor, and Democrat Matthias J. Scholey was returned to office—the headlines were all about Beatrice Welles, the first woman elected to public office in Kenosha's history. After months of fractiousness, the vast majority of the city reacted with pride and joy, and when Beatrice took her seat at the first meeting the following week, she was greeted with bouquets of flowers and a tremendous ovation from a swarm of well-wishers.

Beatrice Welles's school board victory enhanced her local celebrity. On June 1, 1914, Kenosha's only female officeholder gave her first musical performance outside woman's clubs, church events, or the privacy of her home—an "illustrated recital" at the Guild Hall, featuring the music of Schumann, Wagner, and MacDowell with stereopticon slides, to benefit the Girls' Progressive Club, her signature community project. "This is the first opportunity the Kenosha public had to enjoy one of these programs," the *Kenosha News* reported.

That month Beatrice reached another milestone, launching an activist alternative to the Woman's Club called the Kenosha City Club, composed of women "from many walks of life" who felt committed to "civic problems." The club would take up all the issues the Woman's Club had ignored: health conditions, municipal garbage, and growing poverty and inequities in the city. Convening a luncheon of friends and supporters at the downtown Hotel Borup, Beatrice invited Superintendent of Schools Mary Bradford to be the main speaker, and also gave a talk herself, emphasizing "the real need of Kenosha of a strong organization to take the right side in dealing with all great questions in the municipal life of the city." For the second meeting, Beatrice called on her friend Zona Gale to address the activist-minded group.

The emergence of the Kenosha City Club outraged the "antis," who viewed the upstart club as a rebuke of their traditional values. The exodus of suffragist members embarrassed the older clubwomen, especially when it received coverage in the Chicago papers. And now the older, more established club was forced to compete for guest speakers like Gale, Wisconsin's most famous woman. A conciliator at heart, Beatrice tried to mend fences with the Woman's Club, giving a piano performance at its last meeting before the summer. But she also threw sharp elbows, and her personality—viewed by some as self-important—made her a divisive symbol of social change among many of the older members.

For the time being, Beatrice redoubled her efforts for the cause. She and Mary Bradford organized a mass meeting marking National Suffrage Day, with Beatrice conducting the Shubert Club choir in "a song of spring" and leading the audience in a sing-along finale of "America." In June, along with Lottie Jordan, Harriet Bain, and Mary Bradford, Beatrice attended the national suffrage leaders' banquet at the Congress Hotel in Chicago.

Late in the summer, the group launched "Self-Denial Suffrage Day," in which local suffragist leaders trimmed unnecessary household expenses and donated the savings to the cause. The brainstorm of Harriet Bain, the idea was picked up nationally. In the fall, Beatrice, Mary

Bradford, Harriet Bain, and Lottie Jordan took the train to the state suffragist convention in Milwaukee, joining a peace rally at Immanuel Church and attending a special showing of a pro-suffrage moving picture, *Your Girl and Mine*, at the Butterfly Theater. *Your Girl and Mine* was coproduced by William Selig with a company run by suffragist leader Ruth Hanna McCormick, who was head of the congressional committee for the National American Woman Suffrage Association and whose husband was Robert Medill McCormick of the family that owned the *Chicago Daily Tribune*.

The Kenosha chapter of the Political Equality League was neither the largest nor the most militant of the many affiliated leagues that sprang up across Wisconsin, but in some ways it set the standard for the organization. And the leadership's family ties to the thriving industrialists of Kenosha often made it the state's most successful chapter in raising money for the cause.

Summer was always full of pleasant distractions. The circus came to town, and so did Buffalo Bill Cody and his Wild West Show, and a host of barnstorming wrestlers and magicians.

In July 1914, aviation fever swept Kenosha. Dick Welles, the man who had driven the first automobile and the first jitney bus on the city's streets, now brought the first hydro-aeroplane for three days of exhibition flights. In more than one interview, Orson Welles credited his father with having invented a peculiar air-travel machine—"a glider attached to a steam-driven engine," according to Barbara Leaming's *Orson Welles*—with a Negro servant piloting the glider into a crash landing while Dick Welles controlled a wheel from below. But the local press—diligent in covering the Welles family—never made any mention of such an invention, and the claim probably originated with that consummate fictioneer Dr. Maurice Bernstein. (Similarly, biographer Charles Higham insisted that Dick Welles had "presented young fliers at the first air show in northern Wisconsin in 1903, shortly before Orville and Wilbur Wright made their successful pioneer flight at Kitty Hawk." Again: highly dubious.)

But Dick Welles was genuinely smitten with air travel, and air shows were all the rage by 1914. That summer, on behalf of the Kenosha Retailers Association, Welles lured Chicago aviator Charles C. Witmer to the city to headline an aviation festival, intended to promote Kenosha's modern firefighting and lifesaving stations. A private pilot for Harold F. McCormick, another member of the influential Chicago family, who was International Harvester's chairman of the board, Witmer was a pioneer of aviation photography who aspired to be a filmmaker. The aviator brought with him a camera crew and a small group of performers, including Florence Smith, a stage actress well known in Chicago. Witmer planned to involve local citizens and airplane maneuvers in a moving picture comedy set in Kenosha.

The highlight of the three-day festival was a public flight by Dick and Beatrice Welles. Kenosha's "first couple" waved to a crowd as they climbed aboard a plane, piloted by Witmer, which made a ten-mile sweep out over Lake Michigan, circling around the breakwater, city lighthouse, and shore, thrilling thousands of onlookers. It was one of several scenes Witmer shot for his intended comedy, tentatively titled "Her Escape"—making Dick and Beatrice Welles the first Welleses to appear in a film. Alas, "Her Escape" was never completed, and the footage is lost today.

The fall colors were glorious, and in September the Welleses attended a performance by a touring illusionist known as the "Man of Many Mysteries" (a.k.a. Eugene Laurant, based in Chicago), whose specialties included a Chinese Linking Ring trick and something he called "chapeaugraphy," which involved manipulating a piece of felt into many hat shapes while describing the results in verse. They also saw *Twelfth Night* performed by the troupe led by Ben Greet, one of that dying breed of actor-managers who traveled the country tirelessly with their repertory players, bringing Shakespeare and other classical works of the theater to outposts like Kenosha. The Welles children would grow up hearing names like Greet's spoken with awe.

The end of 1914 was dampened by a series of unfortunate occurrences. The elder George Yule, now ninety years old, suffered a stroke in California, where he spent part of each winter. Kenoshans wondered whether Bain Wagon or Badger Brass could continue very long without the head of the Yule clan, who was the boss of one company and the patron spirit of the other.

The Unitarian Church also suffered a crippling scandal. After searching for a worthy permanent replacement for the Reverend Florence Buck, the congregation finally settled on a young pastor who was much admired—until two months after his arrival, when local headlines revealed him as a bigamist who had falsified his ministerial credentials. The disgraced new minister was forced to resign, and Kenosha's Unitarians never really recovered. Beatrice Welles still led the Unitarian choir, but she had already stepped back from the church, bequeathing leadership of the Woman's Alliance to another congregant. She would never again feel the same about the Unitarians, or any religion. Dick Welles's mother, Mary Gottfredsen, quit the board to become a Christian Scientist—and she wasn't the only Kenoshan to abandon the once thriving church.

The holidays had always been a time of hope and joy for the Welles family, and in 1914 Beatrice endeavored to use that spirit to heal the rifts in their larger community. Together with her mother and Mary Bradford, she spearheaded a fund drive featuring Kenosha's first Community Tree, modeled after a similar effort in Chicago. A forty-foot tree from a Wisconsin farm was delivered to Library Park Square, and volunteers from the rival women's clubs filled boxes with candy and gift coupons. Subscribers to the drive were asked to pay anything from one penny to $1, and in turn every Kenosha child between the ages of two and fourteen would receive a coupon for a gift, so none would feel disadvantaged at Christmas. The campaign would culminate on Christmas Eve, with Santa Claus arriving in Kenosha. "Community Christmas Tree Will Recognize No Caste in Distribution of Presents," declared the *Kenosha News*.

It was one of Beatrice Welles's finest hours. She began the week by giving a dramatic reading of Zona Gale's story "The Great Tree" to families at the local Baptist church. On the front page of the *Kenosha News*, she held forth on the true meaning of Christmas, comparing "the literal Santa Claus, with the reindeer and long whiskers," with "the real Santa Claus portrayed in the hearts of the givers," as represented by the Community Tree fund. "On Christmas Eve, every person in Kenosha will celebrate Christmas with every other person," one prominent city banker told the newspaper. "There will be no labeling of this one or that one or the other one. It will be a Kenosha community Christmas in spirit and deed."

As darkness fell on Christmas Eve, with the mercury plunging toward zero and a sharp wind rising from the west, ten thousand citizens thronged the downtown streets. As the crowd sang Christmas songs, Santa Claus arrived at the head of a marching Boy Scout band. "Men who counted their wealth by the hundreds of thousands touched shoulders with their own workmen," the *Kenosha News* reported. Clubwomen old and young dressed as Santa's helpers and handed out four hundred Christmas packages to children, before the shivering crowd, including Beatrice Welles, the mistress of ceremonies and heroine of the day, scurried to the warmth of home.

And there was one more bit of merry Christmas news: ten years after the birth of her first child, Beatrice told her husband she was pregnant again.

Beatrice and Dick Welles sneaked off to the Caribbean after the New Year, leaving ten-year-old Richard with Lucy Ives. The Welleses often rendezvoused in the West Indies with their Chicago pals John McCutcheon, who was planning to buy a private island in the Bahamas, and George Ade, by now one of America's most successful authors and playwrights. In Trinidad, one of Dick Welles's favorite places, they joined up with Ade and his longtime homosexual companion Orson C. Wells, a millionaire stockbroker from Chicago by way of Wisconsin.

The three men smoked cigars and drank rum on the boat as they basked in the blazing sun, marveling at the expectant Beatrice, looking healthy and happy in her swimwear. The Kenosha couple joked about the similarity between the names Wells and Welles, and told George and "Ort" Wells that they would name their new baby after the two men if it was a boy. Orson Welles enjoyed telling this anecdote, which became a staple of Welles family lore, and kept a yellowed clipping of the famous author's obituary for years.

Back in Kenosha, the winter and spring passed quietly, with Dick Welles cutting back on travel and his wife busy with school board duties. Beatrice and her close ally, school superintendent Mary Bradford, continued their push for reform, but progress was slow. The women contrived to disagree in public about certain matters, just to allay any fears that they were forming any sort of conspiracy against the men. But a conspiracy it was: the two never disagreed privately, and Beatrice and Mary Bradford walked arm-in-arm to meetings, reviewing their strategies along the way.

Regardless, the report card on Kenosha's schools was frustrating. The board agreed to build "portable schools" as a temporary solution to overcrowding and buildings in disrepair, but refused by a majority to invest money in either a special school for the deaf or any type of open-air school. Beatrice dashed off an angry letter denouncing the decision, arguing that children with special needs should be "the first aim of the public school," and deserved special help to become "valuable citizens." The *Kenosha News* ran the letter on its front page.

Beatrice took satisfaction in her committee work and interaction with teachers. She was in charge of the teachers' committee, showing appreciation for veteran teachers while recruiting new staff members, and joined a committee that promoted "Wider Use," opening the schools up for community programs and events. She was also the board's emissary to the Parent-Teacher Association (PTA). Beatrice rarely missed a board meeting, and the other commissioners, even those who opposed her initiatives, admired her dedication. Before she was even one year into her term, Beatrice was whispered about as a consensus choice for board president.

But she declined, in light of her new obligations as a mother-to-be. Early in the morning on May 6, Beatrice gave birth to a ten-pound boy. His parents named him George Orson Welles. Of course "Orson" had been the name of Dick Welles's maternal grandfather, whose bequest laid the foundation of his business career. The only real borrowing from the famous Trinidad pact was "George," a name Orson kidded about for years, though he was proud of his connection to George Ade and used it as his first name on official documents. The baby had two godfathers: Ade was one, John McCutcheon the other.

Flash-forward seven months to New Year's Day 1916, when Beatrice and Dick Welles hosted an open house for a grand array of relatives, friends, and neighbors, including the Rhodes, the Needhams, the Jordans, Harriet Bain, Mary Bradford, and Dr. Maurice Bernstein.

Shortly after settling in Kenosha, Dr. Bernstein had been appointed to its new board of health, which was trying to stem a citywide epidemic of scarlet fever and diphtheria among children. The local press noted that Bernstein was the least well-known of the five physicians named to the board, but in the ensuing four years he had ingratiated himself with many of the city's residents, including the Welles family.

By 1916, Bernstein was among the most respected doctors in Kenosha. The *Kenosha News* chronicled his travels to Milwaukee to teach surgery at Marquette Medical College; to Rochester, Minnesota, for tutorial clinics given by the Mayo brothers; and to Chicago for consulting—all while he maintained a full calendar of patients in Kenosha's downtown Gonnermann Building. Bernstein was a demon driver, and local columnists joked about his frequent speeding tickets for racing to his various obligations.

The doctor joined Dick Welles in the annual parade of Kenosha automobile owners, but he also mixed with the Welleses and other Kenoshans on the weekend trains heading to classical music programs in Chicago and on the North Shore. He and the Welleses had many friends in common, including the Rhodes, who owned and operated the Opera House, where Bernstein took orchestra seats for all the touring shows.

In the late fall of 1915, the Kenosha papers were reporting on Bernstein's romantic pursuit of Mina Elman, the younger sister of the Ukrainian-born violinist Mischa Elman. The renowned violinist was one of many musicians Bernstein befriended, often meeting them first when they played in Chicago, where he was known to dash backstage to assist in medical emergencies. The doctor had met Mina Elman when he was visiting her brother at his retreat on Cape Ann in Massachusetts. The violinist had returned the favor, visiting Bernstein in Kenosha and stirring excitement among those who knew his reputation. Bernstein brought Elman to the Welles home for dinner.

Beatrice issued two hundred invitations to her New Year party, which she envisioned as a revival of the old-fashioned custom of open houses. As Booth Tarkington described them in *The Magnificent Ambersons*, open houses involved guests going from one house to the next, "leaving fantastic cards in fancy baskets as they entered each doorway, and emerging a little later, more carefree than ever, if the punch had been to their liking." The open house was Orson's coming-out, and the chubby baby was the star of the party. His mother called him "Georgie-Porgie," and everyone cooed over him. Beatrice's mother, Lucy Ives, cohosted the affair, and a few Watson relatives from Evanston and women friends from Chicago came early to help with the arrangements. The Welleses' sun parlor served as a smoking room for the gentlemen, while the ladies chatted over punch and French cakes.

The Ambersons in Booth Tarkington's novel led a life of fin de siècle grandeur, in a three-story mansion with a black walnut stairway, a skylight dome, and a ballroom, all maintained with the help of liveried servants whom Tarkington called "darkies." The Welleses' celebration was modest by comparison, but their lives had another kind of richness. Dick and Beatrice Welles were widely beloved in the city of Kenosha, and clearly in love with each other. As Booth Tarkington wrote of the Ambersons, the Welleses were "magnificent in their day and place."

Orson would have his own words for it: his parents were "mythically wonderful."

II

ROSEBUDS

CHAPTER 3

1915–1921

The Whispered Word "Genius"

Orson Welles's penchant for rubbing shoulders with royalty—not just show business royalty, but popes and kings and heads of state—was in his genes.

Just as Orson was not the first Welles to direct a stage play or appear in a motion picture, he was not the first Welles to shake hands with an American president. His mother's family knew Abraham Lincoln back in Springfield, Illinois. And although presidents rarely visited Kenosha—at best, a presidential train would idle for a while on the tracks there—when Woodrow Wilson stopped at the station in late January 1916, he agreed to meet with a delegation of female activists. Beatrice Welles and Harriet Bain led a group of five hundred women, wearing yellow sashes and carrying a huge banner demanding a constitutional amendment guaranteeing women's suffrage. Beatrice and the feminist contingent presented President Wilson with a petition and boxes of the homemade cakes known locally as "suffrage snaps," a staple at Kenosha County Political Equality League programs.

Orson's mother was a particularly admirable whirlwind of activity during his first year of life. Although a second woman was appointed to fill a Kenosha school board vacancy, the conservative male majority still blocked most new expenditures. But Beatrice also gave her time to a seemingly endless variety of other concerns: helping to organize a mass meeting on child labor, prodding the City Club to sponsor nursery support and a cooking school, helping to host an annual luncheon of farmers' wives. America had not yet entered World War I—which was then called the Great War—and like many suffragists Beatrice lent her name to antiwar events, including local fund-raising for victims of the genocide in Armenia (Kenosha had a sizable Armenian population). Before one Woman's Alliance meeting, Beatrice presented a recital of Lincoln Colcord's pacifist poem *Vision of War*, offering a "clear voiced expressive rendering" of his graphic imagery. Colcord's humanism and internationalism were values that Beatrice "frankly confessed in many instances embodied her own," according to one newspaper account, and her talent for dramatic recitation foreshadowed her son's rhetorical flair.

As a school board commissioner, Beatrice made the rounds of county schools, even those deep in the countryside. The ties she forged with Parent-Teacher Association (PTA) groups inspired her involvement with other causes, including the temperance movement—though she herself was not a teetotaler, rather a moderate reformer who campaigned against all-night saloons and saloons that were open on Sundays. Similarly, in 1915, Beatrice pushed the school board to crusade against "abnormal and sensational" moving pictures, urging the Kenosha city council to establish the city's first censorship board after PTA members complained about Kenosha theaters that advertised certain fare as "For Adults Only" yet sold tickets to teenagers. Like many young mothers, Beatrice was not against all movies; she opposed only the "sordid moving pictures" that tempted local children. (Indeed, she publicly recommended films that reflected her ideals, such as the pro-enfranchisement *Your Girl and Mine* and Alla Nazimova's pacifist *War Brides*.) Orson's father was a more avid and less discriminating moviegoer, a fan of detective stories, slapstick comedies, and exciting Westerns.

Beatrice bucked the PTAs on other issues, however, promoting "sex hygiene" classes in the high schools and arguing to frame this sensitive subject "in a beautiful, wholesome manner" that would instill in teenage boys "an eternal reverence for all women." Her early embrace of sex education took many Kenoshans aback, and despite her best efforts it was a hard sell.

Beatrice's many talks and recitals for school audiences made her a star on the PTA circuit. Spurred into writing by Zona Gale's example, in January 1916 Beatrice introduced "a story of her own authorship," called "Mother and Child," that became a set piece in the readings she performed for students, teachers, and parent groups at several school venues. Although the "storiette," as Kenosha newspapers dubbed it, has since been lost, contemporary accounts indicate that it dramatized a fictional colloquy between parent and child on delicate matters including sex and death. The moral of the storiette was that it was a mother's duty—"her privilege"—to address difficult subjects while her children were still at an impressionable age. "The mother who withholds knowledge from her child from a sense of delicacy condemns her child to dangerous possibilities," Beatrice cautioned. "There is danger in waiting 'until the child is old enough or until he asks me.' He may never ask."

Her storiette broached the possibility of a child's dying from social neglect, or catastrophic disease. She foretold the passing of a "child dweller in the paradise of earthly innocence, being taken gently by the hand and led by his mother into the other world." Audience members dabbed away tears. "Here and there a stifled sob gave evidence of the emotional power of both the story and its reader," reported the *Kenosha News*.

Despite her local fame, it was not a foregone conclusion that Beatrice would run again for school board commissioner in the spring 1916 elections. But Mary Bradford and Harriet Bain prevailed on her, and she won a second term—though this time her margin of victory was only thirty votes, 394 to 364, reflecting her polarizing effect on people. But the playground tax referendum Beatrice supported, which was voted on citywide, passed by a larger margin; and such direct voter initiatives, which could not be undermined by the city council or the mayor, were proving effective at securing more playgrounds and other school improvements for the city: better school gardens, upgraded toilet facilities, and repairs to aging buildings. Ground was even broken on Kenosha's first open-air school, a longtime cause for Beatrice.

When Beatrice convened the last Kenosha City Club meeting of the season in her home, in late May 1916, it was the largest one yet.

That summer, Beatrice and Dick Welles enjoyed several days at Richard Carle's country estate in Long Beach, New York, heading into

Manhattan for a steady round of theatergoing, museum visits, and concerts. Dick Welles's friendship with Harry Sommers, a well-known theater manager, helped him secure excellent seats for every stage show. Just a year old, young Orson came along for his first trip to New York City, staying behind with a nanny when the couple went out on the town. Beatrice's mother lingered in Kenosha, recovering after a long stay at Chicago's Hahnemann Hospital in 1915. She had a servant to help watch eleven-year-old Richard, though the boy came down with measles during that season's epidemic.

The Welleses returned in time for Beatrice to help prepare for a national assembly of suffragists coming up in Chicago. Among those pitching in was Beatrice's cousin Dudley Crafts Watson, Aunt Augusta's eldest son, who designed yellow-and-white "artistic marching costumes" for the Kenosha contingent. The recently named director of the Milwaukee Art Institute (forerunner of today's Milwaukee Art Museum), Watson was a true character who affected a mustache, round pince-nez suspended by a ribbon from his lapel, and a walking cane. ("Tap, tap, tap, Dudley's coming," people said.)

Braving strong winds and a driving rain, Beatrice and a dozen of her friends donned their uniforms and "Woman's Suffrage Is Preparedness" badges, then met up with their counterparts from Racine before heading off to Chicago. There they paraded through the streets with thirty thousand activists from all the forty-eight states, ending their march at the Coliseum, where the Republican National Convention was in session, presenting a suffrage resolution to the platform committee.

Back in Kenosha for the rest of the summer, Beatrice helped launch public swimming classes at Washington Island beach, met with neighborhood women to bolster the formation of a local drama guild, and christened a "bigger, better" Girls' Recreation Club in a new facility near Lake Michigan. At the Old Settlers' Picnic she spoke on "The Civic Responsibility of Women" and held a lawn crowd spellbound. The whole family took a boat trip to Mackinac Island, and several times Beatrice, Lottie Jordan, and Ray Elizabeth Needham rode the special concert train to Ravinia.

For more than a year Orson's mother had played down her musical aspirations, limiting herself to a few kindergarten performances, while hosting private lessons and summer student recitals in her home. But close friends knew she agonized over her dormant career—she still listed "pianist" as her profession on legal documents—and when Harriet Bain announced a sabbatical from activism to return to painting, her example wasn't lost on her good friend Beatrice.

As fall arrived, Beatrice started telling confidantes that she, too, had reached a turning point. Resolving to limit her future political commitments, she threw herself back into her music—practicing as long as seven hours daily—and stepped up her trips to Chicago to further her studies. She also redoubled her efforts to bring serious music to Kenosha, coaxing her friend Louis Kreidler, a baritone with Chicago's Grand Opera Company, to perform with her at an unusual public recital at her home. She charged attendees $1, with the proceeds going to the Girls' Recreation Club, and told the *Kenosha News* that everyone was welcome. "Mrs. Welles wishes none to feel that a personal acquaintance with her is necessary to make them feel welcome at the concert," the paper reported. "It is her hope that this concert is to take upon itself the proportions of a democratic movement."

Kreidler sang selections from *I Pagliacci*, Brahms, and Grieg, and Beatrice performed solos by Massenet, Moszkowski, and MacDowell. The unusual home recital was guest-reviewed in the *News* by the director of the Milwaukee Art Institute—this was one way Dudley Crafts Watson looked after his cousin—writing that Beatrice performed "superbly."

Flushed with newfound purpose, Beatrice Welles was ready to resume her musical career.

Just a few months later, Dick Welles reached a crossroads of his own.

In the third week of January 1917, the *Kenosha News* proclaimed: "Badger Brass Sold Today." The C. M. Hall Lamp Company of Detroit had purchased the firm outright; at first the Detroit company said it would maintain the Kenosha plant, but that changed soon enough, and the sale of Badger Brass was the first step in the downward spiral of the industries that had fed local growth for decades. The sale price was said to be "in the neighborhood of $400,000," with the bulk divided between George A. Yule, the company's longtime president; and Richard Head Welles, its treasurer and general manager. Although Yule said he would switch over to running Bain Wagon Works, where his frail father, in his nineties, still showed up for work every day, Welles announced his retirement with "no plans for the immediate future," reported the *Kenosha News*, other than "to take a long ocean cruise."

In his mid-forties, with two young sons he doted on and a beautiful, talented young wife, Dick Welles was a rich man—a millionaire in today's dollars—with nothing but blue skies on the horizon.

With a kind of anxious curiosity, the Kenosha newspapers faithfully chronicled the local power couple in their state of transition. Beatrice and Dick Welles seemed carefree on the surface, often spotted on first nights at the Rhode Opera House, enjoying shows such as May Robson's *Miss Matt*, seated in one of the front rows with Dr. and Mrs. Maurice Bernstein.

Dr. Bernstein had married Mina Elman on New Year's Eve 1916. The Welleses did not attend the ceremony, which took place at the Hotel Statler in Buffalo, New York. (Elman reportedly wanted to establish the union on a fifty-fifty basis by marrying halfway between her home in Massachusetts and the groom's in Kenosha.) Some biographers have described Mina Elman, the younger sister of violinist Mischa Elman, as "plain," but the Kenosha newspapers described her as chic and fashionable, "a girlish, round faced young person with claims to beauty." The newlywed Bernsteins moved into a Library Park house around the corner from the Welles family. The Welleses, and Beatrice in particular, were sympathetic to the aspiring classical singer.

Beatrice made her "public reappearance" as a musician at a Guild Hall program in late January. When the management refused to allow her to transport her own full-size concert grand piano from home for the concert—as she'd done before, at great cost and inconvenience to the venue—the new Mrs. Bernstein saved the day by lending her personal grand piano, "a size or two smaller" than Beatrice's. Also on the bill was Sybil Sammis MacDermid, a New York soprano, but it was Beatrice who stole the show and made it the social highlight of the winter. Her selections, including several polonaises and Chopin's Étude in A-flat Major, were "marked by great delicacy and charm and a certain sureness as well as brilliance," according to the *Kenosha News*, and her performance was met with storms of applause.

It was also a Bernstein—this time the doctor—who rode to the rescue the following week, when twelve-year-old Richard suffered another mishap. Some sources say the boy tumbled down the stairs, others that he took a blow to his head while playing football. Whatever the case, the accident was serious enough for Dr. Bernstein to send the boy to a Chicago hospital for multiple procedures, including surgery to reset earlier fractures of his arm and leg. (Kenosha's hospital, built in 1910, was inferior to the many Chicago facilities; a local adage was: "Get sick in Kenosha—go to the hospital in Chicago.") Originally expected to stay ten days in the hospital, Richard lingered there for more than three weeks. His parents shuttled between the hospital and a Chicago hotel, and Beatrice herself was eventually overcome with stress and exhaustion, as local newspapers reported. In those days, doctors commonly prescribed bed rest for women suffering from anxiety or depression, and returning to Kenosha, Beatrice spent several days in bed—the first hint of an Achilles' heel in this dynamo of energy.

Other books have painted Beatrice as preferring to leave the mothering of her children to others, but in private she mentored young Richard—and now little Orson—in art, music, and literature. While her husband taught the boys sports and magic tricks, Beatrice nurtured their cerebral and spiritual side. But eleven-year-old Richard still had trouble in school, and he seemed accident-prone. That winter, after a restorative family trip to Florida, his parents decided it was time for Richard to go to a boarding school in the fall.

With Beatrice and her circle of close friends finally slowing down, the late February 1917 "Suffrage Edition" of the *Kenosha News* served as a kind of valedictory for her generation of feminists in the city. With Harriet Bain as editor in chief, Ray Elizabeth Needham as managing editor, and Emma Robinson as city editor, the paper featured contributions by Drury Underwood and by George Ade, who sent an amusing wire from a Florida hotel: "Once there was a Man opposed to Universal Suffrage because he said Every Woman would Vote just the way her Husband told her to Vote," wrote Ade. "Later on he got Married. He is now a Pacifist." For a feature entitled "How It Seems to Be a Husband of a Suffragist," Dick Welles observed wryly: "Being the husband of a suffragist seems just the same as it did before I made a suffragist out of her."

The keynote of the special section was a four-stanza poem by Beatrice Welles, under her byline "B.I.W.," expressing the common frustrations of the Kenosha sisterhood:

> When the news was circulated
> That male citizens awaited
> The assistance of Kenosha's ladies fair
> To help them in improvement
> Thru their new-formed civic movement
> With twelve dollars we announced that we'd be there.
>
> We had worked in days departed
> In a manner most whole hearted
> For the things we thought would do Kenosha good
> So with flesh and spirit willing
> At this convocation thrilling
> We prepared to do what ever thing we could.
>
> We sat with breath bated
> And thru fifteen speeches waited
> With our ears attuned and listening for our cue
> Till a gentleman, distinguished,
> Said we should not be extinguished
> For in taking care of garbage we might do—
>
> Then a board of men elected
> And committees they selected
> But on not one of them were women asked to be.
> And as we homeward wandered
> We very sadly pondered
> Do men alone make up "community?"

By the time the special edition was in print, however, nearly all the best-known champions of the suffrage movement in Kenosha had moved on. Harriet Bain left for Spain to resume her painting. (She later moved to New York, where she became a founding member of the modernist New York Society of Women Artists.) Emma Robinson suffered a nervous breakdown and departed for California. Lottie Jordan moved to Cleveland, where her husband opened a new car factory. Finally, in April, Ray Elizabeth Needham left for Chicago with her husband, Maurice, who launched his own sales agency there. Of all Beatrice's closest friends, only Mary Bradford—a Kenoshan to the last—remained in the city.

The Welleses' circles were narrowing. Dick Welles had rejected entreaties from Charles Hall, his colleague at Badger Brass, to accept a top position with the new parent company in Detroit. Another longtime crony at Badger Brass, L. J. Keck, used his share of the buyout to relocate to rural New York. And the departure of Edward Jordan and Maurice Needham, Dick's friends and fellow male suffragists, left Kenosha a smaller, lonelier place for the young couple.

Lucy Ives returned early from another family vacation in the summer of 1917, feeling poorly. Her health took a turn for the worse in July, and she died on August 10. Orson's maternal grandmother was not yet sixty when she died. Her death certificate lists the cause as an uncommon, difficult-to-diagnose type of colon cancer. Her attending physician was the all-purpose Maurice Bernstein. She was interred next to her husband in the Welles family plot in Green Ridge Cemetery.

Some historians have depicted Lucy Ives as a nonentity, suggesting that Beatrice Welles was emotionally and intellectually aloof from her mother. Yet Lucy made many friends in Kenosha, and the press mourned her as "a woman of rare personal charm, of intellectual development, of an unusually happy disposition." To many, mother and daughter had seemed like kindred souls.

Grief-stricken, Beatrice took to bed once more, and this time her illness was severe enough that she was taken to St. Luke's Hospital in Chicago. Beatrice and her mother had at one time talked about organizing a major benefit for the Red Cross, which was heavily taxed by

America's entry into the Great War; now, on returning to Kenosha, Beatrice announced that the benefit would go forward in her mother's honor. Channeling her pacifism into war relief, she organized a concert in late October, again with baritone Louis Kreidler, mixing opera and classical music with "La Marseillaise" and "The Star-Spangled Banner." Her piano playing reached a stirring peak with songs that touched on death such as "Mourn with the Sighing Wind" and "Danny Deever," with lyrics from the Kipling poem. But Beatrice did not offer as many solos as the audience had hoped—and a few weeks later, just before Christmas, the city's first elected female official surprised her fellow school commissioners by submitting her resignation from the board, effective immediately. The terse announcement, on the front page of the Kenosha News, offered no real explanation.

Even her opponents on the school board had come to appreciate Beatrice as a tireless advocate of the public welfare. Mary Bradford would miss her loyal co-conspirator, but she knew that Beatrice's artistic ambitions could not be gratified in Kenosha, and she accepted the resignation sadly. By the end of the year, the Welleses were making arrangements to leave their Park Avenue home, and Kenosha.

Beatrice had grown weary of the rancor and struggles that hampered her diverse causes. Her many sideline projects—the Woman's Club drama group, the alternative and populist Kenosha City Club, the activist Woman's Alliance of the Unitarian Church, and the Girls' Progressive Club shelter—would fail rapidly in her absence. Yet Beatrice and her circle of activist friends had succeeded in spurring real change. The following year, when Wisconsin became the first state to ratify the Nineteenth Amendment granting national female suffrage, the credit belonged in part to the suffragists of Kenosha.

One night that January, Dick and Beatrice Welles huddled together on the late Saturday theater train as it burrowed through snowdrifts from Chicago back to Kenosha, finally pulling into town on Sunday at dawn. It was their last such trip. Not long afterword, faster than anyone expected, Kenosha's onetime power couple left the city to take up a new life in Chicago. One of their sons, little Orson, not yet three years old, would move with them. The other, twelve-year-old Richard, was away at the Todd School for Boys in Woodstock, Illinois—an institution that would loom large in the Welles family's future.

The Welleses had many reasons to move to Chicago, but their two boys were significant factors. Richard was complicated: he sang, played piano, and painted with talent, and he had learned a love of magic from his father, but he never settled comfortably into school, and he acted out in worrisome ways. Dick and Beatrice were increasingly uneasy about their oldest child, and they knew that in Chicago they could consult medical specialists if his problems persisted.

With more time on her hands than she'd had in years, Beatrice could also devote close attention to little Orson, as perhaps she never did with Richard. She had fretted that Kenosha would stifle her younger son's creativity, whereas Chicago's artistic and musical offerings would nurture his instincts and intellect as they had nurtured his mother's. In their new home, Beatrice would read to the boy from her favorite works of poetry, drama, and literature. She would speak to him like an adult. She would raise him to explore and express himself. If she was at fault in any way for Richard's quirky and disappointing behavior, then Orson offered her, and her husband, a precious second chance.

By the time the Welles family arrived in 1918, Chicago had mushroomed into a metropolis of nearly three million people. Its mayor was the corrupt, buffoonish "Big Bill" Thompson—often called a "Hearst mayor," as his campaign was pushed heavily by the newspapers of William Randolph Hearst. The city's streets were jammed with streetcars and automobiles; its downtown was filled with tall buildings; its neighborhoods boasted many new single-family bungalows. Ben Hecht was corresponding from Berlin for the *Chicago Daily News*, while his future writing partner, Charles MacArthur (they would collaborate on *The Front Page*), was on sabbatical from the *Chicago Tribune*—volunteering with the Black Watch Highlanders in the Great War.

By Easter Sunday, the Welles family had settled into a spacious apartment on East Pearson, close to Lake Michigan and not far from downtown. Later in the month of May, after Orson's third birthday, the family took a taxi to the Illinois Theater in the theater district, where they saw the actress Sarah Bernhardt in a single afternoon performance of Eugene Morand's allegorical *Les Cathédrales*, which had been a huge success at her theater in Paris in 1915 and at a royal command performance in London the following year. The pacifist stage poem depicted the war-ravaged cathedrals of France as seen in a waking dream by a French soldier. Proceeds from the occasion went to relief of French artists wounded in the war, and to the widows and orphans of those who had died. These were sacred causes for Beatrice—pacifism and the victims of war.

At seventy-four, Bernhardt had an artificial limb—one of her legs had been amputated after an injury—but she still performed and still greeted well-wishers backstage after the show, and that day Dick and Beatrice Welles were among them. Little Orson "touched the hand of Sarah Bernhardt," he recalled years later. "Can you imagine that?" The little boy was "led into a bower of dark-red roses where that marvelous old lady sat in her wheelchair refreshing herself from a tank of oxygen. That hand I took was a claw covered with liver spots and liquid white and with the pointy ends of her sleeve glued over the back of it." This was one of several farewell tours for one of the theatrical legends of the nineteenth century; she went on to play in North America deep into October. The tour included Milwaukee in Wisconsin, though not Kenosha.

Bernhardt had passed the show business torch to the future director of *Citizen Kane.*

Five months after the family relocated to Chicago, in September 1918, Dick Welles registered for the draft. At forty-five, he was nearly too old to serve. (The third national registration was held on September 12, for men eighteen through forty-five, but the armistice would be signed two months later.) Dick was fit and healthy, but on his draft form he listed his occupation as "not employed." Without the routine of work and travel that had sustained him for almost two decades in Kenosha, Dick Welles was unmoored. His wife's days were filled with bustle and ambition. His were filled with empty hours.

His downfall may have been aggravated by drink; it's possible he was drinking steadily all along. But had he drank to excess in Kenosha? "By 1912 he was a hopeless alcoholic," Charles Higham wrote of Dick Welles. But Welles was a much-chronicled public figure in Kenosha, and the local press consistently portrayed him as a model citizen. Even after Orson became famous, when he referred to his father's alcoholism in interviews, longtime Kenoshans and family members insisted that Dick Welles drank normally, not heavily, when living in their city.

In Kenosha, Dick and Beatrice Welles seemed to have been an ideally married couple: standing together at rallies, holding hands and dancing together at holiday events, hosting memorable dinner parties in their home. Yet by the end of their first year in Chicago, there is no question that their marriage had imploded. In court papers, Beatrice was precise about the date: on February 1, 1919, after discovering that he was involved in an adulterous affair, Beatrice confronted her husband, and after a furious argument, the two stopped cohabiting that day.

It was not just one woman, either. Dick Welles had been conducting similar affairs "for a considerable time past," according to her attestation, "with divers other lewd women."

That reference to "lewd women" has led some to speculate that Welles's affairs were with working girls of one kind or another: low-class chorines, perhaps, or even high-class call girls from Chicago bordellos. Court papers confirm that his lovers were not part of the Welleses' social circle, in either Chicago or Kenosha. Their names, said Beatrice, were "unknown" to her.

In the shooting script of *Citizen Kane*, after the famous newsroom scene celebrating the success of the *Inquirer*, there is a scene in which Charles Foster Kane, Jed Leland, and Mr. Bernstein adjourn to a high-class bordello. In the script the bordello is called "Georgie's Place"—an echo of Orson's teasing nickname—but Welles once told John Houseman that the place was akin to Chicago's turn-of-the-century Everleigh Club, where captains of industry like Marshall Field Jr. mingled with clientele like his father, he imagined. When Herman J. Mankiewicz, the script's cowriter, was questioned during a lawsuit about the "Georgie's Place" scene—which was shot but dropped from the film after censors objected to it—he became irritated. "It is my understanding," Mankiewicz huffed, "that this is a customary thing [gentlemen frequenting a bordello] and not violently indecent."

Not everyone would have agreed. Beatrice Welles ordered her husband off the East Pearson Street premises. Her social standing, her dignity, demanded it, but that wasn't all. Her husband was unapologetic, and after he moved into a hotel he continued to see the particular "lewd" woman who had triggered the breakup. But the affair ran its course soon enough, and Dick Welles missed his family and regretted his indiscretion. Banishing painful memories, Beatrice relinquished their East Pearson Street home to her husband, installing herself and four-year-old Orson on nearby Superior Street, "the most fashionable apartment on the Gold Coast," in the hyperbolic words of Dudley Crafts Watson. Still, Beatrice could not bring herself to forgive her husband, and she discouraged and restricted Dick's visits to Superior Street. It was at this juncture, according to her divorce claims, that Dick Welles finally sank into "habitual drunkenness."

The marital crisis coincided with another family emergency that could only have exacerbated the tensions between the couple. At the age of fourteen, Richard Ives Welles was asked to leave the Todd School, his boarding school in the town of Woodstock, sixty miles northwest of Chicago. The reasons have been lost over time. Perhaps Richard had been caught with a town girl, as Orson's later headmaster Roger Hill theorized (though he never claimed to know firsthand). Whatever the case, it's clear that Richard was behind in his course work, and he did not mix well with other boys.

Richard rejoined the family in Chicago around the time that his mother and father started living in separate apartments. At a loss for how to handle their son, both parents sought the counsel of Dr. Maurice Bernstein, who knew Richard well as a surgery patient and who also had mental health credentials stretching back to his first postings after medical school.

Dr. Bernstein was one of the few close family friends who had lingered in Kenosha. His marriage to Mina Elman had ended dismally, however; though Bernstein had tried to foster his bride's musical ambitions—introducing her to musicians including Irish-born tenor John McCormack; soprano Alma Gluck; and her husband, violinist Efrem Zimbalist—Mina lacked professional ability, and her singing career never took flight. The couple lived together for only a few months before Mina moved out of their Library Park house in April 1917. Their divorce was finalized one year later in July. Dr. Bernstein maintained ties to the local Jewish community and the municipal government, and he kept up with Kenosha patients; with his brother, he even briefly launched a soft-drink distribution company from the same Main Street address as his office. But he made increasingly frequent trips to Chicago, and gradually shifted his practice there.

Now, at this critical hour, Dr. Bernstein became not only the family physician for all situations, but also an intermediary between the estranged Dick and Beatrice Welles. Bernstein concluded that Richard had mental or emotional problems, and he told young Richard's parents that he thought the boy should be enrolled in a Chicago preparatory school closer to home and watched carefully.

Together Beatrice and Dick Welles decided on the Latin School of Chicago, the city's premier prep school, on the near North Side. Although Beatrice never forgave her husband's betrayal, their shared devotion to their children kept the marriage together—if in name only.

Striving to regain her artistic footing in Chicago, Beatrice resumed piano lessons with her former teacher Julia Lois Caruthers. She took on a few pupils in piano and spoken-word performance. She built up a fresh repertoire of recital pieces and reconnected with women's club patrons in Chicago and along the North Shore. Her cousin Dudley Crafts Watson, who had encouraged her to leave Kenosha, promised engagements for her at the Milwaukee Art Institute.

Refashioning herself as an elocutionist was part of her plan. Female elocutionists thrived in progressive women's clubs throughout America in the early twentieth century. As the feminist scholar Marian Wilson Kimber has noted, elocution was considered a respectable and womanly art for public purposes, while also serving as a means of entertainment and education in the home. Beatrice had been gravitating toward this specialty during her last years in Kenosha, and in Chicago several of her students, whom she mentored, combined music and elocution in their performance pieces; these pupils included Ann Birk Kuper and Phyllis Fergus. Kuper went on to a long career in dramatic recitals throughout the Midwest, and Fergus became even more acclaimed as a spoken-word diseuse and composer who specialized in "story poems" for speaker and piano. A founding member of the Society of American

Women Composers, Fergus organized concerts by female composers at the White House; her several dozen published works included piano and violin solos and choral music for women's voices.

In April 1920, two years after her last public performance, Beatrice returned in a Lake View Musical Society recital in the Parkway Hotel ballroom. The highlight of the recital was a new piece by Phyllis Fergus blending two violinists, a contralto, and Fergus's piano accompaniment, with Beatrice declaiming the verse of Natalie Whitted Price, a local suffragist and published poet. Beatrice's dark, mellifluous voice was perfectly matched to Fergus's intricate compositions, and the Lake View Musical Society event launched Fergus's career, with Beatrice the star elocutionist of her earliest programs. The Women's League Candlelight Musicale devoted an entire evening to Fergus's compositions in February 1921, with Beatrice reading the poetry of Robert Browning, Edmund Vance Cooke, and again Natalie Whitted Price; Beatrice's vivid rendering of Alfred Noyes's "The Highwayman" was the centerpiece. Beatrice and Phyllis Fergus took variations of this playbill to many ladies' organizations that formed a constellation leading up the North Shore. Their tour brought them to the Milwaukee Art Institute in March 1921.

Their ascent was interrupted in June 1921, when Phyllis Fergus married the Chicago steel and iron broker Thatcher Hoyt and took a several-year break from performing.

Young Orson would celebrate his fifth birthday in May 1920. Short and chubby, the boy had dark lanky hair that fell over soulful brown eyes staring above a snub nose. Although his mother dressed him in cutesy sailor suits, in truth he was already a budding sophisticate.

By some accounts, Orson Welles had first appeared onstage at the tender age of three, in the role of Trouble, the child of Madame Butterfly, in the August 1918 production of Puccini's opera at Ravinia, the outdoor venue in Highland Park. More recently, the boy had pocketed $10 for greeting shoppers at Marshall Field's department store in downtown Chicago; he was dressed as the White Rabbit and exclaimed, "Oh, I must hurry—or else it will be too late to see the woolen underwear on the eighth floor!" He was a born showman, and from the beginning no job was beneath him: $10 was $10, especially to a boy whose parents had separated and who became a pawn in the conflict between them, often a conflict over money.

During Orson's earliest years in Chicago, that rift was often bridged by Dr. Maurice Bernstein. The doctor had an office on Michigan Avenue and an apartment on Chicago Avenue, one block north of Superior, where little Orson lived with his mother. Childless himself, Dr. Bernstein made himself indispensable to Beatrice, joining her and little Orson on regular outings, but he also accompanied Orson on many excursions with his father. In time, the doctor became a kind of bonus member of the family: a companionable fellow, reliably humorous, the king of bad jokes. Everyone liked him, even Dick Welles. Orson was encouraged to call Bernstein "Dadda," a term of affection that has struck some of Welles's biographers as a slight toward Dick Welles, but which may have been the child's contraction of "doctor." As for Bernstein, he dubbed Orson "Pookles," and they were Dadda and Pookles to each other for most of their lives.

Over time, some wondered whether Beatrice Welles and Bernstein ever transcended the bounds of friendship. It was true that Dr. Bernstein "left Kenosha to be near my mother," Welles said. Nostalgic about his early career in Kenosha, the doctor always pined for the small Wisconsin city that was his personal Rosebud, "a paradise he'd lost," according to Welles. "My mother used to make heartless fun of that." Though Dr. Bernstein adored Beatrice, she was merely fond of him, Welles thought.

Later, as he embellished Orson's life story for publicity purposes, Dr. Bernstein had a habit of leaving out the boy's parents. In *his* telling, it was Bernstein who took little Orson to the museum, who bought him his first conductor's baton, puppet show, magic kit. But the truth is that Orson's early years were dominated by Beatrice, who would make the grade as an outstanding mother to her second son. She took charge of Orson's intellectual and artistic development, sharing works of classic literature with him as bedtime reading. These early reading sessions gave him an adult vocabulary, along with early training in the memorization and recitation skills that were his mother's forte. Beatrice loved old-fashioned story poems like Noyse's "The Highwayman" or "Barbara Frietchie" by John Greenleaf Whittier, but also drew her bedtime repertoire from "the poetry of Swinburne, Rosetti, Keats, Tennyson, Tagore and Walt Whitman," according to Peter Noble's *The Fabulous Orson Welles.**

Orson's mother also read to him daily from Charles and Mary Lamb's two-volume *Tales from Shakespeare*, an illustrated English compendium of the comedies and tragedies, simplified for children. (Orson eventually grew old enough to demand "the real thing," Noble wrote, probably exaggerating.) *A Midsummer Night's Dream* was always Beatrice's favorite Shakespeare play, and by Orson's third birthday, Noble claimed, she had switched to reading from the actual text. This play became "my reading primer," Orson recalled, though his mother drummed it into him so thoroughly that he contrived to avoid it professionally throughout his career. It was one Shakespeare masterpiece he never acted in or directed.

Beatrice prized painting too, and so by the time he was five Orson had received his first paint kit, a gift of easel, brushes, and colors from his mother's friend Lorado Taft, the eminent Chicago sculptor. Orson was often taken to the nearby Art Institute of Chicago, where he was encouraged to ponder the works of the masters and mimic them as best he could on his sketch pad. His mother was acquainted with many of the museum's visiting artists, such as Russian painter Nikolay Roerich, who presided over a major Chicago exhibition in 1920, and the painter and stage designer Boris Anisfeld. Little Orson was encouraged to ask the celebrated artists questions about their work, as an adult would, and he drew and painted even on his own time, precociously and happily. "That's what I loved most," Welles told Peter Bogdanovich ruefully. "Always. If only I'd been better at it."

Imbuing her son with a love of music was another of Beatrice Welles's priorities. Orson received regular violin and piano lessons, and attended the symphony, opera, and ballet in company with his mother, or

---

* Noble's 1956 book was the first extensive biography of Welles and the one most influenced by Dr. Bernstein. When speaking to Peter Bogdanovich, Welles debunked it as "a perfect treasury of misinformation," but Noble tried earnestly to interview Welles and others, and the trick, for him as well as readers, became sorting out the facts from the factoids.

Dr. Bernstein, or both together. Beatrice, convinced that Orson should learn piano not from his mother but from an outside teacher, enlisted Phyllis Fergus Hoyt to give him instruction in an upstairs room at the Hoyts' residence on North State Parkway. Orson liked to say that he eventually grew so weary of the "endlessly repeated musical scales" that he threatened to hurl himself out a window. Alarmed, Phyllis rushed to tell his mother, who was waiting in an anteroom. Beatrice rolled her eyes and said, "Oh, just tell him to go ahead!" "She had to kill my act, you see," Welles explained years later to his daughter Chris Welles Feder. But Welles was genuinely fond of Phyllis Fergus Hoyt; decades later, spotting her in a New York hotel lobby, he rushed up and gave her a bear hug.

The beauty of Orson Welles's upbringing, however, may be in how Beatrice filled in her own gaps. She carefully organized and overloaded Orson's time, making sure he was always constructively occupied. Part of her strategy was fobbing him off regularly on childless acquaintances who were "good influences"—friends and relatives who knew her mind and shared her values, broadening the safety net for this boy from a newly broken home.

She counted on Orson's father, and Dr. Bernstein, to expose Orson to boyish interests and popular culture. While his mother read masterworks to him, the two men took him to Kroch's, the big downtown bookstore, and loaded him up with adventure tales, spy thrillers, and whodunits. Dick Welles was devoted to musicals and vaudeville acts and the big touring magic shows that came to Chicago and took over the downtown theaters for a week. Beatrice rolled her eyes at too much magic, but the mentalists intrigued her, and if Orson was happy she was happy.

One of Dick Welles's heroes was the magician Harry Thurston, who performed annually in Chicago. The Great Thurston, as he styled himself, had been on the circuit since before the Great War, working his way up from a one-man card-trick act to the host of an extravaganza complete with scantily clad female assistants, small furry animals that popped out of strange places, and forty tons of apparatus. Harry Houdini's greatest contemporary rival, Thurston considered himself a greater success with the public: "America's most popular magician."

Thurston was small of stature, but one of his achievements was transforming himself into a charismatic spellbinder onstage. His originally affectless midwestern speech was said to have been honed at the Moody Bible Institute, and his hypnotic patter masterfully misdirected the audience's attention as he wove his illusionist wonders. His musical voice rippled, purled, and enchanted, stretching out each syllable to mesmerizing effect. While assuring his audience that he loved them, and that "I wouldn't deceive you for the world" (a line Orson later adopted for his unfinished film "The Magic Show"), the Great Thurston fooled his audiences time and again.

"I idolized him," Welles recalled. "He was the finest magician I've ever seen."

Another favorite of Dick Welles's was the equally formidable Okito, who started out in the Great Thurston's act. Okito was the stage name of Theodore Bamberg, the Dutch-born patriarch of a family of magicians. Billed as "Europe's greatest shadowist," Okito appeared in immaculate evening attire and cape, and dominated the stage entirely with his fingers and hands, projecting fantastic shadow figures on a blank screen—not unlike what Charles Foster Kane does in *Citizen Kane* to amuse Susan Alexander on their first evening together.

Dick Welles always made his way backstage to meet the touring magicians, and to wangle a few magic lessons for his boy. Okito lived in Chicago for periods between his world tours, and from these great magicians and others—later to include Harry Houdini—the impressionable boy eagerly absorbed lessons in bluff and patter and poise.

He was usually able to talk one parent or the other into a moving picture matinee, especially in his mother's case if the show was a literary adaptation or could be otherwise defined as uplifting. Orson never lost his boyhood affection for Allan Dwan's *Robin Hood*, whose stars, Douglas Fairbanks and Mary Pickford, attended the film's 1922 premiere in Chicago. "I was batty about *Robin Hood* and *The Three Musketeers*," Orson told Peter Bogdanovich. "Fairbanks was my idol." He had a similar fondness for the 1923 version of *The Hunchback of Notre Dame*, with Lon Chaney as Quasimodo. "I still see Lon Chaney as I saw him when I was eight years old," Welles told Henry Jaglom. "Everything he did I adore."

It was his mother who took Orson to Robert Flaherty's pioneering

Nanook of the North, the feature-length documentary about Eskimo life in the Canadian Arctic. Welles never forgot how he was bowled over by *Nanook*, and by another Flaherty documentary, set in Ireland, *Man of Aran*, which he saw at a later time. Orson never lost his nostalgia for these and other early silent moving pictures, among the most sophisticated of their era, which he saw in the company of his parents.

Little Orson was scarcely thinking of a stage or screen career in 1920. At the age of five, he was a more likely candidate to be a painter or musician. He had real talent in violin and piano, and friends of his mother treated him as "a sort of imitation musical Wunderkind," in his words. His mother's small ensemble and other music groups rehearsed at their apartment, and the boy stood in front of them as they played their instruments, waving his toy baton. He sometimes performed on his instruments for his mother's dinner guests, who were luminaries passing through Chicago.

Beatrice's many "brilliant dinner parties" featured these luminaries "chiefly of the theater and the music world," according to Dudley Crafts Watson, "sometimes eighteen or twenty in number." By age six Orson was permitted to stay up late and sit in on the luminary dinners, as long as he cooperated by taking an afternoon nap. He sometimes obliged the nap, but he never went down easily at night. After getting a good night kiss, he'd follow his mother into her bedroom, talking a blue streak until she escorted him back to his room with strict instructions to go to bed after he finished whatever poem or sketch he was working on. Then he'd follow her back again, talking and talking until finally she fell asleep, often waking up the next morning with little Orson curled up beside her, snoring.

In April 1922, Beatrice and Dr. Bernstein hosted a dinner in honor of the poet, playwright, and Shakespeare authority Louis K. Anspacher, who was visiting Chicago for a lecture. Orson, almost seven, sat alongside his cousin Dudley, whom he thought of as "Uncle" Dudley, and Russian sculptor Boris Lovet-Lorski, taking in their high-flown conversation. The new Jacques Gordon String Quartet, which his mother championed, performed for the guests.

Recalling the celebrities who passed through his Chicago home in his youth, Welles liked to believe that some of them, such as the opera singer Fyodor Chaliapin, had designs on his beloved mother. "I've always suspected [Chaliapin] was my father because he had a big love affair with my mother at the time when it would have counted," Welles mused in his phone talks with Roger Hill. "He looks a lot more like I do than my father did." It didn't matter that the opera singer was actually nowhere near his mother, or even the Midwest, when Orson was conceived. The important thing was that Chaliapin, who came straight from the opera stage to the Welles apartment wearing his costume, showed a paternal interest in the boy, bouncing him on his knee, at a time when Dick Welles was persona non grata in the household. "While I prayed to God as a little child," Welles mused, "I always prayed to Chaliapin dressed for *Boris Godunov.*"

Welles enjoyed imagining his mother's illustrious flings; and on another occasion, he hinted that Beatrice may have enjoyed a liaison with Enrico Caruso as well. (The filmmaker in him also imagined a possible extramarital romance for Charles Foster Kane's mother: it is there deep in the backstory of *Citizen Kane*, just a hint of Mary Kane's affair with the boarder who leaves her his fortune—a boarder who might well have been Kane's real father.)

Whatever their relationship with Beatrice, the visiting luminaries doted on little Orson, seeing in the exuberant boy a reflection of his charming, talented mother—and, perhaps, of themselves as children. A marvel of a boy, little Orson could draw and paint, play the violin and piano, recite verse and drama, sit and listen to artistic shoptalk, and sometimes chip in thoughtfully during the adults' conversations. He might even crawl into a famous guest's lap and fall asleep. Dr. Bernstein thought the adorable, mischievous boy was a genius, and said so. His mother merely smiled. "The word genius was whispered into my ear the first thing I ever heard while I was still mewling in my crib," Welles said, "so it never occurred to me that I wasn't until middle age."

The other Welles boy, Richard, did not thrive at Chicago Latin, where he was repeating the eighth grade he'd failed to finish at the Todd School. Indeed, in the spring of 1921 another malady struck the fifteen-year-old, and he was sent home to the care of Dr. Bernstein. Richard claimed later to have aggravated his previous leg fracture, but it is hard to know.

Orson's older brother was already a smooth confabulator. Later, Richard would boast that he excelled in his home studies, that his grades in French and Latin should have been solid enough for high school credit. But despite the attention and encouragement that came with home schooling, Richard never did complete his course requirements. "No work done by Richard Welles in the Chicago Latin School could possibly be construed as High School Work," an administrator there wrote in his file. "He missed almost the whole of our Eighth Grade and was never in our High School. It is true that we have French and Latin in our Eighth Grade, but the amount done by him was not enough to constitute a credit in any sense."

His parents placed their last bet on Northwestern Military and Naval Academy, originally located in Highland Park, but operating since 1915 in Lake Geneva, Wisconsin, where both his parents had summered in days past. Richard was enrolled for the fall term at the academy in 1921, but almost immediately he was sent back to Chicago. The problem, it seems, went beyond adolescent maladjustment; surviving medical records suggest the investigation of a cord lesion, or a central lesion contained within the skull, which could cause mood swings and right side weaknesses. To address the problem, Dr. Bernstein recommended an operation, although its exact nature—and, indeed, whether Bernstein performed it himself—is unclear.

In early November, Dr. Bernstein wrote to inform Northwestern Academy that the operation had been a success. "There were no evidences of an organic nervous lesion," the doctor said. "The spinal puncture showed clear fluid, and the electrical tests showed no degenerative changes in the muscles. We have, therefore, made a diagnosis of a functional nerve condition, possibly concussion of the spine. He is making a very rapid improvement regaining function in all his muscles. I expect that he will return to school either at the end of next week, or the beginning of the following week. This will undoubtedly relieve your mind of the contagious nature of his trouble."

The academy furnished a history outline and English and geometry study guides so that the sixteen-year-old could keep up with his education at home. Bernstein assured school officials that Richard was physically sound, though "the muscles of [his] right side have not fully regained their tone and it will be necessary for him to sleep indoors and avoid cold baths or showers." Mentally, however, the teenager suffered from a neurosis or hysteria that combined periods of high excitement with low discouragement. "I am sending him back to school at this early date, because there is a psychological aspect to a condition of this character that requires a care that you and your splendid school are best able to give him.

"The boy has, of course, suffered a severe mental shock [possibly from the operation], and the remedy is to keep his mind absolutely free from dwelling on this illness. I would suggest that even his periods of full time be indefinitely occupied for a while. It is difficult to tell how much actual soreness and fatigue he will experience when he gets into active school life."

It was not to be: Richard never returned to Northwestern Academy, or any other school. After coming home from the hospital, he shuttled between his parents' apartments. Beatrice Welles all but threw up her hands. She was increasingly preoccupied with the boundlessly energetic Orson and her own blossoming career as an elocutionist; convinced that what Richard needed was a father's strong example, she tossed the gauntlet to her estranged husband.

In the spirit of healing and reconciliation, Dick Welles proposed that the entire family spend the month of June vacationing together in Grand Detour, Illinois. Beatrice agreed.

A short drive from Lake Geneva, Wisconsin, the village of Grand Detour—named for the Rock River's loop around it—was an escape from the summer heat for Chicagoans. Artists from hundreds of miles around were drawn to the picturesque river and elm-shaded streets of the town, called the "Hudson of the West" by feminist author Margaret Fuller. The Chicago Art Institute painter Charles Francis Browne presided over summer classes there. Nearby, on the river's east bank, stood Eagle's Nest Bluff, the home of an artists' colony founded before the turn of the century by a group of Chicago artists and architects led by Lorado Taft, whose towering statue of Sauk Indian leader Black Hawk loomed over the compound.

Having made trips through Grand Detour many times on their way back and forth to Lake Geneva, Dick and Beatrice Welles both felt a connection to the place, and the couple took a rental cabin on the north side of the main bridge. Dr. Bernstein came along as an escort for Beatrice and Orson, but also to monitor Richard's behavior. The family was hoping that a summer in peaceful Grand Detour might help Richard regain his physical and mental health. Regular long walks, fishing, and river recreation were arranged, along with day trips to the nearby towns of Oregon and Dixon for circuses, county fairs, and moving pictures. Richard enjoyed painting almost as much as Orson, and because of the lifelong gulf between them, they never spent as much concentrated time in each other's company as during these weeks.

But the vacation was marred by Dick and Beatrice Welles's persistent quarrels, often revolving around finances. Dick Welles controlled the purse strings for Beatrice's household, and she regarded her separation allowance as inadequate. Dick balked at underwriting Beatrice's many dinner parties, music lessons, monthly masseuse appointments, and frequent travel for functions and performances. Nor did he wish to pay for the nanny, Sigrid Jacobsen, who helped her tend to seven-year-old Orson, and also handled sewing and domestic chores.

The couple's attempt at peacemaking failed, and shortly after July 4, Beatrice and little Orson departed for Highland Park, where they often stayed with the *Chicago Tribune* music critics Edward "Ned" Moore and his wife, Hazel—at first just for weekends, but by 1922, Beatrice's stays stretched through most of July and August. Dr. Bernstein, another long-standing friend of the Moores, accompanied Orson and his mother.

This was the first golden age of Ravinia, the beautiful all-purpose park that sprawled across thirty-six woodland acres in Highland Park, twenty-five miles north of Chicago. Since its debut just before the Great War, Ravinia's ambitious summer program of grand opera and symphony performances had attracted classical music lovers from around the world. The 1922 summer season would reach a peak with thirty-one opera productions—a "colossal achievement," Edward Moore observed in the *Tribune*, "even when some are cut to accommodate the Ravinia traditions of time in and time out."

"Uncle Ned" and "Aunt Hazel" spent the summer hosting musicians, opera singers, and other friends in their large house on Kincaid Street in Highland Park, a suburb of lakefront mansions, forested estates, and bohemian hideaways. A Wisconsin native in his mid-forties, Moore was a witty, discerning critic and a composer himself. He and his wife, who had no children of their own, doted on Beatrice and little Orson. Another fixture at Ravinia was the museum director and "art evangelist" Dudley Crafts Watson, Beatrice's cousin, who summered with his own family near the Moores. The Moores' guests included many of the prima donnas, or divas—and their male counterparts—from New York's Metropolitan Opera, who enchanted Ravinia audiences during the summer, when the Met was dark. The leads that summer in Ravinia included Alice Gentle, Claire Dux, Queena Mario, Edith Mason, tenor Mario Chamlee, who had come to the fore in the opera world after Caruso's death in 1921, and Chamlee's wife, Ruth Miller. They gathered at the Moores' dinner table, the mere mortals genuflecting before the divine performers—"diva" derived from the Italian word for "goddess." The divas' elaborate airs and posturing, their scandals and messy private lives, even their tantrums, were all forgiven in deference to their artistry.

Also collecting around the Moores' table were Uncle Ned's Chicago newspaper colleagues, including Charles Collins of the *Chicago Tribune*, Eugene Stinson of the *Daily News*, Herman De Vries of the *American*, Felix Borowoski of the *Record-Herald*, and Ashton Stevens of the *Herald-Examiner*. Stevens was a slender, dashing critic who came from a family of actors and impresarios in San Francisco and Hollywood. A lifelong theater fan, he had seen Edwin Booth's *Hamlet* as a boy and had interviewed all the famous stage artists—Richard Mansfield, Mrs. Fiske, the Drews, the Barrymores, Laurette Taylor, Ina Claire. Also knowledgeable about music, he wrote the *Encyclopaedia Britannica* entry on the banjo, and once gave banjo lessons to none other than William Randolph Hearst, who was spurred to employ Stevens at the *San Francisco Examiner* and the *New York Evening Journal* before anchoring him at the

Chicago Examiner. Stevens had a three-decade store of Hearst anecdotes, replenished several times a year when the publisher stopped by to see his old banjo teacher during his Chicago visits.

Dick Welles's experiment in reconciliation with Beatrice that summer had fizzled—their discord continued and he rarely visited Ravinia nowadays—but in the stimulating atmosphere of the Moore household, full of show business anecdotes, little Orson found a different kind of close family. As at his mother's artistic salon in Chicago, Orson had a seat at the table along with the bright, fascinating adults—provided that he had napped, of course—and he learned to be equally adept at piping up or listening quietly. Uncle Ned loved the boy, and more than one Chicago newspaper would describe Orson as "Ed Moore's protégé." But in a sense, he was everyone's.

CHAPTER 4

1922–1926

A Great Shock

In the fall of 1922, moved by his ardent enthusiasm for singing, juggling, and magic, Orson's older brother announced that he was going to join a vaudeville troupe. In the first of his vanishing acts, teenage Richard Welles packed a bag and went on the road.

Their failed idyll in Grand Detour, and Richard's disappearance, cast a shadow over the family. On October 13, not long after returning from Ravinia and almost three years after she and Dick had separated, Beatrice Welles filed for divorce. Orson recalled listening "quietly the night of their last quarrel," Barbara Leaming wrote, "after which, by mutual agreement, Dick and Beatrice separated forever. Orson was neither surprised nor terribly shaken."

"When they separated," Leaming quoted the filmmaker as recalling, "I felt no partisanship." After all, he explained, the divorce meant receiving "twice the love" from his parents.

In her divorce claim, Beatrice accused her husband of drunkenness and philandering, while affirming her own comportment as a "true, faithful, chaste, and affectionate" spouse who had "treated him kindly and affectionately" throughout their almost twenty-year marriage. But it was Dick Welles's parsimoniousness that had forced Beatrice's hand. In her divorce filing, she estimated that her husband owned "stocks, bonds and other securities" worth $150,000, and collected another $8,000 annually from his investments, while she herself was "possessed of no property, either real or personal," and had "no means wherewith to support herself or children." Closely watched by their friends in the press and high society, the case was reported on page one of the *Chicago Herald and Examiner*'s city section. Tellingly, Beatrice was represented by a Chicago public defender.

If Dick Welles worried about other men pursuing Beatrice, she did little to allay his fears, suggesting that the count grant her an annulment so that she might be "at liberty to marry again" if the opportunity arose. She also threatened to secure "sole care, custody and education" of her two sons—Richard, who had just turned seventeen; and seven-year-old Orson. If her husband refused to accept her financial demands, she said, she would carry through with the suit. But the record of their dispute is one-sided, as Dick Welles filed no rebuttal to the claim. It's clear that he opposed the divorce, but his silence in response is a mystery. Was Orson's father afraid that open-court testimony about his drinking and womanizing would invite scandal? And what bothered him more: the possibility of forfeiting some of his money, or the threat that his children would be taken away from him?

The answer came within ten days of Beatrice's filing, when the divorce petition was abruptly withdrawn and dismissed. Dick Welles had turned over to his wife fifty shares each of Goodrich Rubber and Utah Copper, and agreed to deposit a specified monthly sum into Beatrice's bank account, making her financially stable and independent.

From that point forward, the couple would meet mainly for crises and special occasions. But their divorce was never finalized. Perhaps Dick Welles hoped for one last chance to redeem himself in Beatrice's eyes.

At the Milwaukee Art Institute, among the many programs launched by museum director Dudley Crafts Watson were his own acclaimed "music picture symphonies," a series of informative and entertaining lectures on foreign art and architecture accompanied by stereopticon slides from Watson's travels to European landmarks and more exotic locales including Morocco and Egypt. Watson invited Beatrice to provide piano accompaniment to his main attraction, an opportunity that afforded her a small fee and exposure for her talent.

Their first joint presentation was scheduled for a Sunday in early January 1923, soon after her divorce suit was withdrawn. Beatrice rehearsed long and hard for the program of Wagner, MacDowell, and "very modern compositions by hitherto unknown Spanish and French composers," according to a Milwaukee newspaper, performing behind Watson as he expounded on Montsalvat and the Holy Grail, illustrating his lecture with his stereopticon slides. This event at the Milwaukee museum was greeted so warmly that the two were able to bring it to women's clubs in Wisconsin and the Chicago suburbs. Beatrice adored her erudite cousin, even if others found him stuffy, and for a time the two of them were a happy team on the road, with little Orson and his nanny sometimes tagging along.

Although she eschewed the kind of immersion in women's clubs that had preoccupied her in Kenosha, Beatrice took a growing role in the Lake View Musical Society, a music appreciation organization of well-heeled Chicago society ladies. As leader of one committee promoting the careers of young musicians and another for community outreach, she promoted emerging talent such as the Jacques Gordon String Quartet and the new female composer Aletta Arnold, presenting the artists at home soirees and civic appearances hosted by patrons such as Edith Rockefeller McCormick, the daughter of John D. Rockefeller and the ex-wife of Harold McCormick, head of the Chicago Civic Opera.

Beatrice kept her pledge to stay away from grittier social activism, but Orson recalled that he was not overly spoiled with Christmas presents, while his mother trundled underprivileged children into their home for holiday parties and gifts. The Welles family always sandwiched in a Yuletide trip to Kenosha for awkward reunions at Rudolphsheim. Dick Welles's mother, Mary Gottfredsen, was openly skeptical about Beatrice's artistic "career," and this was one reason that Orson, as an adult, spoke ill of his paternal grandmother.

Organized religion no longer appealed to Beatrice the way it had back in the days of Reverend Florence Buck and the Kenosha Unitarians. Little Orson was never baptized, and though the family went to church at Christmas, the boy did not attend regular services while he was growing up. ("I try to be a Christian," Welles told Merv Griffin late in life, "but I don't pray, really, because I don't want to bore God.") Yet Beatrice's quest for the sacred artistic experience was leading her deeper into spiritual realms. Though she had never traveled overseas, her cousin's tales of foreign cultures opened her eyes to the arts and beliefs of the Far East; and the poetry and stories of Rabindranath Tagore, the Bengali who won the Nobel Prize in 1913, inspired in her a new search for transcendence in her music and recitals.

Influenced by Tagore's mysticism, Beatrice developed "a calm of understanding" about her life, according to Dr. Maurice Bernstein. Turning forty, the woman who once wrote a meditation on a child's death now reflected on her own mortality. "She somehow knew that her life line was not long, and therefore talked constantly about what life had in store for all of us," Dr. Bernstein recalled. She grew interested in "the other world: the world of infinity and the preservation of the spirit. She was a great believer in the order of the universe, its moral and spiritual expressions. She constantly speculated about reincarnation and wondered if people come back to the earth with the experience of a former existence. . . .

"She believed," Bernstein continued, "that we come back richer with each return to this life. When she would hear of someone going on [dying], she would say perhaps it is but they have outlived their usefulness. She did not fear death."

Inspired by Tagore, Beatrice launched yet another artistic reinvention of herself. Early in 1923, she sat for a Hyde Park photographer who took portraits of Chicago musicians and stage personalities. Having her piano tuned by the most qualified expert in the tristate region, who came from Iowa to tune her Steinway grand piano, she plunged into a fresh round of lessons with Julia Lois Caruthers, preparing a novel form of recital that would combine her pianism, her elocution skills, and her newfound identification with spirituality and foreign cultures.

But her plans were interrupted in May 1923 when she went into the hospital for an undisclosed operation. Perhaps she underwent a hysterectomy—a fairly common procedure in those days for women over forty, sometimes as an elective preventive measure, at other times to remove malignant tumors. The operation was performed by Dr. Charles Kahlke, head of the Chicago Surgical Society, and a founder of and chief of staff at Chicago Memorial Hospital, where her surgery took place.

As part of her recovery, and in the spirit of their recent truce, Beatrice accepted Dick Welles's invitation to bring the family back to

Grand Detour for a few weeks in June. Dick, still legally Beatrice's husband, said he was thinking about buying a hotel.

The larger of Grand Detour's two hotels was the Sheffield, at an inter-section of Route 2, the serpentine road connecting northern Illinois with southern Wisconsin, lying adjacent to the John Deere homestead, site of America's first plow factory. The hotel, an L-shaped, two-story wood-frame building with more than thirty guest rooms, was owned by Charles Sheffield, a local character whose big smile and overalls fixed with a safety pin masked the fact that he was among the area's wealthiest citizens. By the early 1920s Charlie Sheffield was getting on in years, and had started talking about selling the hotel, but he was taking forever to make his move, and Dick Welles was trying to nudge him toward the sale. Beatrice, in turn, encouraged her long-idle hus-band, cheered that he was contemplating a return to business.

The hotel arranged boating and fishing for guests, who also had the use of a croquet green and tennis court. There was sunbathing across the highway on the shore of the Rock River, with nearby whirlpool rocks. Artists, business travelers, and farmers came from miles around for the weekend fried chicken and catfish suppers, famous throughout Ogle County.

Seventeen-year-old Richard was back that summer, though no one knew for how long. Dick Welles bunked with his sons at the hotel, while Beatrice and the omnipresent Dr. Maurice Bernstein stayed in a rented colonial house nearby. Richard was an agreeable fellow on the surface, according to people in Grand Detour, and his parents both hoped he would commit to a regular job and begin to support him-self. But the often contrary Richard now changed his mind, writing letters to various colleges pleading for admission. Though his letters were heartfelt, they were also full of misspellings, and when Chicago Latin and Northwestern Academy were asked for his references and transcripts, the schools had no choice but to report that the young man never had satisfied their requisites.

The ten-year age difference between Richard and Orson was like that between Dick Welles and his half brother, Jacob Rudolph Gottfred-sen, with much the same consequences. Their lives barely intertwined during Orson's boyhood, and Richard's problems went over Orson's head most of the time. Although they set up their easels and painted alongside each other, their relationship was not close.

Richard's mysterious afflictions and difficult temperament made his parents all the more anxious to coddle Orson, whose every illness was regarded as life threatening. Dr. Bernstein, who was consulted about the boy's slightest twinge, fostered the impression that Orson was "sickly." Welles told his biographer Barbara Leaming that he was born with anomalies of the spine—Bernstein specialized in these—and his other childhood conditions and illnesses, chronicled with more or less accuracy in other books, included sinus headaches, hay fever, asthma, diphtheria, scarlet fever, mumps, malaria, weak ankles, and flat feet. There was nothing too out of the ordinary about this list, but over time the general preoccupation with his health made Orson an opportunist, more than once faking illness when it was to his advantage.

For Beatrice Welles, who believed in the benefits of outdoor life and physical culture, a stay in the country was a tonic. Orson would inherit his mother's attachment to nature, more than once in his life disappearing into the wilds to recharge himself. Life in Grand Detour was not as stimulating for Richard, however, and as his college prospects dwindled, he started talking about going on the road again. Dr. Bernstein had come to see Richard as delusional, in need of serious medical treatment. His parents hoped the doctor was wrong, but they wrung their hands over Richard. When Beatrice left for Ravinia in July, taking little Orson and Dr. Bernstein with her, Richard quickly fell out with his father, wangled some money out of him, and disappeared again.

When Orson and his mother returned from Highland Park and Ravinia to Chicago in the fall of 1923, Beatrice immersed herself in rehearsals for a Milwaukee Art Institute presentation intended to introduce the bold shift in her career that had been delayed by her operation. This "interpretative concert combining poetry and music" was her first advertised solo recital in years, and the first in which she reclaimed her maiden name in her billing: Beatrice Ives Welles.

A crowd of Milwaukeeans with friends and guests from Chicago and the North Shore gathered that Sunday in mid-November for an afternoon of readings from Tagore and original compositions "of the most delicate and colorful imagination," according to Catherine Pannill Mead, the music editor of the *Milwaukee Sentinel*. The performance featured cantillation—ritual chanting—and "various charming Spanish dance rhythms," Mead wrote. "Mrs. Wells [*sic*] is happily the owner of an exceptionally musical speaking voice," and "is very lovely to look at."

No doubt her eight-year-old son, Orson, was in the audience that day, immaculately suited with garters and a pressed handkerchief, witnessing what would be the apogee of his mother's career. In public, however, Beatrice took care not to favor Orson above his brother. In her only known reference to her son in her entire career as a public figure, she supplied this tidbit for the publicity release about her triumphant solo appearance in Milwaukee: "Her interest at the present time is divided between two very talented sons and recitals in and about Chicago."

After the New Year, Dick Welles brought Orson to New York in what was becoming an annual tradition. Dick took the boy to a matinee of *Hamlet* starring John Barrymore, and after the performance escorted him backstage to greet the actor. Orson's father had known Barrymore for years, through many backstage visits and postshow revels.

When Orson returned to Chicago, his mother was waiting for him with tickets to a tenth-anniversary screening of D. W. Griffith's *The Birth of a Nation*. Her cousin Dudley Crafts Watson, who also wore the hat of film critic for the *Milwaukee Free Press*, where he hailed Griffith as "the genius of his craft," had urged her to go. The sweeping dramatization of events of the Civil War and Reconstruction was playing in her favorite theater, the Auditorium, backed by a full orchestra including many of her musician friends. *The Birth of a Nation* may have been controversial for its racist distortions of American history, but it was also groundbreaking and thrilling for its time, and Orson always spoke admiringly of Griffith.

"Did his films exert an influence on you, do you think?" Peter Bogdanovich asked him.

"He's influenced everyone who's ever made a movie," Welles replied firmly.

Welles was sensitive about the image of his mother as an overly solemn personality—an artist who was serious to the point of pretension. He liked to point out to interviewers that she was also "a great practical joker"—another of her traits that he folded into his own personality. "She used to take a long piece of cord," Welles told David Frost, "and she was such a dignified lady, if she came to a street corner and said to a man, 'Would you hold this, please,' he would hold it. Then she'd go around to the other side of the street corner and find someone and say, 'Would you hold this, please.' That was her idea of a fun thing to do. She was so dignified, the men would be standing there all afternoon thinking, 'She told me I must hold it.'"

The success of her Milwaukee recital fanned Beatrice's ambitions. She brushed up with Julia Lois Caruthers, the Hyde Park man shot new publicity portraits in January, and the tristate piano tuner returned. She had a brochure printed touting a planned fall tour of her Asian-influenced interpretative poetry and music, with dates in the Midwest and prospectively all the way to New York. But before the tour, early that summer, she was hoping to make her first trip to Europe. Beatrice's cousin Dudley Crafts Watson had left the Milwaukee Art Institute to join the staff of the Art Institute of Chicago, and one of his initiatives was organizing overseas tours for art lovers. He planned to lead the first such trip in June, and Beatrice, Dick Welles, and Dr. Maurice Bernstein—demonstrating their esprit de corps—all paid deposits for the excursion.

One of Watson's last days at the Milwaukee Art Institute was April 20, Easter Sunday, and it was announced that Beatrice would appear in his final holiday program there, accompanying a lantern slide lecture reprising his exegesis on the Holy Grail. A few days before Easter, however, Beatrice backed out. She felt unwell.

Almost two weeks passed with Beatrice feeling ill, though she didn't complain enough to raise serious concern, even within her family. With Orson's ninth birthday coming up, she dispatched her nanny and housekeeper Sigrid Jacobsen to buy the boy a pair of ice skates, along with a new Gilbert Mysto Magic Kit as a birthday gift from his father.

Dick Welles wasn't informed of his wife's illness until May 3 or 4. By then, Beatrice had taken to her bed for the last time.

Decades later, in a faux memoir he wrote for *Paris Vogue*, Welles described his birthday celebration that fateful May 6, 1924: the cake candles lit for him in the "black room" where his mother was dying, her cello voice beckoning him to her side. "Well now, Georgie-Porgie . . ." This is the scene that opens *RKO 281*, the 1999 telefilm about the making of *Citizen Kane*.

According to Orson's moving account, his mother recited to him:

These antique fables apprehend
More than cool reason ever comprehends.

These were teasing lines from *A Midsummer Night's Dream*, the Shakespeare play his mother had read to her sweet bright boy ad nauseam during his tender years. "Those great shining eyes looked dark by the light of the eight small candles," Welles wrote. "I can remember now what I was thinking. I thought how green those eyes looked when it was sunny."

That year, however, there were actually nine candles on his birthday cake.

According to the *Paris Vogue* version of events, Beatrice whispered a few more lines from *A Midsummer Night's Dream*, then told Orson that the birthday candles on the cake constituted "a fairy ring" and "you will never again in your whole life have just that number to blow out. You must puff hard," Beatrice urged the boy, "and you must blow out every one of them.

"And you must make a wish."

The birthday boy puffed hard "and suddenly the room was very dark and my mother had vanished forever." Not that she had died— not yet—but little Orson must have sensed that the end was near. "Sometimes, in the dead watches of the night, it strikes me that of all my mistakes, the greatest was on that birthday just before my mother died, when I forgot to make a wish."

Soon after marking Orson's birthday, Beatrice lapsed into a coma. "Ever since," Welles told his daughter Chris Welles Feder years later, "I've never wanted to celebrate my birthday."

Taken to Chicago Memorial Hospital, Beatrice Ives Welles was attended by a team of physicians headed by Dr. Charles Kahlke. Two nurses alternated round the clock as her health deteriorated. Dudley Crafts Watson and Dr. Bernstein took turns by her side. Dick Welles hovered nearby. No treatment helped. Orson's mother slipped away on Saturday, May 10, at 10:30 P.M. She was not yet forty-one.

The hospital physicians were baffled by Beatrice's symptoms, the sudden onset of her illness, and her death. After conducting an autopsy himself, Kahlke convened a meeting of the top doctors in the hospital to discuss the inconclusive results. "Acute yellow atrophy of the liver" was the diagnosis ultimately recorded on her death certificate, and some books on Welles have interpreted that as evidence of jaundice or hepatitis. But acute atrophy indicates a severely shrunken, scarred liver, which makes other scenarios possible, including infection caused by a blood transfusion, or an earlier operation. Even her dentistry treatments were scrutinized.

Beatrice Ives Welles's death was front-page news in Kenosha ("A Great Shock," the *Kenosha News* reported), and it was covered widely in many Illinois and Wisconsin newspapers. Calling her "a pianist of exquisite feeling and polished technique," Catherine Pannill Mead wrote in the *Milwaukee Sentinel* that Beatrice would be mourned by "hundreds of friends." The *Chicago Daily Tribune*'s headline noted that "Chicago Musicians Mourn Passing of Mrs. Welles." The Lake View Musical Society established a fund in her name to benefit aspiring talent and send bouquets to young classical musicians making future debuts.

Dick Welles arranged for his wife's burial in Kenosha in the family plot. The many drama and music critics she knew traveled from Chicago and Milwaukee to attend the funeral. A local Baptist minister who had known Beatrice eulogized her, and Dick also paid $50 for Horace Bridges, a Shakespeare expert and leader of the secularist Chicago Ethical Society, to come by train from Chicago and deliver a meditation.

Nineteen-year-old Richard was conspicuously absent. With his father's help, Richard had recently signed on as an "apprentice fish-culturist" with the U.S. Bureau of Fisheries in Bozeman, Montana, and no one thought it wise to jeopardize his job by bringing him home so soon. Nine-year-old Orson was at his mother's grave, however. Years later, when he told interviewer Joseph McBride that he had only terrible memories of Kenosha, his companion, Oja Kodar, pointed out that his recall was colored by the miserable, rainy day of his mother's funeral.

What to do about Orson was a pressing concern. Dudley Crafts Watson's tour of Europe was on the horizon, and after Beatrice's death the three men closest to her all felt the trip should go on in her memory. Watson and Dr. Bernstein agreed to travel ahead with Orson to the village of Wyoming in upstate New York, where the Watson family spent part of every June at an artists' colony, Hillside. There, little Orson could stay for the summer with Watson's wife and their three young daughters—Augusta, Emily, and Marjorie—while the three men headed off to Europe.

It speaks to the suddenness of Beatrice's deterioration, as well as to her enigmatic relations with her husband, that she did not leave a will. Thanks to the arrangement with Dick Welles, who inherited her estate, she possessed more than $7,000 in stocks and bonds on her death, along with several hundred dollars in a checking account. Her few debts were easily paid. In the flurry that followed her death, Dr. Bernstein ended up with Beatrice's piano and other family belongings, including some Asian treasures. Years later Orson would blame Bernstein for expropriating these objects, but what use did Dick Welles have for them? The Welles family was done with the piano and all that. Orson later insisted that he would never again play either the piano or the violin: not quite true, but true enough.

Orson's father lingered in Chicago, tidying up his wife's financial affairs, before rushing off to join Watson, Bernstein, and a group of Chicago art lovers as they sailed from Boston to England on June 10. From there, the group went on to Spain, France, Austria, and Italy, while Orson spent the first part of the summer with his cousins at Hillside.

"Life and money both behave like loose quicksilver in a nest of cracks," Jack Amberson says poignantly to his nephew George Amberson Minafer, after misfortune has humbled the Ambersons, in Booth

Tarkington's novel. Uncle Jack (played by Ray Collins) says the same thing to George (Tim Holt) in Orson Welles's film of *The Magnificent Ambersons*.

Time and money were the two bogeymen of Welles's career, and he battled both in grand style. His mother's unexpected death taught him about the exigencies of time. From his mother, Welles adopted the view that art was ephemeral, time fickle, and money a mere tool, as mundane as a shovel. Time was not an enemy—it was a waiting game—and he would make an art of waiting and playing the game. Even the life of an artist was not to be glamorized: there were only a few immortal artists, she taught him, and it would be immodest to think of himself as one. Despite his great ego, he never altered this view.

As a child, Orson had been torn from Kenosha and shuttled between the homes of his estranged parents, both of whom he loved and both of whom, in their individual ways, ceaselessly traveled. His rootlessness, his quickness to pack his bags and escape, would turn him into the most nomadic of American filmmakers. "Orson never wanted to face unpleasantness," Dr. Maurice Bernstein observed decades later, and the habit of skirting unpleasantness could be traced to his itinerant boyhood and his quick removal from Chicago after the death of his mother.

A boy's love for his lost mother is a motif that crops up in a number of Orson Welles films. The scenes cited by most scholars occur in his two earliest pictures. One is *The Magnificent Ambersons*, in which George Amberson Minafer visits his mother, Isabel, on her deathbed—the rippling-lace lighting here is sublime. George has behaved abominably toward his mother, yet even in her delirium Isabel thinks only of her son: "Darling, did you get something to eat?" she asks tenderly, "Are you sure you didn't catch cold coming home?" Her eyes follow him as he leaves in shame, and Isabel's ensuing death takes place offscreen, just as Orson must have been too young to have been in the hospital room when his own mother died late at night. Delivering the news, George's aunt Fanny wraps him in a reassuring embrace:

"She loved you. She loved you."

The role Orson assigned to mothers in *Citizen Kane* is even more complicated. "There's just not any connection" between his real-life mother and the mother of Charles Foster Kane, Welles insisted to

Peter Bogdanovich. Beatrice Welles was "very beautiful, very generous and very tough," Welles said, and "rather austere with me." By
comparison, Mary Kane, played by Agnes Moorehead, is a hard-bitten
countrywoman.

But neither Welles nor Bogdanovich mentioned the second mother
to appear in the film: Kane's first wife, Emily Monroe Norton, whom
Kane rejects in a climactic scene at his supposed "love nest." Later, the
divorced Emily is killed along with her and Charles's little boy, Charles
Kane Jr., in an offscreen automobile accident. Emily Kane was played
by Ruth Warrick, who—like Dolores Costello, playing Isabel in *The
Magnificent Ambersons*—evokes the ladylike Beatrice Ives Welles. Charles
Kane Jr. is eight when he and his mother perish in *Citizen Kane*, close to
Welles's age when Beatrice died.

Bogdanovich tried to argue the point with Welles, reminding him
of the sequence when Kane first meets Susan Alexander, his second
wife in the film. Their meeting derails Kane's trip to a warehouse,
where he intends to go through his dead mother's effects "in search of
my youth." Later in the sequence, when Susan and Kane are talking
in her apartment, she tells him that her mother always thought she
should sing grand opera. "It's just what, you know, mothers are like,"
Susan explains sweetly. Kane hesitates, then replies, "Yes" ("in a sad
reflective tone, full of memories," in Bogdanovich's words). Following
an awkward pause between them, Kane asks Susan to play the piano
and sing for him.

Kane really doesn't know what mothers are like, does he? After all,
his own mother sent him away.

"It's one of my favorite moments in the picture," Bogdanovich told
Welles.

"No, Peter," Welles insisted, refusing to nibble. "I have no Rosebuds."

Equidistant between Rochester and Buffalo, Wyoming, New York,
was a picture-postcard village in the heart of Middlebury township
in Wyoming County. Settled as a "water cure" spa in 1851, the Hillside estate was a family vacation home before a daughter, Lydia Avery
Coonley Ward, a Chicagoan, turned it into a summer colony for art-

ists, writers, and musicians. After her death, Dudley Crafts Watson became one of a group of devotees who kept Hillside active.

Hillside was far from Chicago. Orson had been close, from earliest memory, to his Watson cousins Augusta (born in 1910), Emily (1912), and Marjorie (1915)—perhaps especially Emily, who was slightly older than he and a mischief maker. The Watson girls were a captive audience for Orson, who stayed awake long after the grownups, spinning ghost stories enlivened by simple theatrical effects he was already shrewdly mastering: thunder and lightning, a flashlight, and a magician's voice for mind reading and hypnosis. "His [character for the] radio program 'The Shadow' was born that summer under my daughters' bed, after they had gone to bed at night, scaring them to death," recalled Dudley Crafts Watson.

Young Orson had other eye-opening adventures in the girls' bedroom, he claimed later. "Emily Watson introduced me to the mysteries of playing doctor," Welles said. "But she was full of what I later discovered to be misinformation." Limited and "fumbling" though they may have been, in Barbara Leaming's words, these early experiences left the young boy "with a keen appetite for more." A few more years would pass before Dr. Maurice Bernstein tried to explain the facts of life to him. Orson always laughed to recall the doctor's abashed demonstration of the mechanics. "He drew a circle on a blackboard and that was the end of the evening," Welles said.

Besides his girl cousins, Orson's playmates at Hillside included the vacationing children of the family of Aga Khan III, who had come to Wyoming in part to foster Prince Aly Khan's interest in racehorses. Nine-year-old Orson and thirteen-year-old Aly Khan, who crossed paths here for the first time, would grow up to marry the same woman, Rita Hayworth, in the 1940s. "We've known each other all our lives," Welles liked to boast.

By the time Dick Welles returned from Europe, he had spent many days and nights discussing his son's future with Dudley Crafts Watson and Dr. Bernstein. Orson was a demanding boy, and while he was perfectly capable of entertaining himself for long periods of time, he thrived on input and interaction. (In another era he might have been labeled "hyperactive.") He scoffed at afternoon naps, and after his mother's death avoided going to sleep as long as possible after dark.

He play-acted through the night in his bedroom, with magic, puppets, makeup, and costumes to keep himself entertained.

Perhaps Beatrice had indulged her youngest son by giving him such a long leash, and by immersing him in her world of performance and self-expression, yet her constancy and values also had shaped him into a bright and personable boy. Everyone felt beholden to her.

In his early fifties, Dick Welles was feeling the weight of age. His mother, now approaching eighty and living alone at Rudolphsheim (her second husband had died in 1913), would be no help to him in raising the boy; at family get-togethers, she long had made it known that she felt Beatrice was pampering Orson with her dalliance in the arts instead of giving him a more practical upbringing.

The other two men felt that Dick Welles should continue to raise Orson in a way that honored Beatrice's priorities, and they promised to help as best they could. Watson traveled even more frequently than Dick Welles, but young Orson could and did spend long hours in "Uncle" Dudley's care at the Art Institute of Chicago, playing detective with his girl cousins, slipping out into the skylights over the galleries, prowling around the narrow solid flooring while avoiding the expanses of glass. As for Dr. Bernstein, still childless, he doted on the young boy, seeing in Orson the possible fulfillment of Beatrice's artistic promise. According to Welles, Bernstein believed that "I *was* my mother and I kept the flame." The doctor even scolded the boy for not mourning his mother enough. "It wasn't that I didn't love my mother," Orson told Barbara Leaming; it was just that "I didn't love her the way he did."

If Dr. Bernstein carried a torch for Beatrice, he also felt a responsibility toward Dick Welles. Bernstein and Welles had established an awkward friendship, but by now something else bridged their differences. Evidence suggests they also had a doctor-patient relationship.

Peter Noble's book about Orson, which was virtually ghosted by Bernstein, states that "an illness late in his life" had led to Dick Welles's "addiction to gin." This may sound like an overly sympathetic diagnosis, but it was grounded in contemporary medical practice: in the early twentieth century, many physicians prescribed gin as a kind of herbal pain relief, often blending it with bitter medicinal quinine. The famous drink that resulted, gin and tonic, was thought to offer relief from diseases like malaria, and to calm heart palpitations. Orson's father may have been self-medicating to ameliorate his atrial fibrillation—a condition that would recur in his sons half a century later.

Neither Dick Welles nor Dr. Bernstein alone could handle Orson, but together the former husband and the bachelor physician would do their best. After bringing Orson home from Hillside to Chicago, they resolved to preserve the family's summer routine, taking the boy back to Grand Detour, where Charlie Sheffield was finally getting ready to sell his hotel. After a few weeks, Dr. Bernstein picked Orson up to bring him to Ravinia, where Ned and Hazel Moore would take their turn as increasingly important members of his extended surrogate family.

At the end of the summer Dr. Bernstein moved from his East Chicago Street address into an apartment shared with Dick Welles on Cambridge Street in the River North neighborhood. He and Dick never became soul-baring friends, however—in the nearly one hundred pages of cursive notes Bernstein kept for his own planned biography of Orson, he could only write (inaccurately) that "Dick Welles was born in Kansas." But the unlikely roommates were determined to join forces in raising young Orson. Their first major decision was to enroll the nine-year-old in a public school near the University of Chicago. Dick, the senior partner in every way, "felt that by going to a public school, [Orson] would come in contact with boys of his own age and take part in their games," recalled Bernstein. Dick Welles himself went to work every day; he now listed his profession as "stockbroker," though mainly he tended to his own stocks while giving investment advice to friends. Bernstein, according to his own recollection, agreed to drive Orson to school in the morning and "call for him when school was out."

The public school experiment was unsuccessful. "Orson did not fit in with the usual boys," the doctor recalled; he didn't join in sports and games at recess, and he was taunted. And there was another reason Orson didn't last long: "I persistently pretended to be sick," the filmmaker recalled years later. "One afternoon, upon returning from school, I put the thermometer on the hot water bottle, which moved Dadda to send me to the hospital where they took out my appendix. I kept saying, 'Wait a minute, I'm feeling better.' Nobody would listen." Bernstein always insisted that Orson really *did* have appendicitis, and over the years the story led to a running argument between Pookles and Dadda.

Orson went home to stretch out his recovery, and Orson at home was a handful. Before he was old enough to go out on his own, one of the men had to escort him to an art store for paints, brushes, sketch pads, and easels; to a bookstore for the poetry, plays, novels, and works of history and philosophy the boy soaked up; to a magic shop next to the Princess Theatre; to the museum, where he'd clock in with "Uncle" Dudley for a few hours; to the opera, symphony, latest moving pictures, touring plays, and vaudeville shows.

Dr. Bernstein filled Beatrice's role in the partnership. At home, the doctor read Orson's school assignments, or original works—often verse. Young Orson's precocious writing and speaking abilities, so reminiscent of his mother, were all the more impressive to Bernstein, for whom English was a second language. Insecure about his own writing, the doctor needed a collaborator for the one piece of medical research he published, and even when he wrote simple business letters a secretary touched up his imperfect grammar and spelling.

Later, presenting himself as the authority on Orson's boyhood, Bernstein made great claims for the genius of his young charge. Bernstein was undoubtedly sincere, but he was a publicist at heart, and many of his stories were flights of fancy. Young Orson may have been fascinated with the theater and may have been a prodigy, but he did *not* at the age of eight or nine dash off a treatise called "The Universal History of Drama," a piece Bernstein insisted was "something of a masterpiece even had it been written by someone twenty years his senior." Nor did young Orson craft a searching essay on Goethe or Nietzsche. "I'm an anti-Nietzsche fellow, and I certainly never wrote that," Welles told David Frost. "It sounds like one of those stories." Later in life, Welles batted away questions about his supposed boy-genius masterworks like annoying houseflies. "No," he'd simply say.

The boy's artistic abilities must have seemed doubly remarkable to Dr. Bernstein, who revered the arts but was never an artist himself, playing the cello only as an enthusiast. The doctor applauded all the boy's magic tricks and puppet shows, took special delight in his improvised poetry and his artwork, and was rarely bored watching young Orson perform huge chunks of Shakespeare, including all the famous soliloquies.

Dick Welles and Dr. Bernstein were Orson's first producers, surrounding the boy with the finest stagecraft money could buy: high-quality puppet theater paraphernalia, the best magic and makeup kits, with a wide array of face paints, mustaches, beards, and wigs. King Lear was one of his favorite Shakespeare characters, partly because of the elaborate costumes and makeup it required. (The young boy could recite "*any* speech from *King Lear*," Bernstein insisted.) Some Welles experts have seen this penchant for *Lear* as a youthful obsession with growing old and the inevitability of death. "He spent his youth pretending to be old, dying men," Peter Conrad wrote in *Orson Welles: The Stories of His Life.* But Orson was also instinctively following the age-old theatrical practice of building his characterization and performance from "externals." The credo of many actors is that a physical lie begets a psychological lie, and Orson followed this credo as an actor and a director—though hardly unwaveringly. Being a distinct physical type himself, he was acutely aware of the physical appearance of characters.

To balance his mother's "ultra-artistic" influence, Dr. Bernstein later told Peter Noble, Dick Welles introduced Orson to newsmen such as the Chicago-born Bud Fisher, creator of *Mutt and Jeff,* and George McManus, who drew *Bringing Up Father,* both of them syndicated Hearst cartoonists. Oil painting was an admirable high art, but cartooning seemed a more practical career goal, and Orson took his father's views seriously. The boy started carrying around a pencil and notepaper, sketching people he encountered and places he visited. This became a lifelong habit, and Orson frequently adorned his letters to family and friends with funny little caricatures and line drawings of sights and landscapes.

With young Orson in tow, Dick Welles and Dr. Bernstein returned to New York City soon after the New Year. Dr. Bernstein wanted to bring the boy to the American debut of Igor Stravinsky, who was performing his piano concertos with the New York Philharmonic in early January 1925. Afterward, Bernstein took young Orson backstage to meet the Russian-born composer. Still later, after the concert and backstage visit, Bernstein recalled, the nine-year-old "discoursed intelligently on the evening's music" to listeners in the lobby of the Waldorf Hotel. One of those who overheard him that night was a petite young brunette actress, Agnes Moorehead; she never forgot the intelligent boy, with his "shock of black hair" and blue blazer. "He was fantastic," she recalled, "the way he kept explaining his feelings about the concert." A decade later, the actress—who graduated with honors from the American Academy of Dramatic Arts, and forged her career on radio in the 1930s—came to mind as Orson pondered who should play Charles Foster Kane's mother, the hard-bitten countrywoman, but with "a strong face, warm and kind," according to the script. Less than a year after the death of his own mother, he had met her fictional counterpart.

On that same trip, Dick Welles brought Orson to see the famous magician and escape artist Harry Houdini at the Hippodrome on Sixth Avenue. Afterward, father and son paid a visit backstage, and Houdini graciously showed the boy a fundamental card trick known as "the pass" or "the shift," in which a card placed in the middle of a deck resurfaces as the top card.

Houdini, billed that year as the "World Famous Author, Lecturer, and Acknowledged Head of Mystifiers," was at the height of his fame. The highlight of his Hippodrome show was his escape from a wooden box that was pierced by iron rods. Orson insisted on seeing the feat a second night, and Dr. Bernstein took him. This time, when they went backstage, the magician revealed to young Orson the secret of one of his favorite handkerchief tricks, cautioning the boy that a good magician practiced a newly learned trick a thousand times before performing it in public.

Just then, a prominent magic dealer knocked on the door and rushed into the dressing room to pitch Houdini a marvelous new vanishing lamp for his act. As Orson watched with big eyes, the dealer showed Houdini the trick, and after a few questions the magician quickly mastered the moves. "I'll put it in the next show!" Houdini exclaimed, thus contravening his own advice. Nevertheless, Bernstein swore that Orson did practice his magic tricks *thousands* of times.

Thirty years later, Peter Noble reported in *The Fabulous Orson Welles* that Welles was still practicing with Houdini's vanishing lamp, and that he performed the "old Houdini handkerchief trick most effectively" onstage. "I saw him do it at the great Sid Field Benefit Show at the London Palladium in 1951 and again, before the then Princess Elizabeth and the Duke of Edinburgh, in the Variety Club Gala Show at the London Coliseum in 1952."

Houdini was also from Wisconsin—Appleton—as Dick Welles liked to remind Orson. Dick loved magic, and if Bernstein took the lead escorting Orson to opera and the symphony, his father took the lead with magic, buying his son instructional books and taking him to see all the famous magicians in Chicago and New York. Magic was in Orson's genes, Todd School's headmaster Roger Hill once said—it was a boyhood passion closely linked to his father, and a wellspring of inspiration for Orson's future as a conjurer of a snowstorm in a glass ball, a life faked in a newsreel, a palatial tomb, and a hallway of mirrors stretching into infinity.

When they came back to Chicago, Orson talked his way out of returning to public school, and his father and Dr. Maurice Bernstein debated the next step in his education. Unlike Richard, who quit his Montana fishery apprenticeship soon after his mother's death—these days he was in and out of Chicago, driving Dick Welles crazy—Orson had no trouble busying himself constructively, and he easily kept up his studies at home. Welles and Bernstein knew it was best to gain Orson's cooperation first before nudging him down any path.

A year after his mother's death, in May, Orson celebrated his tenth birthday. His father and Dr. Bernstein took him to see the new Michael Arlen stage comedy *The Green Hat*, with Broadway's newest leading lady, Katharine Cornell. Married to the play's director, Guthrie McClintic, Cornell was the talk of the town that spring in Chicago. She proved a delightful comedienne, although over time romantic tragedy would emerge as her true forte.

Orson studied the program, memorizing the names of everyone involved in the comedy, including the lesser actors and even the backstage artists. He prided himself on paying attention to the unsung personalities; he was always recasting plays in his mind, and he returned to these boyhood mental notebooks throughout his career. One weekend in Kenosha, for example, he and his father saw the Theatre Guild touring production of A. A. Milne's *Mr. Pim Passes By* at the Rhode. Going backstage after the show, father and son shook hands with all the actors—including Erskine Sanford, already a whiz at frazzled-old-man parts though he was only in his thirties.

Orson inherited his father's fondness for comic dancers, such as the vaudeville act Durant and Mitchell, and years later he would hire Jack Durant for a nightclub scene in *Journey of Fear.* Another dancer who made an impression on young Orson was the loose-limbed comic dancer Harry Shannon from Saginaw, Michigan, whom he saw cavorting in a Chicago revue. By the time Orson saw him again, in 1940, Shannon was fifty years old, with no serious dramatic credits. Orson was searching for someone to play his character's father in *Citizen Kane*—a role that goes without description, unusually so, in the published script. Shannon was doing uncredited bits in Hollywood pictures until Orson chose him to play, unforgettably, the vaguely ineffectual, possibly alcoholic and abusive senior Kane.

Young Orson would follow Cornell's career after seeing her in *The Green Hat,* and more than once he drew casting from the roster of her ensembles. The next time he saw her onstage, it was several years later in New York, in a drama called *Dishonored Lady* by Margaret Ayers Barnes and Edward Sheldon—the latter a Chicago playwright whose work Orson followed. It was a bit of *guignol,* not really very good, although Cornell was authoritative in her role. And Orson noticed one actor: Fortunio Bonanova, a former opera tenor from Mallorca, who played an oily South American lover murdered by Cornell. Bonanova stole his scenes, and Orson would not forget him. In 1940, as he reworked the scenes in *Citizen Kane* in which Susan Alexander Kane strains to hit the high notes while rehearsing for her opera debut, Orson thought of Bonanova for the role of the frustrated voice tutor, Matisti.

MATISTI

Impossible! Impossible! . . . I will be the laughingstock of the musical world. People will say—

KANE

If you're interested in what people will say. Signor Matisti,
I may be able to enlighten you a bit. The newspapers, for
instance, I'm an authority on what the papers will say,
Signor Matisti, because I own eight of them between here
and San Francisco. . . . It's all right, dear. Signor Matisti is
going to listen to reason. Aren't you, maestro?

Like Shannon, Bonanova had been languishing in Hollywood,
taking walk-on parts as headwaiters and hotel managers. "Sent for
him the minute I wrote that part," Orson told Peter Bogdanovich. "He
was so marvelous. God, he was funny."

In June 1925, Dick Welles took his son back to the Hotel Sheffield in
Grand Detour. The hotel was filled to capacity that summer on most
weekends and holidays. Some writers have scoffed at Welles's recollection that the Sheffield was filled with circus folk, or that the hotel employees included colorful characters like "Rattlesnake-Oil Emery" and
a waitress who performed birdcalls in a tent show. But Rattlesnake-Oil
Emery was a real person—the hotel's handyman and launderer, who
also butchered chickens—and Route 2, which ran past the hotel, was
busy all summer long with circus and festival wagons on their way to
county fairs.

Memorial Day opened the summer season, and Orson and his
father trekked to Court House Square in Oregon, where by 1926 the
parade of Civil War "Old Boys" in their tattered blues had dwindled
to a feeble handful.

With their parents off on another European art tour, the Watson
girls joined them for the month of June. Marjorie Watson recalled
Orson honing his magic act that summer, trying to hypnotize his
cousins. One day, ten-year-old Orson and his cousins Emily and Marjorie managed to slip the noose, as they later boasted, running away
to live the actor's life on the road. County police searched for them
for hours before spotting them in Oregon, ten miles north, with the
girls passing as boys, all of them in blackface, singing and dancing for
pennies on a street corner.

Emily went along fearlessly with Orson's adventures, her father told Peter Noble. "Orson was exceedingly gallant, made her pine-bough beds to sleep on at night in the deep woods and took off his own coat and put it over her. Her only concern was when he threw all the money that he had in his pockets into a stream and said, 'Now we will live on our own talents, or we will starve to death.' "

When the Watsons whisked the girls away, Dick Welles and his son were left to their own devices for a few weeks. Young Orson was an "odd child," in the words of Frederick J. Garner, a Grand Detour resident, "and stories are told of him entertaining people in the evening at the country store." Every now and then father and son took off for Dixon, the biggest town in the county, driving to the downtown air-conditioned theater where the comedies and Westerns were interspersed with vaudeville acts on Sundays. In the summer of 1925 they saw Chaplin in *The Gold Rush*; they also saw the spectacular *Ben-Hur*, and William S. Hart's *Tumbleweeds*.

Dick Welles was finally closing in on a deal for the Hotel Sheffield, and he was hoping to install his restless son at a summer camp for boys during August. Dr. Maurice Bernstein knew of a good one near Borcher's Beach on the north shore of Lake Mendota, the largest and most beautiful of the lakes surrounding Madison, Wisconsin. It was a curious fact about Camp Indianola that it recruited heavily from the Chicago Jewish community, and the majority of its campers were Jewish. The camp stressed resourcefulness and self-reliance, traits young Orson had in abundance. But Orson would also benefit from the outdoor physical regimen.

The dome of the state capitol and the buildings of the University of Wisconsin could be glimpsed several miles away on the other side of Lake Mendota. Camp Indianola had grown, since its humble beginnings in 1907, into a large, well-equipped facility boasting a large two-story cottage with library and music rooms, a canoe house, a mess hall, and a general assembly building with a small stage. By 1925, more than one hundred boys were attending the summer camp, coming largely from Madison, southern Wisconsin, and northern Illinois. The camp was owned and operated by Frederick Mueller, known to his young charges as Captain, and his wife, Mina.

Barbara Leaming's biography of Welles refers to Mueller as a professor of psychology, an "eminent German psychologist who specialized in unusual children." In fact, Mueller was born in Wisconsin—his parents were German immigrants—and the German language was one of his teaching specialties in college and later in Madison-area high schools. When not running Camp Indianola, Mueller was, indeed, a psychology instructor at the university in Madison, but he was not a particularly "eminent" academic; his only advanced degree, then or later, was a master's degree in philosophy.

Camp Indianola was situated on onetime Native American ground, and Captain Mueller ran it like an Indian encampment, with the boys divided by age and size into opposing Onaway and Wendigo tribes for sports and games. Among the pastimes were archery, horseback riding, swimming, and canoeing. The campers could fish for black bass, pike, bullheads, perch, and bluegills in abundance from rowboats a short distance from shore. Older boys lived in large tents on raised wooden platforms, arranged in a semicircle, and smaller tents were available for roadside pitching on overnight trips. The summer culminated with the boys taking a two-week "Gypsy trip" north through the Wisconsin Dells, a popular tourist destination.

Before the new boy arrived, Captain Mueller buttonholed Lowell Frautschi, a university undergraduate serving as the camp athletic director. Mueller told Frautschi that an "unusual child," whose mother had died tragically the previous year, was arriving shortly. The new boy had been raised in a "heady environment and was accustomed almost exclusively to the company of adults," Frautschi recalled Mueller telling him. The boy would benefit from learning "the normal childhood skills." Mueller asked Frautschi to share his barracks room with the boy, and to "keep a close watch on his participation in camp activities."

Many years later, Frautschi vividly recalled the new arrival. "Orson was large for his age," he noted. "He had a pleasing personality and had little difficulty getting along with the other campers, although he was indeed awkward at sports. He entered into things well enough to relieve me of any special effort in having to encourage him."

Besides bunking together, Frautschi and Orson shared a morning art class, which had only one student: Orson. Dick Welles had stipulated that art be added to the program, and paid extra for Frautschi to supervise the class. The new boy arrived with his own easel and paint set, which he told Frautschi had been a gift from the eminent Lorado Taft. "We would usually go somewhere, such as a nearby pasture," Frautschi remembered, "where Orson would put up his easel and proceed to paint while I sat on the ground and read."

Young Orson also got involved with the camp newspaper, the *Indianola Trail*, writing humorous tidbits and verse. One fragment of Orson's creativity survives from that summer of 1925, four lines from a lengthy pastoral titled "The Voice of the Morning," his earliest known published work:

> *From out of the dark and dreary night, a mellow voice did come*
> *A voice of sweetened love and truth*
> *Of passionate love, in sooth.*
> *It said awake, my son, 'tis day.*

The "unusual child" may have fitted in surprisingly well overall, but he did cause a few problems at the camp's evening gatherings, where the boys were encouraged to demonstrate their talents. "Orson volunteered every time!" Frautschi recalled. "He told interminable stories made up from things he had read—and he seemed to have read everything—and from his own active imagination. The other boys soon grew tired of this and became restless, so finally I told Orson he should not monopolize the scene that way."

Dick Welles and Dr. Bernstein took turns visiting on weekends, huddling with Captain Mueller for updates on Orson's progress. "The few comments that I exchanged with Bernstein," said Frautschi, "revealed that he was genuinely interested in Orson's welfare." Dick drove over rough country roads from Grand Detour. "He was thin and rather languid," recalled Frautschi. "As I saw him leaning against the front of the barracks, the thought occurred to me that he looked like a character out of a Joseph Conrad novel of the South Seas."

Decades later, Orson told film historian Joseph McBride that he had few warm memories of Camp Indianola. One night, he claimed, he escaped out his cabin window, rowed a war canoe the five miles or so across the lake to catch a train for Chicago, and never went back. Orson did run away from home more than once in the period after his mother's death, as many boys do, but Frautschi did not recall the great escape, and Orson was definitely back at the camp by the end of August to give a one-man show at the closing ceremonies.

All he needed for his show was a few props, he told Frautschi: eyeglasses, a pitcher, two chairs, a table. Frautschi recalled "being wary" and insisting on a preview of the entertainment. So Frautschi sat alone in the assembly hall watching Orson perform an abridged *Dr. Jekyll and Mr. Hyde*, "making the transformation from one character to the other, altering his facial expressions, voice, and movements in a truly amazing way." Orson was then allowed to perform the show at "a sort of commencement exercise" on the last weekend, with his father and Dr. Bernstein in attendance. "Young Orson played to a packed hall," remembered Frautschi, "and was a stunning success."

Since his son had thrived on Captain Mueller's watch, Dick Welles asked if Orson could stay on with Mueller for the school year in Madison, trying out a school there. By now the deal for the Hotel Sheffield was done, and renovating and expanding the building would keep Dick Welles in Grand Detour for much of the winter. Captain and Mina Mueller were glad to take the boy in, and Dick was happy to pay the costs.

Professor Mueller (he was "Captain" only during the summer) lived at the campus end of State Street, which ran from downtown Capitol Square to the University of Wisconsin campus on the shore of Lake Mendota. The Muellers occupied a first-floor flat on the corner of State and Frances, two blocks from the campus mall. Washington Grade School, where Orson was enrolled in fourth grade, was three blocks away.

In later years, the filmmaker would recall Madison as a "wonderful city." But his time there was also his first experience of living, effectively, on his own, and his fond memories were mixed with discomforting ones. At Washington Grade School, Orson stood out for the way he looked and dressed and carried himself, and he felt targeted on the playground. "The strange plump youngster who talked like a University professor was soon the butt of his classmates," wrote Peter Noble (per Bernstein). The taunts continued until Orson brought his makeup kit to school one day, and in the washroom before recess "painted his face to resemble a bloody pulp. . . . The bully screamed and fled," according to Noble.

At first, as one teacher recalled, the newcomer seemed a "quiet, polite, rather shy little boy who spent most of his time by himself." After a period of adjustment, however, young Orson blossomed, as he had at Camp Indianola. That November he played Squanto in the school's First Thanksgiving pageant; the following month he was Ebenezer Scrooge in its production of *A Christmas Carol*. Orson also designed and helped build a stage fireplace for the holiday show; the prop was tucked away and reused for decades.

According to Dr. Bernstein, one day Orson was invited to address an all-school assembly, and in the course of his lecture on art he lambasted his teachers for their lack of creativity. "You mustn't criticize the public school system!" one teacher called out, to which young Orson rejoined, "If the public school system needs criticizing, I will criticize it!" There was scattered applause. He had made waves—and not a few friends.

In Chicago over the Christmas holiday, Dick Welles and Dr. Bernstein took Orson to the latest edition of the *Ziegfeld Follies*, playing at the Illinois Theater. One of the headliners was the master juggler and pantomimist W. C. Fields, who made a lasting impression on Orson. "I laughed so hard they got worried and took me out of the theatre," Welles told Peter Bogdanovich. "All next day I had to be kept in bed. Quite literally, I'd laughed myself sick. Bill Fields only had to cross a room, you know, and I'd be retching with laughter." He and "Uncle Claude," as he called Fields, became friendly later in Hollywood, and Welles appeared in one movie with Fields—*Follow the Boys*, in 1944—although they didn't share a scene. Orson swore the comedian was funnier onstage than he ever was onscreen.

After returning to Madison, Orson invited a dozen boys and girls to the Muellers' flat for an eleventh birthday party for his friend Stanley Custer, who lived around the corner from the Muellers on Hawthorne Court. Orson, known to the neighborhood as a "bookwork kid" (in the words of Stanley's journalist brother, Frank Custer), donned an orange robe and Oriental turban to perform his "eye-opener tricks" (Stanley Custer's phrase) for his schoolmates, featuring card tricks, colored scarves, and disappearing coins. He even hypnotized one boy, using the classic swaying watch to cast the spell.

Orson presented the guest of honor with a copy of the adventure saga *In the Shadow of Great Peril*, the work of an eleven-year-old Chicagoan, Horace Atkisson Wade, who was publicized as "America's Youngest Author." "I know the author," Orson boasted to Custer, and he may well have known Atkisson: his godfather George Ade had written the preface. "From me to you, Orson," the young magician inscribed the book, adding a caricature of Custer and himself.

Within just a few months, Orson had starred in and designed the sets of two holiday programs and spoken out controversially at a school assembly. His teachers saw no reason to wait until the end of the year before promoting him to fifth grade.

The *Capital Times* caught wind of the "unusual child" from Chicago and dispatched a reporter to profile him for a special section on public school activities. (One wonders who tipped the editors off: Professor Mueller, Dr. Bernstein, even young Orson himself?) Needing a photograph to accompany the article, the newspaper arranged for Orson to pose for a portrait specialist from De Longe's Studio in Madison. The boy phoned Dr. Bernstein to discuss what he should wear for his first publicity still, deciding on "an eccentric Oscar Wilde tie," in Barbara Leaming's words, to "afford a proper image for his public."

The first published photograph of Orson Welles appeared on February 19, 1926, in the afternoon edition of the *Capital Times*, showing a grinning chipmunk-cheeked boy wearing a foppish sort of ascot. "Cartoonist, Actor, Poet and only 10" was the headline of Orson Welles's first newspaper interview. The precocious young student, identified by the anonymous reporter as "Orson G. Welles," was said to be "already attracting the attention of some of the greatest literary men and artists in the country."

This was the first contemporaneous outside account of the boy, and the witness was impressed. Orson G. had a "fluent command of language," according to the *Capital Times*, incorporating "a surprising number of large words equal to those of the average adult" in his

everyday speech. Moreover, he "reads constantly," evincing tastes ranging "far beyond his years," encompassing the "old masters in art and
literature" along with "the difficult subjects of philosophy and history."

The boy from Chicago was "adept at cartooning," but he was also
a natural-born poet and actor, especially gifted "in the art of make-up
and impersonations." Noting that Orson had dominated the storytelling
sessions at Camp Indianola the summer before, the newspaper reported
that he might grow "particularly interested in one of the characters"
when improvising a story—so much so that he felt compelled "to paint
the character," seizing his oil paints and "making a study that, though
it is amateurish in technique, shows a keen insight and interpretation."

The boy had written up one of his campfire stories, which he called
"The Yellow Panther," but the reporter said that the story was too
long to be included in the interview. However, the *Capital Times* did give
readers a sample of Orson's poetry, which was "entirely spontaneous,
with a depth of thought far beyond the ordinary childish jingle." The
sample was a verse Orson said he had dictated to Professor Mueller just
a few nights earlier.

It was titled "The Passing of a Lord":

He sat upon a satin chair.
A Lord was he and had that air;
About his neck was golden fringe,
His trousers ironed without a singe.
At the right of him a table stood,
Made of the finest Circassian wood;

Covered it was with a beaded mat,
and upon it reclined a Persian cat.
His wig was powdered to the last degree.
and silver buckles were at his knees.
The window was thrown open
and let in the air.

The Lord sat still and was unaware.
A moment before there had been a shot.
The aim was true but the Lord knew not;

The next day they found him in a pool of his blood,
His fine clothes torn and bespattered with mud.

Not bad, and within it the glimmer of an idea—"the passing of a lord"—that would open *Citizen Kane.* But the *Capital Times* stopped short of calling the boy a "genius," and the reporter conceded that Orson had at least one flaw: a self-confessed weakness in arithmetic, "which he regard as a serious bugbear in his life." Still, the *Capital Times* feature concluded auspiciously: "Orson has many ambitions. At the present time he cannot decide what he will be when he grows up."

Curiously, the *Capital Times* article did not mention the aspect of the boy's stay in Madison that would later become notorious. While living in the care of Professor Mueller, according to biographer Peter Noble, young Orson spent "many hours" with "eminent psychologists and medical men" who were studying child prodigies. (In another, less sensational account, the experts in question were Mueller's graduate students.) According to Noble, the local brainiacs shouted questions at Orson, such as "What first comes into your mind when you hear the word 'Teddybear'?" To which he reportedly responded: "Oscar Wilde's epigram—'A cynic knows the price of everything and the value of nothing.'"

In her authorized biography, informed by her interviews with the filmmaker, Barbara Leaming wrote that Orson embellished the nightly dreams he shared with the scholars. "Since he'd been brought to town as a prodigy, he'd better have a prodigy's dreams," Leaming wrote. "Afraid that his own would be much too dull, he routinely memorized dreams from the case studies in Herr Professor's library at home."

Published accounts differ on this question of young Orson's time under the watchful eye of Madison's academic elite. According to Noble, the boy was viewed "as an obvious child genius, another Mozart or Menuhin," and he had "the life of a circus exhibit, with his every reaction noted and all his pronouncements filed." But the *Capital Times* article did not refer to Mueller as a professor, and if Mueller was studying unusual children, he never published his research on the subject. (Indeed, he never completed his PhD in psychology; according to university records, his unfinished thesis was on Goethe and *Young Werther*.)

Welles himself later said that he developed qualms about Professor Mueller, worrying that his accounts of his off-color dreams, and perhaps all that talk about Oscar Wilde, had aroused unwonted passions in his host. Mueller studied Orson "a bit too keenly," according to Leaming, and made the boy "the object of homosexual advances." This, according to Leaming, was already "nothing new to Orson who, having been frightened and ashamed the first few times it happened, soon knew just what to say when the bohemians who frequented his mother's salon made their move."

Years later, reflecting on his time in Madison, Welles could not even bring himself to identify Mueller by name. He referred to the head of Camp Indianola only as "Herr Professor." "From my earliest childhood, I was the Lillie Langtry of the older homosexual set," Welles said, explaining that many men had been attracted to him. "Everybody wanted me. I had a very bad way of turning these guys off. I thought it would embarrass them if I said I wasn't homosexual, that it would be a rebuke, so I always had a headache. You know, I was an eternal virgin."

There is always the chance that Orson, at age ten, was reading more into such attentions than was there—that this boy who had lost his dominant mother and seen his father's role in his life whittled down may have felt anxious and insecure about his sexuality as he neared puberty. He may have channeled his fears into intimations of homosexuality—even pedophilia, given the circumstances. But Orson certainly *believed* that he'd been an object of Mueller's lust, repeating the charge more than once in interviews and also in his private conversations with Roger Hill. Though he would have friendships, and work comfortably, with many nonheterosexuals in his long career, homosexual traits were sometimes as much a bugbear for him as arithmetic.

Just a few years after Orson's interlude in Madison, as it happens, Mueller's wife divorced him—accusing her husband of being a womanizer, not a homosexual. Lowell Frautschi, Orson's camp supervisor, agreed that Mueller had an eye for ladies. "During the several years that I knew and worked for Frederick Mueller, usually in the company of males, most of whom were boys of varying ages, I never saw any gesture or expression, or heard any word, which would have indicated a sexual interest in young boys," Frautschi said. Asked directly about Mueller's alleged "homosexual advances" toward Orson, Frautschi said simply, "I don't believe it."

But Orson stuck to his story to the end of his life, insisting that his terror of Mueller finally prompted him to flee Madison once and for all. One day, he said, he climbed out a back window of the Mueller apartment at the corner of State and Frances, ran to the depot a few blocks away, and caught the train to Chicago. The runaway showed up unannounced on Dr. Bernstein's doorstep a week or two before his eleventh birthday in May 1926. The doctor hurriedly wired to Dick Welles, who was vacationing in Trinidad.

By this point, Orson's own sexuality was undoubtedly stirring. Even before his father made it back to Chicago, the boy was caught up in another coming-of-age escapade, this time involving the young daughter of artist Beatrice S. Levy, who was affiliated with the Art Institute of Chicago. Orson and Levy's daughter, who was about his age, were engaged in some "innocent fooling around" in the Levys' basement when her mother came home without warning and discovered them. Beatrice Levy blamed Orson for the episode; the embarrassed Dr. Bernstein was relieved to hand the boy over to his father.

Orson may have contrived his return to Chicago to catch the last weekend of Harry Houdini's run at the Princess Theater. His father was back in time to take him to the show as a treat for his eleventh birthday—but by now, another year older and wiser, Orson cast a more cynical eye on the "Master Mystifier." "A squat little man in evening clothes," Houdini marched onstage and ripped off the sleeves of his tailcoat. "A short sleeved tailcoat?" Welles mused years later. "Even as a kid, I realized the coarseness of it. It was supposed to be a sort of 'nothing up my sleeve' thing. Then, of course, he proceeded to perform a bunch of silly mechanical tricks that couldn't have involved his sleeves at all."

Houdini's style and patter were nothing compared with the Great Thurston's. One third of Houdini's magic was "awful stuff," devices with buttons and sliding compartments. But the other two thirds featured daredevil escapes—including his famous trick of escaping from an upside-down position in a tank of water—which struck Welles as genuinely "thrilling." Houdini also gave lectures on spiritualism and contact with the dead through spirit mediums, and the boy found these "riveting, like a perverse sort of revival meeting." Orson loved the mentalism that the best magicians practiced, and mind reading and clairvoyance were part of his own growing bag of tricks.

Welles couldn't have known it, of course, but this would be Houdini's last Chicago appearance; that fall, he would die of peritonitis from a ruptured appendix.

Not long after they saw Houdini, Dick Welles and his son left to spend the summer in Grand Detour, where Dick was now the owner and proprietor of the Hotel Sheffield. (He had toyed with renaming it the Hotel Welles, but the name Sheffield was well known throughout northern Illinois, too valuable a brand name to sacrifice to ego.) He had purchased only the building—Charles Sheffield retained ownership of the surrounding land—but Orson's father invested ten thousand dollars in a new stairway, a larger fireplace, and a modernized porch dining room. He also bought a general store just west of the hotel and renovated the upstairs to create a ballroom with a dance floor. "When I was little," Orson told Peter Bogdanovich, "I used to sneak up at night and dance by moonlight with the dust rising from the floor." An old stone barn was also remodeled into a stable for horses for the guests.

At first, Dick Welles had announced a grand reopening for Christmas 1925, with plans to keep the hotel open all winter. But the winter weather was harsh, and there were few travelers. The true grand opening came in the summer of 1926, and it was a success. Dick Welles had finally made his fresh start, putting his time and attention into the Sheffield as he once had into Badger Brass. One of his innovations was enticing manufacturing groups such as the Illinois Lumbermen's Association to hold their district meetings at the hotel. The Sheffield had a long-standing reputation for home-cooked food; now, at the height of Prohibition, Welles added homemade wine. Dick Welles made his own red vintage in the cellar for "quite a large and discerning patronage," according to Henry C. Warner, a Dixon lawyer who handled the hotel transaction for Welles and Charlie Sheffield.

Orson would later wax nostalgic over "the sounds of the folks in the bake-house and the smells" in the kitchen when he woke up in the mornings, causing at least one biographer to scoff at his imagination. But along with the basement wine from California grapes, the new Sheffield did offer house-baked bread, fresh vegetables from its own garden, cuts of meat delivered from nearby farms, and "Eastern oysters and Western trout," in Welles's phrase, cured in the yard smokehouse. The menu was overseen by the Sheffield's longtime cook, Frances Wakenight, whose cream pies were beloved by travelers and whose Sunday suppers still drew crowds.

Between Dick Welles's new business recruits, loyal returning customers, and a steady stream of travelers, the Sheffield hosted more than a hundred guests on many weekends. That kept Dick busy, and most of the time Orson was free to roam the place unsupervised. He even had a space of his own: a one-room hut across the road that his father set up as an art studio and clubhouse. Besides drawing and painting supplies, the "art shack" was full of books, costumes, props, and expensive toys from Chicago, many of which the boy was fast outgrowing.

The city boy did not always mix freely with the hotel's rural neighbors. "Most people either disliked the boy or were afraid of him," Peter Noble wrote, quoting Grand Detour resident Frederick J. Garner, "but there is no doubt that he made a tremendous impression."

One reason some townies gave him a wide berth was that Orson had a reputation for practical jokes. On one occasion, he built a stargazing contraption in his "art shack," luring young customers across the highway and charging them a penny for the chance to press an eye against the homemade telescope and view the firmament. When a neighborhood kid, Bruno Catalina, complained "I don't see no stars up there," the rapscallion Orson gave him a kick in the behind, and both Catalina and the contraption collapsed in a heap. "I chased him into the hotel," Catalina boasted to more than one interviewer over the years, "but he was too cowardly to come out. Finally I got my revenge. I stole one of his toy trains."

For others, however—especially his girl cousins from Grand Detour, and the daughters of other vacationers—Orson was good company, a sweet, attentive, and fun-filled boy. He and the Grand Detour girls took over the dance floor above the general store, donning wigs, beards, and hats for their pretend games. Orson was always leading the war against boredom, his own above all.

One school of thought—shared in retrospect by Orson himself—was that he was a deeply serious boy who wished to skip the usual rites of passage through boyhood and go straight to adulthood. "Childhood seemed to me," Welles told Bogdanovich, "a pestilential handicap." But Orson was as much a silly prankster as his mother, and the idea of skipping boyhood was part of his self-mythology. Both boys, the silly one and the serious one, were layers of the same complicated person, who was like a set of Russian nesting dolls.

Orson could make very different impressions on different people. The lawyer Henry C. Warner found him a chameleon: one moment surprisingly adult, the next a boy like any other. That summer, Warner took part in public observances of Memorial Day in Grand Detour. Young Orson volunteered to give a recitation, but "the gentleman in charge asked him not to be bothersome, and that, of course, they would not give him a place on the program," Warner recalled. Skilled at forging alliances, Orson lobbied Warner, who knew his reputation as "quite a celebrated boy wonder." Never mind, Warner assured him; just pop up on the platform next to me after a certain song is done, and I'll introduce you. "Elatedly he did so," Warner recalled.

Orson performed "Sheridan's Ride" by Thomas Buchanan Read, one of those story poems that had been drummed into him by his mother, the kind she used in her recitals. It depicted the Union general's furious ride through the Virginia countryside rallying his troops for a decisive Civil War battle. (A multitalented artist after Orson's heart, Read not only wrote the famous verse but also made a famous painting illustrating the ride.)

Hurrah! Hurrah for Sheridan!
Hurrah! Hurrah for horse and man!

The boy's exuberant performance was the highlight of the day.

Twenty-one-year-old Richard appeared at the Sheffield for a short visit, asked for money, and then vanished again. Orson's brother was capable of stretching a few dollars for weeks, but he also dunned his father endlessly, and Dick Welles was growing tired of it. Reading a newspaper story about a man with a similar name who was killed in a plane crash, Dick Welles made an unhappy remark that Orson never forgot: he wished the dead man were his son Richard.

By comparison, for that reason and many others, Orson was a treasure.

The question hanging overhead that summer was what school Orson would attend in September. After talking it over with Dr. Maurice Bernstein, Dick Welles decided that Madison was the end of their experiment with public schooling. A preparatory boarding school was the traditional answer in the Welles family, but both men knew that Orson would have to be won over. Together they decided on the Todd School for Boys, conveniently located halfway between Chicago and Grand Detour. Richard had foundered at the Todd School, but Dick and Beatrice had never blamed the school for Richard's problems there; in fact, the Todd administrators had shown judgment and caution in sounding early alarms about his behavior.

After receiving a letter of inquiry about the young applicant, the Todd School sent staff member Annetta Collins to Grand Detour to meet with Dick Welles in late August. Collins was the head of the Intermediate Department, the school's four-year program for eleven- to fourteen-year-olds, and part of her job was to screen prospective students. Dick Welles greeted her politely at the hotel before directing her across the road to the "art shack," where Orson awaited her. Collins interrupted the boy as he daubed at an easel. She gave him a précis of the school. He listened solemnly. Orson asked her if boys enjoyed freedom of creativity at the Todd School. He asked about the opportunities for painting and the dramatics program and whether he would be able to practice and perform his magic act without hindrance. After listening to Collins's repeated assurances, Orson told her the school sounded interesting and he would think it over.

To mark the new era in Orson's life, his father planned a quick end-of-summer trip to New York, where they would catch the premiere of *Don Juan*, the first feature-length motion picture with a sound track of sound effects and music. The New York Philharmonic provided the synchronized music, and a real-life Don Juan, Dick Welles's friend John Barrymore, played the title role. But Dick Welles lasted only half an hour into the show, Orson recalled, before the horror of it all drove him up the aisle and out of the theater. "This," he grumbled, "ruins the movies forever." Dick Welles was bothered less by the sound track than by his friend's appearance. "He was a chum of Barrymore's and this must have been the very worst Jack ever was," Orson recalled. "They'd put this little curly blond wig on him—and he just looked diseased."

Back in Chicago, Orson's father handed him off to Dr. Bernstein, who escorted the boy to the Todd School in Woodstock. The two began by inspecting the facilities, strolling around the grounds non-committally until they entered the theater and assembly hall. Orson, poking around backstage, stared at the ancient lighting board. "That won't do," he complained. The theater wasn't perfect, Dr. Bernstein conceded, but perhaps Orson could improve it.

"OK, this will do," Orson said. "This will do."

After arriving at the school, Orson took the Binet-Simon Intelligence Scale Test to measure his intellectual development. Years later, headmaster Roger Hill, as towering a figure in Orson Welles's life story as any person he had yet encountered, reviewed the multiple-choice portion of Orson's test while working on his own autobiography. "Deserts are crossed by Horses, Trains, Automobiles, Camels, or Donkeys," read one question. "Underscore the correct answer." Young Orson had underscored all five choices and added a scribble, "See other side," where he added: "All of these, but the writer of this test was obviously too dumb to know it."

The test established the boy's IQ as 185. Hill entered a dry note in the margin: "140 is considered genius level." The word was beginning to follow him around.

"A genius?" Welles laughingly told the *New York Post* in 1937, shortly after his triumphant Mercury Theatre production of *Julius Caesar* came to Broadway. "Perhaps. I'm either the genius they say I am or the world's godawfullest ham. It's a fifty-fifty split."

It was a word other people used about him, with or without prompting. Orson never used it about himself, he insisted later in Hollywood, after the word had become a millstone. The only real twentieth-century geniuses, he added, were Picasso, Einstein, and someone in China the West hadn't heard of yet.

"It's just one of those *words*," he insisted—a meaningless catchall. Like "love" or "happiness."

CHAPTER 5

1926–1929

"A Paradise for Boys"

Orson Welles liked to deride *The Stranger,* his entertaining if conventional 1946 picture for RKO, as the least significant film in his oeuvre. The in-joke of *The Stranger* is that the provincial Connecticut town where the story takes place is modeled after Woodstock, Illinois—"a picturesque Thornton Wilder small-town setting," as Welles once said. He tried several times to use his films to evoke Woodstock, the home of the Todd School, where Welles started classes in the fall of 1926. The town had a lasting place in his heart: so did the school, "a paradise for boys," he said years later.

The town square in *The Stranger* recalls that of Woodstock, with its bandstand and Civil War statue. Each town revolves to an extent around an elite boarding school. One scene in the film shows a gym blackboard scrawled with names from Orson's schoolboy past: "Puny Hill," gently mocking the height of Orson's beloved headmaster; "Mrs. Collins," the staff member who screened him in Grand Detour; and a dire warning from "Coach Roskie," named for young Orson's archenemy on the faculty. The blackboard displays an announcement from "Wallingford Hall," where Welles was once quartered; and notice of an upcoming basketball game, "Harper vs. Todd."

Set on a ten-acre campus about sixty miles northwest of the Loop, on the outskirts of Woodstock, the Todd School for Boys had been open for business since 1848. "Near enough to Chicago to be easy of access for parents desiring to place their boys with us from any part of the country," as the school booklet described it, "at the same time, it is far enough from the city to be free from the interruptions of too frequent comings and goings, which are very demoralizing to a school of this kind."

The school's buildings included large classrooms and residential halls; an assembly hall and theater; a gymnasium with a bowling alley; a music cottage; a library; a horse stable and riding track; and print, woodworking, and metal shops. ("After we have learned to handle woodworking tools, we can make things needing some blacksmithing," according to the school booklet, "like a sled.") The school promoted physical culture and contact with nature, providing an outdoor tennis court, a running track, and a toboggan slide in winter. About a mile away, students had access to another forty acres of hickory and oak, a place for hiking and spiritual reflection.

The basic tuition from September to June 1926 was $900 to $1,000, depending on whether a boy had a single or double room—this would be $13,000 or more in today's currency. In theory the students were all boys, although a daughter or two of teachers and administrators were often sprinkled among the boys. Some students came from as far away as Europe, South Africa, or South America, but most were from Chicago or the North Shore. (In *Citizen Kane*, Kane tries distracting Susan Alexander by wiggling his ears. "It took me two solid years in the best boys' school in the world to learn that trick," he says. "The fellow who taught it to me is now the president of Venezuela.")

The Todd program began in first grade for some and ended after tenth grade for all. After graduating, the highest achievers were ready for early admission to colleges, though many went on to the upper levels of other prep schools. Most "Todd boys," as they were known, were sons of Chicago-area captains of business, destined to follow in the family occupation, although the school's alumni also included authors, scientists, economists, and lawyers.

A Todd boy wore a suit and tie to classes, and participated in marching drills and flag raisings, but the school atmosphere was more "homelike" than regimented. The assembly hall was used for daily chapel services but it also served for a wide variety of entertainment. The school promoted good citizenship and leadership, but it stressed self-expression over conformity. Boyhood was not a pestilential handicap at Todd; it was regarded as a time to be savored.

"An institution is the lengthened shadow of one man," Ralph Waldo Emerson observed, and the Todd School's founder, Richard Kimball Todd—a native of Vermont who had graduated from Princeton—ran his institution along Presbyterian lines.* His successor, Noble Hill, maintained both the morning religious assemblies and the all-school "crocodile" marches, eyes forward, into town for Sunday services. Hill had been headmaster for thirty-seven years in the fall of 1926. Nearing seventy, he was stern but kindly; boys and teachers alike referred to him as "the King."

"I hear we've got another Welles boy," the King was said to have commented within his son Roger Hill's earshot after Orson was enrolled there. "I hope he's nothing like his brother."

On arriving as an "intermediate boy" in early September 1926, eleven-year-old Orson was ushered into a brightly painted ground-floor room in the Clover Hall dormitory. He was assigned to share it with another Illinois boy, John Dexter, who had been at Todd since the first grade. Along with a small suitcase of clothing, Dexter recalled, Orson lugged into the room a large steamer trunk stuffed with makeup, costumes, and props. That first night, after the lights went out at nine o'clock sharp, Orson stole out of bed and lit an array of candles—strictly forbidden—then plunged into the closet. Just as Dexter was dozing off, his new roommate burst from the dark, weirdly made up and costumed, reciting passages from Shakespeare. "This went on night after night," Dexter recalled years later. While he found the shenanigans amusing, Dexter eventually encouraged Orson to move into a single room.

In his early days at Todd, young Orson marked his territory, challenging a pedantic history teacher on the accuracy of his Egyptology and rebuking an English teacher for dangling his participles. In time, Orson would become more clever about how to get his way.

One educator he kept his distance from, at least at first, was Roger Hill, the headmaster's thirty-year-old son. A Todd School alumnus

---

* Originally, the school was known as the Todd Seminary for Boys.

himself, Roger had gone on to the University of Illinois in Champaign-Urbana, and then to a short stint in advertising in Chicago, before his father lured him back as athletic director of the boys' school. A slender, dapper man with the look of Douglas Fairbanks and what Welles recalled as a "sailor's swagger," the younger Hill sported "rather too much hair for those days, looking artistic and rather brigandish." An avid sailor, he was known as "Skipper" around the school, and he kept a boat moored on Lake Michigan for sailing trips.

To Orson, the really alarming thing about Skipper was his position as athletic director. Skipper was a basketball expert—he wrote a guide called *Let's Go Team!* that was a "local best-seller"—and a believer in acrobatics. Orson abhorred both disciplines. Basketball "intimidated me tremendously," Welles reminded Hill several decades later during one of their long-distance phone conversations, which fill Todd Tarbox's book *Orson Welles and Roger Hill: A Friendship in Three Acts*, while acrobatics inspired "mental pictures of myself engaged in some sort of gymnastic endeavor, not prostrate with physical pain, but worse, stabbed by the pain of hearing the roars of laughter from my peers."

Short and stout, Orson didn't look like much of a basketball player. Skipper didn't particularly notice the new sixth-grader until the Halloween bash. Todd boys were in perpetual lockdown, their "town privileges" limited to special events and Sunday churchgoing; school officials channeled the boys' energies into Saturday night skits and recitals, and one of the big Saturday night events was the annual costume party and variety show for Halloween.

That weekend, a star was born. The new boy worked up a number of routines, in one memorably spoofing Tennyson ("Do you see those gracious meadows?" "No, but I do see the Noble Hills"), but it was his magic act that wowed everyone. Dressed like Sherlock Holmes, complete with deerstalker cap and flowing cape, Orson strode onstage and chewed the scenery, staring disapprovingly through his reading glasses at Sherman Perlman, the upperclassman recruited as his Watson, while he ran through his repertoire of illusions like a young Thurston.

"A terrific show," Hill recalled years later, so much so that even the glitches were memorable. "The miniature building that [Orson] caused to materialize from beneath a handkerchief wasn't aflame," Barbara Leaming wrote. Though the trick had fizzled, "Orson's rapid-fire inventive banter, delivered in stentorian tones and with much accompanying choregraphy, almost entirely obscured what had really happened." Skipper was impressed.

Roger Hill may have been locally famous for promoting basketball, but he harbored a secret: he didn't really care that much for the sport—or for organized sports of any kind. He felt like a fraud as both an athletic director and an educator, having left college for his advertising job without even graduating. His proudest achievements were writing *Boneyard Babblings*, a collection of poems depicting undergraduate life, and serving as the editor of his university literary magazine. He modeled himself after a fellow staffer at the magazine, writer Samson Raphaelson, whose first play, *The Jazz Singer*, had debuted on Broadway in the fall of 1925.

Instead of graduating, Hill had married a university woman from Chicago, Hortense Gettys, and taken a sensible job writing advertising copy for the Montgomery Ward catalog in Chicago. His experience at "Monkey Ward's," as it was called, enhanced his natural skills as a born promoter but made him feel like a traitor to his artistic soul. Skipper had enjoyed music and theater from boyhood, when his mother's brother, Joseph Morgan Rogers, an author and a critic for the *Philadelphia Inquirer*, often took him to operas and symphonies while visiting Chicago. To coax Hill back to Todd, his father put the school's drama and entertainment programming under his aegis.

Orson always needed collaborators—coconspirators—in his artistic endeavors. He needed them more than he needed money or even, arguably, an audience. And he had a positive genius for finding the right partners for his plans. Once Orson realized that Skipper was a reluctant athletic director, their kinship was sealed.

Roger Hill presided over Todd's elaborate dramatics program, which included several tiers based on age and class, as well as two all-school clubs—the Slap Stick Club, and the Paint and Powder Club—that shared responsibility for producing shows on Saturday nights. By 1926, the upper-grade Todd Troupers were staging five or six full-length all-school plays each year under Hill, who wrote many of these plays and directed all of them. After he was won over by Orson's

Halloween show, Skipper promoted the young man to a leading role in the school's traditional Christmas pageant—playing a most unlikely Virgin Mary.

The school went all out for its shows, whatever the tier. A few years later, Orson contributed a description of the school's dramatic offerings for the Todd catalog. "The scenery is in every case original, being designed and built and painted by the boys," he wrote. "The make-ups are also done by the boys. Our stage is completely equipped. The lighting is most modern with all the circuits on dimmers, and a plaster back wall similar to the Goodman's [Goodman Theatre's] in Chicago makes possible very realistic and stunning outdoor effects."

With so much to supervise, Skipper enlisted his wife, Hortense, as his lieutenant. And a former child prodigy, Carl Hendrickson, ran the school orchestra and chorus, composing music for the full-length "foolishments" that dominated the theatrical schedule when Orson arrived at the school. Skipper had discovered the handsome Swede at the Chicago Theatre on State and Lake in 1923, leading the orchestra behind the silent pictures and variety acts. After inveigling Hendrickson to Todd, Hill teamed up with him to create a number of original revues for the school, with the boys dressed up as ingenues, grandes dames, and chorus girls. There was a vogue for lighthearted drag shows in prep schools and colleges. Hill had written one such revue in college, and lyrics for another; he and Hendrickson even sold a few of the Todd foolishments to national agencies for packaging to Kiwanis and Rotary clubs.

Orson appeared in at least three of the Todd Troupers' foolishments in 1926–1927: *Around the World*, *Finesse the Queen*, and *It Won't Be Long Now*. He loved to dance and sing, even if that wasn't his forte, and he loved the songs with their silly lyrics. Years later, while directing his first picture in Hollywood, Welles wrote to Hill to urge him to watch a certain dance scene in *Citizen Kane* for proof that his Charleston steps from *Around the World* were remembered.

The spring extravaganza, *Finesse the Queen*, a three-act play with fifteen musical numbers, was a love story between a prince and a commoner set in mythical Gondolivia. By now Orson had a singing *and* speaking role; he was billed as detective "William J. Spurns, who has a clew." (He never forgot the *Finesse* songs either, and half a century later, on the set of one of his last, uncompleted films, "The Other Side of the Wind," Welles repeatedly regaled cast and crew with snatches: "Everybody loves the fellow who is smiling," he sang. "Ah Gondolivia, Gondolivia, land of melody!")

His first roommate, John Dexter, was the "leading lady" in *Finesse*, and young Orson used his makeup expertise to give his friend an air of femininity. "When he finished with me, he kissed me, said he couldn't help it, but I turned out so good," recalled Dexter. "He had a crush on me every time we did that show." A photograph survives of eleven-year-old Orson, still bantam-size, beaming up at the bigger, taller Dexter.

By the time *It Won't Be Long* was produced, Roger Hill knew he could count on Orson, who was cast as one of six leads—the hero's best friend, "with troubles of his own," according to the program. Offstage, the sixth-grader was making himself just as indispensable, increasingly taking charge of lighting, sets, makeup, and costumes for the school's many varied programs.

The Todd Troupers toured the foolishments to nearby prep schools and small colleges, and the experience sharpened their skills. Music director Carl Hendrickson was a severe taskmaster who insisted on precise timing and cues, but he was also fantastically resourceful—not unlike composer Bernard Herrmann, with whom Orson would forge an alliance a decade later. Skipper Hill was always unflappable in a crisis, a tolerant overseer—his wife, Hortense, less so. "Horty" famously corrected Orson during the spring tour of *It Won't Be Long*, scolding him for laying on his own greasepaint a bit thick. "Just be still and let me do the makeup," she told Orson firmly. "No doubt my fascination, if not obsession, with the art of make-up is an effort to, in some small measure, gain Hort's begrudging approval," Welles told Skipper years later.

Also, in the spring, Dick Welles took Orson and Dr. Maurice Bernstein on another trip to New York for a round of concerts, plays, museums, and motion pictures. Dr. Bernstein and Orson traveled on to New Orleans, sailing from there to Havana and other points in the Caribbean. Dick was called back to Chicago for an unhappy reason: to prepare for a court case against his older son, Richard.

Twenty-two years old by the spring of 1927, Orson's brother was promoting himself as a magician, with a résumé boasting a stint doing magic and singing with a group in a western vaudeville tour. But Richard never held any job for very long without defaulting, and his employment history was no more reliable than his imaginary academic credits. He "was always trying to get some money and he was off some place and nobody knew where," Roger Hill remembered. "'Due to the Christmas festivities, I have contracted gonorrhea' and he would like a little dough for that."

There was something clearly wrong with Richard.

Orson's brother was diagnosed with "dementia simplex"—a broad subtype of schizophrenia characterized by slow, progressive deterioration and mental inadequacy, though the term was often used as a catchall for unspecified mental illness. Simon Callow and other biographers have claimed that Dick Welles "conspired" with Dr. Bernstein to arrange this diagnosis, and certainly Bernstein, long Richard's physician, was the medical authority supporting the determination. In May 1927, Dick filed papers to have his elder son declared incompetent and remanded to the State Hospital for the Insane at Kankakee.

About sixty miles south of Chicago, Kankakee housed nearly four thousand patients in eighty buildings on a thousand-acre campus, which included a working farm. Though state documents record a small number of deaths there every year, some due to experimental drugs and other treatments for hard cases, the general population had the use of a golf course, dances, regular movies, and occupational therapy. Because of his artistic upbringing, Richard was channeled into the arts and crafts program, thought to provide a positive stimulus for "the primitive creative instinct," according to a state report.

But Richard wasn't too delusional to fight his institutionalization tooth and nail. The young man filed suit repeatedly over the next eight years, trying to have his insanity judgment overturned. Court records of institutionalizations are strictly shielded by Illinois law, and Kankakee records have since been destroyed in a fire, so it is impossible to know what drugs or treatments Richard received there, or if these might have contributed to his debilitation.

Young Orson was also cushioned from this latest trauma; he was off with Dr. Bernstein in the Caribbean when his father went to court.

Yet he must have been troubled by his older brother's downward spiral, whether he felt that Richard had disgraced the family, or that the family had failed Richard. Either way, it was up to him alone now to carry the family banner.

Back at the Todd School, Orson took solace in the written word. He was encouraged to contribute to the school's quarterly, *The Red & White*, also overseen by Roger Hill. Orson was a regular presence in the pages of *The Red & White* throughout his first year at Todd. For the Easter issue, he wrote a singsong ode to Chicago that he coyly entitled "Pome."* It was a parody of one of those long poems he had committed to memory—Henry Van Dyke's "America for Me."

POME
Tis fine to see the old school, and wander all around,
Among the knarly oak trees and buildings of renown,
To admire the ancient Clover Hall and the office of our King
But now I think I've had enough of all this sort of thing.
So it's home again, and home again, Chicago town for me!
I want a train that's southward bound, to flit past field and tree,
To that blessed land of "Home" and "Folks" beyond Cook County line
Where movie shows are always good and malted milks are fine.
Oh, Crystal Lake's a hick's town, there's hayseed in the air;
And Woodstock is a factory town, with Dagos everywhere
And it's sweet to dream in English Class, and it's great to march in gym;
But though this student may love Todd, home's now the place for him.
I like our games, I like our shows, with actors nicely drilled;
I like our Beans, I like our Hash, with luscious thumbtacks filled;
But Oh, to take you out my lad, for just a single day,
And eat at Childs or Thompson's (that is, if you will pay).
I know that Todd is marvelous, yet something seems quite wrong,
The teachers like to make you work entirely too long.

---

* The original spellings and punctuation of "Pome" and Orson's other writings are preserved.

But the glory of Chicago is "No parking on the streets,"
We love our town for what she is, the town of "Home" and "Treats."
Oh, it's home again, and home again, Chicago land for me.
I want a train that's southward bound to flit past field and tree,
*To that blessed town where Big Bill's frown has King George on the run,**
Where the hours are full of leisure and the leisure's full of fun.

For the magazine's commencement issue that year, Orson produced a flurry of cartoon sketches and no fewer than four verse offerings. These included a romanticized portrait of an ancient mariner (not far from Captain Ahab in *Moby-Dick*, a character the older Orson Welles would stalk on the stage and screen several times during his career).

THE PILOT—A DESCRIPTION
Staunch he stood, his great grim face, marred by the wrath of the sea,
His burly hands gripped tight the wheel, his pose both wild and free.
The biting wind clawed for his face and kept its fingers there.
And the icicles came streaming down from his gray and sun-bleached hair.

Another was a Longfellow-like ode.

AT NOONTIME—A DESCRIPTION
The sun beat mercilessly upon,
The scorching heat cursed plain;
And the field that lay in sunny wealth,
Was gold with sun and grain.

The toiler sought with lagging steps
The comfort of the great oak trees
And there to taste with hungry lips,
The coolness of long sought breeze.

---

* "Pome" showed that young Orson was already attentive to politics: "Big Bill" referred to corrupt, buffoonish Mayor Thompson of Chicago, and "King George" to George V of England, whom the mayor had denounced as America's worst enemy, threatening to punch the monarch in the nose if they ever met.

The bloodstained sword and the earth stained plow
Now lazy and idle lay;
For all men's number and various tasks
Are left in the great noon day
Close by a knotted oak there laughed
A silvery rippling stream
Whose shining crags and glittering rocks
Cut the water in between

On one moss bank his head in air,
There dreamed a peasant boy;
Who from sun bronzed feet to sun bronzed hair,
Was a symbol of boyhood joys.

His lengthiest contribution recast Camp Indianola's rival sports teams as warring Indian tribes:

THE ONAWAYS AND THE WENDIGOS
The Onaways were hot and mad
And in their war togs they were clad;
Dancing up and down with might;
Dancing in the firelight.
Singing praises to Gods of war,
Of ancient legend and olden lore,
Of how they captured the fearless braves,
And made them serve them as slaves.

Waving scalps with thought of more,
With hopes of hearts they'd have to gore,
When suddenly from the forest trees,
Blown by the gentle waving breeze,
Came the cackling voice of an ancient hag,
Who silenced the braves by the wave of rag;
It is prophecied in the magic sands,
That a terrible curse is upon these lands,
And unless its braves shall turn to the wise,
The almighty spirit his children despise,

You of yourselves must not be talking
Or with Wendigo packs you'll soon be walking.

The warriors knelt down upon the ground,
And with attention most profound,
Promised these things they would not do,
And kept their oath right well and true.
They won the war with the Wendigo braves,
And made them serve them as their slaves.

Orson closed the year with a solemn verse commemorating the terrible battles of the Great War:

AT THE CALL OF THE DRUM AND FIFE
From scorching heat to freezing cold,
The men of whom these tales are told,
Come from every walk of life,
Come at the call of the drum and fife.
From cobblers' boys to rich men's sons,
They came to fight the tyrant Huns,
Entranced by the song of blood and strife,
March to war with the drum and fife,
Thru fiery rain and gorey mud,
The boys who bathed in the cleansing of blood,
Sacrificing more than life,
March to hell with the drum and fife.

When Orson's first year at the Todd School was over, a month after he turned twelve, he left Woodstock for Grand Detour and the last summer he would spend with his father in the small Illinois town that, he told Hill half a century later, came closest to being his private Rosebud.

In his first year, Orson had established himself as a good student, a leading light on *The Red & White*, and an indispensable fixture of the school's theatricals. If some teachers looked askance at the brash youngster, Orson had powerful allies in Roger and Hortense Hill. If some students did not warm to him, others did. While some books have portrayed him as a solitary boy at odds with his classmates, in truth he found boon companions among his peers, often across age lines and other divisions. Among them were Sherman Perlman, two years his senior and his partner in the Halloween magic act, whom he later called "my great pal" and "the closest friend I had at Todd"; and his roommate John Dexter, a talented halfback who later captained the formidable "Todd Eleven," but who also stood shoulder to shoulder with Orson in girlie musicals, blackout skits, and, later, productions of Shakespeare.

"In many a school," Roger Hill explained years later, Orson "would have been very strange and might have had trouble. Todd was nutty enough and unique enough so that the things he could do were appreciated by the toughest football player in the place."

Grand Detour was another story. While many of the football players at Todd were equally comfortable onstage, the youth of Grand Detour kept their distance from Orson because of his lack of interest "in football, baseball, or any other form of athletics," according to Charles Higham, who visited Grand Detour and spoke to a number of locals who claimed to remember Orson. In his overimaginative way, Higham wrote that, by contrast, "the girls fancied Orson because he entertained them with impromptu shows in a tent of his own making, playing every part in Shakespeare, both Romeo and Juliet, Antony and Cleopatra, hilariously changing from male to female clothes borrowed from anyone who would lend them."

At age twelve Orson still found creative solitude in his "art shack" across the road from the hotel. In the river village he spent hours horseback riding, the rare physical sport at which he felt proficient, and took in circuses and county fairs with his father. They traveled to Dixon to watch movies in the best theater in the county—the pictures were still silent, though some, especially comedies, had musical accompaniment—and they loved the vaudeville revues that came there on Sundays. Often they were driven to Dixon by one of the hotel workers, because Dick Welles no longer trusted his eyes at night.

The Sheffield was in its second year under Dick Welles's management, and it was running like clockwork. Travelers spread the word about the hotel's excellent catfish on Saturday nights and the Sunday fried chicken suppers. The establishment drew a steady stream of business groups, vacation travelers, and acquaintances from Chicago. Booth Tarkington very probably dined at the hotel with his friend and collaborator Harry Leon Wilson, a native of nearby Oregon, whose picaresque stories were often set in that part of northern Illinois.

Dick Welles read the Chicago newspapers at his own pace in the slow afternoons, handing the sections to his son as he finished them. But Welles was a night owl, and especially relished his son's company after dark. When the guests retired, the two of them would sit on the front porch of the hotel, chewing over the day. Orson always called Dick "Father" or, on rare occasions, "Dad." Dick Welles's pet name for his younger son was "Lamb." Orson's father still drank and smoked profusely, using "one Virginia straight-cut cigarette to light another," according to Higham.

This last summer spent in Grand Detour was a golden memory for Welles. Not much given to nostalgia, he nevertheless considered the village "one of those lost worlds, one of those Edens that you get thrown out of," and bristled to hear Grand Detour slighted. Years later, when Roger Hill referred in passing to the "little" Rock River, Welles objected but with humor. "I never think of it as *little*," he quickly interjected, "It's great . . . one of the foremost rivers in the world." He would treasure his summers along the river—"the Hudson of the West," as the hotel's ads boasted—as if they had afforded him a portal to the past, "a childhood in the last century."

That golden summer, Dick Welles drew up his last will and testament. He had learned a lesson from his wife's death: Beatrice Ives Welles had died intestate, without even life insurance. Dick Welles, by contrast, maintained a substantial policy on his hotel and considerable personal life insurance, and he added a stipulation to his will that both his sons must carry policies of their own.

This was not simply a theoretical provision. Orson's father was suffering from worsening heart disease, and by that summer he knew his days were numbered.

One of his sons stood to benefit more than the other from his will. Because he had already made "extraordinary advances" to his older son, Richard—still residing in an "insane" ward at Kankakee—and because of Richard's "apparent irresponsibility and ingratitude," Dick Welles set aside only one seventh of his estate for his firstborn.

Six sevenths would go to Orson.

By the time Dick signed the document, on October 20, 1927, twelve-year-old Orson was back in Woodstock for seventh grade.

Dick Welles wasn't the only one passing the baton. Halfway thru the school year 1927–1928, headmaster Noble Hill announced his retirement, and by the end of term his son had assumed full command of the Todd School.

The new headmaster and young Orson had much in common. They were both born talkers. Hill later marveled at "how easily words flowed from [Orson] in graceful prose even as a teenager," matching his own uncanny ability to rattle off famous speeches, poems, songs, quotations from the Bible and Shakespearean passages from memory. But the new headmaster was genuinely self-effacing about his own talent, and perhaps this modesty was what Orson most admired in his mentor.

Orson enjoyed the run of the school. He had a reliable ally in the new headmaster, but he irritated Hortense Hill on more than one occasion, suffering her barbed tongue, then winning her back with humor and kindness. He showed up in the Hills' bedroom after hours, sitting on their bed and talking, talking, talking as the couple tried to wind down and get to bed. Hortense only narrowed her eyes balefully, never daring to get undressed.

Hortense Hill was a sensible, nurturing maternal figure for the boys, hovering over them outside classes, watching over their grooming habits, and monitoring their daily meals. She was also a stunning beauty. They couldn't escape her—but few of the boys wished to. Her wedding photograph, Welles told Skipper years later, was "one of the sexiest pictures I ever saw."

"Our sunshine," Welles wrote upon her death, "the radiant blessing of my life."

The headmaster was less critical of his young charge, and found himself fascinated with Orson's constant patter. They bonded over books such as *Don Quixote*, which Orson had read at an impressionable age, and which was a favorite novel for both of them. Oratory was part of the Todd curriculum, and during his visits to the Hills' bedroom, Orson rehearsed his class assignments, among them the fiery speeches of radical abolitionist John Brown. He would toss off a favorite soliloquy from Shakespeare, then wait for Skipper to answer with a selection from his own vast repertoire. One night, Skipper regaled him with orator Wendell Phillips's eloquent tribute to the Haitian revolutionary Toussaint-Louverture. Orson listened to this with wide eyes—it was new to him—and went away, returning the next evening to repeat it to the Hills. Fifty years later, chatting with his former student by phone, Hill was thunderstruck when the filmmaker delivered the same address from memory. Did Welles remember the words simply because he'd heard them from the headmaster long ago? "More than once," Welles drawled. "You were fond of it." And then Welles did the same, on the phone intoning a celebrated speech by Illinois attorney general Robert G. Ingersoll, nominating James G. Blaine for president at the 1876 Republican convention:

> Like an armed warrior, like a plumed knight, James G. Blaine marched down the halls of the American Congress, and threw his shining lance full and fair against the brazen foreheads of the defamers of his country and the malingerers of his honor.

Hill was second to no one in his passion for American history, but Orson knew Shakespeare as well as his mentor. Hill knew the Bible better, however, and Welles often reached out to his old headmaster in later years when working on a script that required a particular biblical touch.

Not all their banter was high-flown. The headmaster and his wife loved jokes and gossip, and Hill entranced Orson with tales of his gifted and often drunk cousin Jack Rogers, who had preceded him on the Montgomery Ward staff, and who specialized in sly copy for ladies' wear.

At first the Hill children were jealous of Orson's constant presence in the house, and Hortense Hill also wondered why they must indulge this pest of a kid. But the couple were drawn by the boy's good humor and intelligence, and they recognized that, under his showy exterior, he was a sensitive, thoughtful boy. At a time when his mother's death was still a raw wound—and his father was showing signs of mortality—Orson found the Hills to be perfect stand-ins for his parents. But Orson was also perfect for the Hills. When Orson first arrived at the Todd School, Skipper Hill had still been laboring under his father's shadow, feeling like a fake as he promoted the school's athletic program when his real interest lay in the arts. Mentoring Orson gave him a chance to be his own man.

Over time, as Orson spent more time with the headmaster and his family, Hill recalled "that there weren't really the same rules for Orson" as for the other students. Though athletics remained important under Roger Hill's leadership, Orson managed to elude gym and sports classes by faking Dr. Bernstein's signature on a form excusing him from strenuous physical activity owing to health concerns. Not that all exercise was undesirable—Orson made a point of telling classmates what a shame it was that Todd School had no swimming pool, because swimming was his real forte. When the school installed a pool a few years later, Orson felt trapped. "Try to build a mountain for me to get called a liar on!" he complained to Skipper.

By then, though, Roger Hill and his protégé were coconspirators; their devotion to the arts was gradually changing the school's direction. "Every youngster is a creator" became the new headmaster's credo, and his freethinking approach to education was bolstered by his success with Orson.

Woodstock had a convenient downtown train station, and Skipper took the boys to Chicago regularly for lectures, music and theater performances, and museum visits. Like Orson's parents, the headmaster always arranged backstage passes so the boys could meet the artists, entertainers, and dignitaries. Along with the Theatre Guild plays trucked in from New York, the students also saw frequent productions at the local Kenneth Sawyer Goodman Memorial Theatre.

Led by Thomas Wood Stevens, the founder of the drama department of the Carnegie Institute in Pittsburgh, the Goodman was an annex of the Art Institute of Chicago, housing a professional repertory company and a drama school since 1925. The Goodman had emerged as the leader of Chicago's "little theater" movement, a bastion of artistic purity that offered an ambitious mix of classical and avant-garde works. The troupe's standout performers included the Irish actor Whitford Kane, who also sometimes directed its presentations, including an acclaimed spring 1926 production of *A Midsummer Night's Dream* that the Todd boys attended.

Orson's second year at Todd was busier and more productive than the first. Between trips to Chicago, he expanded his sketching and writing efforts for *The Red & White.* He assumed more responsibility for organizing the Saturday night entertainments. And he really began to distinguish himself in the all-school productions. Soon, Roger Hill was handing the seventh-grader starring roles that traditionally had been earmarked for boys in their last year at the school.

Partly thanks to Orson, the school's foolishments were gradually replaced by solid dramatic works. In the spring of 1928 he took one of three lead roles in *Food: A Tragedy of the Future,* a single-act satire by William De Mille set in a future world where ordinary foodstuffs are more precious than money. Orson played a simpering wife who covets the nutritional benefits of an egg; his pal Sherman Perlman played his husband. The program was filled out by Orson's tarantellas on the piano—suggesting, as Simon Callow observed, "that his abandonment of the piano was not quite as complete as he later chose to remember."

On the day Orson turned thirteen, May 6, 1928, his father was away in Grand Detour airing out the Hotel Sheffield for the summer ahead. Early in the morning on May 14, as hotel employees installed a new elbow in a kitchen smoke ventilator, they set fire to a handful of papers to test the draft. The smoke carried a spark upstairs, and the fire that ensued wasn't discovered until 9:30 A.M., by gaining "considerable headway," according to newspapers. The housekeeper summoned firemen, but by the time the pumper covered the six miles from Dixon to Grand Detour, the hotel was engulfed by "a mass of flames." The pumper drew water from the nearby river, but it was too late. Only the chimney survived the blaze, according to local reporters, along with "a few pieces of furniture" from the hotel.

The hotel fire would become one of the most mysterious incidents in Orson's boyhood. Peter Noble, in one of the earliest published accounts of the fire, quotes one local resident as saying that "apparently" Dick Welles was sleeping off drunkenness as the fire spread through the Sheffield. "They had to break down the door of his book-lined and paper-littered room and carry him, protesting bitterly, down the stairs to safety," according to Noble. Charles Higham embellished this account, claiming that Dick had been "sleeping late, heavily hung over after a night of drinking bootleg liquor," and waitresses had to march him out through the smoke. Orson's own version didn't help: in his 1983 *Paris Vogue* piece, the filmmaker referred to his father as "the suspected arsonist," and claimed that Dick Welles "emerged from the flames dressed only in his night shirt, carrying in one hand an empty parrot cage, and in the other, a framed, hand-tinted photograph of a lady in pink tights (an ex-mistress fondly remembered) named Trixie Friganza."* Orson also took liberties with the date of the fire, which he placed after "we'd just returned from China" (a trip two years in the future), and he set the scene with "a nice Christmassy fall of snow on the ground" (there was no such snow).

At the time of the fire Dick Welles said his "valuable library" had been "completely destroyed," according to the *Ogle County Republican.* (Orson added later that the library included his father's precious "jade collection," which was not covered by insurance.) The dazed hotelier guessed that the damages would rise to at least $30,000, and his insurance would cover only "a little over half that amount." He was "undecided" about whether he might rebuild the hotel, Dick Welles told the press, pending "the nature of the adjustment he receives from the insurance companies."

But the Hotel Sheffield was never rebuilt. And as far as anyone recalls, Orson's father never set foot in Grand Detour again.

---

* Trixie Friganza was a vaudevillian who was Dick Welles's contemporary. In his *Paris Vogue* piece, Orson made a conceit of coupling Friganza's first name with his mother Beatrice's supposed nickname, "Trixie." Some accounts say Beatrice Ives used "Trixie" as a stage name. Others say it was Dudley Crafts Watson's pet name for his cousin. Both versions are unlikely.

━━━

Like his mother's death, the Hotel Sheffield fire was a catastrophe that took place while Orson was somewhere else, forcing him to draw on his imagination to fill in the gaps. Like his father, Orson never returned to Grand Detour. In years to come, when Dr. Maurice Bernstein suggested a nostalgic return to the town, or Roger Hill said he thought the site where his father owned a hotel might merit a plaque with Orson's name on it, the filmmaker scoffed.

Orson capped his second outstanding year at Todd School with a mesmerizing recitation, at the commencement exercises, of the final courtroom speech John Brown made after the abolitionist was found guilty of treason. But the Grand Detour fire threw Orson's summer plans into a scramble. Facing months of dispiriting meetings with fire investigators and insurance officials, Dick Welles had no place for him to spend the summer. Instead Orson was plunged back into the world of Dr. Bernstein, moving into Bernstein's Chicago apartment for the remainder of June. He always felt at home in Chicago, where he could stock up on art supplies and books at Kroch's and roam through the Art Institute whenever he liked. He hurried to catch the last plays of the season at the Goodman, where the repertory ensemble was alternating between a new play about India called *The Little Clay Cart*, translated from Sanskrit, straight from its Neighborhood Playhouse premiere in New York, and a studio production of Noël Coward's *Hay Fever*.

Now that he was thirteen, Orson was a welcome guest at the Tavern Club, a prestigious men's club for arts patrons and cognoscenti atop an art deco skyscraper on the south bank of the Chicago River at Michigan Avenue. Ned Moore and Dr. Bernstein, both members, brought Orson along to luncheons there, reuniting him with old Ravinia acquaintances including Charles Collins, the drama critic of the *Chicago Tribune*; and Collins's friendly rival, Ashton Stevens of the *Herald-Examiner*. John Clayton, the former foreign correspondent of the *Chicago Tribune*, now heading public relations for the Chicago Civic Opera, was another Tavern Club regular. The newsmen's table was a kind of club within the club, a regular way station for show business and literary personalities passing through town, and for native sons in touring shows, who were greeted like returning war heroes. Among the latter group, for example, was Preston Sturges, a hometown actor and fledgling writer, who always dropped by while touring with road companies, long before he struck gold as a playwright. Nearly twenty years Welles's senior, Sturges got to know Welles in the latter's prep school days over lunches at the Tavern Club, and Orson avidly followed his career as Sturges became one of Hollywood's first "writer-directors."

The newsmen had always been fond of Orson, and now that he was nearing adulthood—at thirteen, he was almost as tall as the older men—they treated him more or less as an equal. Their talk was freewheeling, ranging over local and national stories, politics and crime, arts and society. They vied with each other, sparring on each new topic; for Orson, listening to them—and jumping in alongside them—it was like sitting at a table of unstuffy professors.

In July, when the "club within a club" adjourned to Highland Park and Ravinia, Orson accompanied Bernstein to a new house the doctor was renting on Kincaid Avenue in Highland Park, near Ned and Hazel Moore's place. Orson had been away from the Ravinia music festival in recent years, but now "Uncle Ned" promoted the teenager as a novelty columnist to Louis Eckstein, the Chicago businessman who bankrolled the Ravinia Festival and published the *Highland Park News.* Eckstein signed up the "thirteen-year-old dramatic critic, cub reporter, and what have you," in the words of the newspaper announcement, for a column called "Hitting the High Notes," with Orson reporting "inside dope on the opera stars."

Orson was uniquely positioned to collect the "inside dope," since visiting Chicago critics and performers camped out at the Moores' place, and these days at Bernstein's house too. Celebrities were as common as clover at Ravinia, where on any given night the audience might include luminaries such as Ethel Barrymore or even Vice President Charles G. Dawes, who had a home in nearby Evanston. Barrymore, visiting Chicago, came to dinner at Dr. Bernstein's house in early August, and young Orson sat across the table from the leading actress of her generation.

Orson's first column, after the Fourth of July weekend, was jokey and polite. But he turned thoughtful in his next piece, offering capsule reviews of four "brilliant" productions: *Lohengrin, Manon, Il Trovatore,* and *L'Amore dei Tre Re.* Of the last, he rhapsodized, "The effects [conductor

Gennaro] Papi got out of his orchestra! Music as Montmezzi wrote it to be. All the beauty and the horror of a great romance wrought from men and instruments by a master of directors. And the encomparable Lazzari. The Mansfield of modern Opera he should be called."* In later columns he gave informed commentary on the productions of *La Juive, Fra Diavolo, Le Chemeneau, Thaïs, Marouf,* and *Tosca,* assessing everything from makeup and costumes to lighting and set design, but always particularly attentive to the actors. ("The acting just got by!" the young columnist complained about *Tosca.* "And that's all! I am afraid, however, that the audience, the largest of the year, was far from disappointed.")

Later in life, Orson viewed "Hitting the High Notes" as one of those youthful indiscretions for which it was his eternal duty to apologize. "I have so many happy memories of you and Mario from the very earliest times," he wrote to Mario Chamlee's wife, the soprano Ruth Miller, in the 1970s. "I have quite forgotten that I was ever presumptuous enough, in those salad days, to attempt a review of one of Mario's performances. But of course I do remember his *Marouf* very well indeed. He was not just a fine singer, but also a superb actor."

Orson attended all the operas that summer and also all the performances of the Chicago Symphony, whose lead violinist, Jacques Gordon, had played in his mother's home and at her memorial service. What he did not already know about opera, he could crib from his frequent concert companions—especially Uncle Ned, who wrote critiques of the Ravinia operas for the *Chicago Tribune*; and Aunt Hazel, who was one of the classical reviewers on her husband's staff. Moore treated Orson like the son he never had, even agreeing to lend his precious collection of music recordings to the Todd School library at Orson's urging. At the time, Moore was preoccupied with his magnum opus, *Forty Years of Opera in Chicago,* a book that would become the definitive source on the notorious story of Ganna Walska, a Polish garden enthusiast with a penchant for wealthy husbands. Walska's second husband was the Chicago Civic Opera's head Harold F. McCormick, who lavished money on her ill-advised musical career, paying for singing

---

* The newspaper preserved Orson's misspellings of "Montemezzi" and "incomparable."

lessons and thrusting her into plays and operas that flopped. Walska would become one of several inspirations for the character of Susan Alexander in *Citizen Kane.*

Besides seeing everything at Ravinia for several seasons, Orson rarely missed the operas that were performed in Chicago, thanks to Roger Hill and John Clayton. In the fall of 1928, Clayton, who had two sons enrolled at Todd, began arranging for the Todd boys to have a block of free seats at the Civic Opera on Sundays, and he made sure the boys met the stars after the performances. Clayton also introduced the boys to Harold F. McCormick, who was still married to Walska; and to Samuel Insull, a public utilities magnate who was a driving force behind the new Civic Opera House, and who also took a sometimes heavy hand in repertoire and casting.

On the Todd boys' opera trips, Orson was everyone's favorite seatmate. "He knew all the operas by heart," remembered John Dexter. "On the train going in Orson would tell us what the hell was going on, what the opera was all about. Kids used to fight to sit next to him at the opera. 'What's going? What's the old broad singing about?' "

But young Orson was also made uncomfortable during this time by the moments—apparently frequent—when one of the male Italian opera singers spied him as "meat for a quick seduction," as Welles told Barbara Leaming. He had a knack of catching the attention of preying homosexuals—like Captain Mueller—or perhaps of blaming them for his own sexual discomfort.

Welles told Leaming that he was forced to rebuff a number of "advances" from male opera stars while keeping secret his embarrassment at their behavior. Homosexual men seemed to trail him everywhere: a classmate he later said he took pains to avoid; a Todd School father who sprang upon him in bed during one weekend sleepover, he claimed. Orson complained of such situations so often that it's hard to believe they're purely fictional, so Simon Callow may be right: "Pretty well everyone must have felt some sort of sexual frisson in his presence."

Orson had been a pudgy boy with chipmunk cheeks, but by the summer of 1928, he had sprung up into a tall (six feet two inches or more, eventually) and strikingly handsome youth with dark brown eyes, unruly black hair, and a high pale arching forehead. To his big, winning smile and characteristic booming laugh was added a voice that was now preternaturally sonorous—a voice like God's, as Roger Hill liked to say—that could fill any room or auditorium.

His personality grew as surely as his body. He was grand and theatrical in his mannerisms. He crackled with energy and ideas. His delight was contagious; his rages were explosive. Hungry for attention, brooding when bored, Orson could also be contemplative and sweetly solicitous about other people. To people who knew him well, he was wonderful, if also, to people who knew him best, a handful—a singular character inside a singular physical package.

As he entered eighth grade in the fall of 1928, Orson was firmly ensconced as the Todd School's shining star of all things literary and theatrical. Promoted to editor of the *The Red & White*, he crafted a Kane-like "declaration of principles," sketching a man with a placard: "Our Platform—a Bigger, Better, Snappier Red and White." Besides writing poetry and a regular column, he now reviewed shows at Woodstock's downtown Miller Theatre. ("The whole piece was rather loosely put together," he wrote of the touring musical *Sweetheart Town*. "The leads were handled by very competent talent but the chorus work was rather pitiful in spots.") And his own theatrical blossoming continued. By now, thanks to Roger Hill, Orson was taking lead roles in most of the all-school plays, and handling much of the backstage work as well. In the fall of 1928, he starred in A. A. Milne's mystery-comedy *The Man in the Bowler Hat*; the following spring he played the main role of the condemned murderer in Holworthy Hall and Robert Middlemass's famous one-act *The Valiant*, a production that toured to other nearby schools.

Orson's third year as a Todd boy culminated in his first Shakespeare production for the school, an abridged *Julius Caesar* presented at the Drama League of Chicago's annual tournament at the Goodman Theatre in late May 1929. The task of adapting the play fell to Orson, who was just turning fourteen; Roger Hill helped—but mostly it was Orson, as the headmaster always said. They condensed Shakespeare's text into a sixty-minute version for a cast of twenty of the school's older, more proficient boys. The direction, too, was a collaboration between Orson and Hill—but, again, mostly Orson, making this the first all-school play he directed. He even handled costume and stage design, draping the cast in bedsheet togas and crafting sets from cardboard boxes. It was an early instance of Welles's career-long creativity with pinchpenny budgets combined with a philosophy of bricolage—with actors *and* sets.

Slathered in makeup, Orson also played two of the key roles in the Todd School production—Cassius and Mark Antony. "As Cassius, I killed Caesar quickly," he recalled, "then ran around, changed my make-up and was back on stage in time as Antony for the funeral oration." The cast included his friends John Dexter and Sherman Perlman, the latter about to graduate.

The Goodman tournament put the Todd boys in competition with other Chicago-area schools, and their annual bête noire was Nicholas Senn High School, which had taken the coveted first-prize silver cup and $25 award for two years running. A third victory would give Senn permanent possession of the trophy. The governor of the panel of judges was the Goodman's leading actor-director, Whitford Kane, whom both Hill and Orson knew personally from backstage visits.

Orson desperately wanted to take the trophy home to Todd, and by all accounts his first public foray into Shakespeare set a high bar. But another contender, Morgan Park High School, surprised everyone with a powerful staging of a one-act play set in China called *Robe of Wood.* Todd's chances were hurt when one of the tournament judges insisted that the "two" Todd boys playing Cassius and Mark Anthony—both Orson—must be ringers because they were obviously too big in size to be high school students. Morgan Park took first place.

When the decision was announced, pandemonium broke out in the theater. Hiram "Chubby" Sherman, a Goodman actor who was Whitford Kane's protégé, leaned over to whisper in Kane's ear. Kane jumped up to propose a face-saving "special award" for Todd School. "For God's sake, Roger," Kane told Hill afterward, "get a rich parent to buy a cup and have it engraved from us." Chicago's Better Speech Association chipped in, offering the Todd boys another special citation for diction. But Orson wasn't fooled: he had lost. His *Julius Caesar* had fallen short. He felt miserable, a failure.

Late that evening, as Orson was licking his wounds, Dr. Bernstein wrote him a letter of consolation. "Applause [means] little in the long run and not all the things we do that are worthwhile receive recognition," he advised. "Look at all the great works of art that slumbered without being recognized and so let this be a lesson to you. There will be times in your life when you will meet up with the same situation. Some day when you will be in the eyes of the world doing big things, as I know you will, you will look back upon this disappointment as having been just a passing experience. We must learn to accept disappointments and profit by them.

"Success is in the silences, though fame is in the song," Bernstein continued, quoting a line from the poem "Envoy" by Bliss Carman, a Canadian poet Orson's mother had loved. "I know your true values and I hope to live long enough to see them grow into fruition.

"I love you more than all else, Dadda."

The 1929 commencement edition of the *The Red & White* was the last issue with Orson as its editor. Along with sketches and musings, the issue indulged the budding maestro's silly side, with a humorous ode to mumps, which had overrun Todd School in the spring, and another happy-go-lucky poem to the summer ahead.

I'D LIKE TO BE A KITE

I'd like to be a kite and sail the skies,
I'd like to see the school building from above,
I'd like to break off all my mortal ties,
I'd like to fly—and gosh I'd love
To just keep sailing and not listen to the bell.
And what an end, to in an oak tree lie,
T'would suit me well—
To soar above the world—and then die!

Orson's bag was packed for the summer, but he would be soaring beyond Chicago. With Grand Detour out of the running, and Ravinia dark until July, everyone in his extended family—his father, Dr. Bernstein, the Moores, and by now the Hills—worried that the inexhaustible Orson would have too much idle time on his hands.

The headmaster had a brainstorm. Carl Hendrickson, Todd's chorus and orchestra director, spent part of every summer touring Europe. Hendrickson was willing to take Orson and another Todd boy along, for a guided art-travel tour much like the one Dudley Crafts Watson had given Orson's father. Dick Welles liked the idea, and promised to meet Orson in Europe at the end of the summer.

Along with the boys, Hendrickson would be bringing along his new toy: an eight-millimeter movie camera. He had become fascinated with motion pictures during his stint conducting the house orchestra at Chicago's most lavish picture palace, and had brought the camera on several school camping trips, filming little scenarios with the boys to project at school on Saturday nights. These "home movies" were Orson's first brush with filmmaking.

The small group sailed from New York in June, for a ten-week itinerary including England, France, Germany, Austria, and Italy. The three traveled "third rate, almost bumming," Orson later recalled, booking cheap train seats and steerage on Mediterranean boats.

The chaperoning was loose. Orson told Barbara Leaming that he enjoyed his first "grown-up" sexual encounter on board the ship with a girl who was two or three years older. Orson was savvy enough to tip a steward to borrow a first-class cabin, but he made no boasts about his lovemaking. "I was, however, not a wunderkind in that department," he said, "merely precocious."

In London, Orson later claimed, he attended a mass rally in Hyde Park, where he met a nice gentleman who took him to a closed-door meeting of militant socialists. In Munich, where the three were quartered with a woodcarver and his family, they visited a beer hall; Orson recalled sitting next to a man with a toothbrush mustache who rose from a bench to deliver a rant. He realized in retrospect that the ranting man could only have been Adolf Hitler.

In Milan, or so Dr. Bernstein later insisted, Orson was roused by police as he slept in a park and was briefly arrested after faking a conniption.

In Rome, as he waited to glimpse Pope Pius XI, he commandeered Hendrickson's eight-millimeter camera and attempted to direct his first motion picture: a sort of documentary featuring St. Peter's Basilica.

"A highly artistic study in 8mm of the big church that bears your name," Orson later told Peter Bogdanovich, "featuring Significant Architectural Detail. This was hand-held throughout, mind you, so it was really way ahead of my time. I got fascinated with that fountain—[Michelangelo] Antonioni at the very summit of his powers never held a single shot so long. Then, to my horror, the very instant I'd run out of film, the great doors of the cathedral were flung open, and with a mighty fanfare of trumpets, out came the Pope on a palanquin surrounded by Swiss Guards and a hundred cardinals."

On his first visit to Vienna, the locale of *The Third Man*, Orson recalled meeting the cigar-smoking Frau Sacher and stuffing himself with her famous Sacher torte at the Hotel Sacher. Orson and his companions also attended the magnificent State Opera House, although Orson was preoccupied by something other than the singers onstage.

"I was just becoming interested in girls," Welles reminisced some years later. "There was a knock on the back of my chair and I looked around, and a very pretty girl was sitting there, a little older than myself, but not too much older. And I gave her a big smile and she didn't react at all. Then there was another little tap on the back of my chair and I looked around and still no reaction. The opera went on, a third tap, and I looked and discovered that she wasn't flirting with me. She was cracking hard-boiled eggs. She'd brought her picnic lunch to the opera."

In Vienna, Carl Hendrickson also escorted the boys to a small playhouse to see a Schnitzler comedy, directed by the Austrian stage visionary Max Reinhardt. Orson spoke little German, but such obstacles never hampered his enjoyment. His father, Dick Welles, met up with the school group in Berlin and took his son to see Elisabeth Bergner in Reinhardt's production of *Romeo and Juliet*—the impresario ran theaters simultaneously in Berlin and Vienna. One of the most important theatrical figures of the early twentieth century, Reinhardt was renowned for his spectacular innovations in staging, breaking with realist tradition to incorporate expressionist and other modern aesthetic influences into his productions. Orson idolized him.

"He was a great, great director," Welles told Henry Jaglom a half century later, "a great master of spectacle as well as intimate comedy. He could do anything."

Stopping in London, Orson and his father would have been on time to see John Galsworthy's *The Skin Game*, later filmed by Alfred Hitchcock with the same star, Edmund Gwenn; and a variety show at the Coliseum featuring George Burns and Gracie Allen. They surely lined up to see the Australian Shakespeare specialist Oscar Asche in his modern-dress production of *The Merry Wives of Windsor* at the Apollo. Father and son returned, through Quebec, in the last week of August.

One curious by-product of Orson's first trip abroad was his maiden venture into public speaking. As a boy, Orson had gladly held forth at dinner parties, fireside gatherings, and school assemblies, but he had never delivered a prepared talk at an event open to the general public. His first opportunity came in March 1930, when he gave an entertaining "travel talk" on his European vacation for members of the Woodstock Woman's Club. Much as his mother and Uncle Dudley once had done with their "music picture symphonies," Orson enlivened his improvised performance by caricatures he sketched on a large pad. His presentation "had all the humor and sparkle of a clever, witty, but thoroughly natural and fun-loving American school boy," reported the *Woodstock Daily Sentinel*. He may not have struck everyone as an all-American boy, but a clever, witty speaker he was. And public speaking would become a lifelong sideline.

CHAPTER 6

1929–1931

A Great Sorrow

In September 1929, Dr. Maurice Bernstein drove Orson to Woodstock for ninth grade.

By now Roger and Hortense Hill had become very friendly with Dr. Bernstein, seeing him as a source of stability in Orson's life. They encountered Dick Welles only fleetingly at school plays, where he seemed subdued. The Hills got along more easily with Bernstein, an extrovert who counted other school families within his practice. When Bernstein and Ned Moore attended Orson's plays, the local newspaper listed them as important out-of-town visitors, providing an extra fillip of publicity for the school.

Although Dr. Bernstein often boasted about "his ability to charm other women," in the words of one of his conquests, no one was ever quite sure how successful he actually was in his love life. This made it all the more surprising when Bernstein suddenly married a glamorous Chicago diva he had been assiduously wooing all summer.

In July, a Chicago court had granted Edith Mason a divorce from her third husband, the Chicago Civic Opera conductor Giorgio Polacco. Bernstein had been waiting in the wings for a year or more. In late October, he and Mason eloped to Antioch, Illinois, a small town in northern Lake County, where they said their vows before a local justice of the peace. Two weeks later, when the Chicago press learned the news, the story of the doctor who won the heart of the famous opera star hit the wire services, appearing in the *New York Times*, the *Los Angeles Times*, and other papers from coast to coast.

Court records of Polacco and Mason's divorce bolster the image of Bernstein as a threat to their marriage. Polacco named the doctor as his romantic rival, demanding justice for the unfair loss of his wife and their four-year-old daughter. Welles later told Barbara Leaming that Dr. Bernstein "had this way of getting himself into triangles as the third party." Bernstein had carried a torch for Beatrice Welles, and Orson told Leaming that the doctor conducted an "on-again, off-again liaison" with Hazel Moore for years behind Ned Moore's back. But other anecdotes suggest that the doctor was a prim, old-fashioned character who was fundamentally clueless about women—and some husbands, including Dick Welles, felt safe leaving their wives in Bernstein's company.

Only a few witnesses received advance word of Dr. Bernstein's wedding. Among them were Orson; the Hills, who drove him to Antioch for the ceremony; and Ned and Hazel Moore. (Dick Welles was absent.) Some members of the Todd School community saw Orson as a "privileged character" (a "p.c.," as Simon Callow put it), and the impromptu trip to Antioch as just one more example of the many ways the Hills spoiled him. Not every teacher at Todd treated him as indulgently as the headmaster wished. One who viewed him with ambivalence was coach Tony Roskie, who had inherited the post of athletic director from Roger Hill. Orson was still ducking the school's fitness regimen, and he and Roskie engaged in a "running fight" over that and other matters, according to Welles.

Orson now had a single room in Grace Hall—single rooms were rare, but there were some—that was full of Oriental knickknacks his father had given him. He perfumed it by burning sticks of incense, a hazard that was strictly forbidden at the school. Roskie saw the room as a challenge to his authority, a veritable den of iniquity in the heart of Todd School. "He hated the Oriental decorations in my room," Welles recalled. "He said they would attract germs."

Worse yet, Orson routinely sneaked off campus to flirt with a girl who sang in a local church choir—another violation that bothered Roskie, though most of the Todd boys also chased town girls when they could. Orson secretly cultivated more than one "townie" girlfriend during his upper school days, he told his former headmaster decades later. "Barking and yelling and all that," Welles laughingly recalled.

"Meaningful. It included everything but penetration. The maiden fair had to remain a maiden until the wedding day."

Of all the dormitories at Todd, Grace Hall was the most difficult to escape. "I was in the main part of the prison," Welles recalled, "It took some ingenuity." Roskie was determined to catch him in the act, however, and one night, when Orson crawled up the fire escape and back in through a window, the coach was waiting for him. Roger Hill waived any punishment, but Roskie boldly confronted the headmaster with Orson's "delinquency" at a meeting of "the entire faculty," Hill recalled, "all of whom thought I was too easygoing." Hill talked his way out of the situation.

Hill's three children "despised" Orson because of the preferential treatment Hill gave him, according to Welles, viewing him as "this gosling in the midst of the chicken run." But he wasn't the only "p.c." at the school. Two years behind Orson, another budding "genius," Hascy Tarbox, was emerging as a vital contributor to many of the school plays Orson dominated. Tarbox would grow up to marry Hill's eldest daughter, Joanne. Despite a strong career as a commercial artist, he sometimes felt he languished in Orson's shadow. Tarbox gave interviews reflecting these tensions ("Orson had no friends," he told Leaming), echoing the sentiments of adults like coach Roskie, who grumbled that Orson "was a good kid, but he wasn't the only one. The school didn't revolve around him."

But if the headmaster had boundless warmth and approval for Orson, he also had boundless warmth and approval for all the Todd boys, and not a few alumni named their children "Roger" or "Todd."

Orson spent almost as much time on the train to Chicago, during the school year 1929–1930, as he did in class. With access to free or discounted tickets to the Chicago Civic Opera, the Chicago Symphony, the Shakespeare Society, the Goodman Theatre, and all the touring Theatre Guild productions, he attended dozens of productions and stored them all away in his mind, crammed with memories like Xanadu's cellar. He'd see a play; make a mental note about a scene that worked, a playwright worth following, or an actor who stole the show; and recall the memory when he needed it—sometimes decades later.

The Todd students paid an extended call to the dressing room of the soprano Mary Garden, "the Sarah Bernhardt of opera," after seeing her in *L'Amore dei Tre Re* and *Le Jongleur de Notre Dame*. They also enjoyed a private audience with Chicago's foremost Shakespearean, the actor and director Fritz Leiber. Orson and the Todd Troupers attended every Shakespeare production offered by Leiber's troupe during its twelve-week run at the Civic Theatre starting in late 1929. A Chicago native, Leiber had played Mercutio in a 1916 silent film of *Romeo and Juliet*, and he became a regular character actor in Hollywood after sound arrived. That season in Chicago, Leiber either directed or starred in ten Shakespeare plays—*Macbeth*, *Othello*, *King Lear*, and *Hamlet* among them. The Todd boys met with Leiber backstage, where they were encouraged to ask him about his interpretations of the plays; the *Chicago Herald and Examiner* ran a photograph of Leiber with Roger Hill, Orson, and the other Todd Troupers.

One Shakespeare play Leiber omitted that season was the comedy *Much Ado About Nothing*, so Hill bused the boys to Madison, Wisconsin, to see it performed by Sir Ben Greet, one of the last great actor-managers, who was near the end of his touring days with his players. "Constant play-going of this sort," reported the Woodstock newspaper, "develops a critical faculty in the Todd Troupers which is reflected in the remarkable excellence of their own productions."

The Todd boys gorged themselves on theater that year, taking in the entire New York Theatre Guild road show schedule, which included *Caprice* with Alfred Lunt and Lynn Fontanne; Eugene O'Neill's *Strange Interlude*; the Czech science fiction play *R.U.R.* by Karel Čapek; a revival of George Bernard Shaw's *Major Barbara*; and a new British drama, *Wings over Europe*. They also attended the Goodman's acclaimed *Romeo and Juliet*—another Shakespeare standard Leiber had omitted—as well as a revival of Richard Brinsley Sheridan's eighteenth-century comedy of manners, *The Rivals*; and a young people's matinee of *Ivanhoe*.

In Woodstock, the school's own drama program was evolving. Carl Hendrickson had lingered in Europe, taking a yearlong sabbatical to get married; and without him to crank out music and songs, the foolishments waned. Orson harbored ambitions to mount important dramatic works, and in Hendrickson's absence the headmaster leaned on the youth increasingly.

Early in the winter, the Todd Troupers mounted a tribute to the Chicago poet and playwright Kenneth Sawyer Goodman, whose death in the 1918 influenza pandemic had led his family to found the Goodman Theatre. The first show to be staged in "Roger's Hall," the newly renovated auditorium named for the popular young headmaster, was Goodman's one-act *Dust of the Road* starring Orson as the restless ghost of Judas, condemned to wander the Earth and implore others not to sell their souls for thirty pieces of silver. To fill out the evening, Orson wrote, directed, and starred in his first original play, *Purple Joss*. The text has been lost, but a joss stick is a type of incense, and newspaper accounts suggest that the play was a one-act Oriental mystery. Orson also presented a satirical sketch, *Skum of the Earth*, poking gentle fun at Goodman's portentous *Dust of the Road*. Orson was the young man of the hour, writing, directing, or starring in every part of the show.

Roger's Hall was part of an extraordinary expansion of the Todd School that was preoccupying the headmaster in the fall of 1929. By the end of the year the school had added a swimming pool and a riding academy, and inaugurated ambitious road trips to American historical sites. Soon after Orson's graduation, other amenities would follow: a radio laboratory and even a small airport, complete with three Piper Cubs, so that the boys could have flying lessons.

Hill liked to say that he turned Todd's dramatic program over to Orson to get the youth out of his hair. Welles liked to say he did so much in so many plays to capture Skipper's attention. But Orson was a godsend, a self-starter, and Hill delegated more and more responsibility to him as the school year wore on. Hill was still listed as director of the all-school plays, but his actual involvement tapered off.

Naturally, as Orson immersed himself in dramatics, his grades suffered, especially in the subjects that didn't come naturally to him. Here again the headmaster was complicit, encouraging Orson to befriend his classmate Paul Guggenheim, whom Hill regarded as "the other genius" in the same age bracket. Hill then looked the other way when Orson paid Guggenheim for assistance with Latin declensions and geometry. Orson was proud of his lifelong resistance to mathematics, and his spelling also stayed weak. But these weaknesses would not be reflected in his Todd School grades.

Orson's schedule was brutal, and by Christmas he had run himself down and developed a bad cold. His father was still away, so Orson headed to Bernstein's house in Highland Park, where the doctor was spending the holiday with his new wife, the opera diva Edith Mason.

Their marriage was fast combusting. At first the newlyweds had shuttled between Bernstein's modest flat and Mason's luxurious Lake Shore Drive apartment. Yet Mason's ex-husband, Giorgio Polacco, dogged their every move—calling to talk to her, turning up to visit, sitting down and refusing to leave. Orson still visited Bernstein on his many trips to Chicago, but now those visits were unsettling, with the three adults always quarreling. Court records prove the truth of this anecdote: Polacco carried a gun, and at one point he showed up and waved it around, threatening to shoot the couple and himself—until Mason grabbed the gun and threatened to kill herself first.

Orson's presence stirred up other layers of complexity. Polacco was sexually omnivorous, according to Barbara Leaming, and lusted after Orson, always trying to "touch" the teenager when no one was looking.

Orson admired Edith Mason's singing, but she was no fan of his. When he arrived in Highland Park, the opera star was greatly "upset" by his cold, according to Chicago newspapers, because she herself "recently had recovered from a cold" and did not want to risk a relapse. When Dr. Bernstein refused to find Orson somewhere else to stay, Mason stormed off, taking a suite at the Belden-Stratford apartments in the city. When reporters got wind of the contretemps and asked Bernstein whether he and the diva had separated permanently, the doctor insisted that he was spending Christmas in the suburbs for peace and quiet. "I visit my wife and see her often," he insisted. "I am very much in love with her, and I think she still is in love with me." But the marriage never recovered, and within months Mason had filed for divorce.

The case took a year and a half to resolve, with Mason leaving the Civic Opera and taking up residence in Dallas, Texas. The divorce proceedings painted "a strange marital mosaic," according to the *Chicago Herald and Examiner*, with a "curious roundelay of charges and countercharges." Mason claimed that the doctor "set about deliberately to obtain money from me, to live off my income, and to spend my income," even borrowing $1,000 from her to buy her a diamond wedding ring. Bernstein countered her charges with a five-thousand-word deposition that presented Polacco as the "arch conspirator against his marital happiness," according to the press, turning up incessantly on their doorstep, threatening their lives, trying to extort $100,000 from Bernstein to compensate him for the loss of his beloved wife and daughter. Polacco even warned Bernstein that Mason was getting fat, urging the doctor to put her on a diet and curtail her smoking, which was ruining her glorious voice. Bernstein attested that Mason had her own faults: she was "extravagant in behalf of herself," according to the *Herald and Examiner's* account of his deposition, "citing as one example her possession of 100 pairs of shoes."

After the divorce came through, Mason reconciled with Polacco, remarrying him later in 1931, then divorcing him again six years later. The enigmatic doctor, meanwhile, had added a second failed marriage to his own scorecard.

Where was Dick Welles throughout this soap opera? Was he traveling constantly for pleasure in the Caribbean, as some accounts suggest? Was he visiting his son Richard in Kankakee? Is it possible that Dick was ill, even in a hospital for tests, without Orson's knowing?

According to Peter Noble's biography, relying heavily on information from Dr. Bernstein, Dick Welles retired from business after his wife's death and devoted himself "to enjoying a life of leisure and travel," with his son as his "constant companion." Barbara Leaming's biography expanded on this travelogue and gave Dick an ulterior motive. "Expressly to steal him away from Dr. Bernstein," wrote Leaming, "Dick took Orson on far-flung travels in Europe, Africa, and Asia." Orson insisted in multiple interviews that his father even lived in China for long spells.

But this appears to be more fantasy than memory. Though available records are admittedly partial, they indicate that after his wife's death Dick Welles rarely traveled outside the United States, apart from his customary vacations in the Caribbean. His two documented trips to Europe were his 1925 excursion with Dudley Crafts Watson's tour group, which included Dr. Bernstein, and his trip to meet Orson in Berlin in the late summer of 1928.

In the summer of 1930, however—in honor of Orson's fifteenth birthday, and perhaps for other reasons—Dick Welles proposed a long voyage to the Far East.

That spring, Orson and Roger Hill cowrote a joke-laden musical revue, *Troupers' Trifles of 1930*, which was performed at Roger's Hall for the student body, then reprised at the Woman's Club and the Woodstock Opera House before touring to a few North Shore towns. Orson designed the costumes, the lighting, and the sets; played the lead role; and, for the first time, officially shared directing credit with the headmaster. After attending a performance of *Troupers' Trifles*, Dick Welles unveiled his plans: in early July, he and Orson would leave by train for Seattle, where they would embark on a boat for Japan and China.

For a young man already fascinated with the Orient, it was a dream trip. Orson arranged to resurrect his *Highland Park News* column as a kind of travel diary, complete with a new title, "Inklings," and his own ink-sketched logo.

His first dispatch came from on board the twenty-thousand-ton *Korea Maru*, off the shore of Victoria, Vancouver Island, in British Columbia. "Gissing would terminate his feverish search for 'where the blue begins' were he here now, for this is where the blue ends," Orson reported ecstatically, "the sky being considerably faded with the heat."*

It would take the *Korea Maru* a few weeks to cross the Pacific. After anchoring briefly in Honolulu and Manila, the vessel reached Japan in late July. Orson gave one account of the crossing in his column, and another later on at a Woodstock speaking engagement; both lighthearted, they formed the basis of accounts of the trip in the earliest books about Welles. Not until Welles retold the story to Barbara Leaming, many years later, did a darker narrative emerge. This tale, supported by Orson's private letters from the time, was colored with anguish.

---

* "Gissing" was a reference to Christopher Morley's 1922 novel *Where the Blue Begins*, which concerned a dog named Mr. Gissing, who makes an exhausting search, traveling vast distances to seek the meaning of life, meeting with little success until he returns home to find solace in the blue of the cerulean flames in his fireplace.

At first, Orson busied himself aboard ship writing a prospective radio script featuring Sherlock Holmes. As the filmmaker later recalled, he began to notice that his father was sleeping through most of the days on board. Forced to fend for himself, Orson whiled away the hours signing chits at the bar "for everybody on the ship," as Peter Noble wrote, quoting Welles. "I was certainly popular on that voyage, and the pile of signed chits grew into an enormous heap. My poor father, who knew nothing about my chit-signing, was obliged to settle up a huge bill when the ship landed in China, gave me his first and only lecture—on the value of money.

"I am afraid that it had very little effect on me."

According to Leaming, Dick Welles spent the voyage repeatedly drinking himself into a "stupor" and once was "drunk enough to lose his trousers" before shocked witnesses on the ship. He made Orson his errand boy, tasked with keeping his father supplied with all the alcohol he could consume. The young man, now fifteen, wrote to the Hills in misery, saying he only wished his father could "find a drink that wouldn't make him sick." Worse yet, Dick grew furious when he realized that Orson was picking up drinks for himself as he raced to the bar to replenish his father's glass, and warned the boy that no member of the Welles family had started out on the road to alcoholism at such a tender age. "There was considerable tension" between Orson and his father, Leaming wrote. "Dick made no bones about being terribly disappointed with Orson, who, he kept sadly repeating, had passed from him."

Stopping in Tokyo, they gazed upon Frank Lloyd Wright's recent Imperial Hotel ("typically Wright with long, horizontal lines and very handsome," Orson reported in the *Highland Park News*), then docked in the ancient capital, Nara. "Picturesque and lovely, one of the most beautiful spots in Japanese Japan and particularly so in the rain," Orson said in his second "Inklings" column. "It started to sprinkle just as we left the station in our rickshaw and increased in violence as we rode. There was a thin green mist hanging over everything as we went scurrying through a kind of three dimensional Japanese print, rattling over little lacquered bridges across willow-bordered streams under huge pines as old as time itself, crunching across temple yards, past age-old pagodas, and on up the hill to our hotel."

After the rain stopped, he left "our Dad to snooze under mosquito netting" and stepped outside, venturing into a park where he encountered a traveling theatrical troupe. "In the park we found an open space," Orson wrote, "in the center of which was a gayly-curtained platform. We guessed correctly that it was a temporary stage erected by some company of strolling players. We parted the drapes and peered in. The actors were clustered about a tiny stove eating their supper. They invited us to join in with them and of course we accepted."

Seated in "the only chair" and presented with chopsticks, at which he was already evidently proficient, Orson proceeded to get "stuffed with rice, raw fish, and 'saki.' And while even our Japanese was more extensive than their English we carried on a successful conversation of three hours duration—entirely with our hands. We taught them a song from a school musical comedy and they instructed us in the art of Oriental theatrical fencing and make-up.*

"It was a truly fascinating experience.

"Late that afternoon we left, promising to return to their show in the evening."

Father and son returned when darkness fell. "We found ourselves alone in the park" with the troupe, Orson continued, the show drawing a sparse crowd. "The moving picture industry is hitting the theatrical world even in the East, and it was raining a little. The players laughed long and heartily, and we had tea. We were shocked by their living conditions, their poverty. They told us that they had enough rice for one more day, if no one came the next night. . . . They felt hurt when we offered them money and laughed at our sympathizing. They would laugh at death. We said good-bye and the last thing we heard as we walked down the road was the sound of their merry voices singing the American song we had taught them."

In China, the two toured more widely, making a memorable visit to the Great Wall near Peking. Whether Dick Welles accompanied Orson on all the side trips is unclear, but Dick must have traveled on land with his teenage son when great distances were covered.

In a conversation with his daughter Chris Welles Feder, however,

---

* The song was probably from Orson's favorite foolishment, *Finesse the Queen.*

Orson implied that he was alone at least one day, probably in Shanghai, when he wandered into a Chinese opera. "I'll never forget the elaborate costumes, the masks, the revolving stages," he told her. He would evoke that moment in *The Lady from Shanghai*, the 1948 film in which a sailor (played by Welles), framed for a murder, hides in a Chinatown theater in San Francisco as Betty Leong and the Mandarin Theatre enact a masque onstage.

As the boat turned back toward America, Dick Welles reverted to sleeping through the days. For the rest of his life, Orson believed that his father was sleeping off his alcoholism, and other biographies accept this conclusion. But there may be more sympathetic explanations. Dick Welles's heart condition had not gone away, and besides his gin and tonics he may well have been taking digitalis, then a popular treatment for heart disease. Digitalis retarded the swelling of body tissue and stimulated normal heart rhythms, and it was often prescribed in combination with lengthy bed rest; for this reason, people with heart disease often took ocean cruises. Digitalis was a difficult substance to prescribe in an accurate dosage, and its effects were notoriously erratic.

One voice that is absent from all this speculation is that of Dick Welles himself. He left no correspondence or other written record of his life. He may have known he was gravely ill; after discussing the trip with Orson, Barbara Leaming wrote that Dick Welles expressed a fear "of dying in the Orient." At one point during the voyage, far from home, Dick Welles made his son promise "he wouldn't be buried in the ground," i.e., on foreign soil. He made Orson vow to have him cremated or buried at sea if he should die during the trip.

Orson returned from his summer in Japan and China rattled by the "terrifying journey" he had undergone with his drink-addled father. Barbara Leaming wrote that the boy complained privately to Roger and Hortense Hill about the voyage, and the Hills "made him vow not to see his father again until he had sobered up." Orson "bluntly" passed on that ultimatum to Dick Welles. "That was the last I ever saw of him," Welles told Leaming.

But when, exactly, was that blunt face-off? The first important production of the 1929–1930 season at Todd was George Bernard Shaw's

Androcles and the Lion, a large undertaking featuring forty dramatis personae—mostly Junior Troupers (underclassmen) but also members of the Society of Learn Pidgins (the youngest Todd boys), all of it "staged by Orson Welles," his first credit as sole director. And Dick Welles was there to see the show.

Androcles was a typical Todd School shoestring operation—the school never had adequate resources for proper costumes, sets, or even rehearsals. Of course the casting was catch-as-catch-can too, and Orson learned to appreciate the Todd footballers who could act, such as John Dexter; William Mowry Jr., who later followed Orson into the Mercury Theatre; and the ordinary-seeming Edgerton Paul, who played Androcles in this production, and who always underwent an impressive transformation onstage. Orson directed Paul in key roles at Todd before he too joined the Mercury. "A funny little fellow," Orson mused years later, "with acne and unfortunate in every way but he kind of cast all that aside when he got into makeup and costumes."

Todd productions encouraged Orson's habit of directing as though trapped in the eye of a storm, herding his fledgling actors, shouting at them, driving them fiercely toward the cliff's edge. "If you had a lead, you did exactly as you were told" by Orson, remembered Hascy Tarbox, then a Junior Trouper. "He choreographed everything. 'That's your mark. Don't move. Don't wriggle.' He was a martinet. The result was extraordinary theatre." Dexter concurred: "Keep it moving!" was Orson's credo, he remembered. Yet when necessary, Orson was also insightful and nurturing: "He would stop and explain to one and all the plot, the feeling he wanted, the mood, the speed, etc. How he knew it I don't know."

As was his wont, Orson took a plum role himself in *Androcles*, doubling as the brutish warrior Ferrovius, whom Androcles describes as having "the strength of an elephant and the temper of a raving bull." He even designed and wrote the production's program, including an amusing discourse on the import of the play: "A mystery surrounds the author of this delightful satire. Just what is Bernard Shaw, vegetarian, socialist, anti-vivisectionist and Irishman, really driving at?"

Roger's Hall filled up with parents and townies, many of them drawn by Orson's growing reputation. Among them was Dick Welles, who arrived by train from Chicago. Was it here and now, at *Androcles and the Lion*, that Orson cornered his father and told him to stay away? Or did he write his father a letter and later dodge Dick's telephone calls?

Leaming and Callow agree that practically everyone in the school knew that Orson's father was an alcoholic. "His father would come out to see almost every play that we would do," Hill said, "but he would go into the back seat and he'd sit there silently and he'd probably leave just before the end." Dick Welles was "usually pretty heavily cocked with alcohol," the headmaster recalled. "According to Paul Guggenheim," Callow wrote, without quoting Guggenheim directly, Orson "hated" his father and made himself scarce whenever Dick Welles showed up at Todd for his performances. "His drunkenness was impossible to ignore," Callow explained, "an unbearable embarrassment in front of his fellow students."

But was it really so surprising that a father would leave a school play quickly, as the curtain fell, if his son had warned him away? If he thought his presence was embarrassing his son, or if he was reluctant to reveal his own deteriorating health?

Just a week after *Androcles and the Lion*, Orson stopped in at the Tavern Club after a Saturday matinee of Fritz Leiber's company performing *Julius Caesar*. According to Ashton Stevens in his "A Column or Less" for the *Herald-Examiner*, Orson came looking for "either his guardian, the distinguished Dr. Bernstein, or the doctor's playmates, the childless but children-loving Ned Moores." When neither could be found, Orson sat down alone and ordered a meal. "Too young to be a member of the Tavern, and too prosperous looking to be a dinner-snatcher, he caused considerable speculation," Stevens wrote. But the headwaiter vouched for the boy: "Why, that young gentleman's all right," the headwaiter reportedly said. "He's the only son of Mr. and Mrs. Edward Moore."

Callow pitied "poor Dick Welles, if he was able to read the piece," with its references to Bernstein as Orson's guardian and the boy himself "as another man's son." Yet Stevens was obviously kidding; as an old friend of Dick Welles, he knew full well who Orson's real father was; and the headwaiter was quoted as part of the joke. Stevens went on to praise Orson's self-assurance, predicting that the youth would become "my favorite actor" someday, though he had "yet to see him act." He vowed to file the column away, betting that Orson would be "at least a leading man by the time it has yellowed."

Orson himself pinpointed the last time he glimpsed his father. It was not at a performance of *Androcles and the Lion*, but at the second major Todd School production of the year: *Wings over Europe*, the British drama the Todd boys had seen staged by the touring Theatre Guild in Chicago the previous year.

Wings over Europe was presented in Roger's Hall one week before Christmas 1930. Again, Dick Welles made the trip from Chicago; again, he left quickly after the last act—because "he didn't want to admit he was interested in my acting career or some damn thing," Welles told Leaming. Orson had the leading role, as an intense poet-scientist grappling with deadly knowledge; Hill was the nominal co-director, but Orson was really in charge, borrowing shrewdly from the Theatre Guild version.

As Orson later recalled, even as his father slouched somewhere in the back row, the Roger's Hall performance came to an unexpected climax. In the story, several government officials have come to meet with the scientist, concerned that he intends to detonate a bomb. Another senior—a boy Orson didn't particularly like, as either actor or classmate—played a Parliament official who is goaded by his colleagues into shooting Orson's character. When the boy pointed his gun at Orson, however, the prop weapon didn't fire. Orson the director was crestfallen—but Orson the actor was thrilled, a moment later, when the other student startled everyone by diving across a table, tackling Orson, and wrestling him to the ground, saving the scene. "I admire him for that," Welles told Hill fifty years later.

By the time the curtain call was over, Dick Welles was gone. Orson had kept his vow to distance himself from his father, although his ambivalence about the decision was never resolved. "I didn't think I was doing the right thing, I simply wanted to please the Hills," he told Leaming in 1984. "I promised," he told his daughter Chris Welles Feder, "not because I agreed with them—I didn't think my father's drinking was a terrible thing—but because I wanted to please them."

Dick Welles returned to Chicago, alone with his thoughts. He no longer had a permanent address; instead he shuttled from one residential hotel to another, and by the late fall of 1930 he was under the regular care of a nurse. His mental faculties may have deteriorated: when he fell behind on his bill at the Harrison Hotel, his half brother, Jacob Rudolph Gottfredsen, had to be summoned from Kenosha to help settle his accounts. His debts included payments to the Harrison Hotel's house physician, as well as minor bills he had left unpaid in Grand Detour. Gottfredsen helped move Welles to the Hotel Bismarck, on Randolph Street in the heart of the Loop.

A few days before Christmas, Dick Welles used the hotel phone to ring Kenosha and speak to his half brother's wife, asking her if she would buy a flowering plant as a holiday gift for his mother, promising to repay the cost. (His half brother would later dun his estate for the expense.)

Also just before Christmas, Dr. Maurice Bernstein visited Dick at the Bismarck, less than half a mile from his office on Michigan Avenue. Bernstein, who must have realized that Dick was clinging to life but failing rapidly, may have cautioned Roger Hill and suggested that Orson stay in Woodstock over Christmas. Bernstein and Dick Welles talked over Dick's will and the future of his sons after his impending death.

Orson's father made it through the holiday, but three days later, in the late afternoon of Sunday, December 28—the last weekend of 1930—he collapsed. In signing Dick Welles's death certificate, Dr. Bernstein noted the principal causes of death as "chronic myocarditis," which is an inflammation of the heart muscle commonly associated with chronic alcoholism (though also linked to certain viruses and prescription drugs), along with "chronic interstitial nephritis," an inflammatory condition sometimes triggered by toxins or prescribed medications (but also a possible sign of autoimmune disease). According to Bernstein's death certificate notes, the nephritis first manifested itself in May 1930—just before the Far East voyage Dick Welles undertook with his son. In Dick's case, unlike that of Orson's mother, no autopsy was performed.

Jacob Rudolph Gottfredsen returned in haste to Chicago. As other books have noted, Gottfredsen filled in several blanks on the official death form with "Don't know"—among them Welles's birthplace; the name of his father; and, most puzzlingly, the name of Dick Welles's mother—Gottfredsen's own.

Bernstein sent a telegram to Orson at Todd School: "Your father's dead. Rush here."

By the time Orson arrived, Gottfredsen—the Wisconsin uncle he barely knew—had prepared the body for the train to Kenosha, where prayers were said over a casket set amid candles and incense in the living room of Rudolphsheim on the afternoon of December 30.

As with his mother's service, the minister was Episcopalian. But Orson said later that he was aghast at the funeral, full of rituals he found unfamiliar and peculiar, and he was haunted by his failure to honor his father's wishes to be cremated or buried at sea. But Dick Welles had spoken with both Dr. Bernstein and Jacob Rudolph Gottfredsen about his wishes shortly before his death, and a plot was reserved for him next to his wife and her parents in the Green Ridge Cemetery. Orson was a teenager with no standing to interfere.

Orson stalked out of his grandmother's living room and returned to Chicago with Dr. Bernstein; he would never shed his resentment over his father's funeral. He never again said a kind, or even an accurate, word about his paternal grandmother, Mary Head Welles Gottfredsen, going so far as to describe her in interviews as a "witch" who made animal sacrifices. For her part, she said nothing at all in public about him, and in her will left him his choice of half the books from her personal library.

Richard Head Welles was only fifty-eight when he died. He was mourned on the front page of the *Kenosha News*, and in the journals of the trades he had left behind. "Old-timers in the industry will regret to learn of the sudden death" of "Dick Welles, as everyone knew him," read a notice in *Automobile Topics*.

In Chicago, when the First Union Trust and Savings Bank, executor of Dick Welles's estate, presented his will for probate, the event made louder headlines than the news of Welles's death. The front page of the local section of the *Herald and Examiner* reported that Welles had left a $100,000 fortune to his fifteen-year-old son, George Orson Welles. The probate court appointed Dr. Bernstein as the boy's guardian *ad litem*, a temporary position until other candidates were reviewed. But the *Herald* glossed over the details: "Dr. Bernstein Made Guardian of Rich Boy," the headline prematurely announced.

———

His mother's death taught young Orson the capriciousness of time. He had learned not to live in fear that time would run out, but rather to thumb his nose at time in every brave and devious way imaginable. His father's death would remind him of this, while teaching a new lesson: money was an abstraction. The headlines called him a rich boy, but those riches were withheld from his grasp. Money, for him, would always be as insubstantial and capricious as time.

In his last years, Welles would come to view his father as an "enormously likable and attractive" human being, adding that "it was a great sorrow to me when he died." He blamed himself for deserting his father in those final days, not the Hills—"momentarily, false gods," he called them—whose guidance, usually so valuable, had failed him at that critical juncture.

"I had followed the wrong adults, you know, and for the wrong reasons," Welles explained to Barbara Leaming. "I've never, never . . . I don't want to forgive myself. That's why I hate psychoanalysis. I think if you're guilty of something you should live with it. Get rid of it—how can you get rid of a *real* guilt? I think people should live with it, face up to it." After his brother, Richard, had so disappointed his parents, he had felt "the burden of achievement" shift to his own shoulders. "I couldn't let them down," Orson told his daughter Chris. "My parents were larger than life to me, wonderful, mythical, almost fantastical creatures, and more than anything I wanted to please them. . . . The wish to please them has never left me."

That desire would come to shape Orson Welles's life and career. He was confronted continually by setbacks, interruptions, and delays, and often he was wounded by problems of time or money—but rarely was he permanently deterred. He rejected obstacles and crises, always pushing on, almost relishing the hurdles. Without the tragedy of his parents, Welles might never have developed his singular drive, his quixotic belief that time and money should not matter.

At school, Orson turned his back on calamity. On a cold winter night just a few weeks after his father's death, he kept a previous appointment to address the Dean Street School Parent-Teacher Association (PTA) on the subject of "China and Japan." Wearing a "magnificent" costume he had purchased in the Far East, Orson strode onto a stage bedecked with his own souvenirs, greeted the PTA audience with "Good evening" in Japanese dialect, and then began to make drawings on a chalkboard as he related off-the-cuff stories about his summer trip. "We traveled with him in mind," reported the *Woodstock Sentinel*, "as he led us along the wide beautiful streets and also through the narrow, poorer districts of both of these countries." Though Dick Welles's behavior, and condition, had cast a shadow over the trip, Orson mentioned his late father only lightly in passing. "Orson is a young man fifteen years of age and already a genius," the *Sentinel* reported, "with poise, expression, and ability beyond his years."

Poise, indeed.

And "genius" again: Orson's senior year at the Todd School confirmed the impression, already recurring in newspaper accounts of his activities. The school year 1930–1931 brought no fewer than five full-scale all-school plays that could have been billed as "Orson Welles productions," in addition to the many Saturday night entertainments he continued to oversee. Although the latter were frivolous, Orson was also starting to express his social conscience. When he and Hascy Tarbox staged an elaborate puppet theater program—long enough to take up half of one Saturday night bill—the villainous puppet was the proprietor of the "J. P. Bloodshed Bank." And the second half of the show, as Todd Tarbox wrote in *Orson Welles and Roger Hill: A Friendship in Three Acts*, "was a lively musical revue performed by puppets resembling faculty members."

His grades, admittedly boosted by the helping hands of other students, now reached honors level. Outside the classroom, he did everything from painting history murals on school walls to editing and designing a publication called *Todd: A Community Devoted to Boys and Their Interests*—a combination yearbook, catalog, and sales brochure that he enhanced with sly personal annotations. ("Every word of this book was either written or edited by him," wrote Roger Hill in a subsequent letter to Cornell College in Mount Vernon, Iowa, enclosing a copy with his letter urging them to admit Orson. "The only 'cheating' I did in this was to make him cut out some of his best bits of writing as they were too completely mature.")

In late February, the Todd Troupers brought new life to one of Orson's old favorites: *Dr. Jekyll and Mr. Hyde.** Billed as "J. Worthington Ham," Orson joined forces with codirector Roger Hill to re-create the atmosphere of the original 1880s stage productions of Robert Louis Stevenson's story. As a candlelighter "lit" the footlights, the student orchestra—wearing vintage costumes—struck up the overture, with Carl Hendrickson back on the podium. A vendor sold peanuts between acts. With a blurb from John Clayton ("This is the best thing the Troupers have ever done!"), the Troupers took the show to venues in Lake Forest and Highland Park.

The headmaster was skeptical about squeezing so many full-scale plays into the school calendar, but Orson could not be talked out of Molière's *The Physician in Spite of Himself*. Orson starred in and supervised this early spring production, which boasted a "full-blown constructivist setting" reminiscent of Vsevolod Meyerhold, according to Simon Callow. Always influenced by what he saw, Orson could recall the similarly modernist production of Elmer Rice's *The Adding Machine*, which had had its Chicago premiere at the Goodman in 1930.

The theatrical high point of Orson's senior year was the last play, which was traditionally offered as part of the Closing Day program. Orson set out to produce an adaptation of *Richard III*, carrying around "a falling-to-pieces one-volume Shakespeare," in Roger Hill's words, which he "marked up with great black-crayon cuts." As his modifications continued, however, he began to draw on other Shakespeare plays, until his *King Richard III* (as he called it) became a stitched-together condensation of all the Bard's history plays covering the War of the Roses.

Orson and Roger Hill reached down into the fifth grade, casting fifty Todd boys of all ages; and they crafted their most elaborate set ever for the spectacle. Orson himself would play the hunchbacked Richard III, "his face unrecognizable, as if made from spare parts of several faces stuck together with huge pieces of sticking plaster," as Simon Callow wrote. "Disturbing and powerful." But Orson's script

---

* Orson also would perform his old Camp Indianola favorite on radio, and he would be very funny as Maurice, the leader of a traveling troupe staging a hapless version of *Dr. Jekyll and Mr. Hyde* in the 1969 comedy film *Twelve Plus One*, a.k.a. *The 13 Chairs*.

was too lengthy for any audience to bear, and he felt under pressure to trim and then trim some more, rather drastically, at the eleventh hour. Even so, the production, which stretched over three hours, was "the most outstanding affair of its kind ever attempted by the Troupers," wrote the *Woodstock Sentinel*, with acting "far beyond that usually found in school plays. . . . Orson Wells [*sic*] outdid himself. . . . Orson today leaves Todd. If he misses his school in the days to come he may be sure that the school will also miss him."

With his three-hour *King Richard III*, a luncheon, a swim meet, a riding exhibition, numerous speeches, and the annual bestowing of laurels, Closing Day ceremonies that year dragged on interminably. Only ten seniors were graduating, with Orson one of four honor students. According to the only extant copy of his report card, for the first semester of his final term, he received unsurprising A's in English, ancient history, and art; questionable A's in algebra and spelling; B in French, and also in neatness and deportment; and C's, finally, in Latin and gymnasium—the former an elective but neither C averaged for honors.

His graduation was attended by Dr. Maurice Bernstein and Ned and Hazel Moore, along with his mother's favorite cousin, Dudley Crafts Watson. "The school did to him," Watson told Peter Noble, "what none of the rest of us could."

Orson's friend John Dexter also graduated that year. "At Todd," Dexter recalled, "the guy was really an unbelievable human being. We had a lot of fun and he was a great guy."

"It was only at Todd that I could be my own person," Orson told his daughter Chris Welles Feder. "My greatest coup," he added poignantly, was not getting good grades, playing lead roles, or staging the ambitious *King Richard III* on Closing Day. It was, simply, "winning Skipper's love."

Shortly before graduation—on May 7, very nearly coinciding with Orson's sixteenth birthday—a Chicago judge formally appointed Dr. Bernstein as the guardian of the boy's welfare and estate. It may be, as Orson later insisted, that Dick Welles wanted his son to be able to choose his own guardian. The judge did consult Orson, although his wishes were nonbinding.

Orson said in later interviews that he would have preferred Roger Hill. The headmaster discussed it with him at Chicago's Union Station, probably over spring break. But Skipper was reluctant to take on the mantle. "I remember we sat down on one of the great seats and talked a long time," Hill recalled, "and he asked me if I'd be his guardian. And I, selfishly in one way, because I didn't want [the] trouble of doing it, but I said, 'Orson, that would be mad. It would break Dadda's heart.' This Bernstein who had been practically his father and he called Dadda."

The precise monetary value of Dick Welles's estate was fluid, dependent on the fate of his oil and railroad stocks (the will directed that the estate be "invested at all times in safe, income bearing or interest bearing properties and securities"), and on the termination value of his insurance policies: accident, home, and travel. According to court documents, Welles owned 200 shares of capital stock and 102 shares of common stock in the Standard Oil Company of Indiana; 100 shares of preferred stock and another 50 of common stock in Chicago and Northwestern Railway; 100 shares each in Illinois Central Railroad and Pullman; 52 shares of preferred stock and 106 shares of common stock in Tex-La-Homa Oil Corporation; 50 shares of preferred stock in B. F. Goodrich; and 25 shares of preferred and 1,400 shares of common stock in Globe Consolidated Oil. There were share amounts of a handful of other stocks—smaller numbers of shares, but not necessarily trivial.

The probate court fixed $42,344 as the determined value of the stock holdings, added to which Orson's father had $21,191.82 cash in his bank account. The court estimated the total value of Welles's estate at $63,535.82. Adjustments for inflation can be calculated in various ways, but it would be reasonable to estimate the value at roughly $900,000 in today's terms. Orson's father also owed debts totaling $8,901.29.

The court's financial estimate did not count Beatrice Ives Welles's jewelry, including a globular crystal necklace and drop earrings, a crystal neck pendant, and seed pearl earrings with drops, all stored in Dick Welles's safe-deposit box. Nor did it include his itemized personal belongings: a gold matchbox, silver lighter, and silver key-winding watch; a complete set of table silver for twelve with teapot, gravy dish, olive forks, platters, and pearl-handled knives; one Iver Johnson revolver (the type of gun used to assassinate William McKinley in 1901); an oil painting of Wild Bill Hickok; and, touchingly, one photograph of "Dick Welles" the racehorse. Nor did it include continued earnings, if any were still forthcoming, from Dick Welles's patents.

Some of these personal belongings may have been sold, but many ended up in the hands of Dr. Bernstein. Orson's father also left a trove of family photographs, his gladstone bag, and a traveling trunk of private items and memorabilia; these too would be held for years in a safe-deposit box at the First Union Trust and Savings of Chicago, which administered his estate.

Orson's brother, Richard, was twenty-five at the time of his father's death, and no longer required a guardian. With Richard institutionalized at Kankakee, however, Bernstein also became the financial executor of his one-seventh share of the estate. It would be Bernstein's job to dole out moneys for support and necessities for Richard until he was released from Kankakee. The remainder of his one-seventh would be paid out to Richard when he turned thirty-five, according to the will.

After allowances as warranted for "support, maintenance and education" of his younger son, the remaining six-sevenths "principal and reserve" of Dick Welles's fortune was to be held in trust for Orson "until he shall have reached the age of twenty-five years." As Charles Higham pointed out in his biography of Welles, "The proviso that this inheritance was to be held in trust until Orson's twenty-fifth birthday was echoed, even to the age, in the discussion of the legacy of Charles Foster Kane in *Citizen Kane*."

Dr. Bernstein quickly drew on the estate funds to purchase a larger house on Groveland Avenue in Highland Park, near the Ravinia grounds, ostensibly to carve out extra living space there for his new ward. Two thousand dollars was set aside for Orson's college tuition. Especially later in life, after souring on his guardian, Welles wondered why Bernstein needed such a big house, and how much of his stipulated inheritance ever reached his pockets. Even in flush times, however—perhaps especially then—Orson's pockets were riddled with holes.

Many tenth-grade Todd School graduates transferred to other elite academies for two more years of high school. Some went straight on to college, or internships. But at Closing Day ceremonies, the school's most illustrious graduate was undecided about his plans.

Roger Hill's opinion was that Orson was a good candidate for an Ivy League university. The headmaster thought his prize pupil should pursue an artistic career that might embrace acting, painting, and writing. Encouraged by Hill and Bernstein, Orson applied to several colleges, including Harvard. Skipper—not because he thought college was the best thing for Orson, he said later, but because he felt the boy should get away from Chicago—dutifully wrote reference letters.

Harvard reportedly offered a scholarship to its famous "47 Workshop" in playwriting, but Hill thought Orson should go somewhere else for a broader education in the liberal arts. Late in the summer, the headmaster wrote to Clyde Tull at Cornell College. Tull, a professor of English, was a noted mentor for young talent and invited poets such as Carl Sandburg to the midwestern campus as artists in residence. Hill urged him to consider Orson, insisting that the boy was "really doing post graduate work with us last year . . . we can very honestly give him credit for three years high school work, work done in the class room with the proper number of hours. Of course, actually his education in all cultural subjects is now beyond that of the ordinary college graduate."

Although this letter stated that Orson was "talented to the point of genius," the headmaster confessed he had one flaw: "I rather doubt if he could pass a college board examination in Algebra, although he passed this course with us. He is rather weak in mathematics."

Unenthusiastic about college, Orson opted to postpone any decisions about higher education while he spent the summer on the stage. In May, the *Woodstock Daily Sentinel* reported that he had signed up with a professional summer stock company in Michigan. Roger Hill operated a Todd School sideline, a summer camp on Portage Lake near Onekama, Michigan, called Camp Tosebo (TOdd SEminary for BOys). Orson had visited Camp Tosebo in prior summers, and thought there might be an opening for him in a nearby summer theater. Yet this opportunity fizzled, and he then took the bold step of advertising in the "At Liberty" section of *Billboard*, a trade paper for the music and entertainment industry:

ORSON WELLES—Stock Characters, Heavies, Juveniles or as cast. Also specialties, chalk talk or can handle stage. Young, excellent appearance, quick, sure study. Lots of pep, expertise, and ability. Close in Chicago early in June and want place in good stock company for remainder of season. Salary according to late date of opening and business conditions. Photos on request.

The response was underwhelming.

Orson met with actor-manager Fritz Leiber and asked to join Leiber's Shakespearean company. Leiber was polite, but he told Orson he couldn't promise anything; his troupe was at liberty until the fall, when the members would start preparing their next season. Orson then placed a second, more desperate advertisement in *Billboard*: "I will invest moderate amount of cash and my own services as Heavy, Character and Juvenile in good summer stock or repertory proposition." Still no takers.

After Closing Day, a disconsolate Orson moved in with Dr. Bernstein in the Chicago apartment. The doctor urged him to do something constructive with his time while he sifted through realistic long-term options. Orson consented to private classes with the Russian scenic designer Boris Anisfeld, now in residence at the Art Institute of Chicago. In June, Anisfeld took Orson "under his wing," recalled Roger Hill, encouraging the young man "to live with him this winter and study art."

Between Art Institute tutorials, Orson lunched with the usual gentlemen at the Tavern Club. The big topic of conversation was the demise of the Goodman Theatre. The board had cashiered its founder, Thomas Wood Stevens, in the summer of 1930. Some members of the original company had quit, including the revered Whitford Kane, but a temporary director had hired replacements and the troupe had completed a respectable season intended to be more commercial. Still, the Goodman board felt that public support was insufficient, and in June 1931 the board announced that the professional company was being jettisoned for the foreseeable future in favor of "student productions."

Everyone was upset. For six years the Goodman Theatre experiment had been the pride and pinnacle of Chicago stage culture. No one was angrier than Ashton Stevens, who had extolled the Goodman in his column as the embodiment of what a small theater company should strive to be. Stevens had divorced his first wife and married a Goodman actress, Katherine Krug, who had stayed on to play several leads with the short-lived new repertory ensemble in 1930–1931.

Meanwhile, in the *Chicago Tribune*, columnist Fanny Butcher, the "Armchair Playgoer," devoted several admiring pieces to the Gate Theatre of Dublin, Ireland, a new company that followed the Goodman formula in building a classical as well as an experimental repertory. Together with the Abbey Theatre, the emergence of the Gate secured Dublin's place as the new center of the English-language theater world, Butcher wrote.

In July, after Orson's tutorials with Boris Anisfeld ended, he and Dr. Bernstein returned to Highland Park for a stellar summer at Ravinia. That season brought Queena Mario, Lucrezia Bori, Mario Chamlee, Fred Vogel, and a host of other performers in no fewer than thirty-four operas. *Peter Ibbetson*, based on George du Maurier's novel, was the consensus hit. As usual Orson attended all the operas and symphony performances and joined the dinner parties, many of them hosted by Dr. Bernstein or the Ned Moores, but his mood was subdued. He begged off his old column for the *Highland Park News*, instead sitting in the backyard, sketching, painting, and jotting notes for a play he thought he might produce himself—somewhere, sometime.

He welcomed visits from the drama columnist Ashton Stevens and his wife, Katherine Krug, newly unemployed after the demise of the Goodman professional company. Krug was charming and vivacious, and especially friendly to Orson, who was much closer in age to her than her own husband. Their rapport endeared the young man to Stevens, whose reluctance to give Orson career advice was itself a kind of advice, implying that Orson should follow his own instincts.

But Orson spent most of his time in Ravinia alone, with no close companions and no concrete objectives. Dr. Bernstein urged him to have a fallback plan: a wage-earning job, college enrollment, even further painting studies with Anisfeld—anything to occupy his time. Ned and Hazel Moore always sided with his guardian. Roger Hill was off at Camp Tosebo, purposely incommunicado.

To Orson, it seemed as though all the members of his extended surrogate family were conspiring to persuade him to go to college, the option that interested him less and less. In mid-August, he and Dr. Bernstein had a heated argument over his apparent stubbornness and stagnancy.

"Three days of particularly vicious domestic war-fare," Orson reported to Skipper in a letter, "during which time I tried vainly to get in touch with you, ended in a roundtable conference which found all the principal powers as determined as ever. Dadda had thought the matter over and decided he could not permit my having ought to do with the diseased and despicable theatre. [Everyone else] was uniformly and maddeningly derisive. My head remained bloody but unbowed, and my nose, thanks to the thoughtful blooming of some neighboring clover (which I assured the enemy was ragweed!) began to sniffle hay-feverishly, and the household was illusioned into the realization that something had to be done."

Scrambling for a solution, Orson had a sudden brainstorm. Drawing on his college fund, he proposed a walking and painting tour of Ireland, Scotland, and England. He would begin in Ireland, sketching the glorious landscape, and by fall wend his way inexpensively to Dublin, where he promised to apply to Trinity College. It was *his* inheritance after all, he argued, and surely both his arts-minded mother and his travel-loving father would have approved. He vowed to write home regularly, and to keep a journal, which would prove to his guardian that he was making good use of his father's money. The journal could serve as the basis of a magazine article later on, he suggested, or even an autobiography.

It didn't take the doctor very long to respond. Orson, bored and brooding, had been driving him crazy. "Dadda arrived at a momentous decision," Orson wrote, "and in the spirit of true martyrdom chose the lesser of two great evils. Going abroad alone is not quite as unthinkable as joining the theatre—and so . . .

"Four days later I was in New York!" On the morning of August 13, he made his way to the West Twentieth Street docks and boarded a White Star liner bound for Galway.

CHAPTER 7

1931–1932

Travels in Ireland

Crossing the Atlantic took ten days to two weeks, depending on weather conditions. Though he was booked in second class, Orson traveled with a cushion of several hundred dollars drawn from his inheritance and borrowed at the last minute from every Chicago friend and acquaintance he could corner. Stockbroker Orson "Ort" Wells, who had laid eyes on him once when he was a baby, saw him again now when Orson stopped by to ask for a $5 loan for his Irish trip. "I never have seen him since," Wells complained good-naturedly to George Ade several years later.

The shipboard days were long, and he had plenty of books to while away the hours: plays by Synge and O'Casey, the verse and fairy tales of James Stephens, Pádraic Ó Conaire's *Field and Fair: Travels with a Donkey in Ireland*. But staring at the waves made him eager for action. "A few months of walking and painting in Ireland and Scotland," Orson wrote to Roger Hill, "and then on to England where there are schools—and theatres!!!!!!"

He composed expansive letters to Roger and Hortense Hill and to Dr. Maurice Bernstein, sometimes writing one household a letter and then copying it, with slight variations, for the other. The recipients typed up the letters and passed them around so that other interested parties—the Ned Moores, Ashton and Katherine Krug Stevens—were kept apprised of Orson's adventures.

"I am unspeakabl[y] lonesome for Todd—which is just another way of spelling your name," Orson wrote to Skipper after arriving in

Ireland. "You know, I think, of my fondness for you and Mrs. Hill. It is a love too great to speak of or describe."

He left the ship impulsively at the first port of call: the city of Galway, in the province of Connacht, the largest population center on Ireland's west coast. At first he had planned to continue to the other side of the island and the sea town of Cobh in Cork Harbour, but he was too excited to stay on board. He felt like Columbus stepping ashore to turn a new page of history.

"I wish I could describe that moment," Orson wrote to his guardian, going on to describe it quite well, invoking various Irish clichés to poke fun at them. The men and women were streaming joyously down the gangplank, he wrote, dropping to their knees, weeping, kissing the earth, and singing "The Wearing of the Green." "People separated for years were locking and unlocking in the intricacies of an Irish jig," Orson wrote. He conjured a cinematic montage of the occasion, complete with a close-up: "A fine tall man with flowing silver hair and a face like Wotan brandished his silver headed cane fiercely over our heads crying in a voice like thunder—'Sure, and it's God's own country.'" Hearing himself murmuring the same phrase, the young American grabbed his luggage and fled the boat without settling his accounts.

"I looked out over the rolling indigo sea to the misty mountains, blue and gold at the horizon," he wrote, and felt at peace.

Galway thrilled him. "Surprise I have had in my travels—countries like Japan and China have exceeded my expectations, but in sixteen short, very full years of living, nothing comparable with Galway—or the West of Ireland—has loomed so unexpectedly—so breathtakingly," he told his guardian in another letter.

After spending three or four days in picturesque Galway, he chucked his oil paints into a haversack and started down the road toward Clifden, a seaside town about fifty miles to the north and west, the largest town in the province of Connemara. "Two miles revealed to me the impossibility of combining art, hiking, and pleasure," Orson recounted in another letter to folks in Chicago, "and the third proved too much on the haversack. With a despairing scream it vomited forth my pigments and succumbed to total physical collapse."

He retreated into a nearby pub for a pitcher of warm Guinness.

Spying a donkey cart, "the commonest sight in Ireland," he felt inspired, and jumping up, offered to purchase the cart from its owner. He was told in no uncertain terms that "everything in the donkey and donkey-cart line had been bought up for use in the haying and gathering of new turf to follow for the next two months." Undeterred, Orson asked for directions to a local shop, McDonogh and Sons, which crafted new donkey carts for sale. By a happy coincidence, Mr. McDonogh, the shop owner, was a relative of Pádraic Ó Conaire, the Galway-born Gaelic-language writer who had died a few years earlier—and whose travel memoir Orson had absorbed during the crossing. McDonogh, in turn, introduced Orson to the writer's brother, a clay-pipe-smoking man named Isaac Conroy.

When Orson said he wished to buy a donkey cart and roam the west of Ireland, painting the countryside in all its splendor, "an adventure-loving, romance-loving, very Irish light" came into the eyes of Mc-Donogh and Conroy, and the two men conveyed him by Chrysler to Galway Racecourse, where he was able to haggle his way into purchasing an excellent donkey, "a three year old Spanish lady with original ideas, and a beauty of face and figure"; and a suitable used cart, "a magnificent creation of blue and orange."

Soon another Ó Conaire relative materialized—Michael, a cousin of Isaac—and the four men became fast friends. "I lived in their houses, danced with their daughters, and swam with their sons," Orson wrote home.

He christened his new donkey Sidheoghe, or Sheeog, which was "delightful Gaelic for a certain specie of fairy," recounted Orson. The Galway citizenry turned out "in thousands for the purposes of instructing Sheeog and myself (both novices in the mysteries of cart driving and pulling)," and one local blacksmith even shod the donkey free of charge. Before Orson could leave, however, horse fever descended on the city in the form of the annual Galway Races, which meant several days of "carousing, fun-making, fighting, gambling, drunkenness, and gaiety of every conceivable description."

The president of the Irish Free State, W. T. Cosgrave, a veteran of the Easter Rising of 1916, arrived to officiate at the races, lodging with the McDonoghs along with the young American. "We grew very friendly," Orson wrote to Dr. Bernstein. "He is a charming, quiet and extremely intelligent man." (To Hill, he described Cosgrave somewhat differently, as "a severe, puritan-looking figure.") Orson took Cosgrave for a ride in his donkey cart and mused about advertising it as "The Cart That Carried the President." Cosgrave etched "a good-luck sun (for good weather) rather like this [Orson drew a smiley sun] on the side" of his cart, but he mused in his letter, "I don't suppose I'd ever get [anyone] to believe he did it."

Finally, Orson tore himself away from the dream of Galway, promising to save his stories for his return—"much shall be recounted at Ravinia firesides." He started down the winding roads to Clifden. ("The roads are literally ribbons," he wrote, "six inches of gravel on an endless peat bog. When autos pass over them they shake and sink under their weight.") Exploring the west coast, he told tales of climbing mountains, escaping quagmires, and even spending a week or so tethered to a band of Travellers (Gypsies).

He often camped on the roadside at night, feeding Sheeog on the mountain grass and cooking over a turf fire before curling up to sleep under his cart. "There were nights too spent in the cottages," young Orson wrote home, and "most of my daytime meals were eaten among the people." Sometimes he joined in "weddings, wakes, and matchmakings." He did a fair amount of painting on the road, with unsatisfying results: "Ten terrible landscapes," six of which were "hideous abortions," he reported. Four of them "paid for lodgings" and now hung in mountain dwellings; the others were ruined by weather and "diversions." He despaired of capturing the island's beauty in oils. "Ireland is really a water-color country," he wrote, "and I have learned to my sorrow that whatever craftsmanship I can lay claim to, lies only in the channels of still-life, composition, design and portraits. . . . The almost unearthly quality of the countryside and the mountains in the West and North completely stumped me."

"Finally at the end of it all," he wrote, lay Clifden, where he took a room at Joyce's Hotel. At the town market he enlisted hotel proprietor P. K. Joyce as his auctioneer, selling Sheeog for ten pounds sterling—a fact Joyce boasted about in local newspapers after the "War of the Worlds" sensation of 1938.

Returning by bus to Galway, Orson scouted out the Taibhdhearc, Ireland's first Gaelic-speaking theater, which the stage designer, writer, and actor Micheál MacLíammóir helped launch with his play *Diarmuid agus Gráinne* in 1928. But MacLíammóir had moved on to the Gate Theatre in Dublin, and there was no place at the Taibhdhearc for an American with meager Gaelic.

He decided on a trip to the Aran Islands. J. M. Synge, the Irish poet and author of *The Playboy of the Western World*, had lived for a while on the three islands off Galway, describing the harsh existence in a famous series of dispatches for Irish newspapers. Irish artist Seán Keating also had made the Arans his subject, painting portraits of their rugged people. Now Orson would see for himself these "three tiny piles of limestone off the West Coast," as he put it in his letters. He hopped a boat to Inisheer, the smallest of the Arans, twenty-three miles west of Galway Bay, and at the end of the hour-long voyage he found himself in an ancient, inhospitable land of fishermen and farmers—"the most primitive spot in Europe," he wrote to Dr. Bernstein, "as it has been for many centuries."

Electing to stay in Inisheer, young Orson found "a wonderful little old thatched cottage by the sea" that he turned into a painting studio, and vowed to create "nothing but portraits now, simple sketches of men and women I have known here. . . . There is a quality in the Erin eye a thousand times more elusive than the blue in the Conemarra hills, a something in the clean, naïve smile that plays on the Aran mouth, a twinkle that dances in an Erin eye—an <u>intelligent candour</u> and something more . . .*

"To paint <u>that</u> is to paint <u>God</u>."

Inisheer was a remote paradise—"a kind of lost Eden," Orson wrote, invoking what was already becoming a signature phrase for him. His letters from Inisheer were timed for the weekly boat—"weather permitting—and it never does!"—that carried mail as well as passengers. Sometimes he wrote them at four in the morning "after a very full evening" at Patch Litman's, "yarning and 'talking fairies,'" followed by a "shindy," fiddling and jigging at John Connelly's. He waxed rhap-

---

* Orson's underlining, here and elsewhere quoting from his letters, has been preserved.

sodic over these shindys, full of "fine Erin men in indigo homespun" with "smiling colleens in nice red skirts and sienna jackets, all whirling about in the intracasies [*sic*] of 'the stalk of barley,' and stamping their leathern slippers on the flaggings as the orchestra plays on." It was all so wonderful. "I am really drinking too deeply of Ireland to write about it," he said in a letter.

During his few weeks on Inisheer, Orson boasted, he became "really intimately" acquainted with all its inhabitants. Though most of them spoke Gaelic, a language of which he'd absorbed the merest smattering, he felt a great kinship with the islanders. "I have lived with these people, farmed, gathered kelp, fished, sang, drank, eaten and even wept with them," he wrote, "when Mourteen's three boys were beaten to death on the rocks almost at my doorstep." His only disappointment was his own painting, which was still "something of a flop." "At the end of three weeks," Orson explained woefully, "I shall carry away with me perhaps a half dozen [portraits]. Some of them will be bad pictures and some fair . . . but as portrayals of that undefinable Erin spirit they will all be dismal failures."

One day, after nearly a month on Inisheer, he woke up "desperately in need of money," Orson wrote. "Yesterday—for the first time, I checked up thoroughly on all my accounts—0." He was almost as helpless with money as his brother, he confessed. "The same blood that flows in Richard's veins," he wrote to Dr. Bernstein, "flows also in mine."

The young American went shooting and fishing with the islanders, and hunted birds with a Catholic priest who made a regular circuit of the three islands. Orson claimed subsequently to have spent a little too much time with the local lasses, his dalliances catching the priest's attention. "These great, marvelous girls in their white petticoats," Welles later recalled, "they'd grab me. It was as close to male rape as you could imagine. And all with husbands out in their skin-covered canoes. All day, while I had nothing to do. Then the girls would go and confess it all to the priest." As they tramped the island together, the gun-toting priest hinted unambiguously that young Orson might consider moving on in his Irish travels—and so he did.

Orson must have had a little money to spare, for after returning to Galway he embarked on a tour of the south and east, visiting Limerick, Kerry, Kilarney, Blarney, Tipperary, and Wicklow before returning to

Limerick. There he purchased a bicycle—dubbing it "Ulysses," a nod to Homer and Joyce—and met up by prearrangement with Michael Conroy from Galway to continue his travels. The two explored on their bikes and hitched a ride on beer barges floating up the Shannon. Orson used his journal to sketch people he met on the road, while chronicling his adventures with Conroy, whom he disguised in the journal as "O'Connor" portraying him as "a more sober counterpart to Orson's madcap self," as Simon Callow notes. "They seemed to have had a delightful time of it."

By October, near the end of his cash, Orson found himself in Athlone, a town on the Shannon about halfway between Galway and Dublin. Roaming Battery Heights, he crested a hill and spied something amusing.

"I came upon three little boys, their bellies flat upon the grass," Orson wrote to Roger Hill, "peeping furtively over the brink. I tiptoed up behind them to see what was the object of their attention and was amused to discover two young persons of the opposite sex reclining in the trench and making violent and enthusiastic love.

"But what delighted both performers and audience was the presence of a matronly lady—fat in a respectable kind of way and obviously the chaperone of the party—stretched out alongside of the delighted lovers, snoring lustily!

"Rather than disturb so happy a scene, I descended the hill on the side farthest from Romeo and his dark-eyed Juliet. This brought me quite near the slumbering chaperone. Imagine my astonishment when upon passing to discover that lady manufacturing the sounds of sleep with her twinkling eyes wide open! Thunder struck, I gazed down at her and as I turned away she closed one of those very Irish organs in an elaborate wink." Next to this Orson drew a long-lashed lady's eyes, one wide open, decorated with Z's and exclamation marks. (This letter was meant for the worldly Skipper Hill alone—not for Dr. Bernstein, prim holder of Orson's purse strings.)

A seventy-five-mile bus trip then took Orson to Dublin, where he was hoping for an infusion of cash from home. He was broke, but as blissful as he would ever be.

"I am riding into Dublin," he jotted, drawing a bus with the sun shining overhead, "thinking glad thoughts about Ireland."

The glad thoughts wouldn't last. When he got to town, Orson rushed to American Express—only to be disappointed. There was no wire from Dr. Bernstein. Crestfallen, he shrieked "so loudly that traffic stopped on College Green," he wrote later. As soon as he settled into his hotel, the electricity failed, preventing him from sitting down to write at length about "the anguish that was in my soul—and it was anguish—the despairing ready-for-the-river anguish one experiences when unknown and alone in a big city."

He was down to only "a few shillings," Orson recalled, which he decided to blow on "a good dinner." And after the dinner he lit a quality cigar, having taken up cigars in Ireland on the theory that smoking them made him look older, like his father or Ashton Stevens.

From the start of his Irish travels, Orson strove—somewhat obviously—to make the adventures he described in his letters seem accidental, to lull Dr. Bernstein into believing all his blarney. But he had a strategy. He had jumped ship at Galway, where the Taibhdhearc was located, with its direct links to Micheál MacLíammóir, and the Gate Theatre. He had insinuated himself into the well-known Ó Conaire family in Galway, where he also met Cathal Ó Ceallaigh, a folklorist and actor who happened to be performing a small role in the Gate's current production. Now with his few remaining coins, Orson purchased a ticket to the evening's program: a new drama by the Earl of Longford called *The Melians: A Tragedy of Imperialism.*

The Melians was an ambitious work that offered a nationalist spin on Thucydides's history of the Peloponnesian War, with Ireland standing in for the occupied island of Melos. MacLíammóir had the lead role—a privilege he customarily alternated with Hilton Edwards, the cofounder of the Gate, his partner in art and, quite openly, in life. (In later years they cheerfully dubbed themselves "The Stately Homos of Ireland.")

The two had met in the mid-1920s as players in the Intimate Shakespearean Company, led by actor-manager Anew McMaster. McMaster's troupe crisscrossed the island, playing country towns and church halls—what Orson called "the smalls of Ireland." McMaster was MacLíammóir's brother-in-law and (possibly) his onetime lover, and he was a mentor to both him and Edwards. Hilton Edwards had occasional affairs with women, MacLíammóir had flings with other men, but the two remained a couple throughout their lives.

Together, in honor of McMaster, they had founded the Gate Theatre in 1928. When Orson arrived the Gate was in its fourth season, presenting original and Irish-language plays from its own core group of dramatists and translators, along with Irish premieres of classical and West End plays. The Gate had recently vacated the Peacock Theatre, a small experimental stage annexed to the state-subsidized Abbey Theatre, in favor of a new four-hundred-seat theater carved out of the Rotunda building on Parnell Square.

The Melians failed to impress young Orson—he called it "stupid" in a letter to Skipper Hill—but he spotted his Galway friend Ó Ceallaigh onstage, and after the show Orson went behind the curtains to say hello. There he contrived to meet Edwards, who was immediately struck by the "very tall young man with a chubby face, full powerful lips and disconcerting Chinese eyes," as MacLíammóir wrote in his autobiography, *All for Hecuba.* "His hands were enormous and beautifully shaped," MacLíammóir continued. "The voice, with its brazen transatlantic sonority, was already that of a preacher, a leader, a man of power."

Waving a cigar, the backstage visitor introduced himself—fudging his age—and babbled haughtily about his experience with the Goodman Theatre and the New York Theatre Guild.* (In fact, Orson *had* performed onstage at the Goodman, and he *had* acted in a play originally produced by the Theatre Guild—albeit both occasions were Todd School affairs.) The Gate partners didn't really care about vetting the young stranger's résumé; they were too intrigued by his look and aura and "some ageless and superb inner confidence . . . that no one could blow out," in MacLíammóir's words. "It was unquenchable. "That was his secret."

The Gate men were "gracious and candid," Orson recalled in a letter home, and Edwards said he might consider Orson for a small part in

---

* The reader might keep in mind that there are as many versions of this first encounter between Welles and the Gate's cofounders as there are accounts of Stanley meeting Livingstone. In one of Welles's, MacLíammóir was not even present.

the Gate's next production, Ashley Dukes's dramatization of the Lion Feuchtwanger novel *Jud Süss*, or *Jew Süss*, as the Gate version was known, which was just then being cast. "You would have to work on amateur's wages," Edwards cautioned Orson, "which are but a gesture. If you care to stick and if we get along together, bigger parts might come and I might even persuade the committee to pay you an extra guinea."

After a night of carousing with Ó Ceallaigh and a morning of quick study of *Jew Süss*, Orson returned to the Gate for his audition the next afternoon. He had focused on "two big parts," both attractive. "One is the Süss, the George Arliss title role, which Matheson Lang made so famous in London last season—and which is dramatic by virtue of its negativeness," he wrote to Skipper, "and the other is the half-Emil Jannings, half-Douglas Fairbanks contrast to the Jew: Karl Alexander, the Duke. It is really the fattest of the two parts—all positives and I prefer dealing in negatives—but meaty from first to fifth acts—it runs the gauntlet of fine temper scenes, drunks, darling seductions, rapine, murder, heart attacks, and death." But he "scarcely dreamed of" playing Süss, a role earmarked for Edwards, and his real goal was to win the part of Duke Karl Alexander. He auditioned for a "committee" of repertory company officials and rotating directors, including Edwards and MacLíammóir.

In a 1946 account of the audition, MacLíammóir recalled young Orson arresting everyone's attention by flinging a table, a chair, and some books around the stage and savaging a plum blossom floral display, stirring up "a violent cloud of dust, like a miniature sand-storm." Orson described his performance differently in his contemporary correspondence. "Being as I was," he wrote to Hill, "terribly nervous and anxious to impress them, I performed a kind of J. Worthington Ham Karl Alexander with all the tricks and all the golden resonance I could conjure up." But his golden resonances proved "a bitter failure." Edwards, for one, could barely control his mirth as Orson struggled to impress the committee.

MacLíammóir, however, saw potential. "An astonishing performance," he recalled, "wrong from beginning to end, but with all the qualities of fine acting tearing their way through a chaos of inexperience. His diction was practically perfect, his personality, in spite of his fantastic circus antics, was real and varied; his sense of passion, of evil, of drunkenness, of tyranny, of a sort of demoniac authority was arresting; a preposterous energy pulsated through everything he did. One wanted to bellow with laughter, but the laughter died on one's lips."

The committee huddled. Edwards beckoned Orson to the stalls. In a letter home, Orson transcribed their conversation "practically word for word":

"Terrible, wasn't it?" asked Orson

"Listen old boy," responded Edwards, "you've been playing Shakespeare and you've learned Shakespearean poise, manner, and resonance of voice. You're very young and you're one of the finest technicians I've ever watched. It's an enigma . . ."

("I glowed," Orson wrote to Bernstein.)

"You have a greater accumulation of manner and technique, more tricks, more subtlety than the average professional first-rater picks up in a lifetime," Edwards continued. "And you can't be very old are you?"

("I told him my age," Orson wrote to Bernstein—though what age he said, exactly, is unclear.)

"God help you!" Edwards gasped.

Young Orson roared with laughter. It was one of his endearing qualities that he enjoyed nothing more than a good laugh at his own expense. And the laugh itself was unforgettable. Milton Berle, meeting Welles a few years later at a New York showing of Chaplin's *Modern Times*, called it a "deep, guttural" explosion. Others, who knew his love of Shakespeare, sometimes described the laugh as Falstaffian. It was a gorgeous instrument, with many uses and meanings, not all of them sincere. As Mercury Theatre actor Everett Sloane later said, Orson was capable of laughing simply because he wanted something. "When Orson calls with a smile in his voice," said Paul Stewart, another Mercury stalwart, "he's already lying." To playwright Tennessee Williams, Orson's laugh was a wonderful thing, "forced and defensive, like mine."

Backstage at the Gate, Hilton Edwards looked kindly on the young American. "It's no laughing matter," he told Orson. "You're at the point a matinee idol arrives at when he has got on in years and people are writing plays around his little tricks and capers. But of course that won't do—nobody's going to write nonsense for you to show off in.

"I tell you frankly you have a gorgeous stage voice and a stage presence in a million and you're the finest *over* actor I've seen in eons, but you couldn't come in and say, 'Milord, the carriage awaits' as well as Art, our electrician; you could put more somersaults in *Hamlet* than John Barrymore and handle theatrical, very theatrical restraint with more delicacy than Matheson Lang, but you couldn't say 'how-do-you-do' behind the footlights like a human being; you handle your voice like a singer but there isn't a note of sincerity in it. You're all flash and finish."

Edwards sent Orson away with valuable advice. "You go back to your hotel and practice acting like a man and not an actor," he said. "You expend a great deal of energy on throwing weight and strength into characterization—forget it—despite your youth, you have all the strength you need. Drop affectation, over-studied grace. Try and make over what you've been doing all your life tonight—learn that art that conceals art—learn restraint and, above all, sincerity. It may take you years, but come around tomorrow and I'll see how you're coming along."

Orson took the words to heart. What he didn't know was that the part of Duke Karl Alexander was his to lose. The Gate's most likely candidate, a member of the ensemble named Charles Marford, had just quit the company. Edwards himself was not only portraying Süss but also directing the play. The casting of Karl Alexander was an urgent matter to him.

In his hotel room, Orson practiced and practiced his lines, trying to muster every ounce of restraint and sincerity he could. When he returned, Edwards spent days putting him through "repeated auditions" and "endless consultations among the producing staff" before finally deciding to roll the dice and cast him in the role of Duke Karl Alexander—the first-billed role in the play.

"I am a professional!" Orson wrote to the headmaster, adding multiple exclamation points and underlining the word "professional" several times. "Forgive the somewhat salesman-like exuberance of this last. It was written immediately after my getting the job."

In the meantime, Dr. Bernstein had finally sent him some money—including a check signed over to Trinity College, where he was expected to apply for admission. But Orson made only halfhearted gestures in that direction, and it was just too bad for Trinity and Dr. Bernstein.

All his energy and abilities were trained now on the Gate.

Orson had other responsibilities besides acting. Edwards also hired him "to fill in the various [other] departments" formerly occupied by Charles Marford, including scene painter and publicity agent. His habitual sleeplessness was an asset. The Gate seemed busy twenty-four hours a day, and Orson had a knack for finding extra time for both moonlighting and pleasure.

Edwards saw the young American as a diamond in the rough. The director and star of *Jew Süss*, in his late twenties, was more down-to-earth than his older partner, MacLíammóir, although Edwards was perfectly capable of fiery displays of temper when the occasion warranted. A short, chubby fellow with small, bespectacled eyes and a prominent nose, he could have been mistaken for a bank clerk. With his common sense and good-heartedness, though, Edwards was the anchor of the company.

Jew Süss—the title is a reference to the main character, a historical figure, a court banker named Joseph Süss Oppenheimer—is set in the duchy of Württemberg in 1776. The story revolves around the enthroned Duke's resentful dependence on the rich, cultured Jew. Duke Karl Alexander, Orson's role, was a villainous rapist and murderer, "beyond any question the most difficult characterization in the entire play," in Orson's words. But whenever he tried to play the character to the hilt, Edwards reminded him of the virtues of restraint and of "absolute and unalloyed sincerity," as Orson noted ruefully in his letters home.

"There are moments in the play," Orson wrote, "when I feel I must make my voice ring and boom and make a gesture simple but studied and stagey, but even in the moments of the most intense comedy or tragedy I must be Karl Alexander without a single tassel or tinsel." Orson sometimes balked at Edwards's direction, but Edwards brought him to heel, giving him detailed instructions and asking him to follow them to the letter: Orson could reflect on the whys and wherefores later. It was a lesson Welles himself would later pass on to other actors.

The Gate mounted one new play every month, so time was short and the company was under constant pressure, with *Jew Süss* rehearsals going on "all day and every day," in Orson's words. It was hard work, but "lots of fun," (another of his by now frequently recurring phrases). "Everyone has such a fine, keen, clean sense of humor and is so easy to work with." Adding to the fun was the fact that the Duke was supposed to be in his fifties—giving the sixteen-year-old actor a perfect excuse to festoon himself with deep wrinkles, false hair, and stomach padding. His towering height and sonorous voice, lowered to bass baritone onstage, would complete the illusion of age.

Orson's primary hurdle in this role, however, may have been learning to speak with an accent the native-born audience would accept ("in the most accent conscious city on the globe!"). "It's wonderful diction training," he wrote to Skipper. "I'm really learning the English language."

Orson made strides during the nightly rehearsals, and by day he juggled his other duties—including publicity-mongering, already second nature for him; he easily dashed off reams of puffery of the sort he'd learned from the likes of Roger Hill, John Clayton, and the master newshounds of the Tavern Club. Best of all, writing publicity for the Gate gave him an excuse to tout himself—the exciting new discovery from America—inflating his age and reputation. Sometimes, as in a column he scribbled fitfully for a tabloid, he offered Gate hype under the pseudonym "Knowles Noel Shane," an anagram of Welles, Kenosha, and, tellingly, "non."

The lesser Irish newspapers gobbled up his breathless handouts, but so did the high-minded press. Even the *New York Times*, reviewing *Jew Süss* later, parroted his publicity handouts, describing "Orson Wells" as an eighteen-year-old who had "appeared occasionally" in Goodman Theatre plays and in "small parts" with the Theatre Guild in New York.

He had to make time for a little scene-painting for local groups of "Gaels," "our deprecating term for the players who—monthly—edify Dublin with Irish plays *in* Irish," in Orson's words. The Gate provided the Gaelic troupes with made-to-order scenery as part of the bargain, and it fell to Orson to "dig out some stock flats" and "mottle" or "finish" them under strict instructions. This he "did with much care," Orson reported to Dr. Bernstein, "being anxious to impress." But he couldn't resist improvising his own touches, and then felt "indescribable shame" when the stage manager complained about the results.

(In his letter home, Orson illustrated this anecdote with a drawing of himself, glimpsed from behind, standing forlornly onstage with arrows pointing to mismatched scenery.) The Gaels "raged and ranted" until Charles Marford himself, "still in town, was hired to do the list over— per instructions!"

Micheál MacLíammóir hovered in the background as preparations for *Jew Süss* continued, keeping a wary eye on Orson and feeling much like a babysitter. When he wasn't acting in the Gate's current offering, the theater's cofounder wrote poetry and original plays, and translated works of literature into Gaelic. (Though a champion of the Gaelic language movement, he was secretly an Englishman born and bred.) And he usually designed the sets—or supervised the design—and this was true of *Jew Süss*.

MacLíammóir was a stylish and expressive stage designer, who achieved tremendous effects on cost-conscious budgets with sets that were typically complemented by Hilton Edwards's atmospheric lighting, both men drawing from whatever was au courant on the Continent. MacLíammóir valued imaginative set design as much as Edwards valued restraint and sincerity in acting.

Thirty-one when Orson arrived in town, MacLíammóir was tall, dark, and charismatically handsome, notwithstanding the feminine powder, thick eyeliner, and toupee he affected offstage. He was not an easy man, and he would not have an easy relationship with Welles, who was on his way to becoming more famous than MacLíammóir would ever be. At first he saw Orson as a dangerously charming upstart— talented, perhaps, but an upstart all the same.

But MacLíammóir was also gracious to Orson, taking him aside to reassure him that Marford had been given a little painting work merely to keep the poor chap from starving. Orson could redeem himself working on the sets for *Jew Süss*. And so he did. "I followed directions explicitly and much against my will," Orson wrote home to Chicago. "I can see already that my artistic conscience is going to lead me into some disastrous and drastic differences of opinion."

Came the momentous occasion: on the night of Tuesday, October 13, 1931, the Gate's production of *Jew Süss* had its premiere. The opening was attended by Dublin first-nighters in their finest outfits, and by drama critics from the Irish and English press. Everyone in the packed theater had read Orson's own publicity: the young American playing a lead in his Gate Theatre debut. "I stood in the wings—my nails digging into the palms of my hands, perspiration bubbling through the greasepaint," Orson wrote to Dr. Bernstein, "and I said a prayer, a long and fervent one, to Tai Tsung, Ming Huang, the patron saint of actors. Never have I prayed like that, and never have I lived so many eons in a second."

The voice of William Sherwood, the durable Gate actor who was portraying the character Councillor Weisensee, beckoned from on-stage: "And here, I think, are our pair of highnesses . . ." That was Orson's cue for the Duke's first entrance. "For one awful moment I tasted of the exquisite torture of crucifixion," Orson recalled in a letter home; "in another, I was at the door, gazing in to the teeth of what [Edwin] Booth so aptly termed 'A crouching and invisible beast'—the audience. A first-night audience in the leading theater of a capital city—critics, celebrities, titles—an audience that spoke a different language than my own—my first audience!"

Nobly costumed, amply bewhiskered and bewigged, he marched out front and center and planted his feet, rumbling his lines. "When Orson came padding onto the stage with his lopsided grace, his laughter, his softly thunderous voice," MacLíammóir recalled years later, "there was a flutter of astonishment and alarm, a hush, and a volley of applause."

So far, so good. Now it was up to Orson to win over the audience and then lose himself in the performance, forgetting the spectators were there. The performing and the forgetting were equally important. "That wonderful something about a play picked me up in its arms and carried me far away to sixteenth century Württemberg," Orson recalled. The Irish audience—reputed to be "the world's most critical and most appreciative," in Orson's words—sat forward, watching intently.

As was traditional at the Gate, Edwards brought the newest member of the company out onstage during the intermission, introducing him to the Dublin theatergoers with warm and humorous remarks. "Orson swelled visibly," remembered MacLíammóir. "I have heard of people swelling visibly before, but Orson is one of those who really do it."

His big moment came in Act Four, when the Duke dies onstage of an apoplectic stroke, just after the exit of the pretty actress Betty Chancellor, who was playing the daughter of the Süss. Orson's business, as the lecherous Karl Alexander, was to stare after Chancellor, chortle suggestively, and remark, "A bride fit for Solomon. He had a thousand wives, did he not?"

Just then, a voice rang out from the back of the theater: "That's a dirty black Protestant lie!"

Orson was momentarily rattled. He was supposed to draw his sword, shouting his final line—"Ring the bells and fire all the cannons!"—before slumping lifelessly on the throne. But his sword stuck in his scabbard, and as he pulled on it helplessly, he garbled his line: "Ring the cannons and fire all the bells!" Finally in despair, he flung himself headfirst down a flight of steps, ending in a backflip. "It was the only thing I could think of," Welles said years later. "I didn't care whether it killed me or not. It almost did—but it also brought down the house."

As he often said himself in later interviews, the sixteen-year-old had stolen the show. "There was much in that performance even now I can see was wrong—but it was my finest work till then," Orson wrote to Dr. Bernstein exultantly. Taking his "first professional bow," hearing his name shouted again and again, "truly, I wept for joy."

The reviewers took notice. "There was a naturalness and ease about his acting, which, at once, caught the packed house on his first appearance," wrote J. J. Hayes, the *New York Times'* stringer in Dublin. While *Jew Süss* was a "somewhat unpleasant play," Hayes noted, the Gate had mounted a "magnificently produced" drama, with an "amazingly fine" display by the Chicagoan. "When the last curtain fell," Hayes wrote, "he had acquitted himself so well that he was given an ovation. Dublin is eager to see him in other roles."

Dublin critics, while generally supportive of the Gate, could be fierce and prickly. Yet the majority of them also singled Orson out, praising him in review after review. "His impersonation was interesting at every moment," rhapsodized "D. M." in the *Irish Press.* "He built a complete and subtle character around his lines. Particularly remarkable was his skill when, silent and motionless, for long minutes in the fourth scene . . . he held the audience tense." The American had lent humanity and simplicity to the Duke, capturing him "magnificently," said the *Irish Independent. The Irish Times* agreed: the "new actor" was "excellent."

The weeks to come would bring wild applause (six curtain calls on some nights, "with the gallery and the pit shouting and stamping and calling out my name," Orson wrote to Hortense Hill), laudatory press notices, and sold-out performances—three weeks, instead of the Gate's customary two-week run. As soon as the curtain rang down on that opening night, however, the company was in a mood to celebrate. They went out on the town in force, eating and drinking, brandishing cigars.

More than once, late in life, Welles would say half-jokingly that this was his only pure triumph, and the rest of his career was downhill.

His success in *Jew Süss* launched him as a star in Dublin. He became "a legend almost at once" there, recalled Lady Longford, the wife of the Earl of Longford—both Gate patrons and investors. "People began to talk about Orson," agreed Micheál MacLíammóir.

The young sensation took a small flat within walking distance of Parnell Square, but he was rarely found at home. Orson spent most days doing publicity, painting scenery, and rehearsing; appeared on-stage as the Duke six nights a week; and went out late after the performances. He was usually the last person to leave the public house, often reaching for the tab. On his rare nights off, he took in the wide range of dramatic offerings in Dublin: the revival at the Abbey of William Butler Yeats's verse lament *The Land of Heart's Desire*; the new musical revue at the Theatre Royal; and a garage production of *Roar China!*— Sergei Tretyakov's attack on Western imperialism.

The Gate thrived on parties, and Orson was high on everyone's guest list. "Orson was a great man at a party," recalled Lord Longford. "When he thought a party had gone on long enough, he would say, 'Take me out to Kilmahogue to see the fairies.' " Perhaps the celebrating got out of hand now and then. "Went to jail in Ireland for rowdyism," Orson claimed, speaking to Henry Jaglom half a century later.

At pubs and parties, Orson crossed paths with more living legends— including Yeats himself and the cofounder of the Abbey Theatre, Lady Gregory, just a year before her death. "Yeats makes me shiver," Welles told Jaglom during one of their mealtime conversations, which Jaglom recorded. (Transcripts were edited by Peter Biskird and published in 2013 as *My Lunches with Orson*.) "He was at every party, and you could see him walking in the park," along the pathways of St. Stephen's Green.

The Irish were beguiled by Orson's hilarious stories about his travels, from his Far East wanderings to his time riding Sheeog across the west of Ireland. (He freely embroidered his tales, adding in parts of the world he hadn't visited.) And he was just as good a listener as he was a talker, most agree. Orson was "as nice and friendly as could be," recalled Lady Longford.

When it came to one subject—the opposite sex—the sixteen-year-old acted his age. He was sweet on his colleague at the Gate, Betty Chancellor. "She was the sexiest thing that ever lived," Welles told Barbara Leaming. "She was one of those absolutely black-haired girls, with skin as white as Carrara marble, you know, and eyelashes that you could trip on." While she was only five years older than Orson, Chancellor had made her professional debut with the Gate soon after its inception and was firmly ensconced on the Dublin stage as a skilled comedienne and tragedienne. Chancellor was fond of young Orson and allowed him to flirt with her. But Orson was "highly immature in any kind of sexual discussion," she told Welles biographer Frank Brady, and even onstage he could not cope with their big "love" scene in *Jew Süss*. This scene preceded the Duke's "rape" of Suss's daughter, which happened offstage. "His extraordinarily mature acting fell apart" during the scene, Chancellor recalled. "He was then obviously embarrassed and unsure and he tried to hide this by gripping me with such violence that I nearly lost my life, but certainly not my virtue."

Orson wangled a few "dates" with the older, more established actress, but Chancellor did her best to cool his ardor. One time, disconsolate after she had stood him up, Orson inveigled another Gate actress, Eve Watkinson, to slip off with him to see the latest Laurel and Hardy comedy, *Pardon Us*. Slapstick foolishness always cheered him up, but after the movie he and Watkinson shared a late dinner, and Orson poured out his heartache over Chancellor.

Yet Chancellor never lost her affection for her young suitor. "With me, Orson was never either loud nor boastful," she recalled in Peter Noble's *The Fabulous Orson Welles*. "He used to talk a lot, but it was interesting. We had long suppers at revolting cafes in Dublin, for which dreadful repasts we usually clubbed together to pay the bill. Once we hadn't enough and Orson had to pay the balance in stamps. When he had any money he was very generous and spent it right away."

Nothing ever made Orson prouder than his breakthrough in Dublin, but after *Jew Süss* a few things happened that, when he was in a certain mood, could dim the glow of his warm memories.

In November, after sitting out a production of Molière's *Scapin* in Gaelic, Orson and the company mounted *The Dead Rides Fast*, an eerie thriller by the Dublin journalist David Sears. Once again Orson caked himself up, this time to play an elderly American millionaire traveling with his daughter in the west of Ireland. The travelers are forced by a storm into a gloomy mansion, which is haunted by a stranger from another world (played by Hilton Edwards). And once again Orson attracted good notices, reverting to his American accent on top of his customary "big gruff voice," in the words of Dublin-born architect and theatrical connoisseur Joseph Holloway, who followed Welles's rise at the Gate in his diaries. The *Evening Herald* praised the "delightful subtlety" of Orson's performance—a notice that must have cheered Edwards.

In private, writing to Dr. Bernstein, Orson was upbeat about his role: "comedy relief in modern dress," he said, "a pleasant change after the rigors of *Jew Süss*." But he was scornful of the overall script, "a rather bad thriller . . . trying desperately at the expense of the thrills to do high-brow." And he made the mistake of airing his scorn in public, speaking ill of the play's bogus American dialogue to Hugh Curran, the *Chicago Daily Tribune*'s correspondent in Dublin: "It was of the pre-Abraham Lincoln period with a dash of gangster talkie thrown in."

From childhood, Orson had always been encouraged to speak his mind, and his remarks about *The Dead Rides Fast* were an early instance of this persistent habit—and its pitfalls throughout his life. Criticizing the Gate's own production, while it was still in front of audiences, piqued his sponsors at the Gate. MacLíammóir, especially, saw it as another sign of Orson's immaturity. (Though Orson may have been right on the merits: *The Dead Rides Fast* ended its run after two weeks when it failed to fill sufficient seats.)

Later in November, the Gate tried to recoup with a more ambitious historical spectacle: *The Archdupe* by Percy Robinson, a "Corkman" living in London. Set in Mexico during the Napoleonic era, *The Archdupe* concerned Napoleon's puppet emperor, the former Archduke Maximilian of Austria. Edwards played Maximilian, while also directing. MacLíammóir was Napoleon, and Orson had a plum role as the audacious General Bazaine, who conquered Mexico and helped set up the puppet regime. Edwards must have given the young actor a longer leash this time: he delivered an outsize performance that sparked "quite a controversy" among Dublin theatergoers, as Orson admitted in his letters home. "I think it's quite poor myself," he added of his performance. But his theatricality also made it watchable. "Impossible not to believe in the Bazaine of Mr. Orson Welles," declared the *Irish Times*.

His controversial behavior was not limited to showy performances and candid interviews. Soon after *Jew Süss*, Orson began moonlighting for other theater groups in Dublin. Decades later, Orson promoted the notion that MacLíammóir grew envious of him after *Jew Süss* and contrived to demote him to lesser roles, forcing him to take gigs elsewhere. Welles insisted that MacLíammóir's rivalry was personal as well as professional—the older actor was resentful of the close bond developing between Edwards, his life partner, and his young American protégé.

"On stage during [*Jew Süss*] curtain calls," Barbara Leaming observed pointedly, "Orson could frequently be seen affectionately putting his arm around Hilton." According to Welles, MacLíammóir reacted with instinctual hostility to "the possibility of Hilton's being interested in anybody else," in his words. "Hilton was a born hetero," Welles insisted, curiously, "and our friendship was the friendship of two men, with no sexual overtones. I think that bothered Micheál."

Orson liked to adopt a flirtatious pretense with homosexual men, he told Leaming, but in this case it may have backfired, spiking MacLíammóir's jealousy and resentment. "It was right back to my childhood, playing parts to keep various people interested," Welles explained. "I had an entire persona for Micheál, which has no relation to anything I was ever like before or since, or with anybody else—but it was what he *wanted*, and what amused him—it was a kind of *camp.*"

But Orson oversimplified when he complained in later interviews that the Gate stopped giving him substantial roles after *Jew Süss.* He played juicy parts in *The Dead Rides Fast* and *The Archdupe*, and soon thereafter he rejected one of the "fattest" parts in the next Gate play, a slice-of-life original called *Youth's the Season.* The part didn't appeal to him, he explained in a letter home—and, besides, he had a "financially more inviting" offer elsewhere.

The extra money wasn't even the main attraction. Orson's newfound reputation for impersonating old men had led to an opportunity to tread the boards at the legendary Abbey Theatre. He was invited to play a sexagenarian, Lord Porteus—"John Drew's original part," as, at sixteen, he was knowledgeable enough to boast—in a limited-run production of Somerset Maugham's *The Circle.* "It will be a real treat and an experience not to be missed to play at the famous Abbey."

The production was a weeklong benefit for Irish youth hostels, and his fellow actors were not the true Abbey players, who were off touring.* But the director, Madeline Ross, was an Abbey veteran, and Orson relished his part, "a terrible, hateful parody of an upper-class Englishman." The newspapers ran photographs of Welles, tickets sold briskly, and the press covered the opening. Once again made up with wrinkles and padded for girth, Orson "proved himself a character actor of unusual merit," in the view of the *Independent.*

Regardless of what he may have said later, at the time Orson felt guilty about leaving the Gate company in the lurch. "I feel rather small in letting Hilton Edwards, who's been so very generous to me, down in any way at all," Orson wrote to his guardian.

But Edwards was indulgent of Orson, so much so that he gave him an excused absence for the Maugham play, shrugging off the defection. And recognizing Welles's drive and energy, Edwards then encouraged

---

* The Abbey Theatre regulars toured Canada and the United States from October 1931 through April 1932, so they were absent from Dublin the entire time Orson lived in that city.

him to join William Sherwood in launching a Gate side project: an "art-theatreish" adjunct company, in Orson's words, that was going to mount plays in the Peacock Theatre. Named for the color of the upholstery on its walls, the 102-seat Peacock adjoined the Abbey complex. This would give Orson a chance to stretch his wings, taking charge of stage design for the new Peacock Repertory Players.

Even as he was playing the millionaire codger in *The Dead Rides Fast*, Orson was preparing the first Peacock production: Herman Ould's *The Moon Rides High*, which opened in mid-November and played for one week, nightly with weekend matinees, in the interval between Gate plays. Ould was a protégé of George Bernard Shaw—his one-act had preceded Shaw's *The Great Catherine* at its 1913 premiere—and he promised Orson an introduction to his famous friend. The supernatural theme of Ould's play would inspire Orson's spooky stage design.

Most of the Peacock players were Gate actors who were interested in supplementing their salaries. Sherwood directed all the Peacock shows, except one. As far as can be determined, Orson directed that Peacock production, while also starring and designing the sets. But was it a potboiler called *Mr. Wu*, with Orson in the role Lon Chaney performed in the 1927 silent film; or was it *The Chinese Bungalow*, a mystery melodrama set in the Malay Peninsula?

Some sources say *Mr. Wu*. ("I've played it once myself," Welles told Peter Bogdanovich when the play came up in conversation.) Others—including the *Chicago Tribune* (in its coverage of Orson's return from Dublin), MacLíammóir (in a letter to Peter Noble), and publicity releases for the Katherine Cornell's tour—say it was *The Chinese Bungalow*. Strangely, though, there is no extant record of Orson Welles's professional directing debut, or of this starring role (in either play he would have appeared as a pigtailed Oriental)—not in the Gate archives, and not in the electronic indexes of the Irish press.

By mid-December, when the Peacock mounted a production of Jerome K. Jerome's farce *The Celebrity*, the sideline operation was drawing regular attention from the Dublin press, and Orson was being praised for his vivid stage designs. "Touches of originality give interest to the settings designed by Mr. Orson Welles," observed the *Irish Press*. *The Celebrity* was followed by a clever adaptation of *Alice in Wonderland* in time for Boxing Day. "Brilliantly produced" by "this gifted little company," according to the *Irish Independent*, the play used twenty-two sets of scenery designed by Orson, which were essential to capturing the "true spirit" of Lewis Carroll. The company also produced, in early 1932, a pairing of Strindberg's one-act *The Stronger* with Jules Romains's spoof of medical arrogance, *Doctor Knock*. "Welles gives the [latter] play a brilliant setting," wrote the *Irish Times*.

Programs from the Peacock Repertory Players have not survived, and Orson never mentioned his "art-theatreish" venture in interviews. But it was an important legacy of his stay in Dublin. First, because he directed professionally for the first time. But the Peacock had to live up to the Gate's reputation, and Orson also had to create the sets within nominal budgets that would live up to the standards set by MacLíammóir. Previous books on Welles have scoffed at the credit he took, later on, for the stage design of certain Mercury Theatre productions, without realizing that he was executing acclaimed professional sets at age sixteen.

Over time, MacLíammóir's ambivalence about the young upstart's success would wax and wane. Some of the anecdotes about Welles in his books were scathing and hilarious. He struck at Welles's Achilles' heel with jabs at his vanity and immaturity in his Dublin days. He told interviewers young Orson was known to hog the stage and step on other people's lines—low blows to any actor. *Put Money in Thy Purse*, MacLíammóir's diary of the filming of *Othello*, added broken financial promises to the litany of Welles's transgressions.

Orson waited until 1985, after MacLíammóir's death, to strike back, dismissing him in Lemming's book as "kind of the less glamorous and extraordinary *sister* of his brother-in-law," the legendary Anew McMaster. McMaster had it all—beautiful blond hair, godlike looks, a marvelous speaking voice, acting genius. MacLíammóir was "remarkable, he was a really great Hamlet, he was a tremendously amusing writer and a formidable personality, but compared to Mac [McMaster] he was *nothing*! Mac had his eye wiped, as they say in Dublin."

The Gate's Christmas play for 1931 was *Mogu of the Desert* by Padraic Colum, a distinguished Irish poet, dramatist, and novelist then living in Paris. An extravagant Oriental saga with crowd scenes, music, and songs, set in mythical Persia, *Mogu* traced a beggar's rise to power. Orson returned to play a fat role, in more ways than one, portraying Chosroes, the last King of Persia, his face augmented by "several pounds of nose-putty," as MacLíammóir recalled, his costume topped with "a white turban at least two and a half feet in diameter and three-inch fingernails of peacock-blue and silver."

In one scene, Mogu (played by Edwards) was meant to whip a dagger out of an assassin's hand, but he accidentally sliced off Orson's fake nose. Welles covered his nose with a hand and played through his next pages, a long love scene in blank verse—another mishap to be treasured.

The Gate plays were not all fabulous successes. Georgie Hyde-Lees, the wife of William Butler Yeats—she was called George Yeats by everyone—thought the *Mogu* sets and costumes were marvelous but the acting was an atrocious jumble of accents. "Hilton Edwards played Mogu as he played the Jew in *Süss*," she wrote to her husband. The second act of *Mogu* had been trimmed without Padraic Colum's approval, and the writer complained to George Yeats after seeing the production with her on a visit to Dublin: "I don't recognize my play." Still, Colum stood everyone to a grand shindig, and Orson once again came off well in reviews, the *Irish Times* seeing his role as "an excellent opportunity to use his fine physique and great voice."

The year Orson graduated from the Todd School and planted his flag in Ireland culminated in the annual Gate Ball, a dinner, dance, and cabaret celebrating the New Year, held in the grand ballroom of the Gresham Hotel and attended by seven hundred invited friends and luminaries, including the lord mayor of Dublin. Hilton Edwards, garbed austerely as the wise patriarch of the Gate family, crooned evocative Irish ballads; Micheál MacLíammóir donned a mermaid's costume and sang bawdy songs like "Milly, the Messy Old Mermaid." The company's "youngest and only American" also sang, this time "without make-up," according to the *Irish Tattler & Sketch*, "and we saw how ridiculously young his genius is."

As the company toasted the New Year, 1932, the "ridiculously young" Orson draped his arms exuberantly around both Edwards and MacLíammóir. Despite their backstage bitchery—a lingua franca among show people—all three men spoke warmly of each other more often than they sniped. (MacLíammóir once described Orson as among "the three deep loves of my life.") The Gate partners did not always approve of their young protégé's behavior, but at times like this—and there would be many such times ahead—their mutual respect and affection were manifest.

January and February flew by, with Orson designing sets for the Peacock shows and closing out his Gate tenure with pivotal roles in several main-stage productions. In January 1932, the Gate offered the Italian romantic drama *La Morte in Vacanza*, translated by Walter Ferris as *Death Takes a Holiday*. Orson portrayed Duke Lamberto, the lord of a creepy castle whose unwanted guest—the weary, lonely figure of Death (MacLíammóir)—falls in love with his daughter (Betty Chancellor). MacLíammóir also designed the sets, and Edwards directed.

Death Takes a Holiday was followed, in early February, by *Hamlet*, Orson's first professional excursion into Shakespeare, with MacLíammóir as a spellbinding Hamlet, and Edwards, who also directed, sensational as Claudius. Orson was third-billed; he doubled as Fortinbras and the Ghost of Hamlet's father, who appears several times throughout the drama. His Ghost especially was "very beautifully played," according to the *Irish Times*. "The Ghost can seldom have been presented more movingly," observed the *Irish Press*. "One of the best [Ghosts] I have ever seen," MacLíammóir himself said years later.

Hamlet was one of the season's biggest successes for the Gate. The theater was filled to capacity during the run, with the standing ovations stretching close to midnight, after which many members of the audience walked home happily, having missed the last public transport.

The Peacock's playbill was winding down. And after *Hamlet*, was there anything else on the Gate main stage for Orson? There was talk, probably stirred by him, of an *Othello* in which he would essay the title role. There were other rumors, perhaps from the same source, that he might be in line for the lead in *Coriolanus*. Some believed the talk, and wondered why it never came to anything. "They wouldn't let him play Othello," Orson's loyal crush Betty Chancellor complained to Welles historian Richard France decades later. "He was so remarkably good," she said in another interview. "I think the management was jealous!"

Writing home to Chicago at the time, Orson grumbled, "I am doomed for a kind of typecasting . . . nothing but roaring villains, old . . . those parts which demand my build and voice." Hilton Edwards saw things much the same way—at least for now. "I know you can do juveniles and so on," Edwards told Orson sympathetically, "but Micheál can do them better, and as a producer am I justified in misusing the best heavy and character actor in the company?"

"When he put it that way," Orson wrote to Dr. Bernstein, "I couldn't kick!"

So *Hamlet* was the end of it: the last Gate play with the impossibly young American taking major responsibilities. Orson did not even lobby for a part in the company's February production of Marcel Pagnol's *Topaze*. By now his sights were set higher. Having heard from visiting English critics and producers that the grass was greener in the West End, he looked ahead to visiting and conquering London.

At the end of February, the company threw an all-night party in Welles's honor, bidding him farewell. There were speeches and cheers and songs, whiskey and cigars. The last thing Orson did before leaving Dublin was visit the Abbey Theatre, where he had thrown together the sets for one last production by the Peacock Repertory Players: *The All-Alone* by Edward Martyn, which involved a scheming mother, a child of the sea, and a ghostly siren. A workman was changing the marquee for the next Abbey production. Individual actors' names never appeared on the Abbey's marquee, as a matter of long-standing tradition, but Orson bribed the man to put his name up there briefly, and take a photograph of him standing in front of it.

By March he was in London, making the rounds of producers, casting offices, and theatrical agents. Despite the reputation he had earned at the Gate, he soon realized that it was futile: with so many British thespians unemployed, a work visa for an American of any age was out of the question.

One day he took the train to a Hertfordshire village, Ayot Saint Lawrence, to knock on the door of one of his heroes, George Bernard Shaw, whose plays he had seen in Chicago and produced at the Todd School. Shaw was also a Dubliner and a stalwart of the Gate, which regularly presented his plays. (For a long time *Back to Methuselah* boasted the Gate's box office record.) Meeting the great playwright was a memory Orson always prized. "I recall the way in which he received me," Welles told Peter Noble, "listened to my ideas on the Theatre, gossiped about Dublin and shared a joke with all the enthusiasm of a schoolboy. I remember his walking me down to his gate and talking to me with the greatest simplicity as if I were as grown up as he."

Orson could not resist a short hop to Paris, where he "wined, drank, and attended parties with exuberance," according to Frank Brady's *Citizen Welles*. Crashing parties in Paris, Orson crossed paths with Brahim El Glaoui, who was the eldest son of the pasha of Marrakesh and served as his father's envoy. Brahim invited Orson to visit him in Morocco one day.

By now, however, Orson was homesick. And where was home for him? It was not Kenosha, and not quite Chicago, and never Highland Park. Graduation, his first professional credits, and eight months away from the United States helped settle the issue.

Several decades later, an interviewer in Paris asked him: Where was home for Orson Welles? "That's a problem," he replied in the filmed exchange. "As a kid I was moved around everywhere. I have lots of homes but I would like to have the one—but I don't . . .

"I suppose it's Woodstock, Illinois, if it's anywhere."

He had told Roger Hill as much in his letters home, hinting that now he felt qualified to teach dramatics at the Todd School, if the headmaster could be convinced to create such a position for him.

On board the ocean liner heading back to the United States, young Orson clasped his arms and leaned over the rail on deck, puffing manfully on his cigar. He felt more like an Irishman than an American, and he had the accent and pixie sayings to show for it. (It was good practice for his later stint as Michael O'Hara in *The Lady from Shanghai*—a film whose working title was "Black Irish.")

He had become a professional in Dublin, taking lead acting roles and being applauded for them. He had designed scenery for several plays and even directed one. He belonged now to acting and the theater, to the ancient dishonorable profession of faking it. It was perfect for him, a profession of scrounging and faking. Whatever else happened to him later in life, he always would be an actor.

For all this, he was indebted to those consummate scroungers and fakers Hilton Edwards and Micheál MacLíammóir. Welles would always consider Edwards his role model as a director, storing the older man's many and varied lessons in his memory—even if he didn't always follow those lessons. And MacLíammóir? Beyond his vaulting standards as a scenic designer, wasn't MacLíammóir just the kind of glorious artiste Orson himself wished to be?

For decades, Welles's plays and films would be stimulated by their great example and influence. "My debt to them can never be measured," Orson said frequently in interviews, adding, "I don't suppose any director ever owed so much to another director as I did to Hilton."

On March 15, he arrived in New York, still two months shy of his seventeenth birthday. He spent a few days shopping his résumé around to Broadway agents and producers, but was neither surprised nor deflated to learn that he was more famous in Dublin than New York.

He boarded a train for Chicago. Thanks to Dr. Maurice Bernstein, the local press was there to greet him and mark the occasion. "Chicago Schoolboy Who Won Place on Dublin Stage Returns," read the headline in the *Chicago Daily Tribune* on March 18, 1932.

When his train pulled into the station, the young actor had a Buster Keaton–like moment. The reporters were waiting for him, but they were on the wrong track. When Orson spotted them, he jumped off the train and raced toward them, shouting and waving excitedly, lugging his cheap suitcase, huge and cumbersome and little better than cardboard. His father had given him a piece of lasting advice: never carry luggage anyone would think of stealing. As he raced down the platform, the suitcase finally erupted under the pressure, spilling Orson's belongings—his writing pads and books and clippings of his Dublin shows—all over the ground. Dr. Bernstein and the reporters scurried to help him grab the stuff as the wind whistled around the depot.

CHAPTER 8

1932–1933

"Hope Rises with the Morning Sun"

Orson's "adopted Irish brogue" was so thick on his return, according to biographer Frank Brady, that even Dr. Maurice Bernstein had "trouble understanding him." His guardian also had trouble understanding why he now smoked cigars whenever he felt like it. When Orson's brogue faded, a manner of speech and gesture often described as mid-Atlantic replaced it—permanently. But the cigars became a lifelong prop for him, useful for dramatic pauses and gesticulation, on- and offstage— even late in life, when doctors' orders kept him from smoking them.

He stayed with the excitable Dr. Bernstein only briefly, which was long enough. Then it was off to Woodstock, where Roger Hill had concocted a job for Orson as second-semester drama coach. Within a week of his triumphant return from the Irish stage, Orson was immersed in the prep school's adaptation of Shakespeare's comedy *Twelfth Night*.

Skipper Hill had chosen it as the school's entry in Chicago's annual Drama League competition, partly because his students had attended Jane Cowl's production at Chicago's Harris Theater in the spring of the previous year. Todd's version would borrow heavily from hers— Orson would even copy Robert Edmond Jones's acclaimed set design, which featured a huge book occupying center stage, arranged against the backdrop of a sea. In Cowl's production, a clown turned the book pages, but in the Todd version, the boys would turn the pages, revealing Orson's series of scene paintings.

Full of adrenaline after his Irish sojourn, Orson did it all. He devised the colorful costumes and settings; he helped condense Shakespeare's text; he played Malvolio, the steward of Olivia's household; and, of course he "codirected" the Todd Troupers. Not all were boys: Roger Hill's eldest daughter, Joanne, played Olivia, the character at the center of the play's setup. Using the school's new sixteen-millimeter camera, Orson filmed the *Twelfth Night* dress rehearsals for the actors to see and critique their performances—similarly, he would later use phonograph recordings for radio show run-throughs and, sometimes, in Hollywood.

In the 1970s, author Frank Brady watched color footage of this rehearsal film, the rarest of the rare in Welles's oeuvre, in the headmaster's living room in Miami. "The print that I saw," Brady wrote, "was still perfectly preserved with rich color and quite professionally focused but without any camera movement, or pronounced flourishes or angles. It was simply shot from one point of view, perhaps from the middle of the tenth row of the theater: an amateur recording of the play on film rather than a piece of cinema. Orson narrated this film by making a phonograph record that was to be played in accompaniment."

Over the years, the annual Drama League contest—the scene of Orson's great disappointment in 1929—had acquired mythic status at Todd School, as an occasion for the slingshot-wielding Todd boys to challenge the bigger, richer Chicago Goliaths. Three years after his failure, Orson was determined to redress the balance. And now the young drama coach led the underdog Todd Troupers through showdowns against Senn High School, with a student body of eight thousand, and Bowen High School, with seven thousand, in the Fine Arts building of the Goodman Theatre.

The two-and-a-half-foot silver loving cup went to Todd School.

Early in May, Skipper had scheduled a two-week history and civics road trip for eighth-graders, and Orson begged a seat on the bus. He was still too young to help with the driving (and didn't care to learn to drive anyway), so Hill made him chief of crew—the crew being all the Todd boys on the trip. Along with assistant-teaching, Orson supervised the daily journals the boys were expected to keep on the trip, and even helped organize the meals cooked on board the school's fully equipped Arrow Coach, which Hill dubbed "Big Bertha."

Orson's connection with Skipper Hill was as strong as ever, and the trip would give him a chance to pursue a hidden agenda: he had talked the headmaster into collaborating on a stage play. Only in his weaker moments did Hill think of himself as a playwright, but Orson was a natural writer, and their long hours together on the road would give them time to discuss Orson's "Big Idea." That was one reason the itinerary took the boys south, through Kentucky, Louisville, and Lexington, en route to Appomattox Court House, Harpers Ferry, and Washington, D.C. Orson wanted to write a biographical play about the radical abolitionist John Brown.

Orson and Skipper Hill both were fascinated by the odyssey of Brown, who had tried to inspire a slave revolt with his attack on Harpers Ferry in 1859, an incident that helped trigger the Civil War and led to Brown's capture and execution. Visiting the historic sites was a way of teaching civics to the Todd boys, but also a way for Orson and Skipper to soak up the atmosphere of places where the great opponent of slavery had lived and breathed. Orson spent hours sitting next to Hill as the headmaster drove Big Bertha through Kentucky and Virginia, both of them talking excitedly about Brown, brainstorming ideas for their play.

From Washington they drove north to New York City, where the Todd boys visited the Empire State Building, which had just opened the previous year. Skipper had brought the *Twelfth Night* camera along on the bus trip, and Orson captured silent footage of the boys gaping at various landmarks. Sometimes the chief of crew went before the camera himself—the ebullient tour guide, gesturing toward the viewers and expounding, always the incorrigible actor. But the trip also exposed Orson to the deepening effects of the Great Depression, now in its third year. In Ireland he had witnessed dire poverty, and now, in New York, he must have seen the droves of unemployed begging on street corners and living in parks. His growing political consciousness would inform his sympathetic portrayal of the radical John Brown.

From the city they swung upstate, stopping at Brown's farm in North Elba, near Lake Placid, and at Niagara Falls before heading back to Woodstock. They returned just in time for Orson to start preparing for Closing Day ceremonies on June 15, which included a reprise of *Twelfth Night*, a musical puppet show, a short French play, and a "home movie" interspersing clips of Todd daily life with footage from their American history bus tour.

The Hills lingered in Woodstock for another week before leaving for Camp Tosebo in Michigan. Orson visited the camp briefly in July, then moved back in with Dr. Bernstein, shuttling between the doctor's residences in Highland Park and Chicago, still corresponding faithfully with the headmaster while taking the lead in researching John Brown.

The Depression had doomed the Ravinia Festival, which underwent a financial crisis and closed that summer. The theater scene in Chicago was also bleak. Charles Collins in the *Chicago Tribune* pronounced it comatose until fall. July was torrid, driving Orson and thousands of other Chicagoans into air-conditioned movie theaters for the matinees. After delving into books and newspapers for a month in the public library, Orson was ready to write—and eager to leave the city, where the heat and dust of August aggravated his asthma and hay fever.

Dr. Maurice Bernstein and Roger Hill were now conspirators in looking after Orson's needs, as Bernstein and Orson's father once had been, and they recommended one of the summer cottages in northern Wisconsin owned by an Evanston colleague of Bernstein's, Dr. J. P. Sprague. The cottage retreat was near Woodruff and Mercer Lake, a vacation destination for city dwellers, 350 miles north of Chicago. Summer camps, cabins, and sparse hamlets dotted the north woods area, part of the vast Lac du Flambeau reservation set aside for the Chippewa tribe.

Seventeen-year-old Orson boarded an overnight Chicago and Northwestern train, carrying his paints, brushes, pads of paper, typewriter, and books, heading for the Wisconsin woods. The train seemed to crawl north in the August torpor. At the water fountain, Orson bumped into James B. Meigs, who was the father of several Todd boys and the business manager of the *American Weekly*, the lurid Sunday magazine of the Hearst newspaper chain. His older son, James Jr., who had just graduated from Todd, was a Trouper in the large cast of *Twelfth Night*; and the younger Meigs boy, William, was also theatrically inclined, with a strong singing voice.*

---

* William Meigs would later have a career as a singer in stage vehicles and as an actor in television and films, mainly Westerns.

Meigs invited Orson to stay with him and his family on their estate near Lac du Flambeau. Orson could have the run of the place and join the Meigses for meals in the main lodge. Orson was tempted, and when he met the driver who'd been sent to bring him to J. P. Sprague's cottage—a "cross-eyed half-breed," in Welles's words, who was "raving drunk" at 6:30 A.M.—he took Meigs up on the offer. Orson got back on the train and accompanied Meigs to Lac du Flambeau, which boasted "a main street like an illustration from somebody's novel of life in the early lumbering and Indian-fighting days," in Orson's words. At the station, he crammed himself into a Packard with Meigs and the rest of the "multitudinous" Meigs family.

The Packard wove past small lakes and through dense pine forest. Arriving at the luxurious-looking lodge, Orson was treated to "as demoralizing a breakfast as has ever been fed to an aspiring co-dramatist," he reported in a letter to the headmaster. A three-day introduction to the north woods followed: the Meigs family took him sightseeing, hiking, swimming, sailing, canoeing, game-fishing, and even for a bit of hunting. "We went out for deer but brought home a mere brace of gamey partridge," Orson recounted.

Eager to buckle down, Orson erected a personal wigwam on a small pine grove island offshore from the main lodge. The wigwam materials, Orson wrote to Skipper, consisted of "wild things, deer skin and bark, soft maple and basswood." He forked $25.50 over to local "squaws and a few antiques of the neuter gender" for help in gathering materials and constructing the "great inverted salad bowl" in which he meant to dwell. He still didn't feel much like writing, and went paddling along the river, recognizing "a portly old gentleman in a mellow panama"—none other than Hortense Hill's father, Arthur Lincoln Gettys, who was vacationing nearby.

Gettys was a prominent Chicago attorney, a partner in a firm with five-term Chicago mayor Carter Harrison Jr., himself the son of another five-term Chicago mayor, Carter Harrison Sr., once a presidential hopeful. The Harrisons belonged to the newspaper family that owned the *Chicago Times*. Orson loved the name Gettys, and he would use it in *Citizen Kane* for Boss Gettys, the corrupt political broker described as "a big heavy set man, a little past middle age" in the script.

"Fate—everything is fate," Orson wrote to Skipper from the

Wisconsin north woods. The people he met, the places he went, all added up to a road map pointing him to his future.

The young man was galvanized by the first letter he received from Roger Hill. Skipper had dashed off an opening for their play about John Brown, a scene set at a town hall meeting in Concord, Massachusetts, where the debate is dominated by abolitionists Henry David Thoreau and William Lloyd Garrison.

Orson was all enthusiasm, but it was Hill whose discipline had started the ball rolling. Feeling "permanently shamed" by his own procrastination, Orson promptly sat down at his typewriter in the wigwam and pecked out a title page—"Kansas Days, Copyright, 1932"—breathlessly summarizing the projected work as "a play of the stirring days just before the civil war, concerning chiefly John Brown, prophet—warrior—zealot—the most dramatic and incredible figure in American history."

Then he wrote his own first scene, setting it at John Brown's farm in North Elba, from where the antislavery crusader set out for Harpers Ferry. (After his death, the abolitionist's body would be returned to North Elba—the place where "John Brown's body lies a-moldering in the grave.") The scenes Orson wrote now would be overhauled later, but, as always with him, when the writing began to flow it gushed. "I have trouble sometimes thinking things out clearly unless I write my thoughts down in some consecutive order," Welles told Peter Bogdanovich years afterward, "so I write myself quite a good deal of disposable prose." He would evolve a lifelong habit of settling down to write late in the evening, after everyone else had retired—"a ten-thirty that feels, even to this inveterate night-hawk, like the cold moment before dawn in a Dublin scene-dock," he wrote to Skipper. Guzzling coffee, he would write until dawn.

Inspired by one scene, then another, Orson often wrote episodes out of sequence—and that may have contributed to the structure of this first script, which would be framed by its opening, Brown's death, and then be driven forward by a clever narrative device: a newspaperman's search for the real man behind the legend. The stage directions called for stereopticon slides of photographs, documents, and newspaper headlines. All of these elements anticipated *Citizen Kane,* noted Welles's authorized biographer, Barbara Leaming. "Long before John Brown actually appears on stage," Leaming observed, "we have examined a variety of conflicting points of view about him."

Hill was older and wiser, but in this teaming with Orson he swiftly became the junior partner, as reflected in the credit on Orson's cover page, which read "by Orson Welles and Roger Hill." Hill understood his role: once he fired the starter pistol, he could step back and watch Orson run the race. The headmaster would complete only a few scenes for the play; the bulk of the work was Orson's.

Even at seventeen, Orson was already a peerless editor of other people's ideas. "Personally I think it's <u>great</u>. Wonderful!" he wrote, critiquing Hill's first pages, before asking tactfully, "With this opinion understood, may I offer the inevitable criticism?" Certainly the headmaster had "made incredibly dull expository material genuinely dramatic. But I <u>do</u> think there's too much Thoreau! Not too many lines, understand, but too wonderful a personality. He completely dominates the off-stage individuality of John Brown, whose shadow should be more real than any of the persons actually presented. All of the characters are perhaps a little too painstakingly <u>characters</u>."

He tempered his critiques with praise. Thoreau's "marching-on" speech in defense of Brown was "superb," Orson noted, "the kind [of speeches] that live because they combine a literary quality with a very real dramatic and practically theatric power." But parts of the other dialogue Hill wrote were perhaps "too good," Orson said. "We don't want to be accused of bombast. I think neat 'lines' are a fault of mine too, we must both beware, for that way lies floweriness."

Another lifelong pattern emerged: alone with his creative impulses, Orson always had too much energy, too many thoughts in his head, to focus exclusively on one Big Idea. Once he plunged into the John Brown script, his mind began racing, and during breaks from writing about the abolitionist he dashed off notes for other projects. He whipped up an outline for a mystery play called "The Dark Room," involving society figures gathered together for a haunted séance. "A natural, a positive honey!" Orson predicted in a letter to the headmaster. "Every English-speaking repertory company on the globe will be doing that show, mark my words!" But he didn't get very far on "The

Dark Room" before he was distracted by another intriguing possibility: "Bright Lucifer," a story that could draw on his own life and the northern Wisconsin locale. But he soon stalled on "Bright Lucifer," and set that aside too.

The "sacred" task of the moment, he realized, was his collaboration with Roger Hill. Orson pined for the "sunshine of your enthusiasm," he admitted to Skipper, and sometimes withheld finished pages for fear of the headmaster's negative reaction. If Hill didn't respond to his work quickly enough by mail, Orson worried that it had fallen short. Orson peppered his letters with the puns and silly jokes that amused them both: "I can ride a canoe, canoe?" ("Skipper brought out the boy in him," Simon Callow wrote.) He signed his letters, "Love without end."

A series of fierce August thunderstorms finally expelled him from his wigwam. He had struck up an acquaintance with another vacationer, Lawrence C. Whiffen, who operated Wisconsin's first archery supply store in Milwaukee, and Whiffen offered to share his pine log cabin for a small stipend. A bow-hunting fanatic, about fifteen years older than Orson, Whiffen spent summers in the Lac du Flambeau region honing his archery skills while working on conservationist tracts. "Larry the Archer," as Orson fondly dubbed his cabin mate, was the strong, silent type, but Whiffen made "a great to-do" pounding on his Underwood through the night—setting a good example for Orson, who sat across the table from him, doing the same.

When not writing, Orson spent time with the multitudinous Meigses. One day James Jr. bagged a deer ("You 'bag' a deer, don't you? Or do you <u>bug</u> it?" Orson joked to Skipper), and it was a splendid animal, "glorious antlered." All feasted on the venison. Orson was friendly enough with James Jr., "a remarkable huntsman" who was nearly his age, though he noted that "his are the huntsman's faults and there is just no halting the tedious, Albert-like inevitability of his tongue."* He preferred the younger, more artistic William, whom the family called Willie.

Orson tried never to miss a John Barrymore picture, and one day

---

* "Albert-like" is probably a reference to Prince Albert of York, later King George VI of England, notorious for his stammer.

he drove with the Meigses to see *Grand Hotel* at the Isle Theatre in Minocqua. Orson bought tickets for the whole family—in honor of Willie's fourteenth birthday, but also as a "gesture made towards repaying all this overwhelming Meigs hospitality," Orson wrote to Skipper. But these movie tickets, along with the rent he paid to Larry the Archer, the cost of the wigwam, and "a general malted milking now and then," as Orson reported to the headmaster, left his wallet shrunken "to the most incredible flatness," engendering "a state of mind not amiably inclined to fertility and the fruitful pen." Orson fired off telegrams to Dr. Bernstein and Skipper, pleading for cash.

When his guardian temporized, the headmaster sent $25 by wire from Michigan, calling it a gift that would not have to be repaid. Orson could have wept. "I can scarcely think of a more perfect workshop," a newly hopeful Orson wrote to the headmaster from Larry the Archer's cabin. "A tuneful country this, here on the reservation, now that noisy outboards have been packed away. Woodland sounds from the wild where the Chippewa hunt bear and deer, silver sounds from the lake, and sunny insect sounds at mid-day. A little sad, perhaps the song the marsh-folk sing, and sadder yet the endless dirging of the wind in the fir trees. At night there are stealthy little sounds, and always the unbelievable: ceaseless in the air, the throbbing of medicine-drums."

The John Brown script had languished briefly as he scrounged for subsistence. Now his spirit was lifted, his creativity recharged. After "a soul-satisfying dinner" provided by the Meigses, he plunged afresh into the script. The night flew by. "Now, through the murky spectacles of early morning (one does keep barbaric hours in this bee-loud glade)," Orson wrote to Skipper, quoting Yeats's "The Lake Isle of Innisfree," "I search in vain for rosy pigmentation. Courage my soul! Hope rises with the morning sun."

September brought Orson back to Highland Park, where he busied himself collating his scenes with the headmaster's, revising as he toiled. He and Roger Hill planned a trip to New York once the fall semester was safely under way. Skipper was genuinely enthusiastic about Orson's script and thought he could pitch it to any number of former Todd boys who were now in show business.

And Orson's script it was. In just one month's time, Orson had written more than two hundred pages, encompassing eleven major scenes and twenty-nine characters. Hill claimed credit for only "most" of one finished scene, the very first he wrote, and even that was rewritten by Orson. After spending the first half of September on revisions, Orson started typing multiple drafts for submission purposes.

Autumn was gorgeous, and the Moores, who still lived near Dr. Maurice Bernstein, had "a heavenly back-yard, sun-flecked and fragrant," where Orson could sit writing, typing, and retyping. ("I doubt if I have ever, even in a class-room, been forced into such stupid, wearing work," he nevertheless complained.) Orson's guardian and the Moores were so closely aligned that today they might be considered "blended households." Orson could never quite figure out what was going on between Bernstein and Aunt Hazel; but he complained in his letters that the two quarreled often and sometimes tearfully, interrupting his concentration and slowing his writing.

For that reason and others, Orson occasionally escaped to Chicago, where the newspaper world was in an uproar. After repeated clashes with a new editor of the *Chicago Examiner*, his friend Ashton Stevens had been threatened with the sack; the respected drama critic eventually accepted a switch to the afternoon Hearst paper, the *Chicago American*. Thanks to Stevens, Ned Moore, John Clayton, and his other well-placed friends, Orson still had his choice of opening-night tickets for the symphony, opera, and theater. He was particularly taken by *Of Thee I Sing*, by George S. Kaufman and Morrie Ryskind (with a Gershwin score), a new hit satirizing a presidential campaign. The play had its Chicago premiere in late September, and Orson agreed with Charles Collins, who wrote in the *Tribune* that it was the "most triumphant show of the year." "Much the swellest thing," Orson wrote to Skipper. "You must see it." He and Hill were already talking about writing a second play—a Big Idea musical about another famous American, perhaps even a president. To Orson, the triumphant *Of Thee I Sing* was both a template and an inspiration.

Still, Highland Park stymied his creativity. When Dr. Bernstein wasn't bickering with Aunt Hazel, he was lecturing Orson about the future. Orson had enjoyed his little fling with theater; now, perhaps, was the time for college. After all, if Orson was still serious about his theatrical ambitions, why was he lolling around in the Moores's back-yard? Orson had "wasted the summer," and now he was "wasting the already started theatrical season," his guardian warned him. If Orson was going to try to sell his play, when was he leaving for New York?

Orson was just as impatient. "Why not now now NOW?" he wrote to Skipper.

Orson's plans and problems and Big Ideas exasperated Bernstein—indeed, nearly overwhelmed him. As Hazel Moore pointed out, when-ever Orson was home Bernstein got lost "in the throes of Orson," and was unable to focus on his own interests.

Aunt Hazel thought she handled Orson better, finding him always "an intensely interesting person, regardless of the element of agreement one may have with him." The boy's feelings about Hazel were harder to discern: in one passage of her biography, Barbara Leaming wrote that Orson "vehemently disliked the autocratic" woman, but elsewhere she wrote only that he found her "somewhat irritating," a kinder analysis. Orson was not quoted directly.

Everyone in the Moore and Bernstein households seemed intent on debating Orson's best possible future. The Moores always sided with Dr. Bernstein, who wanted to point Orson toward a constructive target and dispatch him toward that goal for a fixed and if possible lengthy period of time. The Hills felt the same way: "Anything to get him out of my hair!" Skipper told Leaming.

In late September, Orson had lunch at the Tavern Club with Charles Collins. The respected drama critic had read the John Brown play, and now he "waxed wonderfully human" over its prospects, Orson reported to Hill. Collins also suggested a few possible titles: "The Madman of Freedom," "The Approaching Storm," "War's Pioneer." Collins had known Orson since his adolescence but now treated him almost as a colleague or personal friend. When Orson spoke of his adventures in Ireland, Collins answered with stories of his flirtation with the Dublin-born actress Patricia Collinge when she last passed through Chicago.

In Highland Park, meanwhile, Dr. Bernstein announced disquiet-ing news: Orson's older brother wished to pay him a visit. Richard I. Welles, as he now called himself, had been fighting his institutional-ization at Kankakee since 1927. His efforts were unsuccessful, but he was allowed occasional weekend outings in the company of a hospital attendant, and Richard was hoping to see his brother on his own twenty-seventh birthday, coming up on the first Friday of October. Bernstein had no legal responsibility for Richard, other than doling out small portions of the inheritance for hospital expenses, but he insisted that Orson welcome his brother for a birthday visit, and that Orson offer to pay Richard's travel expenses out of his own allowance.

Orson had not seen his black-sheep brother for at least three years—the last time probably in the company of their father. "Frankly I have no desire to see him for another three," Orson sounded off in a letter to Roger Hill. "He's so upsetting to one's equilibrium. But something has got to be done I suppose, and I do want to be as nice as possible.

"But what the hell? . . . Do I seem callous? Really, Richard is a tremendous strain. Always making off with himself or your silverware, and unbearably overbearing. But I do love him and sympathize—and I will try just this once to be a little unselfish. Incidentally, you must meet him. I'll never feel you quite know me 'till you know my family."

But Skipper never did get to know Richard, who would remain unknowable to all but a few in his lifetime. "After all that worry over Richard, and all that heroic self-sacrifice, the weekend is not to be," Orson wrote a few days later. "Dadda forgot to perform certain Kankakee rites, he's so busy these days, so brother Dick must languish in the institution over his birthday."

Not long after that, the Hills rode to the rescue in Big Bertha, sweeping Orson away to New York. Roger Hill bet the moon on the whirlwind trip, installing his wife and prize pupil in a suite at the Algonquin "suitable for entertaining lucky Broadway producers who would be offered our opus," in the headmaster's words. Hill's top candidate was Dwight Deere Wiman, who'd been his own former roommate at Todd School before coproducing a string of Broadway hits in the 1920s. Also high on the list was his college chum Samson Raphaelson, the New York playwright and nowadays a screenwriter for Ernst Lubitsch. When Wiman took a quick pass, Skipper pinned his hopes on Raphaelson but was unable to track him down—no surprise, as Raphaelson wasn't even in New York. He was in and out of Hollywood.

When Wiman said no and Raphaelson couldn't be found, Hill's confidence faltered. He and his wife had duties in Woodstock, and they decided to leave promotion of the script—now titled "Marching Song"—to Orson. "I peered into an empty purse," Hill recalled, "moved our boy into the cheapest of rooms, to continue sale efforts via pavement pounding, and headed home." Hill dangled the hope that he might return to New York over a long weekend.

Installed at $9 a week in an "efficiency" with kitchenette and bath at an apartment house on the corner of Eighty-First Street and Broadway, Orson hit the pavement with a stack of typed scripts and his own researched list of prospects. His targets included Ben A. Boyar, general manager for Max Gordon, who had achieved his breakthrough as producer of Raphaelson's *The Jazz Singer*; Richard E. French, general manager for John L. Golden, another producer of Raphaelson plays; Samuel French (no relation to Richard), a well-known publisher and producer of plays; and Broadway mainstays including William Harris Jr. and George C. Tyler, whose producing credits predated World War I.

The established producers gravitated toward musicals and light fare, but that wasn't the only hurdle for the young aspiring playwright. Although Orson jumped out of bed earlier than usual every morning, dressed in his best, and spent the day knocking on producers' doors, he rarely got to meet anyone important. And no one had the slightest interest in reading something written by a seventeen-year-old, unproduced, unrepresented writer from the Midwest. After days of polite but steady discouragement, Orson yearned for the bottomless optimism of the Hills. His own ebullience melted into "qualms and doubts," in his words. The occasional inspiring letter from the headmaster enabled Orson to console himself that "'Marching Song' is the goods!" On days without any positive reinforcement, though, he had the "sinking suspicion" that their play was simply "bad." Still, he wrote to Hill ruefully, "We can always write more, can't we?"

In late October came a body blow: the *New York Times* reviewed a "searching" new biography of John Brown that sounded superior to their own work. "My happiness and self-respect seem founded only on an admiration and confidence in that, our play," Orson wrote dismally. "Sometimes I go wandering off into the suburbs of doubt, and journeying too far catch a glimpse of that awful pit, without a bottom, and sickeningly without a vestige of gravitation to take you there—and then there is a great floundering of entrails within me, the nausea of despair—and I go scurrying back to the Times Square of our optimism."

Characteristically upbeat, Hill replied swiftly: Didn't an acclaimed new biography make the abolitionist's story all the more marketable? Orson thrived on such pep talks, no matter how unrealistic. He mailed a fresh version of the script to Hilton Edwards and Micheál Mac-Líammóir at the Gate Theatre, then took out his well-thumbed stage directory and jotted down more names of producers. "I've been pawing through that lousy directory for so long I think I shall go mad," Orson wrote, "mad . . . Mad . . . MAD!" At the urging of Hill and Dr. Bernstein alike, Orson finally agreed to seek a literary agent to represent the script to producers. He tried Leah Salisbury, a onetime actress who had developed an important clientele; and Alice Kauser, a play broker since the turn of the century. "They [literary agents] were much the most difficult," Orson reported bitterly. "Gave one a sense of defeat, just by their manner, obviously youth was a tremendous handicap. Producers are much more folksy" with their rejections.

One day, on West Forty-Eighth Street, Orson ran into Hubert Osborne, the former director of the Goodman Theatre, who had taken over briefly after its founder, Thomas Wood Stevens, was cashiered. When Osborne asked what he was doing in New York, Orson boasted that he was a playwright now, busy trying to interest producers in a serious drama. Serious drama was a long hard road, Osborne observed sadly. "Don't let them forget your face," Osborne advised him. "Which means, I suppose, sitting in offices," Orson wrote to the headmaster. "I can think of . . . nothing in this whole wide world I would like to do less."

Osborne, who knew Orson primarily as an actor, urged him to try out for some acting parts in his spare time. In his quest to find a home for "Marching Song," Orson had almost forgotten he was an actor with professional credits—and acting was indeed his best bet for income. Learning that there was an opening for an understudy in a revival of *The Silent House*, a 1928 melodrama, Orson stopped by the Shubert offices and sat around with a few dozen other optimists, hoping for the part. "Somebody got it days before," he wrote to the Hills. "They always do."

Night was when he felt most positive, his energy infinite. With most of the work on "Marching Song" complete, he dived into another project, a more commercial stage thriller, tentatively called "Where Was Moses?" He and Skipper had sketched out the story en route to New York, but Orson was determined to write "Where Was Moses?" alone. He wanted Hill to produce the show in Chicago before embarking on a national tour, ultimately bringing it to Broadway.

Orson expected to play the lead, another Chinaman to add to his repertoire; the staging would incorporate his penchant for magic. "My part is absolutely marvelous, and will give ample opportunity for the exhibition of my every trick," Orson reported to Hill. "I'm really writing it with your promise to produce it," he reminded the headmaster. "It's a cheap show and should pack 'em in, not only at home but around about, even in Gotham if it takes at all. In fact I'm envisioning a production company by us—limitless possibilities, Skipper, limitless."

Orson wrote the Hills overlapping letters while waiting desperately for mail from either of them. Had Skipper tracked down Samson Raphaelson? Had he seen Of Thee I Sing yet? "You don't know, you can't guess, how my spirits can fade and wilt without you," he wrote to the headmaster. "Particularly in this strange, trying town and in this strange, trying situation."

Most producers' offices were willing to let him drop off a copy of "Marching Song," but few ever responded. "I haven't been phoned, or post-carded, or written to," he reported to Hill. One day, when he missed paying his rent, his landlord virtually tossed him onto the sidewalk. Orson downsized into a fourth-floor flat in a nearby brownstone on West Seventy-Seventh Street, a "sunny quiet friendly old room," shabbier than the "efficiency" apartment but close enough to shops and Broadway. He worried about the $7.50 weekly rent, and whether he should send his mail by special delivery, or settle for a three-cent stamp. He wired to Dr. Bernstein, pleading for money.

Just as his spirits began to plummet, a "cheering letter" from the Hills lifted him up again, pushing him back to work on the commercial thriller and coaxing him to keep looking for producers for "Marching Song." He met with the reader who had "covered" the John Brown play for producer William Harris, who told him the script was "extremely interesting" but not the kind of subject Harris backed.

Again, he despaired. "I went over to the Riverside and stared moodily at the deep black water," he wrote to Skipper. Then one happy day, Orson managed to coax Ben Boyar to the telephone, and Boyar promised to read "Marching Song" and get back to him.

Another "cheering" epistle arrived from Hortense Hill, saying she hoped Orson wasn't feeling too lonely in New York. "No, I'm not lonely," he replied. "Strangely enough I haven't been a bit. A little bitter perhaps, inert rather, and cheerless, but the thriller has kept my nose to its own peculiar grindstone, and I haven't minded. My dread of New York has been supplanted by a half contemptuous affection. Broadway has become for me the most transparent and the least dazzling of all main streets—inclusive of Indianapolis and Kenosha—[and] the desirability of the end for which we are all striving here, grows more and more dubious.

"It's cold out," he ended, "My hands are still numb. Too numb to type properly."

October became November. Orson lived according to his mood swings. Sometimes he pinched pennies; at other times he dined well. "I gotta be comfortable!" he wrote to Skipper. He spent a few precious dollars to join Actors Equity, in case he lucked into an acting job, but warned Hill not to tell Dr. Bernstein, whom he constantly dunned for advances on his allowance.

A wire from Dr. Bernstein bailed him out financially one last time, but Bernstein also scolded him: "I do hope you won't continue to waste your youth aimlessly." His guardian dangled a fresh possibility: John Clayton, out of regular work since the Chicago Civic Opera closed in 1931, was on the verge of signing a contract to produce a twenty-six-episode aviation drama series for WLS, the Sears Roebuck radio station in Chicago, an affiliate of the Blue Network of the National Broadcasting Company (NBC). Clayton had told Bernstein he envisioned a continuing part for Orson. Orson was tempted—it was his first job prospect in months—and yet he knew that accepting it would mean returning to Chicago with his tail between his legs.

Orson stalled before replying, asking for Roger Hill's all-important opinion. He and Hortense had both loved the presidential campaign musical *Of Thee I Sing*, but on learning that Skipper didn't think much of it, he was forced to rethink his own view. Maybe the problem, he wrote to the headmaster, was the play's focus on the political scene. "Nothing could be as funny as American Politics except American Politics," he suggested, musing that perhaps "The Newspaper Business" would make for a better Big American backdrop. "Whoa!" Orson scribbled, "There's an idea! The newspaper business as an operetta. A *Front Page* [set] to Gershwin, only more so!!!!!"

He saw as many plays and movies as time and money allowed. The films he made sure to catch that fall included Ernst Lubitsch's *Trouble in Paradise*, with Samson Raphaelson's script; and Jean Cocteau's avant-garde *Blood of a Poet*. Orson admired Roman Bohnen, who had been a star of the Goodman Theatre in its heyday, and he made a point of getting to Jackson Heights in Queens, where a small left-wing theater group was presenting Bohnen's new message play, *The Incubator*, about a delinquent who is "incubated" as a criminal in a state school for youthful offenders. Also in New York was another player from the Goodman—actress Katherine Krug, the wife of Ashton Stevens—who'd recently been hired as a Broadway understudy and was now using her married name, Florence Stevens, professionally.

Florence Stevens (FloFlo to close friends, including Orson) was "a dear," Orson wrote to the Hills. "She's my salvation. We've been out together a good deal, shows and what-not." He and the actress preferred sophisticated theater- and moviegoing, heading to the Criterion, for example, to watch the sensational German film *Mädchen in Uniform*, with its pro-lesbian storyline and all-female cast.

Ashton Stevens visited New York in mid-November to see his wife on Broadway, where she had stepped into a billed role in the new Edgar Wallace mystery *Criminal at Large*, and to review fall cultural offerings for the *Chicago American*. Orson accompanied him to the Whistler retrospective at the Museum of Modern Art. *Portrait of the Artist's Mother* was on loan from the Louvre, and other major Whistlers were juxtaposed with masterpieces by his contemporaries and the next generation of artists. The two gazed at Whistler's *White Girl*, and the painting that hung opposite from it, Eugene Speicher's portrait of Katharine Cornell in George Bernard Shaw's *Candida*, her signature role.

Orson told Stevens he preferred some of "the later guys" (in Stevens's words) in the exhibition over Whistler, especially the more realistic painters such as George Bellows and Edward Hopper. But Stevens vigorously defended Whistler and the Romantic tradition, and Orson shut up and listened, as he would listen until the end of Stevens's life.

"I hope Orson wasn't too annoying," FloFlo wrote to her husband when he told her about their museum expedition. "He can be sometimes," she added. No, Stevens said, Orson was "very companionable," before and after their debate. "I have a feeling that boy will get somewhere," he confided. "There seems to be a kind of honesty in his precocious smartness." Orson, for his part, recognized that Stevens had gone out of his way to be "very nice" to him, and he felt privileged to have been treated almost like a friend by the great man.

Stevens was nice enough to offer pointers on anything Orson sent him to read. He thought "Marching Song" showed real talent. ("There is splendid stuff in his play," he told his wife.) But he agreed that the market was unpromising for such serious subjects, and he urged Orson to try something more salable. Having read his dispatches from Ireland, Stevens suggested that Orson try his hand at a book about his travels—a sort of early autobiography. Orson embraced the idea, dashing off pages in the last week of November, while Stevens was still in New York. The columnist read Orson's effort quickly and gave him some advice. "I told him it was near-literary," Stevens said to his wife, "and to get down to earth." Orson took heed, writing late into the night on both his stage thriller and his nascent travel memoir.

Come December, and money was tight again. Orson begged Dr. Bernstein for reinforcements, while imploring Roger Hill, "in your official capacity of optimizer," to assure the doctor that his money was being spent on worthwhile objectives. He was full of questions for the headmaster: When did he plan on returning to New York? Orson insisted he could find room for both Hills to stay at his small place. And why was Samson Raphaelson so elusive? "I've seen his name on a lot of big-time movies lately," Orson wrote to Hill. "He's our man! There must be some way of reaching him, of enthusing him."

But Hill threw him a curve in his next letter, saying that he'd spoken with Dr. Bernstein, and Bernstein might be right: perhaps Orson should reconsider college, or acting. "Peddling our play is enough," Orson moaned. "I just can't bring myself to look for a job."

Hill had another, more welcome suggestion: if they couldn't interest a producer in "Marching Song," perhaps they could self-publish the play using the Todd School printing press. Skipper could write a history-minded preface, and Orson could decorate the script with his scene design sketches and pen-and-ink caricatures, which the headmaster loved. Publishing "Marching Song" might make the play more attractive to a potential producer. Leaping at the idea, Orson instantly started adding drawings to the typed copies of "Marching Song" that he was still circulating. But when he handed the illustrated scripts to office intermediaries, he got only baffled looks in response.

The rejections for "Marching Song" were piling up. Ben Boyar finally weighed in: the script made swell reading, and it might make a good play, Boyar said, but not a commercial one. The Samuel French office praised its "passion and good writing," but found it "too sprawling" for practical purposes. After charging him $5 for its report, Maddens issued a rejection: "Not suitable for the market." Samson Raphaelson? Still incommunicado.

"I am now firmly convinced that 'Marching Song,' despite its merits, will never be produced, at least not this year," Orson wrote to Skipper miserably. "I am aware that disappointments, it matters not how many, should in no way affect my confidence, but they do." He would have to settle for the book version of "Marching Song." Meanwhile, using John Clayton's connections, Orson wangled a broadcasting audition at NBC in New York. The tryout was "very favorable," he wrote to Florence Stevens, although he was diffident about radio for the time being. ("I'm not interested in anything but this aviation program," he assured FloFlo.) Orson told Roger Hill to let Clayton know he was willing to return to Chicago for the radio series, but he would accept no less than $100 per episode. "For prostituting myself over the ether, I oughta get paid" well, Orson wrote to Skipper.

At the eleventh hour, however, "Marching Song" was rescued from failure. The veteran producer George C. Tyler wrote to Orson to declare his tentative interest in mounting the play. Nothing definite, but thereupon followed "some very exciting letters of approbation," as Orson wrote to Florence Stevens. Tyler asked to option the script until the end of 1934: an unpaid option—no real commitment—but clear and definite interest. "There are some changes [he recommends,] of course," Orson exulted, "but he thinks a good deal of it."

He had accomplished his mission after all. "Marching Song" was still alive. The headmaster might not make it back to New York any-time soon, but the dream of collaborating with Skipper on a Big Idea musical was still a possibility. He continued to putter away on his Irish travel memoir, and his stage thriller was "shaping up beautifully."

In Ireland Orson had learned to keep his trunk always half packed and ready to go. In New York he learned another lesson: betting the moon on a single script was foolish. At any given time he could and should have a wide range of projects in the works.

By Christmas, he was back in Chicago.

John Clayton's aviation series never got the green light from radio sta-tion WLS, however. And despite the earnestness Orson invested in the Irish travel book, and the encouragement he got from Ashton Stevens, he was dissatisfied with his efforts and shifted this writing project to the back burner. He also set aside "Where Was Moses?" once and for all.

Orson pleaded with Roger Hill to play hooky from Todd and join him for lunch in Chicago, where they could discuss their next Big Idea. "As you love me, do this little thing," Orson wrote to Skipper. "Drive in tomorrow, or at most the next day. Tell Hortense you have confer-ences, auditions, and so on in great numbers." They could even squeeze in a matinee of Cecil B. DeMille's latest picture, *The Sign of the Cross*—a biblical epic "directed by the future director, according to [George] Tyler, of 'Marching Song.' . . . Then coffee, this doughnut or that, and you can be back in Woodstock for vespers. . . . Please, please!"

In early January, Orson organized a reading of "Marching Song" in Highland Park in front of his surrogate family; a sprinkling of Todd School alumni; and invited guests such as John Clayton, artist Helen S. Levey, recitalist Hazel Felman, and drama critic Lloyd Lewis of the *Chicago Daily News*, who was also a Civil War expert. Reciting his own script aloud taught Orson a few things. "Modern dialogue is always dialogue of implication," he wrote to the headmaster, who missed the event. "Mine goes where angels fear to read, hits big mo-ments right on the head, suggesting nothing, which, they tell me, is a method difficult almost unto impossibility." The reading went off with "an emphatic bang," Orson reported, but it was a last hurrah for "Marching Song."

Orson spent that winter with too much time on his hands, shut-tling anxiously between Chicago and Woodstock, debating future projects—*his* future, really—with Skipper. They mulled ideas for a musical about another Big American like John Brown. Only this time, Orson thought, their subject ought to be a contemporary public figure, a fictional tycoon with the story set in Chicago.

Orson had three different real-life tycoons in mind from which they might create a composite: Samuel Insull, Robert R. McCormick, and William Randolph Hearst. His parents had known all three of these men in passing; he himself had fleeting contact with them. Orson pro-posed a drama, perhaps with music and songs, about a typical Ameri-can tycoon with one foot in Chicago's newspaper world and the other in opera or show business.

Orson had met Insull in the corridors of the Chicago Civic Opera House on his Todd School tours. After unscrupulously making his fortune in electrical power, Insull had underwritten the arts and cham-pioned opera in Chicago, sometimes insisting on casting his favor-ite singers in leading roles. Insull had sponsored the comeback of his wife, actress Gladys Wallis, in the leads of plays launched in Chicago and then shipped to Broadway. Though he lived in splendor through the years of Orson's youth, Insull was eventually indicted and fled the United States to evade malfeasance charges. In the end he was captured and tried, and although he was found not guilty, he died almost penni-less. "His opera house and his millions and his baronial estate and his eventual disgrace" made Insull a natural subject for Orson's proposed story about the rise and fall of a Big American, the headmaster recalled years later.

Publisher Robert R. "Bertie" McCormick, known as "the Colonel" for his World War I service, was another local tycoon Orson had en-countered at the *Chicago Tribune* and the Tavern Club. A member of the prominent family that presided over Chicago business and soci-ety, McCormick led his newspaper in early crusades against gangsters, racketeering, and Prohibition, but by the 1930s he had turned into a conservative, even fascist-minded Republican, a bitter opponent of the New Deal. McCormick had a messy private life too: named as the debaucher of a relative's wife in a long-running, notorious divorce case, the Colonel ended up marrying his mistress, Amy Irwin Adams, in a surreptitious ceremony his own newspaper was not allowed to cover.

Orson thought he might also borrow from the story of the Colonel's cousin, Harold F. McCormick, chairman of the board of International Harvester Company, who once was married to Edith Rockefeller, daughter of the Standard Oil tycoon John D. Rockefeller. It was Harold McCormick who, after divorcing Edith Rockefeller, married the Polish opera singer Ganna Walska and attempted to launch Walska as a diva. In 1920, after paying for her singing lessons, McCormick had arranged for Walska to star in the Chicago Civic Opera production of *Zaza*, which ended with his tempestuous wife storming out during final dress rehearsals. Though Walska's abrupt departure doubtless saved her from a critical drubbing, the scandal permanently tarnished McCormick's reputation, and the marriage was short-lived.

Last but not least was William Randolph Hearst, the czar of America's largest publishing and media chain, whose newspapers and magazines typified the "yellow journalism" of the early twentieth century. Hearst was twice elected a congressman in New York, but proved unsuccessful in a series of later campaigns—for mayor of New York City, and for governor *and* lieutenant governor of New York State. Though Hearst still ran his increasingly right-wing media empire with an iron fist, after his political ambitions fizzled he lived openly with the comedic actress Marion Davies in Hollywood, while dabbling in film production as head of his own company, Cosmopolitan, whose pictures were released by MGM.

Orson had caught glimpses of Hearst on his visits to Chicago, where he roamed the offices of his newspapers. But he also knew Hearst from the many stories told about him by the newsmen of the Tavern Club, especially Ashton Stevens, Hearst's longtime friend and employee. Orson also took pride in believing that his father had been chummy with Hearst before he was born.

Orson and Skipper talked long about the Big American Idea, circling it warily. Hill mainly intended to encourage Orson. But both understood that writing another stage play about a Big Idea would mean a mountain of research and a tremendous investment of time, and neither was ready for the commitment.

After arguing about his future with Dr. Bernstein, Orson moved in for a while with John Clayton's family. "Tough days those," Clayton remembered. "Vain job hunting by day. Writing until four or five in the morning." Both Orson and Clayton were at loose ends, unemployed in the depths of the Depression. "No jobs for any of us," said Clayton. "The cash reserves dwindled." Still, Clayton was impressed by Orson's resilience. One day, when Orson was down to $1, he took his money and bought a bouquet for Mrs. Clayton and a cake for the family, bursting through the front door and proclaiming, "Let them eat cake!"

Finally cornered in Hollywood, Samson Raphaelson dutifully read the John Brown play and offered equal parts flattery and discouragement. "Stick with this boy!" Raphaelson wrote to the headmaster. "Any three pages of this script sing. But any 20 pages fall apart. Tell your star pupil to either turn this into a novel or teach him that stage plays are tight little miniatures." When George C. Tyler allowed his option on the play to lapse, Orson briefly went to work revising "Marching Song" as a book, a biography of John Brown, lest all his research go to waste.

While in Highland Park, he tried to find inspiration in Ned Moore's collection of recordings, but grew so weary of listening to "Debussy and others," he wrote, "that another symphonic blue note will find me rolling on the floor." Moore and Dr. Bernstein strongly hinted that, with his sonorous voice and professional poise, Orson might have some success on the women's club circuit, reciting behind music as his mother once did. "We recited over some of my mother's old things inclusive of Oscar Wilde and Phyllis Fergus," Orson wrote Skipper, "and even the pleasing discovery that several numbers were dedicated to me, with my name spelt out at the top in print, failed to keep me from feeling a little disillusioned about musical readings."

Orson thought about earning a little extra money writing detective stories. There were several publishers of story magazines in Chicago, and Orson knew a published fictioneer with the right connections who agreed to partner with him on a few stories under a pseudonym. Very quickly Orson amassed half a dozen linked stories that concerned, as Barbara Leaming wrote, "a young detective who lived in Baltimore with his aunt. A dilettante and a playboy of sorts, the colorful character was based on what Orson imagined his father's youth to have been like."

But Orson was itching to get far away from Highland Park. He needed to go somewhere new and different to find solace and inspiration. "The year is tearing by depressingly swift," Orson wrote to Skipper, "and boats are sailing all over the world. I'm sick of Ravinia: sick and desolate. I want to finish my [travel] book in peace. I want to get going. I'm going mad."

Now, like his father, he proposed a long voyage. "I have decided not to go to college," Orson wrote to the headmaster. With the Depression at its worst, he guessed that the investments tied to his inheritance, managed for Bernstein by the First Union Trust and Savings, were plummeting in value. "Pretty soon there's going to be a powerful inflation or something. And my money, if I still have it, won't be worth anything. I propose to enjoy it now."

But how could he concoct travel plans that would be sufficiently worthwhile to coax the necessary outlay from the parsimonious Dr. Bernstein?

Skipper understood the problem, and when Orson visited him in Woodstock in late February the headmaster came up with a Big Idea all his own. Forget John Brown, Hill said. Instead, he and Orson could collaborate on a compendium of Shakespeare plays annotated for high school teachers and students. All the intelligence and passion Orson had brought to his Shakespeare adaptations at school could be channeled into a practical and inspiring guidebook for staging the plays with young people. Orson could condense the classical works while contributing scene sketches and illustrations, as he'd done with the copies of "Marching Song" that he circulated in New York. Hill would serve as adviser and editor of the Shakespeare book, and perhaps add some writing of his own. And the Todd School could print the book and sell it by mail order.

How well Hill knew his prize pupil! Nothing excited Orson more than Shakespeare, whose body of work he had mastered, committing nearly all the most famous plays to memory. Returning to Highland Park, Orson swept his sundry other projects off the table and went feverishly to work, writing, first, a grand introduction summing up the Bard's greatness.

Shakespeare said everything. Brain to belly; every mood and minute of a man's season. His language is starlight and fireflies and the sun and the moon. He wrote it with tears and blood and beer, and his words march like heart beats. He speaks to everyone.

Orson rushed to the post office and mailed the grand introduction to Todd School, anxious for Hill's response. The headmaster recognized that he had tapped a deep well. "When I read the first few sentences of what he wrote," Hill told Barbara Leaming, "they were absolutely fantastic." He also loved the sample drawings Orson had enclosed. "Kids will love them," he wrote to Orson. "We'll fill the margins of every page."

Orson went into overdrive, pulling together everything he would need—writing tools, sketch pads, a collected Shakespeare, other books—and cramming it all into his cheap battered trunk. He proposed a working trip to Africa. He thought that if he booked an inexpensive passage on a freighter he could visit his acquaintance from Paris, Brahim El Glaoui, in Morocco, and on the return trip he could stop and meet up with Dr. Walter Starkie, an Abbey Theatre man traveling with Spanish Gypsies, who was said to be living in Seville.

Dr. Bernstein was persuaded by the merits of the project, especially since the headmaster had vouched for it. Orson's guardian agreed to release enough of his inheritance to bankroll the trip. The good cop–bad cop routine the headmaster and doctor had going with Orson worked exceedingly well. The two father figures rarely clashed directly, and while Hill was amused by Orson's frequent grumbling about Bernstein, he held his tongue and rarely seconded those complaints. Putting Orson on a ship to Africa, to go off and create an annotated Shakespeare, would suit both the frustrated guardian and the enterprising Todd School headmaster. As Hill told Barbara Leaming, "It would keep Orson occupied and it would rejuvenate the print shop."

Orson took the train to New York and boarded a freighter called the *Exermont*, which departed for Casablanca on March 20, 1933. The ship accommodated twelve paying passengers, but Orson and another person were the only ones on this voyage. He looked forward to two weeks at sea. "It is all very Eugene O'Neill and salty and shippish," Orson reported to Roger Hill. His private quarters were not luxurious, but "I can work beautifully in a two-by-four lounge in the presence of all the officers," he wrote. "The radio won't work, which is another blessing."

A week or so later, the *Exermont* passed within one hundred miles of the Azores. "This morning there was sunlight and a school of turtles, but I slept through," Orson wrote to the headmaster. "Now of course, it's raining. Nary a turtle. ... . I wish you were here. You'd love it. Everybody from the Captain down is a real character, and you can't think how out <u>on the ocean</u> it seems in a tiny freighter wallowing about in the high Atlantic. Here is a crossing that's genuine adventure, fourteen karat. Just the meals are rare fun, chasing the stews and soups around the mess and trying to keep chair and self beside the shifting scene of the table."

Orson "slept through" most days because he worked through most nights, spreading his books and notes around him as he launched into condensation and embroidery of the first play he tackled—*Julius Caesar*. He had seen *Julius Caesar* performed numerous times and even staged it himself for Todd School. But as he worked, he felt the nagging underside of creativity, an insecurity that people didn't always associate with him. Behind the face of soaring confidence, he was questioning himself. "I've gotten some swell ideas about Brutus and the rest, what was going on in the author's mind when he wrote them down, etcetera," Orson wrote to Hill. The work made him feel "much nearer to *Caesar* than I ever dreamed I could. . . . Just near enough to know how far I am. And Skipper, I've always known *Caesar* pretty well, and others, *Hamlet* even, are terribly foreign. What do I know about *Hamlet*? What do I know about Shakespeare? I feel an awful bluff."

Doubt made him cautious, and he slowed down. The first batch of scenes, which he mailed when the ship briefly made port, contained "grotesque word ordering," Orson warned the headmaster, along with

"repetitions and misfirings." At first, he felt trepidation about encroaching on the Bard with his own editing and annotations. "What
right have I to give credulous and believing innocents an inflection for
a mighty line of Shakespeare's? Who I am to say that this is 'tender'
and this 'angrily' and this 'with a smile'?" He cautioned Hill that his
work might require "a little spring cleaning" before it was ready to
show the world. "I wonder, will you think there's not enough, or as I
fear today, much too much? Is our whole idea wrong? I wish to high
heaven you were here to reassure me."

As he did throughout his life, Orson sprinkled little drawings and
verse into his correspondence. In the earliest surviving letter from this
trip, Orson offered Hill an ode to the indelible experience of seafaring:

Days now numberless, it seems to me.
We've lolled and wallowed in the lusty sea.
Careening and squeaking, teetering and creaking.
Curtseying and kicking down the waves.
And screwing through the working waters of the sea.

Time is a thing that used to be.
The order and ascent of days is nothing now.

The March-blown, hail-fretted oceans mawl our bobbing bedlam.
Shiver the empty Exermont *from screw to prow.*
And yet still to Africa there move a million mountains, growing now.
An acreage hysterical for us to plow.
Crash in the galley.
Crash in the shelter deck.
Crash on the bowing prow.
Crash on the bowing prow.

Time is a thing that used to be.
The order and ascent of days is nothing now.

"Today," the letter concluded, "for the first time it's fairly calm and
we're headed Southish" toward the coast of Africa. "There's no hail to
speak of . . . My love, Orson."

When the ship docked at Casablanca, Orson left it for Marrakech, where he hoped to find Brahim El Glaoui, the son of T'hami El Glaoui, the pasha of Marrakech—the "King of the Atlas," as he was known. Orson arrived in time for Aid Al-Kebir, an important Islamic holiday, a four-day festival that marked the end of the annual pilgrimage to Mecca.

"Exciting is the word," Orson wrote from Marrakech. "The pleasure city of the Bedouin, the mountain clansmen and the Graid Caid, the high capital of Islamic fanaticism; frenzied, noisy, wicked, utterly proud, a violent place. I have been lying here in bed brooding over the typewriter which I have perched on my knees in the frantically peach-colored French quilts, trying to frame sentences for you about this wild, swaggering city."

Writing late at night, he threw the shutters of his hotel window open to "a garden-scented, star-populous, moon-bright and very noisy night. . . . A million dogs from the Mella to the Medinah howl without pause: locusts, gramophones, flutes, drums, cymbals, crowing cocks, the sleighbellish ringing of the taxi carriages, hoarse Arabic and nasal French, music and more music . . .

"A night to be out in the streets."

He drank sweet thick coffee and gazed out the window. Whenever the street parade dwindled, his typewriter started up, disturbing the neighbors till they banged on his walls. His goal was to write until dawn and catch a glimpse when the sultan passed on the way to prayer.

Orson spent his first days in Morocco writing—not the Shakespeare book, but a flurry of letters home to Roger Hill and Dr. Maurice Bernstein. "Visiting sunsets and Kasbahs and Souks and whatnot," Orson reported to Skipper. "In a mere week, I've spent most of my money and all of my time doing just what I swore to you I wouldn't. Don't blame me, blame Africa."

The El Glaoui family was not easily located; the members were dispersed among several castles in Fez. After a week Orson left Marrakech by bus, heading for the French protectorate near the Grand Atlas Mountains, expecting to meet up with Brahim El Glaoui there and grow "horribly industrious and economical." Besides passengers the bus was filled with stinking chickens, and Orson struck up a friendship with an elderly curator from the Rijksmuseum in Amsterdam, who was roaming Morocco painting landscapes. Together in Fez, he and this kindred soul knocked on the door of the palatial residence of Brahim El Glaoui.

Orson told Barbara Leaming that Brahim El Glaoui and his family warmly welcomed the visitors, inviting the young American and the elderly Dutch museum curator into their home and then bringing them along on a "two-week picnic" that wove through the Atlas Mountains in a long train with other European guests and a parade of retainers. (It was not unlike the extravagant picnic party led by Charles Foster Kane in *Citizen Kane*.) Every night the two oddly paired travelers were treated to elaborate feasts, singing, dancing, and storytelling. Six guests shared a tent, and Brahim El Glaoui made a gift to his guests of concubines from his entourage, Welles claimed. "Entrancing experience," Welles told Leaming, as usual stingy with the carnal details. The Dutch curator didn't think it was so entrancing, and hopped a bus to Casablanca.

Over the years, Welles would develop a reputation for mythmaking, but he rarely made up stories about himself out of whole cloth; imaginative embroidery of actual events was more his style. The stories he told about his time with Brahim El Glaoui were too fabulous for many people to swallow. "No one believes me," Orson dolefully told an interviewer later in the 1930s, "so I've stopped talking about them any more." Decades later, Welles's biographer Simon Callow made it clear that he doubted the whole business—elderly Dutchman, concubines, and all.

One thing seems certain: Orson neglected his work on Shakespeare in Morocco. "I didn't do much writing at all," he later admitted, "I did a lot of reading." He was probably still in Fez when his eighteenth birthday came—there is a monthlong gap in his surviving letters—but after lingering a while longer in the French protectorate, he boarded a bus to Tangier. From there he took a ferry to the southern tip of Spain, and then traveled by train to Barcelona, where he was expecting to receive money from Dr. Bernstein via Western Union. Barcelona was in the throes of a workers' strike, but the doctor had sent a bonanza: payments from a magazine that had accepted Orson's pseudonymous short stories about a young Baltimore sleuth. He was suddenly flush.

Unfortunately for Welles scholars, neither the identity of his pulp-fiction collaborator nor their pseudonym has ever been discovered. To this day, Orson's short stories remain lost. Pulp fiction historians Sam Moskowitz and Nils Hardin tried tracking them down in the late 1970s, corresponding with Welles when he was living in Los Angeles. "I did indeed write in the pulps," Welles told them, "and earned my living doing it for the better part of a year, but I did this through an arrangement with a pulp writer who had all the proper connections and who sold my stories under various established nom de plumes [*sic*] of his own. I never saw these in print because I was living in Africa and Spain and this long-forgotten partner's name escapes me."

Perhaps it was John Clayton, one of the names Welles dredged from his memory. But he had already forgotten the man's name even by the time of a deposition he gave in 1949. When lawyers for Ferdinand Lundberg, digging for parallels between *Imperial Hearst*—Lundberg's biography of William Randolph Hearst—and *Citizen Kane*, asked Welles what other literary works he had written before *Kane*, Orson volunteered that he had written "two or three novels unpublished" and a number of short stories. What had happened to this early fiction? "All destroyed," Welles told Lundberg's lawyers. "I do not know where the manuscripts for special articles and short stories are, if they indeed exist, and I have no memoranda as to the dates or publication of these works."

"For what it's worth," Welles wrote to the two pulp fiction historians in the late 1970s, "I know we [he and his coauthor] did manage on a few occasions to place stories in *Adventure*—considered then to be the ultimate in its field. Most of my stuff, as I remember, ran in lesser magazines." Besides the "detective series with a rich, young aristocratic sleuth living with his three elderly aunts in Baltimore," the filmmaker said, he also wrote "a good deal of science fiction of the Lobster-Men type and a few novelettes and stories laid in the Far East.

"I'm sorry, but this absolutely exhausts all recollection," Welles concluded.

There were no letters from Skipper in Barcelona. Taking this as a sign of disapproval, Orson booked passage on a slow ship stopping frequently along the south and west coasts of Spain, and rededicated himself to writing.

The only draft he had completed and mailed was *Julius Caesar*. Now he plunged into *The Merchant of Venice*, pushing himself through the nights. By the time the vessel reached Malaga he had made progress— but once again the process of adapting Shakespeare proved daunting. "Besides being a rip-snorting romance, moving and hair-tingling from the first entrance to the last exeunt," *The Merchant of Venice* "is one of the most imperishable collections of poetic writing ever produced. God! I hate gooing it up!"

Dawn was "sweetening the sultry Spanish night" as he labored on *Merchant*, he wrote to Skipper. He had "never worked so hard" and "produced so little. I gave up trips and things, I really did, everything except the most perfunctory sight-seeing; since I left Tangier I've stuck in this wretched little bake-house of a boat and screwed my face into granny-knots." Orson prodded Hill for reassurance, worrying about the "limitation of space, and the kids' lack of a stage vocabulary, and the dangers of scaring them off us with anything, <u>anything</u>, faintly esoteric or syllabled." When his nerves overwhelmed him, or he needed a distraction, Orson toyed with other projects: a one-act play; a Greek tragedy ("with masks and a good company of six actors," he wrote to Hill); a "Big Idea for filming *Treasure Island*." *

Late at night in the Malaga harbor, however, he decided he was closing in on an authoritative approach to *The Merchant of Venice*. His working draft was "messy, pasted, scratched and scribbled," he conceded, the stage directions were "garbagey," the "descriptions of emotions . . . simply bloody, there's no defending that." But his writing had begun to sharpen; the latest scenes evinced real quality. "<u>The drawings are going to be hot!</u>" he wrote proudly. His once tentative grasp of this play was now "very good—O, infinitely better than it was on *Julius Caesar*."

As dawn approached, Orson completed his draft of *Merchant*, just in time to mail the pages to the headmaster ("sailing time, mailing time"). He was still undecided about what the third play should be:

---

* Decades later, Welles would be involved twice in films of *Treasure Island*: a 1965 short, which he directed, and a 1972 feature. In both versions he played Long John Silver.

Hamlet? Twelfth Night? A Midsummer Night's Dream? Much Ado About Nothing?
He would think it over as he sailed on to the river port of Seville, writing a chatty letter to Hortense.

Seville was a travel poster come alive, one of the most enchanting cities in Spain, its ancient culture a patchwork of Roman and Moorish traditions. Orson left the ship to meet with Dr. Walter Starkie, professor of Romance languages at Trinity College, who was on the board of directors of the Abbey Theatre. Orson had heard Starkie speak in Chicago on the beauties and mysteries of Spain, and had met him in Dublin.

A scholar of Gypsies who roamed Spain with them and spoke their Romany language fluently, Starkie was at work on a new volume of *Raggle Taggle*, his ongoing series of picaresque travelogue books. The latest installment would cover his wanderings in Barbary, Andalusia, and La Mancha, and life in the Triana quarter of Seville.

Triana was "the home of song and dancing," as Starkie wrote, with Gypsies, flamenco artists, and bullfighters idling in the parks and cafés. Orson was instantly enamored of the sleepless quarter, with its orange blossom scent and constantly thrumming guitars. With his pulp-fiction earnings easing his financial concerns, he took a flat above a "fuzz castle" (bordello), with money left over to buy drinks for "half of Andalusia," as he told Barbara Leaming.

Just across the Puente de Triana, spanning the wide Guadalquivir River, lay the city proper and its landmark bullring, La Maestranza. Seville was "the city of the bull," and spring was the season for bullfighting fever. Orson had just read Ernest Hemingway's *Death in the Afternoon*, celebrating the rituals and traditions of bullfighting. He mingled "with the bull-fighting set and soon was helping out 'backstage,'" Peter Noble wrote.

Seville was the setting of another of Orson's elusive legends. Did the eighteen-year-old really take bullfighting lessons from a toreador at a local ranch, briefly launching himself in "a succession of pitiful bullfights" (Leaming's phrase) in which he billed himself as "El Americano"? And when he failed as a bullfighter, did Orson really relaunch himself as a picador, who stabs the bull with a lance from on horseback to weaken and goad it? Did the scars he proudly exhibited to interviewers in later years truly originate in the bullring?

Simon Callow, skeptical about the tale, pointed out that Orson's bullfighting wounds "tended to travel a little" from one interview to the next. Welles told Leaming that at one point rowdy audience members had "showered him with beer bottles (from which he still bears a slight scar on his upper lip)." According to Kenneth Tynan, however, it was his thigh that suffered injury. When David Frost interviewed the filmmaker, the injury migrated to his neck—and there were "others" he'd rather not bare, Orson hinted, since Frost's show was "a family type of program."

What to believe? It's true that Orson lived in Seville for only a month or so, but he had already proved he could pack a lot of frenetic activity into the briefest time. Seventy-five years after Orson came to Seville, two European filmmakers spent months chasing the truth, and their documentary *El Americano* insists that Orson participated in at least four bullfights as "El Americano," with bulls he purchased with his pulp-fiction windfall. (Paying for the bulls was one shortcut to becoming a matador.)

There's no question that Seville initiated him into the world of bullfighting and launched his many friendships with the bravest matadors and a lifelong reverence for the sport that soured only toward the end, when he began to feel pity for the bulls. Over time Welles would draw close to Antonio Ordóñez, a top bullfighter of his era, whom Ernest Hemingway chronicled admiringly in *The Dangerous Summer,* and also the Peruvian *torera* Conchita Cintrón, one of the greatest women ever to command the ring, for whose autobiography Welles supplied the introduction.

Years later, while shooting *Mr. Arkadin* in Madrid, Welles habitually stretched out his lunch hour to attend the bullfights of his famous friends. One time, the filmmaker returned after witnessing one of Ordóñez's storied turns in the ring, a riveting bullfight that was already the buzz of the city. His assistant, Juan Cobos, asked Welles about what he had seen. "Juan, you know how much I love bullfighting," Welles answered solemnly. "It was an extraordinary *faena.* Ordonez's art was so great that I was deeply moved. Tears came to my eyes, and for a time I couldn't see well for the beauty of that magnificent performance."

Working on the same film, an elderly assistant producer challenged Welles—saying, as a native Andalusian who prided himself on his knowledge of bullfighting, that he doubted the legend of "El Americano." "In the history of a towering art," he had heard Orson boast, "there can be very few people who were as bad as I was." But if Orson were as poor a toreador as he claimed, the Andalusian said, surely he would have heard of him! Welles roared with laughter.

Orson's one-month idyll in Seville also established his lifelong love affair with Spain. Along with the magnificent food and wine, Spain was the land of Cervantes and Don Quixote. "[Don Quixote] is better than any single creation in Homer or Tolstoi or Shakespeare," Welles once said, "this heraldic creature . . . this tattered, battered, divine old dreaming fool." Spain was the inspiration for monumental painters and artists such as Velásquez, Goya, and Picasso, whom Orson revered, the home of epic explorers like Cortés, Pizarro, Magellan, and Amerigo Vespucci.

Seville was very diverting, and once again the Shakespeare project was put on hold until Orson finally made his way to Lisbon and departed the Iberian peninsula in the first week of June, with just enough money left to fund the voyage home. He would have to make up for the lost time while crossing the Atlantic, and he did. He arrived back in Chicago with solid drafts of the three Shakespeare plays ("edited for reading and arranged for staging") that would form the eventual book: *Julius Caesar*, *The Merchant of Venice*, and *Twelfth Night*.

CHAPTER 9

1933–1934

The Saga Begins

Back in Chicago by mid-June after three months away, Orson planned to spend the rest of the summer revising and polishing the Shakespeare book. The remaining work included finishing the scene designs and illustrations that would accompany the text. "He turned out literally thousands of detailed sketches, most of them crumpled and thrown away in angry frustration by a self-critical young artist," Roger Hill recalled. The headmaster, who was summering in Michigan, consulted with Orson by phone and letter.

Without the Ravinia music festival to attract him to Highland Park, Orson took a room on Rush Street, a few blocks from the Newberry Library, furnishing it with a rug, a daybed, a wicker chair, and a folding table, all from Dr. Bernstein's attic. Orson sketched his designs for the book on a large drawing board, working through the night and sleeping until late morning, when his guardian woke him for "brunch—my lunch, his breakfast" (Bernstein's words) at the Tavern Club.

All the Tavern Club regulars were still in place: newspapermen Lloyd Lewis, Charles Collins, John Clayton, Ned Moore, and Ashton Stevens. In that summer of 1933, much of the talk revolved around the Century of Progress Exposition, a world's fair that had opened on near South Side parkland in May, as Orson was acquiring his bullfighting scars in Seville. The fair's most conspicuous symbol, and one of its most popular attractions, was the Sky Ride, which ran along the shoreline of Lake Michigan and carried passengers up high from one end of the fairgrounds to the other. Clayton was now involved with public relations for the Century of Progress Exposition.

One night in early August, Clayton dropped by Rush Street and coaxed Orson away from his worktable to a party at Hazel Felman's house. The guest list would be a who's who of local arts and society, Clayton promised—including Roger and Hortense Hill, who were passing through Chicago. Felman was a contemporary of Orson's mother and, like her, a star on the women's club circuit. She composed musical settings for the works of Carl Sandburg, Robert Frost, and other well-known poets. Felman had just performed at the Century of Progress.

During the party, Orson found himself squeezed into one end of a room where people were taking turns on the piano. He was discussing his abandoned play about John Brown with Lloyd Lewis, the *Chicago Daily News* drama critic and Civil War expert, when a reedy professorial type eased into the corner with them. The newcomer asked Orson if he was a pianist waiting his turn. "No," Orson replied haughtily, looking the man up and down, he was *not* a pianist. ("Here's another queen!" Barbara Leaming says he was thinking.)

By a surprising "jump of association," the professorial type later recalled, he asked if Orson was "the extraordinary young American actor" who had starred on the Dublin stage, and about whom he'd read so much in the Chicago press. Yes, Orson admitted. "I *used* to be an actor," he added. "Now I am an author." In fact, Orson explained, he was currently working on a new guidebook to staging Shakespeare plays for high school teachers and students. "Let's get out of here and have a talk," said the man, introducing himself as Thornton Wilder.

It seems incredible that Orson did not recognize the tall, bespectacled Wilder, who was as famous as anyone in Chicago, or on the larger American literary scene. Wilder had earned his first Pulitzer Prize for his novel *The Bridge of San Luis Rey* in 1928, and taught English and classic literature at the University of Chicago. Even if Orson had never seen Wilder's photograph, he would have glimpsed the author at the Drama League tournament in the spring of 1932, when *The Long Christmas Dinner*, a playlet telescoping ninety years of Christmas dinners into a single act, had one of its first public performances. This was the same Drama League tournament where Orson directed the Todd boys in *Twelfth Night*, competing (and winning) in another category.

The meeting between Wilder and Welles was probably contrived by John Clayton. Wilder was intrigued by Orson, whose height was towering (he even towered over Wilder), and whom he later recalled as "rather pudgy-faced . . . with a wing of brown hair falling into his eyes and a vague Oxford epigrammatic manner." Wilder bore Orson away to his rooms at the University of Chicago, where the two enjoyed a "galvanizing" talk (Wilder's word). They conversed late into the night, warming to each other as they discovered shared interests and a similar background (both of them were born in Wisconsin—Wilder in Madison). Orson's vaguely Oxonian manner was a pose derived "from his misery," Wilder decided, "and [it] soon drops under a responsible pair of eyes like mine." Orson might have an outsize personality, Wilder thought, but he also possessed depth of mind and character.

They talked about "Marching Song" and Orson's other writing projects. Wilder offered to read the play about John Brown and also the guidebook to staging Shakespeare when it was ready, but he wondered aloud whether Orson could be satisfied as only a writer, keeping his distance from acting. Wilder knew all about the Gate Theatre and saw Orson's eyes light up as the young man talked about his triumphs in Dublin. Orson told Wilder that he despaired of attracting the attention of important Broadway agents or producers. Wilder told Orson not to give up; his commanding physical presence and godly voice gave him natural advantages. "I urged him," Wilder recalled, "to earn his living as an actor and not to despise so acknowledged a gift."

Wilder told Orson to give New York another try. The famous writer knew about several upcoming shows, and offered to introduce him to influential people. Producer Jed Harris, for example, was casting a new play called *The Green Bay Tree*. Wilder said there was a good part still available, and Harris was a friend of his who was also angling to produce Wilder's translation of Ibsen's *A Doll House*.

Another of Wilder's friends was Katharine Cornell, who with her husband, the director Guthrie McClintic, was organizing a touring repertory company. Wilder was even closer to Cornell, for whom he had translated *Lucrèce*, which she had starred in on Broadway earlier in

1933. Cornell planned to lead her company across America performing three plays—one of which would be *Romeo and Juliet*, her first foray into Shakespeare. Cornell was going to play Juliet, and the key supporting role of Mercutio, Romeo's friend, was not yet settled.

One of the other two plays on the tour would be George Bernard Shaw's *Candida*, with Cornell reprising her acclaimed Broadway turn as the title character. The actor playing Mercutio in *Romeo and Juliet* would rotate as Marchbanks, a young poet trying to woo the formidable Candida. Mercutio was a brash extroverted character, while Marchbanks, as Shaw wrote, was "a strange, shy youth of eighteen, slight, effeminate, with a delicate childish voice, and a hunted and tormented expression and shrinking manner." Wilder thought Orson had the right look and the range of talent to play both of these important roles.

Orson's eyes lit up again at the mention of Cornell. Fate, everything was fate.

Wilder said he would write letters of introduction to Harris, Cornell, McClintic, and a few other personages—including Alexander Woollcott, the redoubtable drama critic of *The New Yorker*, "at times Wilder's mentor, at times his critic, and very often his advocate," in the words of Wilder's biographer Penelope Niven. Woollcott, above all, would go the extra mile for Wilder.

When he left Wilder, Orson was in a daze. He never forgot that night, the pep talk from Wilder that brought him back to his first calling.

Keeping his word, Wilder dashed off letters to friends in high places, extolling the young man he had just met. "The whole town [of Dublin] was staggered" by his performance as the Duke in *Jew Süss*, the playwright wrote to Woollcott, so much so that Orson next was persuaded to play Othello, which was also "wonderful beyond belief," and later, "Hamlet's father and stepfather." Never mind the errors of fact, which may have been conspiratorial white lies: "The name is Orson Welles and it's going far," Wilder declared.

A professional encourager, a mentor to many young artists and writers in his lifetime, Wilder was amused to read in later years that he had "discovered" Orson Welles. He saw his role in the matter modestly. But Welles felt he owed Wilder an eternal debt of gratitude.

They stayed friendly and never lost touch. The Pulitzer Prize–winning author had given him a helping hand when he badly needed one and, like an oracle, had prophesied his greatness.

After Wilder performed his favor, Orson tortured himself with worry that he would be betraying Hill if he moved to New York without finishing the Shakespeare book. The headmaster was in Woodstock preparing for the fall term, hard to reach and even harder to pin down—"with no more than a 'wotta-mess-I'm-in' over the telephone—and _my_ phone call too!" as Orson complained in a letter to Hortense Hill. "And me stranded here for some more time with Mercutios streaming into the casting offices of the Belasco and other important things happening when I could just as well be streaming a little myself between periods at my drawing-board in the Algonquin!"

Hortense told him not to fret about the book, and Skipper finally found time to say the same, graciously telling Orson to go and wishing him luck. The young man was packed long before Wilder phoned with auspicious news: Alexander Woollcott had agreed to see him.

Orson "never passed so serene a Pullman night" as when he departed Chicago in "hay-feverish haste," as he wrote to Skipper. "The train was nice with good food in an Edwardian diner, and lots of wonderful people" on board including former Illinois congresswoman Ruth Hanna McCormick and Secretary of Labor Frances Perkins, bound for the intermediate stop of Washington, D.C.

Arriving in New York and checking into the Algonquin Hotel, Orson showered, shaved, unpacked, and made his first phone calls, to Woollcott and Guthrie McClintic. (Katharine Cornell was in Europe.) McClintic could not be coaxed to the phone, but Woollcott was "colossally nice" and made an appointment. "The rest of them," Orson wrote, "are only a matter of time, and not so much of it, they will call me, they will be delighted, even their secretaries are nice." After his first round of calls, his spirits rose higher. "I am a New Yorker now," Orson reported to Skipper. "Broadway is deader than Broadway [ever was] and hotter, but the old tread is still nimble, and they turned to gape at me, I was so fresh and smiling." The support of someone besides the headmaster, his guardian, and the many members of his surrogate family—someone as illustrious as Thornton Wilder—meant the world to him. His letters in the weeks ahead were filled with confidence and good cheer.

"You have given me a whole ring of keys to this city," Orson wrote to Wilder gratefully.

And Woollcott, who put out the welcome mat for the young Chicagoan early the next week, looked to be "the pass key," in Orson's words. The influential drama critic invited Orson to his Forty-Second Street apartment overlooking the East River for cocktails with the humorist Dorothy Parker, before the two men left to dine "salubriously" (Orson's word) at Voisin, the midtown temple of French cooking. Merry, malicious, and sentimental in roughly equal parts, weighing 250 pounds, with large thick spectacles, a small beak, and a droll mustache, Woollcott never went out dressed less than magnificently. His customary evening garb—wide-brimmed black hat, flowing cape, and walking cane with an ivory head—might have given Orson ideas for the future.

As was often the case with people meeting him for the first time, Orson impressed Woollcott initially as a physical specimen. While Woollcott was notoriously acerbic—his barbed reviews were feared in the stage world—he found himself surprisingly at ease in the company of an intelligent young man almost thirty years his junior who appreciated an excellent cocktail and French cuisine. Woollcott had expected to find Orson a hunk of unformed putty. Yet here was an eighteen-year-old who seemed able to hold forth credibly on any subject—and who listened well too. "Conversation was the most important item in Woollcott's life," wrote the critic's biographer, Howard Teichmann. "Writing and eating ran a close second and third, but talk always came first."

Woollcott mentioned that Orson coincidentally bore the same last name as a supporting character in *The Dark Tower*, a play he was currently writing with George S. Kaufman. Considering Orson's mature bearing, along with his résumé of aged and bearded parts, Woollcott wondered if he might care to audition for that role, that of a middle-aged man. "All kinds of people seem to be reading this part," wrote Orson, "and pretty soon, if I can manage to be convincingly paternal to a young lady who is obviously thirty-two, I am to be given my opportunity—maybe even to put on the makeup and drive over and surprise Mr. Kaufman."

New York's most important drama critic made good on his promise to help Orson, taking him out and buying him better clothes for his appointments with producers, including new shoes to replace the worn ones that ill fitted his huge feet. After that first dinner, Orson wrote, Woollcott kept in touch, "calling me up and asking me what he can do for me and being generally pretty wonderful."

It was harder to pass muster with Jed Harris. The Austrian-born producer and director was already a Broadway legend, admired by many, loathed by others, but easily "the most exciting person in the American theater," in Orson's words. Their first meeting, according to Orson, was "an unpleasant ordeal."

"He has a way of putting one on the witness-stand," Orson wrote to Wilder. "On the bench, as though one were guilty of something dastardly, out of which one is to get oneself only by fast talking, and the right answers to Mr. Harris'—permit me—prosecutiating [*sic*] cross-examinations. He shut me up finally with a laugh, and 'All right, we can only take so much!'

"Then he turned to an impressive underling (Jewish) who had been doubling as a sort of rock of Gibraltar behind him—Harris—and clerk of the court—and said to him, 'This boy is the Baron Munchausen of the theatre'—to which suspicious compliment I didn't know the answer.'"

Their second meeting was "very different," Orson wrote. This time he brought a sheaf of clippings to show Harris. "He squinted carefully at the notices," Orson wrote to Wilder. "Squinted carefully at me and began to talk—every now and then he would stop and ask me little disconcerting things, such as—Who were my favorite American actors? When had I seen Ruth Gordon? Did I like Helen Hayes? Did I admire Katharine Cornell? Had I ever played a madman? Had I ever played Shakespeare? What plays had I seen in New York last year?"

Orson was in his element, trading opinions and discussing theatrical esoterica. "In between," he wrote to Wilder, "[Harris] talked and that was magic. Every time that little man stood up—and he was a ridiculous figure in a sports sweater and shirt-tails—his pants were being altered in the next room—it was an exhilarating and exciting experience."

Harris too was won over. Unfortunately, the producer had finalized the casting of his new play, *The Green Bay Tree*, but he said he could arrange for Orson to meet the scenic, lighting, and costume designer Robert Edmond Jones. As leading lights of the American theater, Jones and his wife, the vocal coach Margaret Carrington, were certain to have any number of possibilities in the pipeline. Harris thought Orson would be perfect for Mercutio and Marchbanks in Cornell's company, but he "regretted" that the touring job "would tie me up for the whole season. Mr. McClintic, Harris hoped, would 'have the imagination' to give it to me."

Orson wondered if there might be a part for him in any of Harris's other planned shows in development, if things did not pan out with Cornell and McClintic. "He shakes his head," Orson reported to Wilder, "said he thought I shouldn't be given 'ordinary' parts, that I needed something 'vivid.' He has plans for the future which seem to involve Miss Katharine Hepburn, an Englishman called, I think, Lawrence [*sic*] Olivier, Shakespeare, and it was suggested, me.

"It was stressed that I am not to move very emphatically in any direction without consulting him. After some final and very valuable advice about reading Marchbanks, I was dismissed again."

Another of Wilder's letters introduced him to Edward "Ned" Sheldon, the playwright from Chicago, whose career Orson had followed avidly. Crippling rheumatoid arthritis had ended Sheldon's active writing and kept him bedridden. But he was an informal dramaturg for New York show people, and Sheldon would be a sounding board for many of Orson's projects in the years ahead.

Orson flew through his first week, ushered into the presence of Broadway royalty thanks to Wilder's name. "All of these great people," he wrote to Wilder, tend "to geld me into brain prostrations and hideous impotencies of speech—And what shall I say to them? Always, it seems, the wrong thing. But they are very kind and if I don't cover myself with glory now you've opened up this New York to me—why then there's nothing to cover."

One exception to the overwhelmingly positive reception was director Guthrie McClintic, the husband of Katharine Cornell. When Orson was informed that McClintic wouldn't be able to see him for at least a month—because Tallulah Bankhead, the intended star of his new play, *Jezebel*, had fallen ill, throwing him into a tizzy—Woollcott "executed a hearty sniff and straightaway got on the phone," Orson reported to Wilder. "Read out letter by you to him (Mr. Woollcott), about me, to Mr. McClintic, and won me a presentation at Beekman Place that night." (Woollcott seemed to enjoy waving his magic wand for Orson. "'And anybody else?' he offered the next morning.")

Orson was instructed to phone McClintic after 11:30 P.M., when *Jezebel* rehearsals had wrapped for the night. The night he called, he was told to hurry over to the director's East Side address. He jumped into a taxi. "The great producer himself met me at the door, work-worn, but very cordial and pleasantly folksy in flannel slacks and a Hollywood sport-shirt widely opened to a chest proud with an incredible harvest of black hair," Orson wrote to Wilder afterward. "He waved me up to what is now visible of his apartment—it's shrouded in cellophane for the summer—and offered me drinks and then confidences, one after the other, before I could as much as unleash your letter. It was breathtaking but friendly.

"The confidences concerned many things—his liver, his hopes, his fears; Miss Bankhead's liver, which is keeping her in bed, and the rehearsals in a hospital, and her hopes and fears; you and Nazis, the Nazis and Mr. McClintic; Mr. McClintic and Shakespeare; Shakespeare and the public; the use of mirrors on the stage; the trouble with scene designers; the troubles with the theatre; Mr. McClintic's troubles.—

"And all of this, for some reasons, put me at my ease."

McClintic found himself at ease too, "indeed, so much so I'm afraid I may have overstayed my welcome," Orson recounted. Like Woollcott, McClintic was struck by "this extraordinary-looking young man with his beautiful voice and speech," as McClintic himself later recalled. After a while, Orson told Wilder, McClintic "got his feet under him and we started on me."

McClintic talked about the upcoming tour and "the Mercutio-Marchbanks problems," increasingly implying that Orson's casting was a fait accompli. The director fell to discussing the third show in the rotation, Rudolf Besier's *The Barretts of Wimpole Street*, another of Cornell's Broadway triumphs. He mentioned the role Orson might play, that of shy, stuttering Octavius, the brother of Cornell's character, the poet Elizabeth Barrett. Finally he asked Orson, rather casually, if he wanted the job. "Of course I did and we discussed that at some pleasant length." McClintic said he would phone Orson the next week. "He would wire Miss Cornell and ask her what she thought about a Marchbanks that was six feet one. I went home eventually—very thrilled."

He used the intervening time to jump back into the Shakespeare book project, and to dash off grateful letters to Thornton Wilder, Roger Hill, and Dr. Maurice Bernstein. When writing to Wilder, Orson made abject apologies for his weak spelling. And it *was* writing to Wilder, not typing, because Orson recalled Wilder proclaiming his preference for longhand during their all-night gabfest in Chicago. "I can only say that I am busy thanking my Gods for you," Orson wrote to Wilder. "For the wonderful things you've done for me and more for our friendship—whose growth is my prayer, but which I can illumine only by a very deep devotion."

His thanks to Roger Hill were even more fervent. "My god Skipper, I owe you my life!" As a congratulatory gift, Hill mailed Orson a copy of *On Reading Shakespeare*, a new book by the noted critic Logan Pearsall Smith. Orson said he "gobbled" up the book "the minute I got it," though it "should have been relished, sniffed, savoured and delayed like Hortense's fruit-cake." The gift refreshed Orson's enthusiasm for their own Shakespeare book, which was intended for young people performing—not reading—the Bard. Smith, "bless his whimsical heart," was persuasive on the merits of reading Shakespeare, but couldn't fathom the value of *acting* the plays.

"Only an actor can read a play for all it's worth," Orson told Skipper with born-again actor's fervor. "Acting is fun. Good theatre means entertainment. Our answer to the voice raised in objection is simply, as you've always said, why not begin Shakespeare by having a good time?"

He had dozens of sketches left to finish for their Shakespeare book, and while waiting for word from McClintic he worked straight through several nights in a row in order to catch up, asking Hill to send more of his favorite charcoal paper from his favorite Chicago art store.

At last, McClintic phoned to tell him that Cornell had tentatively approved him to play Mercutio, Marchbanks, and Octavius Barrett. Suddenly, his days were filled with appointments. The book deadline would have to be pushed back, Orson wrote to Hill apologetically.

"Please don't look for any [more] productivity on my part until things settle down a little more."

First, however, Cornell wanted him to undergo voice training with Margaret Carrington. Mrs. Carrington, the older sister of actor Walter Huston, had been an accomplished singer and spoken-word recitalist before becoming the most sought-after voice expert in New York's stage community. She had famously guided a nervous John Barrymore through his first Shakespeare performances on Broadway, his triumphant *Richard III* in 1919, and later his landmark *Hamlet*.

Inviting the young Chicago actor to her Park Avenue apartment, Mrs. Carrington thrilled Orson by brandishing the same copy of the script of *Hamlet* she had used when coaching Barrymore—complete with surviving notes in the actor's hand. Carrington, who projected "physical vitality, psychic intensity and an imperturbable air of authority," in the words of scholar Michael A. Morrison, listened as Orson recited passages from *Hamlet* that he'd long known by heart. "Enthuses pretty much," Orson wrote to Skipper. "Will coach me."

Three weeks after arriving in New York, Orson was officially invited to join Katharine Cornell's repertory ensemble. "Mr. McClintic hasn't even asked me to read!" an amazed Orson scribbled to Skipper on "a night of triumph" after signing the contract. "Biggest and best debut in America for me!" he wired to his guardian.

McClintic ordered up a portrait sitting with Florence Vandamm, the top Broadway photographer, and Orson's casting was announced in the *New York Times* on September 25, 1933. On the same day, Charles Collins devoted a longer article to Orson in the *Chicago Tribune*, touting the young man's forthcoming Shakespeare book, the play "Marching Song" ("which the Gate Theatre has accepted"), and the equally baseless claim (courtesy of Dr. Bernstein) that the eighteen-year-old theatrical "prodigy" was "the grandson of Gideon Welles, secretary of the Navy during the Civil War."

An overjoyed Orson wrote to Hill: "Looks rather like the saga has begun."

The national tour featuring the legendary Katharine Cornell's Shakespearean debut was a big event in the New York theater world. As the

New York Times noted, "the ghosts of past magnificence" hovered over *Romeo and Juliet*. Could Cornell, now entering her forties, her hair silvering, capture the youthful spirit of a Juliet that had been defined by Julia Marlowe, Helena Modjeska, Mary Anderson, Adelaide Neilson, and other great actresses, in performances some living theatergoers had actually witnessed?

Cornell never had performed in repertory—let alone in a repertory troupe under her own leadership; neither had she made a "grand tour of the country," an increasingly rare undertaking for stage companies. The planned itinerary would cover seventeen thousand miles and seventy-five cities and towns over six and a half months. Many of the stops along the way would be one-night stands in places where Cornell had never appeared, with the surefire *Barretts of Wimpole Street* dominating the schedule. The experiment was going to culminate with *Romeo and Juliet* opening on Broadway in the late spring of 1934.

The tour would be a kind of apogee for the marriage of McClintic and Cornell. McClintic was homosexual, as was Cornell, and both traveled with lovers; but their marriage was one of Broadway's most successful partnerships. Tall, slender, with dark eyes and dark wavy hair, always parted in the middle, Cornell was a regal presence. She saved her emotions for the stage and left the shouting to the hot-tempered McClintic.

The distinguished Basil Rathbone, an actor steeped in Shakespeare, was slated to play Romeo to Cornell's Juliet. Rathbone would also portray clergyman James Morell, married to Cornell's character in *Candida*, and poet Robert Browning in *The Barretts of Wimpole Street*. Brenda Forbes, unforgettable as the quirky maid in *The Barretts* on Broadway, would re-create her role for the tour and play Prossy, secretly in love with Morell and jealous of Candida, in *Candida*. The new sets for *Romeo and Juliet* would be designed by veteran Woodman Thompson, with road versions of Jo Mielziner's original Broadway scenery for *Candida* and *The Barretts*. More than sixty performers and crew members were engaged for the duration of the tour—many of them bringing spouses, children, even pets with them on the company train.

Late October was a month of intensive rehearsals. McClintic concentrated on *Romeo and Juliet*, the only production new to Cornell and the most anticipated of the three plays. The tour would open with

Shakespeare, leaving *Candida* until the troupe reached the West Coast. After the delayed premiere of *Jezebel* in New York, McClintic would fly to Duluth, Minnesota, to catch up with the company as it boarded a train for Seattle, where the Shaw play starring Cornell would have its first performance beyond Broadway.

Shaw himself once called Cornell the ideal Candida of his imagination. Her turn as the clergyman's wife was "one of the great performances by an actress that I have ever seen," Rathbone rhapsodized in his memoirs. The third play—in some ways the loss leader—was *The Barretts of Wimpole Street*, but it would be almost a brush-up for Cornell, who had played Elizabeth Barrett for 541 performances on Broadway in 1924–1925.

Orson's voice had mesmerized McClintic at their first meeting, and the director had decided on the spot to award the young actor the honor of speaking *Romeo and Juliet*'s first lines, parting the curtain with a mask held to his face and intoning the prologue: "Two households, both alike in dignity . . ." At the very first rehearsal, Orson later told his guardian, he found a way to stand out among the cast with a bit of mischief: after the first phrase he stopped, pretending to have gone up in his lines. McClintic stared helplessly and everyone else looked embarrassed until they all finally got the joke—the first of many to come—and the theater erupted with laughter. The company was won over.

After conquering an early bout of nerves, Orson performed well during rehearsals, and McClintic was pleased with his Mercutio. Orson was still short of money, however, and wrote to borrow some more from Roger Hill, promising to start paying it back with his first paycheck, while profusely apologizing for the fact that, for the moment at least, he would have to abandon all work on the Shakespeare book. In a touching response, Skipper Hill told Orson—once his prize pupil, now increasingly his friend—to stop worrying. "In the simple acceptance of each other per se lies the beauty of our relationship," Hill replied. "Let's never spoil it with too many words. Or with too little realization. There are some things too solid, too genuine to be made articulate. Lord! Life is so full of explaining ourselves and justifying ourselves and masquerading ourselves before folks. Thank god we each have a friend for whom we need apply no makeup."

The tour was set to premiere on Wednesday, November 29, in Cornell's adopted hometown, Buffalo. (The actress was born in Berlin but raised in Buffalo, where she first fell in love with theater.) Droves of reporters and photographers saw the company off at Grand Central Terminal, and more awaited their arrival in Buffalo. The choreographer Martha Graham traveled with the troupe, directing the dances; Graham was "a tower of strength," Cornell recalled, "equal to any emergency," including last-minute touches for the costumes. After opening with *Romeo and Juliet*, playing it for three nights and a matinee, the company would dish up *The Barretts of Wimpole Street* on Saturday night.

As he would for most of Orson's stage appearances in the 1930s, Orson's guardian made the trip for opening night. Arriving by train from Chicago, Dr. Maurice Bernstein hurried to the Statler Hotel, where Orson was staying. When he discovered that Orson wasn't in his suite, Dr. Bernstein asked to be admitted to the room, only to be taken aback by what he found there: "the remains of two breakfasts and a napkin with rouge," evidence of his ward's first love affair.

The prudish physician quickly returned the room key to the front desk. "I walked out into the street a disturbed man, thinking," Dr. Bernstein remembered: " 'What did she look like? Was she dark, was she a blonde, tall or short?' But what difference did this make? I thought to myself. After all he is not a child, and it is no concern of mine." When Orson materialized later, he relieved Bernstein's anxiety with an explanation: needing fuel for his performance, Orson said, he had eaten for two, and the rouge on the napkins was merely a vestige of his own stage makeup. He raved to Bernstein about the ensemble and Cornell in particular—"a most cheerful person"—but lamented that "the sets were not to his liking," stodgy and old-fashioned.

At the premiere in the Erlanger Theatre, Dr. Bernstein sat in the fifteenth row, but had trouble hearing some of the actors, and wondered whether the acoustics were poor. After the performance, he noticed McClintic in a box seat, looking glum. "As Orson passed him, he turned to Orson and asked him how he thought the performance went," recalled Bernstein. "I was rather surprised since Orson was a newcomer to the company and was its youngest member." To his "horror," Bernstein continued, Orson "opened up, starting first of all with the [voice] projection of scenes and second, criticizing, the balcony scene. 'The balcony on the backdrop looks like a glorified cigar box.'" McClintic shook his head wearily, as though Orson had gone too far, then "called the actors back on the stage," and, echoing Orson, "told them that the audience had hardly heard them, that they must speak up."

The company's next stops were in Wisconsin—not Kenosha, Orson's birthplace, but Milwaukee and Madison, where Cornell had never appeared. Playing these two cities had the added benefit of giving the company an excuse to avoid Chicago and its often ferocious critics. The company did not bypass Chicago entirely, however, stopping there by train long enough for Cornell to have lunch with Ashton Stevens, who spoke fondly of Orson. Many of the Chicago reviewers simply traveled to Milwaukee, anyway, Cornell recalled, and "most [of them] were displeased" by her *Romeo and Juliet*. Charles Collins in the *Tribune* found the middle-aged Cornell deficient as Juliet, but the other players—including Orson, whom he had known since he was in short pants—were "brilliant." ("In his duel with Tybalt and his death scene," Collins wrote, "this Mercutio is a complete realization of Shakespeare's bravest blade.") The Wisconsin critics were even more affirmative, with the *Milwaukee Journal* finding the production "superlative," and the *Sentinel* calling it "superb."

The tour had its first one-night stand at the 1,300-seat Parkway Theatre on Madison's Capitol Square, performing the reliably entertaining *The Barretts of Wimpole Street*. Orson recalled Madison and the Parkway from boyhood, and he was touched when his old friend Stanley Custer from Washington School came backstage to congratulate him. "I didn't think anyone would remember me!" Orson exclaimed.

Next the Cornell company swung north for five days in Minneapolis, then on to Saint Paul and Duluth for shorter stints, arriving at Duluth the week before Christmas. Guthrie McClintic joined the company in time to give *Candida* its last licks of preparation. "We had been rehearsing all the way along with me directing," recalled Cornell, "very badly." McClintic almost instantly regretted casting Orson as the sensitive aesthete Marchbanks, leveling a brusque critique of his introverted performance. Orson would have to improve on the road, and in the next months he did: Cornell would remember him as a "tremendously interesting" Marchbanks, his performance "always provocative."

In two Pullman cars with two baggage cars, the company embarked on the long train trip to Seattle, where *The Barretts of Wimpole Street* was to open in the evening on Christmas Day. The company left during a heavy snowfall, and somewhere around Montana the train ran into tracks that were washed out from steady rain and heavy flooding. With the engines overheating, the train slowed to a crawl, and the actors were informed they might miss their Seattle opening. Making the best of it, the troupe donned happy faces and poured punch over a Christmas Eve roast chicken feast. Orson and the younger players passed out gifts they'd purchased at a ten-cent store in Duluth, and everyone joined in lusty Christmas caroling. All night and the next day the train inched forward, with emergency crews laying trestles and tracks ahead, until it finally limped into Seattle's King Street Station shortly after 11 P.M.—more than two hours past the scheduled curtain time.

They arrived to the news that a packed audience of 1,200 in evening dress was still in place at the Metropolitan Theatre, awaiting the show. Shocked, the company sprang into action. Racing to the theater, the crew prepared the sets and lighting in full view of the audience. Seattle was McClintic's birthplace, and he took the stage as master of ceremonies, narrating the preparations to cheers and applause, urging the stage manager, prop master, and wardrobe mistress each to take a bow as they finished their work. The performance didn't start until one o'clock in the morning, and lasted until four. The cast woke up late and exhausted but proud.

From Seattle, the Cornell tour snaked down the coast to Oakland and then to its only stop in southern California, Los Angeles—Orson's first visit to the motion picture capital.

Katharine Cornell was beloved in the city, having set a record for nonmusical box office receipts there when she toured with *The Barretts of Wimpole Street* in 1932. This time her company's three plays would rotate for two weeks at the downtown Biltmore Theatre, where as usual Cornell was stalked backstage by Hollywood producers bringing her flowers and film offers. But Cornell was a theater purist, and though she regularly promised MGM production chief Irving Thalberg that she would make a screen test, she never did, and she withstood all temptations to play her signature role, Elizabeth Barrett, onscreen. (Thalberg's wife, Norma Shearer, inherited the character for the MGM picture, which would be released later in 1934.) It would be another ten years before Cornell stooped to her only screen appearance: a fleeting cameo as herself in *Stage Door.*

No matter how much they loved movies, most of the cast and certainly Orson felt the same devotion to the theater. Orson may have tried to look up Samson Raphaelson, and he and other young cast members toured the area, gawking from outside at the gated Hollywood studios. The two-week stand was a tremendous success, garnering excellent receipts and reviews (Orson earned his first mention in the *Los Angeles Times* with critic Edwin Schallert writing that he made a "very acceptable" Mercutio). But the collective success was overshadowed by a predawn car crash at the end of the run that involved young cast members and sent three players to the hospital; the company was forced to leave behind another actor, charged with drunkenness.

Road tours, then as now, are remembered for their triumphs but also for their crises and calamities. The car crash in Los Angeles was the worst setback, but not the only one. In Oakland, for example, the scheduled space was divided into a theater and a basketball court; backboard shots and referees' whistles could be heard faintly as the troupe performed. In Colorado Springs, Colorado, Cornell and the other actresses were forced to share a single dressing room that had only one mirror. In Amarillo, Texas, the actors played through a dust storm so loud they strained to hear their cues.

Orson, who loved mishaps and challenges, stored it all away for future reference. Much has been written about his involvement in this storied tour, often focusing on his immaturity, or on his inability to match the performances of more seasoned players in the company. Orson's Marchbanks, Basil Rathbone wrote in his autobiography, was "so fatuously unpleasant that Morell became, by contrast, a deeply sympathetic character, which most certainly was not Shaw's intention." Then again, Orson "was supposed to be a boy wonder verging on the phenomenon of genius. With this type of advance publicity much should be forgiven him."

Another player in the troupe, John Hoysradt, who roomed with Orson for much of the tour and later joined his Mercury Theatre, told author Richard France that "Orson at the time always played to the top row of the third balcony, both in make-up and projectivity."* Welles himself agreed, telling the BBC years later that his performances on Cornell's tour were sometimes "terribly campy" and constituted "one of the poorer moments in the American theater."

The tour's impresario, Guthrie McClintic, later wrote that the eighteen-year-old Welles was "effective" when portraying Mercutio in *Romeo and Juliet*, "but left more than a little to be desired when he undertook Marchbanks in *Candida*. That he got by was by no means enough." But the stage director conceded that he himself lacked experience working with touring repertory companies, and admitted that the overall casting had involved "plenty of compromise." McClintic insisted, "It was not the actors' fault that they were better in some parts than others."

In particular, McClintic lamented his own mistakes in staging the Shakespeare play. The touring version was too somber, he reflected, its emotionalism telegraphed, its heavy scenery oppressive. Gradually, as the tour progressed, *Romeo and Juliet*—less popular with audiences and critics—saw fewer performances, while *Candida* was phased out entirely. *The Barretts of Wimpole Street*, old hat for Cornell, was the most reliable offering for the sticks.

Any criticisms of Orson should be seen in this broader light. Read carefully, his notices suggest an actor who was making shifts and strides on the road, as often happens over the course of a tour. He pleased many critics and most audiences. Wood Soanes of the *Oakland Tribune* found the young unknown "indifferent" as Mercutio when he first saw *Romeo and Juliet* in January, then "appreciably improved" one month later. (He also said that Cornell's Juliet had "matured" during the same period of time.) As for Marchbanks, Orson played him "to the hilt," Soanes wrote. "He looked and acted the sensitive shy poet

---

* In Hollywood, years after the Cornell tour and his stint with the Mercury Theatre, John Hoysradt would change his name and appear in many films as John Hoyt.

without ever suggesting femininity. The choking scene was delight-fully accomplished and the hearth episode was memorable."

Of course Orson also received negative reviews—often enough neg-ative *and* positive reviews from different critics in the same city. "Do reviews ever wound you?" Michael Parkinson asked Welles four de-cades later in an interview on Parkinson's British television program. "Deeply," Welles replied without hesitation. "I can remember every bad notice I've ever had." He went on to recall a particularly caustic critique of his Marchbanks, which one reviewer on the Cornell tour likened to "a sea calf whining in a basso profundo." Welles said the barb still haunted him, and "I'm sure it's an absolutely accurate de-scription of that performance, which must have been abominable, but it still goes through my head before I go to sleep at night."

Offstage, he was certainly full of youthful mischief. On one occa-sion, in a San Francisco restaurant, Orson offended Cornell's dignity when she caught him and John Hoysradt strutting around wearing false beards and tuxedos, impersonating stuffy foreign dignitaries. An-other time, it is said—perhaps apocryphally—that Orson missed the company train and had to charter a plane to make the next tour stop. In Kansas City, with extra time on his hands, he took a room in a cheap neighborhood, put up a sign, dressed like a swami, and told fortunes. In Atlantic City too, he set up a booth and practiced palmistry on vacationers strolling along the boardwalk. He looked for scars on their knees from unhappy accidents when they were children, and wondered if they had undergone a trauma between the ages of twelve and four-teen. Who hadn't? He certainly did.

"About twice a year I wake up and find myself a sinner," Orson sweetly apologized in a letter to Cornell at one point during the tour. "Somebody slaps me in the face, and after the stars have cleared away and I've stopped blubbering, I am aware of the discomforting realities. I see that my boots are roughshod and that I've been galloping in them over people's sensibilities."

All agree that Orson was the touring troupe's livest wire. To McClintic, the young actor was "an arresting, stimulating, and at moments exasperating member of the company." To actress Brenda Forbes—who was six years Orson's senior and who already boasted some New York credits—Orson was "the talk of the company and our favorite piece of gossip. His youth, talent and beautiful voice made up for what he lacked in discipline, and in spite of never knowing what he was going to do next, we became very fond of him."

After Los Angeles, the repertory company looped back to the mountain states before heading down to Texas, then north again to Oklahoma, Kansas, and Nebraska. After wandering for weeks in the plains states and the Midwest, the tour explored the Deep South and then, in late April, headed for final dates in a cluster of cities on the East Coast and in New England.

As with his notices, every negative anecdote about Orson seems balanced by a positive one. He was one of the leaders of the steamboat expedition down the Ohio River, when the company turned south in the spring, sailing from Cincinnati to Louisville and enjoying a picnic lunch on board with friends including Hoysradt, Forbes, Cornell, and McClintic. On Sunday nights, "whenever we could," Cornell remembered, Orson joined her and Hoysradt, listening to Toscanini conduct the New York Philharmonic on the radio. The same small group enjoyed the most beautiful of days in Charleston, sipping mint juleps at the Villa Margherita.

The "low point" may well have been New Orleans, where, according to Forbes, Orson and his friends ordered everything at Antoine's—snails, oysters Rockefeller, lobster thermidor. "Everyone ate and drank too richly," recalled Forbes.

Forbes's memories of her fellow actor varied in interviews, and she saved one story for her autobiography, published in 1994. "The young men" of the company, Forbes recounted in *Five Minutes, Miss Forbes*, paid innumerable visits to the red-light district in New Orleans. "One particular night, when most of us were fast asleep in our berths, Orson Welles returned highly elated and full of mischief. He climbed to my upper berth puffing and wheezing (he was a big man even then) and plunked himself down on top of me. What a situation—both horrifying and hysterically funny. Apparently Orson enjoyed himself. Scrunching up railway bed linen to protect myself, I did not.

"Neither one of us ever referred to that night again."

As much as his stint with the Gate Theatre, Katharine Cornell's tour was a coming-of-age experience for Welles, restoring his belief in himself as an actor, while encouraging him to contemplate an even more ambitious plan for his future.

The idea had been growing in his mind since boyhood. Dissatisfied by the prospect of a career as a mere actor, he was drawn instead to the careers of actor-managers like Hilton Edwards and Micheál MacLíammóir, or one he had met earlier in Chicago, Fritz Leiber. His months on the road with Cornell exemplified the type of actor he wanted to be: the head of his own touring repertory company. Edwards needed MacLíammóir for their partnership, and Cornell needed Guthrie McClintic as her coproducer and director. But they were all actor-managers of the breed Orson had grown up following and admiring and longing to emulate.

As a boy, he had watched classical theater presented by the companies of great actor-managers in the twilight of their lifelong tours, and had been privileged to shake the hands of more than a few. He devoured books about the great luminaries like David Garrick, Henry Irving, Herbert Beerbohm Tree, and Sir Ben Greet, who did it all: played leads; designed the sets, lighting, and costumes; staged and produced their shows. Orson had the skills to pursue that tradition; he had proved it repeatedly at the Todd School. More important, besides these skills Orson also had belief in himself, energy, drive, and willpower.

Before anyone else would have declared such a path possible, Orson was talking about presiding over his own repertory troupe—such apparently idle talk always serving him as a kind of rehearsal for later reality. He talked about his ambitions incessantly during the Cornell tour. Orson could be "gauche and tiresome," Brenda Forbes recalled, "always talking about plans for his own theater."

He would have his chance, sooner than he knew.

By spring, doubt was brewing behind the scenes that *Romeo and Juliet* would be ready for Broadway in the first half of 1934, as originally announced. McClintic was unhappy with the sets and his own ponderous staging; the heavy trappings seemed to be affecting his wife's performance, which lacked charm. In April, when McClintic rejoined the tour in Cincinnati to talk it over with her, they decided to close *Romeo and Juliet* "for the season," according to Cornell. "All one-night stands from then on—and threw away the sets." The company would disperse after the tour to regroup for Broadway in the fall of 1934, when McClintic would reconceive *Romeo and Juliet*.

The decision had little to do with Orson, but he was devastated to learn that his appointment with Broadway had been postponed. Defeat and disappointment often galvanized him, and he speedily contacted the scenic designer Robert Edmond Jones and his wife, Margaret Carrington, who were busy staging an *Othello* starring Carrington's brother, Walter Huston, for the annual summer drama festival in Central City, Colorado. The couple had mused about bringing their *Othello* to Broadway afterward. Now that *Romeo and Juliet* looked doubtful, Orson asked, was there a part for him in their show? Jones and Carrington liked him, but they shied away from promises. "That hurt for a while," Orson wrote to Skipper.

For five minutes, perhaps, but not much longer. By now, Orson's dreams of launching his own repertory company were already urging him in an independent direction. With the summer yawning ahead, the last thing Orson wanted to do was return to his lonely Rush Street writing studio, or, worse, to Dr. Maurice Bernstein's stifling supervision in Highland Park. But there was another potential base of operations, a natural sanctuary where he was bound to prosper: the Todd School. After all, hadn't he been a virtual actor-manager there, even as a student?

Knowing time was short, he sent silver-tongued letters to Roger Hill, hoping to head off the headmaster's usual summer at Camp Tosebo. Together, Orson proposed, they could organize a serious summer theater operation, using school facilities that were vacant in the off-season. They could hire professionals for the leads, supplementing the core company with Todd boys and young apprentices—charging their parents a fee that would help pay for the professionals. They could rent the Woodstock Opera House on the town square, and even use Big Bertha to chauffeur the major drama critics in from Chicago, supplying them with typewriters and "some picturesque black chef," in Orson's words, on board to whip up meals for the scribes.

Orson had managed to put aside a little savings on the tour, and he volunteered $1,000 of his own as the seed money. True, the headmaster and Todd School would be taking the greater financial risk, but they could pay the professionals something like ("here I blush a little") $25 weekly while extracting $300 to $500 per Todd boy from the boys' affluent parents.

Hill was enthusiastic about Orson's latest Big Idea, his wife a little less so. Orson and the headmaster talked it over by letter and phone, agreeing that the "luminous" (Orson's word) Whitford Kane, revered in Chicago for his tenure with the Goodman Theatre, would be a perfect figurehead for the summer theater festival. Orson wrote Kane a coaxing letter, even promising "a job for Chub!"—Kane's protégé Hiram "Chubby" Sherman, one of the Goodman's best comedic actors. Kane tentatively agreed to sign on as "director-in-chief," a scoop that was given to Charles Collins for the *Tribune*.

Still touring the South, Orson stayed up late after the curtain calls writing drafts of the first press material. By early April, as the company arrived in Nashville, booked for several days at the Ryman Auditorium, the Big Summer Theater Idea had begun to take more definite shape.

One of Orson's brainstorms was inviting two of the actor-managers who had inspired him—Hilton Edwards and Micheál MacLíammóir—to come and join his dream, spending the summer in leading roles for his new theater company in the heart of America. "I am trying my hand at production," he told the pair, promising "a kind of holiday and lots of fun." Edwards could direct one or more shows, and both men could be involved in the production designs.

When Edwards and MacLíammóir replied, asking for particulars, Orson sat down in his room at the Andrew Jackson Hotel in Nashville and gave the evolving update on hotel stationery. By their presence alone, the two statesmen of Irish theater would "inspire a professional company of quality, and a school full of eager amateurs of quantity." The Dubliners could count on "a pretty superlative company," among them Whitford Kane (an Irish stage luminary whose name was well known to the Gate's cofounders), Chubby Sherman, Florence Stevens (Mrs. Ashton Stevens), Brenda Forbes, "a couple of more really top-notch stars," and "let us pray, Hilton Edwards and the inimitable Michael . . . quite enough to antidote the effect of Orson Welles in any theater."

The selection of plays, according to Orson's letter of April 12, 1934, was "a question upon which we should like to hear from you." But he listed some tempting possibilities, demonstrating his breadth and sophistication: Christopher Marlowe's *The Tragical History of the Life and Death of Dr. Faustus*; Arthur Schnitzler's *Living Hours*; Charles Dickens's *Bleak House*; and, from Dostoyevsky, stage versions of either *The Idiot* or *The Brothers Karamazov*. While Orson could offer Edwards and Mac-Líammóir only "very literally pin money," he vowed to cover their round-trip travel from Dublin to Woodstock, as well as "all your expenses during your stay," including "very comfortable rooms" and hearty meals ("by an excellent chef"—from the Todd School staff, that is). They would have the run of the school, with its "submarine-lit swimming pool, its riding stables, its machine and print shops, cottages and dormitories, private experimental theater, luxurious land yacht for transportation, and its fifty acres of American woodlands." And the Dubliners were promised "as much free time and freedom as you want" to explore Chicago and the ongoing world's fair there.

The Chicago press corps was already champing at the bit to "boost" the homegrown enterprise, Orson assured the two men, even "three months before its first day of rehearsal." Indeed, even before they accepted Orson's offer, Charles Collins announced "the summer school of the theater" in the April 22 issue of the *Tribune*. Collins identified Whitford Kane as the director of the summer theater, with the Gate Theatre founders "Edwards and MacLinnoir" (not yet famous enough in Chicago for correct spelling) lending the program "a distinctly Irish flavor." The Dubliners did not officially join the operation until a week after that item appeared in print, when their cable of acceptance reached Orson at the Washington Duke Hotel in Durham, North Carolina. It was a closer call than it appeared: Hilton Edwards was wary of the idea, and they had dithered over the prospect of spending their summer at work in the American Midwest instead of sportively in Europe. But MacLíammóir talked his partner into it.

Orson was "overjoyed," promising to bring the Dubliners to New York in plenty of time "to get thoroughly dizzied in that raucous and remarkable metropolis." Orson would greet the two at dockside as they left the ship, enlisting the help of the Cornell tour publicist to arrange press coverage of their arrival. The tour was winding up, presenting

The Barretts of Wimpole Street in Newark and Brooklyn, at the end of the third week of June. "About the 26th or 27th we will all rush together to Woodstock and begin rehearsals," Orson wrote to Edwards and MacLíammóir.

Disembarking with Edwards in New York, MacLíammóir immediately noticed a difference in the young American he had last seen more than two years before. "Now he had added to the [chest] swelling a new habit of towering," MacLíammóir wrote later. "It was not only the jungle that yawned and laughed: a looming tree, dark and elaborate as a monkey puzzle, reared above the head, an important, imperturbable smile shot down on you from afar."

While Orson tended to the plays and players, Roger Hill busily laid the financial groundwork and beat the drums, feeding publicity about the festival to eager arts and society columnists. Hill dealt with the budget, ticket sales, advertising, and promotional plans; he organized the Todd School for cast and crew residency, readied the Opera House for occupation, and prepared Woodstock for the onslaught of people. The reliable Charles Collins dropped frequent mentions of the "brilliant young Chicago actor" Orson Welles and his new summer theater colony.

On paper, Whitford Kane was still "chief director" of the upcoming festival. When Ashton Stevens telephoned Orson on the Cornell tour in mid-June to ask about Kane, Orson told him that Kane was "very enthusiastic about Woodstock. Nothing short of Hollywood can keep him from joining us." The day after he returned from New York with Edwards and MacLíammóir in tow, he was still invoking Kane's magic name. But in reality Kane was always a shaky piece of the plan, and Hollywood had already come calling for the Irish-born actor. By mid-June Kane had a better offer—and Orson knew it, although he was keeping it close to the vest. Kane was heading west to make his screen debut in *Hide-Out*, an MGM gangster film.

All of Orson's tub-thumping about Kane may have been sincere, but it was also classic misdirection. With Skipper's blessing, Orson gladly stepped into the breach, letting only a day or two pass after his return from New York before telling the press that he himself would direct the festival's first production. The travel-weary Dubliners accepted the revelation with mild surprise and pique. (Edwards found the idea "preposterous," wrote Barbara Leaming. "Orson Welles *direct* a play?")

With only two weeks to go before opening night, Orson still hadn't decided on the first play. Swiftly now he settled on *Trilby*, one of those hoary melodramas for which he never lost his affection. Based on George du Maurier's 1894 novel, it is set in nineteenth-century bohemian Paris and revolves around the rogue musician and hypnotist Svengali, who transforms Trilby, a tone-deaf artist's model, into a diva. Besides directing, Orson announced that he himself would play the lead: Svengali.

After a ten-day run, from July 12 to 22, *Trilby* would be followed by two weeks of *Hamlet*, with Edwards directing and MacLíammóir playing the lead. Within a few frantic days, what was first promoted as only "A Third Play" was narrowed down to *Tsar Paul*, Dmitri Merezhkovsky's play about the assassination of the emperor of Russia, which would be presented from August 9 to 19. The Opera House curtain would rise at 8:30 P.M., Thursdays through Sundays.

Hamlet and *Tsar Paul* were both Gate Theatre staples, as Orson well knew, and those choices pacified the Dubliners. *Trilby*, in contrast, they considered inferior, and it bothered them that Orson had arranged for both to make their American debuts in decidedly lesser roles: MacLíammóir as the artist Little Billee, Svengali's rival; and Edwards as Taffy, one of several suitors drawn to Trilby. But it was customary in repertory or summer stock for important actors to take an easy assignment for one play. Orson reminded them that they'd need time to orient themselves, and he emphasized the opportunities ahead: for MacLíammóir, a chance to re-create his famous Hamlet; for Edwards, a turn as Tsar Paul, and the chance to direct both shows. Each of the three actors would star in one play. Ruffled feathers were smoothed.

The stock of the Dubliners rose even higher as it became clearer and clearer that Orson's original dream cast was just that—a pipe dream. Whitford Kane had melted away, and so did Chubby Sherman, Florence Stevens, Brenda Forbes, and every other established professional Orson had envisioned. Another player who turned Orson down was his friend John Hoysradt, who recalled, "I wanted to go to Europe and felt the Woodstock thing was just harum scarum."

The moment required the confidence of a leader, and here Orson drew on the example set by his parents—especially his mother, a superb organizer and network builder, but his father too, with his persuasive smile and hidden steel. Much as he had for Todd School productions, Orson scrambled to assemble a first-rate summer company drawn from his store of friends, relatives, acquaintances, and professional contacts, and no small measure of instinct and chance.

The summer theater needed a reputable leading lady, and Orson was both shrewd and fortunate to find Louise Prussing just when he needed her. On the stage since 1917, the reed-thin, vivacious Prussing had appeared in several silent films opposite matinee idol Eugene O'Brien. In London, in the late 1920s, she had appeared with distinction in notable plays including Leslie Howard's production of *Berkeley Square*, which she toured in America. The granddaughter of Dr. Fernand Henrotin, a founder of Chicago's Henrotin Memorial Hospital, and daughter of Lilian Edgerton Prussing, a onetime society editor for the *Chicago Examiner*, Prussing was living in Chicago for the summer, and welcomed the chance to star in plays in nearby Woodstock. Her London credentials pleased the Dubliners, while her Chicago background made her appeal to local columnists. Prussing was engaged to play Trilby, the Queen in *Hamlet*, and the Princess in *Tsar Paul*.

Orson got a two-for-one deal when he sent Roger Hill as his messenger over to *The Drunkard*, which was being mounted by Charles "Blackie" O'Neal's troupe of traveling players at a Clark Street hall in Chicago.* Constance Herron was a pretty and fetching ingenue in the troupe, but O'Neal was the real find. Even though he was only five feet nine and 160 pounds, he had been a three-year letterman on the winning University of Iowa football team that upset Notre Dame and Red Grange's University of Illinois team in 1925. O'Neal could recite Shakespeare backward and forward, and Orson had a lifelong affinity for footballers with Shakespeare in their veins. Orson had seen *The Drunkard* in Los

---

* "Blackie" was a reference to the southern drawl O'Neal still had when he moved as a youth from Atlanta to Pierre, South Dakota. Local toughs dubbed him "Nigger." O'Neal clobbered the toughs, and his nickname became "Blackie." Even his mother started calling him "Blackie."

Angeles, where it was still pulling in crowds after a six-month run when the Cornell tour arrived in January. Backstage, he had met O'Neal—who would be the father of future film star Ryan O'Neal—and they had stayed in touch as the capable actor-manager barnstormed the show across America, crisscrossing with the Cornell company. O'Neal served as director and master of ceremonies of *The Drunkard* while also playing the weak hero's brother, and spicing up the interludes with offbeat songs. He signed on as Orson's chief lieutenant—playing supporting roles including the trusted Horatio in *Hamlet*—while assisting Orson in casting and rehearsals. He brought Herron with him to portray Ophelia in *Hamlet* and the Empress Elizabeth in *Tsar Paul.*

Orson cobbled the rest of the roster together from hither and yon. He knew the tall, dapper William Vance either from Evanston, where Vance had attended Northwestern, or from Dr. Sprague's camp in northern Wisconsin, where Vance was a counselor the same year Orson wrote "Marching Song" nearby. Born in California the same year as Orson, Vance was raised in Freeport, Illinois. He had staged Shakespeare plays upstairs from a bank while still in high school, and made his own home movies of Robert Louis Stevenson stories including *The Strange Case of Dr. Jekyll and Mr. Hyde.* One day, Orson had helped the Vance brothers shoot a short comedy featuring William putting up screens at his house in Evanston, and being bothered by a fly until he procures an old-fashioned pump-handle bug sprayer—and ends up spraying himself in the face. The credits read, "Assistant Prop Man: Orson Welles."

Orson and William Vance had great rapport, and the actor told Orson he'd bring his movie camera to Woodstock for the summer. Orson could rely on this kindred spirit as his understudy and stand-in, especially when he was directing the first production. And Vance would portray the characters Zou-Zou in *Trilby*, Fortinbras in *Hamlet*, and General Talyzin in *Tsar Paul.*

Other recruits were drawn from Orson's family and travels. John Dunn Martin, an Iowa speech teacher in his late fifties whom Orson had met on the Cornell tour, was hired for the old-man parts. John D. Davies, a high school instructor, had approached Orson for advice about launching a community theater in Kenosha, and now he was engaged for supporting roles. Orson tapped another Kenosha connection, his talented cousin William Yule Jr., for the key parts of Laird in *Trilby*, the gravedigger in *Hamlet*, and the Baron in *Tsar Paul.*

He and Skipper had hoped to supplement their troupe with "a bevy of stage-struck high school kids," in the headmaster's words, who would hammer the sets and sew the costumes while paying for the privilege of basking in the glow of professionals. Orson and Hill convened auditions, "preliminary to extraction of payments from parents," in Hill's words, but managed to scrounge up only about twenty youngsters, even after adjusting the tuition of "five hundred big depression-time dollars" to as low as $250. Among them were former or current Todd boys such as the budding artist Hascy Tarbox, always an exceptional help behind the scenes, and Edgerton Paul, another old hand at Orson Welles productions. Handsome blond William Mowry Jr., from Orson's years at Todd, was another Shakespeare-loving footballer, who was inveigled away from a boring summer in his hometown, Madison, Wisconsin.

Most of the apprentices came from privileged homes in Chicago and the suburbs. Among the sprinkling of girls was Virginia Nicolson, a petite, willowy, blond, blue-eyed eighteen-year-old from Wheaton who had just graduated from the University School for Girls on Lake Shore Drive.* As brainy as she was delicate, she reeled off a snippet from *Henry IV* at her summer theater audition. Orson raised an eyebrow, and Virginia was "in"—though Hill later scoffed that Orson was more impressed by her "shape" than her Shakespeare.

One of Orson's backstage finds was George Shealy, who had studied under Dudley Crafts Watson at the Art Institute of Chicago. Brought on to jump-start the stage design for *Trilby*, Shealy would replicate the period sets and costumes from du Maurier's original sketches. (He went on to prominence as an advertising artist for Marshall Field's before becoming a distinguished art history professor in North Carolina.) The reliable Carl Hendrickson would orchestrate the summer music.

By now, everything was happening at warp speed. As the apprentices and crew beavered away, Orson blocked the cast and rehearsed the

---

* Her family name appears as "Nicholson" in early Chicago newspaper accounts, and in many books on Welles, but over time it became "Nicolson."

staging, trying his best not to shout at the actors. Watching Hilton Edwards in Dublin, and Guthrie McClintic on the Cornell tour, Orson had stockpiled many directing strategies—including vamping and stalling when he was stuck.

At first, Edwards and MacLíammóir watched the novice director warily, unwilling to bail him out. MacLíammóir, for one, sniffed at Orson's initial staging. "It was disappointingly vague and indefinite," he told Peter Noble. "Orson had not yet found his true métier, which was a preoccupation with restless grandeur and intoxication, a view of life, wholly American and welling up from the soil of the huge terri-tory which had given him birth."

During breaks, Orson ushered the Dubliners and Louise Pruss-ing around for publicity appearances at nearby schools and civic clubs, giving talks and interviews, shuttling between Woodstock and Chicago—pledging that "in spirit, at least," the summer theater would be "a combination Bayreuth and a strawberry festival," as Welles told the *Woodstock News.*

Here again, public relations wizard John Clayton proved a valuable ally. When Orson proposed "a great dinner" at the Tavern Club to charm Chicago society, Clayton stocked the guest list with newspa-per columnists and well-married ladies with time and money to spare. Sculptor Lorado Taft, one of Chicago's most prominent artists, was among the donors and patrons. Mr. and Mrs. Dudley Crafts Watson represented the Art Institute of Chicago, and the current heads of both the Goodman Theatre and Chicago's Drama League also were in at-tendance. "You were play-acting when you were scarcely old enough to walk," Mrs. Watson teased Orson as he arrived at the dinner. "And you're still making those funny faces."

The headliners came late: Welles, Edwards, MacLíammóir, and Prussing arriving with a flourish, dressed to the nines. "We had a [car] breakdown," Orson explained to the crowd, many of whom he knew from his youth. He introduced MacLíammóir as the star of the summer theater—"devastating fellow"—then added with a wink, "We all had engagements to lecture at a girls' school. Micheál went up the first week—did a thorough job. Immediately afterward the school can-celled the rest of the lectures. Three girls had run away, they said, to seek stage careers."

"I expect you to shine brightly at that great dinner," Orson had told Skipper, and now the young man's biggest booster came through with a rousing sales pitch. Hill exhorted the society ladies to host dinner parties during the season, and then to lead their guests in a motor parade to Woodstock after dessert. Newspaper folk could travel courtesy of Big Bertha, and expect to be wined and dined en route. "All Roads Lead to Woodstock Opera," the Chicago press trumpeted, and Charles Collins topped all previous pronouncements by declaring Orson, the chief conjurer of the summer theater, "a striking specimen of adolescent genius." By the end of the evening, the Woodstock summer theater had effectively won the endorsement of Chicago's artistic elite.

Thanks to Clayton, Orson even gave midwestern audiences an early taste of his future on the airwaves. During the week *Trilby* opened, broadcasting from the observation platform atop the west tower of the Sky Ride, seven hundred feet above the Century of Progress Exposition, WGN aired a live dramatic sketch with full orchestra backing, which promoted the summer theater. The sketch was written by Orson and performed by him, Edwards, MacLíammóir, and Prussing.

This was Orson Welles's radio debut.

Bright pennants and ice cream vendors dotted the elm-shaded square on July 12, 1934. A red-coated brass band greeted the town cars arriving at sunset from Chicago, Elgin, Rockford, Lake Forest, Winnetka, Wheaton, and Lake Geneva. The festive crowd included Dr. Maurice Bernstein and the Edward Moores; and the John T. McCutcheons and Dudley Crafts Watsons were among the notables who sponsored caravans from their homes to Woodstock. ("Uncle" Dudley, ever supportive of his cousin Beatrice's son, also arranged for Orson to flack for his summer theater by lecturing and drawing sketches in front of an Art Institute of Chicago class.) Outside, as darkness fell, Chicago critics and columnists mingled with patrons in their evening finery. The summer heat was intense.

"It is a gala occasion," rhapsodized India Moffett, a society columnist for the *Chicago Tribune*, "perhaps the most exciting the little town of Woodstock has ever had."

The atmosphere was matched by expectations inside the theater, where the more than four hundred seats, including the balcony, were filled as the curtain rose. The old-fashioned melodrama, with Orson as Svengali, delighted the crowd. The young star and director gave a barn-burning performance. "Ferocious, bewitching and altogether real," proclaimed the *Woodstock Sentinel.*

The first-tier Chicago critics were more guarded. Charles Collins wrote in the *Chicago Tribune* that Orson mustered "sound stage direction," but cautioned that his performance evinced "too much Franco-Yiddish accent and too hurried diction," among other "minor flaws." Lloyd Lewis flatly charged Orson (with whom he was on a first-name basis) with hamming it up, saying that his Svengali costume resembled "a composite photograph of a hoot owl, Abe Lincoln, Ben Hecht, and John Brown of Osawatomie." Years later, when Peter Noble asked MacLíammóir for his own recollection, the actor was decidedly ungenerous. "His fakes were on the Titanic scale," the Dubliner told Noble. "His Svengali lacked grace and humor."

Regardless, Orson was the man of the hour, and he stepped forward after the final curtain to hush the shouted cheers and applause. He had turned nineteen just two months before. Thanking the audience, Orson invoked one of America's greatest actor-managers: "Joseph Jefferson made a curtain speech here sixty-five years ago. Since then the speeches have been of lesser and lesser importance. But I can say, without any maidenly blushing," he finished, deferentially nodding to the Dubliners, "our next play is going to be *really* good."

After more shouts and clapping, Roger Hill led the audience to a buffet hosted by his wife, Hortense, at the school's poolside patio, strung with lights and bunting. Dr. Bernstein, the Moores, and the Watsons, who attended every opening that summer, mingled happily with other people who had known Orson's parents, Dick and Beatrice Welles. Cast members brought out their favorite musical instruments and turned the occasion into an informal nightclub revue. Thornton Wilder, winner of the Pulitzer Prize, was encouraged to stand and toast Orson as his discovery. The celebration ran late, especially for those driving back to Chicago. But it was a proud, proud night, its glow undimmed for Welles and Hill whenever the years ahead seemed less kind.

Not all the drama that summer took place onstage. In later years, Micheál MacLíammóir vented freely (and pettily) about Orson's youthful inadequacies as a director and actor. Skipper later maintained that the Dubliners were "rather mean" to Orson at times, making cracks about the young actor-manager in front of other cast members, or rolling their eyes behind his back. "He revered them far too much to fight back," the headmaster insisted in one interview. "He outwardly pretended that all was as it should be, but secretly he was miserable."

After nearly fifty years, however, Welles was more than tempted to fight back. He told Barbara Leaming that Edwards and MacLíammóir were "busy hating me" during that summer. He didn't complain about anything they might have done to him personally, or about any professional failings. But he wasn't above mocking their sexual orientation—telling Henry Jaglom that "these two wild queens" were known in Dublin as "Sodom and Begorra." In Woodstock during the summer of 1934, he likewise told Leaming, the Dubliners were "at the absolute high pitch of their sexuality" rampaging through the town "like a withering flame. *Nobody* was safe, you know. It was a rich harvest there for both of them, and they knew no shame."

When the company held rehearsals at poolside, MacLíammóir's swimsuit was memorably skimpy, Welles recalled—and the flamboyant Dubliner was even more brazen when cruising the town. "Micheál wore what were then shorts of a briefness unseen on the Riviera," Welles told Leaming, "and up and down the main street of Woodstock went Micheál, you know, with beaded eyelashes with the black running slightly down the side of his face because he never could get it right, and his toupee slipping, but still full of beauty. Hilton couldn't keep his hands off his genitals—he went dancing around, caressing himself and sputtering. Everywhere were these four eyes darting about for the next victim. I felt rather guilty about it."

His "guilt" was surely doubled by the puritanical reaction of Roger and Hortense Hill. Skipper was "shocked" at the Dubliners' open sexuality, while "pretending not to be," said Welles. (Behind their backs the headmaster referred to the two men as "roaring pansies.")

MacLíammóir even made a stab at romancing Charles O'Neal, a "vigorous non-homosexual," according to Welles.

The Hills were a monogamous and chaste couple. Hortense considered it her sacred duty to keep the young boys and girls under her stewardship from engaging in any sexual activity whatsoever. But the Hills had their hands full—especially with Orson, trying to keep him from pursuing the young blond apprentice from Wheaton, who from day one received extra attention and coaching on her few lines from the actor-manager. Soon enough, Orson and Virginia Nicolson began arriving at rehearsals together, late, whispering and chuckling, holding hands.

But these tensions and rivalries seem to have peaked in the first weeks of the theater's operation, and once *Trilby* ended and *Hamlet* began, Edwards and MacLíammóir settled into more significant roles, and the summer company found a happy rhythm.

Looking forward to MacLíammóir as the Prince of Denmark, the press coverage intensified in Chicago, with ripples throughout the Midwest and the nation. "Irish and London critics have been calling [MacLíammóir] an ideal Hamlet," Charles Collins wrote in a stringer piece for the *New York Times*. Having dubbed Orson a "genius" in the *Chicago Tribune* earlier in the summer, Collins now noted that Orson had "a terrible reputation as a genius to live down." This would become a future trend in the press, doubting the hype even when abetting it.

Edwards promised a faithful *Hamlet*, featuring as much of the original text as possible and the same stellar performance MacLíammóir had delivered at the Gate. "By developing stage settings which can be changed rapidly," Edwards told the press, "we are able to include more scenes in our play than has been done by other companies playing this work." Besides directing and playing Polonius, Edwards designed the scenery and effects—simple settings that would be varied with hangings and lights. Orson would play Claudius and the Ghost, as he had at the Gate.

The Dubliners knew *Hamlet* well, but with only three days between the closing night of one play and the opening of the next, they threw themselves into high-pressure rehearsals that often ran past midnight.

While Louise Prussing (the Queen), Constance Herron (Ophelia), and Charles O'Neal (Horatio) were professionals, most members of the sizable cast were apprentices and local pickups, and the ensemble was hard-pressed to master the complexities.

The July 26 premiere of *Hamlet* arrived, with all the fanfare returning to Woodstock—the brass band, the Rolls Royces and Pierce Arrows from Chicago, the Big Bertha round-trip for the press, and celebrity guest DeWolf Hopper reciting "Casey at the Bat" for the after-theater party at poolside. Orson diplomatically lowered his profile, and Edwards gave the curtain speech.

In general, the reviews were positive. Edwards's staging made for "a first rate art theater treatment of the immortal tragedy," Collins wrote in the *Tribune*, and the "graceful actor" MacLíammóir offered an "exceedingly good" interpretation of Hamlet—although Collins did find him "somewhat lacking . . . in the fire and nervous excitement of a high mettled prince," with "slowness of pace" his "handicap."

Orson had conquered audiences in *Trilby*, and now with *Hamlet* he began to win over the Chicago critics. His Claudius was "unconventional," as John Clayton wrote later, "a King that called forth anathema from the traditionalists." Charles Collins was one of those traditionalists, and that would keep him out of the Orson Welles fan club in later years. Conceding that the show's "special virtue" was its local hero, Collins wrote about Orson's dual performance as Claudius and the Ghost in more than one *Tribune* piece, debating the show as though he were arguing with himself.

Orson recited the Ghost's speeches magnificently, Collins felt, but his Claudius was an "unorthodox character study" reframing the King as "a completely detestable fellow," as if in a cheap melodrama. "Sitting with Miss Louise Prussing, who obligingly bared one shoulder to make the most seductive Gertrude in my experience," Collins mused, "Mr. Welles exchanged caresses, ripe plums, California grapes and lawless looks with her, interjecting so much amorous business as to fairly hog the scene. It is brilliant technical character work, but it flattens the drama."

Yet there was no question Orson was also brilliantly watchable, Collins allowed, performing with courage and imagination. Claudius, in previous productions of *Hamlet*, had always been "a great disappointment to me," Collins wrote. Not this time: Orson reveled in Claudius's villainy, and "acts the king with such floridity that he has started a minor controversy. Some of the Woodstock pilgrims have been proclaiming that they didn't like him, which merely means that they didn't like the character. That was young Mr. Welles's intention."

Orson proved himself both a crowd-pleaser and a critical provocateur throughout the run of *Hamlet*. On the final weekend, Dudley Crafts Watson brought a record busload of thirty-eight after-dinner guests from his home in Chicago. MacLíammóir's final performance was his finest, and in his last curtain speech he said he was touched by the crowd's sustained applause.

Spirits were high in the interval between the second and third productions, and Orson organized an afternoon of fun, in the form of improvised filmmaking. He enlisted William Vance and Virginia Nicolson as coconspirators and costars, and Charles O'Neal, Edgerton Paul, and William Mowry as performers in the short film he planned. Vance would handle the camerawork. Orson would direct. The Dubliners took the day off.

The film was intended as a send-up of the avant-garde of the time— films like Luis Buñuel and Salvador Dalí's surrealist *Un Chien Andalou* and Jean Cocteau's *Blood of a Poet*—with, as Welles explained years later, a heavy dose of *The Cabinet of Dr. Caligari*.

There was also a dash of minstrel show in his own central role as a southern plantation owner sporting a bald pate and garish makeup. Twirling a cane, Orson is introduced prancing down a fire escape on one of the Todd School buildings, bending over to leer into a close-up. A blackfaced, white-wigged minion (Edgerton Paul) rings the Todd School bell. A Keystone Kop (not the last in Welles's filmography) darts past the camera. Virginia, garbed as a grosteque old granny, cackling and gesticulating wildly, rides a rocking chair on a rooftop. Close shots of tolling bells and spinning mirrored globes segue into sinister moving fingers, guttering candles, a hangman's noose, a skull, a coffin, a tombstone and finally a screen card: "The End." All of this is intercut with shots of Orson hamming it up on his boyhood instrument: a piano.

But the piano tinkling was not heard. The film was soundless of course, and *The Hearts of Age* was lost and forgotten until 1962, when the young film scholar (later professor) Russell Merritt discovered the footage among Vance's effects in the Greenwich, Connecticut, public library. Though it is plotless and zany, Welles experts have argued that this first conscious filmmaking on his part anticipates much in his later masterpieces. The spinning mirrored ball can be seen as a precursor to the snowy glass paperweight, and the distorted extreme close-ups presage an old man whispering "Rosebud!" The serially repeated shots are not far from the tragic figure of Charles Foster Kane echoed ad infinitum in a row of mirrors. Not only *Citizen Kane*: Welles would carry these devices, this sort of imagery and jump-cutting, over to many future films.

"It was like finding a youthful play of Shakespeare," Welles scholar Joseph McBride reported, when he watched *The Hearts of Age* several years after Merritt discovered it. "We can see," McBride wrote, "through the young man's mélange of styles, the conglomeration of postures both congenial and unassimilated, a vigorous, unguarded, *personal* approach to even the most second-hand of ideas and motifs."

"The signature is unmistakably his," Peter Bogdanovich wrote in *This Is Orson Welles*. "The shots rush at you with amazing speed and variety—complex images of considerable strength; though clearly not a careful or even considered job, it has remarkable spirit and inventiveness."

"It was a Sunday afternoon home movie that we did between two and five in the afternoon," Welles said ruefully years later, "I don't know how it has entered the oeuvre."

Today, the eight-minute film is easily found online.

The most important thing about *The Hearts of Age* may be the inordinate amount of screen time Orson lavished on the young blond apprentice from Wheaton. Virginia Nicolson was "certainly nubile, probably a virgin" when she joined the summer theater festival in Woodstock, Skipper recalled. But the romance between her and Orson grew serious. Hortense Hill desperately tried to preserve "the virginity of a dozen nubile females" placed in her care by "trustful mothers" that summer, but in a few cases, including this one, she may have failed.

The last scheduled play was Dimitri Merezhkovsky's *Tsar Paul*, a drama rooted in nineteenth-century Russian history, with Hilton Edwards as the Tsar; Micheál MacLíammóir as his son, Alexander, the heir to the throne when his father is murdered; and Welles as Count Pahlen, who contrives the Tsar's downfall. Edwards made a triple contribution, starring, directing, and creating the lighting effects. MacLíammóir also designed the sets and costumes. Virginia Nicolson was promoted from apprentice to understudy for Constance Herron, who was playing Empress Elizabeth. Herron took the last night off to introduce "a new star in the making."

By now the Dubliners were giving full service to the summer theater festival, and the Chicago critics continued their praise. The crowd was overflowing on *Tsar Paul*'s mid-August opening night, and grinning cast members hawked peanuts and soda pop between the acts. Edwards drew the longest ovations, and his curtain speech was filled with warmth and humor.

As crucial as Edwards and MacLíammóir were to the quality of *Tsar Paul*, it was Orson whose acting won the greatest praise, winning over his worst big-city doubters. "Mr. Welles hides his nineteen-year-old face behind a makeup that is a cross between the Saracen Saladin and Gen. Pershing, a swarthy, weather-tanned face of sixty, military, stern, zealously patriotic," Lloyd Lewis wrote in the *Chicago Daily News*. "That boyish exuberance which made him caricature Svengali and the Danish king is withheld here by Pahlen's self-discipline. Mr. Welles has, for the moment at least, quit trying to scare his audience to death and is the artist."

Claudia Cassidy, writing in the *Chicago Journal of Commerce*, agreed: "The show belongs to Orson Welles." He topped "previous achievements, none of them negligible," she continued. "He dominates the stage not alone by size and voice, but by sheer ability to create and sustain illusion. His variety and range are literally amazing, and his youth has nothing to do with the matter except to hint at genius." Even the sometimes grudging MacLíammóir later praised Orson's performance in *Tsar Paul* as "outrageously exciting."

The crowds had been good earlier in the summer, but now, in August, they were even better: *Tsar Paul*'s two-week run easily sold out. Not a moment too soon: the festival badly needed the revenue to offset its expenses.

To help pay the festival's mounting debt, Orson and the headmaster added a last-minute weekend of *The Drunkard*. Charles O'Neal whipped up a fresh production of the old-fashioned melodrama—acting and directing—while Constance Herron reprised the role of Mad Agnes she had so ably performed for him in Chicago in the spring. Festival students and apprentices were promoted to the other substantial roles for a four-night run at the end of August.

The four mainstays of the Woodstock Theater Festival—Welles, Edwards, MacLíammóir, and Prussing—gave notes to the ensemble but otherwise stayed out of it, giving free rein to O'Neal, a well-liked colleague and an old hand at *The Drunkard*. "On the last regretful night of *Tsar Paul*, amid the lantern-lit trees in the courtyard of the school," MacLíammóir reminisced later, "we drank [to Orson's] health and swore lasting friendship."

As friends they parted. Prussing headed for New York. Edwards and MacLíammóir went first to Soldier Field in Chicago, where they helped stage *The Pageant of the Celt* for two nights in late August, with MacLíammóir narrating, in Gaelic, a script he had helped write. The Dubliners then boarded the Santa Fe for a cross-country sightseeing tour. As for Orson, he would "take a vacation in northern Wisconsin for the hay fever season," according to the local press, "and no doubt will be again with Katharine Cornell for the winter season."

TOMORROW AND TOMORROW AND TOMORROW

CHAPTER 10

1934-1935

Big Ideas

Orson was among the thousands of Actors Equity members who made ends meet working in summer stock, then returned like homing pigeons to cluster around producers' offices in Times Square.

He may have spent a few days in Wisconsin for his hay fever, but he headed to New York in the last week of August, once again checking into the Algonquin Hotel. Anxiously, he arranged to meet with Guthrie McClintic, who had been elusive all summer, but McClintic had only vague promises to offer: Katharine Cornell was vacationing in Italy, he reminded Orson, and they wouldn't be finalizing their plans to bring *Romeo and Juliet* to Broadway until after her return. Halfheartedly, Orson began to make the rounds of other producers, flaunting the Cornell tour and the Woodstock summer theater on his résumé.

The summer theater had been a critical and popular success, but it was underbudgeted and operated at a loss—this would not be an unfamiliar pattern for Orson Welles in the future. Despite an estimated cumulative attendance of eight thousand people, the company's gross expenses came to around $15,000, according to Chicago press accounts, and Roger Hill was left with about $1,500 in bills. As was typical of him, Orson had paid the professional actors salaries, while paying himself little or nothing. Dr. Maurice Bernstein fronted his travel expenses to New York, but he would have to survive on a $100 monthly allowance while waiting for news from McClintic.

Orson returned dutifully to several writing tasks he had been neglecting for months. The headmaster wanted to bring out their Shakespeare volume by the end of 1934, but the manuscript still awaited Orson's final round of sketches and changes. Orson also returned with fresh enthusiasm and determination to "Bright Lucifer," the north woods stage play he'd begun in the summer of 1932 and worked on intermittently ever since. Building on their summer partnership, Orson wanted Hill to produce "Bright Lucifer" in Woodstock or Chicago. The headmaster was intrigued.

One of Orson's first appointments in New York was with producer George C. Tyler, who remembered him from "Marching Song." Tyler had been tempted by that play, and he was open-minded about "Bright Lucifer." But he wondered if Orson would consider writing a play expressly for him. Orson was willing. "If he'll pay me," he wrote to Skipper, "I'll do it."

Among the unemployed actors Orson bumped into on his rounds of agencies and producers were other veterans of the Cornell tour, along with more recently familiar people such as Louise Prussing, who had preceded him from Woodstock and also installed herself at the Algonquin.

He made new friends, including journeyman actor Francis Carpenter, who was trying to branch out as a producer. Carpenter was five years older than Orson and had appeared as a child actor in silent pictures such as *Aladdin and His Wonderful Lamp* back when Orson was in diapers in Kenosha; he told Orson hilarious anecdotes about touring with the famed actress Maude Adams in the stage version of *Peter Pan.*

By the mid-1930s, though, Carpenter's acting opportunities had dwindled to small parts in unimportant plays. He and Orson talked about coproducing a Shakespeare play, and hit on the idea of a Caribbean *Romeo and Juliet* with a largely black cast. Orson, who knew the play by heart, was just the enthusiast Carpenter needed to help transfer the drama to the new setting. What Orson didn't know about black patois already he could pick up on the street, at Harlem clubs, from books, and from the numerous all-black plays suddenly in vogue in New York.

He and Carpenter imagined a *Romeo and Juliet* set in Martinique, the lovers divided not just by family but by race: one family white, the other black. Orson snared an established scenic designer with Wisconsin roots, Albert Johnson, to sketch costumes and settings for the project. What eluded the partners was what often eluded Orson: the dough-re-mi. The Caribbean *Romeo and Juliet* was announced in the *New York Times*, only to be postponed and announced again.

Most nights Orson was up past midnight, shuffling projects like playing cards: the Shakespeare guide for young people, his work on "Bright Lucifer," the new idea for George Tyler, and the Caribbean *Romeo and Juliet*. He took breaks to write "punk and rambling" letters to Chicago and Woodstock. "Sleep with my asthma, which is pretty bad, is impossible," he wrote to Skipper Hill.

The days were also endurance tests; he waited endlessly for McClintic and hung out with fellow actors who were similarly treading water. "New York couldn't be worse," Orson complained. "It's hotter and emptier and noisier than I've ever known it before." He had dinner with Louise Prussing a few times, reminiscing about the summer. He spent idle time with Dick Ogden, another Woodstock alumnus who amused him, and palled around with George Macready, another veteran of Cornell's ensembles, both still waiting for news about *Romeo and Juliet*.

Orson refused to see himself as an unemployed actor. He had a job pending, and he was also a producer and a writer whose recent summer theater operation had been written up in the *New York Times* and *Variety*. One day, he grudgingly accompanied Macready on a circuit of casting offices—but "unofficially," he wrote to Hill, as "just a friend." Orson was pledged to writing. "I'm still sticking, rather futilely and pathetically, to my high horse."

One thing had changed: important people were no longer dodging him. He was treated like an up-and-comer. "I seem to have an excellent name here," he reported to Skipper. "But no work. Of course I could go after things by sitting in the shoe-stringer's offices, but I haven't sunk to that. I will, though, the way it looks."

Hilton Edwards and Micheál MacLíammóir blew into New York in mid-September, weary from sightseeing and eager to get back to Ireland. Their summer with Orson had recharged their creativity, and when they returned they mounted a new production of *The Drunkard* in the Gate's very next season. "They fell under its spell," reported the *Irish Times*, "obtained a copy of the script, and brought it home with them." In time, they even tried *Trilby* at the Gate. Whatever friction they may have had, their time with Orson had left its mark.

"Very doleful parting, indeed, with a bad little band playing on the practically empty deck of the same ship on which they arrived," Orson wrote to Roger Hill. "It seemed to them that they had never really been to America, but I knew better."

These days, many of Orson's letters went to a new confidante: Virginia Nicolson. The aspiring actress rebuffed Orson's first attempts to coax her to New York, heading home to Wheaton after their summer fling. Her parents sniffed at her theatrical ambitions, at Orson, and at theater in general: her father, Leo Nicolson, a self-made man in industrial real estate, lumped theater people together with "blacks, Jews, Democrats, 'pansies,'" according to his granddaughter Chris Welles Feder. The staid Nicolsons expected their beautiful, cultivated daughter to matriculate in college, or at the very least land a business-minded husband from among the eligible bachelors at the Wheaton Country Club.

After about two weeks in Wheaton, buffeted by letters and phone calls from her boyfriend and constant badgering from her parents, Virginia surrendered to Orson's enticements. He had found work for her assisting Francis Carpenter, helping with research on their upcoming Shakespeare production. (It might not have gone well when her parents learned their daughter was going to New York to work on a Caribbean *Romeo and Juliet*.)

Arriving in mid-September, Virginia moved into Orson's suite at the Algonquin, stealthily evading the maids and room-service waiters so he could still claim single occupancy. Her presence buoyed his spirits. Virginia communed with Carpenter, though without pay; more important, she became Orson's muse, typist, and coconspirator on the Big Ideas. She was game for anything. "She was the essence of innocent youth when she came to New York," Welles told Barbara Leaming, "and it brought out a wonderful spirit of *let's go with whatever's going* in her."

When not dining extravagantly on meals they couldn't afford, the young couple spent their remaining money on plays and films. Watching *Small Miracle*, the new Norman Krasna play staged by George Abbott, Orson was struck by the lead, the onetime opera tenor Joseph Spurin-Calleia, who was electrifying in the role of a homicidal fugitive. "I could never forget that performance" in *Small Miracle*, Welles told

Peter Bogdanovich decades later. One day, Welles vowed to Virginia, he would work with Calleia—and so he did, casting Calleia as Menzies, his own character's corrupt partner in *Touch of Evil*. It was one of the finest roles of Calleia's career. "One of the best actors I've ever known," Orson called him. "You play next to him and you just feel the thing that you do with a big actor—this dynamo going on."

The theater scene was dominated by left-wing plays, and Orson kept up with that movement as well as traditional show business. His politics were instinctually progressive, but he was also interested in the agitprop productions because they featured people whose careers he followed. Roman Bohnen, from the Goodman Theatre, had joined the Group Theatre, and Welles went out of his way to see Bohnen and other Goodman alumni perform in New York.

One of the fall sensations was *Stevedore*, playwright Michael Blankfort's call to action against racial prejudice, produced by the Theatre Union at the Civic Repertory off Union Square. Set in New Orleans, the drama involved labor unrest, a rape, a lynch mob, and a race riot. The play seemed almost as exciting off the stage, with firebrands in the audience jumping up to improvise their own speeches and plainclothes cops on the sidewalk taking down names of attendees.

Several of the leads were African Americans. Orson was captivated by Jack Carter, who had been the original Crown for 367 performances in *Porgy* on Broadway; and by Edna Thomas, a star of the Lafayette Theatre's stock company in Harlem. After the performance Orson attended, one of the supporting players, Canada Lee—a former jockey, musician, and boxer—stepped in front of him to prevent an altercation between Welles and young hoodlums spoiling for a fight outside the theater. Gratefully, Orson shook Lee's hand. Orson would remember Jack Carter, Edna Thomas, and Canada Lee.

Having Virginia with him in New York, of course, doubled Orson's money problems. The couple didn't stint on their nights out, and Orson raised eyebrows at the Algonquin when he ordered two of everything for breakfast and lunch. Dr. Bernstein insisted that his allowance must suffice, but Skipper was more sympathetic to the young lovers, and in mid-October he sent them $50: a godsend.

Hill could do little to salve Orson's wounds in late October, however, when McClintic phoned to say that the role of Mercutio in the

Broadway retooling of *Romeo and Juliet* was going to another actor: Brian Aherne, an older, dapper veteran McClintic and Cornell also wanted for their revival of *The Barretts of Wimpole Street*, which was going to follow the Shakespeare play. (Aherne would play the same role—poet Robert Browning—that he had in the original 1931 Cornell production.) Adding insult to injury, McClintic was also going to cast a new Octavius: Burgess Meredith, whom *Time* magazine had hailed as "the most promising juvenile on the U.S. stage."

McClintic insisted that the decisions had nothing to do with Orson, per se. Meredith was a name, and Aherne, in his early thirties, better complemented the other leads of *Romeo and Juliet* (Cornell and Basil Rathbone, still Romeo, were in their early forties). "Orson's extreme and obvious youth in such an important part" as Mercutio, McClintic told Peter Noble, "might make certain other members of the company appear older than they should." McClintic had only the merest consolation prize to offer: Orson could play Tybalt, rival of Romeo, fiery cousin of Juliet.

Orson had feared the worst, and now it had happened. Tybalt was a good role, but decidedly lesser than Mercutio. Saving face, he told people the casting switch was a joint choice on artistic grounds. "Tybalt seldom gets a notice," Orson wrote to Dr. Bernstein in Chicago. "I want to see if Tybalt can be played so it can stand out." But privately Orson was crushed, and he rationalized the situation endlessly to friends.

Virginia was his salvation. The two young people were very much in love, regardless of what Orson said later. Orson always stressed Virginia's innocence when they met, but he was vulnerable too. "Your father was a virgin when he met me, whatever nonsense he tells his biographers these days," Virginia told her daughter, Chris Welles Feder, years later.

When the Algonquin management figured out that the unmarried, underage couple were cohabiting in the hotel, Orson and Virginia were told, essentially, to produce a marriage license or move out. The couple decided to wed, quickly and quietly, in a civil ceremony in Manhattan on November 17. Orson placed an eleventh-hour phone call summoning Roger and Hortense Hill from Woodstock to stand as their witnesses—Orson seemed "terrified" on the phone, the headmaster recalled—and the Hills brought gifts and cash.

Dr. Bernstein wasn't there, because he was busy comforting Hazel Moore after her husband Edward Moore, Orson's beloved "Uncle Ned," had died of a heart attack at the Highland Park train station, en route to Chicago to review a concert.

To Barbara Leaming, Welles characterized his first marriage as whimsical. "We really got married in order to live together," Welles told Leaming. "It wasn't taken very seriously by either of us." But Orson's letters to Virginia, from love at first sight through five years of marriage, are full of earnest affection, and they belie his later disavowals.

Virginia's mother, Lillian Nicolson, raced to New York to confront the newlyweds. The young couple should submit to a proper traditional wedding, she declared, complete with a gown for the bride and a tuxedo for the groom, an official portrait, an officiating minister, and a guest list of family and friends. Virginia said yes—it would pacify her mother and please her too—and Orson, distracted by his comedown in *Romeo and Juliet*, made no objection. Although many knew the truth, Orson and Virginia agreed to pretend they were unmarried until the traditional ceremony. Within forty-eight hours, "rumors that the young couple were married" were squelched in the *Chicago Tribune*'s society column, and an item appeared in the *New York Times* announcing that the young actor debuting in *Romeo and Juliet* was to be married "after the premiere," around Christmas.

Guthrie McClintic had commissioned a new production design from the leading Broadway stage designer, Jo Mielziner: "In the manner of Giotto," Cornell recalled, "and very beautiful." Martha Graham refreshed the choreography. The stage director reinstated some of the text that had been excised from the stodgy road version of *Romeo and Juliet*, restoring some of the humor and romantic spirit of the original. And McClintic's direction would quicken the pace.

The first performance would occur in Detroit in less than a month. Orson was still despondent, but he tried to overcome his reservations. The McClintic-Cornell's *Romeo and Juliet* would be safe, conventional, tasteful, everything he despised in theater—indeed, the opposite of what he and Francis Carpenter were trying to do with their own revisionist take on the same play. Stewing with frustration, he clashed with McClintic during rehearsals. At least once he hurled a teacup at a stage manager who dared to scold him for arriving late—"an ingrained personality defect of his," wrote Simon Callow, referring to both the tardiness and the tantrums. Several times in the weeks ahead, McClintic would put Orson on notice; once, after *Romeo and Juliet* reached Broadway, the malcontent was even replaced by an understudy for two performances.

Orson shook rival Brian Aherne's hand, but his smiling face fooled no one. Though Orson was "friendly and good-natured about losing Mercutio" backstage, Aherne wrote later, his resentment came out in other ways. When Tybalt dueled Mercutio onstage, Aherne recalled, Orson "slashed at me with unnecessary venom and twice he broke my property sword off at the hilt."

The excitement over *Romeo and Juliet*, Cornell's first Broadway appearance in a Shakespeare play, was so strong that the *New York Times* covered the play's Detroit premiere on December 3. The revamped production was "colorful" and "fast-moving," the *Times* reported, and Cornell made a charming, radiant Juliet. Welles was among the few cast members singled out by name as lending "distinction" to the tryout. Cleveland, Pittsburgh, and Toronto also went well, although McClintic docked Orson's salary at least once before the play made it to Broadway. On opening night, Orson sent Roger Hill a "terribly embarrassed" telegram, reporting that he could no longer afford his wedding ring, the "cutaway and garnishes," or even the fee required for the minister. He begged for another emergency loan, which Hill could consider an advance of $100 on royalties for the Shakespeare book, now scheduled for imminent publication.

UNLESS I CAN GET AT LEAST ONE HUNDRED EVERYTHING IN INDE-SCRIBABLE MESS STOP KNOW THIS IS A ROTTEN TIME TO IMPOSE ON YOU BUT IN PRETTY BAD STATE ABSOLUTELY SOLEMN PROMISE AND ON MY WORD WILL PAY YOU IN ONE WEEK REALLY PROMISE EVERY CENT REPAID IN WEEK.

The New York premiere of *Romeo and Juliet* fell on December 20. It was a milestone in Orson's career, the culmination of his years of yearning to conquer Broadway, but now the great moment felt anticlimactic. Orson had talked himself into a mood as fiery as the character he played, and his Tybalt was another performance that divided critics. John Mason Brown in the *New York Post* called the young newcomer's acting only "passable." (Aherne was ranked among the "best" Mercutios that Brown had ever seen.) But Percy Hammond in the *New York Herald Tribune* declared Orson's Tybalt among the finest performances of the season, and others agreed. "He took an unimportant part," wrote a reviewer for *Collier's*, "got his teeth into it, and made it mean something."

On Sunday, December 23, 1934, the weekend of the *Romeo and Juliet* premiere, another anticlimax was staged for guests crowded into the home of Virginia Nicolson's godmother in a gated community, Llewellyn Park in West Orange, New Jersey.

Demonstrating Orson's growing reputation, the guest list for his official wedding was sprinkled with celebrities. Among the attendees were Thornton Wilder, Alexander Woollcott, and Katharine Cornell and Guthrie McClintic—proving that despite his transgressions Orson was a valued member of their company. Other guests included baritone Mario Chamlee, whose opera performances Orson had reviewed as a teenager, and who made the trip from Chicago along with Herbert Witherspoon, a former opera singer and artistic director of the Chicago Civic Opera, who had known Orson's mother in her student days. Once again the Hills were present as witnesses, and this time Orson's guardian, Dr. Maurice Bernstein—"Dadda"—served as his best man.

Carrying a spray of white orchids, the bride was arrayed in a white satin gown with a tulle veil trimmed with seed pearls. The groom wore a formal dress coat tapering to a swallowtail. The presiding minister was the Reverend Vincent L. Burns of the secular Unity Church in Palisade, New Jersey. After the ceremony, Virginia Nicolson Welles sat down at a piano and played an "informal musicale" of her own compositions—including a piece called "Lengthening Shadows" that was vocalized by the versatile Dr. Bernstein.

Even that was not enough for the Nicolsons. A few months later, they put Orson and Virginia through a private party and reception in suburban Wheaton at Cantigny, the vast estate of Joseph Medill and his grandson Colonel Robert R. McCormick, publishers of the *Chicago Tribune*. After their third marriage celebration, Orson and Virginia strolled around the five-hundred-acre estate hand in hand, taking in the mansion, golf course, and landscaped gardens. Orson had visited palatial residences in Ireland and Morocco, but this was his first American Xanadu.

Brief items in the *New York Times* and *Chicago Tribune* reported that the newlyweds would honeymoon at Blind Brook Lodge in Rye, New York, before moving to a new address in Westchester, the suburban county directly north of Manhattan. Their honeymoon was over by Monday evening, however, when Orson returned to Broadway to play Tybalt. Most nights, after Tybalt was slain at the beginning of Act Three, Orson retreated to a third-floor nook of the Martin Beck Theatre, toiling away on "Bright Lucifer," increasingly hoping to finish it so that Skipper could produce the play in Chicago in the summer or fall of 1935.

During the winter break, Roger Hill oversaw the first print run of *Everybody's Shakespeare* at the Todd School; these copies were finished in time for him to bring them to Orson's wedding in New Jersey and claim 1934 as the year of publication. The 156-page book was handsomely produced, with inside covers featuring a collage of historical posters heralding famous Shakespeareans such as Edwin Booth, Charles Kemble, Helen Modjeska, and David Garrick. The interior was ornamented by Orson's scene sketches and illustrations, used as insets and marginalia. Two witty, thoughtful, and accessible introductions, one by the headmaster and Orson jointly, and one solely by Orson, opened windows onto the edited plays: *The Merchant of Venice, Julius Caesar,* and *Twelfth Night.* (Orson gave his main introduction a jocular title: "Biography of William Shakespeare: No. 1,000,999." Its opening line: "Well, one more will not seriously disturb his ashes . . .")

Orson's favorite bookstore in Chicago, Kroch's on Michigan Avenue, was persuaded to display *Everybody's Shakespeare* in its front window, and the volume was also "fronted" by the well-regarded Boulevard Book

Shop in the Diana Court building. But "[Marshall] Fields hide [the books] back in an uninhabited corner where they have now relegated all drama and they gather dust," Hill reported unhappily to Orson in a letter of early 1935. The Chicago newspapers were slow to mention the book. "Sales too," the headmaster added, "are quite lousy."

For Orson, the long-awaited publication day was yet another in his recent string of anticlimaxes. He couldn't find a single store in New York that carried the book; clerks scratched their heads when he asked for a copy. The headmaster was slow to solicit the commercial trade, focusing instead on a mailing list of schools that might be interested in adopting the book for their classes. "Have not yet plugged the book-stores of the country—waiting for reviews (hollow laughter)," Hill responded in a letter, "but will do so in a few days."

Orson was apoplectic. "Send out a few press releases to the big city newspapers," he countered. "Something is rotten in the publicity department. . . . I'm not scolding you, you old gentleman farmer, and I wouldn't even if I had any right to . . . !" He sketched out a burlesque of the kind of press release he thought they should send: "Todd, the wonder-school. Hill, the wonder-schoolmaster. Welles, the wonder-school-boy . . . The director, actor, author, Shakespeare-script-authority (or something) and general globe-trotting—son of a bitch," Orson wrote to Hill. "By God, I'll write you some publicity!"

With the help of Ray Henderson, Katharine Cornell's accommodating press agent, Orson did manage to land one squib for the book in the *New York Times*. Henderson also helped compile a list of drama and book editors across the nation, and a who's who of theatrical notables to whom Hill should send complimentary copies. Orson asked Hill to send the new book to influential friends such as Thornton Wilder and Alexander Woollcott, who would be sure to spread the word.

Long after Virginia had gone to bed in New York, long after he was done for the night as Tybalt, in the last hours of darkness when Orson really became adrenalized, he brainstormed new strategies for hyping the book. Hill was busy as always at school, and nothing ever happened as fast as Orson wanted. Both men felt disheartened.

But Orson's spirits rose when Ashton Stevens took up his cause in the *Chicago American*, calling *Everybody's Shakespeare* "the gayest Bard book I ever saw." Stevens acknowledged Roger Hill's contribution, but said that Orson, Hill's "prize graduate," deserved the major credit. "Master Welles is never stuffed," the columnist wrote. "He is endeavoring to unschoolmaster the Bard. And I think he goes a good distance to canceling the course of compulsory Shakespeare."

Such moments brought out Orson's humility, and he slaved over a letter thanking Stevens for "the very swellest notice imaginable," carrying a draft around in his pocket for days as he commuted from Westchester to the Martin Beck Theater.

Everybody's Shakespeare was an exceptional piece of work, destined for numerous future editions, but it would always be a footnote in Orson's career. *Romeo and Juliet* would affect him more profoundly, though not in the way he once imagined.

In the audience on the show's opening night was a thirty-two-year-old stage producer, John Houseman. Temporarily unsettled in his own life, Houseman attended the premiere as a guest of stage designer Jo Mielziner, and like most people in the audience he had never laid eyes on the young actor making his Broadway debut. The "glossy" production failed to impress him; he found Katharine Cornell "fervent" enough as Juliet, but Basil Rathbone was "a polite, middle-aged Romeo." It was the newcomer to Broadway, Orson Welles, who mesmerized him.

What struck Houseman about the show was "the excitement of two brief moments when the furious Tybalt appeared suddenly in that sunlit Verona square," he wrote in his autobiographical *Run-Through*, "death, in scarlet and black, in the form of a monstrous boy, flat-footed and graceless, yet swift and agile; soft as jelly one moment and uncoiled, the next, in a spring of such furious energy that, once released, it could be checked by no human intervention.

"What made this figure so obscene and terrible was the pale, shiny child's face under the unnatural growth of dark beard, from which there issued a voice of such clarity and power that it tore like a high wind through the genteel, modulated voices of the well-trained professionals around him."

Backstage after the show, Houseman greeted his friends Katharine Cornell, Guthrie McClintic, and Jo Mielziner, but he could not spot

Orson, who hadn't lingered for courtesies. Houseman could not shake the "overwhelming and unforgettable" impact of Orson's performance. "In the days that followed," he recalled, "he was seldom out of my mind."

Born in Bucharest in 1902, educated in England, Houseman was a sophisticate who spoke three languages (four if you counted his smattering of Italian). His first job was as an international trader in his father's grain business—a fact Welles often noted, with a sneer, after their falling-out in later years. Houseman had gravitated to the theater world in New York, where he became closely associated with a circle of influential artists and show business folk.

"His British, rather wonderfully cool warmth, his considerate good manners, also British, and his elaborate cultural background in foreign letters and languages, all went up to make a hand that he knew he could bid on," said a friend, composer Virgil Thomson.

By 1934, Houseman had written several plays and staged others—including Thomson's opera *Four Saints in Three Acts*, with a libretto by Gertrude Stein, which he had produced and directed earlier that year. Hailed by the New York press as a landmark production, experimental and groundbreaking in its form, *Four Saints* featured black principals and an all-black chorus of singers vocalizing the lives of saints in sixteenth-century Spain.

Not long before *Romeo and Juliet* opened, however, Houseman had been fired as director of Maxwell Anderson's new Broadway play, *Valley Forge*. Houseman was never a great director; rather, he excelled as a sounding board and as the editor and producer of other people's work. His recent setbacks, the trend toward orthodoxy in left-wing theater, and the difficulty of raising seed money for serious drama during the Depression, had all conspired to undermine Houseman's confidence about the future.

In the weeks after he saw *Romeo and Juliet*, Houseman courted another of his influential friends, the poet Archibald MacLeish, for permission to stage MacLeish's new verse play. One of America's leading modernists, MacLeish had won the first of his three Pulitzer Prizes in 1932 for *Conquistador*, an epic depiction of the conquest of Mexico. His new play, *Panic*, was a blank verse autopsy of the U.S. banking crisis of 1933, complete with Greek chorus. *Panic* was guaranteed to be newsworthy and controversial: American intellectuals scrutinized MacLeish's poetry for its nuances, and New York's left-wing arts community skeptically dissected his unaligned politics. *New Theatre* once had branded him an "unconscious fascist."

Panic revolved around a lead character named McGafferty—the "owner of the country's principal industries and greatest bank," as the script described him, "the leading industrialist and financier of his time." McGafferty defiantly battles the panic, but in the end he is brought down by the destructive bank run, and the play shows him to be a pawn of capitalism and a symbol of its demise. Although MacLeish's script described McGafferty as well into middle age ("a man in his late fifties . . . a strongly built man, his face florid, his hair barely grey, his gestures decisive"), Houseman had a relatively obscure young actor in mind for the part.

The producer may not have known how old Orson was, but he did know how to find him. One night, after Orson's final scene in the play—Romeo slaying Tybalt—Houseman tipped a doorman to be led up to the backstage third floor of the Martin Beck Theatre. Houseman found the actor bare-chested, his beard and makeup wilting under the hot bulbs, bent over the counter in his mirrored dressing room and scribbling away on "Bright Lucifer."

Houseman was particularly struck by Orson as a physical specimen. He even noticed the actor's "extraordinary" hands: "pale, huge and beautifully formed, with enormous white palms and incredibly long tapering fingers." Those hands were busy sweeping over "sheets of paper . . . all covered with large well-formed writing, doodled figures and gruesome faces (a play he was writing about the Devil, he explained smiling)."

At first glance, the producer—nearly thirteen years older than Orson—made a similar impression on the actor. Houseman was tall, balding, always elegantly if austerely dressed. He spoke with a plummy accent he inherited from his British mother. Late in his life, in an unproduced screenplay for a movie about the staging of *The Cradle Will Rock*, Orson described his old friend with deliberate consideration: "In his early thirties," Welles wrote, "he conveys an impression of greater age by virtue of a magisterial air, wholly natural and unforced, and already impressive."

Orson agreed to meet Houseman after the curtain call in a tavern across the street. The producer almost did not recognize the tall, dark-suited, clean, well-combed young man who approached his table, until he noticed the "shuffling, flat-footed gait" that he had found so "frightening" in Tybalt onstage. As the two of them drank their old-fashioneds and talked over Archibald MacLeish's play, Houseman studied what he later described as Orson's "pale pudding face with the violent black eyes, the button nose with the wen to one side of it and the deep runnel meeting the well-shaped mouth over the aston-ishingly small teeth."

Houseman explained his goal of mounting a few showcase perfor-mances of Archibald MacLeish's verse play for small audiences of the artistic and political elite. The estimable James Light, who had been closely associated with Eugene O'Neill and the Provincetown Play-ers in the 1920s, would direct the production. Everything, from the scene design to the music and choreography, would be top of the line. Houseman had commitments from Jo Mielziner and Virgil Thom-son; and Martha Graham, who had worked with Houseman on *Valley Forge* (and with Guthrie McClintic and Katharine Cornell on *Romeo and Juliet*), would choreograph the crowd movements.

After Orson agreed to read the script, he and the producer walked several blocks to Grand Central Terminal, where Houseman saw the actor off on the train to Westchester County. "After he had gone I was left not so much with the impression of his force and brilliance," Houseman wrote in his memoir, "as with a sense of extreme youth and charm and of a courtesy that came very close to tenderness."

Over the next several years, Houseman would become Orson's close collaborator and partner. No one, except perhaps his wife Virginia, was closer to Orson during the creative ferment and high points of the mid-1930s. Partly for that reason, and partly because Houseman was such a vivid and convincing chronicler, his books and many published pieces about his onetime friend have heavily influenced other books about Welles. But Houseman's writings were highly subjective, and don't always stand up to the facts; his portrait of Welles was distorted with apocryphal anecdotes, often presenting Orson as an overgrown child capable of monstrous behavior while painting Houseman in a more favorable light.

Fate, everything was fate. As Orson was known to say, luck smiled on him many times in his career. Was it not pure good luck that John Houseman was so struck by Orson's performance in *Romeo and Juliet* that he offered the struggling young actor the lead in *Panic*?

And yet Orson does not seem to have been struck by the same bolt of lightning. Writing to Roger Hill soon after meeting Houseman, Orson barely mentioned the producer. Touring with the Cornell company, he had missed Houseman's production of *Four Saints in Three Acts* in April 1934. Perhaps he also missed *The Lady from the Sea*, directed by Houseman in May, although the Cornell company had returned to the East by then, and Orson would probably have attempted to see an Ibsen revival starring one of his favorite actors, Roman Bohnen. One thing Orson definitely knew about—everyone knew—was *Valley Forge*, with George Coulouris, Erskine Sanford, and John Hoysradt in the cast. Houseman's firing was big news on the Broadway scene.

Orson merely told the headmaster he was excited at the prospect of working on a production that involved so many famous people: an avant-garde circle that included MacLeish, Thomson, Graham, and others whose unconventionality set them apart from commercial theater. Houseman was a member of this circle of bohemian and modernist artists, who gathered for salons in the high-rises of the Upper East Side. Orson wrote Skipper only that the artists and personalities connected with *Panic* were "worth getting in with and swell to be associated with."

Houseman and onetime press agent Nathan Zatkin had incorporated as the Phoenix Theatre, establishing a bare one-room office on a month-to-month lease above a burlesque theater on West Forty-Second Street. Wearing a tweed jacket, Orson arrived at the office the day after his meeting with Houseman, trailed by "a delicious child with blond reddish hair," in the producer's words. Along with his involvement, Orson wanted his wife, Virginia, to have a role in *Panic*. That was okay with Houseman, who introduced the couple to Zatkin and the third man in the room, the tall, aristocratic Archibald MacLeish, who was on hand as both the author and the production's principal investor. A fellow Illinoisian, dressed in work shirt and trousers, MacLeish extended his hand and told Orson, "Call me Archie."

MacLeish was skeptical about the young actor, however, his eyes narrowing "in exasperation" as he took in the boyish fellow Houseman had picked to play McGafferty, a character in his late fifties. "Never heard of Orson! Neither had anyone else." Not only that; Orson would have to master exceptionally complicated blank-verse speeches according to the adapted rhythm MacLeish had created for *Panic*, which the poet-playwright described as "generally trochaic, sometimes dactylic, sometimes spondaic."

MacLeish and Orson's delicious child-wife made themselves comfortable in two chairs; Houseman and Zatkin hunched on the floor, their backs against the wall. At Houseman's request, Orson started with McGafferty's most difficult scene: his breakdown, which is the climax of the play. MacLeish stared in disbelief as Orson read the lines, hearing the actor's voice revealed in all its "infinite delicacy and brutally devastating power." After performing the breakdown scene, Orson started over on page one of *Panic*, reading in his mellifluous tones for the next hour and a half, speaking not only all of McGafferty's dialogue but the lines of all the other two dozen roles and even the Greek chorus. His few privileged listeners were spellbound. "He was wonderful," MacLeish recalled. "He had a beautiful voice. . . . He didn't know how beautiful, so he didn't spoil it."

Hours later, Orson wrote to tell Skipper about the triumphant audition. "A swell break," he told Skipper. "Lead, Star Part, or Protagonist: Orson Welles! I will play a more than middle-aged Babbitt, giving me a chance to show New York that I can (?) play older parts, which alone sells the whole thing to me, besides which the production will get much attention, will draw a superb first night audience, even if it only runs one night (which it probably will)."

But it hardly mattered to him how long *Panic* ran. The play was the thing: it was a worthy effort, and it dovetailed with his evolving political views. "A rich blank-verse belly blow at the Depression," Orson wrote to Ashton Stevens. McGafferty reminded him of a certain Chicago tycoon, he told Stevens: "a gorgeous, juicy sort of Samuel Insull with a lovely mistress and a lovely suicide. The show is all viciousness, vigour and vividity."

Even as Orson was still performing nightly on Broadway, James Light launched daytime rehearsals of *Panic* in the last week of January.

Houseman and Zatkin booked the Imperial Theatre, the jewel of the Shubert organization on Forty-Fifth Street, usually a showcase for musical comedies. The producers obtained an Equity waiver to underpay the cast, including Houseman's ex-wife Zita Johann, who had just quit Hollywood and horror films; the multitalented Richard Whorf, whose first musical revue had just closed on Broadway; and the eminent African American actress Rose McClendon, a cofounder of the Negro People's Theatre in Harlem.

Jo Mielziner crafted a spare stage with raised platforms and beams of light, shot through with swirling dust, that soared into the rafters. Virgil Thomson contributed a sparse score that included a metronome and ticker tape. Martha Graham choreographed swirling movement for the city street vignettes and large chorus, while James Light, the veteran Provincetown director, took charge of the intimate scenes, including Orson's, revolving around the doomed McGaffrey in his sanctum.

Although plagued by alcoholism, Light was patient and sensitive with artistic types, and MacLeish thought that Orson benefited from Light's long experience. "Orson was a wonderful amateur actor," MacLeish recollected. "He was still amateur. He did all the things amateur actors do. I mean, he overdid everything, but he learned awfully fast."

Young Orson, too, was patient with his troubled older director. He remained "understanding and gentle," Houseman wrote in *Run-Through*, "when Jimmy [Light] started to crack up in the final harrowing days of rehearsal. With his fellow actors [Welles] was considerate," he recalled, and, adding one of his poisoned notes, "perhaps for the only time in his life, punctual."

Whereas *Romeo and Juliet* had struck Orson as hopelessly orthodox, *Panic* was everything he valued: thematically adventurous and artistically courageous. He had learned all he could from Guthrie McClintic and Katharine Cornell, and he would borrow ideas and casting from them for years to come. But *Panic* was the brass ring.

As the March 15 opening loomed, Orson arrived at the theater in the late mornings, before the other actors materialized, to spend hours on his age makeup. Virginia served as his assistant. "He was devoted to the play and devoted to the possibility," said MacLeish. "Very excited!"

The anticipation for MacLeish's new verse play built as galleys cir-

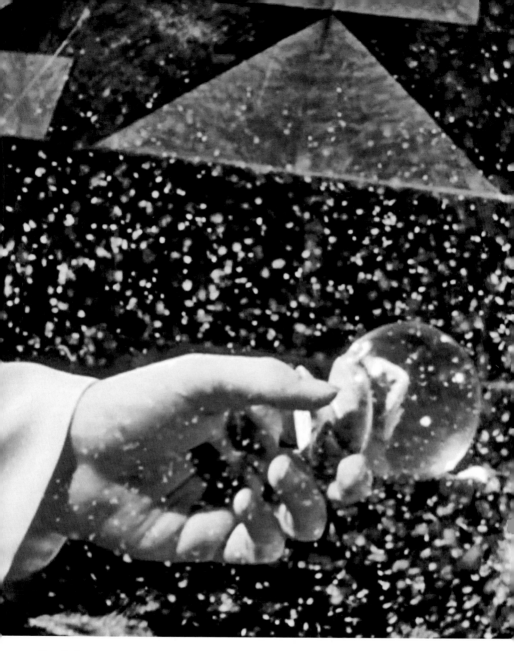

"Rosebud . . . !" The famous first word of dialogue in *Citizen Kane,* the clue to the puzzle of Charles Foster Kane—with multiple meanings for Orson Welles himself. "Maybe Rosebud was something he [Kane] couldn't get, or something he lost," says Thompson the reporter, "but it wouldn't have explained anything."

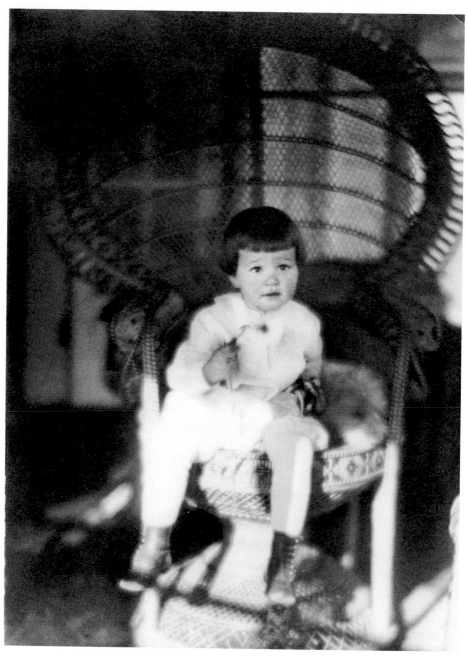

Special from birth, the newborn Orson, son of a power couple, was heralded on page one of his hometown paper in Kenosha, Wisconsin.

The beautiful and multifaceted Beatrice Ives Welles: a prodigy who specialized in classical piano and spoken-word recitals (but wasn't above serving up a Sousa march at parties); Kenosha's first female school board official; and a leading suffragist. In his unfinished early film *Too Much Johnson* (BELOW), Orson included a protest scene (*with Joseph Cotten*, LEFT) that referenced both Beatrice and his father, Dick Welles, who also supported the suffrage movement.

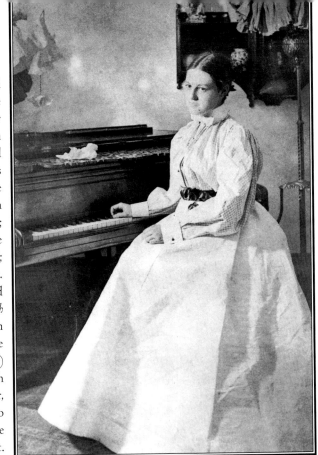

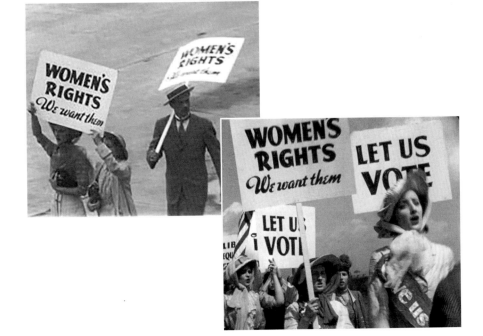

One of the earliest known photographs of little Orson with Beatrice, whose interest in education manifested itself in both her public school reform efforts and her private mentoring of her special boy in art, music, and literature.

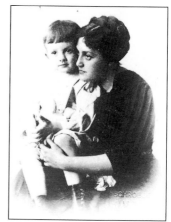

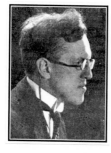

Beatrice's favorite cousin, the artist and Chicago Art Institute teacher Dudley Crafts Watson, a strong and lasting influence in young Orson's life.

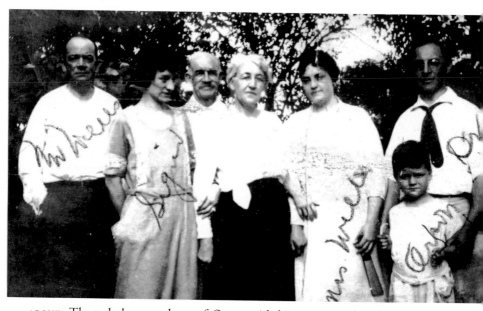

ABOVE: The only known photo of Orson with his parents, taken during a visit to Kenosha after their separation in Chicago. At far right, behind Orson, is Dr. Maurice Bernstein; to Bernstein's right is Beatrice Ives Welles. Businessman and inventor Dick Welles stands aloof at far left, next to nanny Sigrid Jacobsen. The two older people are unidentified.

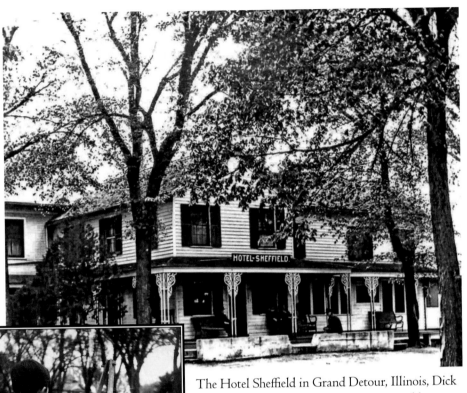

The Hotel Sheffield in Grand Detour, Illinois, Dick Welles's grand experiment. Orson spent golden summers there, painting across the road on the shore of the Rock River (INSET). As an adult, he considered the place one of the lost Edens of his life.

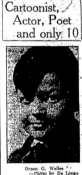

His first full-length profile: *The Capital Times*, Madison, Wisconsin, February 19, 1926.

Cartoonist, Actor, Poet and only 10

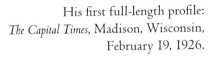

Orson G. Welles
—Photo by De Longe

A POET, artist, cartoonist, and actor at 10 years old.

Orson G. Welles, a pupil in the fourth grade at the Washington school, is already attracting the attention of some of the greatest literary men and artists in the country.

Orson has a background and family history which might partially account for his apparent genius. He is a great grandson of the Gideon Welles who was a member of Pres. Lincoln's cabinet. His mother was a noted artist traveling throughout the country in concert tours. She was also a member of the last state board of

THE CAPITAL TIMES, MADI

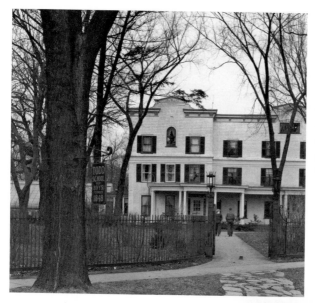

"A paradise for boys": Wallingford Hall, the main entrance to the Todd School for Boys, where young Orson came into his own. "The school did to him . . . what none of the rest of us could," recalled Dudley Crafts Watson.

The earliest known photograph of Orson onstage, performing magic tricks in his detective outfit with classmate Sherman Perlman, Todd School, Halloween, 1925.

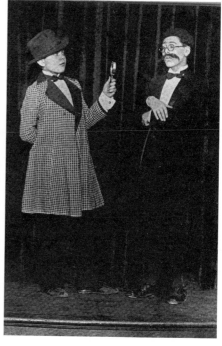

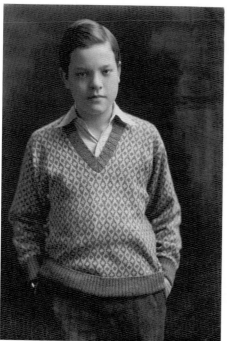

Young Orson, around ninth grade, looking ready for greatness. "The guy was really an unbelievable human being," said his first roommate and friend John Dexter, who graduated the same year as Welles. "We had a lot of fun."

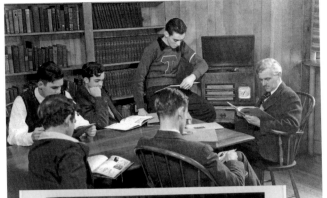

Orson (LEFT, *chin in hand*) and classmates with headmaster Roger "Skipper" Hill—mentor, collaborator, and lifelong friend.

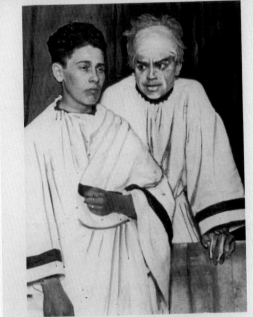

With Hill's assent, Orson virtually commandeered the Todd School's elaborate entertainment schedule. In 1929 he directed and appeared in the school's abridged *Julius Caesar*, staged for Chicago's annual Drama League contest. (The Todd boys took second place.)

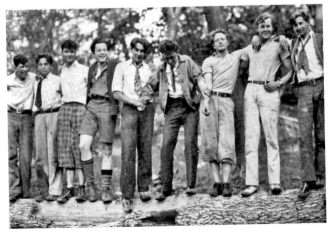

Nearing graduation, Orson (FOURTH FROM LEFT) with his Todd School classmates, among them several other geniuses and footballers capable of reciting Shakespeare on command.

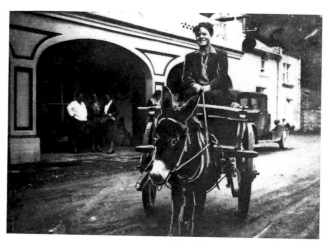

At sixteen, newly orphaned, Orson went to Ireland, where he traveled the countryside on a cart pulled by a donkey named Sheeog. BELOW: Finally landing in Dublin, he met Hilton Edwards (LEFT, *next to Orson*) and Micheál MacLíammóir (RIGHT) at the celebrated Gate Theatre. Three years later, in 1934, he summoned them to perform for his Todd School summer festival, where classmate Hascy Tarbox took this photo.

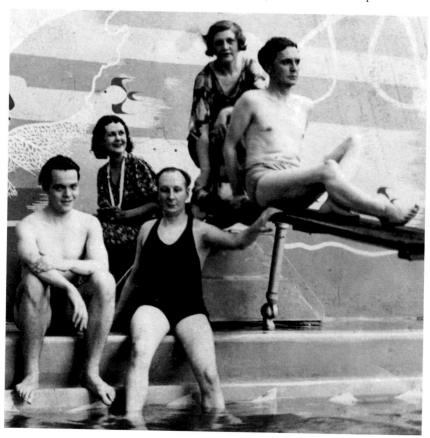

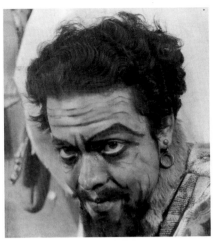

Orson as a flamboyant Mercutio in the Katharine Cornell repertory production of *Romeo and Juliet*. The Cornell tour was a professional breakthrough with a steep learning curve.

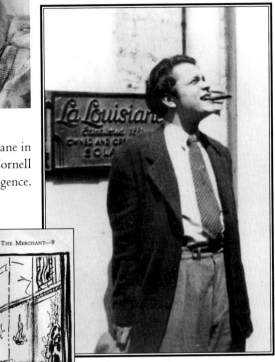

Outside La Louisiane in New Orleans, scene of the Cornell players' overindulgence.

THE MERCHANT—9

RECORD 3
ACT I
Scene III
VENICE—A Public Place

There are countless arrangements for this scene, but many of the most successful settings have employed these elements: a little square with a fountain or a well in the center; to one side Shylock's house, or a part of it, showing the door and a window above. Running along the back is a canal with other buildings visible beyond. Also, if possible, because it has been found tremendously effective in stage-business, a bridge. Shylock, instead of entering after the curtain has risen, might be "discovered" either at his door, or at the top of this bridge. Bassanio, who stands near him, has obviously just been asking, in Antonio's name, for the loan of some money. The old Jew is regarding him shrewdly. Out of the bearded face, cut with hard wrinkles, peer glittering black eyes, surprisingly keen.

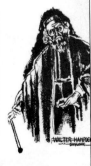

A page from *Everybody's Shakespeare*, Orson's collaboration with Roger Hill; the pages were finally sent off to press after the tour.

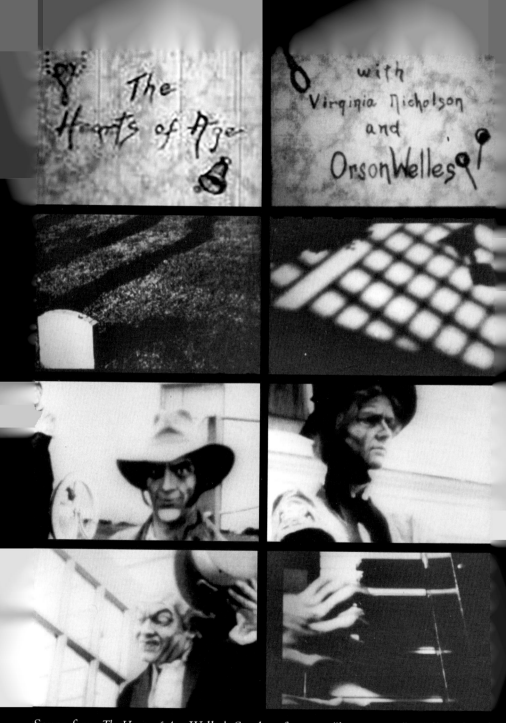

Scenes from *The Hearts of Age*, Welles's Sunday afternoon "home movie": Welles's friend William Vance (*facing camera*), who also served as cameraman; cackling granny Virginia

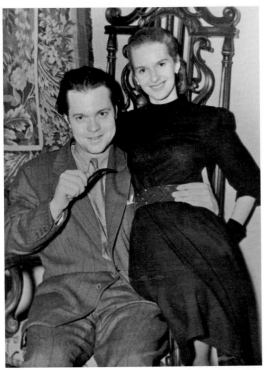

Welles with his wife, Virginia, shortly after their marriage. Regardless of his later comments, the two were very much in love. Orson always stressed Virginia's innocence when they first met, but he was vulnerable too, and she was his salvation.

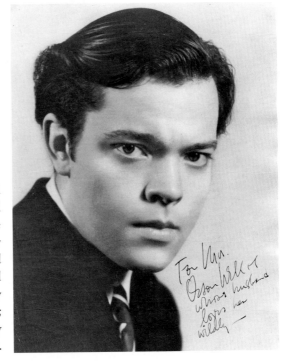

An eighteen-year-old Orson sat for the noted stage photographer Florence Vandamm for a publicity portrait that would be used for the Katharine Cornell tour and his Broadway debut in *Romeo and Juliet*; he inscribed this copy sweetly to his new wife.

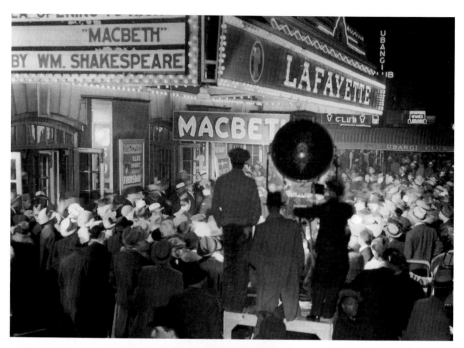

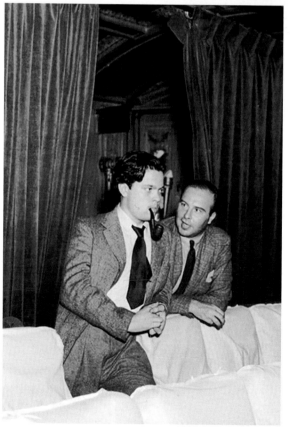

Crowds at the sensational opening night of the Voodoo *Macbeth*: "That was magical," Orson remembered in later years. "It's the great success of my life."

BELOW: Conferring with his partner—and, at first, his loyal booster—John Houseman on the maiden Project 891, the French farce *Horse Eats Hat*.

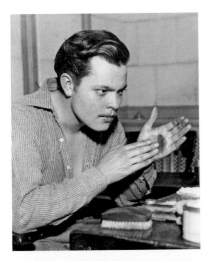

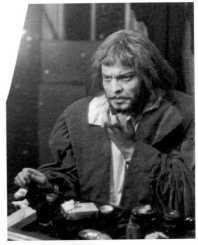

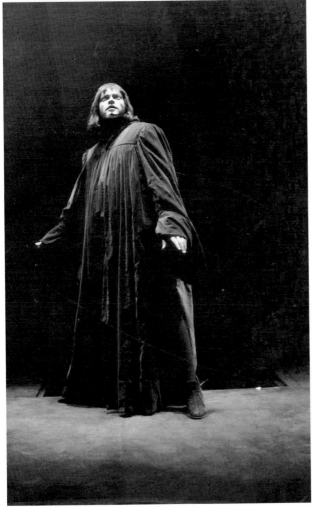

Donning his makeup—a preoccupation with Orson from boyhood—for his defining performance as Faustus in Project 891's 1937 production.

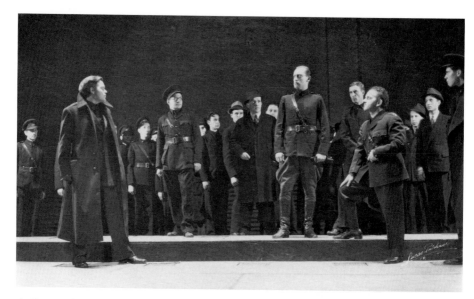

As Brutus (SECOND FROM LEFT) with the cast of the fall 1937 production of *Julius Caesar*. A hit with audiences and critics, it launched the Mercury Theatre like a rocket.

The Shoemaker's Holiday, the Mercury's comedic change of pace after *Julius Caesar*, was its second hit. With Joseph Cotten (CENTER) flanked by Hiram "Chubby" Sherman (LEFT) and Whitford Kane (RIGHT). Also pictured are cast members Norman Lloyd (FAR LEFT), Arthur Anderson, and Marian Warring-Manley (FAR RIGHT).

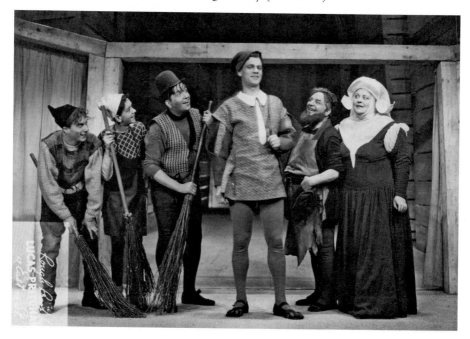

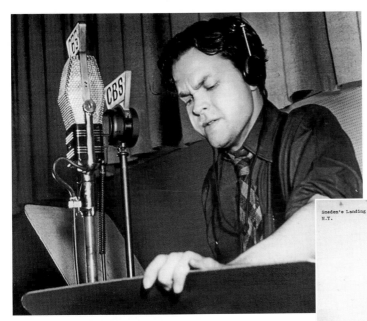

Orson spent several years taking small-time radio gigs for "grocery money" before he finally got his own series to host and produce.

The Christmas card he sketched for friends, 1937.

Sneden's Landing
N.Y.

We hope you are well. Virginia's self-portrait (above) may give you some notion of how we are doing in case you didn't know. In the meantime, Merry Christmas to you from Budget, Orson, Virginia and ....

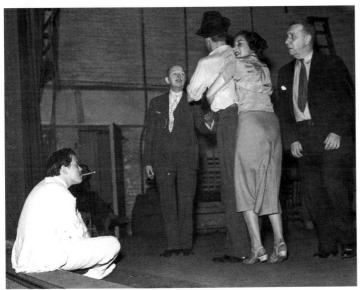

Orson (*with cigar*) with composer Marc Blitzstein (*with mustache*) during rehearsals for *The Cradle Will Rock*. Their deep friendship tested the Federal Theatre Project—and strengthened Orson's left-liberal politics.

Three reputed lovers who were
probably more like soul mates
for sympathetic pillow talk:
ballerinas Vera Zorina (RIGHT)
and Tilly Losch (BELOW LEFT),
and Irish-born actress
Geraldine Fitzgerald
(BELOW RIGHT).

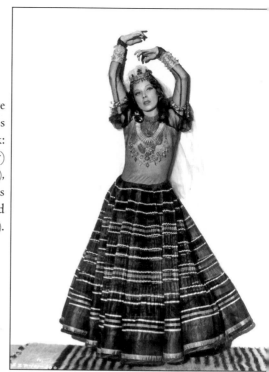

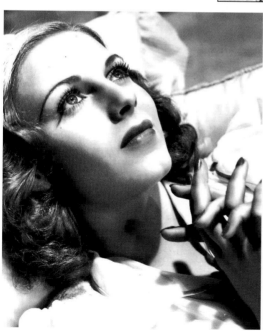

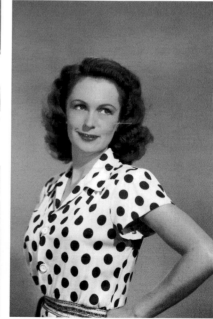

culated among tastemakers. *Panic* divided opinions and unleashed "a storm of controversy in all sections of the radical movement," according to the *Daily Worker*, the U.S. Communist Party's official newspaper. Would *Panic* be sufficiently left-wing and pro-worker? At first, *New Theater* and *New Masses*, two organs often aligned with the *Daily Worker*, agreed to cosponsor a performance for their New York subscribers. But the controversy forced *New Masses* to backpedal; its editors announced that their sponsorship of one performance did "not necessarily imply their endorsement of MacLeish's new work."

Three nights of performances were scheduled, and the Friday, March 15, opening was largely filled with complimentary attendees: subscribers, friends, and drama critics hoping to crunch the weekend deadline. That first night, the audience's reactions were split; the spectators were "mildly admiring and sincerely grateful," as Houseman wrote, but "also worn and confused." At times *Panic* was rousing theater; at other times its message was indecipherable. *The New York Evening Journal*, a Hearst daily, called the production "a pretentious bore," and Robert Garland in the *New York World-Telegram* said the verse play was "better read than heard." Brooks Atkinson temporized in the *New York Times*, noting: "If your mind is constantly searching the verse for meaning, it is difficult to listen to in the theatre, and *Panic*, which is perplexing enough to read in book form, is to this attentive listener, nebulous on the stage."

There was one highlight, Atkinson observed: Orson Welles was "excellent."

In this regard, critics around town were nearly unanimous—the young lead had carried a rather nebulous play on his strong shoulders. Whitney Bolton in the *New York Telegraph* declared flatly: "Orson Welles was the triumph of the hour—he is bluff, defiant, bullock-like and brutal." Gilbert W. Gabriel wrote in the *New York American*, "For such a young actor as Welles to play McGafferty as ruthlessly, as interestingly as he did, was a genuine feat." Gabriel hailed Orson as "one of the most promising artists of our day."

The second-nighters had to pay for their tickets, shelling out $5.50 each; and that stratospheric price, in the depths of the Depression, left the house only half filled. When the curtain rose, and the parable of power and tragedy embodied in Orson's character unfolded, some affluent ticket holders took umbrage at the words of the Greek chorus, which excoriated America's fat cats. There were boos and hisses from the audience.

The final performance, on Sunday, was presold to capacity, to supporters of *New Theater* and *New Masses*. The left-wing publications had solved the problem of whether to endorse the play by scheduling a symposium after the show. Poet Stanley Burnshaw, playwright John Howard Lawson, and the U.S. Communist Party's cultural spokesman V. J. Jerome—three ideologues—would interrogate MacLeish and analyze the play. "The Party's plan was clear, if a trifle ingenuous: to capture alive America's most fashionable poet and put him to work— eager and eloquent on the side of the Revolution," wrote Houseman.

The Sunday crowd was raucous, and Orson delighted in the turnout, drawing on the audience's energy for his outsize performance. With his aging makeup, his strapping presence, and his snake charmer's voice, he beguiled the audience before it could figure out whether McGafferty was good or evil, a symbol or a human being. Whenever he played a "negative" character—one of his great strengths, as he realized— Orson was liberated from pieties. He always refused to dehumanize villainy, and he was a seductive, irresistible villain. He "approached political themes through paradox" in his work, Joseph McBride has written. When François Truffaut wrote that Orson always examined "the angel within the beast, the heart in the monster, the secret of the tyrant . . . the weakness of the strong," he was writing about Welles the director, but the same could be said of Welles's work as an actor.

That night, MacLeish's ringing verse was met with repeated cheers and applause. Onstage afterward, MacLeish faced the symposium panelists, who were hard-pressed to define politically what they had just witnessed. Suffering from flu and a high fever, MacLeish listened politely to their questions, but resisted labels in his elusive answers. The last of the three speakers, V. J. Jerome, declared that the play couldn't be too bad, considering the hostile reaction of the well-heeled audience the night before. "The hiss of the bourgeoisie is the applause of the proletariat!" he proclaimed—a line so good MacLeish should have lifted it for the play.

Jerome did have some nits to pick: *Panic* was not sufficiently pro– working class, he declared. (It was true: like his parents, Orson in his more political stage and screen works always stopped short of blind identification with the proletariat.) Later, in the *New Masses*, Jerome wrote his own critical review: "Capitalism faces destruction [in *Panic,*] but it is necessary to declare who will do the destroying. Will it be the voluntary surrender of life, in the manner of McGafferty?" Jerome's lengthy notice avoided mentioning Orson by name, however.

Orson sat in the back of the theater, listening to the panel. He was a staunch left-liberal, much like Skipper, but never programmatically left-wing; his conversation, letters, and later published newspaper columns all show a resistance to rhetoric or zealotry, which he loathed. Orson later claimed to Barbara Leaming that he disrupted the symposium—"I thought they were talking such nonsense that I began to hoot and holler," he said, until "leftists ordered him ejected from the theater"—but no one else has recalled any such dramatic ejection, and the story seems another "fantasy memory."

That final night seems to have been overwhelmingly positive, however: *Panic* had escaped an ideological auto-da-fé. The third-night audience "did not come to like that play," as MacLeish wrote to Houseman afterward. But "they went away liking it—more than liking it."

Just as important, for three nights Orson Welles reigned supreme in New York, hailed as a major talent by practically every critic in town. For the young actor, *Panic* was a triumph, personally and professionally, to rival *Jew Süss*.

After that glorious weekend, it was back to the future. Halfheartedly, Orson sought other jobs, but he was conflicted about stooping to anything less prestigious. "The truth is my personal success in *Panic* (except in one or two quarters) was so marked I can't get work," Orson lamented to Skipper. "There is the waiting for the big enough part in the big enough play, and the sense of obligation, if you understand."

He spent much of his time working on "Bright Lucifer." When he wasn't writing, he chummed around with Hiram "Chubby" Sherman, a fellow traveler in left-liberal circles, who shared a Greenwich Village flat with his onetime mentor, now life partner, Whitford Kane. Sherman talked about launching a summer stock theater in Springfield, Illinois, where Sherman was born and where Orson had relatives on his mother's side. That sounded like fun to Orson. "It's a chance to do a lot of plays you wouldn't dare to even in a summer theater," he wrote to Skipper. "More than that it's a chance for Virginia to try her wings as a leading lady."

Sherman thought they might offer "Bright Lucifer" as a work in progress in Springfield as part of the summer program. Orson redoubled his efforts to finish the play and get it on the boards—if not in Springfield for the summer of 1935, perhaps at the Opera House in Woodstock. Orson planned to direct and star, and he still wanted Skipper as his producer.

In the two years that Orson had been working fitfully on it, "Bright Lucifer" had evolved into a semiautobiographical stew involving three characters who summer together on Indian reservation lands in northern Wisconsin. One of the characters was an embittered orphaned teenager plagued by hay fever; another was the teenager's adult guardian, an unscrupulous tabloid reporter of the Hearst variety; and the third, a part Orson envisioned for himself, was the reporter's brother, a star of horror films who stirs up trouble with a ghoulish prank on the Indians.

Convinced that Skipper would be won over by the finished product, Orson slaved away late every night, with Virginia as his amanuensis. Despite his first Broadway earnings, he was more than ever financially dependent: although Dr. Bernstein had raised Orson's monthly allowance to $150 after his marriage, the couple needed extra money to tide them over, and now he wrote to ask Roger Hill for a $50 monthly stipend as an advance against the future royalties of *Everybody's Shakespeare*. In return, he offered Hill all the profits from "Bright Lucifer" in perpetuity. He promised the new work would deliver both substance and commercial potential: "a horror play with a literary quality and logic (so far unheard of in this kind of thing), as well as a lot of horror!" He guaranteed: "Tense moments. Screams. Absolutely everything except sex!"

By the time Virginia finished typing the final draft, the couple's finances had deteriorated so dramatically ("situation dire") that Orson felt his best option was to return to the Midwest as soon as possible and stage "Bright Lucifer" as a Todd School production—perhaps in the early spring, he wrote to the headmaster, then reprising it for com-

mencement. Orson could perform triple duty, directing and starring in
the play while teaching drama to Todd Troupers. All Hill, the putative
producer, had to do was supply the teacher's salary. "The Todd Theatre
Festival presents *Bright Lucifer!*" Orson wrote to Skipper Hill. "Think
of the educational value for the boys to be able to attend rehearsals of a
real professional production! The publicity value!" All Skipper had to
do was give "Bright Lucifer" a fair reading. "If you like it, we can start
for Woodstock! . . . It might be a hit. If Chicago goes for it for even a
week we can produce it in New York."

Hill wrote back, enclosing some welcome money, but he said he
hadn't found the time to read "Bright Lucifer" yet; this was puzzling
and dismaying. As the letters from Woodstock slowed down, with
nothing said about "Bright Lucifer," Orson scrambled to hatch other
projects to interest the headmaster. He and Virginia brainstormed a
play that would combine Mark Twain's *Adventures of Tom Sawyer* with his
Adventures of Huckleberry Finn, "probably the grandest stuff ever written
for kids," in Orson's words. Why had no one else ever thought of such
a wonderful idea? "I believe the copyrights have at last expired, hence
the movie of a couple of years ago," Orson explained. "It is ours, then,
for the dramatizing, and it's a gold mine. I'm sure of it. I'll swear to
it!" He was too old to play Tom or Huck, but the Todd boys could
play those parts, and he would find a black actor for the runaway slave
Jim. Orson would portray "the younger, the louder and the funnier of
the two hams [the Dauphin and the Duke], the crooks Tom and Huck
encounter and go down the river on a raft with"; he thought he might
persuade Whitford Kane to play the Duke, "the elder and ginnier"
swindler. Or, if the headmaster preferred, Orson could just write and
direct the show, and the whole thing could be cast "with the cream of
the Troupers."

The Twain play could be readied in time for Closing Day, Orson
assured Hill, and then they could load the Todd boys and sets into
Big Bertha and make a tour "of the summer theatres, country clubs,
halls, movie houses, lawns, churches and swell homes, playing one-
night stands mostly in the summer resort country in the Middle West,
in the East. . . . It's the best publicity ever devised for a prep school.
It couldn't be better!!!!!!" If the tour went well, Big Bertha could take
them all to New York for Christmas shows. "Gas. The boys' meals,

some little change. The production is all paid for . . . No Equity! No Union! Simple! Cheap! A little money on advertising, and a lot of free newspaper space. Amusing to audiences."

Day after day passed, however, with no word from the headmaster. When Hill's next letter finally arrived, it was a shock. The school had suffered a difficult year, Hill explained, straining its resources and finances. He could not encourage any staging of "Bright Lucifer," or of the Mark Twain adaptation. Furthermore, Orson shouldn't count on any reprise of the summer theater festival, whether at the Opera House or as any kind of Big Bertha road tour.

"This summer I must devote to old-fashioned, despised, but evidently necessary salesmanship," Hill admitted. "I'm sure the publicity of last summer has a very genuine cash value to the school in the long run but for the immediate year it was much more offset by my lack of personal work on 'inquirery' follow up. We opened with only seventeen new boys this fall. At no previous opening since I've been in charge have we had less than twice that many."

Deflecting Orson's interest in a school teaching post, Hill advised him to resist the temptation to return home to Illinois at this point in his career. "It would be better for the married couple to be quite far away from either family," Skipper wrote. He urged Orson to think about going away somewhere to do some serious writing, even to consider doing summer stock on the East Coast.

The headmaster's dismissal of "Bright Lucifer" must have wounded Orson, but he moved on with hardly a backward glance; the play that he had worked on for so long was filed away for future Welles experts to ponder. Many of its personal ingredients—the teenager with hay fever, the smothering guardian, the Wisconsin north woods, and a subplot that alluded to adult-child sexual tensions—have encouraged some to view Orson's second complete stage play (after "Marching Song"), as thinly disguised breast-baring. Biographer Simon Callow found "Bright Lucifer" to be "among the most curious and personal documents of his that we have," while scholar James Naremore wrote in *The Magic World of Orson Welles* that it "embodies Welles's major themes," with its mixture of "Midwestern pastoral, grotesque terror, and 'family drama.'"

Joseph McBride, the author of three books on Welles, noted, "The omnipresent 'devil drums' of the north woods Indians are supposed to bring out the diabolical nature (literally) of the cigar-smoking young Orson figure, Eldred Brand, who is described as 'a persuasive little bitch.' Welles's dark self-portrait as a hateful, vengeful demonic youth, resentful of his guardian—sexually, financially, and otherwise—and consumed with indiscriminate rage, make *Bright Lucifer* a disturbing, though clumsily dramatized, glimpse into his nineteen-year-old psyche."

John Houseman had receded into the background for a while after *Panic*, but he saw more of Orson and Virginia in the spring once they abandoned their place in Westchester County for a cheaper apartment on Riverside Drive. Houseman described the Upper West Side flat as a "curious one-room residence" with a huge iron tub where the man of the house lingered for hours, and which, "covered at night with a board and mattress, served them as a marriage bed."

At first the two men met for coffee here and there, trading notes on plays and performers they loved or detested, finding true kinship in their shared enthusiasms and ambitions. After Nathan Zatkin procured a new "temporary headquarters of the catatonic Phoenix Theatre" in the Sardi Building on West Forty-Fourth Street, they began meeting in the Sardi office, "talking, dreaming, laughing and vaguely developing schemes for bricks without straw," as Houseman recalled in *Run-Through*. " 'Planning' is the wrong word for what we did together—then or later. Of the manifold projects we cooked up in the four and a half years of our association—the ones that succeeded and the ones that failed, the ones that were begun and abandoned and the ones that never got started—each was an improvisation, an inspiration or an escape."

The Phoenix office quickly became a haven for out-of-work theater people, with Chubby Sherman, Francis Carpenter, and others dropping by to join in the building of air castles. The big question was what, if anything, the dormant Phoenix enterprise should attempt next. Orson's "dominant drive," Houseman recalled, "was a desire to expose the anemic elegance of Guthrie McClintic's *Romeo and Juliet* through an Elizabethan production of such energy and violence as New York had never seen." But a competing Shakespeare play was too obvious a move for Welles. Instead, he and Houseman narrowed the other prospects down to works by two of Shakespeare's contemporaries: Christopher Marlowe's *Doctor Faustus* and John Ford's *'Tis Pity She's a Whore*.

By April, with support from Roger Hill suspended, Orson was anxious to get a Phoenix production up and going as fast as humanly possible. "It did not matter too much what it was, nor that it was too late in the season, nor that we had no way of financing it," recalled Houseman. Orson chose *'Tis Pity She's a Whore*, and over a weekend spent "in and on his bathtub," in Houseman's words, he whipped up artful sketches of "a handsome and extremely complex Italian street scene (complete with balconies and interiors), in which the stage became a theatrical crossroads where the physical and emotional crises of the tragedy converged." The costume drawings followed, and a short time later Zatkin found a venue: the Bijou Theatre at one end of Shubert Alley, a run-down shell available on reasonable terms.

The partners quickly rounded up a cast and launched read-throughs in Chubby Sherman and Whitford Kane's basement apartment on West Fourteenth Street. Alexander Scourby, who was attracting attention in plays at the New School for Social Research; and Miriam Batista, who had recited Shakespeare in vaudeville, were cast as the incestuous lovers Annabella and Giovanni. The role of Bergetto, the play's ill-fated buffoon, went to Chubby Sherman, "of whose talent," Houseman wrote, Orson "was so fanatically convinced that he would not rest till he had proved it to the world."

On *Panic*, Houseman had been Orson's boss. *'Tis Pity She's a Whore* would be their first real collaboration. With his intense personality and creative drive, Orson led the way, adapting the script, designing the scenery, and directing the play. "I watched him, with growing wonder," Houseman wrote in his memoir, "take as mannered and decadent a work as John Ford's tragedy, bend it to his will and recreate it, on the stage of his imagination, in the vivid dramatic light of his own imagination. . . .

"I was almost thirty-three years old. Welles was twenty. But in my working relationship with this astonishing boy whose theatrical experience was so much greater and richer than mine, it was I who was the pupil, he the teacher. In certain fields I was his senior, possessed of painfully acquired knowledge that was wider and more comprehensive than his; but what amazed and awed me in Orson was his astounding and, apparently, innate dramatic instinct."

Still, the Phoenix faced a familiar hurdle: funding. Francis Carpenter, for whom Orson had set aside a small role in the play, convinced the partners that he had a lifeline to a deep-pocketed angel. "The most outrageous of Orson's many singular friends," as Houseman put it, Carpenter vowed to extract $10,000 from "an aging lady of great wealth," who was his "protectress."

As the play's scheduled May opening neared, *'Tis Pity She's a Whore* was in a heightened state of readiness—"cast, designed, housed," in Houseman's words—but still penniless. No longer able to afford the rent on Riverside Drive, Orson and Virginia sneaked off to join Carpenter on Long Island, where he was squatting at a mansion owned by the elderly "protectress." A devilish character, Carpenter cleverly borrowed what little money the Welleses had and then left them to their own devices, the mansion empty, its refrigerator bare. After three days without a decent meal—or any sign of Carpenter—they surrendered and wired to Dr. Bernstein. The couple moved back into the Algonquin, "signing for things," as Orson wrote to Skipper. "We are broke . . . our income and our heart."

Not long afterward, Orson was supposed to take over the Bijou, launching actor and technical rehearsals for *'Tis Pity She's a Whore*. But the theater and other vendors demanded payments in advance. Carpenter was summoned to a showdown at the Phoenix office. Where was the promised $10,000? Well, Carpenter had good news and bad news. He had just visited the elderly protectress, who had authorized the $10,000. The bad news: it turned out that their benefactor was more passionately devoted to theater *buildings* than to the plays themselves. The $10,000, she stipulated, could be used only for renovating and redecorating the rundown Bijou.

After a long, tense silence, Orson began to laugh. His laughter built into cascading roars. "If Orson had not started to laugh," Houseman recalled, "I doubt if Francis Carpenter would have left the premises . . . alive. His hilarity was infectious. Actors who dropped in to inquire about the start of rehearsals found us, an hour later, still howling, roaring, crowing and slapping ourselves in wild and uncontrollable hysteria." The pair adjourned for an elaborate lunch, during which they decided to cancel the show, vacate the Sardi office, and suspend their partnership.

It was vintage Orson Welles: the fun was in the doing, and the doing was done. He held nothing against Carpenter, who was still welcome in Welles projects as late as 1956, when he appeared among the cast of *King Lear* at New York's City Center. Welles and Houseman parted as friends, promising to stay in touch, but without any real certainty that they would get together again.

With the Broadway season drawing to a close, Orson sent five-alarm telegrams to his guardian and his former headmaster. "The money has a count of three days yet before it's out. And I mean down and out." He pleaded with Roger Hill for a onetime job staging the Todd Troupers' last play of the school year, always a major endeavor. Seeing how downhearted his prize pupil was, Hill drew up "a face-saving offer," in his words, "a very formal-looking document with every-thing nominated in the bond" that pledged $100 monthly to Orson, from May through August, in exchange for his directing the spring play. The Hills also arranged for the couple to lodge in a cottage near Lake Geneva for the rest of the summer. Orson could concentrate on his writing. In return, Hill would take half ownership of the profits of anything Orson wrote.

Within days of the collapse of *'Tis Pity She's a Whore*, Orson and Virginia fled New York, heading first to Dartmouth in New Hampshire to see Orson's Todd classmate William Mowry Jr. play Brutus in an innovative college production of *Julius Caesar*. It was a very unusual production, involving minimal scenery: raised platforms of varying heights, with the main action taking place under pools of light and the rest of the stage plunged into darkness. By the end of April Orson and Virginia were back in Wheaton with the Nicolsons, attending the Chicago Symphony Orchestra's season finale. Orson made a few public appearances in Chicago, addressing groups on "general subjects of the stage," including a presentation at the Circuit Theatre, sponsored by the Round Table of the University of Chicago, that was broadcast locally.

Skipper Hill and musical maestro Carl Hendrickson had already planned the last play of the school year, *Uncle Tom's Cabin*, by the time

Orson arrived in Woodstock just before his twentieth birthday on May 6. Hill's daughter Joan was playing the female lead, Eliza. Although Orson took over the reins of directing, there was little of the publicity fanfare that had marked the previous year's summer festival, and Chicago critics were not bused to the school for performances. *Uncle Tom's Cabin* rarely came up in Hill's later conversations with Welles, except in jokes about the prop gun that misfired in a climactic scene. Orson ghosted a glowing front-page notice in the *Woodstock Daily Sentinel* that gave all credit for masterminding the show to Hill.

After commencement, the Welleses repaired to their summer rental on the south shore of Lake Geneva, half an hour north of Woodstock. Their hope was that they would find peace and inspiration in the idyllic resort community, with the mansions of Chicago industrialists sprinkled around a picturesque lake and beautiful countryside. Lake Geneva was not as rarefied as Ravinia, but the food was excellent, and there were genuine tourist attractions, including the University of Chicago's world-renowned Yerkes Observatory. That summer, the young couple could see Ethel Barrymore's daughter, Ethel Barrymore Colt, and her touring company perform *She Stoops to Conquer*; they also took in productions by a local summer stock group, the Belfry Players.

While in Lake Geneva, the couple were visited more than once by Dr. Maurice Bernstein and Hazel Moore, as well as Orson's mother's favorite cousin, "Uncle" Dudley Crafts Watson, who delivered a stereopticon lecture to a local club. Watson always said that the natural splendors of Lake Geneva, where he was born, inspired his affinity for painting landscapes.

Orson's brother, Richard, had finally been discharged from Kankakee State Hospital, and had taken up temporary residence in Chicago. With almost no money left from his meager inheritance, Richard was working at Hull House, teaching arts and crafts to its impoverished residents. "He got fired from Hull House," Welles told Barbara Leaming, "because he took a hooker upstairs and locked himself in with her and they couldn't get him down for days." Although this anecdote, burnishing Richard's credentials as a Lothario, can't be verified in Hull House archives, Orson must have seen his brother a few times over the summer. Their relationship was strained but cordial. Most people regarded Richard warily; although docile, he was always borrowing money and claiming things he had never done, sparking dust-ups wherever he worked, even at the settlement house.

Orson and Virginia paid occasional visits to Chicago, where they had the loan of Ashton Stevens's apartment on Bellevue Place. They also stole weekends in Wheaton, spending long afternoons golfing, then dining and dancing in the company of Virginia's parents.

To family and friends, Orson seemed unusually subdued. Leo Nic-olson, who hated the fact that his daughter had abandoned her family for the theater, tried to talk Orson into a career as a stockbroker, offer-ing to set him up with friends in the Loop. Orson demurred. Nicolson was insistent, proclaiming that he didn't want his daughter living hand to mouth, married to a failure. Forced into a privileged country-club milieu in the depths of the Depression, holding his tongue while a hard-drinking businessman berated the arts and show business, Orson felt his spine stiffen.

Virginia was on Orson's side. No longer tempted by suburban high society, she felt she had more in common with the black sheep of the Nicolson family: her father's brother, John Urban Nicolson, a poet who had translated Villon's complete works and a modern edition of *The Canterbury Tales* with illustrations by Rockwell Kent.

When Orson had a goal, he pursued it single-mindedly. But that summer, for the first time in a long while, he had no real goal. He and Virginia spent many evenings in Lake Geneva going to films like John Ford's *The Informer* and Robert Flaherty's *Man of Aran*, a documentary re-creation of life on the Aran Islands, which served mainly to remind Orson of the three years that had passed since his time in Ireland, and how stalled he was in life.*

---

* The legend persists in other books that Welles crossed paths with Robert Flaherty on the Aran Islands during his Irish sojourn. Welles fueled this belief with his inter-view for the BBC's *Portrait of Robert Flaherty* in 1952, commemorating Flaherty's death. "By accident, on a trip by curragh," Welles said, "I found myself on Inishmore and in the midst of a long and very rich conversation with Flaherty." But Flaherty did not make his first preliminary visit to the islands until late October 1931, according to Paul Rotha's *Robert J. Flaherty*, by which time Welles was onstage in Dublin. In January 1932, Flaherty returned to Inishmore, which he made his base of operations, but Welles was still being kept busy at the Gate Theatre. Did he perhaps meet Flaherty in Dublin and concoct the rest of it, or was the whole yarn a fantasy memory?

Orson wrote incessantly over the summer of 1935, but he kept shifting gears, and "the literary product of this period was not particularly promising or voluminous," Hill recalled. What little he accomplished has vanished. "Mainly he worked on the old standby, an Irish travel book," Hill remembered. "Also, he turned out a long and rambling piece which was planned for magazine use entitled 'Now I Am 21' or something of the sort. It elucidated in lengthy form his philosophy on life, love, literature, art, the drama, and what not. If his travel book was halted for this, so this was halted for another Big Idea—a daily radio program which would be a sort of super-almanac. 'June 28: This date is famous because of the birth of so-and-so in 1522. Also, the signing of such-and-such a treaty of 1614 etc.' The incidents had to be dramatized.

"A sort of March of All-Time."

There would be many crossroads in Orson's life, but the summer of 1935 was one of the most fateful. What should he do with his talent and profession? He was gifted with a deep vein of creativity—even genius, perhaps, as newspaper clippings reminded him. But did he have the character and discipline to channel that genius into a career?

Living modestly, dining out on the Nicolsons, and collecting the monthlies from Dr. Bernstein and Skipper, Orson and Virginia managed to save a surprising amount of money that summer. The respite breathed new life into them, and by the end of August Orson had made a decision. He would leave the past behind him: the Midwest, his summer projects, and along with them his doubts about his own future. He believed in his own luck, and in the kindness of fate. He would kick away the logjams in his path. He and Virginia would return to New York, and this time they would succeed.

The Nicolsons were not pleased with the decision, but no one else who knew the couple was surprised when they said good-bye at the end of August. They were still so young. Virginia Nicolson Welles was only eighteen, Orson just twenty.

The Hills gave the couple an old Essex motorcar to drive east and then junk. Orson still didn't know how to drive, so Virginia drove the whole way at a safe crawl. Orson talked a blue streak, reciting poetry to keep her alert at the wheel. They pulled into Manhattan and abandoned the car in a hotel lot, and almost immediately their luck—fate—turned.

Orson picked up an "odd job at Columbia [CBS]," he wrote to Hill excitedly, with other radio work promised to follow. The couple moved into "the loveliest English basement apartment on 14th Street you could imagine." The place they found, at 319 West Fourteenth Street, was close to Chubby Sherman and Whitford Kane's place, a bookstore, and a "chink laundry," in Orson's phrase. They committed to a one-year lease, reflecting their freshly sunny outlook. "Space, charm, electric ice-box, garden, and all for fifty-five dollars a month! Virginia's having the time of her life living here. A real home and all the rest of it," he told the headmaster. "There's plenty of room for you when you come."

Moreover, Orson reported, his rapport with John Houseman was paying off: the Phoenix Theatre was resurgent. "'Tis Pity She's a Whore goes into rehearsal in less than ten days!"

The "odd job" was Orson's first appearance on a national radio program. One of his actor acquaintances, Paul Stewart, had recommended him to the producer of *American School of the Air*, a long-running educational series that CBS broadcast into U.S. public schools for half an hour one morning a week. The educational series was a source of small but appreciated paychecks to many in show business, and among the struggling actors hired along with Orson was a tall, dapper Virginian whose gentlemanly exterior concealed the spirit of a scamp.

Ten years older than Orson, Joseph Cotten was a late bloomer in show business. Born in Petersburg, Virginia, the son of an assistant postmaster, Cotten had studied acting at the Robert Nugent Hickman School of Expression in Washington, D.C., where he learned to moderate his drawl and paid for his tuition by selling vacuum cleaners and playing center on a semi-professional football team. Unable to find immediate work as an actor in New York, Cotten retreated to Miami, selling advertising for the *Miami Herald* while writing occasional drama criticism for it. Cotten performed with Miami's Civic Theater for several years before returning to New York as an assistant stage manager for producer David Belasco. The handsome Virginian had begun picking up minor Broadway parts (he had appeared, for example, in Guthrie McClintic's production of *Jezebel*), but *American School of the Air* was his meal ticket.

When he showed up at the CBS studios on Madison Avenue, Welles was introduced to Cotten by Knowles Entrikin, the network's producer. "During our chat Orson put the contents of his pipe in the wastebasket and set the office afire," Cotten wrote in his autobiography, *Vanity Will Get You Somewhere*. "I remember Knowles saying at a later time, 'That young man certainly left an impression!'"

Cotten's experience with a newspaper and as a struggling actor resonated with Orson, and he liked Cotten at once. As talented as he was handsome, Cotten was also self-deprecating to a fault. Though he was serious about acting, Cotten took his profession lightly and never seemed ruffled by the ups and downs. He has been born the same year as Richard Welles, and Orson quickly forged a brotherly relationship with "Jo," as Welles always spelled it. Cotten and Welles were soon grinning across a table mischievously as the cast read through the day's script. "This one was about rubber trees in the jungle," Cotten recalled. "A couple of the lines suddenly took on a double meaning and very rude connotations. Instead of biting our tongues and ignoring the moment, Orson and I lost control and broke into choirboy giggles. Knowles stopped the rehearsal and warned us. He used words like *schoolchildren, unprofessional* and *bad manners*.

"I see nothing funny about the line 'barrels and barrels of pith,'" Entrikin scolded them.

("Thick silence in Studio Two," recalled Cotten. "Eyes of all actors remained glued to their scripts.")

"Will Mr. Cotten or Mr. Welles," Entrikin continued, "please tell us what is funny about the line 'barrels and barrels of pith' so that we may all join in with their laughter?" The air was as dead as Grant in his tomb. Then Entrikin made "the mistake of the day," Cotten recalled. "Now, ladies and gentlemen, if indeed that is what we all are," the director announced with a glare, "we will now go back to the beginning of the scene."

The line "barrels and barrels of pith" belonged to another actor, Ray Collins, and this time Collins too collapsed. "His manuscript simply slid from his helpless fingers," Cotten wrote. "Most of the other actors doubled over, the sound man hid behind his bulky equipment, the orchestra sought refuge in the shadow of the bass fiddle, and the two culprits fled the building in hysterical tears. After a few days, when Knowles's face had lost its angry crimson color, he allowed it to smile as he shook hands and accepted apologies."*

Never again would Entrikin cast Welles and Cotten in the same *School of the Air* episode. But he couldn't keep them apart. It was in the fall of 1935 that Orson first began to round up his future Mercury Theatre. He would never find a better adjutant than Paul Stewart, as sturdy a foot soldier as Ray Collins, as close a comrade as Joseph Cotten.

Stewart was a native New Yorker, educated at Columbia University and Brooklyn Law School. He had quit the legal profession to go into acting, and was playing small parts on Broadway and in radio when he met Welles, seven years his junior. His vaguely sinister looks doomed him as a leading man; he would spend much of his career playing villains or losers, as well as directing prolifically in radio and, later, for television.

If Cotten was Orson's wishful mirror image, Collins was the born-in-a-trunk trouper of show business folklore. Forty-five by the time he met Orson, seemingly ancient by comparison, Collins was another player with a whiff of newspaper background, the son of the drama critic for the *Sacramento Bee*. Collins had performed with the William J. Elleford and Del Lawrence stock companies on the West Coast, and toured in vaudeville and legitimate companies across North America, appearing with his first wife, Margaret Marriott, in everything from musicals to Shakespeare.

In the early 1920s, Collins followed his ambitions to New York, hoping to become a leading man. Held back by his stocky build and avuncular looks, he found a few good parts on Broadway, but in 1929 he began to concentrate on radio, where he gained a reputation as one of the most dependable actors in the business.

---

* Joseph Cotten checked his recall with Welles when writing his memoir, but Orson's version of events, given to Henry Jaglom, was that the fateful *School of the Air* episode, which reduced them to laughter, told the story of the Olympic Games, and "we had to say things like, 'Let me see your javelin. It is by far the biggest in all Athens.'"

As Orson turned this important corner in life, weaning himself from the Midwest and his past, he was starting to assemble a professional family that would follow him throughout his career.

John Houseman and Nathan Zatkin had leased another theatre, the President on West Forty-Eighth Street, and announced a new season for the Phoenix Theatre, featuring plays that "while known, are risky propositions in the commercial theatre," according to the *New York Times.* The ambitious list, posted early in the summer of 1935, included Countee Cullen's all-black revamping of *Medea,* starring Rose McClendon; a translation of the Belgian play *Le Cocu Magnifique;* a night of Cocteau and Strindberg one-acts; and "a couple of new American plays."

By the time Orson returned to New York, however—and largely *because* he had returned—this list was replaced by a single play: *'Tis Pity She's a Whore,* now slated for an early October opening. The interested parties met regularly at the Welleses' new apartment on West Fourteenth Street, or two doors down at Whitford Kane and Chubby Sherman's flat. ("If they borrow another pot from us," Kane wrote to Florence Stevens, "I'll kill them.") But *'Tis Pity She's a Whore* was a chimera, gradually dissolving over the fall of 1935.

Though no one realized it immediately, the play's death knell was sounded in mid-October by a headline in the *New York Times:* "$27,000,000 in Jobs for National Arts." The article announced the appointment of a new regional head of the Federal Theatre Project in New York.

Earlier that spring, the Federal Relief Appropriation Act had allocated $5 billion under the Works Progress Administration (WPA) to create jobs for America's hungry and unemployed. In midsummer, Hallie Flanagan, the director of Vassar College's Experimental Theatre, was named head of the Federal Theatre Project, part of the WPA relief operation, which was tasked with stimulating work for thousands of jobless stage artists. New York was the largest branch of the project, and in October Flanagan appointed the playwright Elmer Rice to head that branch. The president of the Authors League of America, Rice was a respected experimental playwright and an outspoken foe of commercial theater.

Moving swiftly, by the end of October Rice had authorized and allocated funds for several distinct New York units of the Federal Theatre Project: a "Living Newspaper" that would produce news-oriented plays in conjunction with the Newspaper Guild, which also had been hit hard by the Depression; a "Popular Price" theater for experimental works; and a "Negro Theatre," cosponsored by the New York Urban League, that would occupy Harlem theater space and produce plays to employ the many out-of-work black citizens. The Negro Theatre Project—or Negro Unit, as it became informally known—was a particularly urgent mission for the Federal Theatre Project; black theater had suffered a sharp decline even before the Depression, and the Harlem community led the New York neighborhoods in unemployment.

Actress Rose McClendon took the lead in early planning for the Negro Theatre Project, and she was embraced by all factions, including black communists in Harlem, who were numerous and influential in those days. After she was diagnosed with cancer, however, she declined formal leadership of the project, offering instead to work with a white coadministrator who might be helpful in building bridges to both white uptown society and Broadway stage artists. Her recommendation for the job was her friend John Houseman. Widely respected for his diplomatic touch as well as his creative personality, Houseman had demonstrated his sensitivity to black artists when staging *Four Saints in Three Acts.*

Houseman accepted, leaving *'Tis Pity She's a Whore*, the Phoenix Theatre, and his partner Nathan Zatkin behind. He promptly gave orders to refurbish the Negro Unit's planned playhouse, the fabled Lafayette Theatre on Seventh Avenue near 131st Street, which had been in disrepair since going dark in the summer of 1934. Houseman signed federal forms to renovate and modernize the theater with improved lighting and sound. After consulting with Harlem residents and Federal Theatre Project staff members, Houseman announced that the Negro Unit would be divided into two halves: one to focus on plays set in contemporary Negro locales, written, directed, and performed by Harlemites; the other to present classical works featuring all-black casts.

The first Negro Unit plays were announced in the week before Christmas. The lineup included *St. Louis Woman* by Countee Cullen and

Arva Bartemps; an untitled commission by Zora Neale Hurston; *Walk Together Children* by actor-playwright Frank Wilson; and an all-black *Macbeth*. The name Orson Welles was not mentioned.

Once Houseman was ensconced in his position, and the all-black *Macbeth* made the list, however, Orson was in the pipeline. What he always needed more than anything else—money to bankroll his ideas—was suddenly within his grasp. The minute Houseman came to the Welleses' apartment and asked him to direct *Macbeth* for the Negro Unit, Orson said yes.

Later that same night, Orson phoned Houseman to convey a Big Idea for the production: they should set the all-black *Macbeth* in Haiti. The conceit was salvaged from the ill-fated Caribbean *Romeo and Juliet*—but it was Virginia, Orson always claimed, who recognized the play's dramatic parallels to the story of Henri Christophe, a former slave who helped lead the rebellion that brought independence to Haiti in 1804. After purging his enemies and proclaiming himself King Henry I, the autocratic Christophe became increasingly unpopular, and killed himself before he could be ousted in a coup.

Virginia may have had the idea, but Orson was primed for it: He knew Eugene O'Neill's play *The Emperor Jones*, and the 1933 film starring Paul Robeson. In his days at Todd School he had memorized Wendell Phillips's tribute to Toussaint Louverture, the "black Napoleon" who was the military genius of the Haitian revolution and another inspiration for this new *Macbeth*. Orson had probably visited Haiti on his Caribbean trip with Dr. Maurice Bernstein in 1927; he was familiar enough with the island's history to rattle it off on the phone to Houseman. He worked deep into the night, and when the producer returned the next day, Orson revealed a plasticine model of the stage set, spread across his ironing board, for the "Voodoo *Macbeth*"—a castle in a jungle clime.

Orson's size and energy were Bunyanesque, and he sowed excitement like Johnny Appleseed. With contagious enthusiasm, he raved to Houseman about the possibilities: atmospheric tropical scenery, native costumes, spooky lighting, incessant chanting and drumming. If Houseman himself had any genius, on this day it was the kind Orson always preferred in a partner: the genius to believe in him, to be swept along by his vision, and to shout *yes*.

Throughout the fall, as Orson proved himself in *American School of the Air* broadcasts, voicing characters of all kinds—from little girls to Great and Famous Men—word spread about the resourceful young actor. Two weeks before Christmas, CBS gave him his first billed role: a special program featuring scenes from the life of composer Frédéric Chopin, who died of tuberculosis. The fifteen-minute show was a one-off, the annual Christmas Seals promotion sponsored by the National Tuberculosis Association, but nonetheless it was Orson's first starring role in a national radio broadcast, and the first time his name would appear in publicity material fed to scores of newspapers across the country. His mother, a lover of Chopin's music, would have chuckled.

On Christmas Eve, Orson strolled into Saks Fifth Avenue, he told Barbara Leaming, hoping to grab a last-minute gift for Virginia. "To maneuver himself through the crush of last-minute shoppers," Leaming wrote, "Orson arrived in a wheelchair, so that people would step aside to make way for him." The actor went straight for a mink stole, frowning at the price tag and pointing out to the salesmen that this very stole would be going on sale the day after Christmas. Couldn't they give it to him at the same discount now? "Otherwise, I have nothing for my wife," he moaned piteously.

The salesmen huddled and voted to give it to him at the lower price. "It was a flash of Christmas sentiment on their part," Orson said, and "great shrewdness on mine."

CHAPTER 11

1936

King Orson

The surprising news that a twenty-year-old white actor from the Midwest would direct the Negro Unit's production of *Macbeth* broke in the *New York Times* on the first Sunday of 1936. Elmer Rice, the head of the New York branch of the Federal Theatre Project, told the *Times* that the "costumes and settings" of the all-black adaptation of the Shakespeare play would be "suggested by Martinique under the empire." *

Orson Welles's reputation as an actor may have been spreading, but as a stage director he was still an unknown quantity in New York. His only credits were a few prep school plays, a little-noticed program in Dublin, and one play for his own summer theater. But Orson lived by his own clock, which always ticked faster than everyone else's. Whether it was a sprint or a marathon, he was always perched over the starting line, straining at the bit. To him, the three and a half years since he graduated from Todd School felt like an eternity. He was ready.

The Negro Unit was humming along by the time Welles's involvement was announced. The first Harlem production, Frank Wilson's *Walk Together Chillun*, directed by Wilson, a black actor who had appeared in *Porgy* on Broadway, was rehearsing in halls and churches pending the reopening of the refurbished Lafayette Theatre. The unit's second play, *Conjur' Man Dies*, also had a white director born in Wisconsin: Joseph

---

* The eventual setting of the all-black *Macbeth* would be Haiti, not Martinique, which was a detail left over from the Caribbean *Romeo and Juliet*.

Losey, whose New York theater credits dated back to 1933. *Chillun* and *Conjur' Man* fulfilled the program's mandate for Negro-oriented plays, while the third production, *Macbeth*, would be its first classical work.

Orson threw himself into the script, relocating Shakespeare's play in a timeless "mythical place" that could be "anywhere in the West Indies," he told the *New York Times* a few months later: Martinique, Haiti, or elsewhere. The adaptation itself must have come easily to him—after all, he had been tweaking Shakespeare since boyhood—but the finished product was an underrated accomplishment. He shortened some speeches, combined others, altered place names to fit the setting. ("Changing 'blasted heath' to 'fetid jungle' was not as ridiculous as you might think," Welles told Peter Noble.) Shakespeare's three sinister witches became voodoo priestesses, and the chorus was expanded to add as many black Harlemites as possible to the cast. He tinkered with the script throughout auditions and rehearsals, as would become his habit, tailoring scenes to his evolving needs.

At the same time, Orson started assembling a backstage team that would add luster to his Voodoo *Macbeth*. He began with a major figure in modern music, a composer who happened to be John Houseman's roommate: Virgil Thomson. A driving force in contemporary music, Thomson had worked with Houseman on the all-black opera *Four Saints in Three Acts.* Although the job would pay a weekly wage of only $23.86—the same compensation allotted to everyone under WPA auspices—the composer agreed to score *Macbeth* on that modest basis.

Almost twenty years older than Orson, Thomson was educated at Harvard and Cambridge, and had sharpened his classical sensibility while living among cultural expatriates in Paris in the twenties. (Not a few people in Houseman's circle wore their degrees from Harvard, Yale, or Princeton like sheriff's badges.) Pale-faced, with a high forehead, Thomson spoke in a piercing voice; he was a charismatic presence and his opinions were always forceful.

Thomson knew Orson glancingly from *Panic,* but now Houseman brought the two men together for a dinner at their midtown apartment—the first time Houseman had opened his home to his young partner. Orson regaled Thomson with his ideas for the score: a backdrop of near-constant percussion, native chanting, and jungle sound effects that would envelop the stage in an otherworldly atmosphere. Thomson was unsure how to take the younger man's formidable personality, and at first the two crossed swords, with Thomson trying "to beat him down because I felt he was full of bluff," the composer recalled. "His verbalization of what he wanted to do in the theatre was not entirely convincing. I argued hard and not always fairly." When the dueling grew heated, Houseman stepped in, whispering to Thomson to "stop it," reassuring him that Orson was "a very, very good man in the theater." Houseman's endorsement quieted Thomson's nerves, and sealed the composer's involvement.

Welles and Thomson never grew close, but Orson courted the composer over a series of working dinners during the planning of *Macbeth*. Orson was very specific about the musical bridges and noise effects he needed for scenes, and Thomson later took pride in saying that he wrote very little original music for the Voodoo *Macbeth*. "I would not humiliate myself to write precisely on his demand," the composer boasted. Instead, Thomson came up with "sound effects and ready-made music—trumpet call, battle scenes and percussive scenes when he wanted them—and of course, the waltzes for the party scene" after Macbeth has murdered Banquo.

"Orson Welles knew nothing about musical ideas," Thomson insisted in later interviews. As the son of a musician, however, and a knowledgeable aficionado of classical and popular music, Orson certainly knew how to defer to prima donnas. "Instead of telling you in musical terms he'd say, 'This is what I want to accomplish,'" recalled Leonard de Paur, who conducted the orchestra for *Macbeth*. "Ninety-nine percent of the time he was right." Thomson warmed to Orson over time, and the two would collaborate on other projects. Years later, the composer conceded that he'd found the charismatic young man intimidating. "Orson was nearly always likeable," Thomson said. "He was never hateful or brutal with me, though I was a little terrified of his firmness. He was extremely professional and knew exactly what he wanted."

Houseman and Thomson belonged to the same circle, and from the beginning there was a distinction between "Houseman's people" and "Orson's people." Houseman seemed to know everyone in high society and artist-bohemian circles, while Orson had spent his life so far piecing together his own network of show business contacts and artistic personalities.

To design the Voodoo *Macbeth*, the partners gathered a team of rising stars, many of them from Wisconsin or Chicago. Houseman recommended the Milwaukee-born lighting prodigy Abe Feder, another veteran of *Four Saints in Three Acts*. As a teenager, Feder had been starstruck by the Great Thurston, Orson's early idol. He had designed lighting for the Goodman Theatre in Chicago and also styled the lighting for Yiddish theater in the Bronx and minor Broadway plays.

Costume and scenic designer Nat Karson also had Chicago credentials. A well-known caricaturist before turning to theater, Karson had created the mural for the Chicago's Board of Education building; he too had worked at the Goodman Theatre, and more recently had teamed with Feder on the lighting and design of several New York plays. Together, the two designers were tasked with realizing Orson's vision for Broadway-level costuming, scenery, and lighting—all on a thrift budget of less than $2,000.

Karson was an easygoing fellow, and he accepted both Orson's plasticine model and his instructions to dress the set in lush, sinister colors. Feder was more opinionated, and he fell into many shouting matches with Orson, who believed he understood lighting as well as anyone. Orson enjoyed a good shouting match—especially when he was the director, and when he had Houseman, the ultimate boss, backing him up.

At the producer's urging, Orson engaged an assistant director from Houseman's coterie: Thomas Anderson, a black Harlemite who had acted in *Four Saints in Three Acts*. Another *Four Saints* veteran was Edward Perry, who was recruited as stage manager. Leonard de Paur, the music director of the Negro Unit, would orchestrate and conduct Thomson's music.

One of Orson's key conscripts was choreographer Asadata Dafora Horton, who led his own unique African performance troupe in New York. A native of Sierra Leone, Horton had studied and sung at La Scala, and launched a pioneering series of African music and dance concerts with the drumming overseen by the Haitian-born master Alphonse Cimber. Orson had seen Horton's African opera *Kykunkor* at

Carnegie Hall on the last leg of the Katharine Cornell tour, and the witch doctor's incantations and tribal drumming hypnotized him.

Horton was just the man to organize the chanting and drumming for the Voodoo *Macbeth*—even though that meant ordering up "five" (according to Houseman) or "twelve" (Welles) live black goats to be sacrificed in order, according to supposed tribal custom, to furnish fresh drum skins. The resourceful secretary Houseman had hired for Negro Unit operations, Augusta Weissberger, managed to get the peculiar expense billed back to the Federal Theatre Project.

Project guidelines mandated that 90 percent of the cast and crew be unemployed black Harlem residents. In all, about 750 people were registered as active members of the Negro Unit; perhaps a fifth of these were "real professionals," according to Federal Theatre Project historian Wendy Smith, but that proportion included seamstresses and elocutionists as well as stagehands and musicians. The small number of actors who had worked professionally had "scant résumés as extras or chorus dancers."

Casting his leads from this undersized pool was arguably Orson's greatest hurdle, but he had long ago learned how to scour a roomful of dubious casting choices and connect with "the one." Sometimes he cast on sight, believing—as an actor with a distinct physical presence who incorporated "externals" in his own work—that the look of a person went a long way toward building the character and performance. At other times he cast decidedly against type and appearance.

At the beginning of their partnership, Welles and Houseman tried to agree about the casting of their plays, especially when it came to the lead roles. Many of the actors were drawn from either Orson's or Houseman's camp, but Houseman almost always deferred to his director, and if they disagreed about a casting choice, the decision—and risk—was Orson's.

For the role of Macbeth, they needed an imposing actor. Auditioning candidates on the platform of a vast recreation hall that belonged to the Harlem Elks, Welles and Houseman considered Juano Hernandez, a strapping Puerto Rican actor, but Hernandez was so busy in theater and radio that they lost him to an actual paying job. Another promising entry was Cherokee Thornton, who had played a voodoo dancer in *Louisiana* on Broadway in 1933.

Orson eventually brought the casting around to Jack Carter, a giant of a man who rippled with muscles and flashed cold gray eyes. The caramel-skinned son of a black Harlem physician and a white Ziegfeld chorus girl, the handsome, strapping Carter was known, almost more than for his emoting and singing, as a "fashion plate and man about Harlem," in the words of the *Amsterdam News*. Casting Carter was a gamble: the actor had notoriously been indicted for complicity in a murder during a drunken brawl in a Harlem speakeasy in 1933. Carter was accused of holding a gun on the proprietor while a local gangster stabbed a victim to death. Carter was acquitted, but the trial had dominated the front pages of Harlem newspapers.

A reliable stage presence since 1920, Carter had played a wide variety of roles in Harlem shows and on the road with the Lafayette Players, before the Lafayette core ensemble left New York for Los Angeles in 1928. He thrilled audiences as the brutal Crown in the original Theatre Guild cast of *Porgy*. It's unclear whether Orson saw *Porgy*, but he definitely saw and remembered Carter's lead role in *Stevedore*, as a union roustabout framed for an assault on a white woman. "He was beautiful!" Welles told Barbara Leaming. "A black Barrymore."

Carter was a perpetually angry man, and his audition seethed with fury. Carter's brand of "slightly derailed energy," in Orson's words, mirrored the director's own. After the audition, "Orson threw his arms around Jack, his eyes brimming with tears of gratitude and admiration," Houseman wrote. The part was his.

Another performer from *Porgy* was Rose McClendon, who had helped organize the Negro Unit. Early on, McClendon had been penciled in as Lady Macbeth, and she would have played the part if her cancer diagnosis hadn't been complicated by pleurisy and pneumonia after the New Year. McClendon never recovered, and her lingering illness ended in her death in June 1936. Orson replaced her with Edna Thomas, an actress of elegance and gravitas who had appeared in both the 1929 *Porgy* revival and *Stevedore* and was another veteran of the Lafayette Players.

One of Orson's inspirations was to convert the role of Hecate, queen of the witches, into a male character suitable for Eric Burroughs's talents. The product of a New York high school, Burroughs had studied at the Royal Academy of Dramatic Art in London and the Kammerspiele

Theatre School in Hamburg, performing Shakespeare in Berlin before Hitler's rise to power. His natural magisterial aura would be bolstered by the twelve-foot bullwhip Orson gave Hecate for stage business. For the pivotal role of Macduff, Macbeth's killer, the director saw many prospects before deciding on the versatile Maurice Ellis, a frequent radio performer who was already standing out in a comic role in rehearsals for Joseph Losey's production of *Conjur' Man Dies*. Last but not least, Orson saved the role of Banquo for Canada Lee, the former boxer who had saved him from an altercation with hooligans after the performance of *Stevedore*. Even as a ghost, the actor's Banquo always brandished a cigar—Orson's own favorite prop.

Of all the performers in Orson's Voodoo *Macbeth*, these five were the only ones with significant professional experience. Most of the people who crowded onto the stage—more than a hundred in all—were performing before an audience for the first time. "Anyone who could read lines was taken on," remembered Edna Thomas. As he'd done with the Todd boys, however, and with the Woodstock summer theater sign-ons—indeed, as he would do for much of his helter-skelter career—Orson worked with the clay at hand. That ability to find greatness in other people, often people on the margins, was an underrated element of his genius.

After the auditions, Orson had about twelve weeks before the play's mid-April opening. Even as he confronted this uphill climb in Harlem, though, his radio career suddenly exploded. And he was as eager for the work as he was desperate for the money.

Orson had declined his Federal Theatre Project paycheck; he later claimed that he never cashed a government check, and research has yet to prove otherwise. After his years of pleading for bailouts and loans from Dr. Maurice Bernstein and Roger Hill, radio was fast emerging as the quickest way to supplement his income—to pay the grocery bills, as he liked to put it.

CBS offered him his first regular stint in mid-January 1936, just as *Macbeth* got under way. On Mondays, Wednesdays, Fridays, and Saturdays, he recited poetry for fifteen minutes on WABC, alternating with songs by tenor Stuart Churchill and music by Ken Wood's orchestra.

Identified by name on the air for the first time, Orson also plugged a commercial sponsor's product for the first time: Cornstarch. "I got fifty bucks each time," he recalled, "and it was terribly nice money to have, because I just turned up five minutes ahead of time and read a poem and ran away with fifty dollars."

The money was a godsend, and his knack for speaking intimately to housewives led to more of the same. Soon, another station—WEAF, the flagship of the NBC network—was booking him for similar poetry recitals on the *Fleischmann Yeast Hour*, Thursdays at 8 P.M. Then in March, WEAF cast him in a featured role in the popular serial *Peter Absolute*, broadcast nationally on Sunday afternoons.

More important, starting in the late fall of 1935, Orson began to appear with growing frequency on *The March of Time*, a half-hour dramatic re-creation of weekly news events whose "prestige and supremacy," in the words of *Radio Guide*, were "unparalleled in the radio world." *The March of Time* was aired nationally from the WABC-CBS headquarters every Friday at 9 P.M. Eastern time, and Orson relished the work. "Great fun," Welles recalled. "Half an hour after something happened, we'd be acting it out with music and sound effects and actors. It was a super show—terribly entertaining."

Orson was not yet part of the inner circle of *March of Time* regulars, however, and his status in the world of radio was still modest. He shuttled among studios almost daily, auditioning for each new part, and was paid humbly by comparison with the famous radio stars. But radio was a different type of challenge, and a more spontaneous source of fun. While many well-known theater people appeared on radio shows, the field was full of hardworking anonymous actors like Orson, and they formed their own clique.

One of the radio actors he met in 1936 was Everett Sloane, a journeyman performer who was part of this microphone clique. Orson liked a diminutive actor with a voice that could squeak or roar, and the versatile Sloane had been featured in radio soap operas and crime dramas since the late 1920s. Six years older than Orson, with a receding hairline and a long, angular face, Sloane had just made his Broadway debut in the frenetic comedy *Boy Meets Girl*, in a supporting role that would last for 669 performances. But he remained ubiquitous in radio, where a talented voice mattered more than a pretty face. "He liked me," Sloane said of Orson, "I liked him. He was always making me laugh."

Orson was an insatiable workhorse, but he was also a social animal, thriving on interaction with people whose company he enjoyed. As the quality of his radio jobs increased, the medium became more important to him, both as a creative outlet and as a place to make new friends.

Most rehearsals for Macbeth took place at night, sometimes stretching from midnight until dawn. Orson was always packing his date book with commitments—on Fridays, for example, the company had to wait all day while their director finished work on The March of Time—but his schedule wasn't the only problem. The second Negro Unit production, Conjur' Man Dies, was performed nightly at the Lafayette Theatre until April I, and Orson's Macbeth company had to wait until the curtain rang down before they could take the stage for their own rehearsals.

Still, from the earliest read-throughs of his Voodoo Macbeth—held in borrowed Harlem auditoriums, in church halls, even at Orson's West Fourteenth Street apartment—he took charge decisively. One of the first things Orson did to consolidate his authority was banish the man who hired him. Although John Houseman had been crucial in assembling the backstage team and cast, Orson had no desire to be second-guessed by a director with Broadway credits. He shrewdly drew a line between creative and administrative authority that would define and limit his partnership with Houseman from the outset.

At first Orson asked Houseman to stay away for just "the first few weeks," according to the producer's later account. "Jack," Orson cautioned Houseman, "if it is possible for you to be at the rehearsals from the day we start, all the way through every day, you are very welcome. But as an occasional visitor you represent an invasion of privacy, and you disturb everybody." "Overwhelmed" by the managerial challenges of launching the Negro Unit, Houseman agreed to absent himself for the short term—but he never recovered the territory he had ceded.

Some members of the cast and crew would recall Houseman as a benign presence ("so good and nice to everybody," said the actress Rosetta LeNoire), but to others he was a remote, almost fugitive figure. "Houseman never came to [Macbeth] rehearsals unless he had a group of people he wanted to impress," Orson sniffed years later. "On more than one occasion, I asked them to leave."

Macbeth was Orson's mountain to scale, and it was going to be a steep climb. Some of the actors were capable of rising to the occasion, but the vast majority were being introduced not just to Shakespeare but to acting itself. "It was really ridiculous in a couple of instances," conductor Leonard de Paur recalled. "There was no way possible that some of these souls were going to be able to read Shakespeare, but read they had to, because they were told to."

Even as a young man, Orson had an array of strategies for directing and for coaxing performances from actors. He lavished charm and respect on leads, for example. "I seduce actors," Welles boasted to Barbara Leaming, "make them fall in love with me." He said much the same to Henry Jaglom: "I direct a movie by making love to everybody in it. I'm not running for office—I don't want to be popular with the crew—but I make love to every actor. Then, when they're no longer working for me, it's like they've been abandoned, like I've betrayed them."

With the ladylike Edna Thomas, Orson was a consummate gentleman, taking her out to fine restaurants, buying her dinner and murmuring in her ear. He formed an equally ardent but decidedly more macho bond with Jack Carter. The two big men went roistering together after rehearsals, vanishing amid "the late-night spots and brothels of Harlem till it was time to rehearse again," according to Houseman. (This sounds more like the exaggeration of a partner left behind: Orson was never much for gambling or whoring.) Orson liked Carter enormously, and the actor learned to trust his director.

Rehearsing the neophytes individually, Orson could be extraordinarily patient. "Let's try that scene again," he might say, "Try it like it is with your father this time . . . what would you do if you were having the same problem or same discussion? How would you talk to your father?" He'd flirt shamelessly with the first-time actresses. "He would say, 'Listen, Sugar; hey, honeybun'—always started out with something to weaken you inside, warm and lovely," recalled Rosetta LeNoire, who was playing one of the witches—her first job in show business. "Then he'd say, 'Listen, hon, you know what you just said, and you know the way you said it. Were you angry? Well, that line, it's not an angry line, is it? Well, would you say it that way if you were saying that from your

heart to somebody that you loved?' Or, 'How would you say it to somebody you couldn't stand?'"

Orson gave the newcomers to Shakespeare credit for "marvelous"
instincts, as he told Leaming years later. "They preserved the poetry in
a funny way," Welles said, "because they found innately the rhythm of
the iambic pentameter and observed it without any instruction."

Sometimes, because of his mood, or because something was going
badly onstage—or perhaps because he was stalling for time and
inspiration—he unleashed outbursts of Vesuvian proportion. He
fumed at people, hurling the script and anything else at hand, stomp-
ing around the stage. His reputation for tantrums began here, during
the Voodoo *Macbeth*. "He knew what he wanted, and he was darn sure
he was going to get it," de Paur recalled. "He abused people. He yelled
and screamed. I never saw him physically assault anybody, but he always
seemed capable of it."

Orson hated the idea of himself as a shouter. "When I shouted, it
was theater," he insisted to Leaming, still trying to repair his image
decades later. "I *never* scream at actors," he told Roger Hill plaintively,
adding, "maybe at the crew sometimes." De Paur again came to his
defense, however, estimating that 90 percent of Orson's tantrums were
a "posture" designed to win him "the authority twenty-year-olds don't
generally have."

When he wasn't performing on radio or rehearsing the cast, Orson
was beseiged by other responsibilities: he had to confer with Virgil
Thomson about the music, Abe Feder about the lighting, Nat Karson
about costumes, and Asadata Dafata Horton about the voodoo scenes
and drumming. He relied on his wife and muse, Virginia, to catch
what he missed, and on his assistant director, Tommy Anderson, to
run the scenes when he was absent.

The tensions within the company were matched by strong head-
winds from the black community. Among Harlem's many left-wing
activists and avowed communists, the prospect of an all-black *Macbeth* masterminded by a young white nobody was inherently objection-
able. The New York Urban League was forced to issue a statement
clarifying that its support for the Negro Unit was contingent on a
long-term vision of a permanent Negro Theater. But the "prevalent"
view among Harlemites, as the *Amsterdam News* reported, was that the

Voodoo *Macbeth* was shaping up as "a blackface comedy or a satirical skit." At the same time, the WPA and the Federal Theatre Project were being attacked constantly by right-wing congressmen in Washington, and the last thing the program's leadership wanted was to be perceived as appeasing the left—in Harlem or anywhere else.

Orson's *Macbeth* wasn't the first WPA production to provoke discord in Washington. In January 1936, Federal Theatre Project officials had canceled *Ethiopia*, the first production of its Living Newspaper unit, after conservative voices complained that the play—dealing with Italy's October 1935 invasion of Ethiopia—was too leftist. Elmer Rice resigned his New York branch leadership post in protest. Reeling from the *Ethiopia* controversy, Federal Theatre Project director Hallie Flanagan hoped that the Negro Unit's *Macbeth* would turn out to be liberal—but not *too* liberal.

And the risks were not just political but financial. The Voodoo *Macbeth* was turning out to be more expensive and fraught with risk than any other federally funded production to date. Some officials thought the investment wasn't worth the hazards. According to Federal Theatre Project historian Wendy Smith, officials believed that Orson's production was consuming "a disproportionate percentage of the Negro Unit's budget and staff time." Houseman seemed overly deferential to the show's young, white director; the producer himself recalled that project staffers called the show "my boyfriend's folly" behind his back.

And there was one more source of stress: the first two productions of the Negro Unit had both met with trouble. *Walk Together Chillun*, the first of the three plays, was a disappointment to both audiences and reviewers; the second, the unpretentiously entertaining *Conjur' Man Dies*, was pooh-poohed by critics like Brooks Atkinson of the *New York Times*, who labeled it "a verbose and amateur charade." If the Negro Unit were to survive, its third production would have to be all things to all people: popular yet artistic, politically meaningful yet beyond partisan reproach.

It was Houseman's job to tamp down the fires, and he brought all his diplomatic skills to the task. Orson was called on to schmooze with worried souls from Harlem and Washington, D.C., and he was good at schmoozing. But he kept his head down as the pressures intensified—

and when *Conjur' Man Dies* sold out and extended its run, the Voodoo *Macbeth* bought some much-needed breathing room.

In April, the motley cast and crew of Orson's Voodoo *Macbeth* finally took over the Lafayette. Nat Karson's crew erected his sets—a lush tropical jungle, a majestic castle, a seaboard backdrop—and the actors donned their costumes and makeup, which were every bit as fantastical as the stage design. The witches were wrapped in gnarled, woolly hide; Macbeth's officers wore gold-braid uniforms with epaulets and feathers on their caps. And the expressive lighting was gradually integrated into the rehearsals, with Orson and Abe Feder arguing venomously about filters and adjustments. "Orson was constantly on Feder's back," Edna Thomas recalled, "screaming away at him."

To all this were added, for the first time, the hypnotic chanting and drumming of Assadata Dafora Horton's African troupe onstage, with the full orchestra in the pit playing Virgil Thomson's music, plus sound effects—crashes of thunder, bursts of lightning, jungle commotion.

All this ingenious stagecraft, designed to cast a spell on the audience, also colored the mood for the actors during final rehearsals, giving the novice players some cover for their inadequacies. The music and background noise were almost nonstop, with Orson carrying over from his radio experience the idea of "introducing music into a scene as a kind of emotional prelude to the scene ahead," as Welles scholar Richard France has observed. The old-fashioned Lanner waltz heard during the coronation ball scene, for example, was gradually overtaken by voodoo drums rising in the background, as the setting shifted to the jungle and witches.

To casual visitors, the run-throughs sometimes seemed like sheer pandemonium, with Orson barking through a megaphone or angrily dictating notes to secretary Augusta Weissberger or his wife, Virginia. "Orson trusted my opinion and taste," Virginia recalled, "because if I didn't understand a thing, my reaction was fairly typical of the average audience."

Sometimes Orson went too far with his explosive rants, insulting people's dignity, and some friendly cast member would have to rescue him before he sparked a mutiny. Once, Orson was struggling with a few actors grouped on one side of the stage while Edna Thomas waited on a staircase leading up to the castle. "Orson began to get very abusive," Thomas recalled, "until, finally, he said to me, 'Darling, come down here. I'm not going to have you standing there all this time while these dumbbells aren't catching on.' When I came down, I told him, 'Orson, don't do that; those people will take your head off.' And they would have."

Another time, Jack Carter stepped up to defend the director, deriding the complaining victims of Orson's excesses as "no-acting sons of bitches." Carter's invective triggered a brawl onstage, according to John Houseman, resulting in some smashed scenery and injury to at least one cast member. Carter's loyalty to Welles was a key factor in sustaining general morale throughout the production. "Not only was he [Carter] above reproach in his own behavior," Houseman wrote later, "but he constituted himself Orson's champion with the company, scornful of its fatigue, quick to detect signs of revolt and to crush movements of disaffection."

As opening night neared, another factor entered the picture: Orson started drinking more heavily than anyone had ever noticed before. Virgil Thomson, insisting that Orson nipped on the job, boasted of having taught him "to drink white wine, not whiskey, at rehearsals." Simon Callow wrote that Orson, like many athletes and entertainers at the time, chewed energy-inducing amphetamines "as if they were candy."

Orson took pride in the notion that he could work all day and night, whizzing in taxis from the Lafayette to midtown radio studios "sometimes two or three times a day," in Houseman's words. But he frequently nodded off in cabs, and stole naps when he could. "The most sleepless period of my life," Orson told Leaming. "We rehearsed from midnight till dawn. And after dawn would rise, I would walk through Central Park. Imagine what New York was like in those days: I'd walk through Harlem, through Central Park, and with that exercise under my belt, take a shower, and go to whatever studio I had to be at."

The notes for the final weeks of rehearsal for the Voodoo *Macbeth* have survived, and they reflect the high stakes and frenzy, along with Orson's impolitic wrath:

"Light on steps typical Feder pink—terrible . . . Light behind dancers too bright—light stinks . . . Tell Feder light on Edna has terrible green value instead of white or lavender . . .

"What about the goddammed thunder? . . . What happened to Virgil Thomson sound effects between the acts? Why wasn't it started sooner? Thunder ending a little too high . . .

"Jesus Christ, Jack [Carter], learn your lines! . . . TAKE THE WEARINESS OUT OF YOUR BODY WHEN YOU GO UPSTAIRS . . . Jack railroading again . . .

"Christ—first half of scene needs ENORMOUS amount of work."

By April, the buzz from Harlem had reached the offices of the *New York Times*, and drama critic Bosley Crowther paid an unusual preopening visit to the Lafayette to observe a rehearsal of this "geographically irreverent *Macbeth*." Welles was in rare form for the interview, expounding on the Voodoo *Macbeth* as every bit as valid as—perhaps even more valid than—the productions of *Othello* and *The Tempest* he was said to have directed at the Royalty Theatre in London. (He did no such thing, of course; it could have been Crowther's mistake, or one more bit of mythmaking on Orson's part.)

"You see," Orson explained to Crowther, "these Negroes have never had the misfortune of hearing Elizabethan verse spouted by actors strongly flavoring of well-cured Smithfield [ham]. They read their lines just as they would any others. On the whole, they're no better or worse than the average white actor before he rediscovered the 'red plush curtain' style." In another interview, Orson was more politically insensitive: Asked why no serious Negro theater movement had ever emerged in the United States, he answered, "Just a matter of an appalling lack of really good Negro actors." ("It must be remembered that most Negro players are simply Brian Aherne in blackface!" he continued, still stinging from being usurped by Aherne on Broadway.)

Many of the players in Orson's production of *Macbeth* had regarded their imperious director warily, privately nicknaming him "Shoebooty" for his lack of decent footwear. As Carlton Moss, a writer and member of the Negro Unit board, recalled, Orson wore "a shoe on one foot and a boot on the other. . . . He was raggedy." But as the production came together, many enjoyed their first taste of Shakespeare, and no one disputed that Shoebooty pushed himself the hardest. Even in his worst moods Orson seemed to know when to stop just short of landing a permanent insult. He called breaks after midnight and ordered in food and drink for everyone, paying for the sandwiches and beer—and much else—out of his own grocery money.

"A quarter of his growing radio earnings, during *Macbeth*, went in loans and handouts to the company," Houseman estimated. "Another quarter was spent on the purchase of props and other necessities (including a severed head) held up by bureaucratic red tape; a third quarter went for meals and cabs; the rest was spent on the entertainment of Jack Carter."

Outside the theater, things looked far less congenial. Fueled by rumors about the production, local activists started picketing the theater, and skeptical drama critics were already sharpening their knives. One night, as Orson and Canada Lee strolled through the foyer, "four alcoholic zealots" (according to Houseman)—or "one" (according to theater historian Wendy Smith)—lunged at Orson. A razor blade was brandished, and for the second time Lee intervened to save him. "Canada quickly overpowered and disarmed the man, who was allegedly put up to it by a Communist faction," wrote Mona Z. Smith, Lee's biographer.

Most of the cast and crew of the Voodoo *Macbeth* had the same protective feelings for Orson. One night, as rehearsal broke for the predawn feast that had become a nightly ritual—Orson's gift to his hungry charges—an actor stopped and exclaimed, "When I die, if I go to heaven and he's not there—if *Orson's* not there—*I'm* gonna picket!" Everyone in the theater fell over laughing. "That's how much we loved him," Rosetta LeNoire recalled.

The hoopla surrounding the Harlem opening of *Macbeth* was a product of Orson's long experience at self-promotion. Luminous stencils promoting the all-black *Macbeth* were painted on Harlem street corners. When a free preview was held two days before the opening night, it drew an audience of three thousand, and emergency police had to be called out to disperse the overflow. On April 15, the official premiere, two brass bands of the brightly uniformed Monarch Negro Elks marched through Harlem carrying *Macbeth* banners, finishing with a flourish in front of the Lafayette. By 6:30 P.M., an estimated ten thousand people clogged the front of the theater, the crowd spreading for blocks and blocks. The face value of the tickets was forty cents; scalpers outside were asking $1.50.

Limousines arrived from two directions—"Harlemites in ermine, orchids and gardenias," in the words of Wendy Smith, "Broadways in mufti." Theatergoers stepped out of fancy cars, floodlights sweeping around them. The celebrities in attendance included actress Fredi Washington, beloved in Harlem for her role as the light-skinned Negro who tries to pass for white in the film *Imitation of Life*, and Joe Louis, one year away from being crowned world heavyweight champion. Edna Ferber, author of *Show Boat*, came to the opening, along with Harlem Renaissance photographer Carl Van Vechten and playwright Elmer Rice, who had given the go-aheads for the Negro Unit before quitting the Federal Theatre Project. Hallie Flanagan arrived from Washington, D.C., to give newsreel interviews and see for herself the show that had stirred so much alarm. "Excitement," reported the *New York Times*, "fairly rocked the Lafayette Theatre."

An hour later than scheduled, with a crash of cymbals and an overture that quoted from "Yamekraw—A Negro Rhapsody," a 1927 work by Harlem stride pianist James P. Johnson, the curtain rose on the Voodoo *Macbeth*. The sight of its richly realized jungle setting drew a gasp from the sold-out audience, including about one hundred men and women standing in the back and aisles. The three witches launched into Shakespeare's spiel, amid the drumming and voodoo chants. "Within five minutes," Houseman wrote later, "we knew that victory was ours."

With his imperious presence and deliberate manner, Jack Carter commanded the stage. Edna Thomas stood out in Lady Macbeth's sleepwalking scene. Canada Lee made an indelible impression as Banquo's cigar-smoking ghost. The audience was riveted, right down to the final dire prophecy, which Orson in his clever revision had plucked from the first act and shifted to the end: holding up Macbeth's severed head, Hecate proclaims, "The charm's wound up!"

Orson hovered anxiously in the wings, his borrowed white shirt drenched, as the curtain fell and the spectators sprang to their feet, cheering wildly. The actors pulled him onstage to join the bows, and eventually, after many salvos of applause, the stage manager gave up on the curtain, and the audience swarmed onstage to embrace the young director and his company.*

If Orson's Voodoo *Macbeth* was a resounding popular success, it was also, like many of his plays and films in years to come, a Rorschach test for reviewers. The opinions of the white first-stringers ranged wildly; often, there were stray pearls of praise amid reviews that were otherwise racially derogatory pans.

"The production is rather weird," wrote Burns Mantle of the *New York Daily News*, adding, "This is not the speech of Negroes, nor within their grasp." (Yet it was also "a spectacular theater experience," he admitted.) Brooks Atkinson of the *New York Times* described the "darktown version" of *Macbeth* as a "weird, vari-colored, raree show," though it boasted scenes and moments that were "a triumph of theatre art." John Mason Brown of the *New York Post* called Orson's direction "inept," his *Macbeth* the murder of a classic. Robert Garland in the *World-Telegram* said the play was "colorful, exciting, and a good colored show." Percy Hammond of the *New York Herald Tribune* lamented "the inability of so melodious a race to sing the music of Shakespeare," and denounced the show as "an exhibition of deluxe boondoggling" that proved the waste and fraud of the Federal Theatre Project.

This last review, in a Hearst paper, rankled certain members of the *Macbeth* cast, and had mysterious consequences. Soon after Hammond's review appeared, one of the lead drummers, a "dwarf with gold teeth" who encouraged Orson to call him Jazbo, approached the director. "The dialogue, reminiscent of a Tarzan film," Welles told Peter Noble, "went something like this:

"Jazbo: 'This critic bad man.'

"O.W.: 'Yes, he is a bad man.'

"Jazbo: 'You want we make beri-beri on this bad man?'

---

* A Hearst newsreel crew shot about four minutes of the play during its run for the WPA film *We Work Again*. Welles had nothing to do with the filming, but it is precious documentation of the Voodoo *Macbeth*, which survives and can be easily found on YouTube.

"O.W. (slightly bewildered): 'Yes, go right ahead and make all the beri-beri you want.'"

The voodoo drummer marched away purposefully. Ten days later, Hammond, the dean of New York critics, died of pneumonia. *Macbeth* was Hammond's last major review. "I realize on reflection that this story is a little hard to believe," Welles liked to say, "but it is circumstantially true."

The verdict of the black press meant the most to the play's cast and crew, however, and when it came it was nearly unanimous. "Magnificent and spectacular," Roi Ottley exclaimed in the *Amsterdam News*. "Our hosannas are extended to Orson Welles." Harlem could stand proud, Errol Aubrey Jones said in the *New York Age*. "The theatre lives again! Hurrah!" Ralph Matthews declared in the nationally circulated *Afro-American* of Baltimore: "It marked Harlem's cultural coming of age." Even the once doubtful *Daily Worker* loved the show. Decrying an "unjustified prediction of failure" by the capitalist press, the communist newspaper hailed the Harlem version of *Macbeth* "as magnificent proof of the dramatic ability of the Negro people."

As Simon Callow wrote, "Every single notice, good or bad—there were no indifferent ones—makes you long to see the show." The Voodoo *Macbeth* proved a box office success, selling out every performance for ten weeks through June, with audiences of "terribly chic people from downtown," in Welles's words, vying with all "the respectable black bourgeoisie" of Harlem for the available seating. The Federal Theatre Project quickly approved plans to move the show to Broadway and tour it to selected cities.

In a career that spanned more than half a century, Welles had few unqualified triumphs. There was Dublin, when he was just a sprig; there was the handful of *Panic* performances; and then there was the Voodoo *Macbeth*. "That was magical," he reminisced in 1982. "I think it's the great success of my life."

Dr. Maurice Bernstein and Roger Hill traveled to New York to see Orson's headline-making production. The director turned twenty-one in May, shortly after the Voodoo *Macbeth* opened. Around this time, looking like a Byronic art history major, he sat for Harlem Renaissance photographer Carl Van Vechten. One nationally syndicated Broadway columnist, O. O. McIntyre, dubbed him "the newest wonder kiddie of the theater," adding, "The Rialto, always skeptical, expects him to be top man in another five years. Or a flash in the pan."

Never again would he lack for party invitations. His radio work accelerated, and Orson also had the rare pleasure of impersonating himself on a *March of Time* segment covering the sensational premiere of *Macbeth*. "The greatest thrill of my life—I don't know why it thrilled me (it does still, to think of it now)," he told Peter Bogdanovich years later. "I guess because I thought *March of Time* was such a great thing to be on. . . . I've never felt since that I've had it made as much as I did that one afternoon."

Virginia lobbied for a vacation, but Orson was more allergic to vacations than to pollen. *Macbeth* had brought him fame but no fortune. Now more than ever Orson badly needed income. Suddenly, he was the toast of New York, and he believed in projecting the image of success to nurture the reality of it. New radio programming would not begin until the fall, and in the meantime he had to make do with *The March of Time*, his noontime poetry gig, and odd jobs to pay the grocer.

Meanwhile, *Macbeth* played in Harlem until June 20, when Eric Burroughs, clutching Macbeth's severed head, delivered the final line for the last time at the Lafayette, amending it to: "Peace! It's wonderful!" Orson then had to tune up the show for the Adelphia Theater on West Fifty-Fourth Street where the production was to have a two-week Broadway run starting on July 4.

Jack Carter lasted only a week in the midtown rendition before disappearing one night after Act One—either because of "the heat," as the *New York Times* reported the next morning, or because he was besotted, with drink as Barbara Leaming later wrote. ("Harlem simmered yesterday with another version," the *Times* added, "something to the effect that Mr. Carter was annoyed when another principal missed a cue.") The levelheaded Maurice Ellis took over, picking up the role of Macbeth for Act Two and then for the rest of the Broadway dates and the ensuing national tour. Carter's desertion did not seem to bother Orson; he preserved his passionate friendship with the black actor, and would cast him again.

During its Broadway run, Orson and the crew worked to adapt the production for the road. In the months to come, the Voodoo *Macbeth* would visit Bridgeport, Hartford, Dallas, Indianapolis, Chicago, Detroit, Cleveland, and Syracuse, playing everywhere to huge crowds and abundant praise. By the time it was over, more than 100,000 Americans saw Orson's production, and a number of local Negro Theatre groups and all-black classical experiments were inspired by its example.

Orson did not go on tour with the Voodoo *Macbeth*—with one fabled exception. Late in life, he told interviewers that he rushed to Detroit that September to step in for Ellis when the actor fell ill and couldn't take the stage as Macbeth. Orson even seized the opportunity to "black up" for the lead. "The only time anybody's ever blacked up to play Macbeth!" Orson liked to boast. "I was a much darker Macbeth than Jack was. I had to prove that I belonged."*

Although his name was freely used in the show's publicity, Welles received no earnings for the national tour. And while the show was the best possible public relations for the Federal Theatre Project, the production never actually turned a profit—in Harlem, on Broadway, or on tour—largely because of the cheap ticket prices mandated by federal sponsorship. According to surviving records, expenses for the tour came to $97,000—while receipts totaled no more than $14,000.

In most other ways, though, Orson felt richly compensated by the experience. "I would go up two or three nights a week to Harlem where I was the king," Welles recalled. "I really was the king!"

An all-black production of Shakespeare was a rare event in America in 1935, and rarer still were black productions that played to integrated audiences. The races were seated together wherever the Voodoo *Macbeth* traveled on tour, and the Federal Theatre Project management

---

* Did Orson black up as Macbeth in Detroit, or was it Indianapolis? The city varies along with other details of the great moment in differing accounts. And did Welles play Macbeth with the all-black cast "just for publicity," as actor George Coulouris complained in one interview? The fact is that if Orson did play Macbeth in the road show of the Voodoo *Macbeth* it was never mentioned at the time in any known press clipping from a white or black newspaper.

bypassed cities where theaters refused to do this. Orson's *Macbeth* was a milestone for civil rights as well as for theater.

Although Orson had grown up within an elite white culture, his mother was a social crusader, his father a Republican when the party of Lincoln was liberal on race. His guardian, Dr. Maurice Bernstein, was an avid New Dealer, and Roger Hill talked Orson's ears off with his progressive politics. Progressive and populist impulses were as deeply embedded in Orson's background as elitist airs and privileges.

Orson's friendships with the out-of-work black Harlemites who populated his Voodoo *Macbeth*, and the very public crucible of mounting the production, deepened his liberal politics and his sensitivity to black history. He forged a lifelong bond with the black community, initially with organizations in Harlem, supporting theatrical causes, and later with national civil rights organizations on broader issues. First he lent his name; later, when he could, he donated money and time.

Welles would aid in the defense of wrongly arrested Mexican youngsters in the so-called Sleepy Lagoon murder case in Hollywood in 1942; he published a series of articles on prejudice, culminating in his remarkable "Why Race Hate Must Be Outlawed" for *Free World* in 1944 ("a stirring, nearly Lincolnesque speech," in David Thomson's words); and in 1946 he used his ABC radio show *Orson Welles Commentaries* to crusade for Isaac Woodard Jr., a black Army veteran attacked and blinded by South Carolina police. His commitment to fighting racism would outlast his involvement in all other politics.

Regardless, by the time the Voodoo *Macbeth* moved on to Broadway, Orson was done with the Negro Unit. The scrutiny of the factions within the black community inhibited him, and the more militant factions had a point: Why shouldn't the all-black productions have black directors? Having accomplished his goals with *Macbeth*, Orson returned to the idea of forming his own company, one he could shape and dominate as its actor-manager.

Leaving the Negro Unit would also mean leaving behind his sometimes awkward relationship with John Houseman, who was formally tied to the company. There were already spiderweb cracks in their relationship. According to Simon Callow, the partners had "a brief violent, personal row on the sidewalk—a taste of things to come," after the *New York Times* review of *Macbeth* complimented "the staging by Orson Welles and John Houseman." Houseman had next to nothing to do with the staging, and the comment rankled Orson.

Virginia, Orson's closest confidante, was leery of Houseman, sharing Orson's suspicion that the older man was infatuated with her husband. "At first," Welles told Barbara Leaming ruefully, "he fell in love with me." Virginia also foresaw that the producer's possessiveness and rivalry were destined to sour the partnership.

After the premiere of *Macbeth* and all the acclaim for Welles, Houseman was itching to prove his own creativity. Late that spring, he traveled to California to talk with Leslie Howard about staging a new production of *Hamlet* on Broadway that fall, with Howard starring and codirecting with Houseman. When Houseman returned, Orson told him he was quitting the Harlem operation. Yet the men found themselves talking over the future and brainstorming ideas for what they might do as a team if they were able to break away from the Negro Unit.

Orson left the door open for Houseman, who made the decision to follow him. "Already, I was totally committed to that unreasoning faith in his theatrical genius that was an essential condition of our partnership," Houseman wrote in his memoir. "Then and later, friends and intimates, especially women, used to reproach me for what they considered my submission to Orson and for devoting so much of my time and energy to promoting his achievements rather than my own. It was difficult to explain to them (since I was not entirely clear about it myself) that if I did subordinate myself consciously and willingly to a man twelve years younger than myself, it was for a compelling and quite selfish reason: it was the price I was willing to pay for my participation in acts of theatrical creation that were far more stimulating and satisfying than any I felt capable of conceiving or creating by myself."

On July 24, the fourth Negro Unit play opened: *Turpentine*, "a routine play of protest, full of leftist clichés," in Houseman's words. By then Houseman already had pitched to Hallie Flanagan and Philip Barber, the new head of the New York branch of the Federal Theatre Project, the idea of an uptown theater venue for him and Welles, promising a range of classical works targeting the Broadway faithful. Thrilled with the success of the Voodoo *Macbeth*, the officials agreed.

Acting swiftly, the partners arranged for a temporary lease on the Shubert organization's nine-hundred-seat Maxine Elliott Theatre on West Forty-Second Street, where Lillian Hellman's *The Children's Hour* was just closing its run. Houseman took over the rose powder room as his administrative command post, while Orson moved into the master dressing room, which included a bedroom and bath. The Maxine Elliott was the first theater Orson could call his own—his personal "magic box," as he liked to say.

In July, the partners took formal leave of the Lafayette. Orson made a "passionate" departure speech to the Harlemites. Houseman, a founder and leader of the unit, found it harder to bid the company farewell, he wrote later, filled as he was with "sorrow and loss and guilt."

Scrambling to name their new venture, the partners rejected "repertory ensemble" ("inaccurate," wrote Houseman) and "people's theatre" ("pretentious"). When they noticed that the unit was designated as Works Progress Administration Project #891 on a government requisition form, that became the name: Project 891.

The partners talked over possible productions, but the final decision was always Orson's. Eager to shift gears after the heavy solemnity of *Macbeth*, they decided to launch with Eugène Labiche's *Un Chapeau de Paille d'Italie* (*An Italian Straw Hat*), a mid-nineteenth-century French farce full of slapstick and wicked double entendres—a brand of lighter fare for which Orson had a lifelong weakness. "No sooner would you open a Classical Theater than what public you might have would be sure that they were going to have a feast of Ibsen and Shakespeare," Welles explained to the press. "That would provide you with a self-conscious theater full of self-conscious actors, impressed with revering the immortal bard. Damn—he's only immortal only as long as people want to see him! That's why we call it '891 Presents' and are opening the season with a farce."

Labiche's farce had a reputation in Europe, but in the United States it was rarely presented. It had last been seen in New York ten years before, when the American Laboratory produced it as *The Straw Hat*. In 1926, filmmaker René Clair had adapted the farce as a silent picture, which Orson had seen and remembered fondly. The play didn't exactly qualify as classical drama, a fact Project 891 tried gamely to finesse. "The WPA, in a throwaway leaflet, issues a sort of quitclaim," explained the *New York Times*, "pointing out that the original 'has been studied in schools.'"

The overlooked French farce was just the start. Welles and House-man loved debating important and forgotten plays, and they were soon projecting an ambitious future schedule featuring Christopher Marlowe's *Dr. Faustus*, which Orson had considered producing for his summer theater; a modern-dress *Julius Caesar*, one of the plays Orson had adapted for *Everybody's Shakespeare*; and Thomas Dekker's *The Shoe-maker's Holiday*, one of those Elizabethan comedies Orson loved.

The Italian Straw Hat had a thinly stretched plot, rife with absurd compli-cations. The story begins when a horse eats a lady's straw hat, compro-mising two lovers who have been meeting secretly in a park. A frantic search is launched for an exact replica to replace the eaten hat. "It was the kind of action Welles adored," noted Peter Conrad in *Orson Welles: The Stories of His Life*, "a chase or pursuit that races around in a circle."

By transferring the original setting and dialogue to an American milieu, as he had adapted *Macbeth* for a Caribbean landscape, Orson could customize the play in his own way. His first order of business was finding a writer to create an updated vernacular translation of the nineteenth-century play, balancing the French flavor with an American sensibility.

One of the members of the Houseman-Thomson circle of mod-ernist artists, musicians, and writers was the erudite dancer and poet Edwin Denby. An American citizen born in China in 1903, Denby was educated at Harvard and the University of Vienna. He had danced professionally in Europe and spoke fluent French. Returning to the United States after the rise of Hitler, Denby developed a budding rep-utation as a published poet and arts writer. (In time he would become America's leading dance critic.) A witty, self-effacing ascetic, Denby lived with his companion, the Swiss-born photographer and filmmaker Rudy Burckhardt, on West Twenty-First Street, close to Orson's flat.

Denby and Welles met to discuss Americanizing the farce, and they got along splendidly. Denby agreed to handle the basic translation, while Orson would guide the modernized and Americanized touches. "I would read a speech, and he would criticize it for the sound," Denby recalled. "If it blurred, he would rephrase it in such a way that the actual spoken sound was very clear and plain and straight. We understood each other perfectly and worked with a good deal of pleasure."

In fits and starts over the summer of 1936, their collaboration produced a script that followed the twisty French plot while Americanizing the dialogue and the characters' names. To reflect the shift to a modern setting, certain trappings were updated—horse-drawn carriages were replaced with motorcars, for instance. Fadinard, the groom who leads the frantic hat search in the French farce, was renamed Freddy; Helene, the intended bride, became Myrtle Mugglethorpe; the aggrieved Lieutenant Tavernier became Lieutenant Grimshot. To top it off, Orson gave the adaptation a brisk, amusing American title: *Horse Eats Hat.*

As with the Voodoo *Macbeth*, Orson wanted made-to-order music for his new production. To compose the eclectic sound and special effects Welles had in mind, Virgil Thomson recommended the gifted Paul Bowles, another pedigreed friend from Houseman's circle, though more of a free spirit than either Thomson or Houseman. A writer and poet as well as a musician, Bowles had studied under Aaron Copland; he'd also lived in footloose fashion in Paris and Morocco. Orson envisioned almost nonstop music and effects during the production, even through the intermissions; at first Bowles was somewhat daunted by the assignment, and Thomson agreed to walk him through stage conventions and take a credit for "arranging."

But Orson did not intimidate Bowles personally. Like Welles, Bowles was a restless and fecund talent who enjoyed blurring the line between his art and his life, and the two were almost instantly simpatico. Bowles, too, had spent time in Spain, and they talked about the Spanish Civil War, ignited by a fascist coup that July. "Within ten minutes of our meeting," Bowles remembered, "Orson shocked me by remarking coolly that he saw no hope of there being anything but fascism in Spain. How right he was!"

For the scenery, costumes, and lighting, Orson lured Abe Feder and Nat Karson away from the Negro Unit, giving them sketches and detailed instructions. To create the horse of the title, he found another imaginative collaborator in the puppeteer Bil Baird, whose shows he had seen at the 1934 Chicago world's fair. Baird devised a creature made of two halves—a papier-mâché head and a velvety torso with roller-skate hooves—and agreed to play the standing half himself. (Welles had noticed Baird's performing skills one day while trying to coax Chubby Sherman into taking a dangerous pratfall into the orchestra pit. "So I went, 'Whoop!' like that," Baird recalled, "and did a flop and landed on my back in the orchestra pit. Everybody applauded and Orson said, 'Mr. Baird, you're hired.'")

With the script still in progress—it wouldn't be completed until late August—and Houseman off working on his plans for *Hamlet* with Leslie Howard, Orson planned his return to serious acting with a key role in Sidney Kingsley's new play, *Ten Million Ghosts.*

Kingsley, a respected playwright, had approached Orson shortly after the opening of the Voodoo *Macbeth*. Kingsley had the golden touch: his socially conscious tenement drama *Dead End* had filled the Belasco Theatre for nine months, and Hollywood had scooped up film rights. Now he was going to produce a season of three plays, featuring *Ten Million Ghosts*—his first new work since *Dead End*, and the only one of the three plays that he'd also direct.

Ten Million Ghosts was another message play, this time attacking post–World War I munitions merchants whose greed was destabilizing the world. All summer long, as Orson worked on *Horse Eats Hat*, Kingsley wrote furiously, crafting the part that Orson would play: a gallant French aviator who defies politically expedient orders and bombs a German munitions plant.

At first, *Ten Million Ghosts* was announced as the final production of Kingsley's season, scheduled for the spring of 1937. But as difficulties arose with the other two plays in his lineup, *Ghosts* inched forward. Orson welcomed the opportunity. For an actor who was doomed to play heavies, figuratively and literally, for much of his career, *Ten Million Ghosts* afforded a rare chance to play the dashing lead—and at Equity wages, no small consideration for a hardworking young man still paying the grocery bills with small jobs.

Toward the same end—paying for groceries—in August Orson took another step up the ladder in radio, where he was still specializing in character parts. A deep-voiced comic actor named Jack Smart, a charter member of *The March of Time* since 1931, had been slated to host a new ten-week revue series sponsored by Wonder Bread that would be the first full-hour sponsored show on the Mutual Broadcasting System. A few weeks before the first broadcast, however, a Universal scout caught the portly Smart in *The New Faces in 1936* on Broadway and lured him away from radio with a film contract. Smart recommended his comparably deep-voiced friend, Orson.

The money was good, the workload ideal: all Orson had to do was show up at WOR every Sunday at 8 p.m., when most New York theaters were dark, in time for the hour-long broadcast. Besides emceeing the show as the Great McCoy—"a jovial cross between P. T. Barnum and Sir Henry Irving," as Orson wrote to Roger Hill—he would also star in the abridged Gay Nineties plays that had been preestablished as the show's main feature. Although Arthur Pryor Jr. from *The March of Time* was producing the show, Orson had a hand in choosing each week's mustache-twirling melodrama. The post–Civil War *The Streets of New York* was set for the premiere, to be followed by chestnuts such as *Uncle Tom's Cabin* (which Orson knew from the Todd School) and *Around the World in Eighty Days* (the Jules Verne story, which he'd seen at least once onstage at the Goodman Theatre). All the players would be fully costumed, and the episodes would be performed before live audiences; the sponsors were hoping the show could cross over to television, which everyone believed was just around the corner. The series was known as *The Wonder Show*, a title Orson would fondly cadge for his World War II military service revue.

The Mutual network (and the sponsors' ad agency) had booked Carnegie Hall to launch *The Wonder Show* on the last Sunday of August. But Orson then had the idea of bringing the radio show to Chicago, taking over the 3,500-seat Opera House ("Mr. Insull's dream palace," as he described it in a letter to Skipper) for six Sundays in September and October. The two-month run would open with *The Relief of Lucknow*, set in 1870s Chicago, and the show would be broadcast locally by Mutual's affiliate WGN, a *Chicago Tribune* subsidiary.

Alert the "press boys," Orson wrote to Roger Hill; prepare the "strong bally." Working with the show's publicist, Orson arranged to have a Todd School stagecoach trucked into the Loop with local

personalities in Victorian costumes stepping out of horse-drawn vehicles amid floodlights and photographers. The cast included the married couple John McIntire and Jeanette Nolan, who would show up
in future Welles projects (Nolan was Orson's Lady Macbeth in his
1948 film), and his friend Paul Stewart, who would appear in Welles
films from *Citizen Kane* all the way through to "The Other Side of the
Wind."

But *The Wonder Show* alone couldn't keep Orson and Virginia in groceries. Orson also took a small continuing part as "the cad" in a twice-
daily fifteen-minute radio soap opera called *Big Sister*. "God, I loved it,"
he told Henry Jaglom years later. "I had this girl in the rumble seat.
And the suspense was, was I going to make her? And it went on for
about three months. That's the longest session in a rumble seat, you
know."

Between broadcasts of *Big Sister* and *The Wonder Show*—flying to Chicago every Sunday, flying back on Mondays—Orson also plunged into
read-throughs for *Horse Eats Hat*. Then, at the end of August, Kingsley
phoned with news: there were problems with the rest of his season and
he was pushing *Ten Million Ghosts* ahead for an October opening.

In typical fashion, Orson decided he could do it all: prepare two
new Broadway plays simultaneously, while keeping up his schedule of
weekly radio gigs. For Orson, time and money were always elastic and
ephemeral, hard work and enthusiasm ever-renewable from his deep
well.

John Houseman was responsible for organizing the theater building,
staff, and operating budget for *Horse Eats Hat*, but once again he maintained a distance from the creative side of the production, and he was
absent at critical junctures. He disappeared for most of August, heading to Canada to apply for permanent resident status on foreign territory after his five-year work visa as a resident alien had expired.

While Houseman was away, Orson finalized the *Horse Eats Hat* script
and casting. By the time Houseman returned, the launch date for his
production of *Hamlet* with Leslie Howard—early November—was fast
approaching. "Of all the shows Orson and I produced together, *Horse
Eats Hat* is the one in which I was the least involved," Houseman wrote

later. But Orson hardly minded an absentee producer, and *Horse Eats Hat* would be pure Orson.

Squeezing in writing sessions between Orson's radio appearances, Welles and Edwin Denby hurtled toward the finish line with the *Horse Eats Hat* script in late August. "We'd start about 1 A.M. and work all that night and the following day," Denby recalled. "We wrote two acts at a stretch like that. By the time it got to be two or three the next morning, we were falling asleep alternately. He would say something. I'd write it down and fall asleep. Then, he'd take over and write something. I would wake up and go on from there, while he fell asleep for a moment. We finished at 9 A.M., and he went off to do a radio program."

One attraction of *Horse Eats Hat* was the cute role Orson carved out for Virginia, whose career had been languishing while his soared. She would play the shy bride Myrtle, a small but crucial part in the farce—and Orson would be Mugglethorpe, Myrtle's father, with a sly wink at the audience. Mugglethorpe was the kind of "old gaffer" role that delighted Orson, another chance to break out the greasepaint and padding; for fun, he even tossed in a bald dome.

Federal regulations required that no more than 10 percent of actors cast in Project 891 productions could be professionals who were drawing wages from elsewhere. For the leads, Orson relied on stage and radio friends who could afford the moonlighting. He lured his tall, handsome friend Joseph Cotten into playing dumb, charming Freddy, the play's human motor—this was the first time Cotten would perform under Orson's direction. As Bobbin, Mugglethorpe's majordomo, he enlisted the effervescent Chubby Sherman, whom he liked almost as much as Cotten. To play the hat shop owner, he cast a pretty young actress, Arlene Francis, whom he'd worked with happily on *The March of Time*.

Orson also added a role that did not exist in the original play: Augustus, the grandson of the family patriarch, created expressly for his classmate Edgerton Paul, who had played in Todd School and Woodstock Summer Festival plays and *The Hearts of Age*. Although Paul was Orson's physical opposite ("a diminutive actor, almost a midget," in John Houseman's words), he doubled as Orson's stand-in during rehearsals and understudy for performances—joining a long line of doubles and understudies Orson relied on when he was overextended.

The smaller roles and chorus were parceled out to the jobless thespians who showed up for open auditions. Orson gravitated to "aging character actors, comics and eccentrics," Houseman recalled, "middle-aged garrulous ladies with bright colored hair who nobody else seemed to want and a number of bright young' ladies." As with *Macbeth*, the partners had planned the show for maximum employment, and in the end about seventy-four actors, thirty musicians in the pit orchestra, and several dozen crew hands were added to the rolls of the Federal Theatre Project.

Nat Karson designed the principal set as an out-of-control Rube Goldberg contraption, with trapdoors and pop-up pieces and break-away sections. Aided by Virgil Thomson, Paul Bowles contributed a score that consisted of "two long pieces of continuity, three overtures, the horse ballet and several songs," in his words, mingled with strains of standard Americana. Fulfilling Orson's vision, the music would be heard almost continuously throughout the performance, with a uniformed woman trumpeter performing Bowles's "Carnaval de Venise" and Edgerton Paul plunking a mechanical piano to produce "The Song of Hiawatha" during the intervals. An enthusiastic if limited singer, Orson deployed his own baritone in the show's only true song, Mugglethorpe's "lyrical salute to his faithful rubber plant" (as Wilella Waldorf wrote in the *New York Post*), which capped Act One.

Orson insisted on pacing *Horse Eats Hat* like a vaudeville revue, with fast, skit-like scenes bursting with physical and risqué humor. The actors flew through the air, spilled across the apron, and raced up and down the aisles, shouting and laughing.

At the center of the maelstrom, however, was a fierce commander. Watching Welles on the first day of the *Horse Eats Hat* rehearsals, "still thinking we were friends," Edwin Denby recalled, "I called out something or other, some criticism I had in mind. He answered from the stage and put me down completely. Not in a disagreeable way. But it was clear enough to me that, now, he was the director."

Virginia had a similar revelation during an early rehearsal, when she told her husband she didn't think his direction for her was "right" for a particular scene. "I don't care what you think," Orson replied brusquely, echoing sharp advice from Hilton Edwards. "Just do it." Virginia had been sipping on a malted—an ice cream drink—and now she flung it in his face. "It wasn't anything terribly serious," recalled Arlene Francis, "we went right on with rehearsal." From then on, however, Virginia never questioned her director.

The occasional outburst notwithstanding, Orson was a "kind, intelligent, generous director and tireless," recalled Arlene Francis. Compared with the Voodoo *Macbeth*, *Horse Eats Hat* was great fun, and Orson reserved his shouting matches for the irascible Abe Feder. Orson often drew his mood from the material, and his mood during *Horse Eats Hat* was merry and ebullient. The company included many friends, and they were led by the example of Joseph Cotten, whose attitude was beautifully attuned to Orson's. "[Cotten] had a wonderful sense of humor—and such warmth," said Denby. "It's easy in farce to forget the warmth, but that's what has to sustain it."

Orson insisted that the lighting, the music, and the action be timed like fast-action clockwork. The actors should race ahead, improvising to cover any gaffes, just as Orson did the first time he performed sleight of hand at the Todd School. Mistakes forced actors into creativity.

Houseman returned from Canada just in time for the first dress rehearsal—and he found all of Orson's clockwork chaos unsettling. "It was difficult to differentiate the catastrophes which were deliberately planned from the accidental disasters," Houseman observed later, "some of which were so splendid we absorbed them into the show."

Orson had only four weeks to stage *Horse Eats Hat*, even as he was preparing to star in a second Broadway production while commuting to Chicago on Sundays for the sold-out *Wonder Show*. He always had other stray obligations, and sometimes his own clock ran amok.

One day, for instance, Orson forgot the afternoon installment of *Big Sister*. He was "sitting in the barbershop, and I heard the theme song come on." His friend Everett Sloane, who could imitate anyone, stepped in, duplicating Orson's voice. But that was the end of Orson's job on *Big Sister*.

He was pushing his luck—rehearsing two different plays, performing in multiple radio shows, "and living it up in between times too," as Welles told Peter Bogdanovich, "I may as well confess." He was still doing the lunch-hour program, and was in the habit of writing little lead-ins for the daily verse recitations. "Particularly if [the poem] was obscure and I thought the housewives toiling over their stoves needed a little help," Welles said, "I'd make a little remark to 'humanize it,' as they say." One day, the poem was a selection from "Sonnets from the Portuguese" by Elizabeth Barrett Browning. "Out of which I could make neither head nor tail," he said. Reaching for a witty aside to save the day, his mind went back to a line from *The Barretts of Wimpole Street*. "There was a well-received joke made by Robert Browning—a real quote of his, used in the play, in which he was asked the meaning of a poem, and he read it, reread it, and reread it, and finally said, 'When this was written only God and Robert Browning knew what it meant. Now only God does.' It is a good line. . . .

"So I thought I'd say that, because I knew the way I would read this poem would be jabberwocky. So I told the nice little story to the housewives, and when I got to the punch line, what I said was this: 'When this was written only Bravin Drivet Griving—When Grompit Drivet—When this was written only Gropit Drivet—When Gris was Drivet Grinning—' There were twenty account people in the control room and they began waving and turning purple and everything, and I just put down the script and said, 'Good morning, ladies,' and walked out of the studio and was never seen again. I never had the nerve to come back.

"That was the end of my career with Cornstarch."

After the remarkable success of his Negro Unit Shakespeare, the New York theater world eagerly awaited *Horse Eats Hat*. This time, Orson was serving not only as director, but as coauthor of the adaptation and the lead actor onstage. Some critics had their daggers sharpened for him, predicting the end of the one-hit wunderkind.

The audience that streamed into the Maxine Elliott on the last Saturday of September had varied expectations, but few could have matched the reality. When the curtain rose on *Horse Eats Hat*, what the audience saw was a singular production: French surrealism shaking hands with the Marx Brothers. As different from the Voodoo *Macbeth* as night from day, it was a play in which Joseph Cotten rose up in the air on a chandelier and squirted seltzer over the chorus and crowd; in which Bil Baird stood up in a box seat, appeared to trip drunkenly, then caught his foot in the railing, dangling wildly over the audience;

in which the script's coauthor, Edwin Denby, bent over to play the rear end of a horse.

With his false nose, padded stomach, and shining dome, Orson led the exuberance. In one scene, when he was supposed to punch Baird, sending him into a backflip, Orson actually connected, hard. "He loses his mind in a case like that," Baird told Barbara Leaming decades later, laughing. "That's *very Orson!*"

The whole show was very Orson—a wild ride on an exploding merry-go-round—and *Horse Eats Hat* divided the critics even as it consolidated Orson's reputation for risk taking and controversy. Richard Watts Jr., in the conservative *New York Herald Tribune*, declared *Horse Eats Hat* "a dismal embarrassment." The Hearst-owned *New York Journal American* wrote that the retooled French farce "represents a new low in the tide of drama." "Wacky—utterly wacky," opined the *New York Daily News*, "but, paradoxically, not wacky enough." The *New York Times* also equivocated: "Half the audience was pretty indignant, and the other half quite amused."

Some critics were offended by the naughty humor: characters running around in undergarments, all the racy dialogue. An often cited example was the line "It's nice to see a pretty little pussy," which was "spoken to a maid," as Barbara Leaming wrote, who has just "tossed her skirts behind her." "Sewage!" the Hearst papers declared. Everett Dirksen, a Republican congressman from Illinois, took to the *Congressional Record* to condemn the play as another example of "salacious tripe" from the Federal Theatre Project. (Such plays were "full of Communists," echoed Harrison Grey Fiske in the *Saturday Evening Post.*) Nervous Project officials rushed in from Washington to see the show for themselves, forcing a number of minor script changes on Orson ("pussy" became "lassie").

There were plenty of people who enjoyed *Horse Eats Hat*, however, including *Cue Magazine's* reviewer, who saw it as "a demented piece of surrealism which comes perilously close to being a work of genuine theater art." And nothing could dissuade its most zealous fans. The author John Dos Passos ran into playwright Marc Connelly in the lobby one night. The two realized they had been seated on opposite sides of the theater, shrieking the loudest with laughter. "I thought it was the best theatre production I had ever seen in the United States," another Project director, Joseph Losey, said later. Hallie Flanagan herself rated *Horse Eats Hat* as "inspired lunacy," saying that she felt bad for those who missed it, and "even sorrier for those who didn't enjoy it."

Some missed it because of the scarcity of tickets. *Horse Eats Hat* was a box office smash, selling out the ten-week run. "Some New Yorkers came to see it ten, fifteen, and in one case twenty-one times," Houseman wrote. Mere mention of the play usually brought a grin to Orson's face, especially later in his life, when times were harder. "The best of the Mercury shows," he flatly told Peter Bogdanovich (although Project 891 predated the Mercury Theatre per se). When an oral historian asked L. Arnold Weissberger, Orson's lawyer and financial manager (and secretary Augusta Weissberger's brother), which of his client's plays he recalled most warmly, the lawyer answered easily, "The fondest memories are held by *Horse Eats Hat.*"

Around the time that *Horse Eats Hat* was opening at the Maxine Elliott on West Forty-Second Street, Sidney Kingsley was busy over at the St. James Theater, on West Forty-Fourth, with the first blocking rehearsals for *Ten Million Ghosts*. Orson lost weight dashing from daytime rehearsals to nighttime performances six blocks away.

Despite his experience staging *Dead End*, Kingsley was an insecure director. He used a tackboard with thread and colored pins to choreograph the action, shifting the pins contemplatively throughout the rehearsals. Orson was the blue pin, and he didn't think much of the playwright as a director, according to fellow cast member Martin Gabel, who knew him from *Big Sister*. "He didn't like *anybody* directing him," Gabel told Barbara Leaming.

Orson caught catnaps in the St. James Theater during rehearsals for *Ten Million Ghosts*, and at least once he nodded off during an actual performance, according to actor George Coulouris, who was onstage with him. A specialist in cultivated villains, Coulouris shared a dressing room with the Broadway whiz kid, who seemed always to be dozing off, or missing rehearsals, or "dashing off to Chicago" for a silly radio show.

Twelve years older than Welles, Coulouris had started out in his native England performing Shakespearean repertory at the Old Vic.

He had seen Katharine Cornell's production of *Romeo and Juliet*, but hardly viewed Orson as the highlight. (Like Welles, Coulouris had once played Tybalt; "He acts in a very strange way," Coulouris thought, "as if he's chewing gum the whole time.") Coulouris loathed the very notion of an all-black *Macbeth*, and was especially affronted by the story of Orson's trip to assume the lead in Detroit. ("My God, why did he have to do Shakespeare in blackface?!" he complained in later interviews. "Just for publicity!")

So began the relationship between Orson Welles and the man who would put an indelible stamp on the role of banker Walter Parks Thatcher in *Citizen Kane*.

The cast all knew that *Ten Million Ghosts* was a weak play with an unconfident director, and Orson realized he was not entirely convincing as a doomed romantic hero, the poet-aviator who is willing to die for his ideals. It was the sort of matinee idol part that tempted him now and again, but those roles were invariably too pat for him. One day Kingsley dressed Orson down in front of the others, telling him he was the only actor who wasn't doing a credible job. Orson slumped off to his dressing room, fighting back tears. He took failures as a director less personally than shortcomings as an actor.

When *Ten Million Ghosts* opened in late October, Orson ceded the role of Mugglethorpe in *Horse Eats Hat* to Edgerton Paul. The Sidney Kingsley play was not much fun, and the critics laid into Kingsley's script. "The characters are placard stencils," declared Brooks Atkinson in the *New York Times*, calling the dramatic plotting and incident a "cumbersome snarl." The play was "inadequate for the big subject," said Broadway chronicler George Ross. *Ten Million Ghosts* limped along for only ten days before the production was abruptly closed. "We went down," recalled Coulouris, "and the theater was locked up. We hadn't been told."

But none of the reviewers blamed Orson, who looked "unexpectedly handsome" in his pencil-thin mustache, as Richard Watts Jr. observed in the *New York Herald Tribune*. Orson himself later praised the play's "wonderful Donald Oenslager settings and some imaginative lantern-slide effects," and admitted that he'd "learned a good deal from this production"—including "one excellent piece of stagecraft" he'd use later in a film.

"The munitions-makers are in a private theatre, watching newsreels from the battlefields showing wholesale slaughter," said Welles in Peter Noble's book. "As the newsreels show young men being needlessly butchered, I, as the idealistic youngster, rose to my feet and protested against the whole bloody affair. The munitions-makers also rose to their feet and, silhouetted against the scene of butchery, they retorted, 'But this is our *business.*'

"Second Act Curtain."

This echoes the scene early in *Citizen Kane*, following the *News on the March* newsreel about Charles Foster Kane. As a group of newsreel reporters and their editor are silhouetted against the screen, the editor says the news digest needs something—a stronger thrust, an "angle."

"Nobody's face is really seen," the *Citizen Kane* script reads. "Sections of their bodies are picked out by a table light, a silhouette is thrown on the screen, and their faces and bodies are thrown into silhouette against the brilliant slanting rays of light from the projection booth."

Years later, however, Welles rejected Peter Noble's account. "That is one of the biggest pieces of *Schweinerei* I've ever heard in my life," Welles told Peter Bogdanovich, claiming he was in his dressing room during that scene every night before the play abruptly closed, and never once saw the newsreel scene—the rare scene in the flop play commented on favorably by nearly every reviewer who wrote about *Ten Million Ghosts.**

---

* *Schweinerei* can be translated several ways, with "dirt" and "filth" among them.

CHAPTER 12

1936–1937

In Show Business It's Called Friendship

Not without a sigh of relief, Orson returned to *Horse Eats Hat* at the Maxine Elliott. By the time the Americanized French farce closed in early December, the *Wonder Show* radio series had finished its limited run and *Ten Million Ghosts* was a faint memory.

Despite his stumbles with *Big Sister* and the Cornstarch-sponsored show, Orson continued to thrive on the radio. The fall of 1936 found him playing Great Men with increasing frequency on *The March of Time* and the similarly prestigious *Cavalcade of America*, a feel-good historical anthology series sponsored by Du Pont. At times he sneaked his politics into his portraits of Great Men: in a mid-November episode of *Cavalcade*, on "The Story of Rubber," he portrayed a stentorian John D. Rockefeller. He played the part "rather too unsympathetically for the taste of the Du Ponts," he recalled laughingly years later.

Another of his Great Men was the munitions and arms dealer Sir Basil Zaharoff, the inspiration for the greedy death merchant at the center of *Ten Million Ghosts*. When Zaharoff died, on November 27, 1936, Orson played him in the *March of Time* installment reporting his death. The script's fictionalized opening sequence showed secretaries "burning Zaharoff's papers in the immense fireplace in the great hall of his chateau—the secret records (the narrator tells us) of a lifetime's involvement in wars, plots, revolutions and assassinations," scholar Robert L. Carringer wrote, discovering seeds of *Citizen Kane* in the episode. "Other scenes present witnesses who testify to Zaharoff's ruthlessness. Finally, Zaharoff himself appears—an old man nearing death, alone, except for servants in the gigantic palace in Monte Carlo that he had acquired for his longtime mistress. [Zaharoff's] dying wish is to be wheeled out 'in the sun by the rosebush.'" (Orson confirmed this to Peter Bogdanovich: "I got the idea for the hidden-camera sequence in the *Kane* 'news digest'" from the *March of Time* episode, he explained, "in which Zaharoff, the great munitions-maker, was being moved around in his rose garden, just talking about the roses, in the last days before he died.")

Radio producers were now beginning to tap him for showcase productions. CBS launched an experimental series, the *Columbia Workshop*, that mingled dramatizations of classic literary works with original scripts by established authors; Irving Reis and Norman Corwin were the producers. In the fall of 1936 Welles was invited to condense and dramatize his first Shakespeare play for the series.

Was it coincidence or gamesmanship that prompted Orson to choose *Hamlet*, the play John Houseman was staging, almost simultaneously, on Broadway? After out-of-town tryouts, Houseman's version had opened at the Imperial Theatre in early November, collecting polite reviews ("a handsome production," wrote the *New York Times*) that usually found lead actor Leslie Howard disappointing compared with John Gielgud's transcendent Hamlet earlier in the year. Houseman had a trying time with Howard, who was also serving as codirector and who overrode him on major decisions. The production lasted thirty-nine performances before departing for Chicago.

Orson's radio *Hamlet* was spread over two half-hour broadcasts on successive Sundays in November. He had a cast that included Alexander Scourby (Claudius); Rosamond Pinchot (Gertrude); Edgerton Paul (Polonius); Joseph Cotten (Laertes); Hiram Sherman (Bernardo); and his wife, Virginia, in a small part. Although he was not credited for it on the air, the script was his too—Orson's first full-length script to be broadcast. He even oversaw the publicity, which reflected his view of the medium in general, promising an "intimacy of interpretation not possible in stage production."

The radio *Hamlet* was a milestone not only for the medium, but also for himself. At twenty-one years old, he had found another means of bringing classical plays to the masses. Orson made the broadcast, which was one of the rare times in his career when he played Hamlet, a resounding success. "His voice," as radio scholar Bernice W. Kliman wrote in *Hamlet: Film, Television and Audio Performance*, was "a remarkable instrument evoking visualizations as well as clarifying interpretative choices," his whispered asides suggesting "interiority or complicity with the audience."

Also, it was on the *Columbia Workshop* program that Orson first encountered the New York–born, Juilliard-trained composer and conductor Bernard Herrmann, who led the orchestra. At twenty-four, Herrmann already had an estimable career as a symphonic composer when he was not at his day job for CBS. Herrmann was as acerbic and combustible as he was gifted, and just before the *Hamlet* broadcast, when a cue went wrong and he broke his baton, he tossed his script into the air and walked out of the studio. A chuckling Orson dragged him back. "We didn't have time to get the notes back in order on his stand, so he was one cue off all through it," Welles recalled. "So we had the fanfares when it was supposed to be quiet, approaching menace when it was supposed to be a gay party, and all live; it was riotous. Nothing to do [about it]—he just went on. It got funnier and funnier."

Houseman listened to the *Hamlet* broadcast wistfully. Orson's Shakespeare for radio, which had received less hype than Leslie Howard's production, was surprisingly good. Welles's partner returned to Project 891 shortly thereafter, relieved to be back after his dispiriting experience with Howard. "It was pleasant, after the big-time frustrations," Houseman recalled, "to find myself once again in my faded-rose basement [at the Maxine Elliott], with Augusta Weissberger chirping at me from behind her typewriter and the normal bureaucratic agitations of the WPA enveloping me once again."

Houseman believed that Orson viewed his own "juvenile lead" in *Ten Million Ghosts* as the same kind of failure as his episode with Howard, "a sort of absurd and shameful interlude of which the least said the better." As partners, they had soared to spectacular heights in 1936; apart, they had faltered. Now, happily reunited, they plunged into the next Project 891 production: *Dr. Faustus.*

The Tragical History of the Life and Death of Dr. Faustus, by the Elizabethan tragedian Christopher Marlowe, was first performed in the late sixteenth century. Orson had an enduring fondness for *Faustus*, which alternated blank verse with prose to tell the tragic legend of a scholar who sells his soul to Lucifer for twenty-four years of power, during which time he roams the world performing dark sorcery. Charles Gounod's opera, based on Goethe's classic play *Faust*, had been in regular rotation at the Ravinia Festival, and Fanny Butcher, the "Armchair Playgoer" columnist for the *Chicago Tribune*, loved reminding readers that Marlowe's play predated Goethe's by two hundred years. Orson had read Marlowe's play as a youth, and he had floated *Dr. Faustus* as a possible production in the early days of the Woodstock summer theater in 1934.

In his memoir *Run-Through*, John Houseman propounded his often quoted theory that his partner's "deep personal identification" with Faustus-Faust stemmed from a personal belief in Satan. "The first time I met him," wrote Houseman, "he was writing a play about the Fiend and illustrating it with drawings that were, in fact, grotesque caricatures of himself." Faustus's bargain with the devil was "uncomfortably close to the shape of Welles's own personal myth," he wrote. In short, the producer believed, Orson sold his own soul in exchange for acclamation of his genius and a guarantee of fame. Houseman even claimed that Orson's lifelong sleeplessness and frequent nightmares were due to his fear of the devil. "No sooner were his eyes closed than, out of the darkness, troupes of demons—the symbols of his sins—surrounded and claimed him." It was "a very real obsession," Houseman claimed. "At twenty-one Orson was sure he was doomed."

Thanks in large part to Houseman, this notion has become firmly established in Welles folklore. In truth, Welles's interest in the supernatural was far more complicated and unorthodox. He followed no organized religion, and his mother, a Christian who drifted toward secularism and Eastern spiritualism, had shaped his ideas about God and the devil. Welles avoided the subject of religion in interviews, but as a boy who saw both of his parents die at a young age, he may have suffered nightmares, or felt a sense of foreboding, without subscribing to the devil.

Orson believed in evil, however, both as a concrete force in the world—personified, just then, by Hitler's rise in Germany—and as an effective dramatic tool. He was keenly aware of the relationship between humankind and the devil as an ancient thread in storytelling, not least in the Bible. "Many of the big characters I've played are various forms of Faust, and I am against every form of Faust," Welles mused in his interview sessions with Peter Bogdanovich, "because I believe it's impossible for a man to be great without admitting that there's something greater than himself, whether it's the law, or God, or art."

As a student of the theater, Orson had read the legend of Faust and seen it performed in multiple productions. Now, as an actor, he welcomed the opportunity to play a man shadowed by evil. And, as a director, he had found a vehicle that was equal to his greatness.

Working on the script for *Faustus* throughout the time when he was involved with *Horse Eats Hat*, Orson had revised and streamlined Marlowe's text, preserving the high-flown rhetoric while tapering the lengthy speeches. Shaving off lesser characters, shifting around entire scenes, he converted what had previously been a three-hour, five-act endurance test into a seventy-five-minute one-act play with no intermission.

Like *Horse Eats Hat*, this was every ounce Orson's show. Writing decades later, Houseman claimed that it was difficult "to describe the creative workings" of their partnership "with any degree of honesty or accuracy," that their "mutual functions were only vaguely defined." While it's true that their skills sometimes overlapped—Houseman could be an ingenious editor of Orson's ideas—it is *not* hard to say which of the partners repeatedly took the creative lead in choosing and revamping the scripts, designing the shows, and casting the main characters; or which of them *directed* the shows while usually *starring* in them.

Orson would play Faustus, of course, and he wanted his friend the brawny Harlemite Jack Carter as his Mephistopheles, the demon who tempts Faustus with power. ("MEPHISTOPHILIS," Orson emphasized in his unproduced screenplay for the film of about *The Cradle Will Rock*,

"Marlowe's spelling!") Carter agreed to shave his head for the part, and even took up residence with the Welleses in their Fourteenth Street apartment "for ten days before the opening to keep him from going on a binge," as Welles recalled to Barbara Leaming. The personal bond between the men would make for a surprisingly tender and rueful on-stage relationship between Faustus and Mephistopheles.

By the end of November rehearsals for *Faustus* had begun, with some of the cast members coming directly from *Horse Eats Hat* into the poetic tragedy. Orson had earmarked one of the comedic roles for his understudy Edgerton Paul, and another for monologuist Harry McKee, who was among the comedians Orson collected from vaudeville shows. Paula Laurence, an actress from *Panic* who had become a close friend of Virginia Welles, would appear as the masked Helen of Troy. (*Faustus* has a famous line about her beauty: "The face that launched a thousand ships!") Joseph Cotten, already a lucky charm for Orson, would play a scholar loyal to Faustus. (Cotten was billed, wittily, as "Joseph Wooll," to get around Equity rules that prohibited his continued employment in the Federal Theatre Project.) Orson enlisted Bil Baird to craft giant puppets embodying the Seven Deadly Sins, and Paul Bowles to compose eerie music for a small ensemble that included oboe, saxophone, clarinet, trombone, and harp, along with a booming thunder drum.

Easily bored, Orson liked to make the obstacle course harder each time he entered a new arena. His Big Idea for *Faustus* involved draping the stage with black velvet to create a stygian void. Borrowing from the language of magic, he derived the notion from "black art," a technique used by magicians for making people and objects "disappear" into the scenery. Shafts of light would capture the characters as they emerged from the dark anterior of the stage, or from trap holes in the floor, or from under black cones raised or lowered from the rafters. Welles also wanted a lighting grid more intricate and ambitious than that for the Voodoo *Macbeth*, and an innovative loudspeaker system that could envelop the auditorium in music and sound effects.

The more intimate scenes of the play would be presented on a new extension of the Maxine Elliott stage, a kind of ship's prow thrusting twenty feet into the orchestra seats—the first Broadway stage to break the "fourth wall" of the proscenium arch.

In later years, many have debated the originality of Orson's stage designs, suggesting that lighting designer Abe Feder (or, for later plays, scene designer Sam Leve) made decisive contributions to the overall visual look. The controversy was exacerbated by Orson's acrimonious relationship with some of the parties, and by his penchant for taking public credit for the design, in the program and in promotional interviews. It's true that Orson's stage designers were responsible for executing his concepts, but ideas like the "black art" in *Faustus* indisputably came from him. "Everything originated in Orson's head," Paula Laurence recalled. "It was the duty of everybody to fill it out."

Orson's imperious habits continued. For the first time at *Faustus* rehearsals in early December, he addressed the actors and crew through a microphone, part of the public-address system put in place for music and effects. He still preferred to rehearse late at night, often arriving hectically from radio appearances. He tended to work out of sequence, concentrating on certain actors, holding back on problematic scenes, shifting the elements around until time ran out, or he felt inspired. He was notorious for stalling rehearsals, or sometimes interrupting them altogether, to change the mood. He told anecdotes and jokes or imitated the tics of famous people, with Guthrie McClintic a frequent target (though in public he often praised McClintic as a director whose experience as a onetime actor had taught him how to direct actors productively).

Orson also took what sometimes seemed an inordinate amount of time with his own performance. He relied heavily on stand-ins during rehearsals, and was slow even to memorize his dialogue. Fumbling his lines during *Faustus* rehearsals, Frank Brady wrote, Orson would mutter, "Latin, Latin, Latin, down to line twenty-eight."

Early in January, the lighting run-throughs began. Orson had demanded a complex lighting scheme, with hundreds of setups and cues, and it was a nightmare to organize. When the actors went home around 2 A.M., Welles, Houseman, Feder, and the stage managers stayed behind, along with "a few insanely devoted volunteers (usually including Jack Carter) and a handful of girlfriends and wives (led by Virginia Welles)," according to Houseman, "taking turns dozing and 'standing in' for the actors—moving back and forth, up and down on the bare, perforated stage while Orson, Feder and I yelled at them and each other." Around four in the morning they sent out for hamburgers, milk shakes, and brandy from Times Square, finally packing it in after sunrise so that Orson could race off to a radio appointment.

The black velvet stage and deep trap holes posed genuine dangers for the actors. Orson himself was injured during one rehearsal, plummeting several feet through the stage. Some of the trap holes were modified thereafter, although Welles always thought that an injury incurred on-stage was as honorable as a soldier's battle wound.

Hallie Flanagan came to one dress rehearsal and left with nothing but praise for the work in progress. Not every visit was so harmonious: when Houseman arrived unexpectedly with a trio of influential friends—designer Pavel Tchelitchew, the poet and novelist Charles Henri Ford, and a Russian princess—Orson refused to raise the curtain, shouting at Houseman about "Russian pederasts and international whores" until the producer beat a hasty retreat. Sometimes, these pitched battles between producer and director seemed contrived for public entertainment. Usually, Houseman was the loser.

Some members of the cast and crew found Orson's Big Ideas as mystifying as his methodology of crafting his shows in disconnected bits and pieces. His premieres could be as suspenseful for the actors as for audiences. "Welles's dress rehearsals and previews were nearly always catastrophic," Houseman wrote later, "especially if he was performing. I think he enjoyed these near disasters; they gave him a pleasing sense, later, of having brought order out of chaos and of having, singlehanded, plucked victory from defeat." Charles Higham said that as a filmmaker, Orson carried this attitude over into a "fear of completion." Film scholar Joseph McBride has called this "the 'air of frenzy' school of Welles mythology, initiated by Houseman." Yet Houseman never wrote, directed, designed, and starred in a play or film, and his observations later in life were undoubtedly influenced by the eventual rift in their friendship.

As *Faustus* approached its January 8, 1937, premiere, Broadway observers wondered anew whether the genius would fizzle. Posters for the latest Project 891 promised "The Magic of *Macbeth*" with "The Humor of *Horse Eats Hat.*" Most nights, the theater announced, the curtain would be delayed until 9 P.M. to accommodate Orson's numerous radio engagements.

But what a magical show *Faustus* turned out to be! A puff of smoke introduced Orson as Faustus, in a shoulder-length beard and a medieval costume, looking, as David Thomson wrote, "somewhere between Christ and Rasputin." His performance as Faustus—"ravenous, sweating and human," in Houseman's words—did not jell until the premiere. On opening night, however, Welles took possession of the stage in a way New York had not witnessed before. And it wasn't just Orson: ensemble and effects, darkness and lighting—all came together on cue.

Brooks Atkinson in the *New York Times* described this *Faustus* as "brilliantly original." "Arresting originality," wrote Richard Lockridge in the *New York Sun*. "Often startling," said Douglas Gilbert in the *New York World-Telegram*; "ingeniously done." There was plenty of reflected glory to go around: featured players like Jack Carter, character actors like Harry McKee, and even lighting designer Abe Feder were praised by critics. But the lion's share of praise went to the director and star, now acclaimed in both categories. Atkinson applauded Welles as a robust and commanding actor, who spoke the verse "with a deliberation that clarifies the meaning and invigorates the sound of words." Orson supplied "a forthright Faustus, having care for the diction while pacing well his successive emotion," Gilbert wrote in the *World-Telegram*. Richard Watts Jr. in the *New York Herald Tribune* said Welles cut "a striking and eloquent figure in the title role."

The reviews were never unanimous, and the anti-Orson camp was hardening too. Some of the naysayers found Welles a vainglorious actor; others were skeptical of him as an overreaching director. The conservative *New York Daily News* and, the Hearst publications had developed a Pavlovian reaction to the mere mention of his name. Some in the press were suspicious of anything produced under Federal Theatre Project auspices. Gilbert W. Gabriel in Heart's *New York American* called the Marlowe adaptation empty, pretentious, and unexciting. Wilella Waldorf in the *New York Post* found the speeches "pedestrian," with Welles so in love with his own part that he "strangles it to death."

Was it genuine Marlowe? Authentically Elizabethan? Detractors would always split hairs over Welles and his classical adaptations. But with *Faustus*, most critics agreed, Welles had discovered a corpse in the library, a classical drama rarely produced on the U.S. stage, and exhumed it vividly for popular consumption.

Audiences were less divided. According to Federal Theatre Project records, *Faustus* ran for 128 performances, with 80,000 ticket holders and 3,600 standees over a three-month run. And the audiences seemed unusually attentive, as more than one columnist noted: few arrived late for the curtain, and fewer still rushed off without joining the standing ovations at the end.

Faustus was Welles and Houseman's third extraordinary success in a row. The play's director and star could no longer be dismissed as a flash in the pan. The press clamored for interviews. Dinner party invitations surged. Job offers streamed Orson's way.

"The world was treating me so well that I was like somebody at his own birthday party!" Welles told Barbara Leaming.

Orson was never happier than when he was overextended, dashing from his radio gigs in a taxi—or, soon, a hired ambulance—in time to don his costume and makeup before taking the stage. But Virginia was exhausted by the work and trials of the past year and demanded a getaway.

In the second half of March, she left on a Caribbean cruise, with her ultimate destination Paramaribo, the capital of Suriname. The couple vowed not to worry about communicating over the distances, but Orson missed Virginia the moment she was gone. He tried to phone the steamship as it passed through Trinidad. Writing "in the icy, strained light of a late winter's early morning," Orson said he was lonesome and feeling a "big aching vacancy" in his heart. Their dog Bridget—nicknamed Budget as a reminder of hard times—sends "her dearest love with a resounding lick."

Orson assured his wife that he was taking all his meals alone, and doing almost nothing that wasn't related to work. He had dragooned Chubby Sherman into accompanying him to one cocktail party, he reported, but it was "a dolorous little function," from which they escaped after ten minutes. With CBS Radio conductor Lehman Engel, he had just started to "look over talent" for Aaron Copland's *The Second Hur-*

ricane, which he had agreed to stage at New York's Settlement House. But his collaborator on *Horse Eats Hat*, Edwin Denby, had managed to insert a ballet into the script. "A most unfortunate and self-conscious little addition," Orson wrote. "If it stays, I don't.

"Absolutely no more news of me," Orson added sweetly in his letter. "Enough to say I am desperately, wildly, despairingly lonely for my beautiful and wonderful wife."

His letters to Virginia say nothing of his older brother, Richard, who turned up in New York for a brief visit sometime during the long run of *Faustus*. Richard, now thirty-one, was "tattered and incoherent," according to Frank Brady's book *Citizen Welles*, and "the two men barely got on, Orson feeling that his brother, at best, an intrusion, was not to be trusted. Richard was confused as to wanting to become involved in the circle of his now famous younger brother, while simultaneously wanting to asperse, out of jealousy, that same reputation." Augusta Weissberger told Peter Noble that she met Richard around this time. "He was pleasant and slight and rather quiet," Weissberger recalled. After New York, Richard moved on to Washington, D.C.; he claimed brief involvement in Federal Theatre Project productions there—although, as always with Richard, the facts were elusive.

The microphone jobs were coming more easily now, rising in both number and prestige—and Orson channeled a portion of his earnings into Project 891. "I was probably the only person in American history who ever personally subsidized a government agency," he joked later.

One of his most important broadcasts to date came on April 11, 1937, just before Virginia's return from South America. Orson and Archibald MacLeish were still crossing paths, finding themselves side by side at parties, civic occasions, and political benefits, more and more these days for the anti-Franco Republican side in the Spanish Civil War. MacLeish had written another "verse play" especially for radio— for the sophisticated *Columbia Workshop* series. Now he offered Orson the lead role.

The play, "Fall of the City," was a parable of encroaching totalitarianism, the story of a modern metropolis whose citizens gather to hail an approaching conqueror as their savior—topical material for an audience transfixed by the specter of fascism in Europe.

CBS producer-director Irving Reis arranged to broadcast the program from the Seventh Regiment Armory, with hundreds of college students making crowd noises in the cavernous space. Isolated in a soundproof booth, Orson played a radio announcer narrating the disquieting spectacle from his safe perch high atop a tower above a central square in the city. Working alongside Welles for the first time was actor Burgess Meredith, playing the pacifist Orator. Bernard Herrmann was again on hand to conduct the score—four trumpets, four trombones, and eight drums—enhancing the "brilliantly orchestrated cacophony," in the words of Herrmann's biographer Steven C. Smith.

MacLeish's work was followed closely by the New York and national press, and millions of Americans were expected to tune in for "Fall of the City," despite the fact that its Sunday night slot pitted it against Jack Benny's popular radio program. MacLeish had wanted Orson this time not for his booming voice, but for his ability to summon a matter-of-fact tone that would rise to wonder as the drama unfolded. Orson had inherited his mother's gift for recital, and a knack for striking just the right note in performance, often with very little rehearsal.

Orson's narration of the action would guide "Fall of the City" to its solemn climax, the armored conqueror marching into the central square and opening his visor to reveal his face:

There is no one.
No one at all.
No one.
The helmet is hollow.
The metal is empty.
The armor is empty.
I tell you there is no
One at all there.

Welles, hailed now by *Time* magazine as "one of the country's ablest classical actors," lent prestige to the broadcast, one in which radio itself seemed "artistically [to] come of age." One of America's leading cultural critics, Gilbert Seldes, wrote in *Scribner's* that Welles gave his role "the breathless excitement of actuality," and said that the broadcast itself was "so important, in so many different ways, as to make everything else in the field comparatively negligible." The success of "Fall of the City" helped usher in a number of original radio plays commissioned by the *Workshop* from authors such as Maxwell Anderson, W. H. Auden, and Stephen Vincent Benét.

After the success of these two radio dramas—the two-part adaptation of *Hamlet*, followed by "Fall of the City"—the *Workshop* gave Welles a third important opportunity, inviting him to fashion an abridged version of *Macbeth* for radio, this time taking the title role himself. The radio *Macbeth* was scheduled to be broadcast on two consecutive Sundays in early May, coinciding with Orson's twenty-second birthday.

Again, it was Irving Reis, not Orson, who directed. Once more, Bernard Herrmann was in charge of the music. This was the third time Orson worked closely with Herrmann, and each time occasioned a building block in their relationship. Orson arrived late with his *Macbeth* script, the pages twice as long as the time slot. By the time he and the cast had wrestled the pages into readiness, so much had changed that Herrmann had to jettison much of his score.

No problem. "No music!" Orson told Herrmann. "No music at all!" Instead, he summoned into the studio an elderly man sporting a kilt and toting a bagpipe. Standing at the microphone on a podium in the center of the room ("as he always did," wrote Houseman, making it "impossible for anyone to communicate with him on equal terms"), Orson instructed the piper, "Every time I raise this hand, you come in and play!' He turned to the trumpets and drums. "Every time I lift this hand, you play a fanfare!'"

Standing stiffly before his newly marginalized orchestra, Herrmann could barely control his rage. "Trust me, Benny!" Orson coaxed the conductor. "That's how we went on the air," recalled Herrmann. "Every time Orson raised either hand, which he did frequently in the role of Macbeth, trumpets, drums and bagpipe came in fortissimo . . . and so did a whole lot of sound cues, including wind machines and thunder sheets."

While Virginia was still on her cruise, Orson somehow also spared the time to supervise *The Second Hurricane*, an unusual opera by Aaron Copland with a libretto by Edwin Denby, staged at the Neighborhood Playhouse of the Henry Street Settlement House on Grand Street.

Though still at an early point in his career, Copland was on his way to becoming one of the preeminent composers in American history. Motivated by the hardships of the Depression, he had written "a play-opera for high school children," in his words, telling the story of rescue work by an aviator and several children during a flood caused by a hurricane. The opera, written in a self-consciously Brechtian style, upheld "the revolutionary ideals of liberty, equality and fraternity," according to Copland's biographer Howard Pollack, with the songs and spoken dialogue in everyday American vernacular.

For several weeks in April, Orson worked in spurts to shape the much-anticipated Copland production. He contrived a clever set: a bare stage flanked by unpainted bleachers, on which sat two divisions of a large children's chorus. The action would be performed in the open spaces, lit from overhead. On a lofty platform upstage sat an orchestra—twenty musicians in ordinary attire—with Lehman Engel conducting Copland's score and looking out at the audience.

For $10 per performance, Orson inveigled Joseph Cotten into playing the aviator, and he and Chubby Sherman culled the other half-dozen young leads, and something like one hundred young people ages eight to nineteen, from the music and drama programs at the Henry Street Music School, Seward Park High School, and the Professional Children's School. Orson chose many of the students at a glance, then handed the young players and rehearsals over to Sherman.

Orson's letters to his wife suggest he was less than thrilled with the material, and when *The Second Hurricane* was unveiled in late April, the *New York Times* lamented that Copland's opera for youth was saddled with an "innocuous little story" and repetitive choral numbers lacking "melodic inspiration." But "a large and distinguished audience of adults" flocked to see Copland's "opera-play," according to the *Times*, and *The Second Hurricane* rated as one of the theatrical events of the year in New York. "Composers appreciated the work," wrote Copland's biographer, Pollack, "in ways that the casual observer could hardly have suspected." Virgil Thomson, for example, said, "The music is vigorous and noble. The libretto is fresh and is permeated with a great sweetness."

The experimental play-opera hurt Welles no more than it hurt Copland. And it brought him into contact with many young people who would follow him into the future—among them a twenty-year-old budding actor, William Alland, who trailed Welles like a beagle, trying to make himself "useful." Orson invited Alland to look him up next season, when he might need to fill out the cast of a Shakespeare play. A few years down the road, Orson would cast Alland as the reporter searching for the meaning of "Rosebud" in *Citizen Kane.*

From *Panic* to the Voodoo *Macbeth* and now "Fall of the City" and *The Second Hurricane*, Orson's stage career increasingly dovetailed with his left-liberal politics. In the spring of 1937, after his work with Archibald MacLeish and Aaron Copland, he entered into another collaboration, this time with novelist Ernest Hemingway. And although he joined forces with Hemingway only briefly and disastrously, the job brought him into closer contact with New York's left-wing documentary collective, Frontier Films, and one step closer to filmmaking.

Hemingway, born in 1899 in the middle-class Chicago suburb of Oak Park, Illinois, was at the height of his literary reputation. In the late spring, he was working with filmmaker Joris Ivens and author John Dos Passos to complete a propaganda documentary, *The Spanish Earth*, which exalted anti-Franco forces in the Spanish Civil War. Virgil Thomson and another modernist composer, Marc Blitzstein, were organizing a sound track of Spanish folk music, while Hemingway, in New York in May, finished a voice-over script. Behind the scenes, a group of people who included Archibald MacLeish were looking for someone to narrate the film, and MacLeish thought of Welles.

Orson met Hemingway for the first time in June, when he went into a studio to record the narration track. The story of their encounter has been told in almost as many versions as there are tellers. The script had been a source of friction, with Ivens and Hemingway quarreling over it. Now, as Orson undertook the narration, he complained aloud about the "pompous and complicated" language. Where Hemingway's script read, "Here are the faces of men who are close to death," Welles found the comment unnecessary—especially when it was to be read "at a moment when one saw faces on the screen that were so much more eloquent," as he later recalled.

As Hemingway listened to Orson's narration and side comments from a booth, he was appalled. According to Peter Viertel in his memoir *Dangerous Friends*, the novelist found Welle's voice actorly and effeminate. "Every time Orson said the word *infantry*," Hemingway told Viertel, "it was like a cocksucker swallowing."

According to Welles, the trouble began when he tried to persuade Hemingway to drop some of his precious text. "Mr. Hemingway," he said, "it would be better if one saw the faces all alone, without commentary." To Hemingway, this was too much. "You fucking effeminate boys of the theatre," he shouted, "what do you know about real war?"

"Taking the bull by the horns, I began to make effeminate gestures," Welles recalled. "I said to him, 'Mr. Hemingway, how strong you are and how big you are!' That enraged him and he picked up a chair; I picked up another and, right there, in front of the images of the Spanish Civil War, as they marched across the screen, we had a terrible scuffle. It was something marvelous: two guys like us in front of these images representing people in the act of struggling and dying.

"We ended by toasting each other over a bottle of whiskey."

Did all of this happen exactly that way? Welles gave similar accounts every time he was asked about the incident, but at least one of Hemingway's biographers found his version "quite fanciful." Another quoted an eyewitness to the recording session who recalled the two men having a serious, thoughtful discussion of the script, with Hemingway ultimately vetoing Welles's suggested changes.

Whatever the case, no one disputes that Hemingway found Welles's mellifluous narration mismatched to the stark, realistic images, and in the end it was dropped. Orson was miffed, but perhaps Hemingway—who took over the narration himself—was right. And Welles left the studio with an anecdote he would tell for decades, insisting that he and Hemingway remained friendly for the rest of their lives.

The more important by-product of Orson's participation in *The Spanish Earth* was not fighting with Ernest Hemingway but growing closer to composer Marc Blitzstein, who was working on the musical sound track for the film. After the musical warm-up of *The Second Hurricane*, Orson spent the first half of 1937 planning a new Project 891 production: Blitzstein's militantly pro–labor union musical *The Cradle Will Rock*.

The standard version of the events surrounding *The Cradle Will Rock*, as historian Barry B. Witham has noted, makes for "a great theatre story." The mythology surrounding the storied production owes much to John Houseman's book *Run-Through*, which offers a typically colorful but also typically faulty chronicle that has since influenced numerous other accounts.

Though Welles never got around to writing an autobiography, one of his last major pieces of writing was an unproduced screenplay, which he finished a year before his death, about the staging of *Cradle*. Welles frankly conceded that the script took liberties with the reality. "What I have written is not strictly factual," the narration explains, "but it is essentially the truth." He took pains to create sympathetic portraits of key individuals: his wife, Virginia; Marc Blitzstein; even Houseman himself.

To the end of his life, Welles always spoke of Blitzstein warmly and with esteem. "Serious rather than solemn," he wrote in his unproduced script, "he brightens a room when he enters it. His political beliefs are like moral convictions but are held with the most perfect serenity. In the Church he would be called saintly. A total stranger to extravagance in any form, he is mannerly, widely educated, unaffectedly civilized, a man of natural authority and unstudied charm. If he sounds a little too good to be true, he is, almost, just that. It never occurs to him that his mere presence is a kind of rebuke to the rest of us."

The two men had met backstage after a performance of *Horse Eats Hat*, months earlier. From the first, Orson was "personally taken" with Blitzstein—a lithe, dapper man, ten years older than himself, several inches shorter, with sparkling blue-gray eyes, receding short brown hair, and a Gypsy mustache. Blitzstein had been married—he wrote *The Cradle Will Rock* after the death of his wife, novelist Eva Goldbeck, earlier in 1936—but he was open about his homosexuality. A communist who acted and dressed like a boulevardier, Blitzstein had a personality that charmed everyone. "I really loved him very much," Orson told Barbara Leaming.

One of Blitzstein's endearing qualities was his absolute faith in the unproduced musical he'd written, the agitprop *The Cradle Will Rock*, in which downtrodden workers in an allegorical Steeltown, U.S.A., rise up against Mister Mister, the town bully and capitalist boss.

Blitzstein's score incorporated a dazzling array of musical forms and styles, including "recitatives, arias, revue patters, tap dances, suites, chorales, silly symphony, continuous incidental commentary music, lullaby music," as he described it. The music was sung through in the manner of a Kurt Weill–Bertolt Brecht opera, and in fact the composer dedicated the play to Brecht, the German anticapitalist playwright. An early mentor and confidant to Blitzstein, Brecht had urged him to enlarge a pivotal character in the musical, a girl forced into prostitution, extending her role thematically to "figurative prostitution—the sell-out of one's talent and dignity to the powers that be."

Blitzstein had spent the second half of 1936 auditioning his work around New York, pounding the piano and giving one-man shows of his musical in the living rooms of wary backers and producers. When Orson saw Blitzstein give his run-through, however, the composer's zeal won him over, and launched their friendship. At first Orson considered directing *The Cradle Will Rock* for New York's Theatre Guild, but that unlikely idea fell through. Then, although it was far more explicitly left-wing than anything he and Houseman had done together, Orson vowed to produce it for Project 891.

At first, Houseman sniffed disapprovingly, largely because Orson seemed to take *Cradle* for granted long before his partner had even seen Blitzstein's run-through. "He and Virgil [Thomson] were in a huff because of this marriage between Marc and myself," Welles recalled later. While kind to Houseman in his unpublished script, Welles acknowledges their constant rivalry and resentments. The relationship perplexes VIRGINIA (the character as portrayed in the script). "I'm somebody he happens to need," ORSON (the character) explains to VIRGINIA. "And vice versa. In show business we call it friendship."

Eventually Houseman was treated to Blitzstein's demonstration, and he surrendered to the composer's charm. Early in March, Welles, Houseman, Blitzstein, the actor Howard Da Silva, and Federal Theatre Project chief Hallie Flanagan met for a dinner party at the apartment Houseman now shared with Virgil Thomson on East Fifty-Fifth Street. Da Silva, a rising star who'd recently appeared in the Group Theatre's *Waiting for Lefty*, knew Welles mainly from radio gigs, but they had barely exchanged a word until the day when Orson stopped Da Silva and said he wanted his big, loud voice for the lead role of union organizer Larry Foreman in *The Cradle Will Rock*. That night at the apartment, Da Silva and Blitzstein sang big and loud, and Flanagan went "crazy" over their living-room performance, in Blitzstein's words. Though she was "terrified about it for the Project," because of its left-wing politics, Flanagan approved *Cradle* as the next Project 891 show. "Orson and Jack are optimistic," Blitzstein wrote in a letter, "I pessimistic."

Once again, Orson proved a master of catch-as-catch-can casting. Along with Da Silva, he recruited Will Geer, another actor known for his firebrand politics, for Mister Mister. A few players crossed over from *Faustus*, including Chubby Sherman as Junior Mister; Orson wanted Sherman for his light touch onstage and his assistance backstage. Orson also brought in a few powerful singers from the Negro Unit, including Eric Burroughs, the Hecate of his Voodoo *Macbeth*. Olive Stanton, whom he picked to play the Moll, the girl who prostitutes herself to survive, had appeared in a minor role in a previous Federal Theatre Project play. (Her father, the former press agent and producer Sanford Stanton, was a political editor and columnist for Hearst's *New York Journal-American*.) Most of the other actors were newcomers hired not for their experience or political background, but primarily for their clear, strong voices. "To make up our chorus of thirty-two we borrowed or traded singers from other [Project] units," wrote Houseman.

Swept away by the prospect of directing his first Broadway musical, Welles talked Blitzstein into an elaborate stage design calling for fluorescent platforms with glass bottoms that would slide back and forth, amid velour portals, carrying the scenery and props. While he supervised the design, Orson entrusted the bulk of initial rehearsals to Blitzstein, who provided his own piano accompaniment and drilled the singers. Orson dashed in and out, liaising with lighting specialist Abe

Feder and scene designer Sam Leve, a Yale graduate who had joined Project 891 on *Faustus.*

Orson had to learn the music himself before gradually taking over the blocking and performances. "He never tired of going over the smallest details a hundred times in order to have it precisely as he wished it," remembered Lehman Engel, the arranger and conductor for *The Second Hurricane* and now *The Cradle Will Rock.* "He would start at ten in the morning and not leave the theatre. He might dismiss his cast at four the next morning, but when we would return at noon, we would find Orson sleeping in a theatre seat."

For weeks, Welles and Houseman refused to commit to a firm schedule for *The Cradle Will Rock.* Rehearsals were ongoing, and *Faustus* was still drawing overflow crowds. But in the second week of May the partners announced their timetable: on May 22, *Faustus* would shut down for several weeks while *Cradle* moved into the Maxine Elliott Theatre, giving the cast and crew a brief window to rehearse with the extravagant sets, elaborate lighting, and full orchestra. The pro-labor musical would open "in about four weeks, play consecutively for a week or two, and then be joined by *Dr. Faustus* in repertory," according to the *New York Times.*[*]

The production was still rife with challenges—everyone involved was adjusting to Orson's huge sliding scenery and a full orchestra— but as it settled into the theater, *Cradle* slowly began to shape up.

Orson's unproduced screenplay for a film about the staging of *The Cradle Will Rock* should not be confused with *Cradle Will Rock*, a 1999 film

---

[*] Owing to what happened next, *Faustus* would never reopen. But Orson rarely left pet ideas completely behind, and he modernized the legend of Faustus for a one-acter he included in *An Evening with Orson Welles*, presented in Paris in 1950. Duke Ellington supplied the music. Hilton Edwards and Micheál MacLíammóir were involved, with MacLíammóir as Mephistopheles to Welles's Faustus, and singer Eartha Kitt as Helen of Troy. "Photographs of Orson and Eartha at Paris bistros, such as Bricktop's, were being published all over Europe," Frank Brady wrote in *Citizen Welles*, "with the implication that the enticing Miss Kitt was not only his Trilby but also the new love of his life."

dramatizing the same events, based on a later script by writer-director Tim Robbins. The Robbins film re-creates the era from a fondly left-wing point of view, juxtaposing the desperation and suffering of the poor with the smugness of the wealthy in their mansions. The film imagines the involvement of certain famous people of the era, including the painters Diego Rivera and Frida Kahlo, the wealthy young Nelson Rockefeller, and the newspaper tycoon William Randolph Hearst. There is also a key role for the character of Hallie Flanagan, played by Cherry Jones, but the film dwells far more on political camps inside the New York theater world than on Orson Welles, portrayed rather flippantly by Angus Macfayden as a creative berserker.

Welles's own unproduced script offered a more generous portrait of his younger self as a man whose faults might be pardonable given the circumstances. "To those who may find the character of Orson Welles a rather outrageous improvement on the original," Welles wrote for his own intended voice-over, "the director of this film would like to make it clear that this is no accident."

Welles began his script with a narration that frames the story in the context of the Great Depression and the Works Project Administration: "There exists a real treasury of PHOTOGRAPHS recording the desolation, anguish and the curious beauty of Americans standing up straight in the midst of that long storm we remember as the years of our Great Depression," Welles wrote. "The MAIN TITLES . . . and the visual background of most of the OPENING NARRATION will feature a significant selection of these photos." After that, however, Washington politics would be a mere backdrop to his more tightly framed story, referenced only in the character ORSON's gibe about the "little gang of Neanderthals" in Congress who were trying to undermine Franklin D. Roosevelt's public assistance initiatives.

In truth, politics occupied center stage in that spring of 1937. Two years earlier, the National Labor Relations Act, also known as the Wagner Act, had guaranteed the right of private sector workers to organize. By the time *The Cradle Will Rock* took over the Maxine Elliott, the right to unionize was still deeply embattled across the United States, however.

Sit-down strikes at assembly and supply plants swept the automobile industry in the winter and spring of 1937, frequently devolving into picket-line standoffs between striking workers and scabs. Clashes between unionists and police often led to riots, arrests, and injuries. A similar wave of job actions struck the steel industry. The decade-long effort to organize miners in Harlan County, Kentucky, reached a peak of intimidation and terrorism.

Some major companies surrendered to organized labor and signed union contracts, but others refused. In late May, the Ford Motor Company's guards beat the United Auto Workers' organizers (including leader Walter Reuther) on a pedestrian overpass at the River Rouge Plant in Dearborn, Michigan. After smaller companies like Republic Steel refused to follow the lead of U.S. Steel and sign a pact with the union, the "Little Steel" strike on Memorial Day ended in violence, as Chicago police shot and killed ten unarmed sympathizers and injured many others.

Adding fuel to the labor movement was the emergence of the Committee for Industrial Organization, or CIO (later renamed the Congress of Industrial Organizations), a breakaway faction of the more conservative American Federation of Labor (AFL). Aligned with the New Deal, the CIO led militant strikes and engaged in guerrilla warfare in a campaign to assume leadership of the movement. The specter of American communism was everywhere; conservative businessmen and politicians routinely referred to the CIO as "a hotbed of communism." Congressional enemies of the New Deal routinely leveled the same charge at the Works Progress Administration (WPA), the umbrella agency under which the Federal Theatre Project was chartered.

Among those clashing over union tactics and goals were the members of Actors Equity. The union was nominally affiliated with the AFL, but many of the actors in the Federal Theatre Project were resolute left-wing activists who sought a CIO takeover of Equity.

By the spring of 1937, the WPA had been weakened by sustained assaults on its existence from Republican and southern Democratic congressmen. The agency's budget was a hostage in the annual confrontation between the WPA's architect Harry Hopkins, who was FDR's close adviser, and the congressional opposition. One public misstep—such as a federally sponsored militant play waving a pro-union flag—could sound the death knell.

On May 27, three weeks before the first scheduled public previews of *The Cradle Will Rock*, WPA employees in New York joined a citywide work stoppage protesting the impending relief cuts. The CIO-style sit-down tactics quickly spread to theaters across the country; audiences would join hands with Federal Theatre Project actors after the curtain fell on a show. Internally, the Project was divided about how to respond to the actions that incensed opposition legislators.

Acutely aware of the charged atmosphere—and sensitive about the fact that she'd been forced to cancel earlier politically controversial plays—Federal Theatre Project head Hallie Flanagan asked Lawrence Morris from the WPA's Washington headquarters to make an assessment of Project 891's forthcoming proudly left-wing musical. After viewing an early June run-through, Morris reported back: *Cradle* might inflame the WPA's foes, but the production was "magnificent."

All of this came to a head when Flanagan received a blunt directive from Washington on Friday, June 11. Finally yielding to congressional pressure, the WPA announced a prospective 25 percent cut across the board for all arts projects, including all federally funded visual artists, writers, musicians, performers, and stage personnel. At least 1,700 Federal Theatre Project workers would have to be dropped from New York's payrolls by July 15, Flanagan announced to the press. "Amateurs Will Be First to Go," read a subhead in the *New York Times*. New York artists responded by announcing a flurry of sit-ins and work stoppages; and theater folk were among the most infuriated and determined protesters. Under orders from Washington, Flanagan directed New York arts project officials to halt the opening of any new plays, musical events, or art gallery shows before July 1, the first day of the next fiscal cycle.

The first public preview of *The Cradle Will Rock* had been scheduled for Wednesday, June 16. Welles and Houseman pushed ahead with an invitation-only dress rehearsal two nights before. The turnout included show business royalty such as Arthur Hopkins, the dean of New York producers (who was courting Orson about staging a Broadway production of *King Lear*); and George S. Kaufman and Moss Hart, the hit playwriting team—along with left-wing luminaries such as V. J. Jerome, the cultural commissar of the Communist Party U.S.A.

While the invitation-only preview of *Cradle* was a bit of a bumpy ride, the crowd of theater enthusiasts and political sympathizers loved the show's militant message and its rousing spirit. Because of what happened next, this first preview audience and a second crowd who watched a smoother performance the following night were the only people "that ever saw and heard Marc's work performed as he wrote it," as Houseman wrote later.

Welles later claimed that until June 15, the day of the second preview, he had not been apprised of the specifics of Flanagan's prohibition of new openings ("although he had certainly heard rumors," historian Barry B. Witham surmised). Orson and Houseman requested an exemption for one production only, to permit *Cradle* to keep its official opening date. Flanagan was on their side, but it was not her decision, and she could not persuade WPA higher-ups to grant the exemption. Flanagan offered to travel with Welles and Houseman to Washington to plead the case for *Cradle*, to Harry Hopkins himself if necessary.

On the morning of June 16, just a few hours before their first scheduled preview for the general public, Welles and Houseman arrived at the Maxine Elliott to find a dozen uniformed federal guards standing in front of padlocked doors. All the costumes, scenery, and other equipment had been confiscated as U.S. government property. A sign was hung on the box-office: "No Show Tonight." *Cradle* had been closed before it could open.

Suddenly, the Project 891 partners found themselves in a maelstrom not of their own making. That evening's performance had been sold out in advance to boosters of the progressive Downtown Music School, where Marc Blitzstein taught classes. For weeks ahead, the other dates had been sold out to left-wing groups that were using *Cradle* as a fundraiser. Yet the partners were legally prevented from raising the curtain.

A small group of key Project 891 players, including Welles, Houseman, Blitzstein, conductor Lehman Engel, and lighting designer Abe Feder, were allowed to enter the Maxine Elliott building, and they congregated glumly in the basement's pink powder room to weigh their options. Most of them stayed all day, downing coffee and sandwiches supplied by the resourceful Augusta Weissberger.

All of them, including Houseman, looked to Orson for leadership. "Orson had been inclined to obey" the WPA order not to open *Cradle* on June 16, according to Barbara Leaming, until "the sealing off of the theater changed his mind." Now he was furious, and he forged a common resolve with his colleagues in the theater basement. "If they hadn't padlocked the theater, I would never have taken that strong a position," Welles told Leaming. "The padlock was an insult. That's what unified everybody."

Anxious to keep the show in production, the partners called attorney Arnold Weissberger for advice. He told them they had one option: find a theater that wasn't under a federally funded lease. With that, Orson's mind was made up. They would find a theater, he declared, and, "We will have our premiere tonight!" That amazing confidence, that "irrepressible energy and lightning drive," as Blitzstein put it, galvanized the group, keeping their hopes alive throughout the long day.

They telephoned all the influential people they knew, in both New York and Washington, pleading for support. They spoke to critics and newsmen, insisting that the show would go on. They smuggled in a theater broker with a list of prospective venues and started reaching out to other theaters. The Empire? No, it was in mothballs. The Guild? The floor was torn up for repainting. The National? Too expensive. The theater would have to be large enough to accommodate all the advance ticket holders. They considered nightclubs, ballrooms, living rooms. The hours dragged by; hopes dwindled, frustrations mounted.

Finding a theater wasn't the only hurdle. The orchestra musicians were all members of the AFL-affiliated musicians' union, and the AFL informed Lehman Engel, the conductor of the show, that it would prohibit the musicians from playing in a non-WPA theater unless they received full Broadway salaries. Likewise, Actors Equity, also affiliated with the AFL, told the partners that its union members would not be allowed to take the stage in a different theater, because the U.S. government had the same right to postpone an opening as any legitimate producer. Fewer than half the cast members belonged to Equity, but those who did were "the important ones," Houseman wrote.

The amateur cast members—and most of the large cast and chorus were amateurs—depended the most on their WPA paychecks. If these amateurs took the stage in any theater besides the Maxine Elliott, their WPA paychecks were endangered.

This was one of Orson's finest hours. Inspired by the crisis, he sacrificed himself first. Forget the extravagant sets and costumes, Orson told his team—forget all those velour portals and sliding glass-bottomed fluorescent platforms he'd fought so hard to build for the show. Forget the union actors and musicians, for that matter: If the union prevented them from performing, Blitzstein could play the piano and perform a one-man version of *Cradle* from a bare stage, Orson declared. But they still didn't have a stage, or even a piano. Houseman sent Jean Rosenthal, who had joined Project 891 after working as technical director on Leslie Howard's *Hamlet*, to rent a cheap piano for the day, then load it onto a truck and keep it circling in midtown until they'd secured a theater. An unsung heroine of the day, Rosenthal made it happen, at a cost of $10 for the piano, $5 for the truck.

Around six o'clock, Archibald MacLeish joined the powder room cabal. He had tried to reach Harry Hopkins at the White House, but Hopkins would not rescue them. Blitzstein was at the end of his rope. "Marc's despair at this point was ghastly to behold," reported Houseman. "The final, fatal blows had been dealt him by those very unions in whose defense the piece had been written," which were refusing to allow the musicians and actors to perform.

The School of Music, which held the biggest block of tickets for the night's preview, phoned to ask if the show really would go on. "Yes!" boomed Orson, rallying everyone's spirits. "Where?" the caller demanded to know. "Place to be determined later!" Houseman cried.

A crowd of reporters, cast members, and onlookers milled outside, waiting for news. Rumors had spread that a showdown was brewing at the Maxine Elliott, and left-wing activists turned up to glare at the guards and pass out leaflets. At around 7 P.M., without any solution in sight, Welles and Houseman burst through the stage door and headed out front to reassure people.

"Somewhere! Somehow!"

Orson introduced Howard Da Silva, Will Geer, and Chubby Sherman, who teased the outside crowd with highlights from the show— Sherman belting out "I Wanna Go Ter Honolulu," Da Silva and Geer trading tirades about the war between labor and capital.

Returning to the powder room, Welles and Houseman were confronted by the excited theater broker, who had found just what they were looking for: the Venice Theatre, twenty-one blocks north on

Fifty-Eighth Street and Seventh Avenue. Bigger than the Maxine Elliott, with upwards of 1,700 seats, the Venice had housed major Broadway musicals in its prime, but nowadays it was vacant except on Sundays, when it was used by an Italian drama club. They could have it for $100.

Acting with "ingenuity, speed and daring," Jean Rosenthal recalled, Orson summoned the performers, crew, and musicians to a quick powwow backstage, telling everyone that he and the other key production personnel were on their way to the Venice. The curtain would rise at 9 P.M. "You may not appear onstage," he reminded the WPA actors, "but there is nothing to prevent you from buying your way into whatever theatre we find, and then why not get up from your seats, as first-class American citizens, and speak your piece when your cue comes?"

Minutes later, the partners emerged from the stage door to speak to the waiting throng, now larger than the Maxine Elliott could have held. Houseman nervously deferred to Orson, who extemporized with fluency and aplomb—his words so beautifully attuned to the moment that they might have come from a polished screenplay.

Forty years later, Welles wrote down an approximation of just what he might have said:

ORSON
Thanks for your patience. And now we're going to ask you to participate in something that I don't think has happened in two thousand and more years since people have been going to the theater.

(*Low murmur of interest.*)

What we propose (with your consent) is to move an entire play with its audience on its opening night from this theater to another theatre—twenty blocks away.

(*Surprised and bewildered reaction.*)

If you're prepared to make that journey—let's call it a pilgrimage—you're going to the Venice Theatre between 58th and 59th on Seventh Avenue. But those who think

this whole business is as silly as it sounds can have their
money cheerfully refunded at the box-office. The rest can
help to make a little history.

The backstage principals all jumped into waiting cars and taxis to
head uptown. (Later accounts disagree as to who rode in what vehicle:
in his unproduced screenplay, Orson said he rode in a cab with Abe
Feder, Lehman Engel, and stage manager Teddy Thomas; Houseman,
ever the aristocrat, claimed that he, Welles, and MacLeish were chauffeured there in a white Nash.) The sidewalk crowd streamed north on
foot—if not actually marching as though in a parade, as happens with
pardonable dramatic license in Tim Robbins's film.

The hour or so it took for the audience to reach the Venice gave Jean
Rosenthal enough time to get the imperfectly tuned upright unloaded
from the circling truck and installed at center stage. Feder had time to
fiddle with the single spotlight he would deploy for the one-man show.
Lehman Engel had time to consult with the dazed Marc Blitzstein.
Orson took the composer aside, whispering to him, coaxing a laugh
out of Blitzstein between bouts of shouting and pointing and frenetic
last-minute decision making.

In Welles's unproduced script, Chubby Sherman draws Orson aside
to ask, "Suppose it doesn't work? Suppose it's a mess?"

ORSON
The possibility hasn't even occurred to me.

Orson knew he could count on Sherman. The same went for Da Silva
and Geer, who were as professional as they were politically committed.
But no one knew whether any others in the cast would step up and perform their parts, even though most of the actors had made their way to
the Venice and found scattered seats among the civilian audience around
the theater. Tickets and fees were waived, and the downtown crowd
poured into the theater. The mood was celebratory. When the Italian
flag was spotted hanging from a balcony, the despised fascist symbol was
yanked down to cheers and laughter. Orson had told people to spread
the word, and though the Venice was nearly three times as large as the
Maxine Elliott, it was standing room only long before the curtain rose.

Just before 9 P.M., Welles and Houseman shook hands backstage with Blitzstein, then made their entrance from the wings, "like partners in a vaudeville act," in Houseman's words. The audience cheered lustily, then fell quiet. Houseman spoke first, telling the spectators that as artists and men of the theater the Project 891 partners found themselves with no other choice but to defy the WPA and present their musical. But they were making an artistic statement, Houseman stressed, not a political one.

When it came his turn, Orson, "looking tall and boyish," in Houseman's account, began by thanking everyone for coming. In his own unproduced script, ORSON speaks "conversationally—apparently without raising his voice." Lehman Engle thought at the time that Welles gave a "too-long speech," as if to apologize for "the situation, the scenes, the deficiencies of this kind of presentation." But composer Virgil Thomson recalled his words emerging from "the most beautiful voice in the world."

This is what ORSON says in his script:

ORSON

Marc Blitzstein's opera was written for a large orchestra.
The musicians are forbidden to play. Our singers, our
actors are forbidden to perform tonight in their own
theatre. They are forbidden to stand on any stage,
including this one.

(with a faint, slightly conspiratorial smile)

But I understand that most of them came along with you,
our audience, on your famous . . . long march.

Laughter.

And if those members of the audience who happen to have
rehearsed this show would feel an irresistible urge to
stand up where they are, and join the performance—I don't
believe there's any law forbidding that in our free country.

(seriously)

I hope the rest of you appreciate what a risk they will be taking. They earn their living in the Federal Theatre, and they could find themselves tomorrow morning without a job.

Marc's show was meant to have a lot of scenery. But that's all behind us—twenty blocks behind us, and under lock and key. No playwright, no composer since the world began has ever been so lonely.

He's up there, and we're down here—about a thousand of us. But we don't just have to stare at him—

We can keep him company.

Curtain!

———

The curtain rose to reveal the composer, seated at his rented piano in short sleeves and suspenders, with a glass of water and a bowl of peanuts close by for munching during his performance. Blitzstein looked a tad forlorn. He had played and sung his agitprop musical in parlors all over town, but never in front of a packed theater. Bathed in the lone spotlight, Bitzstein announced the setting in what Houseman described as a precise, high-pitched voice. "A street corner—Steeltown, U.S.A.!" Blitzstein began to stroke the piano, nervously singing the first lines of the first song.

Then, to everyone's astonishment, Blitzstein's music was joined by a faint soprano voice—emanating from a "pale and frightened-looking" woman in a green dress, according to Orson's account—who rose from her box seat.

The woman was Olive Stanton, a WPA actress who, everybody knew, stood to lose her paycheck by performing. "It is almost impossible, at this distance in time, to convey the throat-catching, sickeningly exciting quality of that moment or to describe the emotions of gratitude and love with which we saw and heard" the actress, Houseman wrote. Other actors started joining in, standing and speaking and singing from orchestra seats, the balcony, the aisles. Feder swiveled his sole spotlight to catch them. One brave accordionist accompanied Blitzstein from the balcony, flouting the musicians' union. A few cast members watched in stony silence, but Chubby Sherman ably filled in for several of them. Even the Harlem chorus took the gamble and sang their parts.

According to the account of biographer Frank Brady—though no other—Welles seated himself onstage, not far from Blitzstein, reassuring the composer by his presence as he described for the audience "the changes in scenes, the fact that a telephone just rang or an explosion had occurred, or stage business or sound effects that, under the circumstances, could not be produced visually or aurally." In Orson's unproduced script, the director defers to Blitzstein and steps offstage, later sneaking out with his wife to the stage door alley for a break during intermission. In Welles's scripted re-creation, the couple muse about quitting the theater for Hollywood:

"Aren't you just a little bit tempted by Hollywood?" VIRGINIA asks.

"Hollywood," ORSON replies, "is a place where you must never sit down because when you stand up you're sixty-five years old"—an amusing line from an older, wiser Welles.

Blitzstein's performance gained force and majesty, and two hours after it began the first public preview of *The Cradle Will Rock* ended with his thunderous musical refrain:

When you can't climb down, and you can't sit still;
That's a storm that's going to last until
The final wind blows . . . and when the wind blows . . .
The Cradle Will Rock!

"All hell broke loose" when Blitzstein and the cast finished up, wrote Houseman. In Orson's later-in-life script, the show concluded to "that huge Niagara roar . . . that mighty, loving explosion which can be heard but once or twice in a theatre lifetime."

The show ended with wild applause, cheering, dancing in the aisles, exploding flashbulbs, and a "joyous blizzard of leaflets," wrote Orson. Welles, Blitzstein, and Houseman converged at center stage, taking exultant bows. Finally, Orson stepped forward and quieted the tumult, gesturing to a distinguished gentleman in a cream suit who had emerged from backstage to stand beside them. "When you have all sat down," said Orson with a smile, "the one man standing will be the poet—Archibald MacLeish." MacLeish then gave a brief speech telling them all that they had just experienced the dawn of a bright new day in the American theater.

The next morning Orson caught a plane to Washington, where he hoped to make a personal appeal to Harry Hopkins to issue a continuance for *The Cradle Will Rock*. Last night he'd been forced into defiance, but now his only goal was to rescue the production. "I kept thinking we could save the situation, somehow," he told Henry Jaglom decades later.

But Hopkins was unavailable, and Welles had to settle for two high-level Works Progress Administration officials, both of them New Deal liberals: David Niles, a close aide of Hopkins; and Ellen Woodward, who handled women's issues inside the WPA. A secretary transcribed the afternoon conference.

The impasse over *The Cradle Will Rock* had nearly caused "a riot in the streets," Orson began dramatically, and now was the time for the WPA to compromise. To save face, he suggested, last night's unauthorized preview could be reclassified internally as a "dress rehearsal." What he and John Houseman sought was an exemption from the budget freeze that would allow a series of similar dress rehearsals in lieu of an official opening.

Taking the lead, Niles dismissed Welles's suggestion as just a matter of semantics. He did not understand why Project 891 was unwilling to comply with the nationwide order to postpone all arts project openings. Orson and his company could have all the dress rehearsals they wanted after July 1; postponement was neither censorship nor cancellation.

Niles framed the issue as a matter of loyalty to the embattled Federal Theatre Project and the WPA. All New Deal programs were under political assault, Niles explained, and well-intentioned administrators were forced to make sensitive decisions. Project 891 had cast the beleaguered New York branch in an unfair light. "The pressure on them is terrific," Niles said.

Orson countered that postponing *Cradle* hurt his cast and crew just as unfairly. The WPA was not going to keep issuing work-relief checks for rehearsals of a show that no longer needed rehearsing—a show that had now given very public previews.

When Niles was interrupted by a phone call, Welles took the opportunity to ask Woodward if she'd been able to bring the issue before Hopkins. "I had lunch with him," Woodward replied tersely, implying that Hopkins had left it up to them.

After the call, Niles renewed his insistence on loyalty. He stressed that the Federal Theatre Project was "part of a national picture," and the New Deal program had the "right to expect" all its participants to "pull together through this terrible thing." Welles tried to argue, but Niles cut him off repeatedly. "You are hiding behind the letter of what you call a preview performance," Niles scolded him. "Or dress rehearsal—as [opposed to] the public opening. From your point of view there is no difference. The real difference is in the minds of the public—no matter what you call it—it is a theatrical performance for which we have sold tickets."

The argument dragged on, but Niles refused to budge. Backed into a corner, Orson played his trump card. "We are asking for a series of dress rehearsals," he insisted. "If that is of no use, there is another way for us—a commercial theatre. It is not used as a weapon—for us it is a least disagreeable one—last night's affair was a strong argument for the continuance of Federal Theatre. The point is that our gesture did not represent in our minds any form of defiance whatsoever . . . [and] from the point of view of New York City it would be to the advantage of WPA for *The Cradle Will Rock* to open at the Maxine Elliott Theatre in New York tonight."

Niles said he did not like the implied ultimatum.

"I'm telling you, without this being a threat," Orson persisted, keeping his words and tone even, "if we are not permitted to put the play on by a series of dress rehearsals that we will simply put this play on a commercial basis. Mr. Houseman and I have nothing—absolutely nothing—to gain by keeping our WPA jobs. We are sincere government workers as you are.

"However defiant our gesture may be, it was kept within the letter of the law. Since [you] do not believe that our suggestion of instituting a series of dress rehearsals will work, we will put the play on a commercial basis," he said. "We are very anxious not to put the play on a commercial basis, but we will."

Niles then asked Woodward whether the WPA would grant any future support to Project 891 for *Cradle* if Welles went through with his plan to mount the play commercially. "Our position is clear," Woodward said. "If you decide to go ahead with a commercial production of the play, then I see no reason for Mrs. Flanagan not to drop this thing."

The conference ended on this sour note. Orson said he planned to speak to Archibald MacLeish about making a final plea to Harry Hopkins. The WPA officials told Orson they would never reach Hopkins, and he left Washington later in the day knowing the officials were right.

Slumped in his seat on the return flight, Welles tried to collect his thoughts. The work he had done under the auspices of the Federal Theatre Project—the Voodoo *Macbeth*, *Horse Eats Hat*, and *Faustus*—had immeasurably boosted his career and stature. He owed a lot to Hallie Flanagan and her support. Now his defiant stand might harm the New Deal program irreparably. He worried "about the political wisdom of it all," he told Leaming years later.

In the past year, Orson's political convictions had grown stronger and deeper. Even when his plays were not expressly political, he enjoyed many professional and personal relationships with progressives who were devoted to the Federal Theatre Project, and he had committed himself to numerous liberal and left-wing issues, from equal rights to support for the Republican forces in Spanish Civil War to pro-worker causes. His collaboration with Blitzstein had consolidated his beliefs. He would go on to lend his name to progressive causes for years to come, addressing timely topics in his newspaper columns and radio forums, and taking positions that were both antifascist and socially critical of America. Welles would become "the American Brecht," historian Michael Denning went so far as to say in his book *The Cultural Front: The Laboring of American Culture in the Twentieth Century*, "the single most important Popular Front artist in theater, radio, and film, both politically and aesthetically."

The left wing of the 1930s generally embraced the New Deal, the

Works Project Administration, and the Federal Theatre Project, but this was different. Returning to New York, Barbara Leaming wrote, Welles felt he had "failed" in his mission to obtain special permission to continue with "dress rehearsal" performances of *The Cradle Will Rock.* That had been his sincere goal. "But it might be as exact," countered historian Barry B. Witham, "to characterize Welles as victorious in acquiring the undisputed rights to a production" originally underwritten by the federal government.

The Cradle Will Rock now belonged to Blitzstein, Houseman, and Welles.

Curiously, Houseman, usually the diplomat of the partnership, absented himself from the Washington summit. But Orson may have wanted to go it alone, and this was another situation in which his celebrity carried more weight than Houseman's.

When Orson returned from Washington, however, there was little public bluster over the Federal Theatre Project, for or against. Welles and Houseman merely announced that they'd purchased the rights to *The Cradle Will Rock* from Blitzstein in order to present it in a two-week run at the Venice, starting the very next day: Friday, June 18. Houseman obtained temporary financing from affluent friends and supporters. With his elaborate sets gone forever—confiscated by the WPA, they were later destroyed—Orson tinkered minimally with the impromptu staging from their first night at the Venice. Blitzstein still took the stage alone, while the actors and singers fanned out in the auditorium's seats and aisles. The WPA kindly allowed a leave of absence for actors drawing federal paychecks, and in order to perform himself, Blitzstein joined Equity and the musicians' union.

Over the summer, Project 891 was quietly allowed to die. Orson resigned from the Federal Theatre Project first, while his partner lingered in the powder-room office, supervising a skeleton staff until mid-August, when Houseman left to fulfill a one-year appointment, arranged by Hallie Flanagan, as head of Vassar's Experimental Theatre and Drama Department.

CHAPTER 13

1937–1938

Tales of Orson, Real and Imagined

If anything, the brouhaha over *The Cradle Will Rock* added to Orson's professional mystique. Personally, too, it seemed a blessing. He took off more time than usual that July and August, and Virginia later called the summer of 1937 "one of the happiest times in our marriage."

In the late spring, the couple found a country residence on the left bank of the Hudson in Sneden's Landing, a hamlet about twenty miles north of New York City in Rockland County. A longtime haven for artists and entertainers, Sneden's Landing gave the Welleses a chance to live in a proper home a long way from Broadway, with a vegetable garden, a good-sized swimming pool, and extra bedrooms for guests. Orson made regular forays into New York by speedboat, his new indulgence, racing back and forth across the river to the train stop.

In the last week of May, shortly before the crisis with *Cradle*, Orson had been receptive when producer Arthur Hopkins invited him to play the title role in *King Lear* on Broadway in the fall of 1937. While Hopkins decided whether to direct the production himself, Orson could spend the summer adapting the script, which he knew and treasured, and confer on the costume and stage design with Pavel Tchelitchew (last seen being chased out of a rehearsal of *Faustus*).

At the same time, Orson had lined up a surfeit of jobs to pay for groceries, including his first major opportunity as a broadcast writer-director. As an experiment in summer programming, the Mutual Broadcasting System agreed to let him shoehorn Victor Hugo's thousand-page magnum opus *Les Misérables* into seven half-hour broadcasts from WOR, its flagship station in New York, starting July 23.

Set against the backdrop of early-nineteenth-century French history, culminating in a Paris insurrection, *Les Misérables* depicts the struggles of an ex-convict to elude a fanatical police inspector and ultimately redeem himself. Orson wrote a script that ingeniously incorporated disparate narrative devices to streamline the sprawling plot, while remaining as faithful as possible to the literary masterpiece. Directing his first important radio series, Welles demonstrated his inventiveness as well as his command of the medium.

Each of the 10 P.M. weekly broadcasts began with this introduction: "WOR and the Mutual network present Orson Welles, distinguished young author, actor, and director, in an adaptation of this novel, which he has made especially for the radio." Orson narrated the show and voiced the leading role—Jean Valjean—while cleverly differentiating his polished narrator's tone from that of the brusque ex-convict and from the other roles he played in the series. (In one courtroom scene, he even played a man *mistaken* for Valjean.)

Orson wove many unusual sound effects into the show—simulating the echo and ambience of the Paris sewers, for example, by recording in a convenient men's room. His Todd School headmaster, Roger Hill, visiting that summer, always claimed that he was in that men's room, for the occasion, holding the microphone.

Many in the large cast were already old friends; the result was a kind of informal dress rehearsal for the Mercury Theatre. Orson cast Martin Gabel from *Ten Million Ghosts* and *Big Sister* as Javert; and an actress from *Big Sister*, Alice Frost, as Fantine. He made Virginia his Cosette, and set aside good parts for Everett Sloane, Ray Collins, Will Geer from *The Cradle Will Rock*, and his old Chicago friends Chubby Sherman and Whitford Kane. This would be Orson's first time working alongside Kane, and *Les Misérables* would also be his first time directing Agnes Moorehead, who voiced several different characters in the serial.

Les Misérables was a milestone in Orson's radio career. "Well-staged and engrossing," wrote *Radio Daily*, which was the broadcasting counterpart of *Variety* and had first begun to follow him closely in the summer of 1937. His script brilliantly condensed the book; all the acting, his included, was gripping. "Welles has projected his skill into the stellar ranks of dramatic radio entertainment."

Later in August, Orson wrote and starred in another well-received adaptation—this time of John Galsworthy's prison drama *Escape* for the prestigious *Columbia Workshop* series. "A fine piece of entertainment," said the *Radio Daily* critic.

Then, in the first week of September, he joined an all-star cast including Tallulah Bankhead, Cedric Hardwicke, Helen Menken, and Estelle Winwood for an abridged *Twelfth Night*—his third national Shakespeare broadcast in a single year. "It was easy to detect that Helen Menken and Orson Welles had broadcasting experience," a *New York Times* reviewer reported. "They played to the invisible auditors and with intense feeling, as was revealed by their gestures, grimaces and grins." *Radio Daily* called it "the finest broadcast" of the network's summer Shakespeare program.

Finally, by the end of that happy summer of 1937, Orson had caught scent of a real prize: the lead role in a weekly broadcast series.

The Mutual Network owned the rights to *The Shadow*, based on an adventure hero created by the pulp-fiction writer Walter B. Gibson. The series had been a modest hit during its first radio incarnation earlier in the 1930s, with actor Frank Readick introducing each episode with the deathless line, "Who knows what evil lurks in the hearts of men? The Shadow knows!"

The original series had been dropped in 1936 after a five-year run, but New York advertising agencies—representing the main sponsor, Blue Coal—wanted to resume the show in the fall, combining the narrator with the character of the Shadow. They were looking for a high-profile actor to play the Shadow's alter ego, the wealthy and brainy scientist Lamont Cranston, who has "the power to cloud men's minds so they cannot see him," and who "devotes his life to righting wrongs." *The Shadow* was far from Shakespeare, but if he could land the job it would keep Orson and Virginia in groceries for months—and make Orson, for the first time, a national radio celebrity.

Virginia learned she was pregnant in July. The news thrilled the couple, who told Chicago friends and relatives first. "Orson devoted himself to me that summer," Virginia told her daughter Chris Welles Feder years later. "Every day we swam in the pool and lazed in the garden. We paid no attention to Doctor [Bernstein] when he wrote us from Chicago, 'I hear you have a lovely house with four spare bedrooms.' We didn't need any company except each other and Budget."

In fact, the couple had plenty of company. They hosted regular "weenie roasts" for neighbors and friends in Sneden's Landing including Ben and Rose Hecht, and Hecht's writing partner Charles MacArthur and his wife, actress Helen Hayes. Hecht and MacArthur sometimes brought along their friends Charles Lederer and Herman L. Mankiewicz, New York writers who'd gone to Hollywood but still toiled occasionally on wishful Broadway projects. Chubby Sherman, Whitford Kane, Alexander Woollcott, and Marc Blitzstein visited often. John Houseman was "rarely" invited, Welles pointedly informed Barbara Leaming.

Hecht and MacArthur, the former Chicago reporters who collaborated on the defining newsroom comedy *The Front Page*, also wrote for Hollywood studios on demand, receiving high-paying assignments while writing and directing the occasional quirky independent picture for their own production unit. Orson had much in common with both of them, especially MacArthur—including a schoolboy love of practical jokes. One day, MacArthur found himself wondering whether any of the Welleses' illustrious guests urinated in the swimming pool. He and Orson tracked down a chemist who had developed "a clear colorless liquid, which if put in the pool immediately detected urine when anybody would pee," Welles told Leaming. "We put this stuff in and we invited our friends out, naturally, at the weekend, and they were swimming around in raspberry-colored clouds. They were *all* doing it, you see!"

Virginia Welles had initially been wary of *The Cradle Will Rock*, urging her husband to steer clear of its inflammatory politics. Like everyone else, though, she eventually surrendered to Blitzstein's good heart and charm. In his unproduced screenplay about *Cradle*, Orson depicts his wife as performing snippets of the pro-labor musical during their parties at Sneden's Landing, gaily taking over from Blitzstein on the piano.

Virginia was an appealing pianist and a competent actress, who independent of her husband appeared in at least one of Rudy Burckhardt's short sixteen-millimeter experimental films. She also mused about writing a novel someday. But she did not pretend to be "artistic." Nor was she determinedly progressive or bohemian, though so many in their circle were. Orson appreciated the fact that his beautiful wife preserved her debutante "persona," as he put it, her pearl necklaces and cashmere sweaters. "That was part of her great charm to me," he recalled. "If she'd turned into a little bit of Greenwich Village, I would have been horrified. She stayed true to herself."

"My world is just too random for her," the character ORSON confides to BLITZSTEIN in his unproduced *Cradle* script. "Too damn full of surprise. Don't forget that where she comes from the big excitement is the menfolk getting gussied up in pink riding coats to go fox hunting, for Christ's sake, where there aren't even any foxes."

That summer, though, the world seemed the couple's oyster. Their first child was about to arrive, and movie producers came calling with offers tempting enough to drown out any warnings from the cynical Hecht and MacArthur.

One of the first producers to approach Welles was David O. Selznick, who wended his way backstage one night at *Faustus*, then wined and dined the young man at "21." "They got on very well," David Thomson wrote in *Showman: The Life of David O. Selznick*. "David had no doubts about Welles's talent, and they were two equally spoiled boys." Selznick invited the wunderkind to run his story department in Hollywood. Orson took the offer under advisement. He was "intrigued and flattered," Welles wrote to Selznick later, but his "ultimate aim" was to be an "actor-director." In an early hint of his equivocal attitude toward his producing partner, Orson told Selznick that John Houseman was better suited to the Hollywood job and he'd recommend him heartily. Orson was "always interested in being rid of" Houseman, David Thomson wrote in another one of his books, *Rosebud: The Story of Orson Welles*.

Producer Sam Goldwyn was next, chatting up Orson while visiting Hecht and MacArthur at Sneden's Landing. In his script about *Cradle*, Welles quoted a Goldwynism from their brief flirtation: "For Orson, I could write a blanket check."

But it would take more than money to persuade Orson to make the switch to Hollywood. A personal connection with one of his suitors would have helped. While he could wax nostalgic about the moguls, in person they did not beguile him. Selznick: "He thought he was the greatest thing since Jesus," Orson told Henry Jaglom forty years later. He considered Goldwyn "a monster," and Louis B. Mayer "the worst of them all."

Virginia vacillated. "We could try the movies—just for a while," her character coaxes ORSON in the script about *Cradle.* But Welles was still dedicated to the stage, like Katharine Cornell, and besides, he kept telling people he was on a "lucky streak" in the theater. "I *loved* movies," he told Peter Bogdanovich years later. "It just didn't occur to me to want to make 'em. Peter, there are maybe dozens of people scattered over the world who care passionately about films and don't want to direct. I was one of them."·

John Houseman, in his memoir, was precise about what happened next. That version of events, recycled in many books, bolstered Houseman's portrait of Orson as his own worst enemy—often rescued by Houseman.

By late August, according to Houseman, producer Arthur Hopkins had canceled his plans for a Broadway production of *King Lear*, offended by interviews in which Orson grandstanded about the planned production. "The Wonder Boy, without once referring to Mr. Hopkins, had expatiated on his own ideas for the production of *King Lear*," explained Houseman, "and on his personal conception of the old king's progressive stages of madness."

In mid-August, according to Houseman, he stopped at Sneden's Landing on his way back from Vassar, to pay his respects to the Welleses. Orson was in low spirits that day, Houseman claimed, because of the imminent cancellation of *King Lear*. When Houseman informed Virginia that he was a professor now, he recalled, she laughed rudely and excused herself for bed. ("Virginia looks great in pyjamas," Orson observed in his unproduced script about *Cradle.*) Welles and Houseman then stayed up late socializing, reviving their friendship and camaraderie.

At the end of the night, according to Houseman, Orson was walking him to his car and then suddenly wheeled on him, saying, "Why the hell don't we start a theater of our own?"

"Why don't we?" agreed Houseman. They returned indoors, brimming with excitement. When their eyes strayed to a back issue of *American Mercury*, H. L. Mencken's crusading literary monthly, they took the magazine's name as an inspiration for their new organization: the Mercury Theatre. "I did not go home that night or the next day or the day after that," remembered Houseman. "It was mid-August, and if we wanted our theatre for the 1937–1938 season we had not a moment to lose."

But Houseman's chronology, at the least, was off. The two had clearly settled on the theater partnership as far back as August 3, when the *New York Times* announced that Welles and Houseman were planning a fall season "of classical revivals at a popular scale in a small Broadway house." The first show, according to the *Times*, would be *The Merchant of Venice*, performed as "a comedy of manners and not a melodrama."

The very next Sunday, August 8, Herbert Drake, a drama reporter who was a fan of both Welles and Houseman, expanded on their fall plans in the *New York Herald Tribune*. *The Merchant of Venice* had quickly evanesced, replaced now by a fall schedule that would offer "a modern dress" *Julius Caesar*, John Webster's *The Duchess of Malfi* ("the goriest work of Webster," in Drake's words), Ben Jonson's *The Silent Woman*, and George Bernard Shaw's *Heartbreak House*. "And in the spring," Drake wrote, "the whole *Henry IV* cycle, parts one and two, and *Henry V*."

Moreover, in that first week of August, the idea of a new repertory theater would not yet have conflicted with Orson's plans to adapt and star in *King Lear* for Arthur Hopkins—a production the *Times* was still reporting as "due about Christmas time." So what Welles told Leaming is plausible: that Hopkins got cold feet weeks later, not because of Orson's grandstanding, but because the producer had trouble raising money.

Houseman's account of the revival of their partnership in mid-August was a conflation of several meetings throughout August. Houseman himself told the story about the name "Mercury Theatre" differently in 1950, remarking to an interviewer that Marc Blitzstein had suggested it by pointing to a copy of the magazine during a visit to the partners' New York office.

Regardless, by the end of August, the Mercury had been incorporated in the state capital, Albany, with Houseman as president,

Welles as vice president, and the still faithful Augusta Weissberger as secretary. The two principal partners would split 70 percent of the stock equally. (The other 30 percent was set aside for major investors.) By August 29, the plans were solid enough to merit a grand proclamation—issued jointly by Welles and Houseman—on the front page of the weekend drama section of the *New York Times.*

The partners promised to lead New York audiences on "a voyage of discovery" with their new Mercury Theatre. The first production, *Julius Caesar,* would be ready sometime "early in November." Next on their schedule was Shaw's *Heartbreak House,* "his most important play," for which the partners were in the process of seeking the playwright's permission. Other plays they hoped to produce, according to the article, included William Gillette's *Too Much Johnson,* another Americanized nineteenth-century French farce à la *Horse Eats Hat*; English dramatist John Webster's seventeenth-century macabre tragedy *The Duchess of Malfi*; and Elizabethan playwright Ben Jonson's comic *The Silent Woman,* also known as *Epicene.*

"We shall produce four or five plays each season," the partners pledged in the *Times.* "The majority of these will be plays of the past—preferably those that seem to have an emotional or factual bearing on contemporary life. Definitely we prefer not to fix our program rigidly too far ahead. New plays, new ideas may turn up any day."

They would set their top ticket price at $2 (Broadway tickets often ran as high as $4.40), and *Julius Caesar* would run for four or five weeks. "After that, without clinging to the European system of repertory, with its disturbing, wasteful, nightly change of bill, the Mercury Theatre expects to maintain a repertory of its current season's productions."

John Houseman excelled at logistics: setting up a management structure for operations, organizing the theater building and staff. The task of finding adequate financing also fell to him. Working out of temporary offices in the Empire Theatre building, Houseman started lobbying well-heeled friends, trying to scrounge the $10,500 he saw as the bare minimum for the start-up. It all had to be accomplished within two months, with budget strictures that left him constantly "paralyzed with embarrassment and fear."

He found a permanent venue for the new organization in the intimate Comedy Theatre on West Forty-First Street and Broadway, which had a small orchestra pit, two balconies, and 687 seats. (It was identified as the Mercury's likely home in the earliest August press coverage.) The partners enlisted Jean Rosenthal to oversee the renovation, and more care and money was spent on reinforcing the rotting floorboards and upgrading the lighting than on repairing the carpeting or frayed seats. For their first production, Orson demanded an extended apron like that of his *Faustus*, although it meant losing pricey orchestra seats. The woodwork and lobby were given a shine. One day a truck delivered a vertical sign: M-E-R-C-U-R-Y.

As always, Orson took charge creatively. He would give *Julius Caesar*, he vowed in the *New York Times*, "much of the speed and violence that it must have had on the Elizabethan stage. The Roman Senators, when they murder the dictator, will not be clad (any more than were the Elizabethan actors), in the traditional nineteenth century stage togas."

Privately, he announced he was departing for ten days of seclusion in the White Mountains of New Hampshire, to escape the hay fever season and find inspiration for the script. Virginia, now suffering from morning sickness, was offended by the implication that her husband couldn't find sufficient peace and creative emanations at home. The night before Orson left, they quarreled.

Virginia wanted her husband to find a part for her in the Mercury's *Julius Caesar*, no matter how small. "He stared at me as though I'd lost my mind," she recalled years later. "How could I dream of staying up all night in the theater when I was going to have his child? I had to swear on his mother's grave that I'd stay home every night, drink my milk and be in bed by ten o'clock."

What about *you?* Virginia wondered aloud. Her husband was rarely home by ten o'clock these days. More than once she had begged him "to cut back on his radio work," she told her daughter years later, but "he reminded me that if it weren't for the big bucks he was making in radio, we couldn't afford to live in Sneden's Landing or to start a family." Orson said he did his best to get home after late-night jobs, even splurging on the speedboat that facilitated his river crossings. "That was becoming such a rare event that I told him he might as well give up the boat and swim across," Virginia recalled. "I meant it as a joke, but he didn't find it funny."

It was not their first fight, but it was their most acrimonious to date, and the letters he sent from the Crawford House, an inn located in the one-horse town of Crawford Notch, New Hampshire, were defensive if unapologetic. "I eat and sleep and poke around in the mountains, and I have entirely forgotten the sound of my own voice," Orson wrote sweetly to Virginia. "There is only one flaw in my little heaven but it lets in a hell of a draft. I miss my beautiful, beautiful, beautiful wife." With few other guests to distract him, Orson was able to work hard on *Julius Caesar* and—to follow it—the second planned Mercury play, Thomas Dekker's *The Shoemaker's Holiday*, which he'd added to the original announced list as a ribald change of pace.*

Julius Caesar was arguably the Shakespeare play he knew best. He had seen it performed any number of times, in important productions and local versions, like the one at Dartmouth College with William Mowry Jr. among the cast in the spring of 1936. He had mounted his own stripped-down production for the Todd School in tenth grade, and edited Shakespeare's original play for inclusion in *Everybody's Shakespeare.*

Up in Crawford Notch, Orson first breathed life into his own vision of *Julius Caesar.* He envisioned his actors in modern street garb, moving freely across an unadorned stage. He conceived stark, dramatic lighting, and hoped, in his treatment of the assassination plot against Caesar, to echo "the same kind of hysteria that exists in certain dictator-ruled countries of today," in the words of a subsequent Mercury Theatre press release.

As ever, Orson would make a virtue out of the low budget, planning raised platforms and a series of interlocking ramps for different levels of stage action. The brick wall at the back of the stage would be painted an unsettling color: that of dried blood. Marrying ideas from *Panic* and *Faustus*, he called for lights to beam up from holes in the platforms, ramps, and stage floor.

The costuming would also be inexpensive. The character of Caesar would appear first in a black-belted uniform (his first gesture a fascist salute). The bulk of the cast would be dressed in khaki doughboy

---

* *The Shoemaker's Holiday* had previously been on the list of possible plays planned by Project 891.

uniforms dyed dark olive green, with Sam Browne belts and boots, or in cheap hoodlum suits with upturned collars and low-brimmed hats. One exception to the general wardrobe was Brutus, the part Orson had earmarked for himself. An idealist turned betrayer, Brutus would be elegantly dressed in a custom-made double-breasted blue pinstripe suit.

When Orson was alone, he worked swiftly and furiously. Slashing away at Shakespeare's script, he boldly combined and transposed, excising a number of scenes—including the play's battle scenes, believing "there was never a production of Caesar with actual armies in synthetic combat that was less than a little silly." Most of the actors would carry painted rubber daggers, but Cassius and Brutus would carry real steel weapons, which would gleam in the light.

The final script would be "a total reworking of Shakespeare," as the scholar Andrea Janet Nouryeh wrote in her unpublished 1987 thesis, "The Mercury Theatre: A History." "It was problematic," commented Nouryeh, "when students came to matinees with their copies of the play. These performances were always punctuated with the noise of rapidly riffling pages."

Never mind Shakespeare: the big news from Crawford Notch, Orson wrote to Virginia in mid-September, was that he had cinched the role of the Shadow. The ironclad six-month contract for the radio program was his most lucrative yet, including a clause that allowed him to skip the reading rehearsals. The year before, he had been happy to earn $18.50 a shot for appearances on *American School of the Air.* Now he would be guaranteed $185 weekly as the Shadow. "I wouldn't bore you with these technicalities of contract," Orson wrote to Virginia, "except that I think we ought to know we're sure of next winter's bills."

Orson promised to return to New York in time for the premiere of the first show on the last Sunday of September. He also hoped to have the *Julius Caesar* script ready by then, with about two weeks left before the first scheduled rehearsal, allowing him a brief window of time to escape with his wife "somewhere together on a toot," he wrote, "somewhere ridiculous and delightful where I won't even have a script to think about and you won't have a house to worry over." The Caribbean, perhaps . . . but even Chicago was a possibility, if Virginia preferred.

"Let me know and I'll make reservations anywhere," he wrote to her. "I love you, Orson."

The moment Orson returned from New Hampshire, however, his imagined free time evaporated. He plunged into *The Shadow* and urgent groundwork for *Julius Caesar*, spending most of his days at the Mercury Theatre and many overnights at the Algonquin Hotel, writing Virginia love notes on hotel stationery. Despite good intentions, they did not have their "toot," then or ever. When *The Shadow* and the Mercury kept him away from Sneden's Landing, Chubby Sherman and Whitford Kane took the trip in his stead, telling Virginia "tales of Orson."

Along with the script for *Julius Caesar*, Orson returned from New England with a sheaf of drawings and another plasticine model of the stage set, like the one he had presented to John Houseman for the Voodoo *Macbeth*. He handed them over to Sam Leve, whose design work would be supervised by Jean Rosenthal, with instructions to spend as little money as possible. Later, when the program was drawn up, Leve would find his name conspicuously absent, because Orson insisted that the set design stemmed from his ideas. It was the first rude implementation of a Mercury Theatre policy that enforced "Production by Orson Welles" as the one credit that could override all others.

"They were Welles's shows," Houseman himself said later. As a member of the Mercury team, "you were production material," Rosenthal said. "If [Welles] liked you, the association could be pleasant. If not, it was injurious. As a director, he approached other talents as he did his gargantuan meals—with a voracious appetite. Your contributions to the feast he either spat out or set aside untouched, or he ate them up, assimilated them, with a gusto which was extraordinarily flattering."

On this production Rosenthal took over the lighting from Abe Feder, who had moved on after *The Cradle Will Rock*. Orson gave Rosenthal instructions for lighting effects that would create an unusually darkened stage with pools of illumination for the shifting scenes. "Orson dictated clearly and exactly the look he wanted . . . a very simple look based on the Nazi rallies at Nuremberg," Rosenthal recalled. The visual scheme was both dramatic and expedient, with the lighting serving as a curtain to open and close scenes rapidly, reinforcing the fast and fluid pace Orson wanted. Rosenthal was less contentious than Feder, but when he felt like it Welles screamed at her too.

Many writers have described Orson as exploiting people mercilessly, underemphasizing their creative contributions while stealing the credit, as if this were not true of many great directors. "Some of the people around him felt they were being used," Houseman observed later, though for many others "it was a wonderful collaborative experience."

"Orson's people" often fared best. The composer was perhaps his closest backstage ally, and his credit would follow Orson's in the program: "Music by Marc Blitzstein." According to Blitzstein's biographer Howard Pollack, the composer was paid only a modest $200 for his *Julius Caesar* score, but he also was given a small percentage of the box office gross, and an extra $50 per week when *Caesar* went on the road in 1938. His contract also guaranteed a revival of *The Cradle Will Rock*. But *Julius Caesar* was hardly another Marc Blitzstein musical: the composer achieved his music and effects with a union-minimum four-piece ensemble: trumpet, French horn, Hammond organ, percussion. He evoked Mussolini's "Giovinezza" for Caesar's anthem, and sweetened a sonnet for the young page Lucius to sing to the doomed Brutus.

"[Blitzstein's] name could be counted on to help attract that leftist front that had rallied behind *The Cradle* and that Welles and Houseman now hoped might support their new company," wrote Pollack in *Marc Blitzstein: His Life, His Work, His World*. The leftist groups and organizations were crucial to the Mercury's hopes for success. Houseman even wrote a piece for the communist organ *The Daily Worker*, assuring leftwing theater enthusiasts that the new Mercury Theatre was another step toward "a real People's Theatre in America."

Blitztein and Orson remained close friends; and when the *Columbia Workshop* commissioned a half-hour musical from Blitzstein, he wrote an episode that revolved around a composer's search for the right socially conscious lyrics to match his melody. Blitzstein dedicated his first original radio opera, called *I've Got the Tune*, to Welles, who was announced to play the lead role. When Orson's schedule conspired against it, Blitzstein himself stepped into the part—but Welles was there in the booth, along with Houseman and composer Kurt Weill, when the show was broadcast by WABC on October 24, 1937.

Despite its newly hung sign, the Mercury Theatre was still being renovated in early November, when Orson needed to start blocking the cast. For about two weeks the cast had to be transported to the old film studios at Fort Lee in New Jersey, where the ramps and platforms were under construction. For most of the troupe, the journey involved a subway trip, a ferry across the Hudson, and finally a bus ride to Fort Lee. (Orson arrived in a chauffeured limousine—one of his many new perks.)

The Mercury partners had assembled a company that would go down in Broadway history. George Coulouris had thought little of Orson when they shared a dressing room during the short-lived *Ten Million Ghosts*; he changed his mind after seeing *Faustus*, phoning Orson to praise the show. Orson returned the favor generously, offering Coulouris his choice of two parts in the first Mercury Theatre production. "If you want to play Mark Antony, I'll play Brutus, and if you want to play Brutus, I'll play Antony." Coulouris chose Antony.

Chubby Sherman was a shoo-in to be a founding member of the Mercury ensemble, and Orson cast him in the role of "envious Casca," as Mark Antony calls him, one of Caesar's assassins. Another core member was Joseph Cotten, who saw Orson nearly every day in the radio studios, or at the theater. Cotten would play several parts, including Publius, another conspirator. Martin Gabel was not very lean or hungry-looking, as Shakespeare described Cassius, but rather short and stocky. But he was an intense actor with a commanding voice, and his proven history with Orson won him that role.

The part of Caesar went to Joseph Holland, an American-born actor who had trained at the Royal Academy of Dramatic Art in London and toured nationally with Katharine Cornell in Shaw's *Saint Joan* in 1936. John Hoysradt, Orson's roommate in 1933–1934 during the Cornell tour and now a neighbor at Sneden's Landing, became Decius Brutus. John A. Willard (Trebonius) and Grover Burgess (Ligarius) were veteran multitalents. The two female principals were Evelyn Allen as Calpurnia and Muriel Brassler as Portia. "As so often happened in Welles' classical productions," Houseman wrote, the actresses usually played lesser roles, and were "decorative, adequate and hardly memorable." (Houseman failed to mention that the same could be said of the roles as written.)

Actor Norman Lloyd, who was cast as Cinna the poet, was one of "Houseman's people." Houseman had urged Orson to meet with his friend Lloyd, a classically trained actor with a résumé full of small Broadway parts and appearances in left-wing and Federal Theatre Project productions. Orson approved Lloyd for the first Mercury season at the going minimum. Elliott Reid* (Cinna the conspirator) and Arthur Anderson (Lucius the page) were not yet out of their teens, both just starting out in radio, where they had met Orson. Stefan Schnabel (Metullus Cimber) was the son of the Austrian classical pianist Arthur Schnabel and the contralto Therese Behr. A Jewish refugee from Hitler, Schnabel had cut his teeth in the Old Vic company of *Hamlet* starring a British actor Orson was just getting to know, Laurence Olivier.

The twenty-one professionals would earn $40 per week as mandated by Equity. Junior players, less established, were paid $25. More than a dozen extras, young and ambitious, would earn $1 a day playing attendants, citizens, soldiers, and senators—until they threatened a strike during rehearsals and their salaries were raised to $15 weekly. The extras were "the cream of the New York beginners' crop," in the words of Mercury stage manager Walter Ash; they included the strike leader and future film director John Berry. (One supernumerary, George Lloyd, played the "dead" Caesar for a whole scene, breathing through a papier-mâché mask designed by Bil Baird.)

Finally, Orson telephoned the blond, handsome William Mowry Jr., the Todd School football player who knew his Shakespeare, and invited him to make his professional debut as the tribune Flavius, who opposes Caesar. Edgerton Paul, busy in a Theatre Guild production, passed the stand-in torch to Mowry, who had played Brutus at Dartmouth. Mowry obliged, "even [serving as Orson's stand-in] through—this is hard for some people to believe—some of the *dress* rehearsals," he later recalled.

Avoiding rehearsals until the last moment may have seemed a bad

---

* Initially Reid was billed as "Ted Reid" but soon—and for many decades—he became known as "Elliott Reid."

habit, but it served Orson well, helping him avoid the boredom of repetition, while keeping the other actors on edge. He never stood in quite
the same place, or spoke in quite the same manner, as the stand-in.

One day, William Alland—the aspiring actor who'd dogged
Welles's steps during *The Second Hurricane*—caught up with him outside the theater and impressed him by spouting from memory Mark
Antony's funeral oration for Caesar. He was rewarded with the small
part of Marcullus. More important, Alland—or "Vakhtangov," as
Orson dubbed him in honor of the influential Soviet stage director—
became the first of many young people who pledged a kind of informal fellowship with Orson and his genius. Indeed, Alland and others
who followed in his footsteps became known to insiders as "Orson's
slaves"—holding script, running errands, delivering food to his dressing room, and competing to serve his whims.

Though Orson was always, singularly, Orson Welles, his personality seemed to morph and metastasize with each success. The happy
summer of 1937, the time alone in New Hampshire, and the launching
of the Mercury Theatre clearly marked a fork in the road. Orson was
no longer the young unknown dubbed "Shoebooty" by the all-black
company of the Voodoo *Macbeth*. These days he wore expensive shoes.
He had a chauffeur, a speedboat, and a country home. He transformed
himself physically too, nowadays indulging in morning shaves and
manicures before settling in for a long lunch at "21." Dieting to keep
slender and boyish, he adopted a consciously foppish style—"wild
camp," he called it later—modeled after actor-director Alfred Lunt.
("One of the best actors we ever had!") "I see myself in those old stills,"
Welles told Leaming, "and I see somebody that could very easily be
thought of as a faggot."

Orson's carefully presented anecdotes about his womanizing were
often anecdotes about coitus interruptus or fumbling lovemaking in
practice. Indeed, there were so many boastful anecdotes—mixed with
so many disclaimers about dandyism and impotence—that some critics and scholars have raised doubts about his heterosexuality.

In one early French book about Welles, Maurice Bessy described
him as "a Don Juan at heart," adding, "Welles knows—and has openly

stated—that the mythic Don Juan is simply an unsatisfied homosexual, for whom the incessant quest for an ideal woman masks his search for himself." Speaking to Henry Jaglom, Welles claimed he went to court to stop Bessy's book, which is still in print today. "He's a mean, little, crooked fairy," Welles said of Bessy, adding that the author used to join him and Micheál MacLíammóir for meals in Paris during the filming of *Othello.* "Well, when I am with a homosexual, I get a little homosexual. To make them feel at home, you see? Just to keep Michael comfortable, I kind of camped a little. To bring him out. So he wouldn't feel he was with a terrible straight. Bessy might have seen that."

Although he worked often and happily with many gay and bisexual artists onstage and screen—Marc Blitzstein is just one example—Orson too often wielded homosexuality as a blunt weapon in arguments. He made his enemies into egregious homosexuals: Captain Mueller, Micheál MacLíammóir, even John Houseman. Virgil Thomson and Houseman "roomed together," Welles reminded Jaglom, adding, "They were lovers." There is no proof of this, and Thomson had a lifelong homosexual companion, the painter Maurice Grosser. But Orson was convinced that Houseman was a closet homosexual who had a crush on him. About three weeks after they met, Welles went on, speaking to Jaglom, "He said to me, 'I keep dreaming of you riding bareback on a horse.' And I should have taken that more seriously. But I just laughed."

Respected Welles experts such as Simon Callow and Joseph McBride have given some credence to scuttlebutt about the director's affairs with men, while tracing homosexuality as "an increasingly overt theme" in late-career works such as *Chimes at Midnight* (as suggested by the Hal-Poins relationship) and *F for Fake* (whose protagonist is the gay art forger Elmyr de Hory).

According to Callow, who tried hard to pinpoint Orson's sexuality, William Alland "avers that without question" that Welles and longtime crony Francis Carpenter, cast as Octavius in Orson's new production, "had a sexual relationship." But how did Alland know for sure? The author leaves this stone unturned, and for what it is worth, Carpenter—"camp beyond the dreams of Quentin Crisp," according to Callow—was married and had children.

William Mowry Jr. also believed that Welles engaged in the "bisexual chic" that was prevalent in New York artist circles. But Mowry too balked at supplying the details in his Columbia University oral history, insisting, "I know he had [some] men. . . . But I think he did it only to prove to himself that he was [heterosexual]."

Regardless, Mowry believed that Welles spent most of his time chasing women. "Some of the girls in the Mercury Theatre got their jobs through sleeping with Orson," Mowry insisted, adding, "He tried to screw the girl who became my first wife"—a dramatic recitalist named Sherrard Pollard from the Neighborhood Playhouse, who was also involved with the Mercury. Orson "tried" for Pollard simply because he could. Orson was "sadistic in many ways," said Mowry.

But there is scant proof of active bisexuality on Orson's part. Some people prefer their geniuses to be pansexual, and some geniuses may find it useful to be seen that way too. Orson's newly preening behavior in the fall of 1937 may have been deliberate misdirection. Orson cultivated the image of a dandy, even while women constantly fluttered around him. He covered all the assumptions while affirming none.

Gone was the young, attentive Orson, sensitive to the hunger of his fellow actors. Orson shed the egalitarianism of the Federal Theatre Project, dining on steak and mushrooms from Longchamps in front of everyone during the rehearsals. The scent of the food, and Orson's indifference, infuriated some of the actors—perhaps not the worst thing for a play about a conspiracy to bring down an autocrat. The despotic Orson rubbed it in by ordering a magnificent chocolate cake from Schrafft's, contemplating it solemnly, then finally ordering it removed, untouched. "I've had my dessert, my *spiritual* dessert," he'd announce, before turning with a sigh to half a grapefruit.

More than a few films have incorporated Orson Welles as a character, and one of the best is Richard Linklater's *Me and Orson Welles* (2008), which takes audiences behind the scenes of *Julius Caesar* in the fall of 1937. While Linklater's film makes no pretense of strict accuracy, the script weaves the facts into credible fiction, and Christian McKay's performance, as flamboyant as it is loving, is the best fictional Orson on screen to date.

As depicted scathingly in *Me and Orson Welles*, the Mercury ensemble underwent the now customary Welles regimen during *Julius Caesar*: torturous late-night rehearsals, battles royal over the complicated sound and lighting cues, the angry shouting matches between Welles and Houseman that had become ritualized.

Since he was now paying them over his and Houseman's signature, Orson no longer treated the actors like amateurs on the dole. If a performer asked, "Why am I doing this in such and such a scene?" Orson might snap, "Because of your Friday paycheck!" When the actors got distracted, he would settle them down by shouting, "All right, children!" When otherwise disciplined actors started hamming it up, he cried, "Shame on you!" Coming from a twenty-two-year-old, his tactics irked some of the older cast members. Perhaps Orson really exploded only "a few times," as Elliott Reid recalled, but when he did "it was a formidable thing to watch": he popped up like a jack-in-the-box from the back of the theater, streaked down the aisle like a comet, and leaped onstage, screaming all the way.

Orson's directing style provoked a range of responses from the actors, and their feelings about his behavior were often closely aligned with their belief in his genius. Actors recognized an artistic temperament when they encountered one. Orson rarely ruffled Joseph Cotten's feathers, for example. Cotten's customary aplomb, and his deep friendship with Welles, helped sustain their mutual admiration.

George Coulouris, on the other hand, was a "grumbler" by nature, "very temperamental and very barometric," in his own words. "The [*Julius Caesar*] rehearsals were bad," Coulouris recalled years later. "He kept us waiting for hours." Even Coulouris conceded that Orson employed peculiar means to achieve often extraordinary ends. "I think he's a genius," Coulouris observed, "but that is to say he's a genius who has flashes of imagination that galvanize a show, but sometimes the intervals are not galvanic at all."

With *Caesar*, for instance, Coulouris thought Orson wasted too much time drilling crowd movements at the expense of guiding the principals. Welles was "preoccupied with timing and marching," recalled Coulouris, "and had the cast marching around like idiots for hours."

Norman Lloyd, a fastidious man who disliked messy methods and peculiar behavior, was even more grudging in his assessment. "Discipline at rehearsal [for *Julius Caesar*] was not of a model nature," Lloyd complained in his memoir *Stages: Of Life in Theatre, Film and Television*. "Orson might arrive at rehearsal and be amused to talk about something for two hours, or do an imitation of Maurice Evans's Falstaff or of Guthrie McClintic, with whom he had worked. Or he told jokes. Finally, he would get around to the scene, which he would rehearse once over lightly before he left."

Lloyd's perspective may have been colored by the professional psychodrama he underwent during these rehearsals. In his earnest attempt to strike the right note for the part of Cinna the poet, who is murdered by Caesar's followers after they mistake him for Cinna the conspirator, he found himself in a war of wills with Orson. This was not a major scene in the play traditionally—the poet Cinna has only a few lines—and Orson did not appear very engaged by the staging of Cinna's death during rehearsals.

For weeks, in fact, Orson handed Lloyd over to Marc Blitzstein, who had the actor beating a tom-tom to an accelerating metronome while extras playing the murder mob chanted phrases Orson had poached from *Coriolanus*. Lloyd felt his big scene was going nowhere.

He wasn't the only actor in this production who feared that his performance was disappearing down a hole. In some cases literally: as with *Faustus*, the trap holes cut into the stage floor created a dangerous risk of plunging into the basement. Orson was "amazed and indignant," recalled Houseman. "Were they not actors? And were not traps among the oldest and most consecrated devices of the stage? They must stop being amateurish and craven . . ." Until, that is, Welles himself fell into a trap hole flanking the top ramp, plummeting to the cellar floor and spraining his ankle. Then, safety measures were taken.

The actors were also uneasy about Orson's penchant—some saw it as a mania—for aural experimentation. Orson brought in radio man Irving Reis to create recordings of Antony's and Brutus's speeches for the extras to listen to and practice their reactions. He also asked Reis to create a mix of recorded street sounds—traffic noise, police sirens, and air-raid warnings—which would be broadcast as background ambience during certain scenes. Orson worried the actors by spending an inordinate amount of time fiddling with the levels of this "sound track," which seemed to them like a tumult drowning out the import and clarity of their lines.

He drove the cast hard, yet he drove himself hardest. The technical rehearsals, one week before previews, were a hellish experience, with Orson testing the lights and sound "until the stage hands dropped like flies," according to Lloyd, "and the actors became punch drunk." Orson prided himself on staying on his feet all day and all night, but when he wasn't stealing catnaps at a nearby hotel he might be found snoring in the orchestra seats as the company arrived for the morning run-through. The devoted Augusta Weissberger kept him buzzing with fresh coffee; her mother contributed homemade chicken soup.

Rehearsals were always a chance for Welles to try out and refine his ideas for staging. He had intended, for example, to pad the platforms and ramps to muffle the sound of the marching actors' boots, but when the padding proved too expensive, he embraced the resulting thundering-herd effect, which enhanced the tension in the crowd scenes. The lighting design, the sound effects cues, and even his beloved trap holes were adjusted each time he revised a scene.

Originally scheduled to premiere on November 6, *Julius Caesar* had to be postponed until November II, its first public performance to be preceded by one week of invitation-only previews. The Mercury was in a bad financial state, and Houseman, still moonlighting some days as a professor at Vassar, was fast coming unglued. "All our investors' money" had been spent, he recalled, largely on the renovation and actors' salaries. The unpaid bills were accumulating.

Lloyd was not alone in foreseeing a personal and professional fiasco in the making, for him and the nascent Mercury Theatre. Lloyd did not warm to Welles any faster than Welles warmed to Lloyd, and the actor was increasingly flummoxed by the director's seeming indifference to his scenes. Finally, just before the first dress rehearsal, Lloyd confronted Welles, saying he felt unrehearsed and wanted to drop the poet's death scene altogether. "He [Orson] accepted this calmly," Lloyd recalled. "If I didn't want to go on, that was all right."

In his book *Run-Through*, Houseman offered a plausible explanation for the impasse between Welles and Lloyd. "In every production we did together," he observed, "there were one or more moments which came to embarrass or bore [Welles]—either because he had become disillusioned with the performers or because he realized that his own original conception of the scene had failed, and he was uncertain which way to turn. In *Julius Caesar* the lynching of Cinna the Poet had become such a block."

The audience was always the real test for Orson, and he treated previews as a last chance for changes—a derring-do-or-die. When the Mercury Theatre finally opened its doors and performed *Julius Caesar* for its initial invitation-only audience in the first week of November, the lighting, music, and sound cues were a mess, according to most accounts, and the crowd scenes dragged. Still, no one thought the show was terrible—until the curtain came down.

Lloyd was watching in the wings, feeling "really very angry" that Orson had called his bluff and dropped Cinna's death scene from the invitation-only performance. Lloyd refused to come out and line up with the rest of the company for the expected ovation and bows. Then an astonishing thing happened: the ovation never came. Accounts differ, but according to most who were there, a smattering of applause trickled quickly into silence. Then the audience simply stood and filed out of the theater. The cast was in shock, Orson stupefied and humiliated.

The Mercury's publicist Henry Senber darted onstage, sputtering, "Jesus, Orson! We can't even get one curtain call!" Furious, Orson stared down at Senber, "cleared his throat, produced a large blob of phlegm and spat right in Hank's face," according to Lloyd's memoir. As everyone froze in horror, Senber reared back to punch Orson in the face. The publicist would have delivered his blow, too, if Orson hadn't grabbed Senber by the shoulders first. "Spit in my face! Please! Please! Spit in my face!" the director pleaded. "Hank did so," Lloyd reported in his memoir. "The terrible moment had passed, and they were friends again."

Julius Caesar was doomed, unless Orson could save it. Over the next several days, as the date of the true premiere neared, he plunged into round-the-clock salvation. No more experimentation: now was the time for ruthless decision making. Orson's prerecorded ambient sound track, which only distracted everyone, was abandoned. ("What was brilliant on the sophisticated electronic equipment at the radio station," wrote Andrea Janet Nouryeh, "sounded laughable when played on the inadequate sound system at the theater.") The lighting cues were narrowed, simplified.

Returning to the original Shakespeare he knew and loved from boyhood, Welles trimmed scenes, reshuffled others, taking chunks out of certain roles in favor of others. (He subtracted from Octavius and Mark Antony in particular, reducing George Coulouris to "a highly effective but one-dimensional" portrait of Antony, thought Houseman.) Orson had long toyed with the idea of eliminating the intermission, and now he did it.

At last Orson came around to the nagging issue of Cinna the poet, which he had been evading and postponing. In Act Three, Scene 3, of Shakespeare's original, Cinna wanders onstage after dreaming about the assassinated Caesar. He is accosted by a gang of thugs galvanized by Mark Antony to seek out the conspirators and avenge Caesar. The thugs mistake Cinna the poet for Cinna the conspirator. He pleads with them as they close in. No, I am Cinna the *poet!*

Now Welles and Lloyd revisited everything to do with Cinna: his costume, his mannerisms, his line readings. Lloyd had thought all along that Cinna should be dressed as an ordinary clerk, while Orson thought the character ought to have a hint of the Byronic poet about him. Lloyd had an idea: Cinna's death scene could evoke the tragedy of Maxwell Bodenheim, a real-life alcoholic Greenwich Village figure known for handing out poems for spare change in Washington Square. Orson knew about Bodenheim from Chicago, where the poet had once run a literary journal with Ben Hecht. Melding his own vision of the Byronic poet with Lloyd's hapless one, Orson reconstructed the scene. He and Lloyd clashed repeatedly, and Lloyd threatened to quit, but Orson pushed ahead, mediating their differences throughout the long night before the next-to-last preview.

Orson blocked the scene anew. Now the thugs would appear singly onstage, then collect into small groups, edging closer to Cinna as they formed a mob. As he found himself surrounded, Lloyd would desperately pull scraps of poetry out of his pockets as proof of his identity. The mob would grab at the scraps, crumple the poetry, hurl it back into his face.

"At two in the morning," according to Houseman, "the scene began to work, getting tauter and more dangerous as the night wore on. At four-thirty we stopped and it was announced that the Cinna the Poet scene would be in the show for the [next preview] matinee."

Before the performance, the word spread backstage that critic John Mason Brown from the *New York Evening Post* was in the audience, having been granted special permission by Welles and Houseman to attend the preview because a previous commitment kept him away from the premiere. With the hectic revisions of the last few days still drying on the page, not many felt confidence in the production. As Coulouris prepared to make his first entrance from the darkened basement under the stage, the actor was heard to predict ("in a voice loud enough to be heard by the entire front half of the orchestra," Houseman recalled) that this play and the Mercury would fold after the previews.

But Coulouris was wrong. In that desperate moment, *Julius Caesar* came gloriously alive. And the immediacy and universality of Orson's bold, modern-dress vision was capped by his vivid staging of Cinna the poet's death. Lloyd went down screaming, "I'm Cinna, the poet! The poet! The poet!"—blotted out by the mob and Orson's blood-red lighting. The killing was followed by a sustained loud peal from a Hammond organ lasting almost a minute. The audience gaped in shock. "An unforgettably sinister thing," Joseph Wood Krutch later wrote in *The Nation*.

That day at the preview matinee, the ovation was overwhelming. Afterward, the *New York Evening Post*'s critic took the rare step of heading backstage. John Mason Brown shook Orson's hand and congratulated Houseman, telling them what he later wrote in the *Post*: that the Mercury Theatre's maiden presentation of *Julius Caesar* was hands-down "the most exciting, the most imaginative, the most topical, the most awesome and the most absorbing" play of the new Broadway season.

The official premiere on November 11, 1937, came amid the rising tide of fascism in Europe and widespread fear of an approaching world war. The first-night crowd was plunged into a past that eerily seemed to foretell the present day: the stage in darkness, the lone voice hailing Caesar, a figure resembling Mussolini striding forward in military uniform with a fascist salute. Orson's Shakespeare adaptations were never fusty. He had sharpened *Julius Caesar* like an assassin's knife held aloft, amid beams of light that simulated the Wagnerian stage tricks of Hitler's Germany.

The performances peaked on opening night; the actors would enjoy the best notices of their careers. Caesar's spectacular assassination (complete with Orson's real daggers) thrilled the audience, and Cinna's dance of death was lauded in review after review—Cinna's demise was reminiscent of "the hoodlum element you find in any big city after a war," as Welles told the *New York Post*, "a mob that is without the stuff that makes them intelligently alive, a lynching mob, the kind of a mob that gives you a Hitler or a Mussolini."

Welles's own portrayal of Brutus ("a fine patrician type, his face sensitive and intellectual" as Orson described the character in *Everybody's Shakespeare*) added to the opening-night triumph. Almost stealthily Orson had nursed his characterization, committing himself to the character incrementally, while employing his stand-in and juggling his other chores. Welles was often a "king actor," as he once famously proclaimed in an interview—that is, an actor specializing in kingly performances; but the manner in which he played kingly men always revealed—as Truffaut said (and as Welles agreed)—"the fragility of great authority." But he was also capable of playing, as in *Julius Caesar*, a high-minded loser swept away by the dark tide of history.

Dressed to stand apart from the other players in his custom-made double-breasted blue pinstripe suit, Welles offered a ruminative Brutus whose soft conversational manner, in the context of such bombast, allowed him to dominate his scenes. Highlighted by his simple and powerful oration at the forum, his characterization served as "a foil to the staginess of the production as a whole," in the words of John Mason Brown. "There can no longer be any question of his skill as a player," Richard Watts Jr. wrote of his performance in the *New York Herald Tribune.*

The last tableau of the show brought to its feet the capacity crowd that had been privileged to witness the birth of the Mercury Theatre. Fittingly, the final lines belonged to George Coulouris, Orson's doubting Thomas, who now as Mark Antony strode gravely to center stage and stared out over the audience, declaiming in Brutus's memory, "And say to all the world this was a man!"

The Nuremberg lights enveloped the ensemble in white brilliance. The theater broke into a frenzy. People shouted hosannas. Women tossed their hats into the air. Critics risked their deadlines to stand in place fiercely applauding with reddened hands.

John Anderson wrote in the *Journal and American*: "Mr. Welles has schemed it out with resourcefulness and imagination, energy, daring, and perception." Brooks Atkinson wrote in the *New York Times*: "Theatrically brilliant." Richard Watts Jr. in the *Herald Tribune* called it "the great *Julius Caesar* of our time." John Mason Brown spoke for all: "The touch of genius is upon it."

Julius Caesar opened just one day after Broadway welcomed another breathlessly awaited Shakespeare production, *Antony and Cleopatra*, a big-budget star vehicle for actress Tallulah Bankhead. Bankhead's foray into Shakespeare cost an inordinate $100,000 to mount onstage, with Virgil Thomson's score and Cecil Beaton's costumes among the expenses. Brooks Atkinson criticized it as "elaborately encumbered," other critics joined in the mockery, and *Antony and Cleopatra* closed after just five performances.

Bankhead rushed over to see Orson's bargain Shakespeare, then joined the well-wishers backstage. Welles told her the Mercury's *Julius Caesar* had cost all of $6,000. "Six thousand dollars!" Bankhead shrieked. "That's less than one of my fucking breastplates."

As always with Welles, there were skeptics, most of them falling into one of two categories: Shakespeare purists, who were offended; and anti-communists, who were suspicious of the implications of a modern-dress *Julius Caesar* staged by refugees from the Federal Theatre Project. Stark Young in the *New Republic* wrote that he was "on the whole pretty much disappointed" in the production; Mary McCarthy in the *Partisan Review* complained that Welles "cut the play to pieces," then further ruined it with his own "cloying and monotonous performance."

But their voices were drowned out by the Niagara roar of acclaim, and by the sound of ticket office telephones, barraged by eager sub-scribers to the coming Mercury season. The first week of performances sold out, with many standees; the second-night press list rose to 120. "At the box-office as well as in the opinion of the critics," reported the *New York Times*, "the Mercury Theatre . . . has started life with a hit."

But the Mercury also started life with a debt, and it was more than $6,000. Friends of the project pleaded with the partners to forgo their plans for a revolving repertory schedule, which would require deeper investment, expense, and liability. Instead, the Mercury should pay the bills by keeping *Julius Caesar* onstage for as long as the theater could sell out.

At a celebratory dinner at "21," over two bottles of champagne, Welles and Houseman talked things over—and decided cheerily that they were not interested in playing it safe. They were still committed to the idea of a repertory theater. "Neither Welles nor I was primarily interested in money," recalled Houseman. Within days of the premiere, the Mercury management sent out publicity for the second production of the season, Thomas Dekker's *The Shoemaker's Holiday.* "The plan is to open it Christmas week," wrote the *New York Times*, "later alternating it in repertory with *Julius Caesar.*"

During that same dinner, the partners considered other revenue-boosting options. Houseman suggested they might send a second company of *Julius Caesar* out on the road in 1938. Orson initially resisted the proposal, seeing himself "as another Henry Irving or Edwin Booth," as Houseman recalled, who might one day be "leading his company on a triumphal tour of the hinterland, and he wanted no interference with this vision." With a harrumph, however, Welles finally agreed.

Sundays were dark for *Caesar,* and the partners thought of other ways to use the space. The Mercury could open up the theater building to other events and activities. It could present works in progress, with bare staging and a few props, and only work lights. And they could make good on their contract with Marc Blitzstein and revive *The Cradle Will Rock* for a run of Sundays.

For this new incarnation of *Cradle,* Orson adopted an "oratorio" format, with the performers in street clothing and bare makeup, seated in rows atop one of *Julius Caesar*'s raised platforms. Orson asked Blitzstein and Chubby Sherman to fine-tune the staging, and many players from the original cast, including Howard Da Silva, Will Geer, Olive Stanton, and Sherman, agreed to reprise their roles. Blitzstein would still function as the sole maestro on piano, with a small chorus of black singers seated on a second platform. The new version of *Cradle* was up and ready for its first paid preview—a benefit for the striking union employees of a newspaper, the *Brooklyn Daily Eagle*—after the evening performance of *Julius Caesar* on Saturday, November 27.

When *Cradle* then officially reopened on Sunday, December 5, the reviews were so laudatory ("the best thing militant labor has put into a theatre yet," declared Brooks Atkinson in the *New York Times*) that the Mercury Theatre found itself with a second hit on its hands. The Sunday night shows sold out through mid-December, when *Cradle* exhausted its union permissions for the limited run—after which Blitzstein's musical was leased to producer Sam Grisman for another incarnation at the Windsor on Broadway beginning in January 1938.

After a dinner at the photographer Cecil Beaton's apartment, Orson posed for Beaton—one more signpost on the road to Broadway canonization. The portrait shows the twenty-two-year-old actor-director at a worktable, staring intensely over a Roman bust, with scissors, a thick tome, and a human skull draped with beads. Orson returned the favor by inviting Beaton to create the costumes for his conjoined productions of *Henry IV (Parts 1 and 2)* and *Henry V*, now projected as a Mercury offering for the spring of 1938.

Orson was leading a double life in the fall of 1937, reflecting the opposite sides of his persona as a performer: the Shakespearean sophisticate and the cheerful vulgarian. While appearing nightly as Brutus in *Julius Caesar*, he was also appearing frequently (and anonymously) on *The March of Time*, and, more important, purring to life every Sunday night as the Shadow.

The Shadow was his dream role. The job required little forethought, and on this show—unlike *The March of Time* and his other bill-paying radio gigs—he was treated as the most important person in the room. The very first script draft was forwarded to him in New Hampshire for approval, and later episodes were messengered to his Mercury Theatre office, where he marked them up with cuts and improvements. And part of the *Shadow* job was doubling as a pitchman, warning motorists on behalf of Goodrich Tires about roads in treacherous weather.

On Sundays, he often arrived at the studio not having glimpsed the final draft of the script—not even knowing the outcome of the plot. He later said this enhanced the program's feeling of suspense, quickening his performance along with that of the other actors. He sometimes showed up just minutes before the red light blinked on at 5:30 P.M., striding to the microphone with his usual bounce and roll, just as the mysterioso music faded away, to intone the famous opening: "Who knows what evil lurks in the hearts of men . . . ?"

He played the Shadow with a flippancy that kept the other participants on their toes. In the same breath he seemed both to relish and to mock his hokey dialogue. His irony and good humor were infectious. "One time he got to the middle break," recalled actor and writer Sidney Slon, "and he said, 'Hey, this is a hell of a script. How does it end?'" Another time, Orson rushed breathlessly into the studio and dashed up to the microphone, whipping out his copy of the script so fast the pages flew out of his hands and fanned onto the floor. "There was consternation in the control room," recalled series announcer Ken Roberts. "Fear on the faces of the musicians. Everybody was terribly upset. Suddenly, Orson merely smiled, reached into his pocket and took out another script. The whole thing had been planned to frighten the director."

The series pitted the Shadow's powers of hypnosis and telepathy against deadly criminals, who were often deranged, fanatical, or endowed with superpowers. Orson never wrote or directed the far-fetched scripts, but his star contract gave him script and casting input, and *The Shadow* incorporated many actors drawn from Orson's burgeoning theater and radio career: Chubby Sherman, Whitford Kane, Martin Gabel, Everett Sloan, Ray Collins, and Agnes Moorehead, who had a regular supporting role as Lamont Cranston's "friend and constant companion, the lovely Margo Lane."

Although he liked to pretend otherwise, Orson even graced the occasional rehearsal. "I remember him arriving for work one morning," stage and screen director Elia Kazan wrote in *Elia Kazan: A Life.* (A stage player during that period, famous for his role in *Waiting for Lefty,* Kazan also performed parts in radio.) "He'd been up all night carousing but looked little the worse for it and was full of continuing excitement. A valet-secretary met him at the side of the stage with a small valise containing fresh linen and the toilet articles he needed. The rehearsal was never interrupted—Orson had unflagging energy and recuperative powers at that time—and he soon looked as good as new. There was no swagger of aesthetic guilt there.

"*The Shadow* was not patronized, only slightly kidded, and this affectionately," Kazan continued. "It was a way of making a good living at the time and no disgrace. . . . Seldom have I been near a man so abundantly talented or one with a greater zest for life."

Some accounts insist that the network kept secret the name of the actor playing the Shadow in order to heighten the mystery for listeners, but Orson's participation was well known; indeed, it was part of his value to the sponsors. (*Radio Daily* even complained, "Orson Welles does not come up to [other] actors who have played the part in the past.") To devotees of his twenty-six episodes, the season from September 1937 to March 1938—known to fans as "the Orson Welles season"—Orson was the best Shadow. And his one-year stint reinvigorated the series, opening the door to fifteen years of future Shadows.

It seemed miraculous to Orson's friends and coworkers that he was managing to compress so much activity into his life. Young Orson was like a magician, with a top hat and cape full of cards, objects, and furry animals, dazzling you with one trick even as he was barreling on to the next.

The very same week as *Julius Caesar*'s splendid premiere, Orson launched the first rehearsals for *The Shoemaker's Holiday*. He had prepared the production in New Hampshire, taking pencil and scissors to Thomas Dekker's comedy, which wove together earthy humor and sentimental romance in telling the story of a jolly shoemaker's rise to lord mayor of London. First performed on New Year's Eve 1599, *The Shoemaker's Holiday* was rarely produced in the modern era, and it never had been staged in New York. (The play's real claim to fame was the poem "The Merry Month of May," which Orson knew from boyhood.) Orson's revision shrank the play to half its length, breaking up long speeches into bursts of overlapping dialogue, and turning the plot into a locomotive of action and bawdy humor that would last less than ninety minutes.

Orson's set design partitioned the stage into three areas, each screened by its own curtain. A London street would occupy center stage, with the side stages given over to the shoemakers' guildhall and the jolly shoemaker's shop. The set of *Julius Caesar* could be transformed for *Shoemaker's Holiday* by rotating the main platform on wheels. Set designer Sam Leve recalled that the "major design concept" came to Welles one day when they were riding together in a taxi. When the cab stopped at a fruit stand, Orson looked at the boxes and asked him, "Did you ever do a show with orange crates?"

Leve did so now, with natural burlap and canvas too, draping the stage with a cyclorama to conceal the blood-red back wall of *Caesar*. (Again, the program read "Staged by Orson Welles," with no mention of Leve.) The costumes would be homespun too; Orson told designer Millia Davenport that the men ought to wear huge codpieces, a touch actors and audiences alike found hilarious. (In "a downward transposition of his false noses," Peter Conrad wrote, some of the codpieces simulated erections.)

Again, as with *Horse Eats Hat*, Orson wanted plenty of music. Composers Virgil Thomson and Marc Blitzstein were overbooked, so he hired Lehman Engel, who had handled the orchestration for *The Second Hurricane* and *The Cradle Will Rock*. (Engel was also using the Mercury Theatre stage on Sunday afternoons for his New York Madrigal Society recitals.) To honor the repertory theater concept, Orson asked for incidental music—drinking songs and jigs, transitions and effects—composed for the same instruments and musicians involved in *Julius Caesar*.

"Often he tapped out rhythms," Engel said, "and no less often described the quality of the melody and the number of measures needed. The production that resulted from this method was always one very definite idea made up of the scenery he had designed, the play he had revised, the acting he had postulated in great detail, and the accompanying twiddles he had indicated."

While retooling Dekker's play, Orson also created parts for people he wanted to be surrounded by while working on the play. "Have you ever cast a friend instead of the right person for a part?" Peter Bogdanovich asked him during their interview sessions. Frequently, Welles replied. "Would you do it again?" asked Bogdanovich. "Yes," declared Welles.

Whitford Kane, the onetime leading actor of the Goodman Theatre, was someone "we had always thought of as one of the company,"
according to John Houseman, but Orson had never directed Kane onstage. Now he cast Kane as Simon Eyre, the ascendant Lord Mayor.
Chubby Sherman would get a showcase for his buffoonery as the journeyman cobbler Firk, who wore a fool's cap and sagging tights with
an ill-fitting codpiece that swung around when he did. "Firk was promoted to the one who was always going up to the quality and insulting
them, or talking back to his master," Sherman recalled. "Orson built
up my part so that I'd end a scene. Rather than having a thing in the
middle, he made a curtain [closer] out of it. It was all very flattering."

Joseph Cotten was handed the romantic role of the shoemaker pursuing a nobleman's daughter. Good supporting parts were set aside for
George Coulouris, Norman Lloyd, John Hoysradt, Francis Carpenter,
William Mowry Jr., Elliott Reid, Stefan Schnabel, and Arthur Anderson—all from the *Julius Caesar* cast. Smaller billed roles went to
William Alland and to Richard Wilson, another bright young fellow
who had joined Orson's "slave" brigade.

A few new players "from the ordinary marts of the commercial
theater," in the words of the *New York Times*, also joined the company—
foremost among them Vincent Price, who accepted less than his
customary wages to play the ill-fated bridegroom Master Hammon.
Price's star was on the rise after his debut opposite Helen Hayes in
Victoria Regina in late 1935, and his recruitment reflected the Mercury's
growing cachet.

This time, Orson would play no part himself; he was "merely" directing. Whether because he was carrying a lighter load here than on
Julius Caesar, or because the play itself was such a merry romp, the director's mood was playful and contagious. "Whereas *Caesar* depressed
both actors and crew," wrote Andrea Janet Nouryeh, "*Shoemaker* lifted
them up."

As with that other farce, *Horse Eats Hat*, Orson demanded headlong
pacing for the play—a mode that came naturally to him in real life and
that characterized much of his best work (with some contemplative
exceptions, such as *The Magnificent Ambersons*). He wanted the dialogue
to snap and zing. "He loved you to bite the cue," recalled Arthur Anderson, the teenage Lucius from *Julius Caesar*, now "A Boy" in *Shoe-*

maker's Holiday. "Everything had to mesh, go together. You didn't finish a speech that someone else wasn't on top of you—all the time." Orson could be a martinet in enforcing the machine-gun pacing, snapping his fingers and blocking the action so precisely that some of his actors— even Chubby Sherman, who complained about this in interviews— felt he inhibited their comic spontaneity. His staging depended "on the precise machine-like interplay of movement, music, curtains and light," said Lehman Engel. "The actors were his puppets."

Quite a few members of the cast performed double duty, appearing in six nighttime performances (and one matinee) of *Julius Caesar* each week, then rehearsing *Shoemaker's Holiday* after the curtain fell—until dawn. Orson was on a treadmill of his own, with *The Shadow* and *The March of Time* taking up any free time not already devoted to *Caesar* or *Shoemaker's Holiday.* He rarely made it home to Sneden's Landing, stealing sleep in hotels or snoozing overnight at the theater.

Seven weeks after the *Julius Caesar* premiere—late at night on Christmas Day, after a sold-out performance—Orson stepped forward, still in costume as Brutus, and silenced the applause.

"Ladies and gentlemen," he announced in his grand manner, "we are going to give you a full performance, with lights, scenery and costumes, of *Shoemaker's Holiday.* You are all welcome to stay, free of charge." For those who might want a break before the show, he noted, "there's a coffee and donut shop across the way, or there's Longchamps down the street." For the rest, "We'll leave the curtain up and show you how we change the set; perhaps some of the actors will come out and talk to you . . ." The spectators were encouraged to call their friends and invite them to come and join the crowd. The performance would begin at midnight.

So it did, at twelve o'clock sharp, with Lehman Engel's first musical fanfare. Hundreds had stayed and many more arrived, cramming into the theater, including a few critics drawn by the bait. Within minutes of the opening scene, as Houseman recalled later, the company knew they had another hit in their portfolio. The free public preview was the "wildest triumph imaginable," recalled Norman Lloyd, who was playing one of the apprentice shoemakers. "The show was a smash during its run—but never again did we have a performance like that one."

The official opening came a week later, in the evening on New Year's

Day—the 388th anniversary of the play's debut in front of Queen Elizabeth I in 1599, as the Mercury's publicity releases noted. The reviews, if anything, were more exultant than those for *Julius Caesar.* Richard Watts Jr. of the *New York Herald Tribune* hailed the fast and funny adaptation as "the great comfort of the season." Bosley Crowther of the *New York Times* called it "an uproarious comic strip." Sidney B. Whipple in the *New York World-Telegram* found the production splendid and brilliant—declaring it a genuine act of theatrical courage. "Triumph for Orson Welles," read the *Journal and American* headline.

Not only had Orson resuscitated Thomas Dekker for the modern age; he had also fulfilled two long-standing ambitions: to direct Whitford Kane and to elevate Chubby Sherman, Kane's life partner, to stardom. Sherman was the embodiment of the play's rowdy merriment. (Even his character's name, "Firk," sounded like "fuck" when said quickly—a running joke enhanced by the breakneck production.) Sherman proved "a clown of the first order," wrote Brooks Atkinson, and his appearance in *Shoemaker's Holiday* won the actor "with a golden disposition and a continuous grin" his first feature profile in the *New York Times.*

In hindsight, some students of Welles's theatrical career have described the triumphant Thomas Dekker comedy, following closely on the heels of *Julius Caesar,* as the zenith of the Mercury Theatre—"a success never recovered," in the words of Simon Callow. Ticket sales skyrocketed, and for a few weeks the Mercury rotated the two dissimilar plays. By the month's end, however, both of them were moved to the National Theatre, two blocks north, where the Mercury management could sell twice as many orchestra seats to the usual Broadway audiences while still offering big blocks of tickets to the left-wing and educational organizations that were its mainstay.

This was Houseman's practical idea, and at first it was opposed by Orson and just as vigorously criticized by "a voluble minority" of the company, in Houseman's words, including Chubby Sherman. ("I have never been able to decide whether it was wise or foolish" to expand the production to another, bigger theater, Houseman wrote, "whether it aided the Mercury or helped destroy it.") The play schedule now varied slightly every week, depending on ticket sales and Orson's ob-

ligations. He had a night off from acting every time the Mercury performed *The Shoemaker's Holiday.*

Virginia Welles spent most of November and December in Sneden's
Landing. For the few friends who might not have heard their news,
the Welleses sent out a holiday card decorated with one of Orson's
sketches, showing their cocker spaniel, Budget, sitting on her haunches,
with Virginia and Orson standing in profile, gazing off the page into
the future. Orson's figure showed long scruffy hair over his brow. Virginia's showed a tummy bump.

"We hope you are well," read the caption. "Virginia's self-portrait
(above) may give you some notion of how we are doing in case you
didn't know. In the meantime, Merry Christmas to you from Budget,
Orson, Virginia and . . ."

For weeks, Virginia had seen precious little of her husband. Around
Christmastime, Orson sent Irish actress Geraldine Fitzgerald to
Sneden's Landing for temporary safekeeping, and she and Virginia
became fast friends. Two years older than Welles, originally from
County Wicklow, Fitzgerald was a stunning beauty with luxuriant
auburn hair who had started out at the Gate Theatre in 1932, thanks to
an introduction from her aunt, the redoubtable Dublin actress Shelah
Richards. After rising quickly to become a leading actress onstage and
a feature player in British films, she was commended to Orson by his
Gate Theatre friends when she arrived in New York in late 1937. Not
quite twenty, she was married, though her husband—an English baronet, Edward Lindsay-Hogg—distanced himself from show business
and often trailed her like an afterthought.

The date and circumstances of her hiring at the Mercury have been
blurred by varying accounts, but her addition to the company was
not officially announced until the spring of 1938. Houseman was so
floored by how "unbelievably lovely" Fitzgerald was upon meeting her
for the first time that he was reduced to asking "a few routine questions
about her experience in the theatre, to which she gave lying answers."
Ushered then into Orson's presence, she was flattered to realize that the
"boy genius" (as she described Welles years later) was also "absolutely

bowled over by me. He looked at me like Michelangelo's God looking at Adam and Eve before the fall."

On New Year's Eve—the night before the official premiere of *Shoemaker's Holiday*—Orson summoned his wife to dine and dance at the Waldorf Astoria. "Many of our friends couldn't get over how light-footed I was for a woman six months pregnant," Virginia recalled. Such togetherness was increasingly rare for them.

A few weeks later, "fed up with seeing so little of Orson," in her words, Virginia improvised a trip to New York, hoping to surprise him in his room at the Algonquin after the curtain fell on *Julius Caesar*. "It was a very cold night in January and I was in my seventh month," Virginia recalled. Swearing the front desk to secrecy, she took over his suite, waiting for him—waiting, waiting.

"The sun came up and there was still no sign of Orson," Virginia ruefully confessed to her daughter Chris Welles Feder many years later. "I decided there was little point in waiting any longer, but before going home, I wanted to leave a love note on his pillow.

"That's when I opened a desk drawer, looking for some note-paper . . ."

Virginia discovered that Orson's desk drawer was stuffed with what, in her naïveté ("I never dreamed he would go looking for pleasure with other women"), she first took to be fan mail. After skimming the perfumed letters, however, she realized they were "love notes." "That made the shock more terrible," Virginia recalled, "my being so innocent and trusting. It seemed every ballerina in New York had written to him, and there were also letters from my good friend Geraldine. I couldn't believe, at first, that Orson would actually send Geraldine to stay with me when he'd been having an affair with her."

Orson had betrayed their marriage. Feeling suddenly dazed, dead inside, Virginia staggered over to the hotel window, intending to leap out and commit suicide. But she could not pry the window open. "God knows I tried," she told her daughter.

Instead, Virginia returned home to Sneden's Landing, vowing to maintain her dignity and not to confront her husband or Fitzgerald until her child was born. "I wouldn't hold it against her," Virginia told her daughter, "because in those days, you simply fell into bed with anyone who asked you to, especially if you were an actress trying to get ahead."

After a while, however, Virginia began to second-guess her fears. She wondered if the "love notes" meant anything after all, if she had let her imagination run away with her. Orson was attentive and loving whenever she was around, and the rest of the time he was so busy professionally. There were only so many hours in the day. She wondered "how Orson found the time to be unfaithful to me with Geraldine or anyone else."

Indeed, Virginia had jumped to conclusions. And at least when it came to Geraldine Fitzgerald, her suspicions of Orson's infidelity were premature.

Orson was indeed amorously involved with a number of ballerinas, though in his usual indeterminate fashion. "My period of ballerinas," he told Barbara Leaming with a laugh, "and none of them were a disappointment. I got terribly interested in ballerinas. I didn't consciously go out to collect them, but life just worked out that way." Leaming did not name any of these ballerinas; Frank Brady, citing Virginia as his source, listed two: Tilly Losch and Vera Zorina. (In his book about Welles, without substantiation or elaboration, David Thomson enterprisingly added a third: prima ballerina Tamara Toumanova.)

The first, Losch, began her career as a ballerina before becoming an interpretive dancer, an actress, and later a painter (and a countess). Born in Austria in 1903—Welles refers to her as the "older" ballerina among his conquests—as a child Losch trained in dance at the Vienna Opera. Short of stature but amazingly lithe, she had acted for Max Reinhardt in Berlin and London, danced for George Balanchine, and choreographed for her own ballet company in London and Paris. She performed notably in a few Hollywood films, including *The Good Earth*, a Best Picture nominee, in 1937. Losch designed her own clothes and also took them off for art photographers, posing in the nude. A femme fatale with a kitten face ringed by dark red bobbed hair, she collected interesting men, one of whom was Orson. She met him in New York in late 1937.

Leaming, Welles's authorized biographer, suggests an inaccurate time frame for the romance, writing that Orson's tryst with Losch coincided with a broadcast of *The Shadow* in late 1937. Welles approached this infidelity with "enormous guilt," Leaming wrote; then, as he and Losch prepared for "a go at it," Orson was shaken by the sound of his own voice booming from the radio in the hotel room.* "Who knows what evil lurks in the hearts of men? . . ." The coincidence spelled *coitus terminus*. "Imagine what it did!" Welles told Leaming. "The impotence lasted for one night."

In fact, the "love notes" Virginia found in Orson's suite preceded the actual lovemaking, such as it was, by several months, and the date dovetailed with one of the *final* broadcasts of *The Shadow* in the spring of 1938. This rough chronology can be worked out from Losch's archival papers, which include a series of telegrams and messages between her and Welles that track the rising fervor of their relationship through April and May. Most of these surviving communications are brief and coded. (April 23, 1938: OW to Losch at the Ambassador Hotel: "PLEASE.") Most are marked UNSIGNED, and many close with professions of love and devotion from Welles to Losch. One series of telegrams begins in early March 1938 and runs through Orson's birthday on May 6. (OW to Losch at the Ambassador: "I HAVE A COLD THIS IS MY BIRTHDAY LOVE.") The telegrams, which peak with a flurry of activity in mid-May, hint that Losch was the chaser, not the chased. (Unsigned, undated Losch to OW: "I TINK I BETTER GIVE UP.") Their relationship suffered from a number of "COMPLICATIONS" (a recurring word) that interfered with several planned rendezvous—and these complications weren't limited to the threat of discovery by Virginia. Even as his relationship with Losch was drawing to a close, Orson also had begun to pursue the second ballerina identified by Virginia: Vera Zorina.

Losch was a free-spirited, modern woman who apparently tabulated

---

* Among other problems with this anecdote, *The Shadow* was taped "live" with Orson in front of the microphone. Perhaps the show was recorded and delayed for certain markets, but it still raises the question why the incipient lovers were listening to a radio tuned to a broadcast of *The Shadow*.

her lovers on notepaper, listing the number of times she had bedded them. Next to Orson's name, she put only three marks over nine months, from the fall of 1937 to May 18, 1938. And "bedded" does not necessarily mean they had sexual relations; she may have included the night, for example, when *The Shadow* cramped Orson's style.

On that last date, May 18, Losch sailed for Europe. The night before, Orson had telegraphed her: "GOING TOMORROW . . . I CAN'T STAND IT . . . DON'T . . . I MUST SEE YOU TONIGHT, LOVE." Yet the ballerina stayed overseas for the rest of the year, ending their barely consummated affair forever.

CHAPTER 14

January–August 1938

"I am the Mercury Theatre"

Throughout the winter and spring, the curtain for *Julius Caesar* rose nightly at nine, except on Sundays; and most weeks there were two or three matinees. The long run could not help but tax Orson's acting interest. He could stand a long run, he told Peter Bogdanovich, only when he was touring: "then I don't mind being in the same play." He stayed away from the theater until nearly curtain time many nights, sometimes dining out sumptuously beforehand. Composer Virgil Thomson, who was expecting to work on the Mercury's penciled-in production of *The Duchess of Malfi*, recalled arguing on behalf of his musical ideas over a dinner with Orson and Virginia at Sardi's: oysters, champagne and burgundy, red meat and fixings, dessert and brandy. "You win," Orson told him afterward, standing up to go and play Brutus. "The dinner did it. And it's lucky I'm playing tragedy tonight, which needs no timing. Comedy would be difficult."

Perhaps it was hard for him to take *Julius Caesar* quite as seriously, Welles admitted to Bogdanovich, after he dined with Mrs. Patrick Campbell, one of George Bernard Shaw's most treasured actresses, now in her seventies. The original Eliza Doolittle, "Mrs. Pat" was also Shaw's inspiration for the character of Hesione Hushabye in *Heartbreak House*, another play on the Mercury's future schedule. Orson revered Mrs. Pat, a doyenne from another age, and spent hours with her even though she detested his *Caesar*. Mrs. Pat was hilarious on the subject: "They have no reverence, those boys. They speak the lines as if they had written them themselves." Even Orson's performance offended her.

His Brutus was "like an obstetrician who very seriously visits a lady in order to placate her nerves." She was confounded by the modern-dress conceit, Mrs. Pat told Orson: "Why do you have everybody dressed up like chauffeurs?"

"It's true!" Welles told Bogdanovich. "It spoiled it for me. Ever since then, it looked like a whole convention of Rolls-Royces."

At times, Orson's pensive performance as Brutus lapsed almost into muttering. One night, during one of his seemingly endless soliloquies, someone in the theater suddenly shouted out: "Louder!" As often with Orson, accounts of his response vary, and each of them is credible: scholar Richard France wrote that Orson simply glared at the audience before continuing his recitation; biographer Frank Brady wrote that Welles was stricken with humiliation, begging Joseph Cotten to keep him company in his dressing room after the show—"This is awful! Did you hear him? He shouted 'Louder'! I'll never get over this."

One episode everyone remembered—though, again, not necessarily the same way—was the April night when Orson accidentally stabbed Joseph Holland through the chest with his real dagger during the assassination scene. Holland crumpled to the stage floor, lying still and bleeding profusely; the other actors feared the worst. After the scene ended, Holland was rushed into a taxi and driven to the nearest hospital. He would spend a month recuperating, with John Hoysradt taking his place as Caesar.

Perhaps Orson was overcome with remorse, drowning his guilt in Scotch, as cast member Arthur Anderson wrote in his memoir. Or maybe he switched the blame onto Holland, as the play's producer recalled. "When [Orson] learned that his victim was not in danger," Houseman wrote, "he developed an angry conviction that the blame was entirely Joe's for making a wrong move and impaling himself on Brutus's stationary blade." Perhaps, just as likely, Orson did both.

Suddenly, Orson had an abundance of *Caesars* to juggle. He was responsible for organizing the number two company of *Julius Caesar*, casting Tom Powers as Brutus, Edmond O'Brien as Antony, and Lawrence Fletcher as Caesar, then drilling the troupe on the stage of the National Theatre, before they were sent on the road to New England at the end of January. He and Martin Gabel performed the play's famous quarrel scene on radio several times that season. And, in March, Orson led the original ensemble into a studio to record the entire production on a set of five twelve-inch two-sided discs: a mammoth undertaking, the first time any complete play had been preserved for a long-playing album. Around the same time, Orson also took a hand in the Mercury's similarly full-length recording of *The Cradle Will Rock*, one of the first Broadway musical LPs.

No surprise that people wondered when Orson slept, or with whom.

Despite all this activity, the Mercury's home stage was now empty at night—and it threatened to stay that way for weeks, even months. While Welles and Houseman now had three plays on Broadway—*Julius Caesar* and *The Shoemaker's Holiday* alternating in repertory at the National, and *The Cradle Will Rock* licensed to an outside producer at the Windsor—the partners could not nail down the next Mercury production.

As a stopgap, they introduced Worklight Theatre, a series of Sunday night showcases of works in progress. The first of its presentations, staged on the second Sunday in January, was *Dear Abigail*, a domestic drama set in a New England fishing village in the 1840s, written by David Howard, whom Orson knew through radio. A bare-bones offering, one step up from a reading, it featured Joseph Cotten and Agnes Moorehead, with Orson listed as codirector along with radio man Knowles Entrikin. Other works in progress were scheduled for the next several Sundays, but after a month the extra effort proved too much; the Worklight experiment was canceled, and *The Cradle Will Rock* returned to the Mercury after the expensive orchestra-seat sales flagged at the Windsor.

Welles and Houseman hoped to produce Shaw's *Heartbreak House*, but they had not heard from the playwright, who tightly controlled the rights. With foolish optimism, Orson thought he might be able to throw together his envisioned "marathon production" of Shakespeare's *Henry IV* (*Part 1* and *Part 2*) in combination with *Henry V*, first announced in the New York press the previous August. Orson would play Falstaff, with Vincent Price announced as Prince Hal, who later becomes King Henry V. It was a project Orson long had talked about, amounting to another stab at his Todd School graduation play.

By the end of February, this long-standing brainchild of Welles's had evolved into one "evening's entertainment" culled from *Henry IV* and *Henry V*, to be followed by a second evening consisting of a condensed *Richard III*, with one short scene from *Richard II*. Orson would play Falstaff in the *Henry*s and Richard II in the *Richard*s. Together the two nights of Shakespeare would be known as *Five Kings*: "an English cavalcade of the fifteenth century," in the words of the *New York Times*. Though commonplace today, the proposed "marathon Shakespeare" was an audacious concept for American theater in 1938. Welles insisted the two *Henry*s could be ready for audiences as early as mid-April, the *Times* reported.

A fencing expert was brought in to drill the Mercury extras in stage fighting as it was practiced in Shakespeare's day. Orson may have presided over a few read-throughs of scenes as he dived into the text, as some accounts suggest, but when he sank his teeth into something this ambitious, his outpouring of ideas and inspiration kept multiplying the scope and challenges. With all of his responsibilities for *Julius Caesar*, the *Five Kings* script seemed forever "in progress," and Orson couldn't find time to finish it. The tantalizing project was announced, postponed, and reannounced repeatedly in the first half of 1938. "If possible," according to a "progress report" in the *Times* that spring, the "marathon Shakespeare" would debut "early in June and run until July, the Mercury declaring that it recognizes no hiatus between seasons. Besides its house has a cooling system of a sort. . . . There is talk, too, of the whole company going on the road [with *Five Kings*] this summer."

By the first of March, however, Welles and Houseman knew that *Five Kings* needed time to germinate, and they had to fast-track another play, or risk forfeiting the remainder of the 1937–1938 season. At last, they elected to forge ahead with John Webster's play *The Duchess of Malfi*, a rarely produced sixteenth-century tragedy in the mold of *Dr. Faustus*. The partners' enthusiasm for *The Duchess of Malfi* was bolstered when veteran stage and screen actress Aline MacMahon agreed to join the Mercury in the title role, and Pavel Tchelitchew, whose sketches were among the casualties of Welles and Arthur Hopkins's canceled *King Lear*, said yes to designing the show.

Rehearsals for *The Duchess of Malfi* were set to begin at the end of the first week of March. Norman Lloyd wrote in his memoir that Welles convened the first reading of the script after midnight, with "eighty or ninety actors, looking at each other and wondering what was going on; there were only eight parts in the show." Orson took the stage, Lloyd recalled, "fingering the gardenia he was wearing and carrying a large dollar cigar," having arrived breathlessly from Tony's, "a very chic eating club."

"This is only going to please a few friends and myself," Welles announced grandly to the assembly before inviting "eight of us up on the stage to read the play, leaving all the others who had been told they might be in *The Duchess of Malfi* sitting in the audience," Lloyd wrote. Whitford Kane, Chubby Sherman, and Lloyd were among the privileged invitees—"the three madmen, each with about three lines"—as the rest watched in piqued silence.

This is a peculiar anecdote, considering that New York papers already had identified Kane, Sherman, and Lloyd as members of the *Duchess of Malfi* cast—along with George Coulouris, Vincent Price, Edith Barrett (Price's wife), and Frederick Tozere, all from *The Shoemaker's Holiday*; plus Will Geer from *The Cradle Will Rock*. Whatever the case, Lloyd insisted that the first reading "didn't go very well."

According to Houseman, the reading began at 10:15 P.M. "It was a disaster," he said, agreeing on that much with Lloyd. "With the exception of Welles himself, whose fantastic voice seemed ideally suited to Webster's extravagances, the actors seemed incapable of capturing the mood of the piece, which sounded muddled, verbose, and in its wildest moments, merely foolish. Having failed to ignite in its early scenes, it dragged itself on through the night, growing more dreary and embarrassing."

That very night, Orson explained later, he realized for the first time that the Mercury was not a genuine repertory company. It was merely "a group of people" cobbled together for *Julius Caesar* who were being retrofitted, willy-nilly and at random, into roles for the other Mercury plays. "We didn't have a strong enough company," Welles told Barbara Leaming. "I saw they weren't up to it, and I didn't have people for three of the leading parts. They just weren't disciplined classic actors."

When the unfortunate late-night reading ended, the partners convened "a brief, private meeting in [Orson's] dressing room," according to Houseman. "There was no argument. *The Duchess of Malfi* joined *'Tis Pity She's a Whore* in the locked cupboard of our discarded loves."

The Mercury players had been sent a clear signal: they fell short in Orson's eyes. This hardly pleased his band of regulars, and the veteran actor Coulouris, for one, was incensed. Once promised a role, he now felt as if he'd failed an audition for which he'd never volunteered. "There was quite a hullabaloo about the reading and such a bad feeling was created in the company that it was the first and last rehearsal of the play," Lloyd wrote.

The "bad feeling" lingered, and the disgruntlement filtered into press updates about the Mercury. For two weeks, Welles and Houseman dissembled when asked about the future of *The Duchess of Malfi*. Then, out of nowhere, a letter that had been bouncing around from one wrong address to another finally arrived, from George Bernard Shaw. Orson placed a hasty transatlantic phone call to the playwright in England, who did not remember meeting him in 1932, and had not heard of the Mercury. But Shaw was willing to let the partners produce *Heartbreak House* if they met his financial terms and other stipulations.

In the third week of March, *The Duchess of Malfi* was shelved. *Heartbreak House* was swiftly advertised for an April 29 opening, with Welles set to star and direct. Much to the chagrin of the *Shoemaker's Holiday* ensemble, which included the camp of malcontents, the Thomas Dekker comedy would be shut down when *Heartbreak House* was ready, with only three actors moving on into the new production.

Orson's hours, personal and professional, were filled to overflowing. In just two years he had become a Broadway brand name, with multiple products. He bore writing, directing, or acting responsibilities for several ongoing Mercury productions. He was still performing on radio, although nowadays he could afford to be more discerning about his jobs. He relied on a chauffeur to keep him on schedule.

Orson resisted any attempts to make him account for his time, by either his wife or his producing partner. Without letting Houseman know, Welles sneaked off to vaudeville shows, private magic clubs, and romantic assignations. More and more, he was turning up at awards ceremonies, emceeing dinners, gracing the daises at political or charitable events.

In early March, Orson spent most of one day in front of a Senate subcommittee in Washington, D.C., testifying in support of the doomed Federal Theatre Project. (This was also the occasion of his "first adulterous weekend" with ballerina Tilly Losch in the nation's capital.)

Later the same month, egged on by a new friend, Burgess Meredith, Orson stood for a hotly contested Actors Equity election. He ran as one of six members of a "liberal slate" seeking to assume control of the New York branch of the performers' union. Ultimately, the conservative, anti-CIO slate swept the vote, declaring a victory over "communism in Equity." Orson also logged time on the Negro Cultural Committee, which mounted interracial programs at the Mecca Auditorium, and showed up dependably for Spanish Civil War causes. Along with Marc Blitzstein and Will Geer, he hosted an auction to raise funds for medical aid for the anti-Franco side.

Houseman joined Orson on the platform at some civic events, but Orson was more in demand. He also addressed large groups like the National Council of Teachers of English, sometimes asking a fee; and he joined public roundtable discussions, such as a radio broadcast exploring the wellsprings of creative arts, with a panel that included a Columbia professor, a newspaper editor, a music critic, and artist Rockwell Kent.

To help publicize the new touring production of *Julius Caesar*, he made arrangements to appear at its opening in Chicago on Monday, March 7—a date chosen largely so Orson could play the Shadow on Sunday night and fly out the next morning—but at the last minute, the crisis surrounding the cancellation of *The Duchess of Malfi*, and the complicated recording sessions for the *Julius Caesar* LP, forced him to postpone the trip. (He told Chicago reporters that the "impending birth" of his first child had hindered his travel plans.)

When he finally reached Chicago, in the second week of the run, Orson made a flurry of public appearances. He spoke to hundreds of students and educators at a forum on "The Modern Approach to Shakespeare" at the Erlanger Theatre before *Julius Caesar* took the stage. He brought Tom Powers, the touring company's Brutus, to a Cliff Dwellers luncheon, and toured the new Arts Club galleries in the Wrigley Building, which included an exhibit of still lifes and paintings by composer George Gershwin. He squeezed in dinner at Le

Petit Gourmet with columnist Ashton Stevens, who had last glimpsed Orson during the summer of 1936. "He seemed to have developed half a century in the two years since I'd seen him," Stevens wrote. "He was less excited and more exciting. His humor was leaner. He could laugh at himself with more conviction. Whether you agreed with him or not, his opinions were surer and saltier; because they sounded like his own rather than the last he had heard or read.

"He has a magnificent ignorance of the requirements of a snob. He is a restlessly constructive fellow who just won't leave the stage where he found it. I'm afraid he's a genius; but mighty good company nevertheless."

Dr. Maurice Bernstein, still Orson's guardian, was among the other "old intimates" at that dinner, in Stevens's words. Drawing Dr. Bernstein aside, Orson pleaded impending fatherhood, and negotiated a small increase in his monthly allowance, as well as a personal loan of $1,000.

Bernstein insisted that the loan be covered by a promissory note against Welles's inheritance but the doctor was otherwise in unusually generous spirits. Hazel Moore, whom Orson had known since boyhood, had filed a $10,000 lawsuit alleging the wrongful death of her husband, whose heart attack in 1935 had been aggravated by a traffic accident en route to the hospital. After a settlement came through, "Dadda" and "Aunt Hazel" announced plans of their own for the summer of 1938: marriage.

Returning by midnight plane to New York for the Sunday, March 20, final broadcast of *The Shadow*, Orson dashed into the studio, riffling through the script with only moments to spare. The following week, even as he initiated the "first reading" for *Heartbreak House* on the Mercury stage, according to newspaper accounts, a phone call came: Virginia was in labor at Presbyterian Hospital on 168th Street, with her mother at her side. Adjourning the read-through, Orson and the Mercury's publicist Henry Senber jumped into a taxi and raced to the hospital. En route, according to Frank Brady, they reviewed the publicity outlook for *Heartbreak House*: Senber had a feeler from *Time* magazine about putting Welles on its cover to coincide with the opening.

When he arrived at the hospital, Welles later confessed to Barbara Leaming, ballerinas were more on his mind than fatherhood. He could not keep himself from flirting with an attractive hospital nurse, whose lithe shapely figure he correctly identified as that of a former danseuse.

Proudly but uncomfortably, Orson held his baby daughter in his arms. He always said that he'd christened his firstborn while she was still in her mother's womb, and he'd been expecting a boy. That she was a girl did not matter: "Christopher" became her name.

As a little girl, more than once, Orson's daughter asked her famous father, "Daddy, why did you call me 'Christopher'?"

"I liked the sound of it—Christopher Welles. Your name has a marvelous ring to it, don't you think?"

"But I'm a girl, Daddy."

"So you are, and a very beautiful one, too."

"But Daddy, girls aren't called Christopher."

"That's right. You're the only girl in the world who is, and that makes you unique as well as beautiful."

"What does *unique* mean?"

"Different from everyone else."

"But Daddy, I don't want to be different. The kids at school tease me about having a boy's name."

"When you're older, they'll envy you. Wait and see, darling girl. The day will come when you'll love your name and thank your old father."

At that point in the conversation, as Chris Welles Feder recalled in her candid memoir, *In My Father's Shadow*, Orson usually paused to light a cigar, "his eyes twinkling at me through the cloud of horrible-smelling smoke," in her words.

"Do you know what I did right after you were born?"

"No, what?"

"I sent out telegrams to everyone we know. CHRISTOPHER, SHE IS HERE."

More than once, Orson told this anecdote of the wonderful telegram, "how in just four words, a marvel of economy, my father had said it all," recalled Feder. As she grew older, however, she sometimes wondered whether the name "Christopher" wasn't simply her father's excuse for a clever telegram. In 1985, as her plane touched down in Los Angeles for his funeral, it occurred to her that she had never seen one of those legendary telegrams.

George Bernard Shaw's contract with the Mercury Theatre claimed a substantial portion of all the ticket revenue for *Heartbreak House*, starting at 5 percent of $250, with his share rising to 15 percent of all proceeds exceeding $1,500. "For a theater with less than 700 seats and ticket prices between $.55 and $2.20," Andrea Janet Nouryeh wrote, "these royalty figures were astronomical," and virtually guaranteed that the Mercury would never turn a profit on the production.

Moreover, the agreement strictly prevented any deviation from the original script—and this stipulation also applied to the main set, which the script described in detail, including the common room of a country residence, with windows, doors, lockers, benches, bookshelves, and drawing tables of heavy timber resembling "an old-fashioned high-pooped ship." The shiplike setting prompted "the first solid scenery we built," grumbled John Houseman, which "cost us a fortune," because Orson "insisted on genuine paneling indoors and real gravel cemented to the ground cloth for the exterior 'so the footsteps will sound right.'" Ultimately, wrote Nouryeh, "critics universally admired the results" of the costly stage setting.

This shiplike country home belongs to an eccentric retired seafarer, an octogenarian, Captain Shotover, whose "immense white beard," in the words of the script, made the part a natural for Orson. Shaw makes the half-ship home a metaphor for complacent England, adrift amid the brewing storm of World War I. (Society needs a better navigator, someone like crusty Captain Shotover.) Though replete with sparks of brisk Shavian wit, the play is also didactic and pessimistic. Timely when it was written, it was timely again in 1938.

The script featured ten speaking parts, but only a handful of supporting players were drawn from the active Mercury roster: George Coulouris as Boss Mangan; Vincent Price as Hector Hushabye, married to Shotover's flamboyant eldest daughter Hesione; and John Hoysradt as Randall Utterword, married to another Shotover daughter, Ariadne. Again "determined to avoid the stigma of stock casting," in Houseman's words, the partners shopped for fresh faces.

The part of Hesione, the play's lead female character, had been designated for Aline MacMahon as part of her agreement covering *The*

Duchess of Malfi. When that play fell through unpleasantly, however, MacMahon backed out of the Shaw production. Orson wanted Mady Christians as her replacement, but Houseman disagreed, believing that Christians, who had been born in Vienna, would be miscast as a free-spirited Englishwoman. Welles and Christians would prove him wrong, as Houseman later conceded.

Orson picked an old acquaintance from his days with Katharine Cornell, Brenda Forbes, for Nurse Guinness; and the Australian actress Phyllis Joyce as the Captain's less bohemian daughter, Ariadne (Lady Utterword). For Geraldine Fitzgerald he saved the role of Ellie, a rival of Hesione's, who is engaged to marry the business tycoon Boss Mangan. Ellie was the play's pivotal and most likable character.

He asked Theatre Guild stalwart Erskine Sanford to play the seemingly mild-mannered Mazzini Dunn, the father of Ellie, who is actually running Boss Mangan's empire. Sanford had played the same character in the original New York production of 1920, and Orson loved that kind of symmetry. Just as important, he remembered Sanford from the A. A. Milne comedy *Mr. Pim Passes By*, which he'd seen as a boy when it passed through Kenosha on tour. *Heartbreak House* brought Sanford permanently into Welles's fold. He would portray the dethroned *Inquirer* editor in *Citizen Kane* and would be conspicuous in Orson's radio shows, as well as *The Magnificent Ambersons, Jane Eyre, The Stranger, The Lady from Shanghai,* and *Macbeth.*

Orson spent the month between that aborted first rehearsal on March 27, and the play's opening night on April 29, coolly orchestrating the staging of *Heartbreak House*, which would take the place of *The Shoemaker's Holiday* in the Mercury rotation. He and Coulouris ceded their roles in *Julius Caesar* to Tom Powers and Edmond O'Brien from the touring company.

Heartbreak House was a wordy play, but Orson was comfortable with verbosity, and he always had loved Shaw's wordplay. Still, as scholar Andrea Janet Nouryeh has pointed out, his production sneaked changes into the prescribed version. His staging accelerated the play's pacing by discarding ordained exits and entrances, and it broke up and overlapped many passages of dialogue, while creating moments of "great stillness" to enhance its dramatic high points.

The rehearsals were no more chaotic than usual, but time was short, and perhaps there was less team spirit with the new team. Vincent Price, for one, was never "very happy" in his assigned role, Welles recalled. ("He was particularly vexed that he was required to stand still and listen to other actors talking at great length, as actors do in Shaw.") Coulouris clashed with Fitzgerald, patronizing the newcomer and undermining her confidence. They feuded. The other actors liked Fitzgerald, though, and even Price thought Welles directed her "with such affection and care that she stole almost every scene from him."

As much as critics admired the Mercury production, their praise was backhanded, with many feeling that Shaw had painted the typically bold Orson into a tight corner. "There is nothing experimental in the Mercury Theatre's revival," Richard Lockridge wrote in the *Sun*. "This time their experiment is merely the simple, and fine, one of putting on a provocative, stimulating play as straightforwardly and effectively as they know how." John Anderson of the *Evening Journal* called it "an average stock company production, by no means up to the distinguished standard set by the Mercury."

Again the lead player as well as the director, Orson was as always a lightning rod for the reviewers. Wearing nose putty, a white wig, and a full beard and mustache, the transformation completed by liver spots on his hands, he anchored the production. His performance predictably disappointed some critics ("workmanlike," sniffed the *Times*) while pleasing many others ("much better than I have ever seen him," wrote Lockridge in the *Sun*). Even his fellow cast members were divided: Price thought Welles was "not very good in it because he never rehearsed with us," while Forbes thought his performance "brilliant," though she was disgusted by Orson's "outrageous behavior at curtain time" (the first scene was sometimes held up until he had finished dinner in his dressing room).

In any case, audiences flocked to *Heartbreak House*, and, like *Julius Caesar*, the show would entertain packed crowds until its run ended. And on May 6, his twenty-third birthday, Orson could celebrate by pointing to his photograph on the cover of *Time* magazine, where his unmistakably boyish eyes peered out of the caked, bearded visage of ancient Captain Shotover. "George Orson Welles," read the May 9, 1939, headline: "Shadow to Shakespeare, Shoemaker to Shaw."

The five-page spread inside was a promoter's dream. The article declared young Orson a "Marvelous Boy," while reviewing, complete with errors and embellishments, his life story thus far: Kenosha, the Todd School, the Gate Theatre, the Federal Theatre Project, the Mercury. Orson admitted to being the "Caesar (not Brutus)" of the Mercury—that is, "pretty dictatorial" when it came to the stagecraft of Mercury productions. ("Houseman runs the business end," the article noted.) The Mercury's maiden season was only a springboard to the future, said the profile's anonymous author. "The sky is the only limit his ambitions recognize."

The cover story did not delve very deeply into Welles's private life, describing his Sneden's Landing residence as only modestly luxurious ("eight rooms and four nooks, $115 a month") and his burgeoning family in three brief sentences: "Welles met his wife, dainty blonde Virginia Nicholson [sic] Welles, while both were acting in a summer drama festival in 1934, married her that fall. Last month their first child was born. A girl, she was christened Christopher."

The real picture was more complicated. Two weeks after the *Time* story, Tilly Losch took her passage to Europe—and Orson's overlapping flirtations with Geraldine Fitzgerald and ballerina Vera Zorina heated up.

Orson's attitude toward affairs was elliptical, however. Charles Foster Kane does not necessarily make love to Susan Alexander before the scandal that ends his marriage and political career,* and sex and love were often extraneous to the power-and-glory-obsessed characters Orson played most convincingly on stage and screen. (Playing a Nazi

---

* There is a Lubitschean dissolve in *Citizen Kane* from the cheap rooming house where Susan Alexander is living when Kane meets her to the fancier place where she becomes a "kept woman." The showdown between Gettys and Kane takes place in this fancier apartment, in the presence of Kane's wife, Emily. Gettys threatens to give the story of Kane's affair with Susan to every newspaper in the state. But Susan protests, "There isn't any story!" Gettys tells her to shut up. She tries again, "Mr. Kane is just—" She is cut off again, and by then Kane has made up his mind what to do. We never hear Susan's explanation; maybe she has remained the nice girl who, in her first meeting with Kane, insisted on keeping her apartment door open, and Kane is merely helping her out in life—until Gettys calls his bluff.

monster in *The Stranger*, he seems unaroused even by the lovely Loretta Young.) Whatever sexual activity Welles engaged in outside his marriage to Virginia, in those days before *Citizen Kane* it was less than rumored or boasted.

One night during the run of *Heartbreak House*, Welles and Fitzgerald decided to elope—or so the actress told her son, Michael Lindsay-Hogg, many years later.

"Elope?" her son asked. (The word was "an odd one," Lindsay-Hogg wrote in his memoir, *Luck and Circumstance: A Coming of Age in Hollywood, New York, and Points Beyond*, "since they were both married.")

"Let me tell you in my own way," Fitzgerald said. "One Saturday night, after the show, we were going to elope. He'd hired a car and we were going to New Jersey to a motel, and then we kissed in the back seat of the car and I realized it was the kiss of a brother and not a lover and so the car turned around and we went back to the city and Orson came up to the room with me, where Eddy [her husband, Edward Lindsay-Hogg] was asleep, and Orson patted his foot over the blanket and said, 'Everything's all right, old fellow. Nothing to worry about.' And then he left."

Vera Zorina was the second ballerina Virginia identified to Frank Brady as a mistress of her husband's. Born in Berlin, raised in Norway, with intense blue eyes and blond hair cascading to her shoulders, Zorina was even younger than Orson—only twenty-one in 1938.

Her reputation as a dancer had been established in the Ballet Russe de Monte Carlo, where she became the lover of choreographer Léonide Massine, who was married at the time to another member of the troupe. Zorina had starred in the London production of Rodgers and Hart's *On Your Toes* and also in George Balanchine's *Slaughter on Tenth Avenue*, a ballet scored by Rodgers and Hart. Samuel Goldwyn brought her to Hollywood in 1937 for the filming of *The Goldwyn Follies*, in which Balanchine staged her American debut in the "water nymph ballet," rising up from a pool of water in gold lamé. Living in New York since late 1937, Zorina danced with Balanchine's troupe, and was attached to Balanchine himself as his lover.

Captivated by Orson after seeing him onstage in *Julius Caesar*, Zorina gravitated to him at parties and found she liked him even better in person. They started meeting surreptitiously, sharing heart-to-hearts late at night. Welles was still in his Alfred Lunt phase: "a romantic-looking man" as Zorina recalled in her memoir, "somewhat Byronic, with one quizzical eyebrow slightly raised, and often laughing in a special throaty way. I think we would call him 'sexy' today."

Yet, again, there were obstacles to actual lovemaking: not Balanchine, who was "used" to Orson chasing after his ballerinas (as Welles told Leaming), but the dancer's mother, who still traveled with her. Anxious to conceal their "passionate courtship" from the mother, who was on Balanchine's side, the two had to avoid any public displays of affection. "Mama wouldn't have allowed it," Welles explained to Leaming. Orson himself later said that he found such obstacles "a big help" to him, a stimulating test: "It was all very difficult, which was the ideal situation for me because I—thank God—matured before the sexual revolution. I like to be hard to get at!" And Balanchine was not his only competition: also vying for Zorina's affections was "a very famous European actress who liked to fill the ballerina's room with flowers."

Too often, Welles and Zorina were reduced to "steaming up various hired cars around New York," in his words, or meeting in out-of-the-way places. In early April, even before Tilly Losch had left for Europe, Orson desperately tried to arrange a rendezvous with Zorina at a hotel in New Haven, where her Broadway debut, the Rodgers-Hart musical *I Married an Angel*, was being road-tested. Orson devised an elaborate disguise for himself—mustache, thick glasses, raincoat—but the rendezvous went awry when he stepped into the hotel elevator, only to find himself standing next to Balanchine, who was choreographing Zorina's dances in the play. "Hello, Orson, I didn't know you were here!" Balanchine chirped.

Orson relished his dalliance with Zorina, even if Balanchine was her more regular partner. Years later, in his chats with Roger Hill, Welles recalled Zorina confiding in him that Balanchine "was going to a doctor on Fifth Avenue who was lengthening his penis."

"Surgically?" Hill asked Welles.

"No, by pulling it somehow," Welles replied. "That diminished my fortitude because I thought, if this guy has the moxie to have his prick enlarged, I really don't deserve her, he does."

The one time Orson and Zorina managed to escape from prying

eyes was later in the month, when Austrian-born character actor Walter Slezak, who was costarring with Zorina in *I Married an Angel*, offered them the use of his country house on a back road near Mount Kisco, New York. Orson and Zorina were looking forward to a "weekend of pleasure"—but their hopes were dashed when their solitude was interrupted, repeatedly, by a series of loud alarms from hidden locations. Slezak had concealed a slew of alarm clocks in crannies around the house, setting them to go off at random intervals as an elaborate practical joke. "Viennese malice," Welles told Leaming.

Their relationship was fraught with such missed chances. Complicating their romance further, the East Coast tryouts of *I Married an Angel* went so well that on May 11 the musical was rushed into Broadway's Shubert Theatre, where overnight it became a smash hit. Now the two illicit lovers were both starring in Broadway shows, with Zorina committed six nights a week along with Wednesday and Saturday matinees.

In June, after *Heartbreak House* and *Julius Caesar* ended their successful runs, the fault lines within the Mercury Theatre began to shift ominously.

In his memoir, John Houseman was precise about the dramatic series of events. Late that month, he wrote, he was vacationing at a friend's home in the Berkshires when his peaceful breakfast was ruined by an urgent phone call from Augusta Weissberger: the *New York Times* was reporting that Chubby Sherman had quit the Mercury Theatre to join a topical revue that producer Max Gordon was preparing for Broadway that fall. "I accepted this grim news as true the moment I heard it," Houseman wrote, "I did not, then or later, call Sherman to verify it or to try and persuade him to change his mind." Houseman sped to Sneden's Landing, where Orson, Virginia, and baby Christopher were spending "an uneasy summer," in his words.

Orson lay "limp and huge in a darkened room with his face to the wall" and cursed Sherman as a Judas, or an Iago. "To him, Sherman's action was quite simply one of personal, malignant treachery," Houseman wrote. "Coming, as it did, at a turning point in Welles's personal life, Sherman's perfidy hit him with exaggerated force. For the

Mercury, it marked the great divide between our halcyon days and the hurricane weather that followed."

After a couple of days in New York tidying up Mercury business, Houseman said, he drove north again, intending to spend a holiday with his mother, who lived in Rockland County, not far from Sneden's Landing. As his Ford reached a steep hill outside the Palisades, he spied a familiar limousine coming from the other direction, with "Orson's huge face sticking out of the window with its mouth wide open, his gigantic voice echoing through the surrounding woods." The two cars pulled over, Orson yanked Houseman into his limousine, and Orson's car continued on to New York City for an appointment with Columbia Broadcasting System officials. Orson "was about to receive a phenomenal offer—an hour's dramatic radio show once a week for ten weeks on which he could do anything he pleased," Houseman recalled.

Orson, in Houseman's telling, was decked out in his costume as Brutus to make the best possible impression. The officials explained what Houseman referred to as "the network's formula," implying that CBS had conceived the new show. The producer admitted having trouble following the radio lingo ("all of which was Greek to me"), but he sat up straight when he heard that the show would premiere on July 11, "in less than two weeks' time!" ("This didn't seem to bother Orson," Houseman wrote, who "said it would be a tight squeeze but we could make it.")

Orson was revitalized by this deus ex machina, which wiped away Sherman's betrayal. In relating the story, Houseman filled in every detail—settings, costumes, and dialogue—giving it all color, intensity, and an electric pace. Numerous later books would recycle the story.

Unfortunately, Houseman's treasured anecdote was a tall tale. In fact, Orson's new radio series was announced in the *New York Times* a full month before the first broadcast—on Sunday, June 12, the day after the last performance of *Heartbreak House*. After several weeks of negotiations with the network, Orson had agreed to host "First Person Singular," a summer replacement program of nine one-hour dramas for the CBS network. Besides writing, casting, and producing the shows, Orson would narrate each episode and play the "protagonist." "The entire Mercury Theatre company will be at his disposal," according to the *Times,* "and he is to be at liberty to select his own material and technique."

The *Time* magazine cover had spurred the CBS executives into action. The network needed a summer substitute for Cecil B. DeMille's popular Monday night series *Lux Radio Theatre,* which featured dramatic re-creations of motion picture stories, and CBS wanted Orson to take over the time slot for the summer. The network had been sending work his way since 1935, starting him in anonymous, low-paying roles, but nurturing his rise with a series of increasingly important parts in various CBS radio shows and special broadcasts including his breakout opportunities in the *Columbia Workshop* series. Mutual had stolen him away with *Les Misérables* and *The Shadow,* but now CBS wanted him back, promising Orson that the summer series could lead to a permanent engagement in the fall.

It was Welles who brainstormed the concept as an alternative to DeMille's program and a more commercial variation on the *Columbia Workshop.* His series would feature adaptations of literature, and it would be aimed at intelligent adults. To keep costs down, the series would draw largely on stories from familiar or classic works in the public domain. Welles would introduce himself at the start of each broadcast and narrate the show, while also playing multiple characters, as he had done with the summer adaptation of *Les Misérables.* It was this emphasis on his starring *and* hosting that earned the summer series its initial title "First Person Singular," although within weeks everyone was calling it "The Mercury Theatre on the Air."

The contract, negotiated by Arnold Weissberger, gave Orson unusual creative latitude and supervisory control over the program. The series would have a moderate budget, appropriate for a summer program, but the network would pay for the star, for his Mercury actors and associates, and for all agreed-on production costs. CBS staff artists and officials—including Bernard Herrmann, the network's most accomplished arranger and conductor, who had agreed to supervise the music—would be available to assist Orson behind the scenes.

Moreover, "First Person Singular" would be a "sustaining program," broadcast without commercial sponsorship or interruptions—a privileged status afforded to only a few network programs, such as the *Columbia Workshop* series. Everything about Orson's contract was golden, right down to the broadcasting facility at WABC: the famous Studio One, the biggest and best-equipped in the CBS building.

At a press conference to promote the series, Orson told reporters that, while he would bring to radio the same "experimental techniques" he favored in the theater, he would not be drawing on the "stage repertoire" of the Mercury Theatre. "The less a radio drama resembles a play the better it is likely to be," he proclaimed. As he spoke, the scheduled July 11 premiere of "First Person Singular" was still one month away; Sherman's startling resignation from the Mercury was nearly two weeks in the future.

One thing that certainly rings true in Houseman's account is that he himself went through the first CBS meetings in a daze. Houseman knew "almost nothing about radio," he admitted later, "and did not listen regularly except to news." As Orson spoke, his partner merely nodded, "trying to look knowledgeable but understanding little of what was said." The deal with CBS, for all intents and purposes, was a deal with Orson Welles. He was its instigator, and he would have the primary responsibility for its creative fulfillment. And, at the time, there was no one else in radio quite like him: a "first person," a prime mover, writing and producing and starring in a major network series. Orson generously framed "First Person Singular" as a Mercury Theatre venture, but as the deal took shape, Houseman abruptly saw a shift in their partnership. He became Orson's subordinate. "*He* was working for *me*," Welles boasted to Leaming.

The two men had launched their collaboration, with the Federal Theatre Project and the Mercury Theatre, as equals; newspapers and magazines routinely referred to Houseman as the brains behind the operation, Welles as the artistic mastermind. More recent articles revised that description, calling Houseman merely the "business brains." By the time *Newsweek* carried its report of the Mercury's summer radio series, the transition was complete: the name John Houseman was never mentioned. The article was all about Orson Welles.

On the day the series was announced, the Sunday after the final performance of *Heartbreak House*, the partners revisited their earlier declaration of principles with a longer piece in the *New York Times*, called

"The Summing Up." Welles and Houseman compared "our aim with our accomplishment," and declared that they had met most of their original goals. Except for a couple of instances when they'd fudged the "strict observance of orthodox repertory practice" by running two different plays in separate theaters—*The Shoemaker's Holiday* and *Julius Caesar* for a few weeks in January; *Heartbreak House* and *Julius Caesar* for part of May—they had adhered to their original vision of a repertory company alternating classical plays. Claiming they did not "believe that the New York public, accustomed as it is to a specialized system of casting, is willing to accept the sort of company atmosphere that inevitably results from the unquestioned use of the same actors in every play," they noted that they'd picked the "best available actors for each part, even if in special cases we had to go outside" the Mercury company to find them.

They estimated, combining the totals of its Broadway and touring companies, that the Mercury Theatre had played to more than a quarter of a million people, who had paid an average ticket price of slightly less than $1. Only 20 percent of those people came from the "carriage trade." Forty percent were organized theater parties, and another 40 percent had bought lower-priced seats. One third of the tickets had been sold to educational groups. Repertory, the partners had learned, was "an enormously expensive business." The tour of *Julius Caesar* was expensive and lost money. Staff salaries and production costs were crippling. Still, after their first season, Welles and Houseman counted themselves lucky and "a few dollars ahead of the game."

"To sum up," they concluded, "we've played to a lot of people; we've produced a lot of plays; we've enjoyed it. We've made plans, some definite, some still to be worked out for next season, and—we will reopen the Mercury next September."

Even as they issued this proclamation, however, the tension between the two men was growing behind the scenes, as Orson's star eclipsed Houseman's. And, with uncertainty in the air, some of the company's best-known players were on the verge of quitting it.

Norman Lloyd was one. Lloyd had made an indelible mark in his first Mercury role as Cinna the poet in *Julius Caesar*. But now the up-and-coming actor met with Welles and Houseman and told them he had decided not to rejoin the Mercury in the fall. "I had made up my mind," the actor recollected, "partly to get out from under Orson's fantastic personal success, which had resulted in the theatre's total identification with him."

Vincent Price was also disgruntled with Orson's rehearsal and directorial style. After running into Burgess Meredith on the street one day, and learning that Orson had just offered Meredith the part of Prince Hal/Henry V in the ever-postponed *Five Kings*, Price promptly accepted a telegraphed offer from Universal Pictures and left for Hollywood.

John Hoysradt, trying his luck at cabaret, took an engagement at the Rainbow Room.

The Mercury lost three of the players most closely identified with its first season—not quite an exodus, but a blow. The original company had become factionalized. There was a split among the established players: key performers like Joseph Cotten who served as ballast, shrugged off disputes good-naturedly; but there was a less contented group, including Lloyd and Price, who were preoccupied with their own careers. The imbroglio over *The Duchess of Malfi* still rankled some, as did the continued casting of outsiders.

Casting outsiders tore at the actors' delicate egos; compensation was a related issue. The few elite cast members who nabbed the lead roles also drew higher salaries than their colleagues. "We have consistently carried in our company a number of actors receiving full pay but playing only three or four performances a week," the partners noted in "The Summing Up." For most of the Mercury players, however, "full pay" meant Equity minimum, while actors playing concurrent leads in *Julius Caesar* and *The Shoemaker's Holiday*, for example, received double pay—some even received raises—and the top names scored a percentage of the box office. That was one reason George Coulouris, a steady grumbler, hung around: he was assured of leading roles and wages to match. Some weeks, he was paid more than Welles.

The disaffected players blamed the inequities on Welles and Houseman equally: Houseman because he was penurious and dismissive; Orson because he seemed to live high on the hog while others scraped by. Orson's standard of living was, by now, inseparable from his image—he traveled by limousine, dined luxuriously, checked into ritzy hotels—and when his face appeared on the cover of *Time*, the magazine was compelled to ask him about his lifestyle. "Stories of his recent affluence," reported *Time*, "annoy him. First of all, Welles insists, this has nothing to do with his Mercury triumphs; for years he has had these things by virtue of his radio earnings," which the magazine estimated to be in the range of $1,000 weekly. ("Last summer for two or three weeks he hit a high of $1,700.") When pressed on the matter, Welles insisted that his radio earnings were what *enabled* the Mercury Theatre to exist.

Such publicity annoyed members of the company. In interviews later in his life, Orson said he felt guilty about friends like Joseph Cotten, who struggled to get his career going independent of the Mercury. "That was a difficult period for me, as a friend," Welles told Henry Jaglom, "because suddenly I was making a fortune. Jo was still making those smaller salaries, and I was big stuff." Cotten always supported Orson, but their friendship was strained.

When *The Shoemaker's Holiday* was closed and replaced by *Heartbreak House*, a number of the Mercury players demanded a meeting to air their grievances. Welles stood his ground. "Some of you may have thought that . . . the Mercury Theatre owes [you] some obligations," he reportedly declared. "I want to state, here and now, I am the Mercury Theatre." His point was hard to argue—he was the company's undisputed mastermind; the Mercury would hardly have existed without him. But it was a difficult pill to swallow, especially when the much-publicized mastermind rarely mentioned anyone else in his interviews. "How could you feel part of a collaborative effort when Orson took the credit for everything?" Chubby Sherman complained in an interview a quarter century later. "You were supposed to surrender yourself, bask in his reflected glory and be satisfied."

And there were other sources of restlessness—not least the perpetually forthcoming *Five Kings*. The Mercury players were tired of treading water and waiting for the mastermind: they wanted guarantees for the summer and fall. Houseman spoke publicly about taking the innovative Shakespeare production on the road for a summerlong West Coast tour, leading to a fall 1938 opening in New York. He arranged with Lawrence Langer and Theresa Helburn, his friends at the prestigious Theatre Guild, to reinforce the Mercury by coproducing *Five Kings* with "part of the backing and the fat pickings of its 60,000 subscription list," as the *Time* cover story noted. But when the first casting choice was leaked, it was another outsider: sure enough—Burgess Meredith as Prince Hal/Henry V.

On the last day of May, the partners announced that *Five Kings* would be postponed until the fall—and another play would precede it on the fall schedule. Orson had decided to direct a revival of Oscar Wilde's farce *The Importance of Being Earnest*, with Chubby Sherman and George Coulouris as the stars. It was going to be workshopped in August as a "guest attraction" in a summer theater friendly to the Mercury. However, "a sizeable number of the Mercury actors were not too anxious" to commit to the Wilde farce, according to the *Times* account; they had their hearts set on *Five Kings*, whose projected lengthy tryout tour and Broadway run would "insure longer employment."

The lead role of "Ernest," who juggles a double life as a gentleman and a wastrel, was tailor-made for the company's foremost farceur. Chubby Sherman's casting in the role was even reported in the *New York Times*, although the actor would tell Richard France years later, "Orson never so much as mentioned wanting me in anything after *Shoemaker*." By early June, with Lloyd, Price, and a few other Mercury actors bolting from the company, Sherman was torn between the factions. Starring in the Wilde comedy should have pleased him, but it would mean disappointing the other actors who were pulling for *Five Kings*—and make Sherman an unwilling symbol of loyalty to Orson.

Tempted by another producer's fall Broadway musical revue, Sherman stalled. He may simply have been waiting until the Mercury partners were out of town. On June 23, 1938, almost three weeks after reporting that Sherman would be showcased in *The Importance of Being Earnest*, the *Times* broke the news that he was quitting the Mercury.

Sherman was the oldest, most conspicuous of "Orson's people." He and Orson had known each other since the late 1920s, the heyday of the Goodman Theatre in Chicago. In a sense, Sherman, Welles, and Houseman, were three Musketeers, dating back to their dreams of a repertory company in 1936 and their wishful plans for *'Tis Pity She's a Whore*.

Orson had long believed in Sherman's acting prowess ("The Mercury Fuehrer had expected to build his production of the Oscar Wilde work around Mr. S.," the *Times* noted). Sherman had emerged as a valued, versatile stalwart of the Mercury ensemble under Orson's direction—while also serving as Orson's casting director and his assistant director for Mercury plays and outside projects like *The Second Hurricane*. Often an invaluable spokesman for his fellow actors, Sherman was known within the company as its "conscience," Houseman wrote.

One of Sherman's frustrations was he wanted to direct plays for the Mercury. Decades later, Orson insisted to Barbara Leaming that he tried to give Sherman such a chance on a nascent production of Shakespeare's *Measure for Measure* late in 1937. Sherman cast the play, re-imagined in a New Orleans setting, and convened a few read-throughs. From "what I heard," Welles told Leaming, "it was really very good." Welles claimed that Houseman unaccountably canceled Sherman's directing debut, "Orson was terribly puzzled by the cancellation," wrote Leaming—although many Mercury projects fell by the wayside in similar fashion.

The pain of Sherman's defection was compounded when Welles learned that Whitford Kane, who, as an actor and director at the Goodman Theatre, had been his idol—and who was Sherman's life partner—had mounted a whispering campaign against him.

Tension between Welles and Kane had been mounting for some time. From the earliest run-throughs of *The Shoemaker's Holiday*, Kane contributed "the only discordant note" in the production, taking "exception to what he regarded as Welles's lack of respect," said Houseman. Among other things bothering Kane was that his role gradually shrank as Welles's script compressed the scenes involving his character, the shoemaker who becomes lord mayor, in order to shift the focus to Sherman.

The atmosphere during *The Shoemaker's Holiday* was also affected by a generation gap, as the "youthful spirit" of most of the cast "clashed bitterly with the habits of the older performers," according to Andrea Janet Nouryeh. Kane and actress Marian Warring-Manley, playing the lord mayor's wife, led this small older group. When Welles held forth at rehearsals, telling anecdotes mocking the Shakespearean actor Maurice Evans, Kane bristled. He took Orson aside, questioning some of his directing decisions and warning him about eroding the company's morale. Welles was open to outside opinion, if he was in the right mood. Not this time: "He's above taking advice," Kane complained to Ashton Stevens, adding that Orson would be "a much better liked young person" if he listened to his elders.

When *The Shoemaker's Holiday* was closed to make way for *Heartbreak House*, Kane was effectively dropped from the Mercury. "The fate of *The Shoemaker's Holiday*," wrote Andrea Janet Nouryeh, "angered both Hiram Sherman and Whitford Kane."

There was another, more personal factor: in the domestic rift between Welles and his wife, Sherman and Kane sided with Virginia. The two knew all about Orson's late-night carousing—Orson often dragged Sherman on his rounds of parties and nightclubs—and, as homebodies themselves, they empathized with the suffering wife. Besides, Orson was always handing Sherman the check and darting out the door to grab a taxi. "The high-livers were killing me," Sherman complained years later. Orson exploited too much of Sherman's energy, work time, and playtime too. "The pace [for Sherman] had become so wild, the mood so intense and violent," Houseman wrote, "as to be physically and mentally unendurable."

Sherman's departure threw the already splintered Mercury into disarray. And with his featured player gone, Orson lost interest in *The Importance of Being Earnest*.* The company found itself once again on tenterhooks, waiting for its mastermind to choose a new opening play for the fall season. "Coincidental with rumored rifts in the Mercury, several important company members have turned to other managements in order to 'get set' for next season," reported the *Times*.

As he often did at times of crisis, Orson telephoned Roger Hill in the wake of Sherman's departure. The Todd School headmaster knew Sherman almost as well as Orson did, and never lost his fondness for the good-humored actor. In later years, Hill raised Sherman's name with Welles repeatedly—in part because he nurtured a pet theory (influenced by Houseman's memoir) that Sherman's departure was the first domino to fall in the Mercury's ultimate collapse.

"It always seemed to me that Chubby's leaving the Mercury was the reason for its demise," Hill insisted during one conversation. "You

---

* Welles did, however, include a condensation of the first act of *The Importance of Being Earnest* in his *An Evening with Orson Welles* in Paris in 1950.

were so high on him and, all of a sudden, he called you on the phone and said he wanted to make more money somewhere else."

"Yes," Orson replied sympathetically, "he had a good play where he could get a bigger salary. I didn't have a major part for him then, so it was a natural thing to do."

"Yes, but I remember your phone call and you were pretty—"

"Upset," Orson admitted.

"Upset," repeated Hill. "Of course, we all have simplistic answers, but it seemed to me that Chubby killed the Mercury."

"I don't really think so because the Mercury went on to Hollywood fame."

"No, I mean the Mercury Theatre," Hill persisted.

"The Mercury Theatre was killed by lack of funds," Orson parried evenly, "and our subsequent move to Hollywood. Hollywood was really the only choice. It wasn't because of Chubby leaving. I think all acting companies have a life span. The Mercury Theatre came to an end."

But the Mercury Theatre was not dead yet. Orson was never the type to be deterred by catastrophe, or even slowed by it, for very long.

Late in June, on the pretext of escaping from the hay-fever environs of Sneden's Landing, Welles moved into the air-conditioned St. Regis Hotel to concentrate on the launch of the radio series. Just two months had passed since the birth of his daughter, Christopher, but Welles was content to leave his troubled domestic life behind for the summer; while not unloving, he was destined to be an absentee father who left child rearing to the mothers of his children.

One of Orson's masterstrokes was placing John Houseman in charge of scripts for the new radio series. Orson had long viewed Houseman as a shrewd script editor—commending him to David O. Selznick for just that purpose on one occasion—and now he gave his partner a lightning tutorial in writing and editing for radio.

Orson chose Robert Louis Stevenson's pirate story *Treasure Island* and Bram Stoker's vampire tale *Dracula* for the first two shows, announcing *Treasure Island* first but later switching to *Dracula* for the premiere. He loved the fact that the Irish-born Stoker once served as an aide-de-camp to the legendary English actor-manager Henry Irving, and he considered *Dracula* "the most hair-raising, marvelous book in the world." Orson could play two principal roles: solicitor Jonathan Harker, who narrates the horror story, and Count Dracula himself. As for Stevenson's novel, he knew the text almost by memory from boyhood—and that play, too, offered him two important parts: the innkeeper's son (the story's narrator) Jim Hawkins, and the colorful pirate Long John Silver. Both novels thus allowed Orson to fulfill the concept behind the "First Person Singular" series.

Since Orson was the star of the show, the script discussions tended to involve building a structure around his favorite scenes. Orson always wanted an unconventional approach, with subjective narrative passages—diary excerpts, letters, stream of consciousness. *Dracula* is an epistolary novel with multiple narrators, and he wanted the radio adaptation to honor that conceit. Equally important, the radio scripts all had to be punctuated with music and sound effects; like lighting in theater, the music and effects served to accent the mood and heighten the drama. For the radio version of "Dracula," Welles taught Houseman to be creative with these effects, inserting cracks of thunder, whistling wind, clopping hooves, crashing waves, and more.

Orson could sometimes get mired in effects, going to such lengths that he drove the technicians crazy. But time and again, that summer and throughout his radio career, his imaginative efforts enhanced the shows. To attain the ambience of the Château d'If for a summer adaptation of *The Count of Monte Cristo*, for instance, he again arranged actors and microphones in a men's room. For a version of *A Tale of Two Cities*, he expended an inordinate amount of time trying to capture the sound of Sydney Carton's decapitation, which had to simulate the head being severed and dropping into a basket. A sound specialist experimented with a melon, a pillow, a coconut, and a leg of lamb before Orson finally chose a head of cabbage.

After talking the stories over with Houseman, Welles left his partner to his own devices. Orson would drop in regularly to make criticisms and changes in the scripts, but the first drafts were Houseman's responsibility. Houseman worked much the way Orson himself often worked on scripts, lying in bed in his apartment that summer, surrounded by copies of the book they were adapting, samples of usable scripts for reference, and an array of tools: scissors, a paste pot, a supply of pencils. It was an important job, and Houseman mastered it.

Though the story may be apocryphal, Houseman claimed that the partners stayed up all night at Reuben's Delicatessen on East Fifty-Eighth Street, brainstorming the "Dracula" script, after Orson shuffled it ahead of "Treasure Island" "two days before rehearsal." Fueled by coffee, cognac, and two meals (the second one of "large steaks, very rare, followed by cheesecake and more coffee and brandy"), they finished with breakfast at dawn, Houseman wrote. They certainly pulled similar all-nighters several times that summer to meet deadlines for the radio series.

As producer of the program, Orson always had other business to mind, casting major roles even as the script was in progress, molding the parts to available actors. For "Dracula," Orson turned to the Mercury stage ensemble: Martin Gabel would play Professor Van Helsing, Dracula's archenemy; and George Coulouris would be Dr. Seward, Harker's romantic rival. Orson lured his radio colleagues Agnes Moorehead to play Mina, Harker's fiancée; and Ray Collins to portray the Russian boat captain transporting Dracula's body to England.

This was the first time Orson was in charge of a true broadcast series—rather than a one-off serial like *Les Misérables*—and every major decision was his. Whereas in the past he had relied largely on Houseman's extended circle of bohemians and artists—Virgil Thomson, Paul Bowles, Aaron Copland, Lehman Engel—to provide music for his productions, now he was working with Bernard Herrmann, not just as an actor but for the first time as Herrman's boss. It was an adjustment for both men. Herrmann had to align his musical ideas to the scenes as Orson described them, before the script for "Dracula" was actually completed, preparing not only main themes and recurrent motifs, but also the incidental touches and musical bridges that would bolster narrative transitions throughout the radio drama. According to his biographer Steven C. Smith, Herrmann created a sparse but "thrilling" score, with a stinging theme "for muted brass and graveyard bell, and a crackling variant of the Dies Irae for Jonathan Harker's driverless coach ride up the Borgo Pass."

Published anecdotes tend to emphasize the tempestuousness of the relationship between Welles and Herrmann, who had been thrown together awkwardly on several previous radio programs. But even before the replacement series, and increasingly over the summer, the two men developed mutual warmth and appreciation. "Both men deeply respected the other's strong will, nonconformity, and old-world romanticism," wrote Smith.

Both believed in radio and its potential for artful popular entertainment. Like Orson, Herrmann was a connoisseur; his own symphonic work was distinguished and original, but he was obliged to earn his daily bread creating musical pastiches. When outlining the music he wanted for specific scenes, Orson was quite a pasticheur himself; he sometimes behaved "almost as a precocious child," Herrmann recalled, with "an instinctive, intuitive understanding of what should be done." When Herrmann did not like one of Orson's musical ideas, he would cross his arms, frown, and say, "I don't know how I would do that . . ." Orson would trot out every means of persuasion he had: charm, negotiation, shouting, and cursing. But Herrmann knew those tactics; he used them himself. And while Welles was more musically literate than most nonmusicians, he loved being able to count on Herrmann's superiority.

One of Welles's essential characteristics as an artist, Herrmann recognized, was that "Orson was an improviser," who never settled on "one way to do anything" but enjoyed tinkering right up to air time. For Herrmann, Orson's creative, extemporaneous spirit made the mundane work of radio music far more stimulating. "At the start of every broadcast Orson was an unknown quantity," Herrmann remembered. "As he went along his mood would assert itself and the temperature would start to increase till the point of incandescence. . . . Even when his shows weren't good they were better than other people's successes. . . . Horses' hooves are horses' hooves—yet they felt different with Orson—why? I think it had to do with the element of the unknown, the surprises, and the uncomfortable excitement of improvisation.

"He inspired us all—the musicians, the actors, the sound-effects men and the engineers. They'd all tell you they never worked on shows like Welles's."

Radio, Welles's longtime associate Richard Wilson once observed, was "the only medium that imposed a discipline that Orson would recognize . . . and that was the clock." The script, actors, sound effects, and music had to be ready for the live broadcast every Monday at 9 P.M. The show had to start on time, and it had to fill a precise block of time. Otherwise the network signal would go dead from coast to coast.

On Monday, July 11, 1938, the Mercury Theatre went on the air for the first time. From one corner of the studio, Bernard Herrmann led the network orchestra of moonlighting symphony musicians in the series theme—the opening strains of Tchaikovsky's lushly romantic Piano Concerto No. 1 in B Flat Minor. Wearing earphones, Orson raised his own baton as he stood in front of the main microphone on a podium in the middle of the room. He would preside grandly over the acting ensemble, twisting and gesticulating as he guided the actors' pace and intensity; cueing the dialogue, sound effects, and music. Besides directing, narrating, and playing Dracula and Jonathan Harker, Orson voiced several smaller parts.

For the first time Welles signed off on a radio show in his own name and voice, supplying a brief valedictory to end the episode. From the first, his trademark sign-off was sly, and he was intimate with the invisible audience. "When you go to bed tonight, don't worry," he murmured, "put out the lights and go to sleep . . . (A wolf's howl is heard.) It's all right, you can rest peacefully, that's just a sound effect . . . it's nothing at all . . . I *think* it's nothing . . ." As his voice faded, the genial host reminded viewers never to forget that vampires *do* exist.

Asked by Peter Bogdanovich which of the Mercury Theatre radio episodes he remembered as among the best, Orson replied quickly, "'Dracula' was a good one."

The reviews were uniformly excellent. *Newsweek* pronounced it "adventurous" radio. "Luscious radio fare," wrote syndicated radio columnist Richard Murray, with "Broadway's boy wonder" and his Mercury cast "terrific. We think that Columbia deserves a whack on the back."

On July 10, the day before the "Dracula" broadcast, the Mercury partners finally announced Orson's choice for the new opening play of
the fall season. Banishing the memory of Chubby Sherman, Orson
replaced *The Importance of Being Earnest* with another turn-of-the-century
French farce in the manner of *Horse Eats Hat*. His best friend in the
company, Joseph Cotten, would perform the lead.

Originally, this farce, by Maurice Ordonneau, was called *La Plantation Thomassin*, but the actor-manager William Gillette had Americanized it, in 1894, into a breakneck comedy called *Too Much Johnson*.
When Orson was a boy, Ashton Stevens had often regaled him with
tales of Gillette, who was best known for touring in the role of Sherlock Holmes. (Gillette's costume of deerstalker hat, cape, and curved
pipe would forever fix the image of Holmes in the public imagination.)
Gillette had died in 1937 near Stony Creek, Connecticut, where the
Mercury company would mount an August tryout of his farce at the
Stony Creek Playhouse, a summer stock theater. William Herz, who
had served as Chubby Sherman's casting assistant for the Mercury, had
taken over management of the venerable playhouse, and several of the
Mercury players had signed on for the summer.

Among them was Orson's wife. At this juncture in their strained
marriage, Virginia Welles adopted a stage name: "Anna Stafford."
Orson fooled himself into believing the couple had a mature "understanding" for the summer. Indeed, Virginia appears to have been carrying on her own side romances. In his unproduced script about *The
Cradle Will Rock*, the ORSON character is tortured by the unwelcome presence in his life of an Irish sculptor, KEVAN KILDARE, a summer stock
actor with aspirations. "A sexy young man," VIRGINIA calls KILDARE;
the script describes him as "startlingly beautiful," with "something of
an early Brando" in his persona. The man of the household suspects
KILDARE, who is moonlighting as an ice sculptor at his Sneden's Landing parties, of pursuing VIRGINIA.

Too Much Johnson was a similar pinwheel of furtive lovemaking and
mistaken identity. The plot follows a philandering New York lawyer
(Joseph Cotten's role) who is chased to Cuba by his mistress's vengeful
husband. The philanderer, who adopts the name "Johnson"—its phal-

lic innuendo is part of the running joke—is beguiled by a fresh beauty on the island, and finds his fate intertwined with another "Johnson."

For his production of the farce, Orson came up with another of his Big Ideas: he would turn *Too Much Johnson* into a half-film, half-play. To introduce each of the three acts, Orson would direct a set of three filmed slapstick sequences featuring the same actors in the play; projected onto a screen, accompanied by live sound effects and music, the filmed sequences would entertain theatergoers until the live actors burst onstage and picked up the story as though they'd leaped out of the screen.

Moving swiftly, Orson had a pile of editing equipment hauled into his St. Regis suite and threw himself into the hybrid production. Everything always seemed to happen simultaneously with Orson: the script, casting, the first rehearsals, the plans for filming. He offered his wife the plum part of the pretty mail-order bride in Cuba, while drawing most of the rest of the cast from Mercury regulars and friends. Besides the devil-may-care Cotten, who had been so light and charming in *Horse Eats Hat*, as "Johnson," Arlene Francis, also from *Hat*, would play the unfaithful wife caught in flagrante. The capable Broadway veteran Edgar Barrier, already on the Stony Creek roster, was hired to play the outraged cuckold. Erskine Sanford from *Heartbreak House* also took a supporting role. There were smaller parts for Orson's "slave" Richard Wilson and for Mercury actresses Ruth Ford and Mary Wickes; Wickes was also persuaded to put a little of her family money into the production. Orson sprinkled the cast with old-time vaudevillians like pratfall specialist Howard Smith, who amused him endlessly. (When Orson told Smith to sit down in a scene, Smith asked whether he wanted the "Fast Sit" or the "Slow Sit.")

Pulling together a team that included technical director Jean Rosenthal and production manager Walter Ash from the Mercury staff, Orson commandeered a midtown screening room and invited people to watch Mack Sennett comedies such as *Love, Honor and Behave* and *The Lion and the Girl*, along with Chaplin's *The Kid*. Orson and his creative team trooped over to the Paramount-Strand to watch Harold Lloyd's new release, *Professor Beware*. Welles adored Lloyd and his masterwork, *Safety Last*, celebrated for the image of Lloyd dangling from a clock on a skyscraper. Orson considered it "one of the greatest, simplest films ever made." Lloyd, another amateur magician, was passing through New York at the time, promoting his new picture, and Orson contrived to meet him at a private magicians' club.

All this homework bolstered Orson's ambition to shoot the film sections of *Too Much Johnson* as an homage to golden age comedy, with its daring physical stunts and intricate gags. He loved arguing about the relative merits of the great silent comedians—Lloyd, Chaplin, and Buster Keaton—but always insisted that Lloyd was "the greatest gagman in the history of the movies," and disliked the vein of sentimentality in Chaplin's work. He admired Keaton's film *The General*, calling it "almost the greatest movie ever made," and "the most poetic movie I've ever seen."

To simulate the look of classic silent film, Welles needed a capable photographer, and in Harry Dunham he found a remarkable successor to William Vance, who had been the cameraman on *Hearts of Age*—and a precursor to Gregg Toland, who would be the cameraman on *Citizen Kane*. Paul Bowles, who was writing the music for *Too Much Johnson*, recommended Dunham. "A bit of a wild man," in Bowles's words, Dunham was born into affluence in Ohio and in 1931 graduated from Princeton, where he had appeared in drag in college theatricals. Later he briefly tried ballet in New York, where he befriended Bowles, pouring his inheritance into Bowles's career. No one was ever quite sure if they were friends or lovers. (Both genders were attracted to the dashing Dunham.) Together Bowles and Dunham traveled through Morocco and lived in Paris, where they were part of the circle including André Gide, Man Ray, and Gertrude Stein. (Dunham even had a stint as Stein's dog washer.)

Dunham eventually abandoned dance for photography—contributing to *Life*—and then film, making several experimental ballet shorts scored by Bowles and shooting an ethnographic documentary, *Bride of Samoa*, spotlighting native dancers, that played in New York on a bill with the French film *Fantômas*. Two years before *Too Much Johnson*, Dunham had returned from the communist strongholds of China with footage of Mao Tse-Tung and the Red Army, which the left-wing Frontier Films documentary collective turned into the seminal *China Strikes Back*. Dunham then joined the Communist Party, creating campaign films for its American presidential candidate, Earl Browder.

Dunham was not only a young master of verisimilitude who could work on the cheap; he was a reckless personality, eager to dangle from rooftops and cliffs alongside the actors. He gleefully accepted Orson's edict to re-create the old-fashioned derring-do of golden age comedies, with their pristine black-and-white imagery and sometimes jerky, exaggerated action. Orson planned old-fashioned film sequences linked by intertitles; heavy, old-fashioned makeup for the actors; and Gay Nineties–style costumes and props, including Keystone Kop uniforms for the wild chases.

With a furiously scribbled script that left much in the scenes open to improvisation, Orson was ready to begin shooting by the latter half of July. Small crowds gathered to watch the initial filming in New York, and not all the curious onlookers realized they were witnessing the famous Mercury Theatre at work. Nor did they realize that they were eyewitnesses to film history: Orson Welles was directing his first professional motion picture, the first outside the confines of his Todd School experiments: the stagebound *Twelfth Night*, the send-up *The Hearts of Age*, the assorted other home movies.

Press interest in the project was high—several reporters, including Herbert Drake of the *New York Herald Tribune*, volunteered for cameos—and news items confirm that the first shots filmed for *Too Much Johnson* involved Orson exhorting Cotten to take dangerous risks for Dunham's camera, while hanging from the top of a five-story building on Albany Street.

The first of the three filmed segments would begin with Edgar Barrier interrupting Cotten's tryst with Arlene Francis. Frantic, Cotten dives down a fire escape and flees madly across rooftops before hoofing it through busy New York streets. Mere steps ahead of his pursuer, Cotten arrives at the docks and leaps aboard a boat sailing for Cuba. Grabbing a railing, he clings to the ship as it sails out of the frame. This sequence was originally meant to last about twenty minutes before Act One of the live play began.

Welles incorporated dozens of extras from the crowd into the street scenes—including one amusing vignette that alluded to his father's days as a male suffragist. Desperately trying to escape from the cuckolded husband, Cotten joins a right-to-vote parade, marching with the banner-carrying women while shifting places to keep ahead of Barrier, who is following close behind. At one point the two men stop to salute an American flag, before resuming the chase.

"[Welles] would bellow his instructions—no megaphone needed for him—from camera to set, urging his actors in the chase scenes through New York streets to more daring," Frank Brady wrote. "At one moment Welles was behind the camera establishing a shot, and the next he was gathering his extras together and placing them where he wanted them. He also was marvelously patient with the actors, gentling and then cajoling them into a style that would look spontaneous."

While in the city, Orson also staged the incident in the first filmed sequence in which Arlene Francis is startled by the arrival of her husband (Barrier) and must stuff a photograph of her lover (Cotten) down the décolletage of her black corset. In an often retold story, Orson requested a revealing closeup of Francis's bosom, only to be disappointed by her modest proportions. He then entreated the Mercury's Augusta Weissberger to step forward, "amidst the catcalls of the cast and crew," according to Brady, and offer her more ample charms to the lens.

Orson expropriated an empty lot in Yonkers for this scene; following standard silent-era procedure, cameraman Dunham shot it as an interior within a three-walled set, leaving the room open to natural sunlight. Future Hollywood director John Berry, still a cog in the Mercury machine, stayed up all night with a small crew erecting the "indoor" set to have it ready for the morning call. (Berry also did some utility work onscreen, for example, driving the cabbage wagon into which Cotten leaps from a rooftop.) "We got the sets built," Berry recalled years later, "the limousines with the cast started to arrive, it was maybe eight-thirty or nine A.M. Then the wind came up and blew them down. Orson said, 'What are we going to do?' I said, 'We'll get them up, Orson.' So I organized the crew, and we sat there and held the sets up, sitting in this vacant lot, one of us in the corner of each piece of the set.

"Lunchtime—twelve, one o'clock," Berry continued. "We'd been there all night. We'd been holding the sets up all morning. A caterer drove up and a long table was set up. Everybody was fed but the poor fuckers holding up the sets. Finally I said, 'That's it, guys.' We all stood up, and the sets fell down. Orson said, 'What's going on, John?' I said, 'We're going to eat, Orson, because we've been here all night.' He had this enormously shocked and aggrieved look across his face. He said, 'You haven't been fed? You must take my seat. Sit!' He got up. I said, 'I don't want your seat.' He said, 'You must!' Of course we all went back and continued to hold up the fucking sets. Orson did that all the time—operate, manipulate, function . . .

"But it was great fun and excitement."

Later in the day, summoned by straitlaced neighbors alarmed by the sight of a beautiful actress prancing around in undergarments, a gaggle of real city policemen appeared and demanded to see the crew's permits. Orson had not bothered with any official paperwork (or the attendant fees), so they swiftly dismantled the set and fled the location, laughing. It was all a lark; no one gave a thought to posterity.

The second film sequence would incorporate the miniatures that were being crafted to Orson's specifications on the Mercury stage. The resourceful art director James Morcom was busy constructing a mock Cuba, complete with a papier-mâché volcano that would be encircled by a water tank on which floated a model steamship. "The first image on the screen" for this second filmed portion for *Too Much Johnson*, according to Brady, whose account is based on his interviews with Welles, would be that "of the boat sailing the Caribbean. There was then a dissolve as the hand-held camera moved around . . . to the coast of the island where, from the boat's perspective, one could see the jungle. . . . The camera continued moving slowly along the coast . . . until from a distance, through mist, appeared an imposing Georgian plantation house."

Orson handed out bit parts to any and all comers. Some claim that a plucky receptionist in the Mercury's theater party sales department, a blond teenager named Judith Tuvim, can be seen in the footage; years later she would change her name and become famous as Judy Holliday. Marc Blitzstein appeared recurrently, trying for a French flair in his mustache and turtleneck. "The most energetic of the extras," reported *Stage*, "he appears practically all the time." Houseman and Welles themselves donned costumes for turns as, among other things, Keystone Kops.

The third filmed sequence, set on the faux Cuba, involved the volcano exploding, and Cotten galloping off on a white horse, chased by whooping islanders. For these island sequences, the cast, crew, and director adjourned to the countryside near Sneden's Landing, where, in a rock quarry outside Haverstraw, Orson created a Cuban-style backdrop for the horseback footage. The jungle atmosphere was deliberately phony: a wooden sign, "Santiago de Cuba," established the setting, and crew members waved palm fronds to simulate tropical breezes. The foolishness was a joke meant to be shared with the audience. Orson's producing partner was on hand to fill any demand: "Lying on the ground, holding a palm in one hand and the sign [for Cuba] in the other, is the dignified, scholarly co-director of the Mercury, Mr. John Houseman," the *Stage* observer reported.

Although Houseman did not see it clearly at the time, by now his relationship with Welles had changed permanently. First with the radio show, now during the filming of *Too Much Johnson*, the "dignified, scholarly" Houseman found himself subordinated to his young partner, prone on the ground, holding up props. *Too Much Johnson* was almost entirely Orson's baby. ("It was not my favorite piece," Houseman sniffed in *Run-Through*.) Preoccupied with the scripts and planning for the radio series, now more than ever he ceded all the creative impetus to his partner.

Houseman's main job for *Too Much Johnson* was raising money. The Mercury had started the summer with very little cash, and the situation never improved. This was Orson's first real experience with professional-grade film stock, which was one of the primary expenses for any motion picture during that era. Shooting like crazy for ten days, Orson had accumulated roughly 25,000 feet of film, according to Frank Brady. When the bills for the film and lab work began to stack up ominously, however, he had to halt the filming without completing all the planned shots. The Mercury couldn't even afford to process all the footage it had; Orson had the available reels delivered in relays to his suite at the St. Regis, where they formed wobbly piles, with the rolls uncurling like snakes. The Stony Creek preview of *Too Much Johnson* had already been announced for August 15; he would have to scramble like mad to edit what he had into a workable final product.

The editing process did not intimidate him. For one thing, according to Frank Brady, Orson had absorbed V. I. Pudovkin's recent *Film Technique and Acting*, still today a bible of editing theory and practice. And he had been watching and absorbing the best and most popular motion pictures, U.S. and foreign, since boyhood. As always, the real problem was time: he had just two weeks to assemble his first professional film, or half-film, while polishing the script for the live play and holding rehearsals.

Welles's unpaid "slaves" filled his suite. "Vakhtangov" Alland raced in and out, running errands as Orson shouted at him. John Berry hovered nearby, eager to learn how editing worked. Houseman popped in and out for high-level consultations. They all waited on Orson, hoping the mastermind would make sense of the snips and piles of footage.

"On nights when he was not on the air or with his paramour," as Houseman wrote in his memoir (never ceasing to hint more than he knew about Orson's love life), "Orson would sit for hours at the Moviola, laughing at his own footage, while the slaves hunted vainly for the bits of film that would enable him to put his chases together into some kind of intelligible sequence."

More than once that summer, the off-camera goings-on—the actors chased by police off the set in Yonkers; Orson's "paramour" racing down the back stairs as his wife rode the elevator up to his suite— mirrored the farcical nature of *Too Much Johnson*. "To reach the bed [in Orson's suite], the slaves, when they arrived to rouse Orson for rehearsal or for the radio show, had to wade knee-deep through a crackling sea of inflammable film," Houseman wrote in his memoir.

Inflammable it was: the film stock of the time was manufactured with a volatile nitrate base. "One time the film caught fire," Berry recalled. "What I remember, most remarkably, is me running with the projector in my hand, burning, trying to get out of the door and into the goddam hallway, and Houseman racing for the door at the same time—so we had one of those comic who-gets-out-first moments. . . . While Orson, with absolutely no concern whatsoever, was back inside, standing and looking at some piece of film in his hand, smoking his pipe."

Some Welles experts believe it was while compiling the film sequences for *Too Much Johnson* that Orson first became hypnotized by the cutting and splicing of celluloid pieces into endlessly rearrangeable mosaics. Unlike human actors, the film clips could be moved around endlessly, with no complaint, interrupted only by incoming platters of food and gallons of coffee or brandy. This school of Welles scholars has suggested that the young director lost sight of the stage play *Too Much Johnson* in favor of the film portion, the two halves never quite cohering as they might. But editing was central to his artistry. The Mercury coffers were seriously depleted, Orson's time was sorely divided, and on Monday nights he still had to arrive according to the clock in front of the microphone for the radio shows, which he supervised on a weekly basis.

Barbara Leaming, building, like many other accounts, on John Houseman's memoir, wrote that Orson took his suite at the St. Regis so he "could conduct affairs easily and discreetly." Leaming does not say how these plural "affairs" could have been either easy or discreet when so many associates were streaming into and out of his pied-à-terre on a daily basis. And Orson also saw Virginia practically every day, since his wife was deeply involved in *Too Much Johnson*.

According to Stony Creek Playhouse manager William Herz—who had met Welles years before when the Katharine Cornell tour passed through his college town, Pittsburgh—Orson campaigned hard for Virginia to get a role in the summer theater's program. "It was simply to get rid of her," Herz told one interviewer. "He was having a 'do' with Vera Zorina—there was always another dame involved in one way or another. . . .

"Also, he said, 'You know [Virginia] has a car?' I didn't have a car in those days so it was a big help to have somebody with a car. I had to go into New Haven quite frequently."

But Stony Creek was part of a scheme to launch Virginia, or "Anna Stafford," as an actress in her own right. Orson made frequent trips to Stony Creek to see his wife's summer stock performances. He brought her roses on July 4, when he came to see her in a supporting role on the opening night of *Caprice*, a comedy made famous by Lunt and Fontanne on Broadway. And he returned often to review the facilities and visit the Mercury players, including Edgar Barrier, Arthur Anderson, and William Mowry, whose future wife Sherrard Pollard was also in the troupe.

By August 1, Orson was commuting almost daily from midtown to Stony Creek, a small shoreline hamlet east of New Haven, almost one hundred miles up the coast highway. Many of the New York actors made the same daily trip, though a few took summer leases in Stony Creek. Until the second week in August, Orson rehearsed the cast of *Too Much Johnson* on the bare Mercury Theatre stage in New York, with the scenes mutating as the mastermind flogged the script. Houseman found the live rehearsals "desultory," and Simon Callow tsked: "Rehearsals on the play were fitful. When they did take place, they were spent developing routines, sections of stage business, which Welles typically worked and worked, ignoring character, relationships, or the life of the play.

"Andrea Nouryeh [in her unpublished thesis on the Mercury Theatre] describes a sequence in which three of the men enter from three different doors singing 'Swanee,' exiting and entering with perfect rhythmic and harmonic coordination," Callow continued. "This was gone over again and again and again, finally attaining the perfection Welles sought."

By the time the cast arrived at Stony Creek, suspense over the film footage, and renewed anxiety over the actors' summer salaries—"shamefully low," in Houseman's words—sharpened the collective anxiety. Some, but not all, of the cast members involved in the summer tryout of *Too Much Johnson* were able to supplement their income by regular appearances on the more lucrative (and more reliable) *Mercury Theater on the Air*. The actors were paid unequally for the play, depending on the importance of their roles. And some of the actors felt they had been paid unfairly for their work on the film: because they were acting in scenes being photographed for a stage play, they were paid rehearsal rates for a theatrical production, not "performance rates." Nine of the actors filed a complaint with Equity, arguing that the Mercury had not compensated them adequately for the sometimes laborious ten days of photography. The action was still pending as *Too Much Johnson* opened; it would not be resolved until after the premiere, when a special union committee granted the complainants an additional increment of one-eighth of one week's salary.

Adding to the accumulating pressures, at the eleventh hour a lawyer from Paramount popped up with a stern warning. Mercury might have leased the stage rights to *Too Much Johnson*, but Paramount had a claim on its screen rights, having produced a film version of Gillette's play in 1919. "If the play reached Broadway with the film in it, payment, perhaps substantial, would have to be made," wrote Frank Brady.

The last manic week of preparations and rehearsals involved erecting the sets and hanging the lights. Orson brought a work-in-progress version of the film sequences to show to the cast and friends. The length of the first and longest portion of the action kept shrinking in press mentions (the pre–Act One footage was now down to "five minutes," according to New York columnists), and some footage was still being held by the lab, but for the first time Orson projected all three segments on a screen erected onstage for the private audience. None of the Mercury insiders were thrilled with what they saw. And there was one big technical problem: the playhouse's low ceiling obstructed the view of the stage for many in the audience. This was "the last straw," wrote Brady, and "the film portion" of *Too Much Johnson* was abandoned in favor of hastily prepared expository additions to the live script.

Orson felt he had let everyone down, even himself. On the Sunday night after the last dress run-through, he and the cast drowned themselves in champagne, on his dime.

The actual premiere of *Too Much Johnson* came two days later, on Tuesday, August 15, the night after Orson played Abraham Lincoln in his radio adaptation of John Drinkwater's play chronicling a day in Lincoln's life. In his signature fashion, Orson took the Stony Creek stage before the curtain was raised to apologize to the audience, because what they were about to experience had not yet "jelled" in the preferred manner. By the time *Johnson* made it to Broadway in the fall, he promised, the farce would be augmented by filmic material he was unable to project in the playhouse, along with more elaborate sets and musical orchestration. (Scholar Andrea Janet Nouryeh reported that Marc Blitzstein supplied piano accompaniment, at least for the premiere).* Welles asked the local audience to be patient with the actors and with the work in progress.

According to some accounts, the crowd was not a model of pa-

---

* Paul Bowles's more elaborate score and effects would be confined to recordings and were never performed "live" with the play. The composer released his suite, in 1939, as *Music for a Farce.*

tience. "We never integrated the film with the play, so when we put on the play but didn't show the film, of course, the audience had no idea what *Too Much Johnson* was all about," recalled Mercury actress Ruth Ford. During a subsequent performance, the audience grew so "furious" at the half-baked show, Ford insisted, that some spectators threw "everything in their hands at us on the stage. Apples, bananas, every single thing they had, they threw at us. They didn't understand what they'd seen. We were just all going in and out, opening and slamming doors." *

"The [opening night] curtain went up at nine with two intermissions and came down at ten thirty and the audience didn't know what hit them," said the summer theater manager, Herz. "It was an absolute mess. I had no idea what was going on on that stage and I can tell you, neither did the audience. They were absolutely appalled. The actors were also in the dark."

One of the first-nighters was John Houseman, who later recalled that on the "small dreary" Stony Creek stage, the filmless comedy seemed "trivial, tedious and under-rehearsed, and I set myself firmly against its coming in as the opening production for the Mercury Theatre's critical second season. This led to an ugly scene with Orson, who secretly agreed with me but who needed to play out the sabotage scene to salve his pride."

There is good reason to doubt this version of events, since echoed in multiple other accounts. For one thing, *Too Much Johnson* was already no longer in contention as the opening play of the fall schedule: as far back as July 30, the *New York Herald Tribune* had confirmed that Georg Büchner's *Dantons Tod* (*Danton's Death*) would be the Mercury's "first fall production," with Martin Gabel as Danton and George Coulouris being eyed for Robespierre. "Orson Welles will direct." This was two weeks before the Stony Creek premiere and the supposed "ugly scene" over whether *Too Much Johnson* should open the Mercury season.

---

* The anecdote about audience members hurling fruit at the actors sounds suspiciously as though Orson staged the incident in the spirit of the farce. Or did the summer audiences really come to the play with apples and bananas to nibble on and to throw at the performers?

And these doomy accounts of the audience reaction are balanced by other, far kinder reports. Connecticut summer resident Katharine Hepburn, for one, saw the Stony Creek show and liked it enough to pluck Joseph Cotten from the cast to play her ex-husband in the planned Broadway comedy *The Philadelphia Story*, a big break in his career (taking him away, eventually, from Mercury Theatre plays). And though New York critics did not cover the tryout, the local press turned out in force. Local reviewers may have been inclined to be supportive, but their notices were surprisingly unanimous and favorable. The *Hartford Courant* said that Orson had directed "with all the flair and originality of the superb theater technician he is. He uses rhythmic motion and dialogue in spots to gain unexpected humor, many doors in various sets for hurried comic entrances and exits, unusual costumes and trick lighting, shades and nuances of all sorts." The critic from the town of Branford (within which Stony Creek was a small community) found *Too Much Johnson* original and promising, and predicted that the film footage would improve it. "I think it's going to be screamingly funny," wrote the reviewer, "before Mr. Welles gets through with it."

It was not a perfect debut for Orson's innovative hybrid—but then his previous foray into farce, the frenetic *Horse Eats Hat*, had also divided audiences. Orson made many adjustments to *Too Much Johnson* throughout its extended two-week run, during which time the local word of mouth was positive enough to fill the summer playhouse every night. In any case, Welles was not finished with his half-film experiment: he was determined to keep editing the footage and bring the production to life on Broadway as the second offering on the Mercury's fall schedule.

CHAPTER 15

September–December 1938

War of the Worlds

Reflecting his growing estrangement from Welles, John Houseman viewed the downfall of *Too Much Johnson* as apocalyptic. In *Run-Through* he portrayed his partner as severely depressed, taking to bed after the Stony Creek premiere to lie in darkness "for a week surrounded by twenty-five thousand feet of film, ministered to by Augusta Weiss-berger and the slaves, rising from his bed only for the radio show or for one of his amorous sorties. The rest of the time he lay there, like a sick child, convinced that he was going to die, racked by asthma and fear and despair . . .

"On the seventh day he rose from his bed and returned to the world."

On Monday September 5, Orson did rise for the final radio broad-cast of the summer series. The replacement program had proved a re-sounding success, following "Dracula" and "Treasure Island" with a series of further triumphs: a clever condensation of Charles Dickens's *A Tale of Two Cities*; an elegant episode of short stories by Saki, Sher-wood Anderson, and Carl Ewald; an adaptation of John Buchan's *The Thirty-Nine Steps*, faithful to the novel, not Hitchcock's famous film; and praiseworthy versions of John Drinkwater's *Abraham Lincoln*, Alexandre Dumas's *The Count of Monte Cristo*, and Arthur Schnitzler's *The Affairs of Anatol*. Even the increasingly demoralized Houseman saw it as a bright spot: "the summer's leading dramatic program on the air," and "an-other bright feather in the cap of the Mercury."

The last episode of the summer was G. K. Chesterton's *The Man Who Was Thursday*, a philosophical thriller about a Scotland Yard undercover agent. Though Orson often accepted Houseman's scripts "with minor corrections," in Houseman's words, "once in a while, out of caprice or ego, because he really felt he had a superior idea, he would make substantial changes. . . . He also counted on me for the drastic, last-minute editing which took place every week just before air time."

The Man Who Was Thursday, though, was "a work long dear to Orson's heart, but not to mine, and this time, Orson said, he would write his own script; he wanted none of my cosmopolitan pussyfooting; this would be pure Catholic-Christian Chesterton as only he could understand and express it."

Regardless of all the hectic activity surrounding *Too Much Johnson*, Orson had made it to the radio mike on time every Monday at 9 P.M., to lead his band of players and coo and roar his way through one of the most shrewdly crafted radio drama series yet produced. Now, at the last moment, according to Houseman, Orson reneged on his pledge to write the "Thursday" script. He surrendered to Houseman his copy of Chesterton's novel, "uncut and immaculate except for a few mysterious markings and some doodled sketches of the celebrated ballerina [Vera Zorina]," Houseman wrote, "three days before air time." Houseman frantically cranked out the final pages in a CBS office—but the resulting script fell twenty minutes short in dress rehearsal.

Even assuming all this to be true, Orson the performer had a remarkable knack for stretching or squeezing a script to fill the hour of airtime, capable of closing a gap of ten or even fifteen minutes with his sleight of drama. Twenty minutes was a tall order, however. Houseman dashed to the network library, he recalled, scooping up books he and Welles had discussed as possible episodes for the fall. The summer replacement series had been renewed for September, and Orson was saving that announcement for his coda at the close of the Chesterton episode.

When the last broadcast concluded ("one of the finest shows of the series," according to Frank Brady), Houseman handed the library books over to Orson one by one. "Without turning a hair, as his own master of ceremonies," remembered Houseman, "he used the remaining time to thank his audience for their loyalty and to give them a foretaste of pleasures to come."

After first reciting the funeral oration from *Julius Caesar*—set as the first broadcast of the fall season—Orson turned to bookmarked pages in several classics: *Jane Eyre*, *Oliver Twist*, *The Hound of the Baskervilles*. He read the excerpts "with deep feeling and great variety," in Houseman's words, "until the hour was up and he was able to sign off." The last thing Orson did was announce that *The Mercury Theatre on the Air* (as the series was now officially renamed) was moving to Sunday nights at 8 P.M., with the first new show to be broadcast in five days, on September 11.

Houseman's frequent references to Orson's affair with the "celebrated ballerina" reflected his belief that Welles was distracted, overextended, even self-destructive. He thought that Welles's frivolous affair with Vera Zorina was ongoing, and that it would persist for months to come. Evidence available today, however, suggests that when the summer of *Too Much Johnson* and the first season of the Mercury Theater radio series ended, Orson's involvement with Zorina ended with it.

Was Zorina really a lover or was she more of a soul mate, someone who admired Welles without hesitation, a woman to whom he could pour out his heart? Was their friendship more of an escape than a hot, dangerous distraction? Were his boasts about the romance merely an elaborate misdirection by a man devoted more to his artistic pursuits than to his sex life?

The telegrams preserved by Zorina in her archives suggest that the two carried on a passionate yet idealistic flirtation not unlike Orson's fling with Tilly Losch. The first telegram Welles sent Zorina is dated shortly after they met, around Christmas 1937, when he was in Chicago and she was in California:

HAVE NEVER WANTED DELIBERATELY TO HURT STOP TROUBLE WAS THAT IN GENERAL CONFUSION TRIED TO PLEASE TOO MANY PEOPLE I WARNED YOU I WAS DIFFICULT BUT PLEASE BELIEVE MY GOOD INTENTIONS AND ONCE AGAIN FORGIVE MY INCONSISTENCE AND BAD ACTION. He signed it with a pun: OCEAN.

Usually terse, the telegrams proliferated in the spring of 1938. The messages run the gamut from the one-word YES (from Orson to Zorina at the Imperial Theatre on April 7), to I LOVE YOU I LOVE YOU I LOVE YOU I LOVE YOU I LOVE YOU I LOVE YOU I LOVE YOU I LOVE YOU (undated, unsigned). Welles ran out of the auditorium between the acts of her Broadway play, sending her telegrams to praise her performance in each act; he sent her telegrams when he knew she was asleep, wishing her sweet dreams; he sent her telegrams saying simply I AM ACROSS THE STREET. Most of his telegrams ended with the professions of love that came easily to him and that concluded many of his letters to friends of either gender.

A few actual letters saved by Zorina bared Orson's soul more painfully. "I have many, many troubles and I feel awful and I need you," he wrote to her at the Ritz in September 1938.

The next letter, later in the fall, is among the last items in the correspondence she saved.

"Dearest," Orson wrote, "For a time at least, I am afraid I have no more to offer you than my unhappiness.

"So when I come to you again it will be only when my life is such that there can be no misunderstandings.

"You are a wonderful and truly great woman.

"You are my own love.

"I have told you these things before and you have not believed me.

"I cannot hope you will ever entirely understand.

"Always, O."

Zorina herself insisted that she and Orson never moved beyond hand-holding and ardent embraces. Zorina "admired him enormously," she wrote in her autobiography, and for a fleeting moment in 1938 she did experience "all the symptoms of having fallen head over heels in love" with a man "as imaginative in love as in the theater. On days when we did not meet he bombarded me with telegrams, spaced to arrive every few hours." Yet their relationship was destined to remain "platonic and short-lived," Zorina wrote. "Orson was married, and though we never talked about it, I understood that there were problems."

Women have been known to speak coyly about their out-of-wedlock lovers—yet Zorina confessed openly to other such entanglements, writing candidly about her involvement, at age eighteen, in a London ménage à trois with choreographer Léonide Massine and his wife, Eugenia Delarova. Her platonic relationship with Orson was deeply gratifying, Zorina wrote in her memoir, but within months of their "breakup," on the day before Christmas 1938, she married her choreographer, George Balanchine.

＊

Meanwhile, Orson still promoted his wife's professional acting career. "Anna Stafford" had performed credibly in *Too Much Johnson* and other plays at Stony Creek. Now Orson cast Virginia in another small but noticeable role, as Julie, Danton's wife, in *Danton's Death*, the Mercury's fall opener. Orson no longer needed a hotel suite for his asthma, or for editing the footage of *Too Much Johnson*, so when Virginia found a spacious apartment on West Fifty-Ninth Street, close to the Mercury, Orson moved back in with her and five-month-old Christopher, giving family life another try as he prepared *Danton's Death*.

The Mercury radio series had soared to impressive heights during its first season, but the Mercury Theatre's stage operation was plummeting toward insolvency. After months of expenditures with no substantial return, the partners had to start from scratch in raising money for their second Broadway season. Fund-raising was neither man's forte. Welles wanted as little as possible to do with the money side of the Mercury, except for spending as he desired, and Houseman, by his own account, was forced to rely on emergency infusions from his upper-crust friends, or from surprise investors blowing in without warning.

For both men, outward gratitude toward their deep-pocketed benefactors conflicted with underlying resentment. Both felt like children reliant on stern parents, and for Orson "those emotions were so intense as to make it virtually impossible for him to be civil to [investors] on the rare occasions when he encountered them," according to Houseman.

Budgeting for the Mercury still fell to Houseman, and it was his most important job. Wary of returning to their few original stockholders, he planned to raise funds from fresh investors for the 1938–1939 season with a scheme that spread the risks over the company's three envisioned productions, promising a share of 50 percent of the overall profits to the participants. He estimated that *Danton's Death* and *Too Much Johnson* would cost $10,000 each, with another $10,000 required for the Mercury's share of the entire cost of the more expensive *Five Kings*, which Houseman had leveraged as a Theatre Guild coproduction.

Preoccupied with radio scripts, Houseman, by his own admission, neglected fund-raising. By the summer's end he had amassed only several thousand dollars, including $2,000 pried out of "a bootlegger's son from Brooklyn" on a promise that he could work on the Mercury radio series. But "for all our triumphs," Houseman recalled, the Mercury "remained an 'art theatre'—poison to the smart money and the regular Broadway angels." By chance, in September, the Mercury bank account was suddenly boosted by $10,000 from "the most hardboiled outfit in show business," a producing syndicate run by Marcus Hyman and Max Gordon that put a little money into various shows. "I never quite understood why they did it," said Houseman.

Seventeen thousand dollars was all the Mercury had, starting out its second season. Before salvaging *Too Much Johnson*, it had to mount *Danton's Death*, its biggest, most difficult, perhaps least commercially attractive production yet. The theater building would have to stay dark until the premiere, optimistically announced for late September, as the partners poured out money to pay for sets, costumes, lighting, and the salaries of the returning staff and actors. Low on cash and without any revenue stream, they had to work fast and cheap and hope to succeed wildly.

Notoriously complicated—for both stage companies and audiences—Georg Büchner's 1835 play was set during a lull in the French Revolution and revolved around events leading up to the guillotining of Danton, a disillusioned advocate of the death-dealing revolutionary Tribunal. It had found its way onto the schedule, according to Mercury lore, when actor Martin Gabel brought a volume of Büchner's collected plays to a July radio rehearsal, urging Orson to read *Danton's Death* and consider it as a vehicle for Gabel in the title role.

But Orson was already familiar with *Danton's Death* for a number of reasons. His paramour Tilly Losch had choreographed a famous German-language production of *Dantons Tod* for Max Reinhardt in New York in 1927. The celebrated and hugely influential Reinhardt, whose plays Orson had seen as a boy on his first trip to Europe, was a recurrent topic of conversation with both Losch and Vera Zorina, who also had danced for Reinhardt. Although he never mentioned it in any of his interviews, Orson may well have seen the New York production of *Dantons Tod*, which occurred during the period when he regularly visited the city with his father.

After agreeing to *Danton's Death*, Houseman was taken aback to learn that Orson was going to let Gabel play the larger-than-life Danton. Houseman was convinced that the character's "heroism, magnanimity, lethargy, and great personal magnetism" were better suited for Orson (who was also the bigger marquee name). At least that's how Houseman told the story; Welles told Henry Jaglom that it was Houseman who preferred Gabel as Danton. "Houseman kept saying, 'These plays are not vehicles for you. Remember, we're an ensemble company, not the Orson Welles Players,'" he claimed. Either way, the partners argued about the casting, as they often did, with Orson ultimately prevailing, as was usually the case, after pointing out ("not unreasonably," in Houseman's words) that he couldn't very well play Danton, and later in the season alternate as Falstaff in *Five Kings*, while directing both of the plays and also guiding the radio series.

They agreed to an "unsatisfactory compromise," with Orson accepting the "brief but flashy" role of Saint-Just, a ruthless ally of Robespierre—they were both champions of the guillotine—in which role Welles could be "replaced without damage when the *Five Kings* rehearsals began or," as Houseman liked to add, sneaking in another mention, "whenever the ballerina summoned him."

Gabel was thrilled, George Coulouris not so much. It was bad enough that Gabel had been anointed as Mark Antony in *Julius Caesar*. Now Gabel (whom Coulouris considered his inferior) was being placed on an even higher pedestal as the titular lead of the Mercury's second season opener. Coulouris resented the snub—and the likely pay cut. When Houseman instead offered him the role of Robespierre, Coulouris "took it coolly," and a few days later turned the role down as "monolithic and the play turgid." Houseman angrily told him to go to hell, and Coulouris left the stage company indefinitely. To replace him, Orson contacted the Russian-born Vladimir Sokoloff, who had been Reinhardt's Robespierre in the earlier German-language production, and Sokoloff agreed to return to New York to re-create his role.

Coulouris was a major defection, but a few stalwarts from the original Mercury ensemble helped preserve continuity. Besides Virginia Welles (still billed as "Anna Stafford" in the program), the cast of *Danton's Death* included trustworthy Joseph Cotten as the politician Barrère and Arlene Francis as Danton's friend Marion, a prostitute. (Francis and Martin Gabel would fall in love during the long rehearsals, and they later married.) Featured parts went to Erskine Sanford, Edgar Barrier, Eustace Wyatt, Guy Kingsley, Ruth Ford, and Mary Wickes, all from the summer tryout of *Too Much Johnson*. Also back in the troupe were former Todd boys William Mowry Jr. and Edgerton Paul, and three "slaves"—William "Vakhtangov" Alland, Richard Wilson, and Richard Baer.

Marc Blitzstein also returned to compose an imaginative score for "voices, clarinet, trumpet, percussion and piano/harpsichord," according to his biographer Howard Pollack. The music included arrangements of three famous revolutionary-era tunes ("Ah! ça ira," "La Carmagnole" and "La Marseillaise") and two original songs, including a "folkish number," sung by Cotten and Wickes, with lyrics adapted from Büchner. Another familiar behind-the-scenes contributor was technical director Jean Rosenthal, who would oversee the design and lighting by Stephen Jan Tichacek, a veteran of the Federal Theatre Project.

Danton's Death called for hundreds of extras, but Orson proposed a budget-minded alternative: a background cyclorama of masks that would evoke the faces of the bloodthirsty mob of the revolution. Rosenthal purchased a slew of buckram masks—accounts put the number anywhere from 1,700 to 5,000—and had them colored by hand and glued to a curved wall of canvas enveloping the back of the stage. As Orson's brainstorms often did, the hydra-headed wall caused headaches in other departments, requiring the creation of an elaborate lighting scheme that would allow the faces to be illuminated when needed, but hidden from view when the mob was not supposed to be present. Individually controlled lights were scattered throughout the auditorium, each numbered and with a dimmer, shining onto the stage from the front balcony, the boxes, the ceiling, the pipes behind the proscenium, and along and behind the cyclorama covering the back wall. Speaking with Peter Bogdanovich decades later, Welles readily admitted that his lighting schemes for Mercury productions were "tremendously complicated," with *Danton's Death* the most, or worst, complicated—"over 350 cues."

No less troublesome was a huge elevator contraption Orson sketched out to occupy the center of the stage, which would rise to several levels during the drama, as high as twelve feet above the stage floor. The elevator could hold half a dozen people, and in the course of the play would become a rostrum, a prison cell, a bourgeois salon, and finally, at the climax, the dread guillotine. Orson conceived of the device as a way to change scenes swiftly without using a curtain, but Rosenthal and Tichacek struggled with the contraption, which creaked and groaned alarmingly; and it was surrounded by Orson's beloved, treacherous trap holes, from which actors and lighting would spring.

Under the circumstances, Orson did less rewriting initially than usual, basing his script closely on the English translation of *Danton's Death* from the edition Gabel had handed to him, which had been published to coincide with Reinhardt's 1927 production. During rehearsals, though, he indulged in his usual tinkering, "endlessly shifting the order of scenes and the sequence of speeches," Houseman recalled. The solemn play certainly *seemed* long, but Orson's editing brought it down to ninety minutes.

The costs mounted, regardless of Orson's cost-cutting ideas, and neither the rickety set nor the underrehearsed actors were ready by late September. The Mercury partners were forced to make the first in a series of highly publicized, increasingly anticlimactic postponements.

Perhaps miscast, Martin Gabel struggled to capture the Danton of Orson's imagination. "In *Caesar*, there had been mutual understanding and faith" between Gabel and Welles, Houseman wrote accusingly. "None of that was evident now. Gabel was aggressive in his insecurity: he knew that he was not ideally cast and that Orson should have been playing Danton. This suspicion hung between them, unspoken and corrosive, all through rehearsal."

Sokoloff was a consolation, onstage and off; Orson reveled in the older man's anecdotes about Max Reinhardt and the glory days of Berliner theater—now, with Hitler in power, gone forever. The whole company stood in awe of Sokoloff's reputation, and Orson left his Robespierre virtually alone—too much so, because Sokoloff had a thick, nearly impenetrable accent. To Houseman, Welles seemed to be going through the motions. "The show was prepared in an anxious mood that fluctuated between uneasy inertia and almost unbearable tension," the producer wrote.

Orson did drive the actors mercilessly at times, and when he lost his temper Virginia sometimes took the brunt of it. "He was very beastly to her anyway," recalled actor Guy Kingsley. "He shouted at her, and I suppose it's all right, because they [were] married, but I don't think any other actress probably would have put up with the treatment that he gave her, which was rather severe and excessive."

There were still obvious tensions in their marriage, and the couple did not always go home together. Pushing himself to the limit, Orson moved a bed into an aisle of the theater in October, a step that was turned, like much of what he did, into advantageous publicity. "Actors Often 'Live in Theater,' but This Actor Actually Does," read the headline in the *New York Herald Tribune*. ("For six days and nights recently he never stepped outside of the Mercury Theater," the article claimed.) After the actors left for their homes, Orson drove the technical rehearsals relentlessly, until the crew could no longer keep their eyes open. Only when they finally crashed did Orson dismiss them and follow suit.

By now John Berry was billed as an actor, but he was also Orson's first assistant and "green man" ("That means I was in charge of the plants—the prop man and set builder"). Often he was the last man to leave before Orson let them all go. One late, late night Orson stood onstage demanding chalk. Berry told him he didn't know where to find chalk at two in the morning. "He looked at me with that wonderful, noble, aristocratic hauteur," recalled Berry. "He said, 'Why? Must you betray me too, booby?' Berry grabbed the fire ax, went downstairs to the men's room of the theater, broke the wall, dug out some plaster, and came back and handed it to him. "Thank you," said Orson.

Orson counted on strong soldiers like Berry, and on the eleventh-hour inspiration and good luck and serendipity that had blessed his career ever since he and Houseman had teamed up in 1936. But none of their previous productions were dogged by the extraordinary missteps and irredeemable crises that afflicted *Danton's Death*.

In prospect, Orson had viewed the political and historical context of the play—the quandary of revolutionary violence, as represented by the gulf between Danton and Robespierre—as comparable to *Julius Caesar* in its contemporary immediacy. But left-wing ideologues might see the play differently, Marc Blitzstein pointed out. The composer brought the partners' attention to an October 20, 1938, article in *The Daily Worker*, describing *Danton's Death* as a distortion of the revolutionary impulse, a play that loomed about as radical as the glossy *Marie Antoinette*, the new MGM picture covering much the same terrain. The communist newspaper demanded that the planned Mercury script "be changed or the show dropped from the repertoire."

Blitzstein himself agreed with this jaundiced take on the play. Danton, he explained patiently to Welles and Houseman, could be viewed as a stand-in for Stalin's enemy Trotsky, who by 1938 was exiled to Mexico City. Stalin, in this analogy, was the tyrannical Robespierre, while Danton's demise could be taken as a reflection of the dictator's ongoing "purge" trials of purportedly subversive government officials and creative artists in the Soviet Union. New York's left-wing and labor groups had supported the Mercury Theatre since its inception. Now Blitzstein warned that *Danton's Death* could be perceived as political backsliding.

Blitzstein arranged emergency parleys between Houseman and V. J. Jerome, the commissar of the cultural wing of the U.S. Communist Party, whom both Welles and Houseman had first crossed swords with when the New York left publicly dissected *Panic*. Politely, over tea, Houseman and Jerome debated the play's symbolism, which Jerome felt was fraught with reactionary implications. The men agreed to disagree, but Houseman consented to remove "a few of the more obvious Trotsky-Stalin parallels" from the script. "In exchange, the Party agreed not to boycott us."

Blitzstein wasn't Welles's only associate who was close to the Communist Party. Although he was progressive politically, Orson was complex ideologically in his stage and screen work, consistently displaying the human side of monsters and tyrants, for example. In this period, however, he was also careful to avoid making an enemy of the communists. He made the changes to mollify the New York leadership of their party, and at the same time he moved a key speech by his character, Saint-Just, to the very end of the play. The speech could be interpreted as validating the revolution: "Mankind shall emerge from

this blood-bath like earth from the waters of the deluge—with new giant's strength, with limbs born for the first time." Its ambiguity would
"please the Party," as Richard France wrote, and "in fact Orson was
delighted to have a chance to bring down the curtain [himself]." A
press release assured Mercury's left-wing base that "it is a characteristic
of Danton's own personality and not a characteristic of revolution or
revolutionaries which brings him to his decadence and fall."

Even apart from the Communist Party input, the script was ever-
changing, and never more than a day or two ahead of rehearsals. At one
point Welles declared he was going to revise it sweepingly and conclu-
sively from start to finish. He sent the cast home before midnight with
a call for late morning. After pulling an all-nighter, Orson decided he
needed another twenty-four hours, and the cast enjoyed a rare extended
break before gathering at noon on the third day. Arriving late, according to Houseman, Orson vanished into his dressing room, then rushed
out with a howl moments later, having discovered he had left the newly
revised script in a taxi. After "an hour" spent phoning the police and
trying in vain "to trace the missing cab," Houseman said, "rehearsal
resumed exactly where it had left off thirty-nine hours before"—with
the previous version.

Troubles with the actors, the sets, the lighting, and New York
communists kept stalling the premiere. Originally scheduled for September 24, the first previews of *Danton's Death* were reannounced for
October 24, with advertisements running in New York papers on October 16. One hour after the first public preview was due to begin,
however, Welles refused to raise the curtain. He and Houseman argued
ferociously, but Houseman was forced to step out front and announce
that the show was canceled, meekly sending ticket holders home with a
vow to honor their stubs during the future run. The producer remembered the disappointed theatergoers as "a friendly middle-class group
that had seen all our shows and would forgive our imperfections," but
the previews had been sold for weeks in advance as benefits for antifascist groups aiding victims of Nazi oppression, and for Manhattan
physician Bella V. Dodd's campaign for a seat in the assembly on the
trade unionist American Labor Party ticket.

The delays continued. On the night of the second scheduled preview,
Welles and Gabel stalled with recitations from *Julius Caesar* before finally

deciding the scenery wasn't ready and canceling again. Then, before the next scheduled preview, at the end of the third week in October, disaster struck—actual, physical disaster. Orson's huge center-stage elevator contraption collapsed during a run-through, sending several actors to the hospital, including Erskine Sanford, who broke a leg and had to be replaced in the cast. Welles and Houseman canceled all future planned previews as Jean Rosenthal scrambled to fix the "technical difficulties," working feverishly to construct an improved elevator. The premiere then was moved into the first week of November—in part "because the cast and technical staff bordered on sheer exhaustion from intensive rehearsals," as the *New York Times* reported.

"Orson continued to rehearse while morale deteriorated," Houseman wrote later, although the producer conceded that he himself attended only "a few rehearsals." (His "people" kept him informed.) Houseman was busy with his futile fund-raising efforts (the entire season's $17,000 was by now nearly exhausted) and with supervisory work on the scripts for the fall radio series.

Finally, on Friday and Saturday, October 28 and 29, the Mercury offered two "perfectly smooth" previews of *Danton's Death*. At last, it seemed, the jinx was behind them. That Sunday, the cast would gather for rehearsal after the *Mercury Theatre on the Air* radio broadcast. Several days remained before the press opening, plenty of time for Orson to pull a rabbit out of his hat, as he always seemed to do.

It was also the day before Halloween, one of Orson's favorite holidays.

The fall season of *Mercury Theater on the Air* had been launched grandly on September 11 with a condensed *Julius Caesar*. The series had continued with radio versions of Charlotte Brontë's *Jane Eyre* (September 18); several of Arthur Conan Doyle's Sherlock Holmes stories (September 25); a concise version of Charles Dickens's *Oliver Twist*, with Orson playing both the fate-tossed orphan Oliver and the villainous Fagin (October 2); Edward Ellsberg's *Hell on Ice*, the saga of a famous nineteenth-century arctic voyage (October 9); Orson's first adaptation of a Booth Tarkington story, the 1916 best seller *Seventeen* (October 16); and Jules Verne's *Around the World in Eighty Days* (October 23).

The original "First Person Singular" conceit had involved Orson narrating each episode; that conceit was dropped for the new season, but the host still introduced and closed each show with his own musings. And the schedule was still stocked with his favorite authors, some of them—Charlotte Brontë, Arthur Conan Doyle, Booth Tarkington, and Jules Verne—destined for return engagements in his career.

The program now aired at 8 P.M. EST on Sundays, opposite the number one show in that time slot: *The Chase and Sanborn Hour,* informally known as "The Charlie McCarthy Show" after its star, the wisecracking dummy voiced by ventriloquist Edgar Bergen. The Crosley Index of radio ratings showed *The Chase and Sanborn Hour* drawing 34.7 percent of possible listeners, while *Mercury Theater on the Air* attracted only about 3.6 percent. After ten or twelve minutes of opening banter with the puppet, however, Bergen usually yielded the microphone to a popular singer, and the Mercury show got a bump in ratings as the audience turned the dial to see what else was available.

Having been upgraded from its summer replacement status, the fall series was allowed a deeper budget for staff. Paul Stewart, who had directed most of the summer shows, was now better salaried as director of the series. Houseman took the lead on the scripts through September; but when the difficulties with *Danton's Death* overwhelmed him, he hired Howard Koch, a tall, spindly Columbia Law School graduate turned playwright, to take over the main writing responsibilities.

Koch had written a short-lived Broadway comedy in 1929, but since that time, he had carved out a reputation for earnest drama. *The Lonely Man,* which Koch wrote for the Federal Theatre Project, posited a reincarnated Abraham Lincoln as a college professor mediating a labor strike. When *The Lonely Man* was produced in Chicago in mid-1937, with Walter Huston's son, John, playing Lincoln's surrogate, critics acclaimed the production and the playwright. Hardly a dewy-eyed novice (he was older than Houseman), Koch signed a six-month contract with Mercury with a clause giving him the future rights to any radio script he wrote. His capable assistant and secretary Anne Froelick, a onetime actress, was hired with him. Koch did his first writing on "Hell on Ice" in the second week of October.

On Sundays, Orson typically spent all day at CBS, overseeing final changes to that night's script while deciding with Houseman on the next week's story. On October 23, during rehearsals for the broadcast of "Around the World in Eighty Days," the partners agreed on a Halloween Eve adaptation of *The War of the Worlds*, H. G. Wells's 1898 science fiction novel about a Martian invasion. Their decision was halfhearted, Houseman insisted later. "Neither Orson nor I remembered it at all clearly. It is just possible that neither of us had ever read it."

Although there is disagreement about the origin of key ideas in the script, it's hard to believe that Orson did not outline the basic concept, as he always did, or that in a roomful of people he did not collate the best ideas and decide on the approach. The original novel was set mostly in London, in the year the book was published, with the story narrated in the first person by a scientist who is one of the two protagonists. Orson wanted the story relocated to present-day America, a tactic he often adopted with adaptations, and he asked for it to be reworked as a routine radio musicale interrupted by urgent bulletins from newscasters.

The conceit may have been partly indebted to Archibald MacLeish, whose new verse play for the *Columbia Workshop* series "Air Raid," was scheduled for broadcast by WABC the following week. Welles had doubtless read advance galleys of the "Air Raid" script, which "four days before the famous 'War of the Worlds' [broadcast]," in the words of MacLeish's biographer Scott Donaldson, "used the same technique of apparently reliable reportage by an announcer" to recount the advent of a conqueror, raining death from the skies—a narrative device that echoed MacLeish's earlier "Fall of the City." And Orson's friend Ray Collins played the on-the-spot announcer in "Air Raid," when it was broadcast on October 27.

But Welles was also inspired by the fact that many radio programs of the day, including his own September 25 broadcast of "The Immortal Sherlock Holmes," had been interrupted by bulletins about overseas crises and catastrophes. His radio scripts were always built around his own performance, and in the case of "War of the Worlds," it was established early in the conception that he would play Professor Pierson, a noted astronomer who is interviewed during the news bulletins, and who would be the only character to survive to the end of the story—and the broadcast.

Although it was only his third script assignment, Howard Koch would handle the heavy lifting on "War of the Worlds," while Welles and Houseman coped with the crisis-filled days of final rehearsals before the long-delayed first public previews of *Danton's Death*. Koch took that Monday off to refresh his muse, traveling upstate to visit his family. On the way back to New York, he stopped at a gas station on Route 9W. This stop—plus perusing a local map—gave him the idea of having the Martians launch their attack on a place he called Grovers Mill, an unincorporated village surrounded by farmland near Princeton, New Jersey.

Yet Koch felt uninspired by the assignment, and he phoned Houseman on Monday or Tuesday, amid hectic rehearsals of *Danton's Death*, complaining that the tale of the Martian invasion was silly beyond redemption, and they should switch to *Lorna Doone*, another option on the table. Houseman said later that he ran Koch's objections past Welles, then phoned back: "The answer is a firm no. It is Orson's favorite project."*

With the shrug of a professional, Koch embarked on six feverish days of grinding out the script, which he recalled in his autobiography, *As Time Goes By*, as "a nightmare of scenes written and rewritten, pages speeding back and forth to the studio, with that Sunday deadline staring me in the face. Once the Martians had landed, I deployed the opposing forces over an ever-widening area, making moves and countermoves between the invaders and defenders. After a while I found myself enjoying the destruction I was wreaking like a drunken general."

Working in close phone consultation with Houseman, Koch turned out the first draft of the sixty-page "War of the Worlds" script by midweek. (A single page of radio script corresponded roughly to one minute of air time.) Usually the first drafts were ready by Wednesday night, "when Orson was supposed to read it but seldom did," as Houseman said in *Run-Through*, "particularly during the last month's re-

---

* Note the interesting discrepancy: that neither Houseman nor Welles might ever have read *War of the Worlds* in its entirety (according to Houseman in his 1972 memoir), with that same book metamorphosing a few days later into "Orson's favorite project" (as Houseman wrote in his revised 1988 book *Unfinished Business*).

hearsals of *Danton's Death*." Come Thursday, Paul Stewart, whom Orson trusted from his earliest radio days, oversaw a dry-run rehearsal with a makeshift cast while "Koch and I," Houseman said, "made whatever adjustments and changes seemed needed in the script." An acetate recording was made of the dry run for Orson's critique on Thursday night. This input "we would accept or dispute," Houseman wrote, and the script was "reshaped and rewritten, sometimes drastically" over the next forty-eight hours.

Even when Orson ignored the first draft, he closely heeded the practice recording. Listening "rather gloomily" to the recording "between *Danton* rehearsals, in Orson's room at the St. Regis, sitting on the floor because all the chairs were still covered with coils of unrolled and unedited film," according to Houseman, the "dead tired" star and host of the series pronounced the show dull and corny. "We all agreed," Houseman said, "that its only chance of coming off lay in emphasizing its newscast style—its simultaneous, eyewitness quality."

Exactly how Orson suggested punching up the script Houseman does not say, although he frequently mentions the contributions of others, including himself. "All night we sat up—Howard, Paul, Annie and I, spicing the script with circumstantial allusions and authentic detail."

On Friday, the script went to network censors. This was standard operating procedure for radio programs, with censors, for example, requesting changes to the names of actual entities ("New Jersey National Guard" becoming "state militia," and so on) to avoid any risk of offense or lawsuits.

On Saturday afternoon, Stewart, who also acted in many of the *Mercury Theatre on the Air* broadcasts, including "War of the Worlds," convened another rehearsal. After closely consulting with Welles, Stewart added preliminary sound effects during the Saturday rehearsal, again conducted at the CBS studio while Orson was readying the second public preview of *Danton's Death* sixteen blocks south.

On Sunday, October 30, Orson arrived shortly after noon for the customary daylong preparations for the evening broadcast, and in the studio he was the leader beyond dispute.

For the program's musical element, Bernard Herrmann was constrained by a script that called for his classically trained musicians (many of them from the New York Philharmonic) to devote themselves to such popular chestnuts as "Stardust" and "La Cumparsita." Herrmann also contributed solo piano snippets to fill the tense intervals before the newscaster broke in to announce "We now return you to our New York studio . . ."

Apart from Dan Seymour, the announcer who introduced the program on behalf of the network, the cast was drawn from the Mercury stage company and Orson's coterie of radio friends. The theater contingent included the all-purpose William Herz, who was the Stony Creek theater manager; and several of Orson's young "slaves," such as William Alland and Richard Wilson. Orson gave Howard Smith, who had been reliably hilarious in *Too Much Johnson*, an apposite, dramatic, and moving part as a valiant bomber pilot who attempts to delay the Martian onslaught by sacrificing himself in a suicide mission. From radio came Frank Readick, who had preceded Orson as the voice of the Shadow and appeared in *Les Misérables* and other shows with Welles; Carl Frank, also from *The Shadow*; Kenny Delmar, who had acted in "Fall of the City"; and the always dependable Ray Collins.

Readick had a crucial role as newsman Carl Phillips, who reports the alien invasion before perishing. Frank played the second announcer, who interrupts the musical broadcast with breaking news about the Martians. Delmar, a former child actor in D. W. Griffith films, voiced three parts, including a standout turn as the U.S. Secretary of the Interior. Collins played Farmer Wilmuth (who owns the land where the Martians crash), then Harry McDonald (a radio executive), and finally a rooftop radio announcer (whose dire fate is shared by all Manhattan).

Orson trusted these actors and sought their reactions to the script, their opinions about what worked and what fell flat. "Orson railed at the text, cursing the writers," recalled the newest young "slave," Richard Baer, who assisted in the studio that day. The first rehearsal with the cast occasioned many small changes in dialogue, with all hands contributing feedback about tone and characterization, trying to knock all the corniness out of the draft. "Oh Kenny, you know what I want," Welles told Delmar, who was known for his dead-on impersonation of President Franklin D. Roosevelt. Delmar met his suggestion halfway with his portrayal of the interior secretary, his grave proclamation about the "national emergency" slyly evoking FDR.

The first full afternoon rehearsal incorporated all the music and special effects that had been prepared with Orson's involvement during the week. His sometimes exasperating perfectionism when it came to ambient sound fell heavily on the shoulders of sound engineer John Dietz and special effects engineer Ora Daigle Nichols, one of the few women at the top of her field. (Nichols had trained as a musician, and her experience included providing live accompaniment to silent motion pictures.) Among Nichols's storied contributions to the "War of the Worlds" broadcast was the sinister reverberation of the Martian hatch opening up for the first time, which she achieved "by slowly unscrewing the lid of an empty pickle jar in a nearby toilet cubicle," according to John Gosling in his authoritative *Waging the War of the Worlds.*

The second full rehearsal of the day was for timing, with station break announcements added. The goal was to reach sixty minutes precisely—although, as always, Orson made so many alterations during each run-through the length of the show was elastic until it was performed live. And "War of the Worlds" was especially slippery to calculate. The script called for action-packed re-creations of Martian attacks, followed by long stretches of dead air, suggesting that the speaker's live feed had been cut off by calamity. The silences segued into the piano tinkling, as though the radio station were on automatic control.

As the afternoon wore on, Orson daringly dragged out both the silences and the music (the orchestral excerpts of popular standards and Herrmann's piano tinkling) along with his own rumbling impersonation of a Princeton professor who seemed fond of his own brilliance. Houseman complained vigorously, insisting that suspense was giving way to tedium, but Welles shook him off. "Over my protests, lines were restored that had been cut at earlier rehearsals," Houseman recalled, "I cried there would be no listener left. Welles stretched them out even longer."

Everyone took breaks except Orson. He busily ironed out wrinkles, huddling with Herrmann and the musicians, the sound team, the actors. The cast and crew gulped milk shakes and sandwiches as evening fell. Orson sipped pineapple juice, soothing his vocal cords. Frank Readick wandered downstairs to the CBS library, where he listened to recordings of Herbert Morrison's anguished eyewitness reportage of the *Hindenburg* disaster in 1937, which would inform the shocked and heart-piercing tone of his own eventual performance.

However divergent the eyewitness accounts of this radio production, they all agree on their portrait of the single-minded and clearheaded Welles, shaping the evolution and quality of "War of the Worlds" in spite of the staff's continued opposition and skepticism, thoroughly in command of the show's concept and details. Every important decision was his to make; he was the producer and star, and the highest artistic executive. Influenced by Houseman, later critics made a concerted effort to disparage Orson's writing contribution to important scripts such as "War of the Worlds" and *Citizen Kane*; Pauline Kael, for instance, claimed astonishingly that "by the time of the 'War of the Worlds' broadcast, on Halloween, 1938 Welles wasn't doing any of the writing," and Simon Callow in his multivolume biography insisted that Welles had "barely thought about the program, being wholly occupied until the very last minute by his losing struggle with *Danton's Death*."

A network spot before the broadcast advertised "Orson Welles and the *Mercury Theater on the Air* in a radio play by Howard Koch suggested by the H. G. Wells novel *The War of the Worlds*." But Koch himself, while steadfastly defending the importance of his own contribution to the script, never denied Welles his share of credit. Orson's actual writing on the radio scripts often took place at the eleventh hour on those crazy Sundays, but while it "may have been brief," Koch told Richard France, "it was very important. He could do wonders in a few minutes."

Indeed, many say Orson performed wonders on that Halloween eve, as the rehearsals gathered momentum and the show snowballed into readiness. Most say that no one, not even Welles, had the slightest inkling that this episode was different from any other. Despite the eight-hour workday he had already put in, Orson was still in a state of high excitement when, a few minutes before eight o'clock, he took one last swig of pineapple juice and stepped onto the podium. In suspenders and shirtsleeves, holding a baton, Orson raised his arms to cue the musical theme.

The "War of the Worlds" broadcast began like all the others, with the lead-in announcer introducing Orson as the producer and star of the show. Then Orson leaned into the microphone and spoke, some of his eloquent words drawn straight from the novel:

"We know now that in the early years of the twentieth century this world was being watched closely by intelligences greater than man's and yet as mortal as his own. We know now that as human beings busied themselves about their various concerns they were scrutinized and studied, perhaps almost as narrowly as a man with a microscope might scrutinize the transient creatures that swarm and multiply in a drop of water. With infinite complacence people went to and fro over the earth about their little affairs, serene in the assurance of their dominion over this small spinning fragment of solar driftwood which by chance or design man has inherited out of the dark mystery of Time and Space.

"Yet across an immense ethereal gulf, minds that are to our minds as ours are to the beasts in the jungle, intellects vast, cool and unsympathetic, regarded this earth with envious eyes and slowly and surely drew their plans against us.

"In the thirty-ninth year of the twentieth century came the great disillusionment. It was near the end of October. Business was better. The war scare was over. More men were back at work. Sales were picking up. On this particular evening, October 30, the Crosley service estimated that thirty-two million people were listening in on radios."

The episode then shifted into "the first of the banalities that had so worried John Houseman," in John Gosling's words: the tail end of a prosaic weather report, which segued into a dance number emanating from the fictional Meridian Room "of the Hotel Park Plaza in downtown New York," where the Ramon Raquello Orchestra was leading off with "a touch of the Spanish." A news flash interrupted the tango number—"La Cumparsita"—to announce that explosions of incandescent gas had been reported on the planet Mars. The report was followed by a return to music, this time "Bobby Millette playing 'Stardust' from the Hotel Martinet in Brooklyn," interrupted by a brief announcement that "in a few moments" the "noted astronomer"

Professor Pierson of Princeton Observatory would be on hand to comment on the phenomenon.

Then it was back to the orchestra music playing on and on . . . until, at long last, six minutes into the show, reporter Carl Phillips (Frank Readick) materialized at the Princeton Observatory ("a large, semicircular room, pitch black except for an oblong split in the ceiling") to interview Professor Pierson (Welles), who has observed the blasts on his giant telescope.

The sage professor was unalarmed.

PHILLIPS
You're quite convinced as a scientist that living
intelligence as we know it does not exist on Mars?

PIERSON
I should say the chances against it are a thousand to one.

Then, interrupting the interview, a telegram was rush-delivered to the professor, and Phillips asked permission to read the wire aloud to listeners. A shock of "almost earthquake intensity" had struck "within a radius of twenty miles of Princeton," Phillips reported. It was probably a meteorite, the professor interjected reassuringly, "merely a coincidence." Phillips signed off and the faux broadcast returned to "our New York studio," where solitary piano playing faded in.

By now, almost twelve minutes into the broadcast, Nelson Eddy had begun to warble "Neapolitan Love Song" on NBC's top-rated Charlie McCarthy program, and its listeners were beginning to twiddle the dials to see what else was on. Six million people eventually listened to "War of the Worlds," social scientist Hadley Cantril later estimated— and a sizable percentage of them tuned in to CBS just in time to hear the bulletins about the Martian invasion, without having absorbed the disclaimers.

Suddenly, "a huge flaming object, believed to be a meteorite," was reported to have fallen on a "farm in the neighborhood of Grovers Mill, New Jersey, twenty-two miles from Trenton." Eyewitnesses Phillips and Professor Pierson, materializing within seconds at the Grovers Mill farm—already thronged with police and onlookers—described a huge rocket cylinder protruding from a vast pit. As they extracted a local account from the hayseed proprietor (Ray Collins), the top of the rocket rotated like a screw, and out of the shadows wriggled large glistening monsters with tentacles, shooting jets of flame.

PHILLIPS

... It's spreading everywhere. It's coming this way. About twenty yards to my right ...

(CRASH OF MICROPHONE . . . THEN DEAD SILENCE . . .)

Other bulletins reported the aliens as an invading army, piloting huge metal tripods emitting a poisonous gas that wreaked death and devastation. The rocket cylinders and tripods had begun to sprout all across America, slaughtering brave police and soldiers and civilians. Any resistance seemed futile, according to the bulletins. A radio announcer (Collins), "speaking from the roof of the Broadcasting Building, New York City," described the advancing tide of "great machines" on America's greatest metropolis, the smoke and gas, fleeing people, "thousands of them, dropping in like rats." At last, the Martian enemy reached Times Square.

An eerie silence was then followed by a quavering on shortwave.

OPERATOR FOUR

2 X 2 L calling C Q.
2 X 2 L calling C Q.
2 X 2 L calling C Q New York.
Isn't there anyone on the air?
Isn't there anyone on the air?
Isn't there anyone . . . ?
2 X 2 L . . .

This was followed by five seconds of absolute silence. At this point, more than forty minutes into the show—later than usual, because of the long slow buildup—there was inserted a "middle break" or intermission of roughly twenty seconds for station identification, during which time the audience received the courtesy of a routine reminder that the episode was an "original dramatization" by Orson Welles and the *Mercury Theater on the Air*.

By then, it was too late for the audience members who had tuned in after the opening, or had listened distractedly without heeding the program's disclaimers. The next day, newspapers across the country carried reports of people panicking in response to the broadcast. "A wave of mass hysteria" swept America, according to the *New York Times*. The broadcast "disrupted households, interrupted religious services, created traffic jams and clogged communications systems." Calls lit up police switchboards; citizens rushed out of their houses with wet towels covering their faces; traffic accidents, heart attacks, and suicide attempts were reported.

In the control booth on the twentieth floor of the Columbia Broadcasting System building, just before intermission, network official Davidson Taylor took the first phone call from the outside world. When a shaken Taylor insisted that the show be stopped, Houseman blocked him physically from leaving the booth and interrupting the broadcast. Soon the network switchboard was lighting up, and blue-uniformed security guards were swarming the floor.

Having no clue why guards had suddenly appeared, Orson waved them off as he plunged into the second half of "War of the Worlds," a searching conversation about the prospects of a difficult future between a surviving stranger (Carl Frank) and the professor (Welles). The latter makes a lonely and eerie journey through the Holland Tunnel, arriving to paint a doomsday picture of New York City. But the Martians are all dead, the professor reveals. Earthly bacteria have defeated them.

Then the professor turned host, signing off in his usual confidential manner: "This is Orson Welles, ladies and gentlemen, out of character to assure you that 'The War of the Worlds' has no further significance than as the holiday offering it was intended to be, the Mercury Theatre's own radio version of dressing up in a sheet and jumping out of a bush and saying Boo."

Only those people who weren't busy panicking heard it.

Drenched in sweat, Orson finished with a flourish and a cheeky smile. But he and Houseman barely had time to exchange glances before building guards whisked them into a room to be debriefed by agitated studio officials. CBS staff members scurried around confiscating the incriminating scripts and props and recording equipment. Welles and Houseman were amazed to hear accounts of the ongoing nationwide scare. "I've often wondered if you had any idea, before you did it," Peter Bogdanovich asked Welles decades later, "that 'The War of the Worlds' was going to get that kind of response." "The *kind* of response, yes," replied Welles. "That was merrily anticipated by us all. The size of it, of course, was flabbergasting."

A half hour later, Welles took the lead in facing the first newspaper reporters who had rushed to the studio. The reporters were "looking for blood," in his words, and they were disappointed "when they found I wasn't hemorrhaging." He was peppered with disconcerting questions about fatal traffic accidents, stampedes of people, suicides— all of which later proved to be "the worst kind of hyperbole," in the words of John Gosling. Still half disbelieving, Welles was meek and mild, explaining apologetically that the story was clearly a dramatization. They had chosen the Martian invasion only reluctantly, in fact, because "it was our thought that perhaps people might be bored or annoyed at hearing a tale so improbable."

Hurrying to the Mercury for their scheduled stage rehearsal, he and Houseman pushed past another pack of reporters. Inside the theater, the cast of *Danton's Death* waited—including several actors who had participated in the "War of the Worlds" broadcast and arrived before them. The actors were incredulous at the news, and some went outside to see the news ticker in Times Square: ORSON WELLES CAUSES PANIC. "Needless to say," recalled Guy Kingsley, who acted in both *Danton's Death* and "War of the Worlds," "the rehearsal came absolutely to a dead halt."

Welles had a rare night of sleeplessness not of his own devising. He spent much of the night on the phone with Roger Hill and other confidants and supporters, checking on news reports from around the country. He spoke with his lawyer, Arnold Weissberger, who told him that, although his CBS contract assigned legal responsibility for the broadcasts to the network, which had vetted the script, the reported accidents and fatalities were a gray area with regard to his liability.

The next morning, he woke to accusatory headlines. "Radio Listeners in Panic, Taking War Drama as Fact," was on the front page of the usually staid *New York Times*. In the *Daily News*, the banner headline was "Fake Radio 'War' Terrorizes N.Y.," with a subhead: "Scores Flee Homes; 15 in Hospital." The same type of coverage, emphasizing Welles's name as the responsible party, appeared in dozens of smaller cities and lesser newspapers.

Orson huddled with Henry Senber, the Mercury publicist, and a representative from the network, which was anxious to limit the legal implications and any public relations damage. The press was clamoring for a statement from Welles. Both he and Senber thought that offering only a tidy publicity release would antagonize the newsmen. A press conference was a better idea.

So Orson appeared at the CBS building in the late morning—pale and unshaven, in a conventional suit and tie, looking more like a door-to-door salesman than a national bogeyman. He faced a thronged room of reporters and photographers anxious for his explanation.

For a decade, newspapers had gradually lost ground to radio in both advertising revenue and timely reporting—owing precisely to the innovation of flash news bulletins of the type Welles had dramatized in "War of the Worlds." Among the old-school newsmen there was a distinct "anti-radio" sentiment, as *Variety* noted in its account of the broadcast and the panic, and this in turn lent an anti-Orson slant to the press coverage. "Editorials ranted about how irresponsible CBS and Welles were, insisting that I would never be offered another job in show business and how lucky I was not to be in jail," Welles recalled. "Most self-serving of all, they assured their readers that newspapers would never sink to such reckless disregard for the public's welfare."

Biographers writing decades after the "War of the Worlds" broadcast have suspected Welles of cleverly concocting the national panic, or of being secretly unrepentant as he apologized to newspapermen on the next morning. Although his (and Houseman's) first reaction to the panic had been astonishment and laughter, this had been swiftly overtaken by legitimate fears and concerns for himself, his career, and the future of the Mercury Theatre.

In newsreel footage of his Monday press conference, the young mastermind looks "palpably shaken," in the words of Simon Callow. He first reads a prepared statement, in a voice "nervously high-pitched and slightly adenoidal." (This was Orson's true voice, without pretense or bluster.) "If I'd planned to wreck my career," he told the journalists (some of whom "looked sympathetic," according to *Radio Mirror*, "and some who didn't"), "I couldn't have gone about it better." He insisted the show was meant as a Halloween prank. "I'd every hope people would be excited, just as they are in a melodrama," Welles said. A reporter asked, "Were you aware of the terror such a broadcast would stir up?" and he answered, "Definitely not." But Orson was also sarcastic about gullible listeners, and when another reporter went too far, demanding if in hindsight Welles thought he should have toned down the language, he bristled artistically. "You don't play murder in soft words," Orson averred.

His show of contrition won over many of the newsmen, but the Federal Communications Commission (FCC) opened a government investigation into the episode. Columbia Broadcasting System vice president W. B. Lewis announced that, henceforth, simulated newscasts would be banned from network radio dramas (some weeks later, the FCC cited this new policy as one reason for dropping its inquiry). Lawsuits filed against Welles and CBS rose to nearly $1 million, though none was ultimately actionable. And Welles received anonymous death threats; one promised to kill him during his curtain speech on the opening night of *Danton's Death.* "For a few days," he recalled, "I was a combination Benedict Arnold and John Wilkes Booth."

The cause of the hysteria among listeners would be studied for decades to come, and still is debated today. The *New York Times* thought the nationwide panic stemmed from the "war scare in Europe" (the Munich agreement permitting the German annexation of Czechoslovakia had occurred earlier that month), and because "radio frequently had interrupted regularly scheduled programs" to report on the crisis abroad. Rabbi Jonah B. Wise of the Central Synagogue on Lexington Avenue theorized that people were susceptible to panic because of the human Frankenstein monster running Germany: "Last Saturday night," Rabbi Wise was quoted, "people in the whole of the United States were running away in panic fear from Adolf Hitler." Other experts thought the Martians' poisonous vapor evoked for many horrifying memories of the deadly gas used in World War I, and the widespread apprehension that this weapon would return in the next war.

The panic was routinely cited as a product of radio's sweeping power, although the *New York Times* was among the outlets that patiently pointed out the role of willful ignorance. Any listener fooled by the drama would have had to ignore the clear newspaper listings for the show ("Today: 8:00–9:00—Play—H.G. Wells's 'War of the Worlds'—WABC"), its explicit introduction, and three additional announcements during the broadcast "emphasizing its fictional nature." The freethinking journalist and broadcaster Dorothy Thompson, named the second most influential woman in the United States (after Eleanor Roosevelt) in a poll the following year, spoke for America's more sophisticated citizenry when she declared that Welles and his actors had "shown up the incredible stupidity, lack of nerve and ignorance of thousands." Or as Orson's early booster, Alexander Woollcott, teased him in a telegram: "This only goes to prove, my beamish boy, that the intelligent people were all listening to a dummy, and all the dummies were listening to you."

One undeniable result of the panic was that Orson Welles was suddenly a household name. Heretofore, his name had been known only to Broadway aficionados and readers of the theater press and *Radio Daily*. Even when Orson had appeared on the cover of *Time*, the profile was relegated to the magazine's theater section. Now the broadcast and panic had made front-page headlines not only in every state of the union but around the globe. (According to Welles, even Adolf Hitler referred scathingly to the "War of the Worlds" panic in a Munich speech, offering it as evidence of the corrupt and decadent state of democracies.)

Orson's fame had spilled beyond the realm of show business; the potential audience for his future projects had grown exponentially. For the first time, his name became grist for editorialists, political columnists, humorists, and even sports reporters, who now compared the odds in horse races to the odds of Martians landing in New Jersey. "On Broadway, he was well known, all right," wrote *Radio Mirror*. "But Broadway isn't America, and it's doubtful if all his excellent work on the New York stage would ever have made him matter much to the rest of the country. And then, an accident, an innocent mistake, a blunder . . . And everybody in the country knew who he was.

"Overnight."

Fate. Everything was fate.

The days leading up to a Broadway premiere were always make-or-break for Orson. They were a time for final adjustments and improvements. That was true of many Broadway shows, but especially of Mercury productions. Could Orson have worked some crucial eleventh-hour magic to save *Danton's Death*? We'll never know. The "War of the Worlds" maelstrom took over. Three days after the broadcast, on the day of the opening that would seal the Mercury's fate, he and Houseman were still unsure if they would be jailed, sued, or fired by CBS.

The critics and columnists covering theater in New York, who were all loyal to print, saw the "War of the Worlds" controversy as another episode in a fractious year for the Mercury, after the summer of rumored discontent, the changing of the guard among the actors, the widely reported crises causing the postponement of *Too Much Johnson*, and the months-long problems and delays plaguing *Danton's Death*. The broadcast and panic enlarged the bull's-eye that had hung on the boy wonder's back since the Voodoo *Macbeth*.

At the end of the November 2 premiere, the huge elevator contraption rose to its highest level above the stage floor, the guillotine blade emerged under the gleam of a single bright light, and the blade fell on Danton. The stage went to black, the curtain fell, and the play ended—as dead as Danton.

Reporting their negative verdicts, some critics referred to the broadcast and panic. "Having loosed the Martians upon us," the previously supportive Richard Watts Jr. began in the *New York Herald Tribune*, "Orson Welles and his Mercury Theatre now attempt to turn us over to the blood-letting leaders of the French Revolution." Watts went on to describe the production as mannered, stately, and artificial, and its message as fuzzy. Welles the actor was "merely oratorical" in his role. "For the Mercury," Watts said (a self-fulfilling prediction), "the honeymoon is over."

Some aimed mockery at Orson himself. Beginning his review by joking about the boy wonder's actual age ("Orson is 23 years old. Or is it 22. No, he was 22 last year . . ."), Arthur Pollock of the *Brooklyn Daily Eagle* turned his review into a meditation on onetime prodigies past their prime. "He has grown tired of being spoken of as a slip of a boy, treated as a phenomenon and a prodigy," wrote Pollock. However, Welles remained "a little precious" and *Danton's Death* therefore seemed "the product of a boy playing with blocks, doing stunts with them."

As for *Danton's Death*, Sidney B. Whipple wrote in the *New York World Telegram*, "Its only purpose . . . was to demonstrate the undeniable talent of one man." "Except as a director's holiday," John Mason Brown complained in the *Evening Post*, "it proves a bore." Richard Lockridge in the *New York Sun* said the Mercury production was "all switchboard and no soul."

The left-wing press, already wary of *Danton's Death*, threw the Mercury overboard. "It is dull as ditch water and completely muddled," wrote Ruth McKenney in *New Masses*. "Unless you are a specialist in the French Revolution, which I'm not, it's practically impossible to figure out what all the guillotining is about." She questioned the production design—the elevator platform, the stage holes and dark lighting—saying it all made her as nervous as the actors must have been.

Not all the notices were poor. The play and Orson's direction and performance came in for praise from several noted reviewers, including the usually influential Brooks Atkinson of the *New York Times*. Atkinson declared the production tingling and theatrical, crackling with relevance. Welles had vividly staged the production, while acting his role "with some of the melodramatic solemnity of The Shadow." Atkinson too prefaced his review with a mention of the "War of the Worlds" broadcast, and closed it with a gentle gibe: "Ladies and gentlemen, you have been reading a review of a performance. . . . There is no occasion for harm."

But *Danton's Death* could not turn back the tide of adverse publicity. The play itself was part of the problem ("Actually, it's not a great play, a piece of shit, really," cheerfully admitted leading man Martin Gabel years later, though with "some wonderful things in it"), and the Mercury's customary audience stayed away. "The ticket agencies ignored us," wrote Houseman. "Half of our theatre parties were canceled." The partners held on by their fingernails for a few weeks, their finances in free fall, until the final dagger was plunged—by one of Orson's idols.

After one performance, the legendary Max Reinhardt came backstage to make the rounds of people he knew, including Vladimir Sokoloff, who had played Robespierre in his 1927 production. Slowly,

Reinhardt made his way over to the director, forty years his junior. Before his idol, Welles felt acutely aware of the Mercury production's shortcomings, and of his own limitations as an actor.

"You are the best *Schauspieler* in America," Reinhardt told Welles.* "You must do the great parts."

A wonderful compliment—but only for his acting. "Nothing about the production," Orson told Jaglom. "All he could do was tell me what a great actor I was."

"So he didn't like the production," Jaglom remarked.

"Of course not. Couldn't blame him."

The partners closed *Danton's Death* on November 19 after just twenty-one performances. Budgeted at $10,000, the production cost close to $50,000, Andrea Janet Nouryeh estimated. Two weeks later, after glumly talking it over, Welles and Houseman announced that the Mercury would lease its building and stage to other producers. The partners still intended to coproduce *Five Kings* with the Theatre Guild after the New Year, planning rehearsals to start in mid-December. A new Marc Blitzstein musical was also possible, and "that harum scarum production *Too Much Johnson*," as the *New York Times* reported reassuringly, "has already been rehearsed and can be put on the stage very quickly when the auguries are propitious." For now, though, the auguries were dismal.

Yet, in typical fashion, Orson managed quickly to shift gears. He, Virginia, and baby Christopher left for a monthlong stay on the Todd School campus. Barbara Leaming wrote that Welles was "exhausted and depressed, his personal and professional life [a] shambles," although this assessment came from Roger Hill—not Welles, who relished the chance to get away from the defeat and recharge. He could please Virginia, who wanted to spend Thanksgiving in Wheaton with her family. He could find solitude on the Todd School grounds while working on the script for *Five Kings*. He could see his friend Ashton Stevens and hear Stevens's advice. He would see his guardian and wrangle with the bank overseeing his trust fund.

---

* *Schauspieler* is German for "actor."

And each week he could head to Chicago and fly back to New York for the radio show.

The *Mercury Theater on the Air* was in the doghouse at CBS for several weeks after the "War of the Worlds" controversy. But the curse was lifted after an advertising agency representative, Ward Wheelock, approached Welles and Houseman on behalf of the Campbell soup company, with an offer to take over the series and sponsor it commercially, as a promising venue for advertising. The company wanted to rename the series *The Campbell Playhouse.* The program would stay on CBS but move to Fridays, with a prime one-hour slot at 9 P.M. The partners would still control the series creatively, but under new strictures. In return for "big money" for salaries and productions, the sponsors wanted to reorient the radio show toward popular plays and novels, with guest stars from Broadway and Hollywood. The new budget would accommodate the rights to the stage hits and current best sellers that had previously been beyond the reach of the *Mercury Theatre on the Air.*

Wearing their "most conservative suits and stiff collars," according to Houseman, he and Welles visited Campbell's New Jersey headquarters, touring the plant and lunching with company officials in the executive dining room, where the partners "smacked their lips over the thin, briny liquid of which we were about to become the champions."

America's greatest *Schauspieler* charmed the soup sellers, flattering their product and telling them, according to Frank Brady's account, "This is a great big chance for me and a great big challenge. With my faith in radio and your display of confidence in me by becoming the sponsor we can possibly create something important. Let's hope nobody's mistaken."

Orson declared radio to be "the best storyteller there is," and when someone in the room referred to a radio script as similar to a stage play, Welles hastened to correct the remark. "It's not a play," he said. "It's a story. Radio broadcasting is different from motion pictures and the theater and I'd like to keep it that way. The illusion I'd like to create is the illusion of the story." (A version of this exchange would be incorporated into his patter for the first new broadcast.)

The deal with Campbell, which was consummated and announced

before *Danton's Death* had closed officially, tempered the demoralizing effect of the stage debacle—and opened a new channel of revenue for the strapped Mercury operation. Orson alone stood to rake in "approximately $1,500" weekly, Brady wrote, "depending on other fees and expenses."

The *Mercury Theatre on the Air* continued on the air for only one month after the "War of the Worlds" episode. While Orson oversaw planning for the new *Campbell Playhouse*, he also hosted and starred in the final shows of the original series. Among them, on the Sunday after the broadcast and panic, was a program offering selections from both Joseph Conrad's *Heart of Darkness* and Orson's "especially funny and unbuttoned" turn (in Frank Brady's words) as the patriarch in Clarence Day's *Life with Father*. This was followed by "three first-class works": another take on Charles Dickens, *The Pickwick Papers*; another Booth Tarkington, his 1919 stage hit *Clarence*, which had starred Alfred Lunt; and the last show on December 4, a powerful treatment of the Pulitzer Prize–winning *The Bridge of San Luis Rey* by Thornton Wilder, Orson's early champion.

The *Campbell Playhouse* was launched five days later, on December 9. With the enhanced budget now available to him, Orson scored a coup by arranging for the first dramatization of Daphne du Maurier's thriller *Rebecca*, a best seller then in its ninth printing. (Producer David O. Selznick had just purchased the screen rights.) Margaret Sullavan, whose performance in *Three Comrades* would be nominated for an Oscar in 1938, flew from Hollywood to play the nameless wife of Maxim de Winter, who is haunted by the death of his first wife, Rebecca. Orson took the plane from Chicago to host the show and play de Winter.

The sponsor's announcer for the renamed series introduced Orson as "the white hope of the American stage," a young man who "writes his own radio scripts and directs them, and makes them live and breathe with the warmth of his genius," and whose "magical" life story "combines the best features of Baron von Munchausen and Alice in Wonderland." There was more such hyperbole, of the sort that both Houseman and Simon Callow would disapprove of in their later accounts of Welles's career. In truth, Orson didn't mind.

The show itself was excellent, with Orson broodingly romantic as de Winter and Sullavan touching as his fearful second wife. Mildred

Natwick was the sinister Mrs. Danvers, the housekeeper fanatically loyal to the dead wife, and other Mercury players acquitted themselves well in supporting parts. In addition to joining in the soup advertisements, Orson bantered with Sullavan at the end of the drama; brief interviews like those in Cecil B. DeMille's *Lux Radio Theatre* were a new feature of the show. Then, via transatlantic shortwave, Welles and Sullavan conversed with du Maurier live from England, where the author had stayed up till three o'clock in the morning to listen in.

The Campbell Playhouse was off and running—fast. "A good start," the *New York Times* radio columnist wrote, if "marred by too many commercial interruptions." A few months later, when Louis Reid reviewed the first months of weekly broadcasts in the high-toned *Saturday Review of Literature*, he hailed "the fabulous Orson Welles" as "a radio dramatic talent of an unusually high order" who had raised the intelligence quotient for "the armchair audience."

Orson never made so much money having so much fun. At this low point of the Mercury Theatre, and many other times in years ahead, radio paid untold dividends, and not only financially. Years later, during a long discussion of screen acting ("You shouldn't play *to* the camera at all," Orson insisted), Peter Bogdanovich asked Welles how he rated radio as an acting medium.

"I was happy in it, Peter," Welles responded quickly and unambiguously, "the happiest I've ever been as an actor. It's so . . . what do I want to say, impersonal? No, *private.*

"It's as close as you can get, and still get paid for it, to the great private joy of singing in the bathtub. The microphone's a friend, you know. The camera's a critic."

John Houseman did not share his partner's happiness. In his memoir, he complained that after the premiere of *The Campbell Playhouse* the grunt work was left to him, director Paul Stewart, writer Howard Koch, and "a flock of slaves and piece workers," while Orson gave orders, took bows, and then flew back to the Midwest to toil away mysteriously on *Five Kings.*

CHAPTER 16

December 1938–July 1939

"I Had a Lot of Fun"

Five Kings was fated to be the great white whale that Orson chased across miles and years. From its first incarnation at the Todd School, through the ill-fated Mercury Theatre production of 1939 and several makeshift stage and radio versions, climaxing with his 1966 film *Chimes at Midnight*—"perhaps the greatest adaptation of Shakespeare that the cinema has yet produced," in the words of scholar Dudley Andrew—Orson, like Ahab, pursued his Moby Dick obsessively.

Between his flights back and forth to New York, he camped out at the Todd School in early December, working on his script and staging plans for the marathon Shakespeare production. With the New Year fast approaching, the Theatre Guild's agreement with the Mercury Theatre, which stipulated the dates for out-of-town tryouts before a Broadway opening in the latter half of the 1938–1939 season, dictated full speed.

Welles returned to New York in time for the December 23 radio show, "A Christmas Carol," in which he played both Tiny Tim and Ebenezer Scrooge. Lionel Barrymore had traditionally performed the holiday classic on radio for Christmas Day, and Orson had announced during the "Rebecca" broadcast that Barrymore would play Scrooge for *The Campbell Playhouse* this year. But Barrymore, fighting an illness, dropped out of the broadcast, giving Orson his blessing to go ahead without him. Orson would give the eminent actor another chance the next Christmas.

Orson presented radio adaptations of Dickens's stories as often as those of any author. And while he was generally averse to sentimentality in his plays and films, he loved the Christmas spirit and would produce many Christmas broadcasts over the years. He and the Mercury players offered a "Christmas Carol" of great warmth and atmosphere, featuring Joseph Cotten as Fred, Scrooge's nephew and only living relative; and Virginia Welles as Belle, the lost love of Scrooge's past.

For the final show of 1938, Orson joined Katharine Hepburn in a December 30 broadcast version of Ernest Hemingway's World War I novel *A Farewell to Arms*. (Perhaps Hemingway wasn't so horrified by Welles after all.)

In the week between "A Christmas Carol" and "A Farewell to Arms," Orson used the ballroom of the Claridge Hotel on Times Square to finalize the casting of *Five Kings*.

Back in June, Orson had chosen a Mercury Theatre newcomer, Burgess Meredith, to play the young Prince Hal, who would become King Henry V. After making his debut in Eva Le Gallienne's 1930 production of *Romeo and Juliet*, Meredith had become one of Broadway's most admired young actors. He and Orson were friendly whenever their paths crossed. In late spring, just as Meredith was about to sail abroad after a painful divorce, Orson wined and dined him to discuss the lead in *Five Kings*. Orson was "one of the most persuasive and entertaining males I ever knew," Meredith recalled. Welles brought him to Sneden's Landing and set him up with "a lovely French girl who made me forget my marital troubles," Meredith remembered, and even hired a five-man Harlem band to serenade him as he boarded his ship for Paris. The contract Meredith signed gave him top billing and a paycheck above Orson's—a reported $1,000 weekly.

Almost as good a catch was the tall, dashing John Emery, who agreed to portray Hotspur, Prince Hal's rival. Otherwise known (unfairly) as "Tallulah Bankhead's husband," Emery came from a distinguished English theatrical family who had graced the stage since the early eighteenth century. Gifted with a lustrous voice, Emery had played several significant Shakespearean roles, including Laertes to John Gielgud's Hamlet on Broadway in 1936. Both Emery and Burgess Meredith had also figured prominently in the 1935 revival of *The Barretts of Wimpole Street* starring Katharine Cornell.

Welles also ranged outside the established Mercury ensemble for other principal characters. As Henry IV, he cast Morris Ankrum, whose Illinois background gave him a foot in the door with Orson. Welles fondly remembered Ankrum, a veteran of Broadway and Hollywood Westerns, from the road show of *The Green Goddess*, a thriller he'd seen in Chicago as a boy in the fall of 1922. An actress and playwright, Margaret Curtis, was engaged to portray Princess Catherine, the French consort of Henry V. Robert Speaight, a longtime poetry recitalist and a Shakepearean with a powerful voice, had created the role of Archbishop Thomas Becket in T. S. Eliot's celebrated verse drama *Murder in the Cathedral*; Orson gave him the important role of the Chorus in *Five Kings*, a part that would combine the plays' narrative prologues with selections from Holinshed's *Chronicles of England, Scotland, and Ireland* to knit the play's sections together.

Gus Schilling, one of the burlesque comedians Orson palled around with, was brought on board to play Prince Hal's friend from his wild youth, the former soldier, thief, and coward Bardolph. Orson also found a role for "Mrs. Schilling," though some doubt that she and Schilling were married: a stripper usually billed as "The Ball of Fire," her name was Betty Rowland, and she would play the knife-wielding prostitute Doll Tearsheet, one of Falstaff's companions at the Boar's Head Tavern.

Orson cast Mercury players Edgar Barrier as the Archbishop of Canterbury, Guy Kingsley as Gloucester, Eustace Wyatt as Northumberland, Erskine Sanford as the Lord Chief Justice, and William Mowry Jr. as the King of France. Stage and radio regulars George Duthie, Frank Readick, Francis Carpenter, Edgerton Paul, John Berry, William Herz, William Alland, Richard Wilson, and Richard Baer helped fill out the sizable cast.

"All of a sudden, the Mercury Theatre has come to life," the *New York Times* reported excitedly on December 29, 1938. After *Five Kings*, the Mercury partners told the press, both *Too Much Johnson* and the rumored new Marc Blitzstein musical were in the hopper.

By this time, the casting was nearly complete, and after the New Year Orson launched the first read-throughs and rehearsals. The Welles family moved into an apartment on Fifty-Seventh Street, near the East River, and Orson let his beard grow for Falstaff. Boston would host the first out-of-town performance, but the marathon Shakespeare play would touch down in several other cities before its scheduled February opening on Broadway—a tight deadline set months earlier by John Houseman and the Theatre Guild, which sold advance tickets to subscribers.

Welles returned from his sabbatical in Woodstock with a vision for staging *Five Kings* on a huge revolving platform that would occupy almost the entire stage, shifting scenes and actors from castle to tavern to battlefield without blackouts or interruptions. "Again," Jean Rosenthal wrote, "Orson was startlingly lucid about what he wanted and how it should look." James Morcom, who had worked on the abortive *Too Much Johnson*, was handed the daunting task of the scenic design. Rosenthal would supervise the lighting and technical effects. Millia Davenport returned for the costuming, codpieces and all. Back in the spring, Virgil Thomson had been hired to compose music for *Five Kings*, but he had given up waiting for a script and left for Paris. The assignment was handed to Aaron Copland, who knew Orson from *The Second Hurricane*. For $1,000 plus royalties—which he would never see—Copland wrote incidental music for voices and chamber ensemble (including a Hammond organ), enhancing the production's "period flavor" by drawing on "English and French folk songs, traditional sacred music, and [Guillame] Dufay and [Jean-Baptiste] Lully," according to Copland's biographer Howard Pollack.

The deal Houseman had struck with the Theatre Guild gave the Mercury creative autonomy and a $30,000 investment from the Guild in what the producer had projected as the $40,000 budget needed for *Five Kings*. As Houseman conceded in his memoir, however, he had bluffed about the budget ceiling and, at the time of the deal, he had no idea of the production's scope.

"The two things they kept asking me were how long the performance would run—to which I had no answer—and how we expected to produce a hundred thousand dollar show for forty thousand dollars," Houseman remembered. "Since my estimate was based on the wildest of guesses, I could only reply that the Mercury had its own way of doing things."

Moreover, the rehearsals began when the Mercury was "without a cent in the bank and still owing money on *Danton*," according to House-man. The Guild demanded a good faith deposit toward the Mercury's $10,000 share of staging costs, and Houseman had to extract "several thousand dollars" from a loyal stockholder. Never a gifted fund-raiser, Houseman was now a weary one. Too long had he stood in Orson's shadow. While the producer described his behind-the-scenes manipulation of funds as "ingenious and tricky," this was the last money he managed to magic.

The sets had to be constructed in available space, while Orson rehearsed his magnum opus in "various empty stages" the Guild rented on behalf of the Mercury, in Houseman's words. The director ranted and raged over the accommodations. ("Not without reason," recalled Houseman. "For if ever a play needed ideal physical conditions to rehearse in, this was it.") Once the rehearsals were under way, and the carpenters went to work on the set, the clock started ticking. Everything had to go according to schedule because the money spigot was turned on for materials and salaries.

Orson did not like being confined by schedules, and he always resisted being pinned down on his rounds. Fridays were inviolate—they belonged to the *Campbell* radio show—but he vanished at other times, forcing the company to wait for him before starting rehearsals, or to carry on under the direction of subordinates. In the second week of January, for example, Orson flew to Chicago for a Monday lecture at Orchestra Hall for Northwestern University, a lucrative engagement that would help defray the costs of *Five Kings*. He also appeared at several benefits for charities and liberal causes, emceeing at an auction of rare books to benefit writers and artists exiled from fascist nations (donating to the auction his director's copy of the "War of the Worlds" script, inscribed with doodles of Martians). Houseman often was the last to know Orson's whereabouts, and in his memoir the producer complains vociferously about Welles's extracurricular activities but never mentions Orson's busy schedule of public events in the first half of 1939.

The *Five Kings* rehearsals, which again the producer attended only fitfully ("I was made to feel uneasy and unwelcome"), were "undisciplined and desultory from the start," Houseman wrote decades later. He heard "increasingly disturbing" reports from people—"Houseman people"—about their progress.

"Some came from the directors of the Theatre Guild," Houseman remembered. "Orson had announced that he did not want them at rehearsal; when either of them defied this interdiction, a bottle of scotch, especially kept for that purpose, was produced and Orson would call a break and entertain the cast with jokes and anecdotes until he or she had withdrawn."

Orson did enjoy telling stories at the beginning of the rehearsals, or during a break, to enliven the company's mood and establish his control over the proceedings. By Houseman's account, he was such a "prolific raconteur" that he often delayed rehearsals with long whoppers about himself and his boyhood, and "fantasies that were invented on the spot out of sheer exuberance or to cover up some particularly outrageous piece of behavior." One time, Houseman wrote, Welles arrived "more than two hours late" for a rehearsal, wearing an extravagant dinner jacket, and regaled everyone with the yarn of his hair's-breadth escape from "a celebrated gangster" whose wife he had romanced in Harlem, before fleeing his lover with the gangster "and his torpedoes in hot pursuit." Two of Orson's "slaves" had to be deputized to guard the building, Houseman added.

Houseman had begun to view Orson as a "Champagne Charley," given to behavior of "growing wildness" and "conspicuous extravagance." His every meal was "a feast," Houseman remembered, "his consumption of alcohol between one and two bottles of whisky or brandy a night; for his new apartment, which had a living room the size of a skating rink, he acquired furniture so huge that it had to be hoisted by a crane through the double windows; his sexual prowess, which he was inclined to report in full statistical detail, was also, apparently, immense."

Houseman thought the challenge of *Five Kings* intimidated Welles. It presented the specter of "*Danton* all over again," the Mercury producer wrote, "and with a lot more alcohol . . . he seemed unable to organize either his material or himself," adding pointedly, "This time I was of little help to him."

With growing jealousy and resentment, Houseman had read Russell Maloney's extensive profile of Welles in the October 8, 1938, issue of the *New Yorker*, part of the avalanche of publicity that preceded the opening of *Danton's Death*. The *Time* cover story on Orson had referred politely to Houseman as running the "business end" of the Mercury; now the *New Yorker* described Orson as the "inspiration" behind the company. Houseman had his own artistic aspirations, and he was frustrated by this public portrait of Orson as the artistic wellspring and himself as the Mercury's business mind—when he knew better than anyone else that the business side of the company was a mess.

The *New Yorker* profile was one of the first lengthy features to dwell on Orson's boyhood, with passages about his father, characterized as "one of the oddest souls ever to come out of the Middle West." Full of rewritten publicity language and Dr. Bernstein's hand-me-down tales ("[Dick Welles] invented one of the first automobiles in America, but never bothered about patents because the thing seemed impractical," wrote Maloney), the profile depicted Orson as a boy in thrall to his father, "vicariously" sampling the "wine, women and song" of Europe, the Far East and "Dixon, Illinois," where the article inaccurately located the Hotel Sheffield. The profile reinforced Houseman's sense that Orson behaved so extravagantly because his father's example haunted him, and that Orson was subconsciously compelled to imitate his father's path to self-destruction.

"Much of what he had accomplished so precociously had been done out of a furious need to prove himself in the eyes of a man who was no longer there to see it," Houseman wrote years later. "Now that success had come, in quantities and of a kind that his father had never dreamed of, this conflict, far from being assuaged, seemed to grow more intense and consuming." Simon Callow took this idea a step further, saying that it took "no trained psychologist to recognize the figure of Richard Head Welles" in the character Orson chose to play in *Five Kings*: Falstaff, famous as "a drunkard, a trickster, a braggart, a womanizer." Charles Higham claimed that Orson's womanizing was one key reason he "seemed to have lost control" during the rehearsals for *Five Kings*, his many affairs "further dissipating his energies."

In *Rosebud: The Story of Orson Welles*, David Thomson praised Houseman for "concentrating on the radio shows so that Welles could do *Five Kings*," and claimed that Welles "was going on memory of the plays alone. He had little notion of the dramatic properties of the text he had adapted himself." And his absences didn't help: according to Callow, Orson "simply stayed away for a great deal of the allocated five weeks" of rehearsal, employing one of his slaves, Richard Baer, as a stand-in while he sneaked away with Burgess Meredith, the two rascals "roaring their way through the night in various dives and various arms." "There was no script," wrote Callow. "There had been no read-through; no one had seen the complete adaptation, for the good reason that there wasn't one."

If there was madness in Orson's behavior, there was also method.

There is no end to the negatives in the accounts by Houseman, Callow, and others—and yet, somehow, despite Orson's supposed dissipation, and the alleged lack of a workable script, the *Five Kings* company made it to the Colonial Theatre in Boston in February. All of Orson's tall tales; his late-night carousing; and his bonding, like Falstaff, with his chosen Prince Hal—these may also have been clever bits of strategy, a kind of Method approach to directing.

Once in Boston, Orson carried on with the rehearsals in lobbies and cellars while waiting for the crew to install the massive rotating scenery onstage: "towering" and "impressionistic rather than realistic," in the words of one Boston correspondent, "built of plain, unpainted boards, roughly nailed together." The complicated lighting had to be hung and tested ("perhaps the biggest power plant ever installed on a theatre stage," reported the *Boston Globe*). The array of dangerous props included huge mortars, real gunpowder, and flaming arrows.

With such ambitious staging came the inevitable problems. The rotating stage platform was supposed to move as the actors marched around the stage alongside it, revealing the next setting. But the platform was as troublesome as the huge elevator in *Danton's Death*: it rotated ponderously, when it turned at all, and when they tried accelerating it, the apparatus had a nasty habit of throwing itself into reverse, hurling off chunks of scenery that landed in the orchestra pit. The front rows were blanketed with noxious smoke and gunpowder fumes during the fight scenes; the flaming arrows went astray, threatening to cause a blaze. After rehearsing for long, stressful hours with the actors, Orson sent them home to bed, then worked even later hours with the crew trying to solve one technical foul-up after another.

When the cast joined the scenery onstage—with the actors still uncertain, and the sets and the props still misbehaving—the production seemed hopelessly unwieldy and chaotic. But a *Boston Globe* reporter who watched hours of the rehearsals came away with no doubt as to who would win the war of wills. "Orson Welles," read the headline of the Sunday feature, "Is an Amazing Personality, with Limitless Energy, Startling Audacity, Bombast, Patience, and Humor."

After three days of nonstop rehearsals, however, Welles decided it was best to postpone the much-ballyhooed opening. "I explained to Orson, as I had frequently over the past month," Houseman recalled, "that we were now involved in the commercial big time with the Theatre Guild subscription involving tens of thousands of people and specific theatre bookings." Welles swore at Houseman ("in that moment I was his father and every other enemy he had ever known"), then tore a phone off a nearby wall and threw it at him. "Such scenes," Houseman wrote later, "took place almost daily during the final agony of *Five Kings.*"

While every scene had been rehearsed, the company still had yet to run through the entire script of *Five Kings* continuously from start to finish. (The *Richards*, originally intended to be produced simultaneously for a two-night show, had long since been deferred.) Several days before the scheduled February 27 premiere, Orson launched the first public preview. The stage platform groaned into action, then ground to a halt. Orson had to commandeer several dozen Harvard students, who had been invited to fill the preview seats, to rush "to the cellar and push the stage around by hand," as Burgess Meredith recalled. Supplied with beer to keep them happy, the students did a sometimes too enthusiastic job, with the unfortunate effect that "the loudest voices in the house" were coming not from the stage, as Meredith remembered, but from the cellar, shouting "Push! Pull! Forward! Halt!" The run-through went on for several hours, with interruptions for mishaps and miscues and lighting and technical fixes. The same thing happened when Theresa Helburn, a Theatre Guild official, attended another *Five Kings* rehearsal before the premiere, smiling patiently through the "first few hours." The set "was impressive," Houseman wrote, "and the transitions looked as though it might work." At 3 A.M., though, they had still not gotten to the closing lines.

Orson loved impossibilities. He never lost hope. He counted on luck and genius—of all sorts. "How'd we get ourselves into this frigging nightmare?" Burgess Meredith asked his director on the night of the official Boston opening. "Don't worry," replied Welles, as he calmly donned his suit of rubber padding, gray wig, beard enhancements, greasy rags, and heeled boots to play the elderly man-mountain Sir John Falstaff. "There is a thing called theater magic—it's here—wait and see! Now take this pill. It's potent. It's called Benzedrine."

The curtain ascended for *Five Kings*. Apart from being lowered twice for brief intermissions, it stayed aloft for four and a half hours—until thirty minutes past midnight. Props went amok; actors bumped into scenery while searching in vain for their spotlights. But little of what went wrong onstage mattered to "a crowded audience, representative of the city's highest culture in play patronage," as the *Boston Globe* reported, which "was present and followed with courteous, if not always rapt attention." Led by actress Gertrude Lawrence and her troupe, on a night off from their *Susan and God* tour, the audience offered "tremendous" applause and a dozen ovations ending with Orson's "brief speech of grateful acknowledgment."

The *New York Times* closely followed the out-of-town tryout, reporting a "mixed" reaction among Boston reviewers. The *Times* cited one prominent local critic who found the marathon Bard ponderous and dull. But the city's two most important newspapers—the *Globe* and the *Herald*—championed *Five Kings*. "Stupendous," "singularly novel," "comprehensive and satisfying," declared the *Globe*. "Most impressive and ambitious," "long and spectacular," "splendid," and "brilliantly colored," Elinor Hughes wrote in the *Boston Herald*, although she admitted that "the length of the play forced us to depart after the second intermission."

The huge revolving set was impressive if cumbersome. ("Like Ol' Man River," wrote John K. Hutchens in the *Boston Evening Transcript*, "it threatens to engulf the show as it 'still keeps rolling along.'") The battle scenes—with cannons firing, arrows flying, broadswords and chain mail clashing in hand-to-hand struggle—were believable to the point of being frightening. All of it was wondrously enhanced, as the *Globe* reviewer wrote, by the production's "amazing" lighting canopy.

Many cast members were singled out for commendation—including Welles, whose performance, as usual jelling at the eleventh hour, was hailed by the critics as the acting highlight of *Five Kings*. His meticulous makeup was "marvelously amusing and effective," the *Globe's* reviewer commented. "It seems incredible that so young a man could give so robust and mature a performance," wrote the *Herald*. "He misses neither the slyness, the grossness, nor the good fellowship, yet in his downfall his unstressed pathos is most moving."

One of Shakespeare's favorite characters—he appears in three plays—Falstaff was also one of Orson's. Shakespeare describes Falstaff as fat, arrogant, and cowardly, but the character is also comic and wise. "He is almost entirely a good man," Welles told British television interviewer Leslie Megahey several decades later. "He is a gloriously life-affirming good man." Although he himself was only twenty-three, Orson foresaw the wreck of old age and good intentions gone wrong in such a gloriously life-affirming man. He played Falstaff's key scene, after Prince Hal ascends the throne, for sublime tragedy. Falstaff intends to exploit their friendship for privileges, but Prince Hal, now King Henry, rebukes him in front of his friends with a long, humiliating recitation of his bad habits. "I know thee not, old man!" the King declares, before leaving Falstaff alone onstage with Shallow, Pistol, and Bardolph.

In that moment, as Falstaff is forced to save face with lies, Orson turned toward the audience and stammered proudly through tears: "Well, he's just saying that now . . ." Actor Martin Gabel, who attended the Boston premiere of *Five Kings*, said: "Not Henry Irving, not Beerbohm Tree, not anybody could have done this scene as effectively as Welles did it." The same humiliation scene, in Welles's later film *Chimes at Midnight*, is the highlight of that Shakespearean masterwork, and arguably also of Welles's screen acting career.

Yet even its staunchest admirers allowed that the marathon production needed cutting and refinement. And within days of the premiere, Boston newspapers were reporting that Welles had "materially shortened the performance and it now ends at a reasonable hour. Scenes that were not of vital importance to the continuity of this condensation of Shakespeare's *King Henry IV*, parts one and two, and *King Henry V*, have been eliminated, and the changing of the amazing settings has been speeded up."

The changes would continue throughout the thronged two-week

run in Boston, but neither Houseman nor the Theatre Guild team would be heartened by Welles's public declaration, made to the *Boston Herald* and recycled in the *New York Times*, that it would take "at least a year" on the road before *Five Kings* could be presented on Broadway the way he wished to present it—with the *Richards* lagging far, far behind.

During the Boston run, Virginia Welles visited the Colonial Theater for two nights. John Houseman called the trip "a strange, sad attempt to recapture the past," adding that "on the third morning she left for New York, and in due course, for Reno." But Virginia was in Boston partly to help firm up a plan for "Anna Stafford" and other Mercury players to take over the Bass Rocks Theatre in Gloucester for the summer, much as they had done at Stony Creek the year before. After Boston, moreover, Virginia headed to a getaway with her parents in Palm Beach, Florida, and she would turn up at Orson's side repeatedly in the first half of 1939. His letters to her make it clear that he believed they had reached a truce in their marriage. Reno and divorce did lie ahead, but only after further dramatic developments, and not for another year.

Orson's more pressing relationship troubles involved not Virginia but John Houseman. By this time the Mercury partners were barely on speaking terms, and Houseman's grasp of Orson's doings came from brief sightings, reports, and gossip from the "Houseman people." Houseman had embarked on another declaration of independence, signing a contract with the new American Lyric Theatre to direct the premiere of an opera based on Stephen Vincent Benét's *The Devil and Daniel Webster*. "I did not tell Orson of my decision," wrote Houseman in his memoir, "and when he read about it in the *New York Times* he said nothing about it either."

In his book Houseman dates this "decision," taking on a project that would steal time from the Mercury, to *after* the last performances of *Five Kings* in Philadelphia in April. In fact, the *New York Times* carried news of Houseman's project on March 5, the week of the Boston premiere of *Five Kings*. In the tense days leading up to the premiere, Houseman's announcement that he would be directing another play for a different company could not have sent an encouraging signal about *Five Kings* to the Theatre Guild principals. And it also might have had something to do with that phone-throwing incident.

The partners still met every Friday night for the *Campbell Playhouse* broadcast. The radio season was going smoothly under the steward-ship of Houseman, Paul Stewart, and Howard Koch, using stories and casting approved by Orson. Not every episode boasted an Oscar-nominated costar like Margaret Sullavan (who returned, months after "Rebecca," for "Show Boat"), but the series did feature Helen Hayes in "Arrowsmith" on February 3, Madeleine Carroll in "The Green Goddess" on February 10, and Laurence Olivier and Wallace Beery in "Beau Geste" on March 17. The Mercury Theatre regulars in the revolving cast included, often enough, "Anna Stafford," and perform-ers from the *Five Kings* cast. The emphasis on popular plays and novels continued with stories such as Elmer Rice's "Counsellor at Law" (Jan-uary 6); "Mutiny on the Bounty," with Orson as a convincingly sadis-tic Captain Bligh (January 13); Dashiell Hammett's "The Glass Key" (March 10); and Ben Hecht and Charles MacArthur's "Twentieth Century" (March 24).

By plane, train, or limousine, Welles and Houseman traveled to the weekly radio appointment together—from Boston, then later from Washington and Philadelphia—but their conversations grew increas-ingly uncomfortable, until finally only silence stretched between them.

Another source of irritation for Welles was the English actor Maurice Evans, who toured several weeks behind *Five Kings* in the same cities, performing an uncut *Hamlet* (with Whitford Kane as the gravedigger) and a faithful *Henry IV,* in which Evans also essayed Falstaff, "a part which Orson regarded (as he did every great classical role)," Houseman wrote, "as exclusively his own." Reviewers couldn't resist comparing the two actors' approaches to Shakespeare—the traditional versus the revisionist—along with their takes on Falstaff. After *Five Kings* left town, Elinor Hughes mused in the *Boston Herald* that Welles's Falstaff was "the most striking figure" in his production, and that Orson had succeeded in creating a "Falstaff in decline, old, shabby, a little fearful, looking forward to a dreary old age and trying to feather his nest while he could. He did not rouse much laughter, but he succeeded in evoking pity." Evans's Falstaff, by comparison, was the traditionally "jolly, cheerful old rascal, as full of tricks as of sack, fond of a good joke, a merry companion and a frankly unscrupulous but amusing rogue." Orson's greasy ragtag getup as the fat knight may have attracted more attention, Hughes observed, but Evans's physical transformation and makeup were also "truly astonishing."

The comparisons, while not always unfavorable to Orson, were irksome just the same. Never shy in his opinions, he was known to pillory other Shakespearean actors in interviews and conversations, singling out everyone from Dame Judith Anderson and Margaret Webster (Evans's director) to even, on rare occasions, Laurence Olivier, whom he normally admired. ("The first two scenes" of Olivier's *King Lear* for the BBC, Welles told Henry Jaglom during their talks, "are the worst things I ever saw in my life, bar none.") And Evans was one of his recurring targets. "Almost any bum can get a crack at Boris [Godunov] or Lear," Welles told Peter Bogdanovich. "Sometimes the bums even make it with the public. Look at Maurice Evans. He took on practically everything in Shakespeare, the critics raved, and the people packed in to see him."

"And he was bad?" asked Bogdanovich.

"Worse!" Welles roared back. "He was poor."

But Orson was fascinated by Evans's undisputed success with critics and crowds. As late as January 1940, when he was developing *Citizen Kane* in Hollywood, he sneaked off to Evans's sold-out Los Angeles opening of *Hamlet*, leaving the theater after the performance shaking his head in disgust and wondering how the old smoothie got away with it.

By the time *Five Kings* arrived at the National Theater in Washington, D.C., for dates during the second week of March, there were still technical jams and delays on some nights, including the opening night. But ticket sales were brisk, and the ovations continued. Welles had chopped forty minutes from the play in Boston, and even Houseman admitted that "a dramatic form had begun to appear." The reviews were as good as could be expected, considering that certain critics still pined for more orthodox Shakespeare and a merry old Falstaff.

But the production had been woefully underbudgeted from the

outset: it took ten boxcars just to transport the scenery and equipment from city to city, and in Boston the overtime expenses for the stagehands and performers had taken the Mercury already more than $20,000 over the original total estimate of bringing *Five Kings* from the road to Broadway. The undue costs included a $1,400 bill for damages from the Ritz-Carlton Hotel, after Welles threw a party, ostensibly in honor of the straitlaced Robert Speaight, complete with burlesque entertainers and—though the extent of the destruction varies wildly from account to account—furniture tossed out a twelfth-story window.

Theatre Guild officials held Houseman "personally responsible" for the steep production costs, which augured a mounting financial disaster, and they insisted that the Mercury pay its share of the overages. ("In their mouths," Houseman wrote pointedly, " 'genius' had become a dirty word.") Although Orson announced his plans to tune up the show further in Pittsburgh, Detroit, and Chicago before bringing it to Broadway, the Guild agreed to pay the production's bills only through Philadelphia before reassessing its involvement. The Guild insisted that Orson's all-night overtime rehearsals must cease. When Houseman protested that his partner was "incapable of working by day," the Guild responded that if he wanted to work at night Orson could pay the extra expenses out of his own pocket. "Which he did," Houseman noted drily, "during the next ten days, to the tune of several thousand dollars, borrowed against his future radio earnings."

The standoff with the Guild reached the ears of the press. "Guild officials have been burning for weeks," *Variety* noted. "Theatre Guild and Welles May Phfft, It's Reported," read the headline in the *Washington Daily News*. The *New York Times* reported more sedately that the Guild was "unwilling to meet additional expenses incurred by carting around a cumbersome production on the road and other charges resulting from whipping a show into shape." The press painted a grim picture of opposing camps inside an embattled production, with "certain members of the *Five Kings* company growing more allergic to twenty-three-year-old director Orson Welles every day," according to the *Washington Daily News*. "Backstage ruffs are constantly being raised when Welles turns what the actors call 'prima donna,' and they growl that while insisting on long rehearsals he offers little constructive advice." The other camp, including many Mercury loyalists who would go on to work with Welles repeatedly in years to come, saw their leader as a valiant artist willing to expend all the goodwill and capital at his command in order to fulfill his impossible quest.

He was a maddening egotist to some, but a likable hero to others. "Enormously likeable," recalled Burgess Meredith. "He laughed uproariously and constantly and made you laugh with him. And he was an appreciative listener." And, regardless of their feelings about Orson himself, most in the company felt that *Five Kings* had finally begun to hum and click by the time the company left Washington, D.C., for Philadelphia.

But the production met its match in Philadelphia's Chestnut Theater, ill-suited in every way to Orson's vision. It wasn't just the fact that the actors had to use dressing rooms in "an adjacent theatre, taking a bridge to get them back," in Callow's words—an exercise that did little for the company's morale. It was something worse, which Orson could not have foreseen, though perhaps John Houseman or Jean Rosenthal should have: inexplicably, no one had scouted the theater carefully enough to learn that its stage was raked—tilted—precluding the use of the Mercury's massive revolving platform. Before the show could go on, the stage had to be made level, at considerable added effort and cost, with the entire rotating platform shoved upstage (away from the audience) to adjust for sight lines and the fire curtain.

And not until they arrived at the Chestnut did the stage managers learn for the first time that, "for technical reasons which I never even tried to understand," in Houseman's words, the electric current in Philadelphia was "incompatible with the wretched little motor that drove our turntable." The Philadelphia opening had to be postponed for at least a day while the backstage team corrected the pitch of the stage and desperately sought expert advice for the electrical conversion.

Orson was apoplectic. For the Theatre Guild, which was still footing the bill, this glitch in the proceedings was the last straw. The Guild demanded that *Five Kings* go on at the Chestnut according to schedule, even if it meant having the actors themselves rotate the scenery.

Was there ever a nobler folly than the opening night of *Five Kings* in Philadelphia? When the electric converter failed to arrive in time,

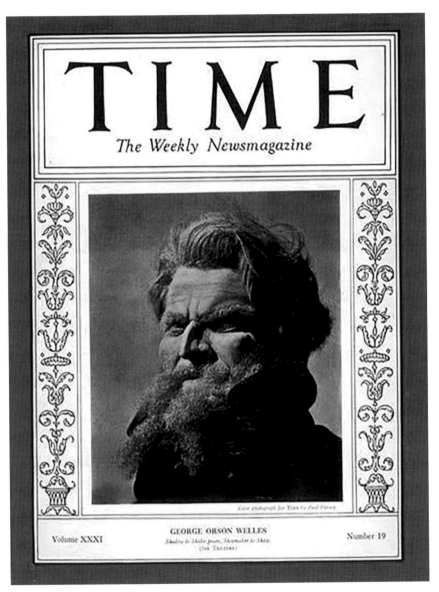

Orson made the cover of *Time* magazine on May 9, 1938, at the age of twenty-three—in an era when that distinction signaled the arrival of true celebrity (though the profile was relegated to the magazine's theater section).

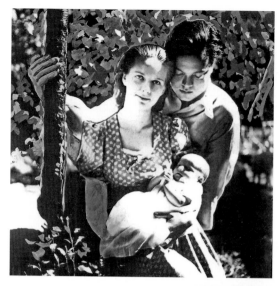

A (retouched) family
publicity photograph
with new baby
Christopher, born
in 1938. By now, the
relationship between the
little girl's parents was
deeply strained.

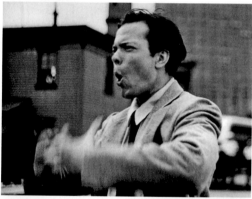

The surviving segments of
the never-completed *Too
Much Johnson* reveal Orson's
filmmaking savvy and his
slapstick soul. FROM TOP: the
ebullient director; Mercury
partner John Houseman,
rapidly fading in importance
at the Mercury, as a Keystone
Cop; and Joseph Cotten in a
Harold Lloyd–type scene.

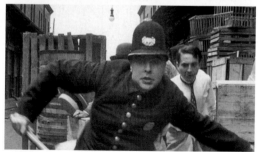

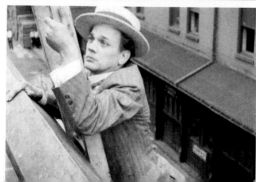

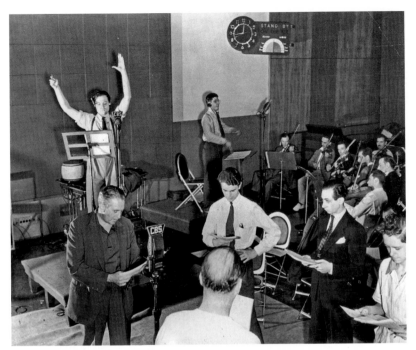

Orson, arms upraised, during the *War of the Worlds* broadcast. Composer Bernard Herrmann conducts the orchestra at right; actor Ray Collins is in the foreground near microphone. The clock says 9 P.M.: the broadcast is nearly over. The next morning, Welles explained himself to a gaggle of reporters.

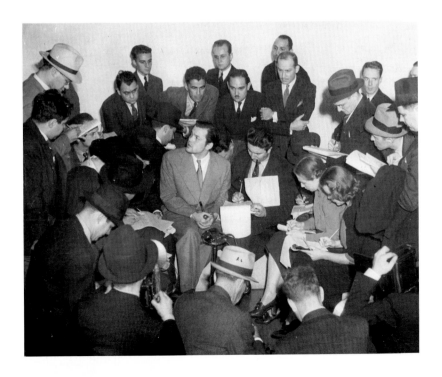

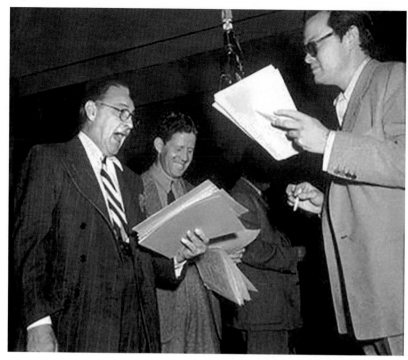

With the legendary actor John Barrymore (LEFT), whom he went out of his way to befriend, on Rudy Vallée's radio show. Barrymore died the following year.

Orson (LEFT) relished his brief vaudeville stint hamming it up in *The Green Goddess*.

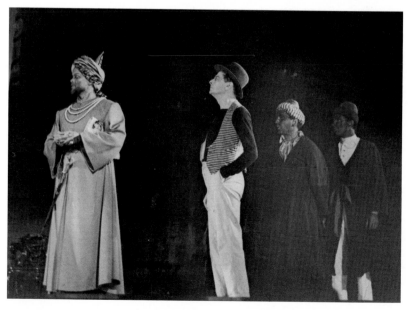

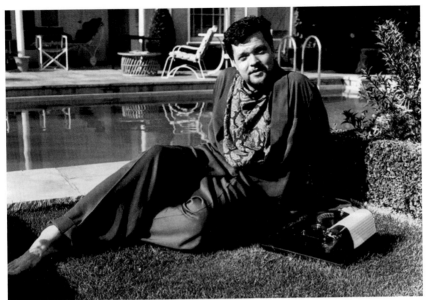

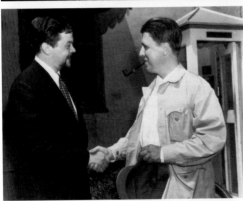

Poolside with typewriter
at his Brentwood
mansion, sporting his
notorious beard.

Despite the sniping of the
gossip columnists, Orson
was warmly welcomed to
Hollywood by old-guard
filmmakers, including RKO
director George Stevens (*with
pipe*), the nephew of Orson's old
friend Ashton Stevens. Ashton
later visited the set of *Citizen
Kane* with his wife,
Florence (FloFlo).

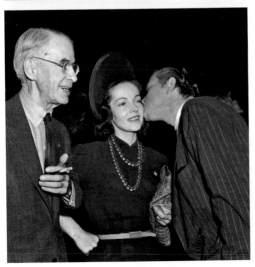

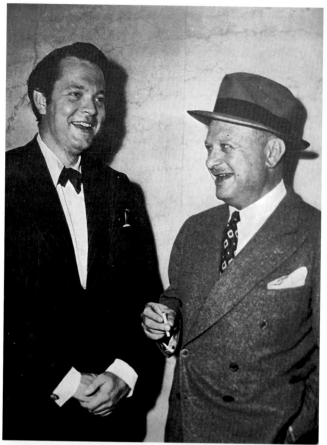

A rare photograph of Welles with screenwriter Herman Mankiewicz. To Welles, the cowriter of *Citizen Kane* was "a great, monumental, self-destructing machine" whom he loved and admired.

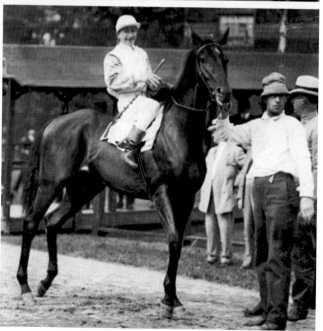

Old Rosebud, the Kentucky Derby–winning horse of 1914, was the inspiration for the mysterious mantra of *Citizen Kane*.

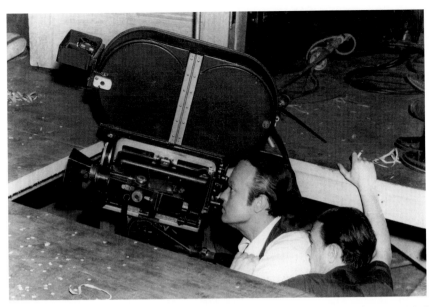

Welles with fellow Illinoisian Gregg Toland, whose work on *Citizen Kane* humbled the director and elevated the film. Welles made the rare gesture of sharing his directorial credit card with the cinematographer.

The director and Toland cavorting with the female extras in the "Georgie's" brothel scene, deleted by censors before *Kane*'s final cut.

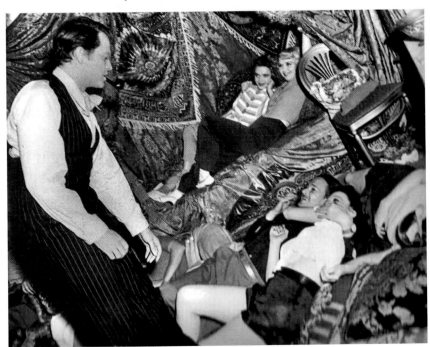

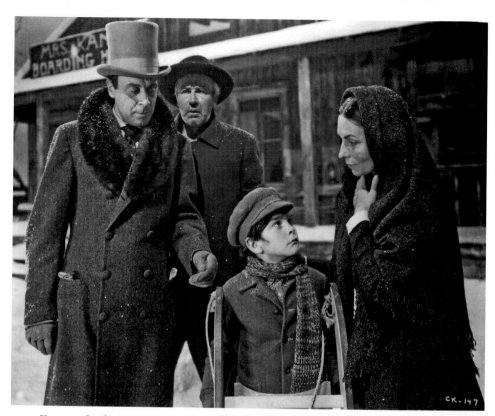

Kane was built, in part, around the stories of two mothers. The first was the boy's mother, Mary Kane, played by Agnes Moorehead (ABOVE RIGHT), whom young Orson met less than a year after the death of his own mother. Her unforgettable scene, in the film's deep backstory, also featured the banker Walter Parks Thatcher (George Coulouris), Kane Sr. (Harry Shannon), and Kane as a boy (Buddy Swan).

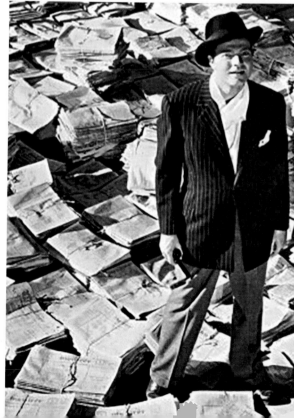

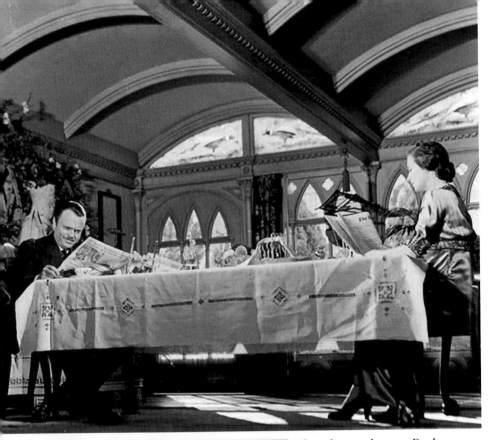

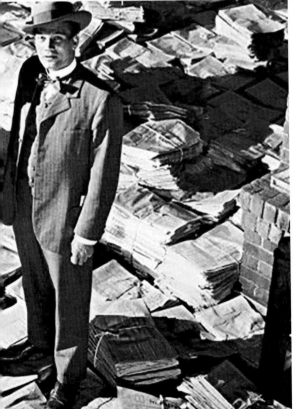

The other mother was Ruth Warrick, whose son Charles Kane Jr. is also ill-fated in the story. Warrick is seen here in *Kane*'s famous breakfast-table sequence, an idea indebted to a Thornton Wilder play that Orson saw in Chicago as a youth.

Joseph Cotten, for whom the part of Jed Leland was closely tailored, was the brother Orson wished he had. They were chuckling companions long before *Citizen Kane*, and remained so until the end of Orson's life.

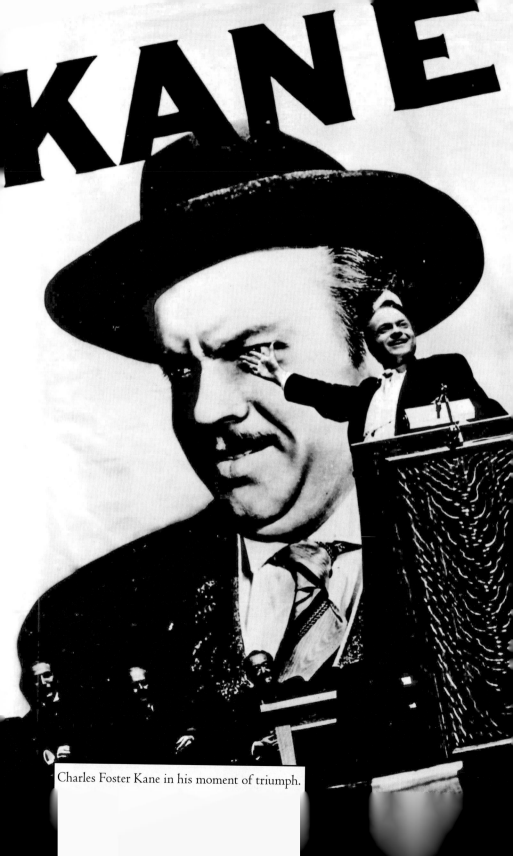

Charles Foster Kane in his moment of triumph.

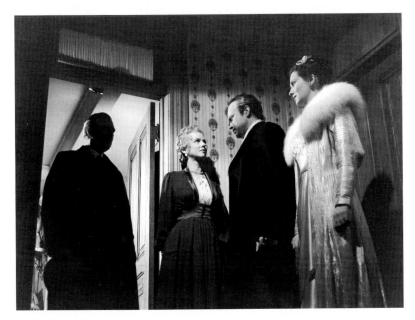

The "love nest" confrontation scene, a pivotal moment in the story, brought together four important characters: (FROM LEFT) Boss Gettys (Ray Collins), Susan Alexander (Dorothy Comingore), Kane (Welles), and Emily (Ruth Warrick).

Dorothy Comingore was the true leading lady of *Citizen Kane*. Here Susan Alexander Kane makes her dismal opera debut—one of the film's most magnificent concoctions.

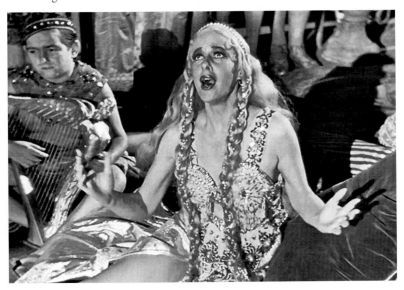

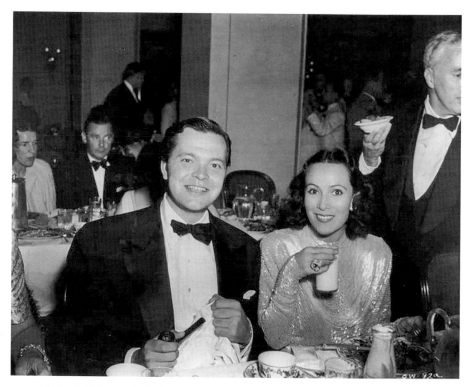

Nightclubbing with Dolores Del Rio, the actress who became his girlfriend.

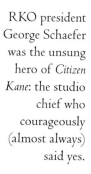
RKO president
George Schaefer
was the unsung
hero of *Citizen
Kane*: the studio
chief who
courageously
(almost always)
said yes.
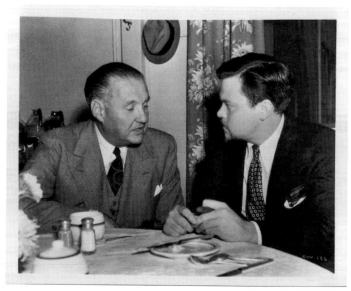

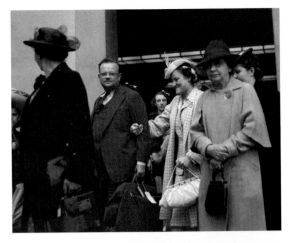

Richard I. Welles, Orson's older brother, returning from Reno and his marriage to Mildred Bill in 1941. When photographers confronted him at the airport, Richard demanded their plates. "Welles grasped the camera and a tug-of-war ensued before amused spectators," reported the *Los Angeles Times*. "The photographer won."

After *Citizen Kane*, Orson would go on to direct *The Magnificent Ambersons* for RKO. Although the picture was truncated by the studio, students of film prize Welles's adaptation of Booth Tarkington's novel, starring his Mercury family of players. (Welles even found a place for brother Richard as a carpenter on the set.)

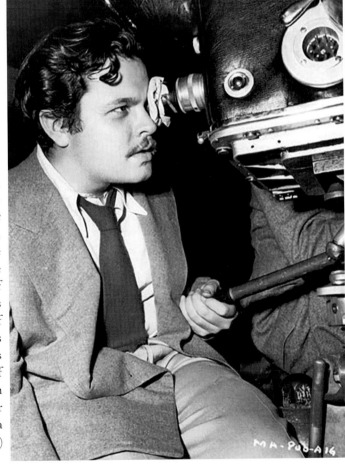

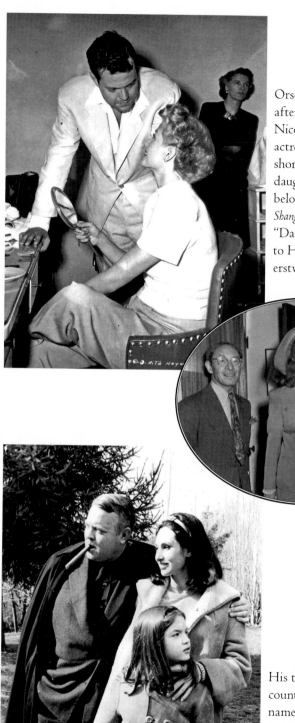

Orson married twice more after his divorce from Virginia Nicolson. His marriage to actress Rita Hayworth was short-lived, though it yielded a daughter, Rebecca, and one film beloved by fans: *The Lady from Shanghai*. BELOW: The couple with "Dadda" Bernstein, who moved to Hollywood to be closer to his erstwhile ward.

His third wife was an Italian countess who acted under the name Paola Mori, playing a lead in *Mr. Arkadin*. They vacationed in Spain with their daughter, Beatrice, in the early 1960s.

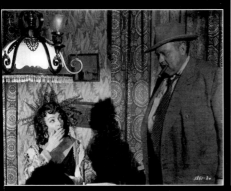

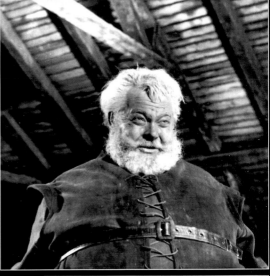

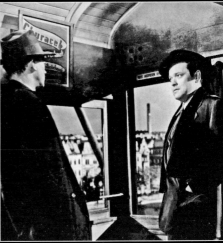

SCENES FROM A LIFE ON CAMERA:
With Marlene Dietrich in *Touch of Evil*; as
Falstaff in *Chimes at Midnight*; with Joseph
Cotten in *The Third Man*; with Oja Kodar
in *F for Fake*; on the last day of his life
(BELOW), reminiscing with talk-show
host Merv Griffin.

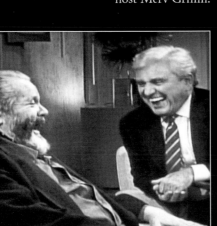

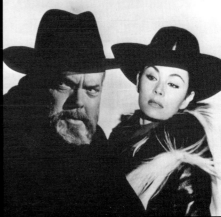

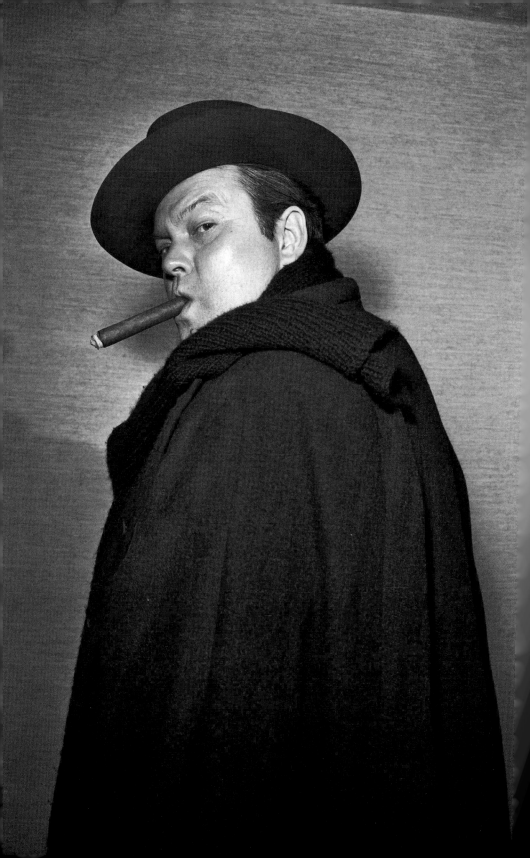

the actors stepped in, hand-cranking the iron windlass, torturously turning the stage, with Orson lashing them on like grunting sailors crowded into a rowboat amid a terrible storm, struggling to align their oars as their vessel crashed through waves toward the great white whale, always just out of sight ahead.

"As a stage colossus," J. H. Keen wrote in the *Philadelphia Daily News*, *Five Kings* "is something to gape at as one might a prehistoric creature brought back to life. But as an entertainment, it has something to be desired." In the *Bulletin*, Robert E. P. Sensenderfer described the production as "a gigantic Shakespeare vaudeville" performed "without particular inspiration." Edwin H. Schloss in the *Record* found the drama strident, the comedy overly juicy, and—the unkindest cut of all—Orson's Falstaff inferior to that of Maurice Evans.

The best notices came from a few New York scribes who descended on Philadelphia for what might be their last chance to witness the audacious Shakespeare production. "The Welles flair for spectacle" was intact, cheered the loyal Herbert Drake in the *New York Herald Tribune*. "The battle scenes are the best I ever saw on any stage." Ashton Stevens and Maurice Bernstein traveled together to Philadelphia and told Orson he had done his finest work. But the handwriting was on the wall: even before the reviews hit the newsstands, the Theatre Guild organization had quietly withdrawn its backing.

Orson was almost relieved. He had felt from the start that the Guild was too tasteful for the Mercury Theatre. And he was a true believer who always took the long view. Waiving his salary for the Philadelphia run, he got "up at dawn," Houseman wrote, "rehearsing all day, replacing actors, pouring in his radio money, trimming and vitalizing *Five Kings*" with Broadway still in mind. Before the company broke for Easter, Welles threw another shindig for cast and crew, reassuring everyone that *Five Kings* would go back on the road and arrive in New York before summer. He would find the money somewhere, somehow.

After the play closed in Philadelphia, Orson rushed to New York to knock on the doors of supportive, well-heeled friends. After hearing Welles sketch his air castles past midnight one night, Tallulah Bankhead—the wife of cast member John Emery—brought him to see her neighbor Marc Connelly, a playwright and director who had loved *Horse Eats Hat*. Connelly was sympathetic, but neither he nor Bankhead had the deep pockets—or nerve—to bail out such a problematic production. "It's [Welles's] optimism I remember most," Connelly recalled. "He fully expected somebody to come up with twenty five thousand dollars in cash at that hour of the morning."

Looking for a savior, Orson chatted up at least one restaurateur whose establishment he could be counted on to frequent in years to come. According to Frank Brady, Marc Connelly phoned Sherman Billingsley, the proprietor of the Stork Club, and the three of them—Orson, Bankhead, and Connelly—"coaxed and wheedled him and cajoled" him "until dawn broke over Manhattan." But the effort was futile: "even Orson's promise to turn over his inheritance from his father failed to convince Billingsley to invest in Shakespeare." Barbara Leaming wrote that the young Toots Shor offered Orson "several thousand dollars" he'd been saving in hopes of starting his own place one day. "As desperate as he was, Orson turned down his friend. Shor would not have been able to open his famous New York restaurant had Orson accepted." Whatever the case, Orson failed to find a wealthy New Yorker to make the kind of investment he needed. "In this desperate attempt to salvage *Five Kings* he received no help from me," wrote Houseman, now busy with rehearsals for *The Devil and Daniel Webster.*

Stage manager Walter Ash had stayed behind in Philadelphia, watching over the scenery, costumes, and equipment until he received word of where to ship the stuff. On April 5 Welles telegraphed a pitiful surrender:

DEAR WALTER WE HAVE MORE MONEY TROUBLES THAN WE DREAMT STOP THERE IS NO LONGER ANY CHOICE FOR US FIVE KINGS CANNOT COME IN THIS SPRING OF COURSE IT MUST THIS AUTUMN STOP TERRIBLY SORRY NOT TO HAVE BETTER NEWS AND NOT TO HAVE BEEN DEFINITE BEFORE NOW STOP PLEASE UNDERSTAND AND COME BACK TO US AND THANKS WALTER FOR EVERYTHING

ALL MY LOVE ORSON.

All the production material was addressed to a New York warehouse—"seventeen tons" of it, according to Houseman. The storage charges would accumulate for the next twenty-plus years.

Welles was emotionally and physically drained. For the first time, during the *Five Kings* tour, the press had begun to remark on his drawn appearance and weight gain. In Washington, D.C., a newspaperman described him as "puffy," and when Orson stepped off the train in Charleston, South Carolina, alone on Easter Sunday morning, a local reporter described him as "portly." When he paid an emergency visit to a doctor in New York, on the Saturday before Easter, he was told that he needed a break from the grueling work and pressures, and that "if he didn't take an immediate vacation of a few days, soon he would be forced to take one for a couple of years."

With his wife, Virginia, in a hospital recovering from a routine procedure (or so Orson's letters suggest), Welles followed his doctor's orders and headed south. His Sneden's Landing friends Ben Hecht and Charles MacArthur often stayed at the elegant Villa Margherita in Charleston, where the writers had established a tradition of retreating for inspiration when they were stuck in the middle of a script. MacArthur and his wife, Helen Hayes, had just returned from a Jamaican vacation and were now spending the Easter weekend there before heading home to New York. In a letter to Virginia, Orson said he thought the celebrated actress, his onetime neighbor and a frequent guest on his radio shows, "looks better than I've ever seen her," adding that it "makes me think how much my lovely wife needs and deserves the sun."

"There were two trains coming south," Welles told the local press, "one of them to Charleston. I got that one, because Charleston is the most beautiful city in America." He remembered Charleston fondly from the Cornell tour three years before. "The people are different [here]," Orson said. "The first thing I did when I arrived here was to go to church. During the day I went to five parties. That isn't the way to rest, is it?"

Initially at the train station, Orson was taken aback by the newsmen waiting for him and by their stream of questions about the "War of the Worlds" broadcast, which had taken place months before and was ancient history to him. "If your questions are to be about that, the interview will have to end now," he snapped. ("He almost shuddered when the Martian invasion drama was mentioned," one reporter observed.) Softening later, Orson met with the same newsmen. The local press saw him as a radio celebrity and was principally interested in "War of the Worlds"; he didn't have to field a single question about *Five Kings*. Orson explained that nothing he could say could dispel people's impression of the controversial broadcast and the ensuing panic, which had surprised him as much as anyone. "Anything I say will render me flippant in the minds of other people," he said.

On the Monday following Easter, Welles said, he had "rented a book" and headed to the Middleton Place, a plantation with famous landscaped gardens, "to read and to rest. Tomorrow I am going to get another book and go to another garden." He lunched more than once with Charlie MacArthur, who got Orson excited about his plans for a script telling the story of Gavrilo Princip, the young Bosnian assassin whose killing of Archduke Ferdinand triggered World War I. As they sat drinking mint juleps and brainstorming, MacArthur told Orson that the story could make either a play or, perhaps better, a film. With encouragement from Orson, MacArthur promised to start writing.

"It's all pleasing but not restful," Orson admitted in a letter to his wife. He attended the Dock Street Theater production of *The Beaux' Stratagem* and, accompanied by Atlanta attorney Henry A. Newman, another guest at the Villa, paid courtesy calls on local civic figures and personalities in the arts. "I know all this visiting sounds unlike me," he wrote to Virginia. "I guess a vacation ought to make you feel as much unlike yourself as possible." He addressed all his letters to "Dearest," and invariably closed with "I love you." In the letters he sounds genuinely warm toward Virginia: "I miss you," he wrote. "Please don't be blue in the hospital—and please get well sooner than you're supposed to."

On the Thursday following Easter, after several days of solitude to ponder the future, Orson flew back to New York.

With John Houseman busy on the Stephen Vincent Benét opera, Orson was alone in trying to salvage the future of *Five Kings*. He still needed to raise an extraordinary amount of money, but that wasn't his only challenge: he also had to fight a rearguard action against nervous actors being tempted by job offers promising more stability and reliable pay.

Burgess Meredith, for one, was flooded with offers from other producers; he had spoken informally with Guthrie McClintic and Katharine Cornell about joining one of their planned late spring productions. For Welles, this was a double blow: Meredith was both a friend and an example to the other cast members. Orson begged Meredith to give him a little more time to dig up some money. John Emery, too, was worried enough that he began making inquiries to other producers. Besides Welles himself, Meredith and Emery were the production's only real drawing cards. And how could *Five Kings* go on without its Prince Hal and Hotspur?

Orson announced that the show's New York opening would have to be postponed—but only until the fall. He would not shave his beard, he vowed, until he played Falstaff on Broadway.

That was more than bluster. Welles intended to deplete his own trust fund to keep the show alive on the road in tryouts. Until now, he had enjoyed only limited access to his trust fund—he hardly even knew how much money it contained—but Orson had convinced himself that the bank would advance him a loan on the principal. But he still needed Dr. Maurice Bernstein's cooperation, and his guardian was skeptical. Orson resolved to fly to Chicago to reassure Bernstein and then meet with the bankers. His powers of persuasion would carry the day.

Before he left New York, however, Orson agreed to make a screen test for RKO.

The studio was planning a remake of *The Hunchback of Notre Dame*, and officials were tempted by the idea of having Orson play the title role. Hollywood had grown more persistent, and earlier in the year, Welles had said no unequivocally when producer Sam Goldwyn dangled the part of Hindley, the enemy of Heathcliff, in *Wuthering Heights*. The reason he declined, reportedly, was that he also wanted to write and direct the picture—but the direction was already in the capable hands of William Wyler, and Hindley was hardly a leading role. Orson was still ambivalent about Hollywood. He still saw himself, first and foremost, as a man of the theater.

Victor Hugo's Hunchback was tantalizing, however. One of Orson's idols, Lon Chaney, had played the role magnificently in the silent era, and the part would appeal to any actor who relished makeup and metamorphosis. This time, the *New York Times* reported, "Welles has indicated that he may be willing to settle for less" than a writing and directing deal.

Of all the studios, RKO had become his most stubborn Hollywood suitor. The company's new president, George J. Schaefer, had started out before World War I as secretary to the film pioneer Lewis J. Selznick, who was the father of agent Myron Selznick and producer David O. Selznick. Schaefer had risen through the sales and management ranks of Paramount in the first half of the 1930s, during which time he had paved the way for Ben Hecht and Charles MacArthur to establish their own autonomous production unit on the Paramount lot. Schaefer had permitted the team to write and direct a series of quirky comedies that no other studio would have dared to bankroll. MacArthur spoke highly of Schaefer as a man who stuck to his word.

Schaefer specialized in marketing difficult and artistic films. He prided himself on familiarity with smaller theater chains, on knowing, for example, the difference between audiences that could be expected to attend one theater in Boston, and those at another theater across town. After a few years at United Artists, where he expanded the company's relationships with independent producers, Schaefer had assumed the leadership of the struggling RKO in October 1938. He was moving aggressively to attract new talent, giving top directors such as Howard Hawks and John Ford leeway on pet projects, hoping their films would raise the studio's profile artistically and commercially. His first meeting with Orson was probably in April in New York, when Schaefer was back east to testify routinely in front of a U.S. Senate subcommittee. Welles, to his own surprise, liked Schaefer in person: he was a pure businessman, like Orson's father, and a man's man who loved sailing, like Roger Hill. Schaefer liked Welles, too, and—after receiving encouraging memos from RKO's New York staff—took a personal interest in recruiting him. He watched Orson's screen test for *The Hunchback of Notre Dame* with interest.

The impasse with *Five Kings* had softened Orson's resistance to Hollywood. But he also had been gravitating toward a cinematic style for some time. He had been using blackouts and onstage curtains to minimize the time between scene shifts. The revolving platform of *Five*

Kings, as critic Nelson B. Bell wrote in the *Washington Post*, was a type of "motion picture technique," bringing mobility to the settings and characters "in such a way that the effect is one of continuous action and dialogue with a revolutionary blending of scenes." The revolving stage also reminded the *Philadelphia News* critic J. H. Keen of "an old-time motion picture." The actors in *Five Kings* noticed the same cinematic quality: "The battle of Agincourt was staged like a long dolly shot, the set turning full circle and thirty or forty extras running in full heat, cannons booming, smoke billowing, trumpets blaring," Burgess Meredith wrote in his memoir *So Far, So Good*.

In April 1938, however, *Five Kings* was still Orson's top priority, and after the screen test he rushed to the First National Bank in Chicago, where he made an impassioned pitch for a loan against the inheritance he stood to receive at age twenty-five. The money would go to alleviate the crippling debt the Mercury owed to its cast, crew, and suppliers, which Andrea Janet Nouryeh estimated at $36,000 in outstanding bills for *Danton's Death* and *Five Kings*, plus $2,000 still outstanding from the Mercury's first season. Dr. Bernstein was also in the room, having agreed in advance not to oppose Orson. The bankers listened politely.

During the meeting, the telephone rang: Hollywood calling. (The call was relayed from Dr. Bernstein's office, according to Bernstein, who later reported the incident to the *Chicago Tribune*.) An RKO representative was on the line with another offer, raising the ante. "Well, $250,000 is a lot of money, but I can't consider it," Welles said as the bankers listened, "No there's no use your flying here. I'm definitely not interested in the movies." Not yet.

The bank would consent to a loan, but only $10,000. Orson grabbed at it, though he knew it wouldn't be enough to save *Five Kings*. He quietly passed the word to people in New York, and soon his cast moved on. John Emery stepped into the role of Heathcliff in the new Broadway production of *Wuthering Heights*. Burgess Meredith accepted a screen offer that would take him to Hollywood throughout the fall. It was hard to imagine *Five Kings* without him.

Orson blamed everyone for the demise of *Five Kings*, especially himself, but he took Meredith's abandonment personally. Years later, running into him after a long silence between them, Orson wheeled on him accusingly. "Do you know why we closed that show? The only reason?" Meredith said, "No. Why?" Welles told him, "Because you quit, you ran out."

"I felt physically and mentally unable to go on," Meredith wrote in his memoir. "Very little went right in that production. For years I relived it in my nightmares. Orson had too many responsibilities. . . . You can blame Orson only in the sense that he should have demanded the kind of help he needed. The confusion threw us all—befogged everyone who was in it. We will always remember it as a towering drama that almost came to pass, but that finally turned into a nightmare. It was a brilliant concept of a great man, but the mechanical problems were never solved. None of us came up to the vision."

Orson's twenty-fourth birthday was just around the corner in the spring of 1939. Chastened by his setbacks, he had no impulse to celebrate, but neither did he care to leave Chicago, apart from flying back to New York every Friday for *The Campbell Playhouse*. He had many reasons to linger in Chicago: he had friends there, and favorite bookstores and restaurants and magic shops. He could roam through the Art Institute. Chicago gave him solace.

Welles repaid a favor to Gertrude Lawrence, conspicuously attending her new road production of *Skylark* in the last week of April, and leading the standing ovations that welcomed her to the Harris Theatre downtown. *Skylark* was one of Samson Raphaelson's hit plays, and the Roger Hills happily accompanied Orson and Virginia to the opening.

The road company of *I Married an Angel* had been playing in Chicago since early March, and Orson also led the applause for Vera Zorina in the last weeks of its acclaimed run. John Houseman interpreted one of Welles's visits to Chicago as an excuse to spend a night with "the ballerina," but in fact Zorina was happily ensconced in a suite at the Ambassador East with her new husband, George Balanchine. The couple greeted Orson as a friend: he always sincerely praised Zorina's performances, and she always listened sympathetically to his heartaches.

Recovered from her operation, Virginia spent most of May and June in Chicago; she and Orson socialized with her parents and made excursions to Woodstock, staying on the Todd School campus. Virginia, like Houseman, was still suspicious of Zorina, but nowadays Orson behaved sweetly and attentively to his wife whenever they were together, and she accepted his reassurance that he and Zorina were merely friends.

Despite his setbacks, Orson did not seem especially downhearted. "Like any genius he must have had his share of demons but he handled them well," Burgess Meredith mused in his memoir. "I never heard a word of despair from Orson." Instead, he quietly threw himself into a personal crusade that was as important to him, in its way, as *Five Kings*. He intended to save John Barrymore.

Shuttling to New York for the radio show, Orson heard from a friend, the bedridden dramaturg Edward Sheldon, that Barrymore was behaving erratically in a road show of the comedy *My Dear Children*, in which he parodied himself as a ham actor who is also a great lover. Part of the in-joke was that Barrymore's fourth wife, Elaine Barrie, was playing one of his three insubordinate daughters. (Indeed, his character literally spanked Barrie at one point in the play.) But after Barrymore consistently disrupted performances with missed lines and antics, his wife withdrew after the Saint Louis engagement, announcing she was going to file for divorce. Otto Preminger, who was directing the Broadway tryout, hastily rehearsed a new actress in her part for the next city on the tour, Chicago, where *My Dear Children* was due to open on May 8.

Barrymore was drinking more heavily than usual, and Sheldon feared that the great actor was at death's door. Hurrying back to Chicago, Welles rushed to the Ambassador East, where Barrymore's older siblings, Lionel and Ethel, were waiting for their miscreant brother. They had come to Chicago after hearing the same news. Orson knew all three of the fabled Barrymores, having dined with Ethel at Ravinia, acted with Lionel on the radio, and accompanied his father to meet the legendary John backstage in various Shakespeare productions. With his encyclopedic knowledge of theater, Orson had an almost scholarly knowledge of the Barrymore family tree, and loved talking about the Barrymores as exemplars: their real family name (Blythe); their American father, Maurice Barrymore ("an aristocrat"); and their maternal grandmother, Mrs. Drew ("the greatest actress-manager in America before the days of Fanny Kemble").

With Orson taking the lead, the three rescuers scoured the South Side in search of the youngest Barrymore, only to find him "pie-eyed in a cathouse," in Orson's words, though quite alive. "He wasn't dying at all—of course he *was* dying, but he wasn't dying any *more* than he was any other day." With the siblings reunited, "there followed a great warm weekend," after which the rescuers entered into a rehabilitation pact, taking turns sitting in the front row at *My Dear Children* for the next few weeks, reminding the black sheep of his obligations.

When Orson spoke of John Barrymore in later years, he grew misty-eyed about their bond. "He was so generous to a young theater man like myself, and so kindly and so gentlemanly and so warm," he told Barbara Leaming. "He was such a good man!" In terms that echoed the stumbles of his own career, his own mixed legacy as an actor, and the lowbrow turns of his later career—touting California wine, off-brand bourbon, and English peas in TV commercials whose scripts he berated—Orson insisted on Barrymore's courage and greatness as an actor.

Barrymore's habitual drunkenness at the end of his life was a masquerade, according to Welles. The celebrated actor feared he was losing his mental faculties, and Orson believed that Barrymore may have suffered from what would later become known as Alzheimer's disease. Barrymore worried that he was following in the steps of his actor-father, Maurice, also a hell-raiser, whose death was preceded by a mental breakdown when he was onstage with his nineteen-year-old son John. Welles was convinced that Barrymore exaggerated his drunkenness to get through "terrible" plays like *My Dear Children*, in which he was portraying "an over-emoting Shakespearean actor, past his prime and debt-ridden. It was a painful self-parody," in Welles's words. But Barrymore worked "as a man of honor because he owed debts," and always performed as best he could under the circumstances. "He knew he was prostituting himself and that everybody he cared about was ashamed of him, but he managed to play it as though it were a great lark, and to bring the audience into it as though they were at a party. A great performance, really."

Barrymore repaid Orson's devotion with mutual admiration. Once, discussing acting with Peter Bogdanovich, Welles described how Barrymore pulled himself together during an otherwise banal B movie to give a wonderful recital of Hamlet's most famous soliloquy. The picture's director gushed compliments after the take, saluting Barrymore as "the greatest actor in the world." Barrymore supposedly snorted his reponse: "There are only two great actors—Charles Chaplin and Orson Welles." Although "I've never felt any sort of secure pride in that department," Welles continued, he prized that compliment above any other he ever received.

Bogdanovich then asked if Welles believed he was "as great an actor" as Chaplin.

"We aren't in the same league, Peter," Welles replied. "Or even the same game."

"Are you a greater actor than Barrymore?" Bogdanovich persisted.

"Of course not. In his time and mine, nobody in our language was ever as good as Barrymore . . . or as bad."

He then added this intriguing observation about his own acting talent: "What I really have in common with Jack," Welles went on ruefully, "is a lack of vocation. He himself played the part of an actor because that was the role that he'd been given by life. He didn't love acting. Neither do I. We both loved the theater, though. I know I hold it, as he did, in awe and respect. A vocation has to do with the simple pleasure that you have in doing your job. Charlie [Chaplin] was a happier actor because he was born for it."

Orson had turned twenty-four by May 19, the day of the "Bad Man" episode of *The Campbell Playhouse*, costarring Ida Lupino. He stayed in New York into the following week to announce the official world's fair poem, winner of a nationwide contest, reading the poem to an audience of several hundred at a meeting of the Academy of American Poets in the Federal Building.

Orson had returned to the weekly radio show to find that actor-director Paul Stewart had instituted some modest changes and improvements that helped keep the show running smoothly while the *Five Kings* tryout preoccupied Welles. Welles erupted in anger at Stewart, dismissing him in front of the cast and crew, according to John Houseman, only to appear later outside Stewart's apartment door at 3 A.M., "prostrate with remorse," successfully persuading his old friend and vital associate to return to his job on the program. In later interviews, Orson would sometimes grumble that Stewart exaggerated his contributions to the radio show. But for posterity, Welles described Stewart to Peter Bogdanovich as "a lovely man. For years he was one of the main pillars of our Mercury broadcasts; he can't be given too much credit."

Houseman, who had marched out of the studio in solidarity with Stewart, also returned for the very next broadcast. "Orson and I saw little of each other that spring except on Fridays," Houseman remembered. The two men had not discussed the future of their partnership other than to agree to forfeit their long-term lease on the Mercury Theatre building, for which they had no real concrete plans.

Taking Houseman aside now, Orson said he had been fielding offers from various movie studios, but he was not ready to accede to Hollywood. (In mid-May, his agent, Albert Schneider, rebuffed another offer from RKO's George Schaefer, wiring him that "new developments regarding Welles make it impossible to consider films at this time.") Orson told Houseman he was still counting on his help in bringing *Five Kings* to Broadway early in the fall. The Mercury Theatre associates at Bass Rocks were moving ahead with plans for summer theater in Cape Cod, but without Orson and Virginia's participation. The Mercury would lend its brand name to Bass Rocks, while making it clear that neither of the partners was creatively involved.

When Orson announced what he was planning instead for the summer, Houseman could scarcely believe his ears. Welles had decided to strike out on his own—in vaudeville. The year before, according to Barbara Leaming, Orson had sprung onstage at a Forty-Second Street burlesque house, playing the straight man to a baggy-pants comedian friend, and this spontaneous lark convinced him that there was fun and money to be had on the dying revue circuit. For a while, Welles told Houseman, he'd considered whipping together a solo act as a magician, but Virginia had nudged him in a different direction. He was going to star in a stripped-down, tabloid ("tab") version of William Archer's *The Green Goddess*, an old-fashioned tingler from 1920 that the Mercury had already adapted for radio. *The Green Goddess* was already booked for a string of midwestern theaters and would open in Chicago.

His earnings would depend on the size of the crowds, he told

Houseman, but he planned to recycle the money he made into the Mercury Theatre's fall season. From the Mercury troupe itself, Orson would borrow only his three "slaves"—William Alland, Richard Baer, and Richard Wilson, the last of whom would help launch the vaudeville tour before joining the Bass Rocks summer theater. Although publicity would link the vaudeville act to the Mercury, nothing really was required of Houseman—which was for the best, as Houseman (who was flabbergasted by Orson's plans) had been looking forward to a restful summer.

Whenever Welles and Houseman talked about the future, however, their mutual regard and shared aspirations were renewed. Although Houseman was skeptical, he took the surprising news to the New York press. After opening in Chicago on June 9, Welles would play vaudeville theaters in a condensed version of *The Green Goddess.* "The tour will probably continue on into the summer," reported the *New York Times,* "depending, of course, on the show's reception and the stamina of Mr. Welles."

The show business columnists lapped it up: "Orson Welles Goes into Vaudeville!" Was there any better way to thumb his nose at the New York theater establishment, which still doubted his promises about *Five Kings?* Or to prove he was one of a kind, once and for all?

On Friday, June 2, Orson was back in New York for the last *Campbell Playhouse* of the season: "Victoria Regina," with Helen Hayes reprising her role from the Broadway hit of 1935.

With the *Campbell* series suspended for the summer, Orson was able to appear in other radio programs. Two days after "Victoria Regina," he stepped in for John Barrymore in the romantic comedy "Business Before Pleasure," offered by the *Knickerbocker Playhouse* on WABC. Barrymore, still performing in *My Dear Children,* had fallen off the wagon again, though the official word was that he had been "stricken" with illness.

In more ways than one the shadow of Barrymore hung over the *Green Goddess* tour, right down to the young actress, red-haired Susan Fox, whom Orson cast as the damsel in distress: later Fox would marry a Barrymore on the Drew side of the family tree. If the Great Profile could pay his grocery bills with *My Dear Children*, why shouldn't Orson perform hokum in vaudeville?

Part of the attraction in doing *The Green Goddess* was that, like *Too Much Johnson*, the twenty-minute vaudeville act gave him a chance to employ film footage to supplement the performance. "Using stock footage from a New York film house that had a library of scenes and situations that could easily be spliced into any motion picture, and shooting just a few insert shots himself," according to Frank Brady, who researched this "lost" footage as diligently as that of *Too Much Johnson*, Welles "created a four-minute introduction" to the plot of the play, opening on a map of India and narrowing in on Mount Everest.

"Next," wrote Brady, "the film cuts to an airplane, flying at night, lights ablaze in its windows, in the midst of a terrible lightning storm, and being deluged with torrential rains."

The plane crashes spectacularly. "There was no soundtrack incorporated into the film, but a recording of an airplane motor accompanied by thunder, wind, rain, and then the boom of the airplane crash was to be synchronized with the film and played on the public address system." Again, as with *Too Much Johnson*, when the film footage ended, the "live" show began.

Wearing a bejeweled turban and long flowing robe, coated in dark pancake makeup, Orson would enter after the crash footage. He portrayed the Rajah of Rukh—"a tall, well-built man of forty dressed in the extreme of Eastern gorgeousness," according to the script. Welles had played the same character in the *Campbell Playhouse* broadcast earlier in the year, recalling the performance Morris Ankrum had given in the Chicago road show Orson had enjoyed as a boy.

The plot of *The Green Goddess* concerned the survivors of the plane crash, who are brought before the evil Rajah, the ruler of a remote mythical kingdom. The Rajah takes an unsavory interest in one of the survivors, the beautiful wife (Susan Fox) of a British officer, who is another passenger on the downed plane. While attempting to seduce the beautiful wife, the Rajah threatens to sacrifice the foreigners to the idol of the kingdom, the Green Goddess.

One week after the season's last *Campbell Playhouse* broadcast, Orson's vaudeville act opened at the RKO Palace at Randolph and La Salle.

After "One Man Swing Band" Vic Hyde, the musical comedy duo Arren and Broderick, the acrobatic Variety Gambols, and the precision-dancing Six Grays, Welles took the stage in full regalia: "The Man Who Scared the World and Then Charmed It," as he billed himself. Four or five times a day, Orson and his patchwork troupe performed *The Green Goddess* as a lead-in to the new MGM romantic comedy *Bridal Suite.*

Virginia sat in the front of the theater for the premiere. The next week, she attended a luncheon at the English Speaking Union featuring her husband as guest of honor. Dr. Maurice Bernstein, Ashton Stevens, and the Roger Hills all came to see the show, shaking their heads at Orson's cheek and the show's glitches. John Barrymore stopped by the Palace to pay his respects—and repay his debt to Welles—by leaping onstage for a cameo. "Imagine the two of us, clowning around up there in front of those poor, bewildered little gatherings of people," Welles told Barbara Leaming.

Not everyone was bewildered. A Chicago teenager, who "thought Orson the most fascinating and sexy actor," cut high school classes with friends to sit through the show twice. Rita Myers Gagnon wrote a letter to the *Los Angeles Times* in the days following Welles's death in 1985, reminiscing about the thrill of it. At one point in the drama, Gagnon recalled, Orson was supposed to fire a gun at an enemy standing across the stage. "During the second show, the gun failed to go off," she recalled, "and without losing a beat, Orson dashed across the stage and beat the villain to death with the gun butt." She and her friends were "enthralled."

Since he "disapproved" of the whole embarrassing idea, John Houseman waited until the troupe's very last Chicago performance before making his reluctant pilgrimage from New York. Though the *Green Goddess* cast included professionals with fine credentials (one of them was Stephen Appleby from his own disastrous *Valley Forge*), Houseman remembered only "a troupe consisting of Wilson, Vakhtangov and Baer in pith helmets and plain turbans and a girl whom I had never seen before in white riding breeches. The audience was puzzled and apathetic." After the performance, heading back to the hotel with his partner, Orson stopped the taxi and pointed toward the back entrance of a downtown building. "That's where they brought my father out—feet first," Welles told Houseman.

After Chicago, it was off to sleepy Steubenville, Ohio, for an all-day Sunday gig. Then "Orson Welles and Co." traveled on to the Stanley Theatre in Pittsburgh, where the *Green Goddess* troupe joined a new series of revue acts, including the comic duo Jack Talley and Terry Howard, the dancing Statler Twins, and the Coon Creek Girls (hillbilly singers who had entertained the king and queen of England at the White House). *Captain Fury*, starring Orson's old rival Brian Aherne, was the onscreen attraction at the huge picture palace.

The special filmed opening of *The Green Goddess* made the show almost as much of a wild card on the road as *Five Kings*, and in Pittsburgh, on opening day, "everything—but everything!—happened to Welles" and his vaudeville act, as the trade paper *Variety* amusingly reported.

"First the screen prolog came on upside down with the sound accompaniment blasting the ears of the customers to pieces and even extended for a minute or so into the sketch itself; then the noise effects went haywire when the boys remembered to put them on at all, and finally the stage mikes picked that particular time to go berserk and sound off a series of buzzing blasts right through the dialog.

"Welles stepped out of character at the outset, begged the audience's permission to start all over again. The mike buzzing promptly stopped and then started anew. By this time, Welles and his company had gritted their teeth and decided to go through the motions anyway. Half the lines were lost completely and the others were meaningless. At the conclusion, 'the man who scared the world, then charmed it'—that's his current billing—mopped a furrowed brow and apologized profusely for the fiasco, and a more earnest, gracious apology has never come from the tortured despair of any actor. Welles was plainly sick about it, so much so that he even told the patrons they could get their money back at the box office and that he'd stand personally responsible for the refunds. He meant it, too, but a checkup revealed that not a single return was made, a tribute to Welles's sincerity.

"All in all it was a performance no performer could have possibly ever conjured in the dread of his wildest nightmare." And *Variety* added this grace note: "Welles took the whole thing like a major, had a heart-to-heart talk with the crew after the performance, told the boys it was just one of those things and by the second show everything was going smoothly."

By the end of the week in Pittsburgh, Orson was livening things up by portraying the Rajah as though embodied by different celebrities. Mercury publicist Henry Senber spread news of the feat. "At the first show he was Charles Laughton," according to the *New York Times*, "at the second John Barrymore, Alfred Lunt for third, and Herbert Marshall fourth."

The crowds were thinning out, however, and after "Orson Welles and Co." left Pittsburgh the Stanley dropped variety acts altogether, switching over permanently to film exhibition. The *Green Goddess* tour tapered off somewhere in the Midwest, but Orson never regretted his impulse to join vaudeville during the last whisper of its heyday, wearing the kind of exotic costume and makeup he loved. "Nobody had ever done worse business than I did," Welles boasted inversely to Leaming. "You could shoot deer on the main floors of all the great vaudeville houses of America. But I had a lot of fun. It was great to be a vaudeville headliner even if there was nobody out front."

By July 4, Orson was back in New York, exhausted and exhilarated. He had a few spot radio jobs coming up, but nothing much else, and July and August stretched emptily ahead.

George J. Schaefer, the president of RKO, had not given up. He had been impressed by Orson's *Hunchback of Notre Dame* screen test and by the unfinished footage for *Too Much Johnson*, and he was coming around to the idea of letting the young Broadway mastermind form his own film production unit, where he could produce, direct, write, and star in stories of his own choosing. Little by little, Welles's lawyer, Arnold Weissberger, managed to stoke RKO's interest, so that the deal was becoming irresistible at just the moment in time when Orson was staring ahead at a hole in his summer.

By early July, Schaefer was crafting an acting, writing, directing, and producing deal covering two pictures. Prospectively, Orson would stand to receive $30,000 as an actor and $35,000 as a producer, along with 20 percent of the net profits. The first picture would have to be completed by the end of 1939. For the second picture, to be shot in 1940, he would receive $35,000 for acting and $25,000 for producing, with 25 percent of the net profits.

Although Schaefer discussed possible stories with Welles, he put off any decision on the exact material until after Welles took up offices at RKO in Hollywood. The studio reserved the right to refuse any story, and Orson had an equal right to refuse its suggestions. If no story could be agreed on, Welles's contract would be "annulled." After a story had been approved, however, the contract gave Orson leeway to depart "substantially" from the initial outline as he crafted the final script. Welles agreed to show rushes of his film productions to studio officials, and to confer with the studio on editing, but he was allowed to supervise his own editing of the two films. As always, the studio reserved the right of final cut, but Schaefer assured Orson that he would go to great lengths to back his subject choices and support his final cut.

Schaefer also gave Orson assurances that he could hire John Houseman and other valued members of the Mercury Theatre—both cast and production staff—under his film unit's budget. Orson could draw on his New York circle in casting his pictures, although the studio had to approve all individual hires.

One of the most appealing aspects of the contract was unwritten. In their several meetings, Orson had come to trust Schaefer. Orson had not personally liked David O. Selznick, Samuel Goldwyn, or Louis B. Mayer. But Schaefer was a businessman who was buying an artistic product that he believed he could promote with his expertise into small, niche, and foreign markets. If Schaefer was a nonentity by comparison with the more famous studio moguls, he was a nonentity who was willing to gamble big on Orson.

Welles talked the decision over with Houseman, inviting him to renew their partnership in Hollywood. Houseman had no better prospects; he said yes. "In the excitement of the new contact and the exhilarating prospects of fresh worlds to conquer," wrote Houseman, "the rancors and miseries of recent months were hastily buried in a shallow grave."

Orson had already talked the decision over with his wife, who had long encouraged him to test the Hollywood waters. With no summer plans of her own, Virginia sorely wanted a vacation. Orson had no interest in vacationing. He made a fateful decision, telling Virginia it would be best for her to wait until he established a beachhead in Hollywood before she moved to California with him. His first days would be spent in hotels, and they would be full of haggling. Wherever he went, initially, studio officials, his own retinue, and the press would trail him. Let Orson settle the details of the contract, find a house for the family, and start preparing his first film production. That would take only a few weeks. Then Virginia and one-year-old Christopher could join him.

Meanwhile, he offered to send his wife to Ireland, where Virginia could spend the rest of the summer with Geraldine Fitzgerald and her husband, Edward William Lindsay-Hogg. The nanny could bring Christopher by train to join Orson in California. Orson saw Virginia off at the New York docks on July 15. The wire services carried a photograph of him, in suit, tie, and beard, kissing his smiling wife as she boarded the *Aquitania*. The caption read: "No Act."

He made the rounds of his New York friends, promising to bring Joseph Cotten to Hollywood and into motion pictures as soon as he had firmed things up. They joked about George "Shorty" Chirello, a talkative and diminutive driver they sometimes shared in New York. Who would inherit Shorty if they both moved to California? One of them would have to take Shorty with him. They playfully flipped a coin to decide the matter, with Orson winning.

Two days after Virginia's departure, the news broke in the *New York Times*. Orson Welles, "who for two years spurned" film offers, had "capitulated" to Hollywood. On July 17, he would leave for the West Coast with his "associate," John Houseman. Welles would captain his own production unit at RKO, the item read. "The subject of the [first] film was not disclosed." Although the press announcement, "approved formally by Houseman and Welles," noted that Welles had rejected previous Hollywood offers because they might interfere with his "primary interest in the Mercury Theatre," the announcement "made no mention of *Five Kings*," the newspaper observed. Newsman Herbert Drake had resigned from the drama desk of the *New York Herald Tribune* to serve as Welles's West Coast publicist. Mercury secretary Augusta Weissberger would stay behind in New York, to oversee the company's East Coast business and bookkeeping.

Orson made one final whirlwind stop in Chicago. Roger Hill met him at the Tavern Club, and brought along a lawyer friend whose specialty was tax avoidance; Orson was so taken with the man that he booked him on the flight to Hollywood. The headmaster viewed Hollywood as a golden opportunity. Dr. Maurice Bernstein, whom Orson also saw, was more conflicted about the sudden events; he loved New York: its art, music, theater. He had no feeling for California.

Once Orson made an important decision, however, he didn't waver. "When you don't really want to go to Hollywood—at least this was true in the old days, the golden days of Hollywood—when you don't honestly want to go, then the deals got better and better," Welles reflected many years later. "In my case I didn't want money; I wanted authority. So I asked the impossible, hoping to be left alone; and at the end of a year's negotiations, I got it, simply because there was no real vocation there—my love for films began only when we started work."

Joined by the tax lawyer, John Houseman, and Richard Baer—the youngest and best-educated of the "slaves"—Orson flew out of Chicago on July 18. RKO had booked the Welles contingent into the Town House, a large hotel on Wilshire Boulevard, which was adjacent to Lafayette Park in central Los Angeles. But they found the facility to be "an almost unbearable bit of Evanston," in Orson's words, and quickly the four of them moved into bungalows at the decidedly more raffish Chateau Marmont on Sunset Boulevard.

IV

SEVENTY YEARS
IN A MAN'S LIFE

CHAPTER 17

July–December 1939

"The Greatest Railroad Train a Boy Ever Had"

The week Orson arrived in Los Angeles, President Franklin Delano Roosevelt called for a special emergency session of Congress to deal with the developing war crisis in Europe.

William Wellman's *Beau Geste* was previewed at the Carthay Circle, Frank Capra's *Mr. Smith Goes to Washington* was in the cutting room at Columbia, and Ernst Lubitsch was directing *Ninotchka* at Metro-Goldwyn-Mayer. All three directors had careers stretching back to the silent era. "Need Fresh Pix Directors," read the headline of an article in that week's *Variety*, which began, "New directorial talent today stands as picture industry's most pressing need."

Three days after his arrival, Orson posted his first letter to Virginia ("My Dearest One"), care of Geraldine Fitzgerald and her husband at their country home in County Kildare, Ireland.

"Well, Hollywood turns out to be just exactly like Hollywood," he began chirpily. This was his first Saturday night in Los Angeles, Orson reported, and he was keeping a low profile. "Still incognito," he had spent all his time thus far dealing with "enormous quantities of rigmarole" involving his contract. "Today at lunch I signed," he announced—a tentative pact, to be formalized later. After the weekend, he would pay his first visit to the RKO studio.

"After a good deal of scurrying around the countryside in an open Cadillac," Orson wrote, "I finally found a nice house—not a piece of cheese-cake—very tastily designed and decorated with pool and bathhouse, together with terrific Capehart hook-up throughout, some [Auguste] Rodin drawings, and a Lincoln [automobile] thrown in.* Pretty cheap considering."

The address was 426 N. Rockingham Drive in Brentwood. North of Sunset Boulevard and the University of California, Los Angeles (UCLA), Brentwood was an exclusive preserve, inhabited almost entirely by Hollywood royalty. Greta Garbo's estate adjoined Orson's new address, and Shirley Temple was his closest neighbor. The new tenant could move in at the end of the month. "I am tolerably certain you will adore it," Orson wrote to his wife, promising to have a fence built around the swimming pool before Christopher arrived with her nanny from New York.

"Hollywood, as I predicted, is not a nice place to go out in," Orson informed Virginia. For the first few days he kept close to the hotel, he wrote, although he did venture out to see the new movie *Clouds over Europe*, starring Laurence Olivier and Ralph Richardson, on nearby Sunset Boulevard. The Chicago columnist Ashton Stevens was in Los Angeles, visiting his ailing older brother, the actor Landers Stevens; and Orson and Ashton dined together, with Welles listening as intently as ever to the older man's advice. The newsman urged him to look up his nephew George Stevens, a top RKO director currently shooting the new Carole Lombard picture *Vigil in the Night*.

Orson wrote to Virginia that he hadn't yet seen "your friends here like [Herman] Mencowitz"—the worse-than-usual spelling was a joke—"and Burgess [Meredith] . . . because I haven't been out." There was still no hint of discord between the couple in these letters of July and August. Thinking of Virginia in Ireland, Orson wrote, "my emotions are mixed and complex. . . . First of all, I miss you, and then I envy you. I would love to see Ireland again, much as it scares me. . . . Please have a wonderful, wonderful time, and let me hear from you soon."

On Monday morning, Welles, Houseman, and Richard Baer trooped over to the RKO studio at Melrose and Gower in Hollywood, where executives greeted them with smiles and open arms. They were given

---

* The "Capehart hook-up" refers to a state-of-the-art Capehart radio-phonograph instrument and sound system.

the keys to the kingdom: a grand tour, introductions to department heads, and new offices already bearing their nameplates. Later in the day, the VIPs made an excursion to the RKO ranch in Encino, where *The Hunchback of Notre Dame* was being filmed. It may have been here, at the RKO ranch, observing Van Nest Polglase's lavish reconstruction of fifteenth-century Paris, with thousands of extras waiting around for a nod from director William Dieterle—a onetime Berliner who had acted under the great Max Reinhardt—that Welles made his famous exclamation about filmmaking: "It's the greatest railroad train a boy ever had." *

The notion that Orson felt isolated in the "strange and hostile town" of Hollywood, as John Houseman put it, is a simplification. Hollywood was only partly strange and partly hostile.

Another member of the Welles family, Orson's older brother, Richard, had preceded him to California, living in the state, off and on, since 1935. Still a flibbertigibbet, thirty-four-year-old Richard held mysterious jobs that kept him shuttling between southern and northern California. Soon he would move to Los Angeles. He and Orson rarely spent quality time together, but when Arnold Weissberger began crafting a new tax profile for Welles to accommodate the RKO contract, he noted that Orson had long provided his brother with a monthly stipend.

Wherever Orson went, he saw old friends and forged new relationships. Burgess Meredith was on the Culver City lot at the same time as Welles, playing George in the screen adaptation of John Steinbeck's *Of Mice and Men.* ("His first real Hollywood break," Orson wrote to Virginia, "and I am very happy for him.") At the Warner Brothers soundstages in Burbank, Vera Zorina was working in *On Your Toes*: her first picture with top billing. Ben Hecht and Charles MacArthur were in Los Angeles trying out their new courtroom drama *Ladies and Gentlemen*, directed by MacArthur and starring his wife, Helen Hayes.

---

* There are many variations of this often-cited phrase, but the original, which is quoted above, appears in Alva Johnston's and Fred Smith's series of articles in the *Saturday Evening Post*, January 1940.

On the night after his first day at RKO, Orson and Houseman went with Welles's agent, Albert Schneider, and Schneider's wife to see Hecht and MacArthur's premiere at the Biltmore. They were "appaled [sic] at the thousands of people and klieg lights, the photographers taking pictures in the aisles," Orson wrote to Virginia. The opus itself suffered from "an overabundance of Ben Hecht philosophy," while MacArthur's direction was "often excellent but never consistently adept," and costar Herbert Marshall, whom Orson normally liked, came off as "simply foolish and flat." Hayes drew Orson's only glowing notice.

After the premiere, Welles went with Hayes and MacArthur to his first Hollywood gala, hosted in the actress's honor by Norma Shearer at the Café Trocadero, the Sunset Strip nightclub near the Chateau Marmont. Orson said a warm hello to actor Franchot Tone, an old friend from New York, who was escorting Loretta Young. Among the guests were Janet Gaynor and her fiancé, costume designer Gilbert Adrian; Jack Benny and George Burns, whom Orson knew from radio; and the MGM boss Louis B. Mayer and a bevy of actresses under contract to MGM, including Hedy Lamarr and Greer Garson. "You can just imagine how many wonderful, wonderful people I met and talked with," Orson wrote.

The important (and self-important) screen industry columnist Hedda Hopper, whose home paper was the *Los Angeles Times*, spotted the newcomer and made a beeline over to him. "Orson Welles, properly bearded, wide eyes bulging, looked like a bird in its first peek at a big, juicy worm," she wrote cleverly in the next "Hedda Hopper's Hollywood," which was widely read both locally and nationally. "Says he's scared of Hollywood—likes the town. If he doesn't make a success of film it will be fun anyway."

At least that was a positive mention. Herbert Drake, the Mercury's new publicist, had not yet arrived from New York, and Drake and the RKO publicity staff were anxious to shape and control Orson's press image. Hollywood was rife with columnists, and the pecking order among them had to be observed. Now that Welles had encountered Hopper, however accidentally, they would have to offer an equivalent "exclusive" to her competitors, especially her chief rival, Louella O. Parsons, who reigned over the *Los Angeles Examiner*, the Hearst morning daily.

It was important that the "gossip queens," as Hedda and Louella were dubbed in the industry, should *like* Orson. Their likes and dislikes could determine ticket sales around the world. Louella had the statistical edge, as her column was carried in many more newspapers—more than four hundred at its peak. And Louella's annoyance at her competitor Hedda's scoop was obvious in her first column devoted to the young arriviste at the end of his first week in town.

The twenty-three-year-old "genius" (Parsons put quotes around the word, setting a pattern others would follow), with his "superior attitude," had "condescended to honor Hollywood with his presence." Louella was particularly rankled by his "record-breaking" contract, which she complained gave Welles "carte blanche" in a city where such privileges were rarely granted even to proven veterans. "He stars, produces and directs his first picture without a soul to say aye or nay. When you consider that the boy who threw the country into a panic with his Martian farce has never had one minute's movie experience, such a contract baffles science. No other man or woman has been able to wangle such a ticket from our film producers."

"I can well understand the bitterness of some of our actors who have had years of experience," Parsons continued. "No such privileges have been extended them."

Months later, when Louella finally got an exclusive interview with Welles, however, she fell victim to his charms. Knowing that the influential Hearst columnist hailed from Dixon, Illinois, Orson regaled her with memories of nearby Grand Detour, and soon enough Louella was putty in his hands. In the column she wrote reporting their interview, Parsons removed the quotation marks from "genius," and assured her readers that Orson was "indeed a brilliant youth."

Orson had developed a sophisticated understanding of newspaper folk since boyhood, from his first press interview at the age of ten to his years in the company of grizzled columnists and newsmen in Chicago. Critics could be dangerous; columnists, on the other hand, had an allotment of space to fill, and they had no reservations about dropping a mention to serve a performer's publicity purposes. Orson knew the columnist breed well; he had mixed comfortably with the worst of them in New York. One "big enemy" was the Hearst papers' Broadway columnist, Lee Mortimer—a notorious right-winger, later a champion of the blacklist—"who used to print awful things about me every day," Welles told Henry Jaglom. "And I always greeted him effusively so that he would think that I'd never read a word he wrote." The *New York Daily Mirror*'s columnist Walter Winchell was also a "terrible" man in many ways, Welles told Jaglom, "but I was very fond of him, because he had great charm. And he was such an egomaniac that it was funny to be with him."*

Hedda and Louella were like weather vanes, and it was foolhardy to try to control the weather. They also held sway over dozens of other lesser Hollywood columnists, who followed their shifting allegiances religiously, echoing them as closely as possible. Louella's skeptical first column about Welles set the pattern for a chorus of remarks about the "boy genius," his exorbitant salary (often conflated with his unit production budget), his Bunyanesque size, and, especially, the novice's "four-way" power, as writer, producer, director, and star.† The week following his arrival in Hollywood, RKO offered the first sit-down interview with Orson to Edwin Schallert, the dean of local film critics at the *Los Angeles Times*, and even Schallert marveled at the "all-encompassing contract," which made Welles "perhaps the first 'free man' in movieland, not bowing to anyone of necessity though he may always do this on grounds of politeness."

The rest of Orson's first week in Hollywood was devoted to more substantive matters. The subject of his first film had to be decided, and a series of studio meetings were held to sift the options. One faction within RKO felt that Welles should capitalize on his reputation for "War of the Worlds" by directing a screen version of the H. G. Wells story, but George Schaefer fought the idea off. "The only way I was

---

* Winchell repaid Orson's fondness. "After the *Kane* thing," Welles told Henry Jaglom, "my name was never, ever printed in a Hearst paper. The Hearst paper in New York was the *Daily Mirror* and Winchell was forbidden to write my name. So he called me G. O. Welles, George Orson Welles, and nobody ever noticed it. He deliberately put me in almost every day, just for the fun of it."

† Frank Brady plausibly theorized that the notions of "genius" and "carte blanche" were intentionally planted by RKO press agents, "to promulgate his [Welles's] image as a boy wonder and creative insurgent." Perhaps for that reason, Orson himself rarely challenged the hyperbole.

able to secure Orson originally," Schaefer told executives, "was because of my sympathy with his viewpoint that he did not want to go out, and be tagged and catalogued as the 'horror' man. . . . He was anxious to do something first, before Hollywood typed him." Schaefer convinced his officers that Welles's first picture ought to be "serious" and artistic, a film that would put Orson in line for critical praise and industry awards. The studio president was confident that he could promote domestic exhibition to the hilt, while international revenue for an acclaimed film would balance out RKO's investment.

Meeting with Schaefer and other RKO officials, Orson ran through a list of projects that interested him. He proposed a film about Cyrano de Bergerac, the lovelorn, nasally endowed dramatist and duelist; this prospect had the advantage of an already completed script by Ben Hecht, based on Edmond Rostand's classic 1897 play. The independent producer Walter Wanger had paid for Hecht's script, but then developed qualms; now other studios were pursuing the property. A film about Cyrano would allow Orson to exploit the Paris settings left over from *The Hunchback of Notre Dame*, while exploring the backstage world of French theater; it would also give him a chance to wear an outsize nose. Welles assured RKO that he could revise Hecht's script quickly, getting a running start on his January 1 deadline for finishing his first film. "He even offered to put up some of his own money if RKO's bid for the script was lower than competing offers," according to Frank Brady.

The studio officials thought there were too many unknowns. Wanger might demand too much money for Hecht's draft. Or the script might be inferior; that could be why Wanger had fumbled the project. Or a bidding war might rekindle Wanger's interest in the script, causing him to pursue it himself after all. RKO and Welles might invest a lot of time and money and find themselves out in the cold.

One of Welles's great strengths in meetings like these was his ability to rattle off endless story possibilities with the speed and knowledge of an auctioneer. He carried around a mental trove of favorite stories he knew from boyhood, or had encountered in previous iterations on the stage or radio. Now he proposed an adaptation of Joseph Conrad's 1897 novella *Heart of Darkness*, about an English ivory trader, Marlow, who travels up the Congo River in search of the mysteriously evil

Mr. Kurtz. Orson loved Conrad's novella, told in a frame-flashback, with its unforgettable last glimpse of Kurtz dying with the enigmatic phrase "The horror! The horror!" on his lips. "The story is marvelously interesting," Orson told Peter Bogdanovich, with "one thing which is in *Kane*, and which is a thing I like very much in pictures, the search for the key to something."

Orson envisioned setting an RKO film version in the present day, opening it in New York harbor with Marlow as an American dispatched to the Congo in search of Kurtz on behalf of his trading company. He told Schaefer and the studio officials that he would craft "a kind of parable of fascism" in the script, drawing parallels between Kurtz and contemporary European dictators.

Serendipitously, he reminded the studio executives, *Mercury Theatre on the Air* had performed a version of *Heart of Darkness* on the Sunday following "War of the Worlds," squeezing it into one half of the hour-long program. John Houseman, now part of the RKO family, was available to convert the radio script into an upgraded screenplay. All this Welles announced "without consulting me," Houseman later wrote irritably.

Orson had his admirers and detractors among the RKO brass, but the studio that gave birth to *King Kong* had a soft spot for jungle pictures. Schaefer, the studio boss, defended Welles against doubters who thought *Heart of Darkness* might be *too* literary and *too* expensive for his directing debut. "This is what was said about all of Welles's productions," Schaefer said, "and look what happened with the Voodoo *Macbeth* and *War of the Worlds.*"

Schaefer thought Conrad's reputation would make *Heart of Darkness* particularly attractive in Britain, the second most lucrative market after the United States. He gave Orson the go-ahead to draw up plans and projections. The studio would commission the Gallup organization to explore the viability of both *Cyrano de Bergerac* and *Heart of Darkness*, surveying a cross section of moviegoers to test their interest in adaptations of these literary works, but such surveys were standard practice, and RKO was free to ignore the findings. (As the studio did, after the poll ranked both titles near the bottom of a list of prospective projects.)

Delighted, Welles put Houseman to work on the concept of a fascist parable, which Schaefer had approved. Houseman began applying himself "like a little soldier" to the *Heart of Darkness* script and other duties, Orson wrote to Virginia, somewhat condescendingly.

The masterstroke that helped win over Schaefer was Orson's idea that he would play both leads: Marlow and Kurtz. In this approach, the audience would never see Marlow clearly; the camera would move subjectively through Marlow's scenes with very few cuts, the lens revealing only the character's viewpoint, while now and then glimpsing his furtive shadow or distorted image. The "camera eye" (or "camera 'I,'" as Orson put it), represented just the kind of original thinking Schaefer was expecting from his new employee, though it would call for unusual measures in the writing, preparation, and filming.

The studio made appointments with department heads for sessions in which Welles could explore his ideas for camerawork, production design, costume, editing, and so forth. RKO delegated an employee of the story department, Miriam Geiger, to create an informal guide to standard camera shots, movement, and juxtaposition for Welles, although *Too Much Johnson* and even *The Hearts of Age* demonstrated that he had long since transcended the basics of camera language and editing technique.

A veteran continuity or script girl, Amalia ("Molly") Kent, was also assigned to help Orson with the pagination and budgeting of his first script for the studio. "Welles found Kent's work so valuable," wrote scholar Robert L. Carringer in *The Making of Citizen Kane*, "that he insisted on her for all his subsequent projects while at RKO. She would see a script completely through its written development, then serve as continuity supervisor during the shooting."

By the end of Welles's first week at RKO, his coterie of assistants, secretaries, and transplanted Mercury staff had begun to multiply like rabbits. Herbert Drake and William "Vakhtangov" Alland checked into the Chateau Marmont before moving to the Brentwood mansion with Welles and Houseman in late July. Arnold Weissberger was in and out of Los Angeles attending to contract minutiae (the final form would be signed later in August) and conferring with Orson's agent Albert Schneider. Welles handed out assignments to everyone on the staff. Richard Baer, for example, was dispatched to libraries and museums to compile a portfolio on the jungle habitat, to enhance the verisimilitude of the planned film of *Heart of Darkness*.

To his joy, Welles learned that he could order up almost any film in the world: an RKO picture from the studio vaults, a loaner from another studio, even an obscure foreign film could be tracked down and shipped to Hollywood for his pleasure and study, to be screened at any time of day or night. He made lists of the pictures he wished to see; lists of ideas for the script, and visuals for its key scenes; lists of other possible subjects for the second film on his contract.

"I am learning thousands of things about the moving picture business every day," Orson wrote to Virginia in Ireland, with a humility that was rare in his public persona, "and I am tremendously impressed by the efficiency and cooperativeness of moving picture people."

On the last Saturday afternoon of July, at the end of his first full week in Hollywood, Orson attended an exclusive lunch and tea at the home of English author Aldous Huxley, who lived in nearby Pacific Palisades. Huxley had turned forty-five earlier in the week, and the lunch was one of several fetes celebrating both his birthday and his latest novel, *After Many a Summer Dies the Swan*, which he'd just completed.

The astronomer Edwin Hubble and Huxley's fellow English expatriate, the writer Christopher Isherwood, were sprinkled among the picnic guests, along with show business luminaries such as Lillian Gish, Paulette Goddard, and Charles Chaplin—Hollywood's previous model of a powerful, truly independent actor-writer-director-producer, though skeptical columnists rarely raised his name in connection with Welles. Charles MacArthur and Helen Hayes, who helped to facilitate Orson's invitation, were also present. Goddard brought an eight-pound English cake, MacArthur a case of Mumm's Cordon Rouge.

The talk that afternoon dwelled on Hitler's depredations in Europe—at least until Chaplin delighted the group by performing his hilarious balletic globe dance from *The Great Dictator*, his mistaken-identity comedy about a Jewish barber who looks like Hitler (with Chaplin in both roles). Chaplin and Goddard had been filming *The Great Dictator* for months.

Huxley teased the crowd with hints about his new novel, whose main character was inspired by William Randolph Hearst. The rich and powerful publisher was well known in Hollywood, where his

movie company, Cosmopolitan, produced vehicles for the deft comedienne Marion Davies, his mistress. Huxley's novel was set partly at
a castle-like estate mimicking Hearst's grand castle, San Simeon, and
involved a millionaire and his mistress.

The tea-party picnic was the kind of sophisticated, artistic gathering that made Welles feel almost at home in Hollywood, despite the
blazing sun and the canyon vistas beyond the Huxley garden, which
also made the place slightly surreal.

Attending significant industry events, parties, and premieres was
part of the job in Hollywood, and the next weekend, the first Saturday
of August, Orson attended his first such diamond-encrusted gala. The
literary and artistic elite he encountered at Huxley's tea were a minority at this glittering occasion: a joint birthday party for mogul Jack
Warner of Warner Brothers and actress Dolores Del Rio.

The ballroom, garden, and grounds of Warner's Brentwood estate
were dressed like a Venetian carnival. Tap dancer Paul Draper and
harmonicist Larry Adler entertained the hundreds of partygoers,
including first-echelon directors (Ernst Lubitsch, William Wyler,
Rouben Mamoulian, Raoul Walsh, Fritz Lang), top producers and
studio heads (Harry Cohn, Darryl Zanuck, Walter Wanger), and the
highest-paid actors and actresses in the business (Errol Flynn, Joan
Crawford, and Claudette Colbert among them). Welles's old friends
Vera Zorina and George Balanchine were there, along with the ubiquitous Hedda and Louella.

Despite being a newcomer, Orson felt at ease in this glamorous
Hollywood fishbowl. He was eager to meet Del Rio, who was cele-
brating her thirty-fifth birthday, which fell on August 3, the day after
Warner's.

A black-eyed goddess born into an aristocratic family in Durango,
the Mexican actress had been in Hollywood since 1925. Some of the
pictures she starred in were fluff, but Del Rio had also worked with respected directors. Welles recalled her vividly in *Bird of Paradise*, a steamy
South Seas romance directed by King Vidor, which Orson enjoyed
in the late summer of 1932, shortly before taking "Marching Song"
to New York. In one famous scene from the movie, the actress was
shown swimming, apparently nude. "That's when I fell in love with
her," Welles recalled. "She was as *undressed* as anyone I'd ever seen on

the screen, and *maddeningly* beautiful! I had some young lady in the back row with whom I was fumbling. It changed my life!"

Del Rio looked equally ravishing at the birthday party, in a white chiffon gown with rose stripes. A sophisticated woman who counted Mexican muralist Diego Rivera among her friends, Del Rio knew of Welles's reputation in radio and theater. Their eyes met—"that sightless beautiful look of hers which was a great turn-on," in Welles's words. The two talked easily; she found him sweet, likable, and unpretentious. Del Rio, who frequently served as a tabula rasa for the men in her life, enjoyed listening to Orson almost as much as he enjoyed listening to himself.

The hundreds of guests dined buffet-style under tents until midnight, with another buffet at ten in the morning for those "who had enjoyed themselves too much to go home." Two of the latter were Del Rio and Welles, who joined other revelers for a late-night dip in Warner's swimming pool. "Oh, she swam beautifully!" Welles recalled.

Del Rio's husband did not seem to mind. For nine years the actress had been married to Cedric Gibbons, the design and decor guru who supervised the look of the MGM studio's pictures. Their marriage was childless, however, and rumored to be unstable. Perhaps this was because it was in some ways a sham: Gibbons's "sexuality was questionable," wrote Linda B. Hall in *Dolores Del Rio: Beauty in Light and Shade.*

Though Orson wrote almost daily letters to his wife, Virginia, in Ireland, he mentioned neither Huxley's lunch nor the lavish birthday party where he met the gorgeous Mexican actress.

Orson's first days in Hollywood were smooth sailing. But the honeymoon ended abruptly.

Suddenly, he found himself beset by problems that were not of his own making: issues both personal and professional, some connected with his new career in film, but others emanating from New York and afar.

Though Welles apparently never expected it, Ward Wheelock, the New York advertising agent who represented the Campbell soup company, took umbrage at the fact that the star of his client's radio program had decided to move to Los Angeles and go to work for a movie studio. When Arnold Weissberger proposed that *The Campbell Playhouse* shift its broadcasting operations to the West Coast, to accommodate Welles and the Mercury players joining him in California, Wheelock hotly refused. The New York and Broadway orientation of *The Campbell Playhouse* was a vital counterpoint to what the agency saw as its principal rival, Cecil B. DeMille's *Lux Radio Theatre*, which was based in Los Angeles and featured Hollywood stars re-creating their movie roles for radio. Wheelock also resisted the idea of having the scripts for *Campbell Playhouse* written and rehearsed three thousand miles away from agency oversight. In the first week of August, he threatened an injunction against Welles and RKO, arguing that the studio had usurped the Campbell contract.

In New York, Houseman had served as a buffer with Campbell's representatives, but now Welles shielded his partner from the drama with Wheelock, ordering him to focus on the *Heart of Darkness* script. Orson opted to handle the matter himself, and Wheelock's "dissension and general unpleasantness" forced him to devote "several hours a day to letters and wires" trying to mediate the crisis, as he wrote to Virginia. Hoping he could placate Wheelock in person, Welles booked his first flight back east, looking forward to "one of the really outstandingly wretched weekends of my career."

At the last moment, however, Weissberger's diplomacy defused the crisis. He had negotiated a clause in Welles's RKO contract that excused him from the studio for radio work for one weekday each week, and that commitment moderated Wheelock's anger and dispelled his threatened injunction. Orson agreed to launch the new *Campbell Playhouse* season in New York, paying the transcontinental travel expenses himself, and he promised to liaise more closely than ever with the agency over every aspect of the show, from script to casting to production. Wheelock assigned a new agency minder, Diana Bourbon, to work with Welles in New York; Orson liked Bourbon and expected to be able to work productively with her. Another agency representative, Ernest Chappell, would consult with him on the West Coast.

In return, Wheelock agreed that the broadcast could gradually shift to the West Coast, later in the season, once the show's rhythm had been reestablished. After all the contretemps, the new season premiere on September 10 would be practically an anticlimax: an adaptation of

George du Maurier's twice-filmed novel *Peter Ibbetson*, starring Helen Hayes in her third guest appearance on Welles's radio show.

Howard Koch and other writers working on the radio show had stayed behind in New York, so Welles and Houseman had to engage a few West Coast writers to initiate scripts for the series—a move that would have long-term repercussions. One of the journeymen Orson hired was Roger Q. Denny, a veteran Hollywood rewrite man who specialized in narration for nature documentaries, making him a natural to chip in with authentic touches for *Heart of Darkness*.

More important, MGM had just laid off the estimable screenwriter Herman J. Mankiewicz, owing to his long slide into alcoholism, insubordination, and nonperformance.

Of medium build, with a beefeater face, a lofty brow, blue eyes, and a mischievous grin, Mank would turn forty-three in November 1939. The son of a stern professor of education, he had grown up in Wilkes-Barre, Pennsylvania, and graduated with honors from Columbia College in New York before he was eighteen. He was then already a chain-smoker (Camels), was known to classmates as "Mank the Tank" for his capacity to absorb alcohol (Scotch), and even in college was an inveterate gambler (poker, horses, anything), perpetually trailed by IOUs. Drunk or sober, broke or flush, Mank was a nonpareil conversationalist, a scathing debunker of anyone and everyone, and a spellbinding recitalist who could reel off pages of Shakespeare and verse from memory.

After dropping out of graduate school, Mank wrote theater reviews for the *American Jewish Chronicle*, then joined the Marines and served in Germany and France during World War I. After the war he worked in the press office of the Red Cross in Washington, D.C.; married his wife, Sara Aaronson; and moved to Berlin, the birthplace of his father. In Berlin, Mank strung for the Associated Press, *Women's Wear Daily*, the *Chicago Tribune*, and the *New York Times* (feeding "News of the Berlin Stage" to the editor of the drama section, George S. Kaufman). He moonlighted as a press agent—including a brief stint for dancer-choreographer Isadora Duncan.

Returning to New York in 1922, Mank accepted an offer from Kaufman to work as a literary and drama critic for the *Times*, and was soon elevated to Kaufman's assistant editor. Kaufman also sponsored

Mank's membership in the Algonquin Round Table, a sparkling circle of New York scribblers who met for lively lunches at the Algonquin Hotel, trading vicious barbs and witty maxims. The circle included the likes of Dorothy Parker, Ben Hecht, Charles MacArthur, and Alexander Woollcott. Although he was younger and lower on the ladder of success than the others, Mank fitted right in: Woollcott once described him as "the funniest man in New York."

One October night in 1925, Mank returned from a revival of Richard Brinsley Sheridan's *School for Scandal.* In the role of the "young" Mrs. Teazle was the superannuated Gladys Wallis, whose husband, Samuel Insull, the Chicago utilities and railroad tycoon, had bankrolled the Broadway show. "Outraged" by the spectacle of a million-airess cavorting as an ingenue in a production gift-wrapped by a shady magnate—and "full of fury and too many drinks," according to his biographer Richard Meryman—Mank passed out at his typewriter after launching a damning critique of "an aging, hopelessly incompetent amateur." This vignette, with certain alterations, would figure prominently in *Citizen Kane.*

Kaufman sent Mankiewicz home in anger, and the *Times* went to print without his notice. But Mank survived the episode, which formed a cornerstone of his legend in the New York press world. Mank's vitriolic tongue, and his drinking, would get him fired more than once—at the *Times* and later as one of the founding members of the *New Yorker,* where he got himself dismissed again after pushing editor Harold Ross to the limit.

By 1926, Mankiewicz had relocated to Hollywood, where he was paid handsomely to write title cards for Paramount silent pictures. He brought with him his gift for effervescent one-liners and synoptic summary. For Clara Bow's picture *Three Weekends* in 1928, for example, Mank wrote this title card: "Paris—Where half the women are working women," followed after a beat by the punch line: "And half the women are working men."

Mank wired his East Coast pals, including fellow newsmen Louis Weitzenkorn, Samuel Hoffenstein, and Ben Hecht, urging them to come to Hollywood; his famous invitation, "MILLIONS ARE TO BE GRABBED OUT HERE AND YOUR ONLY COMPETITION IS IDIOTS," captures his opportunism and superiority. Many of his friends hopped trains at his urging, and most had Mank to thank for prosperous Hollywood careers.

After lighting up the skies with his intertitles for two dozen silent pictures, Mank served as an uncredited producer on the early 1930s Marx Brothers comedies *Monkey Business*, *Horse Feathers*, and *Duck Soup*. But one day Mank offended the usually unflappable Harpo with a sarcastic put-down—and once more he was let go. He had bounced around the studios for years, accumulating a checkered history of brilliance, disaster, and resilience, but when MGM rendered him newly unemployable, he announced he was heading east to pursue his lifelong ambition of writing a Broadway play. Welles and Houseman, who both knew Mank from New York, agreed to help him—and themselves— by hiring him to work on the *Campbell Playhouse* series, pitching in on the scripts in Hollywood and helping with rewrites in New York.

On the first weekend of the new broadcast season, though, Mankiewicz and fellow writer Thomas W. Phipps were driving east when their car skidded on a wet stretch of Route 66 and overturned near Grants, New Mexico. With a badly fractured leg, Mank spent a month in the hospital, and even after he was sent home to his Tower Road residence in Beverly Hills, he was encased in "a heavy cast from under my armpits to my feet," in his words. Now Mank had little to look forward to except lying in bed for months.

Broke even before his accident, Mankiewicz had to lease out his home and move to a smaller, cheaper place in Beverly Hills. His medical bills were piling up, and the Mercury partners resolved to give him as much radio work as possible at $200 a script. Mank soon turned "demanding and impatient" about the assignments, according to his biographer, Richard Meryman; but Houseman supervised the writer tactfully—first in person and later by phone from New York—while Welles also treated him "with consummate and disarming charm."

Mankiewicz's first job for *The Campbell Playhouse* was Agatha Christie's "The Murder of Roger Ackryod" (broadcast November 12, 1939)— "not an unqualified success," according to Simon Callow, as the still-green radio scenarist "left out one of the crucial clues." Mankiewicz was hired to work ahead on adaptations of Sinclair Lewis's *Dodsworth* (the November 26 show), William Makepeace Thackeray's *Vanity Fair* (January 7, 1940), and Mark Twain's *Huckleberry Finn* (March 17, 1940).

Mankiewicz had a pet idea for a Broadway play or a feature film, and he talked about it compulsively whenever Welles or Houseman dropped by to visit. The script he envisioned would offer a kind of composite portrait of a well-known public figure, recently deceased, as viewed through the contrasting reminiscences of friends, family, and associates.

"A certain man can be a whirling pagoda," Mank liked to muse. "You look this way and see one side; turn your eyes away, look again and see another side, so that people looking at it from different angles see ostensibly the same man but not the same man at all."

Mank had worked forever on just such a "whirling pagoda" script, focusing on a criminal in the mold of John Dillinger. The story began with the news of the criminal's death, brought by reporters to the Kansas farmhouse where his parents still lived; then the entirety of the man's life was revealed through the eyes of his mother, his father, his sweetheart, the girl he almost married, and so on. The idea had captured the interest of a Hollywood producer, but when the producer dropped the project and moved on, the script was shelved, unfinished.

At the same time that Welles was fending off Ward Wheelock's complaints about the radio series, he was being bombarded with phone calls and letters from another unexpected petitioner: Dr. Maurice Bernstein. The doctor, who had been ambivalent about Orson's moving to Hollywood, suddenly felt bereft after Christopher Welles passed through Chicago with her nanny on the train heading west. Deciding he missed Orson terribly, Bernstein expressed an overwhelming curiosity about his ward's new life in Hollywood. A summer trip to see father and daughter together in their new surroundings would cheer him up. Didn't Orson owe him that much?

A visit from the exhausting Dr. Bernstein did not rank high on his wish list, but Orson still felt fondness for his guardian—who also happened to control his inheritance until Orson turned twenty-five in May 1940. Welles sent the Bernsteins a night telegram with two air tickets and a booking at the Chateau Marmont. The doctor "became a different man" when he received the telegram, Hazel Bernstein reported back to Orson, "the sun breaking thru the clouds in effect."

The Bernsteins arrived inconveniently on a Monday, August 14, and Orson had to interrupt all work on the radio series and *Heart of Darkness* to arrange the day and most of his week around their vacation. Ashton Stevens and his wife, FloFlo, were back in town looking after Ashton's ailing brother, and the Stevenses joined the Bernsteins along with *New York Post* columnist Leonard Lyons and his wife, Sylvia, for a get-together at Welles's Brentwood mansion. "The whole caboodle stayed on all day and had a lovely time," Orson wrote to Virginia. The next day Orson arranged a car for the Bernsteins ("as insurance against this kind of thing") and set them off on a round of sightseeing, hoping to get back to the studio without interruption and make up for "lost work."

Throughout the Bernsteins' two-week vacation—which included a guided tour of RKO; the studio premiere of *Nurse Edith Cavell*, followed by a party for executives and stars at the Trocadero; an Arthur Rodzinski concert at the Hollywood Bowl; and another Brentwood dinner party with Ashton and FloFlo Stevens and the Mario Chamlees—the doctor oohed and aahed about Hollywood. Orson couldn't really begrudge him his enjoyment, especially after Bernstein, with his remarkable timing for such accidents of fate, recognized symptoms of appendicitis in the "pale lemon yellow" appearance of William "Vakhtangov" Alland, then rushed the "slave" off to Cedars of Lebanon Hospital, where the Chicago doctor performed a successful appendectomy.

Bernstein kept dropping hints about moving to California, which Orson pretended not to hear. Writing from Chicago afterward to thank Orson for the "most wonderful vacation," Hazel Bernstein apologized if they had monopolized his time. "I hope you didn't feel inconvenienced, and I don't believe that Dadda talked out of turn too much either," she wrote. "The trip did make him realize that you are not his little Pookles, but Orson and a personage in your own right."

Everyone doted on Christopher Welles, who had arrived in Hollywood the week before the Bernsteins after three days of cross-country train travel. Not quite a year and a half old, Orson's young daughter was his sunshine, her arrival "the most important event you can imagine," he wrote to Virginia. He and Christopher would share precious little father-daughter time in their lives, and even during these first weeks in Hollywood, Orson spent most of each day at the studio. Writing to Virginia from RKO in mid-August, he admitted, "I haven't seen your daughter today, but hope to before she's put up for the night." Life was hectic at the house, with its incessant flow of visitors and newcomers from the East taking up temporary quarters. Even so, Orson cooed over Christopher in letters to his wife, perhaps to keep Virginia's attention.

"Your daughter is behaving like a famous beauty," the proud father wrote amusingly. "Good tempered only, I suspect, because it becomes her, independent, and shamefully fickle. Her big, beautiful, gray eyes have the serene look of a lady who confidently expects to get what she wants for the rest of her life."

Orson wrote to Virginia often that month, decorating his letters with blazing suns and hearts stabbed with arrows and doleful sketches of himself alongside the swimming pool looking bleary-eyed. ("The pool, beside which I am sitting at this moment, is deep and blue. The sky is blue and I am blue because you aren't here with me.") With all the grueling work at RKO, he reported, and regular bouts of swimming in the pool, he was "getting thin" and tanning up, though his wife shouldn't expect "the [Johnny] Weissmuller effect."

His letters were chock-full of his usual endearments. He urged his wife to splurge on an escape to Paris for a couple of days with Geraldine Fitzgerald and buy herself "some pretty things," adding, "You will never be entirely happy until you have a couple of evening gowns by ALIX who is just right for you."* Orson promised to buy Virginia a stylish new Mercury, the kind she had always coveted, once she came to join him; he pleaded for more letters from her, and complained good-naturedly when their elaborately arranged phone calls went awry.

"I do very much wish you were here," Orson wrote to Virginia, "and see now to the fullest extent how wrong I was in suggesting that it would be better for both of us if my first few weeks out here were spent without benefit of wife. As far as I am concerned, this was a complete mistake, and one which I beg you to rectify as soon as you can conveniently manage it."

More than once he reported that he spent most of his nights as a homebody, and when he told her about his social engagements it

---

* The French haute couture designer Alix Grès.

was usually to mention their old friends, or to emphasize the business side of his activities. Orson gave an amusing account of attending—at Grauman's Chinese Theater on August 8—his first real Hollywood movie premiere, the Twentieth Century-Fox production of *Stanley and Livingstone*. The event drew one of the largest crowds in recent years, and the *Los Angeles Times* reported that a "near riot" involving hundreds of frenzied film fans had to be broken up by motorcycle policemen.

The film itself was not nearly so exciting. Set in Africa (like *Heart of Darkness*), *Stanley and Livingstone* starred Spencer Tracy, "who somehow managed to be very poor," and Cedric Hardwicke, "who was poor without any effort at all," Orson reported.* "Everybody applauds the appearance of screen favorites during the course of the movie, just as though it were opening night on Broadway or any old-fashioned stock company, and afterwards, everybody streams out of the theatre saying loudly, that this picture will undoubtedly make screen history. These words sound hollow enough, I can tell you. However, I am given to understand that *Stanley and Livingstone* will make a million dollars. Certainly that is the only possible excuse for it."

After the premiere, Welles freely confessed, he debauched himself at the soiree held at the Café Trocadero, mingling with the likes of Leland Hayward and Margaret Sullavan, Douglas Fairbanks Jr. and Mary Pickford, and other Hollywood celebrities. Later the party moved to Victor Hugo's at the corner of Beverly and Wilshire, where Benny Goodman's jazz orchestra was holding court, incorporating African drumming for the revelers on the dance floor. Orson confessed to Virginia that he didn't get home to bed until "as late as one-thirty, which in Hollywood is practically dawn." However, sleeping late the next morning allowed him extra daylight time at home for a "visit with your daughter" and "a good deal of work on the script," he wrote.

The *Los Angeles Times* ran the first local photograph of Welles at the *Stanley and Livingstone* premiere with this caption: "Hollywood Convert—Orson Welles, goateed at 24, learns what a Southern California premiere is like. Stage, radio and (soon) film star, official chronicler of Martians' comings and goings, he is seen here accompanied by Lucille

---

* Still a poor speller, Orson wrote the actor's last name as "Tracey."

Ball, screen actress." The studio had arranged his "date" with Ball, then a single and attractive starlet in B movies, but Orson's interest in her was purely professional. Ball made him laugh, and he pondered using her in a film. No reason to worry Virginia by mentioning his night out with Ball—or, the following week, by mentioning the premiere of *The Wizard of Oz*, which he attended with another date, a discovery of Charles Chaplin's named Linda Winters (a.k.a. Dorothy Comingore).

Now and then Orson supped at the Mankiewiczes' home, one Saturday night joining a stellar group that included the Leland Haywards, the James Thurbers, and the Max Reinhardts. "Mankiewicz spoke of you constantly," he wrote to Virginia teasingly, "and with almost excessive affection." He invited Burgess Meredith to Brentwood repeatedly, but was always stood up. ("Spent all morning apologizing on the phone," Orson wrote. "He sends you his love.") Sometimes, after dining at home alone, Orson got into his "nice Buick roadmaster" and was chauffeured back to the RKO studio to run films or watch a nighttime shoot of *The Flying Deuces*, starring two master clowns, Laurel and Hardy, who always cracked him up.

"My life is equally divided between your delightful Hollywood household and the RKO studio," Welles wrote to Virginia not long after Christopher had arrived, "which are equally homelike and just about as old fashioned and friendly as Liederkranz Hall"—a humorous reference to the home of Columbia Broadcasting's Studio X on West Fifty-Eighth Street in New York.

More than once, Orson lost track of the hours during these late-night sessions at RKO, calling up films and footage in the projection room, "picking out what is known as 'atmosphere' and 'keys' for 'process,' and indulging myself in some of the really good moving pictures. All of which is enormously educational and valuable." One night, he paid a visit to a nearby set where filming was in progress and fell into a deep discussion with "a sound man I hadn't met before," Orson reported. "There went the evening." Although the sound man "used to work for Disney and although he is probably the Dean of his Department, he is the freshest spirit and the greatest enthusiast. We got along wonderfully, and I am arranging to have him for [my] picture.

"This is the procedure, day after day," Orson continued, writing to Virginia, "I talk with people and stumble around in their departments, and every once in a while, I find somebody that should belong to the Mercury. In this way, I am slowly recruiting a crew. It is a slow, but a tremendously important procedure and I am learning a lot along the way."

By the summer's end, Welles had learned a great deal and made enormous progress on his first project for RKO. Between the two of them, Welles and Houseman had finished an "actual shooting script" of *Heart of Darkness*, Orson wrote Virginia, "which may turn out to be very bad, but is certain to be quite remarkable, in any case. Frankly I am a little scared."

Unfortunately, he had to interrupt work on the *Heart of Darkness* project to travel back east. The "Peter Ibbetson" premiere of the new *Campbell Playhouse* season was fast approaching, Orson wrote to his wife, and "time marches on toward the inevitable commencement of the regular weekly grind. I must say I am not looking forward to it. I would just like one week with nothing to do before it all starts again, and of course, as usual, I need a lot more weeks than I have, just for work.

"I envy you [in Ireland], almost as much as I miss you."

Then, on September 1, 1939, Germany invaded Poland.

On the same day, RKO president George Schaefer, who was traveling in Europe, sent a telegram to Welles. Within days, England and France would declare war on Germany. Beyond the general destabilizing effects of the coming war, Schaefer realized that the news was bad for RKO: Hollywood already had lost its foothold in Germany, and now the studio would lose distribution in England and the other nations of Europe, where it had been earning reliable profits in recent years.

RKO WOULD HAVE LOST MONEY ON EVERY IMPORTANT PICTURE IN THE LAST FIVE YEARS IF WE ELIMINATED THE MARKETS OF GREAT BRITAIN, FRANCE AND POLAND, Schaefer informed Welles in the telegram.

ALL THIS SEVERE BLOW AS YOU KNOW AND PUTS US IN A POSITION WHERE I MUST MAKE PERSONAL PLEA TO YOU TO ELIMINATE EVERY DOLLAR AND NICKEL POSSIBLE FROM HEART OF DARKNESS SCRIPT AND YET DO EVERYTHING TO SAVE ENTERTAINMENT VALUE. . . . OF

COURSE THIS IS NOT ENCOURAGING TO YOUR GOOD SELF BUT BELIEVE
THERE IS NOTHING ELSE I CAN DO.

Welles's reply, which came swift and strong, was almost touchingly dutiful:

YOU HAVE MY WORD BECAUSE OF CONDITIONS EXPLAINED EVERY
CENT WILL BE COUNTED TWICE IN HEART OF DARKNESS NO SINGLE
LUXURY WILL BE INDULGED. . . .

PLEASE BELIEVE EVERY POSSIBLE EFFORT WILL BE MADE TO JUS-
TIFY CONFIDENCE EXPRESSED IN TIMES WHEN CONFIDENCE IS
EXPENSIVE . . .

I AM TRYING VERY HARD TO BE WORTH IT.

The onset of a world war could not shake the bond between Orson and his new patron. Schaefer further earned the younger man's trust when he read the formative script draft of *Heart of Darkness* and diagnosed its faults.

Houseman had not excelled as a screenwriter. ("I was an editor and an adapter rather than writer," he wrote later.) He had been uncomfortable from the start in Hollywood, where his name meant little or nothing to the columnists, and the press treated him as simply another anonymous member of Orson's entourage. He saw himself as a "failure" in the new arena of motion pictures. "Frightened by the necessities of an unfamiliar medium, worried by the ambivalence of my own feelings for Orson and in my anxiety to give him what he wanted, I found myself unable to give him anything at all," Houseman wrote years later. When his initial draft of *Heart of Darkness* was found wanting, he was certain that Welles felt personally "betrayed" by his inadequacies.

Yet Orson's letters at that time suggest nothing of the kind. When Houseman decided to return to New York, he was paid a generous $15,000 for his rejected draft. Orson himself then took over the writing of the new draft.

Moreover, Orson gave Houseman a golden send-off: his partner was put in charge of the *Campbell Playhouse* series back east, "arguing with the agency, getting the scripts written and watching preliminary rehearsals," in Houseman's words, in preparation for the Sunday night broadcasts. Orson may have foreseen Houseman's retreat to New York as early as his August negotiations with Ward Wheelock, and used his partner's return as a bargaining chip to alleviate Wheelock's concerns.

Orson began his weekly commute to New York on the second weekend of September, usually taking the sixteen-hour transcontinental sleeper leaving Los Angeles late Saturday afternoon for Newark, New Jersey. (New York's La Guardia Field did not open until later that year.) The trip cost several thousand dollars, and the thirteen other passengers on the DC-3 were usually important businessmen or show business figures like himself. He would always regret how Hollywood forced him to leave behind his life of frequent train rides, his favorite means of travel.

Orson was driven directly from Newark to the studio in Manhattan, where he'd listen to the rehearsal recording while eating breakfast. After final rehearsals, the 8 P.M. broadcast, and a full second performance of the show at 10 P.M. for the West Coast, Welles and Houseman shared long dinners while they discussed the next week's episode, or plans for *Heart of Darkness*. The next morning, Houseman sometimes drove Welles back to Newark for the return trip to California. If Welles's schedule became jammed, he took a plane or train to Chicago, connecting there with another flight to the coast, and sometimes rendezvousing with an increasingly plaintive Dr. Maurice Bernstein, who waited for hours in his car at the airport for a few minutes with his ward.

There were many perils in this tightly organized itinerary. One day, as Orson was speeding back to Newark, his car broke down on the Pulaski Skyway, and he and two Mercury players climbed out and stuck out their thumbs. The only vehicle to stop for them was a garbage truck, but that was good enough to get them to the airport on time. When a guard at the airport gate asked what kind of cargo he was carrying, the truck driver barked, "Actors and garbage!" ("At least he gave us top billing," Orson liked to say.)

Herbert Drake doled out tales of the cross-country commute to columnists, and the incident with the garbage truck, for example, was widely covered at the time. But not every story was so flattering. Syndicated radio columnist Jack Sher, visiting the CBS studio for a Sunday broadcast, offered what he said was a verbatim account of one of Orson's characteristic meltdowns:

"'Don't tell me what I can do! Tell me what I can't do and I'll do it!' So screams Orson Welles at his stand-in and stooge.

"'But you can't possibly make the plane, Mr. Welles,' Backpangoff [William Alland] says nervously, brushing the straight black hair out of his eyes.

"'Don't stand there and tell me what I can't do!' Welles screams again. *'Find out what time that plane will get me to Hollywood!'*

"Backpangoff scurries away. A girl comes running up.

"'Florida wants you on the phone, Mr. Welles.'

"Welles stands up and roars, 'I'll be there! Coming! Coming! Backpangoff! Backpangoff! Where is that guy!'

"Backpangoff appears suddenly again.

"'There you are!' Welles yells. 'Find out what time I can get a plane to Florida. I may go to Florida.' And so saying, Mr. Welles rushes for the phone booth."

Orson considered purchasing a private plane to make his East Coast trips more convenient, but Arnold Weissberger told him he couldn't afford to own a plane. In truth, he couldn't even afford his air tickets, which were paid out of an advance on his radio salary. By the end of the year, he had logged enough miles on TWA to be awarded a plaque as its most traveled customer of 1939. This made another feel-good publicity item, but from September to December, before the show relocated for the rest of the season to Los Angeles, the travel took a physical and financial toll on Welles and everyone around him.

The show was a headache in other ways. Diana Bourbon proved more assertive than Ward Wheelock ever was, badgering Orson constantly to consider actors and stories she preferred to his selections. The agency controlled the purse strings, so he had to listen, but he and Bourbon tangled incessantly over the gray areas in every creative decision. Bourbon sent a stream of memos to West Coast representative Ernest Chappell, warning him against Orson's seductive personality ("He sings a siren song to anybody who listens to him") and offering unvarnished critiques of the *Campbell Playhouse* shows after they were broadcast.

On October 8, for example, the series offered "Algiers," with Orson as the French jewel thief Pepe le Moko, who is hiding out in the Casbah—a role made famous by Charles Boyer in the 1938 movie.

Orson's romantic interest in the show was Paulette Goddard, as the character Hedy Lamarr played in the film. Ray Collins was the detective Slimane, played onscreen by Joseph Calleia. After the broadcast Bourbon sent a corrosive memo complaining that Collins had given an inadequate performance; that the sound effects were "overproduced"; and that Welles had spent too much time in his after-show banter plugging Goddard's next picture, Chaplin's *The Great Dictator*. "We're not in the business of giving away free commercials," Bourbon lectured.

Welles dictated an eight-page reply, furiously defending Collins as "wonderful," adding, "I must protest against aesthetic discussion between you and Chappell about performances by actors, over whose efforts mine is the sole authority." He said he was not crooning siren songs to Chappell. "Any 'siren song' I've sung in New York you can lay down to my very real affection for you," Orson wrote to Bourbon. "I'm not a wheedler or charmer. My fault as a personality, as you must know, is that I am somewhat arbitrary by inclination and often unreasonable. I have complete control and absolute jurisdiction over almost every point brought up in your letter to Chappell. I rejoice at criticism but I do not and I will not submit to unreasonable interference." As for *The Great Dictator*, he said, he had plugged it simply because "I wanted to plug it." And "please remember," Orson finished with dignity, "that whatever gives our format individuality beyond regular interest attaching itself to our guest is my own extremely personal rather particular style which must needs express authentically my own enthusiasm and tastes."

Orson chafed at Bourbon's micromanagement, but he strove to react responsibly. Sometimes he was defiant and outraged; at other times he tried to be diplomatic. Some shows were personal triumphs, such as the October 22 presentation of "The Magnificent Ambersons," a rough draft for the future film, with Orson playing the spoiled, tragic George Amberson Minafer. But too many were battles royal, and the fun and joy of the Campbell series were soon bled out of it.

Hollywood had greeted Welles politely, if not warmly, on his arrival in the summer. By September, though, the camps had begun to form. The inflated references to his contract took their toll, as did frequent mentions of his "innumerable yes-men" (by columnist Jimmie Fidler), the "strolling players from New York" always trailing him (by Sidney Skolsky), and his pack of "stooges" (by E. V. Durling). Offbeat publicity events staged by RKO (such as a press party at Shirley Temple's house where he and the child star played croquet) vied with columns like Jack Sher's reporting his tantrums.

In his first interview with the *Los Angeles Times*, Welles spoke less about film than about theater, insisting that the money he earned in Hollywood would be invested in "the further development of the Mercury Theatre." His attachment to theater made him seem almost averse to motion pictures. More than once Welles floated the likelihood of rejoining Broadway after he finished his first picture, as soon as January 1940, and producing *Five Kings* and other favorite plays such as *Peer Gynt*, *'Tis Pity She's a Whore*, and *The Playboy of the Western World*.

Orson had arrived in Hollywood with a beard he'd been cultivating for Falstaff and *Five Kings*, and now he continued to grow it for his role as the evil Kurtz in *Heart of Darkness*. The press seized on his beard, without always explaining the reasons behind it, and many columnists treated it as satirical fodder. F. Scott Fitzgerald was not alone in referring to Orson as "That Beard," as he did in his short story "Pat Hobby and Orson Welles" in *Esquire*. ("What's he done to draw one hundred and fifty grand a picture?" Pat Hobby complained.) Even the *New York Times* dubbed Welles "the bearded bogeyman of Hollywood."

If he hadn't intended the beard as a provocation, later he changed his tune. "You mainly kept the beard for its irritation value?" Peter Bogdanovich asked Welles.

"Let's say," Welles answered, "that I didn't fancy the idea of collaborating with prejudice."

As in New York, differences in cultural sophistication and political coloration helped define the factions squaring off for and against this newcomer to Hollywood. The relatively high-minded *Los Angeles Times* was officially friendly to Welles. The Hearst newspapers, the more flippant correspondents, and defenders of the film world's status quo like the *Hollywood Reporter* were never less than wary of Orson, and often openly hostile. At the end of September, the *Hollywood Reporter*'s powerful publisher, W. R. Wilkerson, used his high-visibility column to blast George Schaefer for taking "too much of a gamble" on Welles "in these critical times."

Orson wasn't entirely innocent with regard to the widening schism between his defenders and his detractors. He and Diana Bourbon often crossed swords over the casting of guest stars—particularly leading ladies—on the radio show, and Orson's private memos were full of unflattering opinions about prissy missies (in his view) such as Irene Dunne, whom Bourbon kept pushing for appearances on the *Campbell Playhouse*. Orson could be just as blunt in interviews, offering "candid, uninhibited opinions of everything," in columnist Sheilah Graham's words, after she spoke to "the bearded boy-wonder" for her syndicated column—and he cheerfully handicapped the leading ladies of Holly-wood.

"There is no great actress of the screen," Welles declared.

What about Bette Davis? Graham asked.

"She's good," Orson answered, "but not great in the sense that Helen Hayes is great. Garbo is the closest approach to a big personality here, but even she falls below the standard set by the men—with Spencer Tracy at the head of the procession." Mickey Rooney ("the George M. Cohan of the future") Orson ranked up there with Tracy, Chaplin, and Emil Jannings.* But forget Katharine Hepburn, whom Welles had disliked since their appearance together in the radio adaptation of *A Farewell to Arms*: Hepburn is "an amateur who is talented, but even though she tries to be a professional for the next hundred years, she'll still be an amateur. She embarrasses me."

Such remarks, harsh toward individuals and sweeping in their preference for Broadway over Hollywood, did not endear Orson to many in the screen colony.

One night early in the fall, talk of "The Beard" and his contempt for certain leading ladies combined with rumors about the "all-male population of the house in Brentwood," in the words of John House-

---

* Welles never backed off his admiration for child star Rooney. "Mickey Rooney was one of the most talented people in Hollywood," he told Henry Jaglom in their 1980s conversations. Rooney appeared in Welles's eight-minute "Vienna" from 1968, included in his unfinished compilation film, "One Man Band," which started life as a CBS television special but was completed as a documentary, *Orson's Bag*. At one point, Rooney was also supposed to play the Fool in a 1980s film of *King Lear* with Welles as Lear and Oja Kodar as Cordelia.

man, to spark a confrontation in which Welles was taunted as a "queer" by one of the screen community's less desirable elements. According to Houseman, the incident occurred at the Brown Derby. Welles said that it was at Chasen's, and the instigator was "Big Boy" Guinn Williams, a burly Western star who had been a rodeo performer before entering silent pictures. After slashing off Welles's tie with a steak knife, Williams challenged Orson to a fight in the parking lot. "Good friends pulled us apart," Welles remembered. "The whole thing was a formal affair, really, without much conviction on anybody's part. Errol Flynn sicced him onto me."

Flynn was "one of the leaders of the anti-Welles faction," Welles told Peter Bogdanovich. "Ward Bond was another." Bond was a right-wing bully with a long memory; twenty years hence, he would get Welles blackballed from John Ford's *The Last Hurrah* on political grounds.* Flynn, on the other hand, was more rogue than ideologue, and in time Welles would easily win his friendship. After the tensions between them cleared, Welles went out often with Flynn, his wife Lili Damita, and her friend Dolores Del Rio. Ten years later, Flynn let Welles use his sailboat in *The Lady from Shanghai,* and late in Flynn's life—in 1958—they appeared together in *The Roots of Heaven,* directed by John Huston.

The "barrage" of anti-Welles sentiment, according to columnist Graham, was "verbal and written." Orson was well aware of all the jeering, she wrote, but it didn't bother him much at the time. "I get a little sad sometimes when they print that I smashed a camera when I actually had posed for everything the cameramen wanted," Welles told Graham. "But I really don't mind." (He would touch on the subject of friends versus stooges in *Citizen Kane:* "Maybe I wasn't his [Kane's] friend but if I wasn't, he never had one," says Jed Leland, played by Orson's own best friend, Joseph Cotten, to the reporter searching for Rosebud. "Maybe I was what you nowadays call a stooge.")

In his letters to Virginia, Orson showed genuine enthusiasm about

---

* Ford, always cagey about politics, blamed this non-casting on Welles, telling John Wayne in a letter Orson had missed a key meeting because "of a slight fever upset etc. So fuck him," adding, "Fuck Bond too." Welles blamed his own agent, not Ford.

RKO and Hollywood, though he recognized the divide between the many, many people he liked and admired, and the others. "The old-fashioned movie people who grew up with the industry and who know what makes a picture move on the screen are all very nice," Orson wrote to his wife in Ireland. "There is nothing horrible about this town if you avoid the horrible people."

RKO offered Orson a refuge as well as a workplace, with plenty of work always left to be done. At the end of August, RKO formally confirmed *Heart of Darkness* as the first Orson Welles production, and Orson started casting ahead of the final screenplay, as he had done in New York with his Mercury stage and radio shows. The script would be prodded and guided by the casting.

In late August, studio publicity revealed his first selection: Gus Schilling would play a German doctor in *Heart of Darkness*. Schilling's name was almost completely unknown in the motion picture industry, except to frequenters of the downtown burlesque houses. Having proved himself to Welles in *Five Kings*, the rubber-faced comedian Schilling would now make his Hollywood debut in a dramatic role. "Orson Welles's popularity in Hollywood is due for a decline," warned columnist Jimmie Fidler, "when our local actors learn that members of his own Mercury Theatre troupe are slated for almost all the assignments in his first picture."

Welles also thought of his old soul mate the strapping Harlemite Jack Carter, the Macbeth of his Voodoo *Macbeth* and the Mephistopheles of his *Faustus*. He cast Carter as the Steersman, the native African ("as proud as a wild, great beast" in the words of Welles's script) who meets his demise in the story while guiding Marlow up the river. Anytime a black man was cast in a billed role in a major studio production, it was newsworthy during this era, when prejudice ruled the screen trade; and in this case it was all the more so because Carter's was another name new to Hollywood.

Setting past misunderstandings aside, Orson reached out to Chubby Sherman and Norman Lloyd, both of whom agreed to come to Hollywood and play featured parts in *Heart of Darkness*. Welles signed George Coulouris, Ray Collins, John Emery, Everett Sloane, Erskine Sanford, Edgar Barrier, Frank Readick, and Vladimir Sokoloff for other speaking roles. Orson's staff of assistants—his yes-men, stooges, and slaves—had to juggle the different schedules of all the incoming performers, arranging their various appearances on *The Campbell Playhouse* in New York around the studio's needs for tests, contracts, and fittings on the West Coast.

Welles devoted part of every day to researching, interviewing, and testing actors for the dozens of parts. Conrad's story had one significant female character—Elsa in the novella, who joins Marlow's river journey—and Orson intended to build up her role in his script. Orson wanted Elsa to be played by a foreign-born actress: someone with an exotic aura but without Hollywood baggage. (This gave trade columnists another reason to snipe.) At first, Orson gave the inside track to the accomplished German actress Dolly Haas, who had only recently emigrated to the United States. He made a stab at Ingrid Bergman, who was new to Hollywood, but producer David O. Selznick, who controlled her contract, wouldn't budge. Finally, after watching Jean Renoir's *La Grande Illusion*, Edmond Gréville's *Mademoiselle Docteur*, and Jean Vigo's *L'Atalante*, he decided on an actress who appeared in all those films: German-born Dita Parlo, who was currently residing in Paris. He sent Parlo a telegram making an offer, she tentatively accepted, and he penciled her in for Elsa.

On and off the lot, Orson respectfully sought the advice of established Hollywood directors. Almost uniformly, to his surprise, this was one segment of the industry that reacted to him with graciousness. If the veteran filmmakers resented the "boy wonder" at all—his youth, the overblown talk of his golden contract—none of them showed it. Rather, they gave him useful tips and confidences. "Logically, they should have been envious and bitchy," he recalled. "They were wonderful."

W. S. Van Dyke, who was best known for his *Thin Man* comedies but whose long career harked back to the silent era, told Orson, "Just keep [the camera] close, and keep it moving."

"Did you follow [that advice]?" Peter Bogdanovich asked Welles.

"Not really. I stay away from closeups when I can, you know—and when my actors are good enough."

King Vidor, whom Welles came to know through Dolores Del Rio, became a particular friend. Orson would attend the Hollywood premiere of *Citizen Kane* with Del Rio, Vidor, and John Barrymore, afterward attending a small dinner party at the Vidors' home. Orson would write most of the script for *The Magnificent Ambersons* aboard Vidor's yacht, sailing to Catalina Island. Vidor told him, "A good director is a fellow who doesn't go on trying to get everything right, who knows when to walk away from something and when to stay with something."

"I think that's a wonderful definition and I never forgot it," Welles recalled years later. "I leave some things rough, and I stay on other things because I think he's absolutely right. If you paint a picture, you're not going to spend the rest of your life on the lower left-hand corner. And there are so many directors of the [William] Wyler and [Fred] Zinnemann school, who paint the lower left-hand corner with so much intensity and good taste that they're left with shlock."

It was as though the old-time directors ("they weren't all of them so old then, of course—but at that epoch they looked a bit old-time to me") were rooting for the new kid on the block. "I took a lot of trouble getting to know them, and it was worth it—sort of rubbing movies into my pores," Welles told Bogdanovich. Besides Van Dyke and Vidor, Welles's other friendly mentors included Lewis Milestone, Victor Fleming, Frank Capra, and John Ford.

While they could have felt the most resentful, the RKO directors seemed the kindest of all. Orson could be amusing on the subject of how *unedifying* it was to actually observe some of them at work, as when he visited George Stevens, Ashton's nephew, on the set of *Vigil in the Night*. When he arrived one morning, Stevens was in one of his notorious trances, completely motionless, his head in his hand, no one speaking, everyone tiptoeing around him, waiting for something to happen—what, Welles had no clue. Maybe Stevens had gone batty. Orson waited "fifteen minutes. Nothing. Stevens didn't move. I waited half an hour, forty-five minutes; eventually I realized he was sleeping! Finally, after an hour I left the set. He was still asleep."

When Stevens dined privately with Welles, however, the veteran director talked expansively about directing, and the two developed a rapport based on their shared love for Ashton. Orson also enjoyed long talks with former Broadway actor and director Garson Kanin, with whom he had many New York ties in common. Kanin, only a few years older than Welles, had just made the leap from scenarist to RKO director. Kanin was "as sweet as ever," Orson wrote to his wife, and brought "a really fine enthusiasm and discrimination to his work. He was very helpful and generous, as indeed is nearly everybody else."

The best way for Orson to rub movies into his pores was at the screenings he conducted constantly, day and night, at the studio. Sometimes, Orson watched pictures looking for possible actors (he spotted the capable Englishman Robert Coote in rushes for George Stevens's *Vigil in the Night*, for example, and promptly engaged him for *Heart of Darkness*). Sometimes he watched pictures for specific technical reasons, with a department head or specialist sitting close to him and answering his questions about techniques unfolding on the screen. Sometimes, Orson watched pictures for African atmosphere, or possible stock shots.

To a degree, Orson wanted an ethnographically realistic *Heart of Darkness*, befitting his appreciation for the documentary style of filmmaking represented by Robert Flaherty (not to mention the South Seas films made by the cameraman on *Too Much Johnson*, Harry Dunham).

Frank Brady's book offers the most comprehensive list of the films Welles watched. Orson sat through *Chang* from 1927, a silent documentary by the *King Kong* team of Merian C. Cooper and Ernest Schoedsack exploring the jungles of Siam. He also saw the 1929 silent *Four Feathers*, directed by Cooper, from which Orson thought he might use footage of the hippo stampede. He watched Belgian documentarist Armand Denis's *Kriss* from 1932, shot in Bali, and *Magie Africaine* (a.k.a. *Dark Rapture*) from 1938. Orson took a look at *Wings over Africa* from 1934, an African travelogue using aerial photography by an American couple, Martin and Osa Johnson. He also screened W. S. Van Dyke's *Trader Horn* (1931), F. W. Murnau's *Tabu* (1931), Victor Fleming's *Red Dust* (1932), and Zoltan Korda's *Sanders of the River* (1935). When he asked to see Robert Wiene's German expressionist masterpiece of 1919, *The Cabinet of Dr. Caligari*, the Museum of Modern Art in New York sent its deluxe print to RKO.

Sometimes, Orson took a break and watched a picture just for the sheer delight he took in its craftsmanship. Over the weeks and months he watched many pictures directed by John Ford, even if they had little to do with *Heart of Darkness* or any other project Orson might be considering. He knew Ford's greatness from boyhood. "*The Iron Horse*," Welles told Bogdanovich, recalling Ford's 1924 railroad epic; "I'll never forget the effect that had on me as a child." He ordered up screenings of *Arrowsmith* (1931), set partly in the Caribbean jungle; and *The Lost Patrol* (1934), about British solders stranded in the desert during World War I. He sat through *The Informer* (1935), Ford's Oscar-winning drama about violence in sectarian Ireland in the early 1920s. "What a sense [Ford] always has for *texture*," Welles said, "for the physical existence of things." But Orson also screened less relevant Ford pictures, such as the mistaken-identity comedy *The Whole Town's Talking* (1935), which was light years from *Heart of Darkness*. "He's such a fine comedy director," Welles told Bogdanovich. "People tend to forget that."

The single film he watched most often in the run-up to *Citizen Kane* was Ford's landmark Western *Stagecoach*, which had launched John Wayne as a bankable star earlier in 1939. (It would eventually receive seven Oscar nominations, including Best Picture and Best Director.) He watched this film "as many as forty times," Welles estimated. Perhaps the journey of stagecoach passengers through embattled Apache lands overlapped with his project encompassing a dangerous Congo River trip, but Welles valued it not for its script pointers but as a textbook of visual vernacular. "After dinner every night for about a month I'd run *Stagecoach*," Welles recalled, "often with some different technician or department head from the studio, and ask questions, 'How was this done?' 'Why was this done?' It was like going to school."

In 1967, when an interviewer for *Playboy* asked his opinion of the current crop of American directors, Welles scrounged for contemporary names and ended up genuflecting to Ford. "Stanley Kubrick and Richard Lester are the only ones that appeal to me—except for the old masters," Welles said. "By which I mean John Ford, John Ford and John Ford. . . . With Ford at his best, you feel that the movie has lived and breathed in a real world—even though it may have been written by Mother Machree." Ford was the director he tried hardest to rub into his pores.

Despite the indignity of being called a bearded nonconformist, Orson half-enjoyed the notoriety and fitted in well with the studio regimen throughout the fall. Again and again, he proved equal to the personal and professional hurdles strewn before him. He pushed *Heart of Darkness* ahead of the agreed-on timetable, solving numerous problems as they arose, dealing shrewdly with concerns that were standard for every Hollywood project.

After Orson tossed out Houseman's draft of the script, he started in on the rewrite himself. Writing in late September to Leonard Lyons at the *New York Post*, Herbert Drake described Welles's progress. Borrowing from the methodology that had served him well in creating his radio adaptations, Welles had taken a copy of Joseph Conrad's novella and pasted every page of it into a large portfolio, Drake said. Then he went through the novella page by page, scratching notes in the margins, crossing out unnecessary scenes, inserting others he concocted, delineating those that would be preserved or modified. By the end of September, Orson had executed a 254-page scene-by-scene breakdown of the new scenario, incorporating his preliminary camera movement and shot notes.

"Supplementing this was a discussion of each character in which he not only described the physical appearance of the actor or actress but went into details about their past life and their future," Drake informed Lyons. "Supplementing the whole thing was a sketchbook which consisted of alternate pages of description of each scene and a line drawing."

After the breakdown, according to Drake, Welles produced a rough script of between seven hundred and eight hundred double-spaced typed pages. These had to be reduced to somewhere between 100 and 120 pages (film running times were estimated at a rate of one minute of screen time per page). Constant interruptions, including his weekly trip to New York, slowed the script work, but progress was steady nevertheless. George Schaefer, whose opinion Orson valued, pointed out the "excess of dialogue" in some scenes, and felt the parallels with contemporary politics were too explicit. "When Kurtz begins to talk of dictators in Europe, you are tying in one world with another world," Schaefer wrote. "At that point it loses something."

HONESTLY AGREE WITH ALL POINTS IN YOUR LETTER, Orson wired the RKO studio chief. URGE YOU TO BURN THAT SCRIPT, AND BELIEVE THAT REWRITES AND REVISIONS UNDERWAY WILL ACCOMPLISH EVERYTHING AND MORE.

One budget item that worried studio officials was Welles's initial demand for three thousand black extras for a spectacular scene in the jungle, in which the natives would be seen bowing down to the evil Kurtz. The day costs were one concern, but so was the challenge of rounding up so many black extras when the studios had only several hundred local black performers on its books. Moreover, Orson insisted he wanted native extras with "very black skin," in his words. If the extras were too light-skinned, he said, he would have to coat their bodies with black greasepaint. Under pressure from the studio, Welles kept reducing the number of extras, finally dropping it to eight hundred—a financial as well as a creative compromise.

To properly convey the jungle atmosphere, Welles argued for shooting parts of *Heart of Darkness* in a tropical climate. RKO was reluctant. In those days, location filming was restricted to rural studio ranches; anything farther afield was frowned on because of the vicissitudes of weather, and the enormous expense entailed in flying a professional cast and crew into distant territories. But the studio did agree to dispatch a second unit to the Florida Everglades, operating on Welles's instructions, for test photography of the wilds in late September. If the studio ultimately rejected extensive location filming (which it did), the second unit footage would at least assist the design and effects departments (which it did).

Before long, Orson's Mercury players from radio and stage started arriving at RKO for testing and contract rituals. Some, like John Emery, who was touring through Los Angeles with the Lunts in *Taming of the Shrew*, just happened to be in the right place at the right time. Everyone was anxious for Welles to direct something besides a camera audition—a scene with setups, lighting—"really just seeing what would happen with me in a movie studio with a camera," in his words. Orson was every bit as anxious.

Several days of preliminary photography were set—probably beginning on October 18—for the first motion picture sequences Welles would direct in Hollywood. According to Frank Brady, Welles planned footage of a few available actors "in costume and makeup, with himself marvelously disguised as Kurtz." There would also be "actorless rehearsals involving only the moving vision of Marlow-camera, such as a pan shot across a process screen, registering the hill and settlement."

Orson had talked RKO officials into letting him try shots with a makeshift handheld camera, "which was unheard of then," in Welles's words.

Linwood Dunn, who was RKO's expert on the optical printer and a special effects wizard (he had helped to create King Kong and the illusion of a leopard frolicking with Cary Grant and Katharine Hepburn in *Bringing Up Baby*), was on hand to supervise the visual tricks. One scene showed "the boat and wharf in miniature, combined with rear-screen projection," in Frank Brady's words, while the actor Everett Sloane, Orson's longtime radio colleague, spoke directly into the camera as though he were speaking to Marlow. The recently signed Robert Coote was among the players in another "big scene," Welles recalled, "Coote and two or three other people." (Coote would be left behind by the time of *Citizen Kane*, but Welles remembered him for Roderigo in his 1952 film of *Othello*.)

"How did it look?" Peter Bogdanovich asked about the preliminary footage.

"I don't know," Welles replied. "I guess it looked all right."

Orson sounded dissatisfied—then, and at the time. He thought the experimental filming was a "dud," according to Brady, and called "for more precision on everyone's part: the camera operators, the miniature technicians, the actors and himself."

While the test footage fell short of Orson's highest expectations, the experience of taking charge on a Hollywood set and commanding the actors and camera was exhilarating. "Had my first night with the movie cameras a few hours ago," Welles wrote in a memo of October 18, 1939, that he dashed off to publicist Herbert Drake, "and I am wildly enthusiastic about this business."

His dreams of returning to Broadway with *Five Kings* were quickly fading away.

In November, Welles had to buckle down to the writing in order to have a proper shooting script ready by Thanksgiving at the latest. The final draft would have to go through censorship channels at the Production Code office and be cost-estimated by the studio departments. Although special effects and postproduction would lag behind, the cameras had to roll by December 1 at the latest in order for Orson to make his January 1, 1940, deadline for completing his first film.

Herbert Drake, who liaised daily with Orson, kept Dr. Maurice Bernstein apprised of the pressures he was under. "The demands on Orson's time are enormous," he reported. "The Budget Department is after him all the time. The assistant director demands his attention. I am always heckling him for the newspaper boys. Houseman requires all of his attention for the radio scripts, and on top of it all he [Orson] is rewriting the movie to tighten it up and shorten it a little, and directing the actors in tests."

Orson's weekly flights to the East Coast may have been taxing, but they also served to give him much-needed "alone time." Throughout his life—whether stranded in a tepee in the Wisconsin backwoods, sailing on a freighter around the Iberian Peninsula, or flying eleven thousand feet above the clouds—Orson needed such moments of peace and solitude to draw from the deep wellspring of creativity that would sustain him for the rest of his life.

He began his draft of the *Heart of Darkness* script in singular fashion: after the appearance of the RKO logo, with its beeping radio tower perched atop a rotating globe, the screen would fade to black, and his radio voice would come in. "Ladies and gentlemen, this is Orson Welles. Don't worry. There's nothing to look at for a while. You can close your eyes if you want to, but please open them when I tell you to. . . . First of all, I am going to divide this audience into two parts— you and everybody else in the theater. Now, then, open your eyes."

As Welles narrated, "the camera would adopt the points of view, successively, of a bird in a cage, a condemned man about to be electrocuted and a golfer driving a ball," as Robert L. Carringer wrote in *The Making of Citizen Kane.* "Then it would take Welles's point of view from the screen, looking into a movie audience made up entirely of movie cameras. In the final shot [of the opening], an eye would appear on the left side of a black screen, then the equals sign, then the pronoun 'I.' The eye would wink, and a dissolve would lead to the opening shot of the film."

After that, the script got even more inventive, with many "experimental tableaux," in Frank Brady's words, and mobile camera scenes that would run as long as twelve minutes on the screen without a cut.

Welles planned to shoot the long takes fluently with a newly fashioned "gyroscopic camera," while incorporating a device he called a "feather wipe," which, as Carringer explained, "involved panning the camera to a stationary point, repositioning the camera but directing it to the same point, then continuing the pan in a new shot." (RKO technicians were busy trying to keep up with Orson's ideas, devising equipment that could do what he wanted.)

Staying "terribly loyal to Conrad," in Welles's words, while thumbing his nose at Hollywood conventions, the script preserved Kurtz's interracial romance with his mistress, an enigmatic native woman ("a real black type," Orson wrote). Welles wrote exciting scenes involving a great fire, an apocalyptic storm, a deadly stampede of animals and Africans.

Even biographer Simon Callow, often measured about Welles's work, described the *Heart of Darkness* shooting script as "a fearless, provocative and immensely talented achievement." When it arrived at the Production Code office, well before Thanksgiving, it was passed with "minor cavils," according to the censors' report. Chief among them were the film's treatment of natives—care should be taken with their costumes; there should be no hint of nudity, no implications of "miscegenation"; and so on. How Welles would have dealt with these thorny issues will never be known; surely they would have posed problems for RKO. But the film Orson envisioned was intended not for the Deep South, where undoubtedly it would be banned in part if not altogether, but for the major cities of the Northeast and Midwest, the awards circuit, and the fast-disappearing European market.

Never was Welles more productive than in the months of October and November 1939. As he completed the shooting script, though, he was also wavering in his determination to play both Marlow and the evil Kurtz. "I decided I was a little too obvious for Kurtz, and it should be a more romantic kind of personality, less of a heavy man—even a young heavy man," he recalled. "I think it should have been a more surprising person as Kurtz than I would have been."

At the same time, to keep up with the fine print in his contract, Orson initiated a second project that was intended to follow *Heart of Darkness*. He had considered and floated several prospects before settling on a new English thriller: *The Smiler with the Knife*, by Nicholas

Blake (the pen name of the English poet Cecil Day-Lewis). Someone in the RKO story department, prodded by studio president George Schaefer, may have guided Welles to the galleys of this suspense novel, published in the first week of November. Its topical plot concerned the wife of an English detective, who agrees to infiltrate a secret right-wing conspiracy threatening to take over the government of Great Britain.

Orson saw *The Smiler with the Knife* as another cautionary tale about the spread of fascism. His script would relocate the story to the United States, turning it into an American political parable. The wife of the English detective would become a madcap American heiress recruited by her father-in-law, a federal secret agent, to join the organization of a right-wing playboy industrialist who is active in the aviation industry. ("Welles told me he modeled this character after Howard Hughes," Carringer wrote. "This is the source for the puzzling claim in Welles's film *F for Fake* that Hughes was his target before Hearst.") The thriller would also incorporate elements of screwball comedy, with a cross-country chase sequence touching down at the Todd School.

Some of these ideas would be recycled in *The Stranger*, but as both Carringer and Brady pointed out, *The Smiler with the Knife* also informed the not-yet-conceived *Citizen Kane*. Orson described one character in the script as "a great newspaper publisher, also to be avoided in dark alleys." And there was "a newsreel sequence based on 'The March of Time,' showing the decaying world situation," Brady wrote. "As the segment ends, the camera tracks back from a movie screen in the film to show the young couple [the heiress and her husband] seated in a smoky theater."

Joseph Cotten was penciled in as the fascist playboy; Orson would direct and play the lesser but showy role of the heiress's husband. The starring part of the heiress was intended for an established leading lady who could pull off screwball comedy, such as Orson's friend the platinum blonde actress Carole Lombard, a queen of the RKO lot.

After the more costly and challenging *Heart of Darkness*, an inexpensive thriller with comedy was instantly attractive to the studio. Quickly writing a synopsis and scenes, Orson had a rough half-script ready for Schaefer by the end of November. The studio chief loved the basic idea—Lombard's involvement went a long way toward convincing him—and he met with Arnold Weissberger in New York to incorporate *Smiler with the Knife* into Welles's contract.

Both men wanted to extend Welles's completion deadlines, and the financial details of payouts and percentages had to be adjusted in the contract. The original document was so confusing that it was revised and annotated almost monthly. Welles did not receive an actual salary until a picture went into production, and RKO paid out a lump sum to Mercury in stages of about $100,000 per film, which was billed back to the production budget. Welles—now it was always Welles, not Houseman—dispersed the money, according to the Mercury's needs.

By the end of 1939, Welles had cost RKO about $106,000—near the agreed-on amount set aside for the Mercury unit's first production, and not an exorbitant start-up cost. True, no finished scenes had yet been shot; no production was yet under way. But Schaefer had a strong shooting script for *Heart of Darkness* in hand, along with about half the script of *The Smiler with the Knife*. Schaefer recognized that Welles was working hard, and he was pleased by the test sequences he'd watched for *Heart of Darkness*. In only four months, Orson had his first film project ready to go. Pundits be damned: Welles was a prize employee.

"Schaefer was enthusiastic about the work you are doing," Weissberger reported to Orson after his meeting with the studio president, "and is apparently wholeheartedly behind you. He told me that he had instructed the crew never to say that anything you wanted done could not be done until every possible means had been exhausted. He said that in most cases it turned out that what you wanted could finally be accomplished."

CHAPTER 18

November–December 1939

The Hardest Worker in Hollywood

Orson's letters to his wife in Ireland fall off in September 1939. His letters suggest she wrote back to him less frequently than he wrote to her. They tried to connect by phone, but that was tricky to arrange. Virginia, in her subsequent divorce petition, listed the date of their final separation as August I—perhaps the day she originally intended to return to the United States, but did not.

From sympathetic friends in New York and Los Angeles, Virginia heard that her husband had been spotted frequently in the company of the beautiful actress Dolores Del Rio. The *Los Angeles Times* ran a photograph of Welles, Del Rio, and Lili Damita—with Orson looking boozy and beaming—at "one of the gayest tables" at the Cocoanut Grove club one night in early September. Louella Parsons also spotted the couple out and about, reporting that Welles had "gone Hollywood with a vengeance," often "Troccing it" (at the Trocadero) with Del Rio, Damita, and Errol Flynn.

Such items bothered Del Rio more than Orson at the time, and she went directly to Parsons in mid-October to deny the rumor that she and husband Cedric Gibbons were "planning a divorce" because of her infatuation with Welles. Yes, she and Welles had attended the opening of the Los Angeles concert season at the Philharmonic Auditorium, but only because Gibbons had been detained at MGM. "I asked Mr. Welles to take me," Del Rio informed Parsons. "When Cedric works I have always gone out with other escorts—with his permission of course. I am heartsick over the rumors."

Orson nightclubbing with another woman was one thing; Virginia was used to that sort of column item from New York. More unsettling were the items saying that Orson had gone on another spree of Alfred Lunt–style dandyism, adopting a healthy diet (only "boiled food"), attending classical concerts, and sneaking off with Del Rio to foreign films such as Julien Duvivier's *La Fin du Jour* at the Esquire, when he could watch anything he wished at RKO. Virginia had been her husband's loyal muse in New York. Now it appeared that Del Rio had stepped into her shoes as Orson's West Coast soul mate.

The rumors were burning in Virginia's ears by the time she returned from Ireland on the S.S. *Manhattan* in the fourth week of October. The *New York Times* ran a homecoming picture of "the wife of Orson Welles," identifying her as "actress Anna Stafford." According to the paper, she and other "notables," including her friend Geraldine Fitzgerald, who joined her on the voyage, had been "marooned" in Ireland longer than anticipated because of the war in Europe, which delayed her safe passage home.

This was Sunday, October 22, the day Orson was in New York preparing the weekly *Campbell Playhouse* broadcast. Yet it does not appear that Welles was at the docks to sweep his wife into his arms; the newspapers do not mention his presence. He was busily engaged with all-day rehearsals before two performances for the East and West coasts. This week it was a version of Ferenc Molnár's *Liliom*, which Orson had reset in the Deep South. Helen Hayes, again his star, always recalled that particular show because "I got the impression that we sounded like an *Amos 'n' Andy* broadcast," and "I was finally moved to protest." Orson put her down "firmly," she recalled. "This is the way I want it, and this is the way we are going to do it!" he declared.

Just before going on the air for the second show at 11 P.M., Orson showed Hayes an anonymous telegram sent to him in the interval by a New York listener. "IT'S A GOOD THING MOLNÁR IS DEAD," the telegram read. "THIS SHOW WOULD HAVE KILLED HIM OFF."* Hayes was right after all, Orson told her with one of his rolling guffaws. "A quality which

---

* Molnár in fact was not dead then. He lived until 1952.

endeared Orson to all," she recalled, "was his ability to laugh at his own mistakes."

When Orson and his wife finally reunited in New York, Virginia confronted him with the rumors about Del Rio. Orson was his usual innocent and flabbergasted self. He indignantly insisted his relationship with Del Rio was platonic. His friendship with her had kept him sane in periods of unimaginable stress. But Virginia was unmoved. During the voyage, she announced, she had decided to delay moving to California while she pondered her future as Mrs. Orson Welles.

The argument only stiffened Orson's attitude against Virginia, but still he walked away believing his marriage would survive. Roger Hill and his wife were fond of Virginia, and when they heard of the discord, they encouraged him to reconcile with her. "I urge you now to give Time, that great mellower, a chance, and don't rush now into a final decree," Skipper wrote to Welles. Dr. Maurice Bernstein, a veteran of two matrimonies and quick divorces, had less credibility on the subject but also preferred to see Orson's marriage healed.

Virginia elected to stay in New York for several weeks. Orson believed he would see her whenever he was in the city for the radio series and gradually talk sense into her. But the wire service photographs of "Orson Welles's wife" out on the town with friends like Franchot Tone and the writer Charles Lederer drifted back to Hollywood, and the press began to wonder in print about the state of their marriage. Still, as late as December 7, Orson was denying the gossip about an impending divorce. "There is no truth to it," he told columnist Sidney Skolsky. "She will continue to be Mrs. Welles." ("I only quote," Skolsky added straight-facedly.)

About her own fidelity, Virginia was "untruthful," according to Mercury actress Paula Laurence, who was her close friend. Orson was "relentlessly unfaithful" with other women, Laurence granted, but Virginia also privately admitted to "an affair or two of her own." Welles's script, written late in his life for the film about *The Cradle Will Rock*, suggests that he suspected as much.

It may have been Geraldine Fitzgerald, as much as Del Rio, who lit the fire of divorce under Virginia. Geraldine and Virginia were good friends, and all summer long in Ireland and then all during the voyage home, they talked about Orson, whom they both adored, sometimes in spite of everything—the wonderful, impossible Orson.* The two women almost competed in their professions of love for him, topping each other with their respective anecdotes about his outrageous behavior. Orson was genuinely enamored of Fitzgerald, but she liked to exaggerate their intimacy. What if Fitzgerald told Virginia the same anecdote she later told her son, about nearly eloping with Orson one night? What if she exaggerated more, telling Virginia that she and Orson had had a torrid affair?

As it happens—and as Virginia knew—Geraldine was pregnant on the ship returning from Ireland, according to her son, Michael Lindsay-Hogg. Who was the father? During her lifetime, Fitzgerald played games in clarifying his identity—even when speaking to her son. Sometimes, she told him that his father was her husband, the English baronet Edward Lindsay-Hogg, and that her pregnancy was an "accident" that summer, spent in County Kildare. At other times, however, she hinted to him and many others that his father was Orson Welles.

"The story got started, maybe gossip at first, and juicy gossip it was, or because others thought it," Lindsay-Hogg wrote. "She embraced it, but subtly, for she was clever. Her denials were contradicted on her part by glancing hints, innuendo, maybe giving some clues to some people in Hollywood, which would keep the story going, and hard no's to others. It gave her cachet."

The questions about his paternity haunt Lindsay-Hogg's memoir, *Luck and Circumstance.* He grew up to become a television and film director, acclaimed for episodes of the dramatic series *Brideshead Revisited* and for crafting the Beatles' final film, the documentary *Let It Be.* Lindsay-Hogg spent years wondering who his actual father was and trying to coax the elusive truth from his mother. After her death in 2005, he sought clues and opinions from people who had known her. After a long soul-searching quest, he ended up believing Welles was his father.

---

* Only later would their friendship founder, after Fitzgerald started a whispering campaign against Virginia's second husband, screenwriter Charlie Lederer, claiming falsely that Lederer was homosexual. Fitzgerald's son, Michael Lindsay-Hogg, suggests in his book that Geraldine started the rumor after Lederer rebuffed her advances.

Since the publication of his book in 2011, this has become widely accepted folklore. The Wikipedia entry on Lindsay-Hogg, for example, states that Orson Welles was his "biological father." Imdb.com describes Lindsay-Hogg as the "biological son" of Welles from Orson's "brief affair" with Fitzgerald "during her marriage." Welles's paternity has been reported as an established certainty in both the *New York Times* and the *Times* of London, and their endorsement has emboldened many other accounts to follow suit.

Surely, Virginia must have heard Fitzgerald drop the same hints about their beloved Orson and about Michael, who was born just six months and two weeks after Fitzgerald's return from Ireland, on May 5, 1940.

"What does Orson say?" Michael Lindsay-Hogg once asked his mother.

"He likes the idea that people think he has a son," Fitzgerald replied. "And the whole intrigue of it, and so he'd probably give you his little smile and not say anything, or he'd say . . ." Lindsay-Hogg continued: "And here my mother put on an affronted bass male voice, as though from a melodrama, 'How dare you suggest I'd ever betray my friend Eddy Lindsay-Hogg. Humph.'"

Perhaps understandably, given the emotional content of the issue, no one seems to have traced the incontrovertible chronology. Fitzgerald departed from New York for her summer stay in Ireland on May 17, 1939. She was gone from the United States for five months. During that time, Orson was in the Midwest, Hollywood, and New York, but he never traveled overseas. By the time she and Virginia landed in New York in late October, Fitzgerald was already pregnant.

The idea of Welles as Michael Lindsay-Hogg's father is a biological impossibility.

Orson always acted in a fatherly way to Lindsay-Hogg whenever their paths crossed over the years. The younger man, early in his career, had some brief tutelage in acting under Welles, when the stage version of *Chimes at Midnight* was presented in Dublin and Belfast in 1960. But there is no record of Welles addressing, privately or publicly, the rumor that they were father and son—except once, in 1983, when Henry Jaglom asked about it during the lunches with Orson.

"It's extremely unlikely [that I'm his father], which I've never told anyone, because I never slept with his mother," Welles said, adding, "She was not my type."

According to the transcript, Jaglom responded, "It's true, you like the dark, Mediterranean types. People say, 'I didn't know that he was such an extraordinary Don Juan.'"

"I used to love everybody thinking I was having sex with everyone," Welles rejoined. "But in this case it would have had to be an immaculate conception. . . ."

"Maybe you just forgot," Jaglom offered amusingly.

"There's just a chance that he is [my son]," agreed Welles, willing to magic away the impossibility. "He believes it. I have no idea. He's a talented fellow. He acted in a play that I did in Dublin [*Chimes at Midnight*] when he was a young boy. I also saw a television movie he made. Awfully well done. He's a very good director. And he smokes cigars well."

In public, Orson made light of personal problems, especially romantic entanglements. But November was another month when the problems came at him from all sides.

As Orson's marriage unraveled, Dr. Maurice Bernstein started inundating him with letters and phone calls, pleading for help with his own career, insisting he was "very unhappy and losing weight and strength from loss of sleep and worry." His Chicago medical practice was stagnating. "I have no important hospital connections and have no teaching position," Bernstein wrote.

First Dr. Bernstein asked Orson to use his influence with George Schaefer to arrange a position for him as RKO's studio physician. When Orson did as little as possible to advance this unlikelihood, Bernstein took the initiative himself, announcing that he would fly to San Francisco to take the oral medical exam for California certification, preparatory to moving his practice and his home to Beverly Hills.

There was one hitch in the doctor's plans: his bank account was so low that he could not afford the air ticket to San Francisco. But if Orson would advance the cost of the ticket and provide Bernstein with financial assistance for "one year" in order for him and his wife to restart their lives in California, Bernstein wrote, "I will pay it back as soon as I am established."

"People with arthritis and other bone and joint conditions go to California on account of the climate," Bernstein explained. "If I had the proper backing I would go there without hesitation. But I must make a real showing in California. I cannot come there looking down in the heels, as far as living and office is concerned. . . .

"Don't think that I want to go to California because of your being there, though that is no draw back [*sic*]. We tried to be out of your way when we visited you and I don't expect to hang on you now. I never stood in your way and never imposed on you and will not start now. But I know that you are in a position to help."

The many letters Bernstein dashed off to his ward were long and "effusive" in tone, he wrote, because he was practicing his spelling and vocabulary in case he had to take any kind of written exam for his California medical license. His wife, the former *Chicago Tribune* music critic, edited his letters as she typed them. "P.S.," Bernstein scribbled on one, "You have helped many stranded actors who meant nothing to you. I hope that I mean more than they did to you."

The doctor faithfully listened to all of Orson's *Campbell Playhouse* broadcasts, as he often reminded Welles, enjoying the little in-jokes inserted just for him (Orson sometimes worked in the name of the doctor's beloved pet dog). He relished his occasional opportunities for time together during Orson's stopovers in Chicago—and was crushed if Welles passed through town without contacting him. "Need I tell you how disappointed I was when I got home and found that you flew past our house, and I was not there to wave a fond greeting," Bernstein wrote in one letter. "I sat for hours at a time in the hope you would call."

Welles still felt grateful to Bernstein, and fond of him, though he did sometimes elude him during the rush through Chicago, and he evaded Bernstein's phone calls whenever he could. But Orson surrendered to this midlife cri de coeur, bankrolling Bernstein's trip to San Francisco, and from San Francisco to Los Angeles for a short booking at the Chateau Marmont. Perhaps Orson was faintly amused when the doctor, a poor writer, announced that he was crafting a play that might also have possibilities for the big screen. "It is what they call a natural," Bernstein told a third party, "but after all who am I to judge."

By mid-November, though, Orson was pleased to put Dr. Bernstein on a plane home. He could ill afford to spend time or money on his guardian: although Orson hopped planes, frequented clubs, and lived in a mansion, his finances by now were a jumbled mess. Every dollar of salary and expense RKO paid him and his staff went to his film work, charged to the budget of *Heart of Darkness.*

Meanwhile, the Mercury maintained separate offices at CBS Columbia Square in Los Angeles for its other operations: radio, recordings, books, future plays. The West Coast office liaised with the marginalized New York office (now down to Augusta Weissberger) in apportioning the non-RKO Mercury income, as well as channeling prospective radio, stage, and screen projects. The Columbia Square staff was paid separately, often by Orson himself, out of his and the Mercury's earnings from RKO. By the end of November, the situation was complicated by the small army of Mercury players who were waiting around for the filming to begin and for their own RKO paychecks to kick in. All the while Orson flew back and forth between New York and Los Angeles, with the travel costs mounting and being deducted from *Campbell Playhouse* advances. And throughout this time he was also making substantial payments on the Mercury's debt and loans.

Richard Baer, in charge of the West Coast ledger, saw disaster coming. Welles paid for his day-to-day existence "solely on money earned from radio," Baer warned the attorney Arnold Weissberger in late November, and "a good deal of that is going to pay both his back debts and Mercury back debts." Orson's weekly non-RKO expenses amounted to $800, "exclusive of rent," Weissberger estimated. It had become Baer's "full-time job," Baer complained, to find that money somewhere and pay the bills.

Yet Orson refused to cut back on costs, demanding, for example, that his household staff be compensated at the going rate, as a matter of honor and reputation, and insisting on his own right "to live in a better style than he did previously," reported Baer. The lavish lifestyle was vital to his image of success, Welles said, and to launching his career in Hollywood.

To make matters worse, Orson gave money away whenever he felt the urge. Besides the handouts to Dr. Bernstein, he lent significant sums during his first months in Hollywood to Burgess Meredith, Charles MacArthur, and other friends. When Harper and Brothers republished *Everybody's Shakespeare* as *The Mercury Shakespeare* in late 1939, he signed over all future royalties to Roger Hill, as repayment for past assistance and loans and as a permanent token of their friendship. (A remarkable ninety thousand copies had been sold by this time.)

Weissberger sympathized with Baer, while urging him to stay strong. "The essential problem is Orson's psychology in spending," the attorney wrote. "He has never consulted his exchequer to see whether he could afford an expenditure. The expenses are incurred first, and then we have to see that payment is made in the best possible way. All along the chief difficulty has been that Orson's expenditures have anticipated his income so that he has always been in the red."

The only way Orson saw of alleviating the financial crunch was to create an additional revenue stream, separate and independent from both RKO and *The Campbell Playhouse*—with the inevitable risk of further taxing his energy and subdividing his creativity.

In December, RKO delivered the worst financial blow to Orson, when the studio departments reported their official cost projection for producing *Heart of Darkness*: an estimated $1 million. Orson's initial contract with the studio had called for him to direct two films, each budgeted at half that outlay: $500,000. Studio president George Schaefer had kept an open mind as Orson hatched his ambitious plans for *Heart of Darkness*. But $1 million for one picture was a Rubicon that the studio rarely crossed, and it was an even more alarming figure for a serious, artistic film by a first-time director—given the loss of the European market.

Orson had long since abandoned his hopes of shooting *Heart of Darkness* in a real jungle. "I lost my battle to go to the swamps and do it in a real place," Welles said later. "That was at the height of the period when nobody left the studio. The studio had to have *control*—as it was called—the famous *studio control*. . . . Well, I was more a victim than an authoritative pro like [Howard] Hawks would have been, because I was the stage actor and director *who didn't know what he was doing.*"

Schaefer said that RKO might be able to float the film's budget if Welles could find a way to shave $50,000 to $100,000 off the $1 million projection. Orson proposed using special effects rather than constructed sets for certain scenes, but that would require him to shoot the mattes and miniatures first, postponing the work with the actors for months while the special effects footage was prepared and photographed.

In early December, Orson met with Schaefer in New York to work things out. Orson suggested moving *The Smiler with the Knife*, which could be budgeted at less than $500,000, ahead of *Heart of Darkness*. As a cost-saving (and face-saving) gesture, Welles offered to direct and act in *The Smiler* without a salary, taking only his contractual 20 percent share of profits.

A grateful Schaefer tore up Welles's two-picture contract and rewrote it for three pictures, so that Orson would have two paying jobs on the back end of the deal. Welles could still direct *Heart of Darkness* down the road, along with a third picture for RKO, the subject of which would be determined later. Only later did Orson realize that his 20 percent share of profits would not be paid until *after* the studio had earned back the budgets of both *The Smiler with the Knife* and *Heart of Darkness*, which would be jointly accounted. As usual, however, Welles did not dwell on his money.

RKO announced the postponement of *Heart of Darkness*. "I did a very elaborate preparation" for the Joseph Conrad film, Welles told Peter Bogdanovich wistfully, "such as I've never done again—never could. I shot my bolt on preproduction on that picture. We designed every camera setup and everything else—did enormous research in aboriginal, Stone Age cultures in order to reproduce what the story called for. I'm sorry not to have got the chance to do it."

Welles never wasted something he could reuse, however, and Peter Conrad is not the only authority to have noticed him "by stealth, distributing [parts of *Heart of Darkness*] through other films—*Citizen Kane*, *The Lady from Shanghai*, *The Third Man*," continuing until forty years later, when he smuggled references to it into his script for *The Big Brass Ring*.

Although Orson had made his script and production budget deadlines on time—and the film's downfall was, at least in part, due to political circumstances beyond anyone's control—the postponement, combined with the announcement that Orson Welles had been re-signed to direct *three* RKO pictures, escalated the mockery from his ill-wishers in the business and the trade press. The *Hollywood Reporter* predicted that the deal would fall through without Welles's "ever doing a picture." *The Smiler with the Knife* was jokingly referred to as "Mr. Welles's latest forthcoming picture." Columnist Jimmie Fidler cracked: "Ha! They're saying Orson Welles has increased his production schedule. Instead of *not* making three pics for RKO, he'll *not* make five!" Spotting Orson at an event, Ed Sullivan described him as "chic in a silver fox beard trimmed with old RKO scripts." Hedda Hopper weighed in: "Looks like the only hair-raising pictures Orson Welles made out here are the stills showing him wearing a beard."

While in New York, Welles also learned that Virginia had met with Arnold Weissberger to initiate divorce proceedings. Under prompting from her father in Chicago, who had never warmed to Welles and suspected his son-in-law of salting away money from his inheritance and Hollywood windfalls, Virginia sought steep terms Orson could not easily afford: several thousand dollars monthly in alimony and child support, or 50 percent of his annual income, whichever was greater. As a footnote, Virginia presented a $500 bill for personal items purchased at Orson's insistence—such as the Parisian gowns—for which she had never been reimbursed.

Returning to Hollywood from New York, Orson had mixed emotions about the postponement of *Heart of Darkness* and the imminent end of his marriage to Virginia. The geographical and emotional distance he put between himself and his wife over the summer had become an unbridgeable gulf. Divorce would be a mercy for the couple. And while *Heart of Darkness* had temporarily fallen through, he thought he could launch the less demanding *Smiler with the Knife* expeditiously after the first of the year. Now he could even shave his beard, which had recently assumed "Assyrian proportions and type," in the words of columnist Sidney Skolsky.

One of the first things Orson did on returning to Hollywood, late in 1939, was narrate a voice-over for RKO's adaptation of an adventure classic, *The Swiss Family Robinson*. Orson did it as a return favor to a friend, scenarist Gene Towne, who had been helpful with advice on *The Smiler with the Knife*. *Swiss Family Robinson* was Towne's first picture as a producer, and it was also Orson's first true "appearance" in a Hollywood production. Despite his growing financial woes, Orson accepted only a nominal fee of $25, which he donated to charity.

Facing an intense month of work on the script for *The Smiler* over the holidays, he turned to Herman Mankiewicz. Once the king of Hollywood screenwriters, Mank was still out of work, "discredited at all the studios," according to his sympathetic biographer Richard Meryman, and subsisting on his paychecks from the Mercury.

"For Herman, a self-destructive personality, who worried that he was a washed-up hack," wrote Meryman, "the chance to deflate this boy wonder was irresistible." Mank shifted his habitual animus onto Orson, determined to show him up at the movie script game, arguing over every word Orson had written. "He destroyed my confidence in the script," Welles recalled, "sneering at everything I did, saying, 'That will never work.'" But Orson enjoyed butting heads with superior intellects, and little by little he regained his equilibrium with Mank.

Meanwhile, Herbert Drake and the RKO publicity department were launching a rearguard action against the poisonous barbs flung at Welles, persuading Edwin Schallert to write in the *Los Angeles Times* that the script for *The Smiler* was nearly ready for filming to begin, and that the production was expected to go before the cameras by the end of January. "Working practically day and night," Schallert reported, Welles may well be "the hardest worker in Hollywood." "Practically day and night" was not strictly true—Orson was visible attending premieres and parties for *The Hunchback of Notre Dame*, *Of Mice and Men*, and *Gone With the Wind*, among other occasions, often with the married actress Dolores Del Rio as his companion. But she always appeared to go home alone at the end of the evening, and Orson returned to Brentwood to work until dawn.

Compounding the pressures of time and money was a problem left over from the postponed *Heart of Darkness*: Orson had enticed more than a dozen Mercury players to Hollywood, welcoming them with an extravagant party, then stowing them in his mansion and various other places while helping them land spot acting jobs to keep them busy and solvent. In December, the radio series shifted to the West Coast for most future broadcasts; that eased Orson's logistics and opened up more radio work.

But now that *Heart of Darkness* had been replaced by *The Smiler with the Knife* as his first project, Orson was confronted with a smaller budget and a smaller cast to fill. Some of the transplanted actors, such as

Orson's Harlem friend Jack Carter, would not be transitioning to *The Smiler*. And even the actors who were promised a part in *Smiler* now looked at weeks or months of waiting before their work (and paychecks) would begin. Hollywood actors routinely coped with such vicissitudes, but the Mercury players were new to film, and Orson felt responsible for them.

The week before Christmas, John Houseman drove from New York to California. He felt as irrelevant as ever in Hollywood—"I had little to say about Welles's film activities," he wrote, "yet I remained president of the Mercury and Orson's partner"—but he joined the Mercury's West Coast team for a celebratory year-end summit at Chasen's, the chic Hollywood eatery. Besides Welles and Houseman, the attendees included Albert Schneider, Herbert Drake, Richard Wilson, William Alland, Richard Baer, and "our new California secretary (a dark girl with wonderfully long, narrow crimson nails)," in Houseman's words.

After steaks and too many drinks, Orson got down to business discussing the emergency: RKO had sent word that actors' salaries would not be paid until a final script, budget, and schedule had all been authorized. In the interim, Orson declared, it was the Mercury's sacred duty to carry the actors out of reserve funds. When Schneider lamely informed him that there *were* no reserve funds, Welles exploded.

"He had absorbed more than his normal quantity of alcohol," Houseman wrote in *Run-Through*. "His eyes were bloodshot, his face damp and white."

Orson turned to Houseman, pointedly asking, "What would *you* do?"

"Tell them the truth for once," the producer replied.

Orson took the bait angrily. "I don't lie to actors," he declared, according to Houseman. "I've never lied to an actor in my life! You're the one who lies! That's why they hate you! You're a crook and they know it! Everybody knows it! Everybody!"

Houseman had reached his personal "Götterdämmerung," as he put it. He stood up, collected his belongings, and started for the door. Welles picked up one of the "burning Sterno dish heaters" on the table and hurled it after him. "It missed me by a yard and landed at the foot of a drawn window curtain behind me. Another flaming object flew by me."

Returning to his leased apartment, Houseman took to bed. A knock came on the door—it was "the girl with the red nails"—but he refused to answer. Later came Orson himself, ringing the doorbell, to no avail. At dawn, "a four page telegram" from Welles was delivered by hand. That afternoon Houseman got into his car and headed east, he said, listening on the car radio to "the last *Campbell Playhouse* I had written."

Stopping in a small town in New Mexico, he composed two letters. "The first, formal and typewritten, was to Orson." Houseman excerpted the formal letter to Orson in his book: "Nothing that has happened recently affects the very deep affection I have for you and the delight I have found in my association with such a talent as yours," the letter began. "What happened the other night merely brought to a head a situation I have seen growing worse for some time—the situation of my false position with the Mercury. . . . It is true that in the past year my position with you and with the Mercury has become something between that of a hired, not too effective manager, a writer under contract and an aging, not so benevolent relative.

"Besides which, there has been something between us, lately, which instead of being intense and fruitful merely succeeds in embarrassing and paralyzing us both."

But it wasn't quite a high-principled resignation. While insisting that "the present situation is hopeless and must be changed at once for both our sakes," Houseman signed the letter "Love," and concluded with, "Let's have dinner together" the next time Welles was in New York.

His second letter, "in longhand," flew to composer Virgil Thomson in Paris. This too was excerpted in Houseman's memoir. "I have decided to end my association with Orson," Houseman told Thomson, putting a more conclusive spin on the news. Reviewing the history of the Mercury, Houseman wrote that it was a chronicle of "failures that were sometimes honorable, sometimes idiotic and ignominious—but constant and uninterrupted." Too often, according to the letter, "feelings of grandeur and what-is-expected-of-the-Mercury completely supplanted the simple desire to put on a good show. I allowed Orson (and the fault is mine as much as his, since by failing to control and influence him, I was betraying my most useful function in the Mercury) to use the theatre as an instrument of personal aggrandizement."

Orson's publicity-mongering was a thorn in his side, Houseman continued in his letter to Thomson, "snowballing to the point where Orson has become a public figure only less recently and massively projected into the news and the national consciousness than Franklin D. Roosevelt, N. Chamberlain and A. Hitler. This new fame has grown in inverse proportion to the success of our recent artistic endeavors. It is unrelated to our work. In fact, it is just about fatal to our work. It is an appetite that grows as it is fed: in a creative artist, it becomes a compensation and a substitute for creation. . . .

"I am fond of Orson still," he finished, "and I retain much of my admiration for his talent: but our partnership is over for good and with it an exciting chapter of my life. It has been very wonderful and very painful and I am very glad that it is ended."

The famous Mercury Theatre (and film) partnership had "ended."

But not quite, not yet, and not in this fashion: once again, Houseman's action-packed account, which burnished his own integrity and advanced his theme of Welles gone amok, looks different when measured against other versions of the events.

Orson told Barbara Leaming that he had realized, long before the Chasen's showdown, that Houseman was miserable in his subordinate position. ("He was working for me," Welles said. "That's why he hated me so.") Houseman was no longer as useful to the radio show either, and the top salary he was drawing was needed elsewhere.

Houseman himself had other irons in the fire. On Mercury time, he was preparing a stage play that Howard Koch and John Huston were writing about Woodrow Wilson's presidency. Orson knew about the play, which was announced a few weeks later, in the *New York Times* on January 22. According to that story, Houseman "is not associated with Mr. Welles in the latter's controversial film activities," but the producer denied that there had been any "formal parting" with Orson, and said that the Wilson drama "may or may not be a Mercury Theatre offering" in the fall.

Though he mentioned Welles's four-page telegram in *Run-Through*, Houseman did not quote its contents, nor did he give the date of his longhand letter to Virgil Thomson, which could only have been written weeks or months after his letter to Orson. In later court testimony involving *Citizen Kane*, Houseman gave a different account of "the night of the flaming Sternos"; he told the court under oath that the objects Orson hurled in his direction that night at Chasen's were flung "not at me but around the room." And Simon Callow, in his intriguing section on "the night of the flaming Sternos," points out that Houseman's original typed letter to Welles was "subtly different" from the version excerpted in the producer's memoir, and that the letter to Virgil Thomson also was "rewritten for publication." In his memoir, Houseman edited out several damning self-criticisms that appeared in his original letters—including this from his letter to Orson: "I have found myself accepting this new position of mine not always with good grace, and I have found myself far too frequently buttressing my position with a kind of cynical, destructive passivity." And he omitted this particular sentence, which undercuts his supposedly concurrent letter to Virgil Thomson: "I do not consider this a divorce from the Mercury." As Callow noted, Houseman's memoir also misrepresented Welles's progress on his film projects. "He was wrong about the amount of work Welles had done," Callow wrote.

By the time of the final confrontation at Chasen's, it seems, both men were seeking an excuse to sever ties. According to Callow, "Houseman had been looking for an occasion to precipitate their rift, and the meal at Chasen's had served well for the purpose." According to Welles, the impetus was his. "The whole purpose was to get Houseman to quit and go back to New York," Welles insisted to Leaming. "It was a total piece of theater. I didn't throw the Sterno within ten feet of him. He'd been sitting at that dinner table cutting me up for an hour, but I didn't get mad. I thought, 'I've just got to get him away.' I couldn't say, 'You're not working for me anymore' after all our time together and all. So that's why I turned over the table. It was cold-hearted. It wasn't a big end of it [the relationship]; it just got him off salary for a while."

Welles's time and money pressures intensified as the holidays approached. December marked the fifth anniversary of his and Virginia's formal marriage ceremony in 1935. In the week before Christmas— the week of "the night of the flaming Sternos"—Virginia flew to Chicago, spending time with her parents while waiting for a flight to Reno, Nevada, where she intended to live temporarily for six weeks, the prescribed state residency for a divorce decree. Chicago reporters recognized Virginia and extracted a terse interview from her before she left. "This is no new story," she said. "We have been separated for a year."

Arnold Weissberger, who understood Orson's financial morass better than anyone else, urged his client to leave the Brentwood mansion for a more affordable house in the Hollywood Hills above Sunset Boulevard. Orson said he would think it over.

Herbert Drake redoubled his efforts to point out that Welles was working "practically all day and night" and to get good publicity to offset the items about Orson's divorce that were sweeping the press. Drawing on Dr. Bernstein's dubious version of Orson's life story, Decla Dunning wrote the most extensive profile yet of Welles in the *Los Angeles Times*, telling readers that the controversial tyro was "distressed by stories of his whimsies, his temperament, his thunderous anger and sullen silences."

In the face of his marital breakup, which she downplayed, Dunning emphasized what a loving father Orson was. "When it comes to holding the center of the stage, he bows to only one other individual, his 18-month-old daughter," Dunning wrote. Her piece perpetuated the "carte blanche" canard, calling "the unprecedented elasticity of his Hollywood contract a subject of controversy." But Orson was not anti-Hollywood, as the PR campaign insisted. "I've been a movie fan all my life," Welles was quoted as saying, and it was true.

"He has stirred public imagination to the extent that people may like or dislike him, resent or admire him, but not ignore him," Dunning concluded in her flattering profile, timed for release on the last weekend before Christmas. "He won't be able to slip by under par. He has to be good. And he is quite sure, with his unfailing optimism, the unquenchable, yet inoffensive ego which have marked his past ventures, that he will be."

On December 23, Orson was photographed at the annual Screen Actors Guild holiday party, slender and smiling, his beard trimmed but not yet shorn, sharing a table with Dolores Del Rio, Fay Wray, and Cary Grant. Del Rio was personally popular with Hollywood columnists, and it helped Orson now that their romance could be out in the open. If it was a romance: Del Rio still denied that it was, and after the parties she still went home to her husband.

Toward the end of the Screen Actors Guild party, Orson found himself in a corner standing next to sixty-four-year-old D. W. Griffith, the pioneer of the silent picture era. Griffith was all but washed up in Hollywood: he was then working as an adviser to Hal Roach, who was producing the prehistoric epic *One Million B.C.*, but Griffith hadn't directed a full feature since 1931.

Orson never wavered in his admiration for Griffith, whose faults— the old-fashioned David Belasco touches and Victorian melodramatics, even the race prejudice of *The Birth of a Nation*—Welles preferred to see as unfortunate by-products of their time. Asked by *Cahiers du Cinéma* in 1964 what directors he revered besides John Ford and Jean Renoir, Orson said that his answer was not going to be "very original," and that his idols were always the "same ones." "The one who pleases me most of all is Griffith," Welles said. "I think he is the best director in the history of the cinema."

Welles edged into a conversation with Griffith, trying "to express what the older man meant to him and the art of film," as Frank Brady wrote. Uncharacteristically, Orson found himself hemming and hawing. Aware that Griffith might have read the nonsense published about the "boy wonder" having a "carte blanche" contract, he imagined the pioneer disapproving of this young whippersnapper. "We stared at each other across a hopeless abyss," Welles recalled.*

Perhaps, too, Welles saw in Griffith a presentiment of his own future in Hollywood. "There was no place for Griffith" in the film industry by 1940, Welles said years later. "He was an exile in his own town, a prophet without honor, a craftsman without tools, an artist without work.

"No wonder he hated me."

---

* But if D. W. Griffith was disapproving at the Christmas party, he admired Welles later after seeing *Citizen Kane*. "I loved *Citizen Kane* and particularly loved the ideas he [Welles] took from me," Griffith told Ezra Goodman in an interview in 1948, the year of the director's death. The interview was originally published in the New York newspaper *PM* and reprinted in Goodman's *The Fifty-Year Decline and Fall of Hollywood* (New York: Simon and Schuster, 1961).

On Christmas Eve, *The Campbell Playhouse* broadcast its final episode of 1939 from the studios of KNX in Los Angeles. The production was "A Christmas Carol," and Lionel Barrymore played Scrooge, just as Orson had promised when Barrymore was ill the year before. With Orson narrating, the cast included one newcomer—the young actress and Radio Guild activist Georgia Backus—along with longtime Mercury "henchmen" (Decla Dunning's word) George Coulouris, Ray Collins, Everett Sloane, Erskine Sanford, and Frank Readick.

After the broadcast, Orson headed to a nightclub to spend Christmas Eve with Richard Baer. When the two men bumped into a young fellow with a hard-luck story, Orson opened his wallet and offered him the contents: a grand total of $31. Welles promised the fellow "a couple more payments," Baer wrote ruefully to Arnold Weissberger.

'Twas not a season to be very jolly. But celebrating the New Year was a long-standing Welles tradition, and Orson attended Errol Flynn's annual holiday bash on Linden Drive in Beverly Hills. Among the glamorous revelers that night were Dolores Del Rio and her husband, Cedric Gibbons. Orson's date was Richard Baer.

The Smiler with the Knife had a shorter shelf life than anyone expected. In mid-January, Orson's quick-and-easy substitute for *Heart of Darkness* suffered a crippling blow when Carole Lombard begged off. Already overcommitted for the year, she could not—or would not—squeeze in another starring role for RKO. And Orson was stuck with his deadlines.

Though some accounts say Lombard vetoed Orson as a director, Welles himself insisted otherwise. "We became tremendous friends," Welles told Peter Bogdanovich, "saw a great deal of each other, and performed many practical jokes. And she was all *for* me. She simply couldn't get released" from productions already scheduled. Another RKO leading lady might have leaped at the chance to play the "madcap heiress" who infiltrates an American fascist movement, but the rush job under a first-time director found no takers among the studio's top tier. "Rosalind Russell may well have turned me down," Welles said. "I seem to remember somebody did."

Orson's fallback choice was Lucille Ball, his first publicity "date," who had recently worked her way up from uncredited glimpses and lesser roles to leads in low-budget pictures. A dozen years before she entered the television pantheon as the producer-star of *I Love Lucy*, Orson was a lone voice hailing Ball as "the greatest female clown around," he recalled. "She would have been just superb in this picture." To RKO, however, Ball was simply a B player without box office clout. "Imagine how idiotic they were," Welles said. Though her name was dangled in public, by mid-January the *Los Angeles Times* confirmed that Ball had "no chance" of landing the part. Orson tried to wangle Dita Parlo or Uta Hagen for the lead, but RKO was no more enthusiastic about either of them—they were not marquee names. Though choices were announced for the supporting cast—Vladimir Sokoloff, Robert Coote—without a star the film's momentum stalled.

If *Heart of Darkness* had been completed, or *The Smiler with the Knife* launched, the three-part profile of Welles that started in the January 20, 1940, issue of the *Saturday Evening Post* would have been a well-timed publicity coup. By now, Mercury's publicity man, Herbert Drake, was doing the kind of thing Dr. Maurice Bernstein once did, in this case supplying the reporters—Alva Johnston and Fred Smith—with a steady stream of colorful anecdotes, as well as Orson's letters and newspaper clippings from Bernstein's scrapbook. While the tone of the *Saturday Evening Post* article was patently tongue-in-cheek ("He talked like a college professor at two. . . . At eight, he started making his own highballs"), later pieces cribbed from it, and Welles spent a lifetime rebutting its effusions. In 1970, when David Frost asked Welles whether it was true that at age ten the "child genius" engaged "in a critical analysis of *Thus Spake Zarathustra*," Welles sighed. "I'm an anti-Nietzsche fellow and certainly never wrote that. It sounds like one of those stories . . ."

The article mostly focused on his boyhood and his youthful conquest of New York. His nascent career in Hollywood and his two unfilmed projects were scarcely mentioned. When Hedda Hopper mocked the *Saturday Evening Post* series, reminding her readers that Welles still wore the beard from his first unproduced film project, Welles invited her to lunch to win her back. He assured her he was trimming his beard "scientifically an inch a day," and that he was still looking for a leading lady for *The Smiler with the Knife*. When was Orson going to direct one of his three promised pictures? "When I'm good and ready," he declared, but charmingly. Orson invited Hopper to join his radio series one of these days and see how well he directed *her*. Hopper readjusted her thinking: "Orson Welles, as I said months ago, has a shrewd head on those shoulders and I think he'll make the critics eat their words. And I for one hope he does."

Regardless of the troubles he was having mounting his first two projects, Orson was still on the hook to find a third story RKO would approve to follow *The Smiler with the Knife* and *Heart of Darkness*. In interviews and studio meetings after the first of the year, he revived the possibility of *Cyrano de Bergerac*; he talked about directing the first screen *Macbeth* since Sir Herbert Beerbohm Tree's silent version in 1915; he floated a *Pickwick Papers* starring W. C. Fields. But the kinds of established literary properties Orson loved faced the most stubborn opposition from some RKO studio officials, for whom familiarity with a title bred contempt. George Schaefer was open to *Macbeth*, sensing the publicity value of revisiting the Harlem production, but Shakespeare was an uphill slog with other studio muck-a-mucks. Orson was unable to overcome the persistent doubts about *Cyrano*, and the splendid notion of Fields as Mr. Pickwick was scuttled by the comedian's firm contract with Universal.

Orson found sanctuary, increasingly, at Herman Mankiewicz's rented residence, ostensibly working on the script for *The Smiler*, although it was fast losing its viability and allure. Lying in bed in a room whose air conditioner had been rigged by their friend Margaret Sullavan, Orson relished the boon companionship of the cranky, abusive, hilarious Mank. "When the bitterness wasn't focused straight on you," Welles told Peter Bogdanovich, "he was the best company in the world."

The common wisdom about Mank was that his loathing for Hollywood and its crass commercialism had paved the way for his downfall. But what Mank really despised about Hollywood was not the machine itself, but his own fall from the machine's grace. His major credits after the silent era tended to be adaptations of Broadway hits such as *Dinner at Eight*, which came complete with sharply chiseled dialogue by his old friend George S. Kaufman and Edna Ferber. One of his best-known pictures, *John Meade's Woman*, from 1937, did contain "elements of a criticism of riches in the story of a tycoon who suffers from personal isolation and loneliness," according to Richard Meryman; and many later critics have characterized it as a precursor to *Citizen Kane*. Simon Callow saw *John Meade's Woman* as a "savage assault" on the lumber baron at the center of the drama; Pauline Kael called it "a trial run on the tycoon theme." But the original story of that B picture was the work of another Chicagoan, the staunchly left-wing scenarist John Bright—not Mank. Indeed, few of Mank's sixty-plus credits before *Kane* were his originals, and the vast majority of his credits were comedies or romances. He was, most often, an uncredited polish man, brought in to touch up dialogue in other people's scripts just before filming. He worked on assignment. He rarely started and finished a script alone.

What haunted Mankiewicz most of all was his failure as a playwright, the source of a lifelong chip on his shoulder. Like many writers of his generation, Mank had grown up regarding the theater as an honorable profession and movies as a form of prostitution; according to Meryman, Mank dreamed of the day Americans would ask, "Have you seen the new Herman Mankiewicz play?" Among his few original screen credits were *The Good Fellows* and *The Wild Man of Borneo*, adaptations of two plays he had cowritten in the 1920s, both of which failed on Broadway but were revived for the screen after his Oscar for *Citizen Kane*. A third play he'd written on his own—*The Meal Ticket*, a satirical portrait of a vaudeville family in Hollywood—closed on the road after blistering reviews. Mank had a stack of unproduced plays. One was a satire about American politics called "We the People." Another was "an uncompleted play about [William Randolph] Hearst," Meryman wrote, without further elucidation. A third was the script about John Dillinger, "The Tree Will Grow," of which he'd written only about enough to constitute the first act.

Mank was the underachiever of the Algonquin circle, which was one reason the others rooted so hard for him. In Hollywood, he gave free rein to his faults. He drank to excess, privately and publicly. Time and again he gambled away his earnings. A know-it-all about history and politics, he scolded inferiors. And his anticommunist beliefs were so intractable that he perversely opposed the struggle to form a Screen Writers Guild, led partly by a faction of communist writers. He sided instead with the right-wing Screen Playwrights, a group that was beholden to producers and, many believed, sympathetic to fascists. Mank himself voiced pro-German sentiments too often and too strenuously in the long buildup to World War II—making people wonder. (Mank himself was proudly Jewish, though, and had married his wife in an Orthodox ceremony.) On top of it all, the playwright's younger brother, Joseph L. Mankiewicz, was rising fast in Hollywood as a writer and producer, and threatening to eclipse his sibling's reputation.

Mank's admirers overlooked his faults or cherished them as evidence of his iconoclasm. To them, he was the perfect symbol of what was wrong with Hollywood: too brilliant for the industry that had cast him aside, he was forced to save his best wit for private conversation, dinner parties, and soirees. Yet anecdotes about him often turned on bad behavior and crude humor: once, purportedly, when he vomited at an elegant dinner, he hastened to reassure his hostess: "It's all right. The white wine came up with the fish." And some of his best-known bons mots were apocryphal or borrowed, including his supposed crack about Welles that appears in Pauline Kael's essay "Raising *Kane*": "There, but for the grace of God, goes God." As Orson himself was at pains to point out in a 1972 letter to the London *Times*, the quip "was made not by Mr. Herman Mankiewicz of me, but by Sir Winston Churchill of Sir Stafford Cripps," a World War II–era British Labour politician. (And, doubtless, by many others.)

Yet Welles counted himself, fervently and forever, among Mank's admirers. When Peter Bogdanovich confronted Welles with "the list of [Mank's] other credits," many of them unimpressive, Orson responded with a flare of anger: "Oh, the hell with lists—a lot of bad writers have wonderful credits." He did not care what other people said about Mank, or, ultimately, what Mank said about *him*. Alcoholism usually brought out Orson's sympathy—it reminded him of his father and of John Barrymore too—and alcoholism allowed him to rationalize all manner of outrageous behavior. Mank was like a writer's Barrymore.

"Mankiewicz was some sort of tremendous performer in a Hieronymous Bosch landscape of his own," Welles said elegiacally when Meryman interviewed him. "There was always the feeling that you were in the presence of thwarted violence. It was this thrashing of some great creature, some beached creature. Some magnificent creature. You didn't know what it was because you had never seen one of those before. It was Mank. . . .

"He liked the attention he got as a great, monumental, self-destructing machine. That was his role, and he played it to the hilt. He was a performer, as I think all very successful personalities are. He couldn't be affectionate or loving outside his family. You never felt you were basking in the warmth of his friendship. So it was his vulnerability that brought out the warmth from his friends. And people loved him. *Loved* him.

"That terrible vulnerability. That terrible wreck."

By the end of January 1940, Orson was eager to get another studio project going. Having vetted Herman Mankiewicz with his work on the radio scripts and *The Smiler with the Knife*, he now enlisted the writer to start batting around the possibilities for an original script.

Mank was still hipped on "The Tree Will Grow," his idea for a multiple-viewpoint portrait of the gangster John Dillinger. Orson identified with "the many-sided gimmick," as he put it, having nursed a similar notion ever since his abortive play about John Brown from 1932—"the idea of telling the same thing several times," as Welles explained it to Bogdanovich, "and showing exactly the same scene from wholly different points of view." But Welles had no interest in making a gangster picture. He wanted to make "a more important movie than that," as John Houseman later noted in Lundberg's lawsuit over *Citizen Kane*.

Welles and Mankiewicz held long, passionate debates about the strategy of the many-sided structure. Orson thought it would be more interesting for "the man to seem a very different person depending on who was talking about him," in his words, while Mank wanted the subjective viewpoints to fit together like a jigsaw puzzle, eventually cohering into a whole. Mank won that argument, but Orson won the debate over "a more important movie."

Orson wanted a Big Idea concerning "a man of large affairs and much influence in the world," as he testified in the Lundberg case, an "American sultan." Setting *The Smiler with the Knife* aside, he and Mank started rummaging through possible Big Ideas for their American sultan story.

They considered a politician, even a president—as in *Of Thee I Sing*, the presidential campaign musical that had excited Orson in the fall of 1932, when he was finishing "Marching Song." They talked for a while about choosing a statesman like William Jennings Bryan, who ran unsuccessfully several times for president. Mankiewicz's family had hosted Bryan at their home in Wilkes-Barre during Mank's boyhood, and he considered himself an expert on Bryan's life. Another idea they "fooled around" with was the life story of French novelist Alexandre Dumas *père*, a pet subject of Orson's, according to Mankiewicz. They also mulled the possibility of a famous soldier, or "an industrialist," recalled Houseman, "but that had been done before in *The Power and the Glory*," a famous film about the life of an industrialist. Orson and Mank even discussed "a shop picture about Hollywood," Houseman testified in the Lundberg case, but the "recently made *A Star Is Born*," starring Janet Gaynor and Fredric March, was "as good a picture of its kind as you could get."

Eventually, the two men came around to William Randolph Hearst, the publisher and media business magnate. Both men had read *After Many a Summer Dies the Swan*, Aldous Huxley's recently published new novel, with its portrait of a wealthy, eccentric empire-builder modeled on Hearst. Huxley's fiction was largely allegorical and philosophical, however, and the novel offered little narrative inspiration beyond reminding them of Hearst.

Not that they needed reminding: Hearst was constantly in the news. After decades of dominance, the publisher had overreached and fallen on hard times. His media chain was shedding newspapers and radio stations; his famous art collection had been pieced off for auction; he had just sold the twelve-story apartment house at the corner of Riverside Drive and Eighty-Sixth Street in Manhattan, where for a quarter century he had stored art treasures and occupied the upper floors and penthouse. (A photograph of that building, well known to New Yorkers, would be incorporated in the "News on the March" sequence in *Citizen Kane*.) Hearst's once mighty empire was shrinking.

"Welles himself had always been interested in mass communications and the power of propaganda," as Houseman testified in the Lundberg case, "so [Welles and Mankiewicz] arrived, by fairly logical steps, at eliminating all these other public figures and ended up with the picture of a man of great power engaged in the molding and the swaying of public opinion."

Hearst was deeply embedded in both men's consciousness. But the idea of "a man *like* Hearst" may have been Mank's specific suggestion for the central figure, as Welles admitted to Mankiewicz's biographer Richard Meryman. "I suppose I would remember if it had been me," Orson wistfully told Meryman.

Hearst, "the outstanding whirling pagoda of our times," in Mankiewicz's words, was the perfect choice for Orson's American sultan who lives to a "ripe age." This would give Welles the *Schauspieler* a chance to indulge his penchant for playing aging kingly men, and Welles the director the opportunity to create a sweeping panorama of the early twentieth century. Not only would *Citizen Kane* tell the tale of "seventy years in a man's life," as one of the *News on the March* reporters says; it would immerse that life in seventy years of American headlines and history.

They were both aware of an earlier film about an American sultan: *The Power and the Glory*, which opened with the death of a Chicago railroad magnate and then unfolded in flashback. Preston Sturges, the fellow Chicagoan whose career Orson had followed since boyhood, wrote the screenplay for that film, his first original for the screen. The story line of the 1933 picture was unusually mature fare for Hollywood, with two suicides and a child whose illegitimacy is kept from his father. But Sturges's script had featured a single narrator; it had no multiple viewpoints, and not much else from which to draw inspiration—except perhaps the performance of Spencer Tracy, who aged through four decades in the film, as Orson intended to do.

Their own many-sided story would also begin with the American sultan's final breath. Welles would introduce three of his films this way, with the death scene of a public figure: *Citizen Kane, Othello,* and *Mr. Arkadin.* Why did he repeat that conceit? asked Peter Bogdanovich.

"Just shows a certain weakness of invention on the part of the filmmaker," Welles replied.

"You can give me a better answer than that," prodded Bogdanovich.

"Peter," Welles returned, "I'm no good at this sort of stuff. I either go cryptic or philistine. All I can say is, I thought it was a good idea: Whether you get me in the morning or evening, I'm always going to say that."

The American sultan's last, mysterious words would tease the audience, much like Kurtz's last phrase in *Heart of Darkness*. Then the film would jump abruptly to a *March of Time*–style newsreel—a long-nurtured idea of Orson's—anchoring the narrative before it fragmented into viewpoints. He knew the mock newsreel would be a snap to create, and great fun, giving him a chance to show the deceased public figure against the backdrop of historic events the great man had participated in or tried to manipulate. Presenting the fake newsreel would "invest this dead man with the atmosphere of reality," as Welles said in the Lundberg case, and "suggest that Kane was a real person."

Mankiewicz, in his testimony in the case, conceded that the *News on the March* framework was entirely Orson's idea, dating back, as far as he could say, to something similar in *The Smiler with the Knife*. "I was very pleased to be able to borrow this from Orson's previous picture script," he said.

As for William Randolph Hearst, over time he had become a personal fixation for Mankiewicz. A former newsman himself, Mank had followed the "finagling, calculating, Machiavellian figure" since his New York days, delivering many "dinner dissertations on Hearst and Tammany Hall, Hearst maneuvering to be Governor [of New York in 1906], ballot boxes floating down the river," according to Richard Meryman. First in New York, and later in Hollywood, Mank knew Hearst personally. "There were two castes in Hollywood," Meryman wrote, "those who had been guests at San Simeon and those who had not. Herman and Sara [Mrs. Mankiewicz] went several times."

The members of the Hollywood upper caste were entertained in style by the magnate: picked up by limousine, shipped by special train car to the formal dinners and lavish costume parties he hosted at the Hearst Castle in San Simeon, 250 miles north of Los Angeles. A hotel-size mansion on an expansive estate, the castle boasted upwards of four dozen bedrooms, several tennis courts and swimming pools, a movie theater, the world's largest private zoo, and an airfield for Hearst and the guests who flew rather than rode the train there. By the early 1930s, Mank had become one of Hearst's pet invitees, visiting "very frequently," in Mankiewicz's words, "from a day . . . to two weeks at a time." Along with his writer friend Charles Lederer, Mank even churned out parodies of Hearst front pages to amuse the publisher and his mistress, actress Marion Davies, who was Lederer's aunt. Over time, however, Mank had been dropped from the elite invitation list, banned from San Simeon for drinking and belligerent behavior.

Mank thought the script should focus on Hearst and Davies—"a love story between a publisher and a girl," in Meryman's words. To this end, Mank wanted to build an important subplot around the story of Hollywood producer Thomas H. Ince, who fell mysteriously ill aboard the Hearst yacht in 1924 and later died, with rumors abounding that Hearst had an accidental hand in the death because of jealousy over another yacht guest's dalliance with Davies.

"I just kept on telling [Welles] everything" about Hearst and Davies, Mankiewicz recalled. "I was interested in them, and I went into all kinds of details."

Orson had never made a calculated study of Hearst; nor had he ever visited San Simeon, as far as anyone knows. He did not know Hearst personally. "Any knowledge I have of his career is gained from general and sociological surveys of his times," Welles testified under oath in the Lundberg case. Orson said he knew what the general public knew and what he had "gained from conversations with people who know him personally or who have worked for and with him."

Moreover, Orson considered it essential that the central role *not* be Hearst, per se. Rather, Orson wanted to craft a fictional "composite" that would borrow elements from many public figures: a type, an archetype. "There were and are Americans who want to be kings or dictators or leaders," in Welles's words. For such men, those he dubbed American sultans, "politics as the means of communication, and indeed the nation itself, is all there for his personal pleasuring."

Too much Hearst would lock in the script and actor, and create legal problems besides. A fictional archetype, on the other hand, would give Welles broader leeway "to make a serious film," he believed, "about a certain type of wealthy American and of his impact on his times in America." Largely for that reason, Mank agreed to fold in allusions to other tycoons, such as *Chicago Tribune* publisher Robert R. McCormick and Chicago business magnate Samuel Insull—not just to make the character more of a composite, but because Orson knew their lives from Chicago. For that reason too, Orson wanted the film's San Simeon, Xanadu, located not in California but in Florida, where many midwestern and East Coast millionaires preferred to build their ornate palaces.

Making Charles Foster Kane the ward of a banker, the heir to a fortune who enters publishing on a whim, gave Orson a crucial means of relating to the character from his own life story, and another way of differentiating the archetype from Hearst. "It was an essential point we wanted to make about his type of wealthy and influential citizen," Welles explained in his deposition in the Lundberg case. "We did not want our character to have the resourcefulness and hardness that goes with an industrial leader who has fought his way from the bottom to the top. It was also necessary for the psychological device with which we tied together the story that Kane should be removed from the care of his mother at an early and impressionable age."

Again drawing on his own experiences and background, Orson wanted the mistress of the American sultan to be pushed into a humiliating opera debut in a Chicago auditorium, which would further distance the script from Hearst (and from screen comedienne Marion Davies), while playing to Orson's strengths. (Mankiewicz's opera background was mainly limited to the Marx Brothers film.)

Throughout January, the two men discussed the composite American sultan and the half dozen or so other key characters whose viewpoints would depict the great man's life story in flashback. They argued and shouted at each other, and Mank often prevailed, but when Orson cared to win there was no question who was the boss.

It was Orson who named the central character, as he would later name most of the major characters in the film. The last name was Orson's final gracious nod toward the Irish-born actor Whitford Kane, his boyhood idol. He had offended Kane during their Mercury Theatre days, but Orson had a way of crawling into people's laps to apologize for his bad behavior, and Kane would take pleasure in boasting to the *New York Times* that cinema's most famous character was named for him.* (Mankiewicz had wanted and argued for the name "Craig," insisting that audiences would misread "Kane" as a reference to Cain

---

* Yet it was also true that the Welles genealogy ran through the town of Kane in the county of Kane, in Illinois.

and Abel. "Do you suppose anybody's ever thought of that?" Welles teased Richard Meryman. "How could you? Kane. *K.* Nice Irish name. With a *K.* You never fail with *K* in a name.")

By the end of the month, they had the lead character's name, the frame of the story, the narrative line, and certain incidents in the plot. Mankiewicz was a night owl like Orson, and sometimes the two men talked deep into the night, with Mank reclining in his bed and Orson perched on the edge of Sara Mankiewicz's matching bed. On the couple's nightstand, according to Meryman, was a snow-globe paperweight "containing a minute and wintry Swiss chalet," which Mank sometimes picked up and shook, watching "the snow swirl up inside and settle down on the tiny scene."

Like Roger Hill's wife, Sara Mankiewicz endured these late-night bedroom planning sessions, propped up on pillows, reading a magazine until she fell asleep. If the hour grew dangerously late, Orson would say, "Move over . . ." and lie down next to her. As he and Mank carried on, "goading each other with sarcasms, laughing uproariously, Welles would reach over and massage Sara's neck," according to Meryman.

"He was fun," Sara Mankiewicz told Meryman. "Magnetic, absolutely."

On February 1, 1940, Virginia Nicolson Welles gained her divorce and custody of Christopher. She emerged from a closed-door hearing in Reno with "only praise for her husband," according to the wire services, explaining that while her complaint had charged extreme mental cruelty—boilerplate divorce language in those days—"the word 'cruel' didn't fit Welles in the least." The problem was more simple: "genius and matrimony" did not mix. "Truly," she said, "I have no plans for another marriage and so far as I know neither does Mr. Welles. He works twenty hours a day and hardly ever sleeps."

Virginia immediately boarded a plane to San Francisco, en route to Hollywood, where she told the press she was planning a weeklong stay with her friend Geraldine Fitzgerald before returning to New York to resume her acting career under the name Anna Stafford. Orson, meanwhile, was headed in the opposite direction; he was on his way to New York to meet with RKO's George Schaefer, attorney Arnold Weissberger, and his estranged professional partner, John Houseman.

Only Schaefer, who gave few interviews in his career, could have said how it felt to hear the very first pitch for the project Orson was calling "John Citizen, U.S.A." It was the life story in flashback of a bigger-than-life newspaper publisher who loses his way in the American dream. Doubtless buoyed by Orson's infectious enthusiasm—and wholehearted identification with the story—Schaefer instantly recognized the story idea as both serious and sensational. Orson vowed to keep the budget under $1 million and to have the script ready for filming by the first anniversary of his arrival in Hollywood the previous July.

Without a blink, the faithful Schaefer quietly tabled *The Smiler with the Knife*. RKO would say nothing to the trade press for a few months, still touting *The Smiler* as Welles's initial opus and *Heart of Darkness* as next in line. "John Citizen U.S.A." would be kept secret for the next three months. But Weissberger could go to work on new contract clauses, and Schaefer would authorize the transfer of seed money from *The Smiler* to "John Citizen, U.S.A.," to underwrite script development and preliminary planning.

Next, Orson approached Houseman. The producer dodged Welles's calls at first but finally agreed to meet him for lunch at "21." "As the two men downed several dozen oysters, Orson filled the room with his enthusiasm and vitality and air castles, and Houseman felt himself softening up. When Welles finally presented his story idea, Houseman had much the same reaction as George Schaefer: his partner had "finally figured out that he had the right kind of picture for himself to make," as Houseman recalled.

Mankiewicz was on fire to write the script, Welles told Houseman—but that was both good and bad. Mank "was a very prolific writer," as Houseman testified in the Lundberg suit, who "unless he is carefully controlled tends to turn out a script that is three or four times as long as what you can finally shoot. This is a great waste of time for all concerned and is not a good way to work." Orson was planning to send Mankiewicz to the California desert, for secrecy and solitude, but Mank needed a minder to keep him from going off the rails with drink or digression—and the only chaperone Mank would accept was Houseman. Orson knew Houseman would be flattered, but it was true: after working with Houseman on the radio, Mankiewicz much preferred the producer's laissez-faire approach to Orson's constant second-guessing. "I had gotten along with [Houseman] better," the screenwriter later told the courtroom in the Lundberg case.

Orson offered Houseman a munificent $1,000 weekly for ten weeks. The contract called for him to fulfill "a very special function," Houseman explained in the Lundberg case, which he described as a combination "writer" and "associate producer." In truth, he was being hired to serve as a dramaturg, a story and scene editor, for Mank.

"It was an absurd venture," Houseman recalled, "and that night Orson and I flew back to California together."

Houseman's contract was with Mercury, which was synonymous now with Welles. Mankiewicz's contract was also with Mercury, and it "assigned all claims of authorship to the corporation," as Robert L. Carringer has noted. In other words, by agreeing to the terms of the deal, Mankiewicz forfeited any claim to screen credit. "I had no intention of Mank being the coauthor" at the outset, as Welles explained to Meryman years later. "None. Rightly or wrongly, I was still without self-doubt in my ability to write a film script. I thought Mank would do that anecdotal kind of thing about Hearst, give me a few ideas, fight me a little—and mainly would be as destructive as he had been in *Smiler with the Knife*."

Before he was fired from MGM, Mankiewicz had been earning as much as $2,250 a week. Out of the funding authorized by Schaefer, Orson offered to pay him the same salary as Houseman: $1,000 a week for ten weeks, officially starting February 19. Over the next five months, Mankiewicz's earnings, plus bonuses, would add up to $22,833.35. Over the same period, Orson paid himself $25,000 for his collaboration on the screenplay—money that was also derived from RKO, but like all the salaries was charged back to Mercury as part of its budgetary allotment for the picture.

A good deal of work had been done before the February 19 contract date, with Mank receiving small sums that Richard Baer managed to extract from the coffers of *The Smiler with the Knife* and *Campbell Playhouse* through creative accounting. The lawyers in the Lundberg case were mystified by the complicated, interwoven financial machinations. "The money that I received was always from Mercury," Houseman tried to explain to the court, "and therefore in essence out of Welles's pocket . . . the same was true of Mankiewicz." Orson *was* the Mercury, as he had boasted, and for him money was always a means to an end, paid out liberally whenever he could pay it.

But Baer's shell games weren't enough to keep Orson afloat. He had to find ways to stretch the preproduction allotment of "John Citizen, U.S.A." *The Campbell Playhouse* would make its final broadcast in late March, depriving Welles of his only reliable source of non-RKO income. And now he had his monthly obligations to Virginia as well. Largely for these reasons, Albert Schneider and Herbert Drake had begun to plan a spring lecture tour that would take Orson to several cities around the country, bringing in up to $1,000 weekly in April and May, the anticipated nadir of Mercury's finances. By late May, then, Orson hoped to have the first draft of the script, which would mean the release of another chunk of preproduction money from RKO.

Yet May 6, which was his twenty-fifth birthday, was also fast approaching. Orson could not help wondering how much money remained in the trust fund bequeathed to him on his father's death ten years before, in 1930. The inheritance might change his predicament altogether, even saving him from having to give up his Brentwood mansion. He asked Arnold Weissberger to ask the Chicago bank for an advance report on the expected final distribution.

Ten years after the making of *Citizen Kane*, John Houseman told the courtroom in the Lundberg case that on returning to Los Angeles he held "numerous conversations" with Welles and Herman Mankiewicz concerning both the script and his own supervisory role. "We were not starting from scratch," the producer said. Then, "almost immediately," Houseman and Mankiewicz set out for the small desert town of Victorville, California, one hundred miles northeast of Los Angeles, about halfway between San Bernardino and Barstow. Richard Meryman estimates their departure date at "around February 1." Houseman told the lawyers it was "early" February or even possibly "the middle of February," which was closer to reality.

Their destination was the Kemper Campbell Ranch—run by a Los Angeles lawyer couple—"a sort of dude ranch which Mankiewicz had been to before," according to Houseman, and a "very quiet" and "suitable place to work." The first car in their small caravan, a studio limousine with a professional driver, carried a German nurse and her patient, Mankiewicz, "excited and groaning cheerfully" in his leg cast. Houseman followed in a sporty convertible, accompanied by a freshly engaged secretary, Rita Alexander, "a patient, efficient, nice-looking English girl," in Houseman's words. Mank would reward the secretary's patience and efficiency over the next months in Victorville by lending her name to Kane's mistress and second wife—Susan Alexander. It was the only major character's name that can be traced unequivocally to him.

Houseman testified that "Mr. Welles had given me to understand in New York that nothing had been written" before their departure, but this could have been Orson cheering Houseman on as just the man for the challenge ahead. Orson insisted in later interviews that before the men left he had created a foundational script, "a mammoth, 300-page version" with mostly dialogue and some description, and with what was always meant as a working title—"John Citizen, U.S.A." "Though everything was reworked throughout, that contained the script as it developed," Welles told Meryman. "But apparently Mank never showed it to anybody."

Even Meryman, attentive to every claim of authorship, conceded in his biography of Mankiewicz that "it would have been strange if Welles had not put his *Kane* ideas on paper before Herman began writing," since that had been his consistent practice since boyhood. Even when collaborating—*especially* when collaborating—Orson wrote his ideas down.

Arriving in Victorville, the visitors from Hollywood took over an adobe bungalow on the ranch. Mankiewicz's nurse took up quarters in a room next door to his suite. Houseman moved into rooms a few doors away in the same bungalow, while the secretary was housed in a separate building.

Before long, they had established a working routine. Most mornings, Houseman recalled, he went for an early horseback ride. Mank slept in, for as long as possible, then took breakfast in bed before the arduous task of dressing and bathing with his broken leg and cast. After a late breakfast, Mank and his secretary debated "a horrendous decision," according to Meryman's account. "Should the dictation take place indoors with Herman in bed? Or now that Herman could hobble on crutches, should he sit in the airy, sunny little patio with his leg up on a stool? . . . In either spot, Herman still contrived to procrastinate."

Late mornings, Mank usually got together with Houseman, reviewing and critiquing the previous day's pages. Then, after lunch, Mank indulged in his customary afternoon nap. His most productive time was at night, after dinner, when he dictated passages to Rita Alexander until midnight or 1 A.M. She typed up the pages before retiring.

Booze was verboten, except for "the great adventure of the day," in Houseman's words—implicitly every day—which was their joint visit to a bar called The Green Spot, near the railroad tracks, "where we slowly drank one scotch apiece and watched the locals playing the pinball machines and dancing to the Western music of a jukebox." Once a week the two men took in whatever new picture was playing at the only movie house in Victorville.

"In that desert limbo," wrote Meryman, "Herman found the perfect circumstances in which he could function. He was quarantined from everything that had always plagued and immobilized him. Trapped in his cast, he could not go drinking. Studio ignoramuses were not degrading him. His family was not riddling him with guilt.

"There was little to do except write."

Rita Alexander, for one, was impressed by Mank's great creativity, and her account of the trip to Victorville would be used by Pauline Kael in her later argument against Welles's authorship of Citizen Kane. (Although Alexander was among the few eyewitnesses Kael consulted, Kael did not learn—or care to mention—that another secretary substituted for Alexander for several weeks in Victorville.)

"He began with the title," Alexander recalled, "the description of the scene, the indications of the camera movement, the dialogue and so on. It was really extraordinary. It all came out not fast, not slow—at a continued pace as though he had it all in his mind."

The word "Rosebud" came at the end of the scene.

"Who is Rosebud?" the secretary asked innocently.

"It isn't a who, it's an it," Mank replied gruffly.

"What is Rosebud?" she said.

"It's a sled."

CHAPTER 19

February–May 1940

"The Script Is a Source of Some Gratification"

"Rosebud" is the first word of dialogue in *Citizen Kane*, the word barely whispered by Charles Foster Kane, his giant lips filling the screen, as he takes his final breath before dying.

There is no mention of those giant lips in the published shooting script of *Citizen Kane*, nor of literally hundreds of other visual embellishments and dialogue alterations that substantially distinguish the published version of the script from the finished picture. When the *New Yorker*'s critic Pauline Kael sought authorization to include the shooting script by Mankiewicz and Welles in her 1971 *The Citizen Kane Book*, Welles gave his necessary permission—in return for a pittance, because he badly needed the money, as he told Peter Bogdanovich—little suspecting how drastically Kael's book would undermine his reputation.

Yet even in its published form, the script's opening sequence reads as though it was devised primarily by Welles, who from his earliest talks with Mankiewicz conceived of scenes in terms of the camera as well as of the story. The fade-in of exterior shots reveals the faded glories of Xanadu in the faint dawn. This "series of setups," in the words of the script, reveals golf links, a zoo, a monkey terrace, an alligator pit, a lagoon, a huge swimming pool, cottages, and a drawbridge, "all telling something of . . . THE LITERALLY INCREDIBLE DOMAIN OF CHARLES FOSTER KANE." Moving slowly, the camera rises to an illuminated window, "very small in the distance."

"All around this," the published script continues, "an almost totally black screen. Now, as the camera moves towards this window, which is almost a postage stamp in the frame, other forms appear: barbed wire, cyclone fencing, and now, looming up against an early morning sky, an enormous iron grillwork. Camera travels up what is now shown to be a gateway of gigantic proportions, and holds on the top of it—a huge initial 'K.'" Dissolving inside the window, the camera reveals Kane's enormous bed, then a snow scene inside a glass ball ("big impossible flakes of snow" with "the jingling of sleigh bells in the musical score"). The music freezes, and "Kane's old voice" speaks the single word. After the word is murmured, Kane's hand relaxes visibly. "The ball falls out of his hand and bounds down two carpeted steps leading to the bed, the camera following."

Kane has died a lonely death in the fairy-tale mountaintop castle, Xanadu, his final utterance the mysterious "Rosebud." Then the screen explodes with footage from *News on the March*, "a typical news digest" that establishes the man's life story against a parade of tricked-up American history. After the end of this newsreel—which Mankiewicz described as an idea left over from the unfilmed *Smiler with the Knife*, but which might just as reasonably be described as left over from Welles's life and earlier career and as inseparable from *Citizen Kane* as "Rosebud"—an editor complains about the newsreel's conventional approach. "What it needs is an angle."

A reporter is assigned to dig into the meaning of "Rosebud."

After this compelling prologue—which composer Bernard Herrmann would treat as an overture—the reporter seeks out five or six key characters to offer their reminiscences of Kane in flashback.

The death of Kane, "Rosebud," and *News on the March*—the opening sequences of the film—all this had been agreed on by Welles and Mankiewicz before Victorville. But what happened next would depend a lot on the five or six key characters, who took over the film for long sections of subjective memory. Welles and Mankiewicz had discussed the characters, but the different personalities had to be fleshed out, and their accounts had to fit together and overlap just a little, without too much repetition or contradiction—a point Orson conceded to Mank.

The structure of the narrative was tricky, because the story had to be chronological, with the thread passed like a baton to each of the key characters as the reporter visits them to hear about Kane. The sequencing was a major challenge, and although Welles and Mankiewicz had discussed the through-line, this was Mank's biggest job. And with each successive draft the difficulties would multiply, as changes in their evolving conception of Kane's story forced them to invent new plot ideas, reshuffle the sequencing, and "re-characterize" the various narrators.

The order in which the reporter called on the key characters would guide the sequencing. Thompson, the *News on the March* reporter assigned to investigate "Rosebud," was the first running character—albeit the only one who never knew Kane. Orson envisioned him as a cardboard figure, a man without background or individuality: "Not a person," as Welles told Peter Bogdanovich, but simply "a piece of machinery" used to tease the audience through the story.

Even Raymond, Kane's butler, who is the last of the witnesses to talk to Thompson, has more color. John Houseman insisted that Raymond, who looms importantly at the end of *Citizen Kane*, was based on Welles's own vaguely sinister butler in Brentwood, although Orson's butler there was French, and Raymond was effectively the kind of stock butler character glimpsed in hundreds of Hollywood films, the household servant who observes and hears all and whose loyalty is unquestioned unless a gratuity is involved. "If you're smart, you'll talk to Raymond," Susan Alexander tells Thompson the reporter. "He knows where all the bodies are buried."

The first source Thompson approaches is Susan, but she is drunk and morose and throws him out. (She will return to the film later through a shrewd bit of structuring.) Thompson then visits the hushed archives of the banker Walter Parks Thatcher, Kane's guardian. Thatcher plays a crucial role as the sole, if biased, eyewitness to Kane's boyhood.* Though Thatcher has long been dead by the time Kane dies, the film uses a device that harks back to Orson's original concept for "First Person Singular": Thompson reads out loud from the banker's unpublished memoirs in the vault of his library, "a room" with a repellent personality much like Thatcher's, "with all the warmth and charm of Napoleon's Tomb," in the words of the script.

---

* The "Thatcher" looked back to Orson's boyhood piano teacher, Phyllis Fergus—and her husband, Chicago businessman Thatcher Hoyt.

Arguably the most transparent character is the next witness, Mr. Bernstein—who has the same last name as Welles's guardian. (His first name is never mentioned.) Bernstein, the comptroller who has risen to become general manager of Kane's empire, tells Thompson that he was at Kane's side "from before the beginning, young fellow . . . and now, it's after the end." Bernstein is devoted to his boss; he never stops rooting for Kane, even after the tycoon's death, with a viewpoint that is nonjudgmental—indeed, for a businessman, profoundly sympathetic, even loving.

One thing the writing team happily agreed on, after the film was done, was that Bernstein's was the one character most indebted to Mankiewicz. Although "I sketched out the character in our preliminary sessions," Welles remembered, "Mank did all the best writing for Bernstein. I'd call that the most valuable thing he gave us."

Mankiewicz had a professional exemplar in mind: Louis Wiley, the business manager of the *New York Times* from 1906 until his death in 1935. Wiley, along with publisher Adolph Ochs and managing editor Carr Vattel Van Anda, formed the triumvirate that made the *Times* "what it has become," in Mank's words. As a former newsman Mank knew all three men from his days in New York. Houseman concurred: "Bernstein was [Mank's] favorite character in this whole script."

THOMPSON

If we can find out what he meant by his last words—as he was dying—

BERNSTEIN

That Rosebud, huh? (*Thinks.*) Maybe some girl? There were a lot of them back in the early days and—

THOMPSON

(*amused*)

It's hardly likely, Mr. Bernstein, that Mr. Kane could have met some girl casually and then, fifty years later, on his deathbed remembered—

BERNSTEIN

Well, you are pretty young, Mr.—(*Remembers the name.*)—
Mr. Thompson. A fellow will remember a lot of things you
wouldn't think he'd remember. You take me. One day, back
in 1896, I was crossing over to Jersey on a ferry and as we
pulled out there was another ferry pulling in—(*Slowly.*)—
and on it was a girl waiting to get off. A white dress she had
on—she was carrying a white parasol—I only saw her for
one second. She didn't see me at all—but I'll bet a month
hasn't gone by since that I haven't thought of that girl.

"That was all Mank," Welles told Bogdanovich of the above exchange.
"It's my favorite scene . . . the best thing in the movie . . . I *wish* it was
me . . . If I were in hell and they gave me a day off and said, 'What part
of any movie you ever made do you want to see?' I'd see that scene of
Mank's about Bernstein.

"All the rest could have been better but that was just right."

Bernstein also frames Jed Leland sympathetically, but he has fallen
out of touch with "Mr. Leland," who emerges as Kane's oldest, most
conscientious friend, though the film makes clear that Kane has betrayed him. At the end of his talk with Bernstein, Thompson tells the
comptroller where Leland is: "In case you'd like to know . . . he's at the
Huntington Memorial Hospital on 180th Street," adding thoughtfully, "Nothing particular the matter with him, they tell me. Just . . ."

"Just old age," Bernstein says, finishing with one of Mank's sublime
one-liners. "It's the only disease, Mr. Thompson, that you don't look
forward to being cured of."

This leads Thompson and the film to the next witness to Kane's
past: Leland, "wrapped in a blanket . . . in a wheelchair . . . on the
flat roof of a hospital." To block the sun he is wearing a visor, which
helps call attention to his baldness. Although Leland already has been
glimpsed in Bernstein's flashbacks, the betrayed friend looks old and
feeble now. This was crafted as a shocking moment for the viewers,
who had previously glimpsed him as a carefree, debonair young man.

Because Mankiewicz had been a newsman, and because of the scene
where the drunken Leland collapses over his typewriter (as Mank had
done when writing his abortive denunciation of Gladys Wallis for the

New York Times), some sources have credited the development of Leland more to Mankiewicz. From the get-go, however, the Leland character was "founded on a personal friend of Orson's who had been a newspaper man," as Houseman testified in the Lundberg case.

That was Ashton Stevens: "practically my uncle," as Welles told Bogdanovich. "The last of the dandies—he worked for Hearst for some fifty years or so and adored him. A gentleman . . . very much like Jed." In addition, Orson wanted Leland to be a *Southern* gentleman— like Joseph Cotten, his close friend, the actor he imagined for the role from his first talks with Mankiewicz. "As author of the film," Welles said, he regarded the character of Leland "with enormous affection. . . . He's the only true aristocrat [in the story]. . . . He's talking my language. I have deep sympathy for him."

As with most of the key characters, Orson even put his stamp on this character's name, changing it from Bradford Leland in Mank's first draft to Jedediah "Jed" Leland for the film. The name was an amalgam of Broadway producer Jed Harris and agent Leland Hayward, Margaret Sullavan's husband, both of whom had made forceful impressions on Orson during his rounds in New York in 1934. (Mankiewicz knew both men, too, and this made it easy for him to agree.)

Three women loom importantly in Kane's life, but Thompson visits only two of them. The first is seen only in flashback, as part of Thatcher's archival reflections. She is Kane's mother, known only as "Mrs. Kane" in the published version of the script, although she is Mary in the film. In 1870, Mrs. Kane inherits the Colorado Lode from a former renter who once skipped out leaving his bill unpaid. Implicitly sparing her son a provincial upbringing and removing him from an abusive father, Mrs. Kane signs five-year-old Charlie (his middle name, "Foster," is a master touch) over to Thatcher in the parlor of her boardinghouse. In exchange for $150,000 a year, she will never see him again.

MRS. KANE

I've got his trunk all packed—(*She chokes a little.*)
I've had it packed for a week now.

(*She can't say any more. She starts for the hall door.*)

The second female character, chronologically, in Kane's life story is Emily Monroe Norton, his first wife, whom he marries in 1898. The niece of the incumbent president of the United States (in real life, this would have been William McKinley), Emily would have more scenes than Kane's mother and would participate in major events in Kane's adult life. This was particularly true of Mank's first script draft, generated at Victorville: that draft—which included a honeymoon scene on a Wisconsin lake, and various other family tableaux—saw Emily survive her husband to tell her side of the story.

But it was Susan Alexander, Kane's mistress and second wife, who would emerge as the film's most prominent female character as the script evolved. After becoming a powerful press lord, Kane meets Susan, "aged twenty-one, neatly but cheaply dressed," outside a drugstore in 1915. When a passing carriage splashes mud on his finery, she can't help giggling at his offended dignity. Her reaction diverts Kane from his errand: sifting through his deceased mother's possessions in a Manhattan warehouse. "In search of my youth," he jokes—the wistful joke of a man who never really had a childhood.

Although the good-hearted Susan has no idea who Charles Foster Kane is, even when he mentions his famous name ("I'm awfully ignorant, but I guess you caught on to that"), she invites him to her rented flat to wash up. His "shadowgraphs" (a quaint word in the script for finger puppetry on the wall) and joking help to alleviate her painful toothache.

One reason Houseman was an important choice to supervise the writing in Victorville was that he knew the actors—many of them Mercury Theatre stage and radio players—whom Orson had cast in major roles even before the script was written. Since Mankiewicz lacked that awareness, Houseman was there to prod him toward their strengths. For example, as Houseman explained in the Lundberg case, casting George Coulouris as Thatcher helped shape the writing of that character: "We might have made Thatcher differently if this rather lean-faced man had not been going to play it. These are intangibles. It is hard to know at what point you are trying to accommodate the actor and at what point you make the actor fit the part."

The part of Bernstein—undersized but spry, Jewish with intense eyes, as the script dictated—was molded for the similarly undersized (and Jewish) Everett Sloane, another member of the Mercury family. "It was extremely desirable, because Sloane had been a faithful collaborator of ours, that a good part be found for him," Houseman explained in his testimony in the Lundberg case, "and undoubtedly the particular coloration and particular character of Bernstein was affected by the fact that we knew that Everett Sloane was going to play the part."

Houseman noted in his deposition, "The same is true of Joseph Cotten" as Leland. "He had never done anything [in Hollywood], and Orson had long been convinced that Cotten could be a star if he were properly cast as a rather aristocratic, moral, but not very active man." Although the character of Leland sprang from Ashton Stevens, he was also consciously "tailored after the personality of" Cotten, in Houseman's words.

The part of Kane's mother likewise was molded for one of Orson's favorite underrated actresses: Agnes Moorehead. As often as possible in his career, Orson created roles for Moorehead, whose persona combined grace and steel. Who should portray Wilbur Minafer's sister Fanny, hopelessly in love with Eugene Morgan (Joseph Cotten), in the film of *The Magnificent Ambersons*? "There wasn't any question about it," Welles told Peter Bogdanovich. "How could there be? She'd been all those years with us—it was going to be her great part." Moorehead, known to her Mercury friends as "Aggie," would cavort onstage (and even play the calliope) in the Mercury Wonder Show during World War II, and she would also appear in *Jane Eyre* and *Journey into Fear*. Moorehead even would have starred as the Nazi-hunting federal agent stalking Welles's character in *The Stranger* if RKO hadn't insisted on a more bankable and conventional choice, Edward G. Robinson.

But as Houseman and Mankiewicz rolled up their sleeves and got down to work in Victorville, Welles had no early idea of whom he might cast as the first and second Mrs. Charles Foster Kane. With the Mercury stage company low on leading ladies under long-term contract, he was forced to rummage through his former radio costars and the familiar Hollywood casting pool for these two actresses—a circumstance that helps explain why they were the most mutable characters as the script progressed.

While Herman Mankiewicz and John Houseman were toiling away in Victorville, once again Welles was beset by unexpected crises, both personal and professional.

After securing her divorce in Reno, Virginia Nicolson Welles had lingered in Hollywood, staying with Geraldine Fitzgerald for weeks; then, shortly after the writing team left for Victorville, Virginia had fallen ill, with acute abdominal pain. Entering a Los Angeles hospital on February 21, she was diagnosed with potentially life-threatening peritonitis. After emergency surgery, she remained in the hospital for about a month. Her slow recovery complicated the arrangements for the care of Christopher, and placed an additional strain on Orson's time and finances. Virginia's medical bills piled up even as his alimony lagged behind.

Orson was solicitous about his ex-wife's health, however, visiting her often at the hospital (where he often crossed paths with a friend, writer Charles Lederer, who was visiting Virginia even more faithfully). At one point Orson volunteered to pay Virginia's long-range hospital bills if she would accept a temporary cut in his child support payments. When the medical costs continued to mount, however, Orson retracted his offer, insisting that he'd been misunderstood. Virginia was furious, and her hospital debt became the cornerstone of financial grudges she nursed against Welles for years.

Orson and Dolores Del Rio made a decision to keep a low profile while Virginia was in the hospital. "Welles and his Hollywood love are chilling," wrote columnist Walter Winchell. But when the beautiful Mexican actress abandoned the home she shared with Cedric Gibbons in March 1940, publicly declaring the end of their "nine-year perfect marriage," Hollywood columnists speculated that she and Welles were headed for the altar. Del Rio was still denying any heated romance between her and Orson, though, and when the couple traveled together to New York, on at least one occasion, Del Rio's mother stayed with her daughter in the same hotel room, adjacent to Orson's.

In the early weeks of 1940, actress Marlene Dietrich, a friend of both, went out on the town frequently with the two rumored lovers.

"Marlene was the 'beard,' you see, for Dolores when she was married," Welles boasted to Barbara Leaming. "I would take out Dolores by taking out Marlene too. Who would guess with those two girls what I was up to?" Orson also went out alone with Dietrich often enough to make columnists wonder if he was wooing her. He wasn't, although their "dates" launched a lifelong close friendship. (Welles, who dubbed Dietrich "Super Marlene," revered her above all other screen goddesses—with the exception of Garbo, although he rated Dietrich as more intelligent. He would later relish the chance to saw "Super Marlene" in half for delighted servicemen at the Mercury Wonder Show, and he gave Dietrich an unforgettable part in the twilight of her career as the clairvoyant prostitute Tanya, in love with Welles's corrupt Quinlan, in *Touch of Evil.*)

Another of Del Rio's close friends was the actress Fay Wray, who suspected Del Rio—raised as a proper Catholic—of using her chaste dalliance with Welles to force Gibbons into a divorce. "She apparently didn't consider having an affair with Orson, but thought she must leave Cedric, get a divorce," Wray recalled. "She seemed herself a lady of purity."

In any case, Del Rio's divorce suit would not go to court for another six months.

Orson gained time and lost money as the radio series wound down in February and March.

With Paul Stewart in New York and John Houseman in Victorville, Orson had to organize the season's last *Campbell Playhouse* programs himself, with the assistance of the West Coast staff. Keeping on the show business columnist Hedda Hopper's good side, Orson gave Hopper a showy part in his radio version of *Dinner at Eight*, broadcast on February 18; Hopper played the character Billie Burke had played in the 1933 movie. Lucille Ball, who had watched her chances for *The Smiler with the Knife* go down the drain, was consoled with Jean Harlow's role.*

---

* Orson and Lucille Ball stayed friends over the years, however, and the "Lucy Meets Orson Welles" episode was a hilarious highlight of the sixth season of *I Love Lucy* in

Many of the *Campbell Playhouse* shows in 1940 made use of screen stars who were willing to moonlight on radio, and some were simply radio renditions of Hollywood pictures. Loretta Young starred opposite Welles in an adaptation of the screwball comedy *Theodora Goes Wild* (broadcast on January 14, 1940). William Powell and Miriam Hopkins played the leads (with Orson playing Hopkins's father) in a freewheeling rendition of Frank Capra's *It Happened One Night* (January 28). Joan Blondell was paired with Orson, essaying the Cary Grant role, in an abridgment of Howard Hawks's *Only Angels Have Wings* (February 25). And Orson played second fiddle to Jack Benny in Ring Lardner and George S. Kaufman's *June Moon* (March 24).

Helen Hayes made more appearances on Orson's radio show in its first two years than any other star, and she returned to the series for "Vanity Fair" (January 7) and "Broome Stages" (February 4). Orson's friend Geraldine Fitzgerald, not quite a movie star of the first magnitude, then or ever, acted with Welles for a radio version of A. J. Cronin's *The Citadel* (January 21).

Orson would host the final broadcast on March 31, with mixed feelings. The sponsor, Campbell, had grown fond of tinkering with the stories and the stars, taking a special interest in the lead actresses, and for months it resisted Orson's attempts to schedule Charlotte Brontë's *Jane Eyre*. The story was "absolute sockeroo," he told the sponsor in a memo, and he wanted to play Edward Fairfax Rochester, the unbridled master of the manor who falls in love with the lowly servant Jane. In the memo he was reduced to painful pleading: "This may seem a foolish point," he finished, "but I do think it would be generous to give me opportunity to do something worthwhile myself on last show rather than supporting an actress in a negligible character part."

Campbell finally relented and gave Orson the chance to play Roch-

---

1956. In the episode, Lucy has contrived to join Orson's appearance at Club Babalu, believing it will give her an opportunity to show off her Shakespeare skills. She winds up as Orson's assistant in his magic act, but rebelliously, and while suspended horizontally in midair recites the balcony scene from *Romeo and Juliet*. The same year, Ball's Desilu company produced Orson's imaginative television pilot *The Fountain of Youth*, which was intended to launch an anthology series (the series never aired); the pilot won a Peabody Award, and helped get Welles off the blacklist.

ester. For the part of Jane, Orson turned to actress Madeleine Carroll, who had performed for him in broadcasts of "The Green Goddess" and "The Garden of Allah." He got his wish to play Rochester again, claiming the role in Robert Stevenson's atmospheric big-screen version of 1943, with Joan Fontaine as Jane. Orson preferred Carroll to Fontaine, whom he called "just a plain old bad actor," in his conversations with Henry Jaglom. "She's got four readings and two expressions."*

Orson's real interest in *Jane Eyre* was the opportunity to play Rochester: if he was given the chance to direct sixty films of his choice, Welles told Peter Bogdanovich, not one of them would be *Jane Eyre*. Welles did so much script and production work on the 1943 film version, produced by Twentieth Century-Fox, however, that the studio offered him a credit as an associate producer. He declined.

"Parts of the film looked as though you had directed [them]," Bogdanovich said.

"Oh, I invented some of the shots," Welles commented. "That's part of being that kind of producer. And I collaborated on it, but I didn't come around behind the camera and direct it. Certainly, I did a lot more than a producer ought to, but [director Robert] Stevenson didn't mind that. And I don't want to take credit away from him."

Robert Coote and Edgar Barrier, among the actors Orson was courting for film work, were behind the mike for "Jane Eyre," the last *Campbell* show of the season. But Coote and Barrier booked themselves up with Hollywood jobs too quickly afterward; neither would appear in *Citizen Kane*. Another player in "Jane Eyre" was George Coulouris, who took a role in the Warner Brothers melodrama *All This and Heaven Too* after seeing *Heart of Darkness* and *The Smiler with the Knife* fall by the wayside. But he remained Orson's first and only choice to play Walter Parks Thatcher.

---

* Fontaine got back at Welles in her autobiography *No Bed of Roses*, complaining about his demands, his lateness, his melodramatics "on and off the set," his second-guessing of the director of *Jane Eyre*. "Everything about him was oversized, including his ego," the actress wrote, adding, "Oddly enough, Orson wanted very much to be liked. We could only think of him as someone to handle carefully, to avoid as much as possible."

Every day and most nights Orson showed up at RKO, making sketches and preparations for *Citizen Kane.* And as usual he had a wealth of other activities and projects on his plate.

Orson spent a day with documentary pioneer Robert Flaherty, who had impressed him with his films *Nanook of the North* (which Orson had seen with his mother in Chicago in 1922) and *Man of Aran,* documenting life on the Irish islands. Afterward, Welles announced plans to collaborate with Flaherty on projects set in the South Pacific and the arctic. (The projects didn't work out as planned, but Flaherty did contribute story material and ideas to part of Welles's uncompleted *It's All True* in 1942.)

Orson also found time to make a test recording for a proposed new radio series featuring selected stories from the Bible. A throwback to his afternoon poetry recitals on radio in New York, the pilot episode was cobbled together with a few Mercury regulars, backed by a symphony orchestra; Orson narrated the origins of Adam and Eve. But the project found no takers and was stillborn.*

Other Hollywood studios contacted Orson about possible acting jobs, and there was fleeting industry buzz that he was in line to play the acerbic critic Sheridan Whiteside—a character based on his early booster, Alexander Woollcott—in the planned screen version of the Kaufman-Hart play *The Man Who Came to Dinner.* But that film was a Warner Brothers production, and his home studio nixed the idea; his starring debut was reserved for RKO.

In interviews, Orson was constantly spooling out plans for future projects; he even went so far as to register a few titles with industry groups, including a film based on *The War of the Worlds* and another focusing on the Borgias, a sweeping (if less likely) Hollywood subject reflecting his longtime fascination with the Italian Renaissance. And when he wasn't talking with show business columnists, he was keeping up his profile in radio: in late March, for example, he repaid Jack Benny

---

* Later, during the production of *Citizen Kane,* Orson briefly explored the idea of a film about the life of Jesus.

for his stint on *The Campbell Playhouse* by appearing on Benny's own radio hour. He and Benny had an easy friendship. In 1943, when Benny fell ill, Orson hosted *The Jack Benny Show* for six weeks, performing some of his funniest bits as himself, spoofing his own genius.

Some of these activities might seem random, but Welles had to tread water while Mankiewicz was working on his draft of *Citizen Kane*, and the radio paychecks helped to replace his income from *Campbell Playhouse*. Albert Schneider and Herbert Drake were hard at work promoting Orson's national speaking tour. "Lecture is informal," Drake said, touting the tour in a telegram sent to Sam Zolotow at the *New York Times*. "Welles invites hecklers from outset . . . besides talking, reads speeches, *Hamlet*, *Richard III*, Congreve etc. . . . opens and closes with jokes."

On April 3, shortly after the final *Campbell* broadcast, Orson opened the intended national tour at the Pasadena Civic Auditorium, addressing a full house of more than two thousand. "The New Actor" was his topic, and although he spoke off the cuff from notes, his comments were serious and thoughtful. "The business of the actor is to increase the awareness of each person in the audience of his being alive," Welles declaimed. "It is a great Christian and a great democratic obligation to remind them of themselves as a part of the human race."

Interspersing his lecture with readings from Shakespeare, Welles addressed the Pasadena crowd for two hours "almost without pause," according to press accounts. Later, he delivered "virtually a second lecture backstage" to "at least one hundred and fifty young students of the drama and some older ones," who lobbed questions at him for another half hour. The audience got its money's worth, and so did Orson— earning $1,000 to $1,500 per lecture—with Albert Schneider's agency, Columbia Artists, taking a 25 percent commission. The Pasadena date was a dress rehearsal for a full itinerary—Kansas City, Portland, Seattle, Vancouver, and beyond—and Welles even volunteered to pay his own travel expenses in order to encourage further bookings.

The second lecture date on April 11 in Kansas City, however, backfired. The problem wasn't the size of the turnout—there were nearly five thousand people, twice as many as in Pasadena—it was the reaction to negative comments Orson purportedly made about Hollywood during the lecture, which were sent out across the country by the wire services. "Of the movies," the United Press quoted him as saying, "I will speak only in terms of contempt." "The average American only goes to movies," Welles supposedly said, "because it is better than drink."

By the time Welles arrived back in Hollywood, a firestorm was raging. The United Press account—headlined "Hollywood! Orson Welles Does Not Approve of You!"—was excerpted over Radio KFI in Los Angeles, and Hedda Hopper commented acidly on the story in her column. Orson quickly took out a half-page advertisement in the *Hollywood Reporter*, insisting that he'd been "grossly misquoted," and offering a recap of his lecture that was intended to correct the "misstatements." He had been upbeat about Hollywood in his speech, he insisted, actually telling his audience: "A movie today is a better bargain for your money than a play. The motion picture medium is populated with ninety per cent of the world's theater talent. It is healthier, livelier, more inventive. It has yet to discover its limitations." His comment about speaking of Hollywood "only in contempt" had been nothing more than a misunderstood joke.

For many, the advertisement ended the controversy, but for a couple of weeks Orson's alleged diatribe against Hollywood became grist for the mill of snide columnists and pundits not only in Hollywood but across the nation. The United Press kept feeding the story, asking other stars about Welles's insult to filmdom. "He is just trying to imitate a Harvard undergraduate," actress Ann Sheridan was quoted as saying. Some wouldn't nibble. "I know it sounds awful screwy," Pat O'Brien said, "but I met Orson once and he's a really nice kid."

Unhappy about the negative publicity, RKO pressured Welles to halt his lecture tour. Orson gave interviews to explain himself, telling Fredrick C. Othman in the *Hollywood Citizen-News*, "Every time I open my mouth, I seem to say too much." He'd launched his lecture tour only to make a little extra money, he explained, having paid out $80,000 of his earnings toward Mercury's debts and projects in the past year. "Everybody seems to think I'm on one of those salaries you read about," Welles added. "RKO isn't paying me a cent. I don't get any money until I start making pictures."

Welles was forced to cancel all the dates outside Los Angeles, where he saved face with two lectures at UCLA in May. Those lectures were more quietly successful, by all accounts, although Orson still couldn't keep all his opinions to himself. When a questioner at UCLA asked what he thought about the recent Broadway hit *Key Largo*, Orson snapped, "Nothing in the world can induce me to see a Maxwell Anderson play, and vice versa."

He had counted on the tour for cash to keep Mercury operations alive, but the controversy was "a really scurvy trick" played on him by irresponsible reporters, Herbert Drake wrote to Ashton Stevens. The effect was "really disastrous. . . . More and more it becomes apparent that the only thing Orson can do to keep these screamers quiet is to buckle down and do that movie."

Even as the controversy about his contempt for Hollywood played out disastrously in public, privately another issue arose to blindside Orson, distracting his attention and threatening his reputation.

A new book due in stores, called *The Invasion from Mars: A Study in the Psychology of Panic*, analyzed the national reaction to the "War of the Worlds" broadcast. The author, Hadley Cantril, an associate professor of psychology at Princeton University (the home of Orson's character in the broadcast), had sifted polling data and conducted interviews with the general public to study the spectrum of responses to the broadcast. Early on, Professor Cantril had corresponded with Welles, who referred him to John Houseman for background about the making of the program. As advertised on its cover, the book would also include the first publication of the "War of the Worlds" script.

In late March, Cantril sent galleys to Welles, hoping for his support with publicity when Princeton University Press brought out the book in mid-April. When Orson read Cantril's prefatory material, however, he reacted with horror. Cantril thanked Howard Koch for his permission "to publish for the first time his [Koch's] brilliant adaptation of the 'War of the Worlds.'" And although the cover credit promoted "the complete script of the Orson Welles broadcast"—a more accurate description of the script, which had been transcribed from the broadcast—inside the book the phrase "script by Howard Koch" leaped out at Welles repeatedly.

Orson unleashed a volley of heated telegrams and letters to Cantril. Crediting Koch "to the exclusion of myself as the dramatist," Welles wrote, was a "grave" error that would be "detrimental to my reputation" in radio and Hollywood. "The idea for the 'War of the Worlds' broadcast and the major portion of its execution was mine," he insisted. "Howard Koch was very helpful in the second portion of the script [which centered on the character Welles himself played] and did some work in the first, most of which it was necessary to revise." While he "always worked with a fairly large complement of writers," Welles went on to explain, "the initial emphasis and attack on a story as well as its ultimate revised form have in almost every instance been mine." Among the writers "of much greater service" than Koch to the ultimate "War of the Worlds" script were Houseman ("my partner" and "chief collaborator") and Paul Stewart, who "also did a great deal of writing." And there were indispensable contributions from the chief engineer John Dietz; CBS production executive Davidson Taylor (helpful with "news dispatches, mobile unit pickups, special interviews etc."); and "my director of music," composer-conductor Bernard Herrmann.

Professor Cantril was taken by surprise. Until that moment, on the eve of publication, he had had no idea that he might be transgressing by crediting the script to Koch. Cantril replied that he had affidavits and correspondence from Koch, Houseman, and Koch's assistant Anne Froelick attesting to Koch's authorship. "The testimony of Mr. Houseman is no more valid than that of Miss Froelick," Welles replied testily, "for the simple reason that Mr. Houseman is about to produce a play by Mr. Koch on Broadway," which Froelick was also involved in planning.

Cantril offered to add a last-minute errata sheet to *The Invasion from Mars*, affirming Welles's overall supervisory authorship. But Orson insisted this was inadequate.

WAR OF THE WORLDS WAS NOT ONLY MY CONCEPTION, Orson telegraphed to the professor, BUT ALSO, PROPERLY AND EXACTLY SPEAKING, MY CREATION. VERY HAPPY TO HAVE ALL MY ASSISTANTS CREDITED BUT THIS IS MEANINGLESS WITH THE FINAL LINE "AND WRITTEN BY HOWARD KOCH." ONCE AGAIN, FINALLY, AND I PROMISE FOR THE LAST TIME, HOWARD KOCH DID NOT WRITE 'THE WAR OF THE WORLDS.'

It was indeed the last time, because *The Invasion from Mars* was published as scheduled on April 15, with the full script of "War of the Worlds" permanently attributed to Howard Koch. Koch held the copyright according to the terms of his contract, and he would republish the script multiple times in the decades ahead. (As of this writing, it is still in print.)

The nuances of authorship were lost on reviewers, who routinely referred to the famous episode as "the Orson Welles broadcast" and rarely mentioned Koch. But it was an untimely defeat for Welles, already feeling beset and beleaguered in Hollywood while struggling to launch *Citizen Kane*. And he might have felt a premonition: the dispute over the credits for "War of the Worlds" foreshadowed the controversy over the writing of *Citizen Kane*.

The published scripts of "War and The Worlds" and *Kane* both drew from a common source: John Houseman. Back east in New York, nursing a grudge against Welles, Houseman was Cantril's primary informant, as he would be years later for Pauline Kael. "After the notoriety he had achieved with 'The War of the Worlds,' how could [Welles] let it be known that a $60-a-week scribbler had, in fact, been responsible for the script?" Houseman wrote in *Run-Through*. "Following a year of false starts and international suspense over his entrance into motion pictures, how could he acknowledge that his first film was based on the work of a well-known Hollywood hack?"

Seven years after Kael's book, in Richard Meryman's corrective account in his Mankiewicz biography, published in 1978, Welles is quoted as saying he believed that Houseman carried his grudge to Victorville, planting seeds against him in Mank's mind as the two worked on the first draft of *Citizen Kane*. Houseman encouraged "Mank's latent hatred of anybody who wasn't a writer," Welles told Meryman, "directing it at me. When Mank left for Victorville, we were friends. When he came back, we were enemies. Mank always needed a villain."

Houseman and Mankiewicz delivered the first official draft of "John Citizen U.S.A.," which they gave the new title "American," in the same week that *The Invasion from Mars* appeared in bookstores.

Run-Through cattily compressed Orson's contribution to the first draft. "Orson telephoned at odd hours to inquire after our progress,"

Houseman recollected. "On the appointed day, at the end of six weeks, he arrived in a limousine driven by Alfalfa [his chauffeur at the time], read a hundred pages of script, listened to our outline of the rest, dined with us at The Green Spot, thanked us and returned to Los Angeles. The next day he informed the studio that he would start shooting early in July."

In fact, eight weeks would elapse from assignment to delivery of that first draft. There were several crucial later script drafts that Houseman glossed over in his account. And, as Houseman told the lawyers in the Lundberg case ten years later, "during that time [in Victorville], we received *several visits—I can't remember exactly how many**—from Orson Welles, and then I went down to Los Angeles at least once or twice and spoke with Welles, and reported our progress to him." Welles said consistently through the years that he spent much of the Victorville time working on a parallel script draft at home, combining his original pages with revisions of their output.

Yet Orson was pleased by the first draft of "American," dated April 16. The self-destructive Mank had proved himself "extremely constructive," Welles said years later, contributing exceptional material "even where I didn't agree, either at first or later." He always bent over backward to give Houseman credit for the groundwork done at Victorville as well. "Actually [Houseman] was a junior writer," Welles told Peter Bogdanovich, "and made some very important contributions. But for some curious reason he's never wanted to take that bow. It gives him more pleasure just to say I didn't write it."

Possibly because he was concerned about legal repercussions to himself in the Lundberg case, Houseman insisted in his testimony that he himself functioned only as a dramaturg in Victorville. "I did not originate any scenes or any of the text," Houseman told the court. "I corrected it, edited it, I made suggestions about it. I did not originate any script."

What Houseman surely did not originate were any of the incidents and character traits patterned after the life of William Randolph Hearst, which lawyers for Ferdinand Lundberg insisted had been

---

* Author's emphasis.

cadged from Lundberg's 1936 book, *Imperial Hearst*. If Houseman knew most of the Mercury Theatre players intimately, he was blithely ignorant about Hearst.

Mankiewicz, on the other hand, had read dozens of books about Hearst; his private library of more than two thousand books was full of volumes on the tycoon, many of them written by personal or professional friends of Mank's. Of course, Mank told lawyers in the Lundberg case, he had read *On the Great Highway: The Wanderings and Adventures of a Special Correspondent* by the former Hearst reporter James Creelman, one of the progenitors of "yellow journalism"; Creelman's book contained a definitive account of the telegram about the Spanish-American War—an incident Mank referenced in *Citizen Kane*. Creelman's son James Ashmore Creelman was a Hollywood scenarist, a contributor to *King Kong*, who had collaborated on several scripts with Mank. And of course Mank had read Oliver Carlson and Ernest Sutherland Bates's *Hearst: Lord of San Simeon*; Carlson had once worked under Mank as a movie critic for the *New Yorker*.

Mank had read Lundberg's *Imperial Hearst*, too, he admitted, largely because a Columbia professor, Charles A. Beard, whose seminar he had taken, wrote the introduction. Though he respected Beard, he could not understand why the distinguished American historian praised Lundberg's book, which Mank found "a tendentious, one-dimensional tract," bent on proving Hearst an "exploiter." He could not explain the odd fact that there were *two* copies of this book in his library, but Mankiewicz declared repeatedly that he did not derive a single incident in his script from it, nor did he bring a single book pertaining to Hearst to Victorville. Mank had no need to consult books about Hearst, he said: testifying in court in 1950, he discussed Hearst knowledgeably and in detail, furnishing names and dates from memory.

For his part, Houseman said he read only one nonfiction book in Victorville: *Forty Years, Forty Millions: The Career of Frank A. Munsey* by George Britt. The name of Munsey, an eccentric early twentieth-century publisher of pulp fiction, had come up in the pre-Victorville discussions with Welles and Mankiewicz. Intrigued, Houseman packed Munsey's biography with his belongings. The *News on the March* footage alluded briefly to Munsey's ownership of grocery stores ("An empire upon an empire. The first of grocery stores, paper mills, apartment buildings, factories, forests, ocean liners . . ."), the rare line by himself that Houseman recalled surviving into the script—and proof, he said, that Kane was not Hearst, who owned nary a grocery store.

Houseman had never read a single book about Hearst, he said, and claimed no expertise on the subject. According to his testimony, he and Mankiewicz discussed Hearst no more than they did "many other famous people," who were folded into various characters in the film.

Mank crafted Walter Parks Thatcher, for example, to bear an intentional resemblance to corporate financier J. P. Morgan, especially in the scene when Thatcher is the target of a congressional hearing. In 1933, a press agent for Ringling Brothers had taken advantage of a lull in similar proceedings to pop the midget circus performer Lya Graf onto the lap of the astonished J. P. Morgan Jr., son of the celebrated banker. In the *News on the March* footage, "a baby alligator has just been placed in [Thatcher's] lap," according to the published *Citizen Kane* script, "causing considerable confusion and embarrassment." If this scene was ever filmed, though, it was cut—and at any rate, Houseman testified indignantly, it would be "obviously absurd" to link Thatcher too closely with Morgan. Morgan was merely one of several models for Kane.

Still, Mankiewicz admitted in his testimony that Hearst was directly or slyly evoked in many scenes of *Citizen Kane*, and he was proud of it. Details were borrowed from numerous sources, Mank insisted, often dating back decades; many of the tidbits were common knowledge, none of them unique to Lundberg's book.

As for Houseman, who prided himself on knowing little about Hearst, he was ill-equipped to spot the script's many real-life references and inside jokes. In Victorville, for example, Houseman wondered aloud whether the idea of a publisher like Kane running for public office would strain credulity. Were there any "precedents" of "a molder of public opinion running for public office"? Yes, Mankiewicz told him: William Randolph Hearst. And Houseman marveled at the clever scene Mank devised for the composing room, after Kane has lost his gubernatorial race—it survived every draft—with Bernstein ("actually crying," according to the published script) as he chooses between two newspapers with rival headlines held up by the composing room foreman: KANE ELECTED or FRAUD AT POLLS! "I thought this was an extremely amusing episode," said Houseman, "and I asked him if he had thought it up; and his reply [was that] this was a true story," another actual Hearst anecdote.

Reading the scene Mankiewicz had written, in which Kane sends a wire to a reporter covering the Spanish-American War—"You provide the prose poems, I'll provide the war"—Houseman again was vastly "amused." Once more he asked the writer if the dialogue was "original with him," and Mank replied that it was a paraphrase of Hearst's legendary telegram to illustrator Frederic Remington: "You provide the pictures, I'll provide the war." (In his own deposition in the Lundberg case, Welles said that the telegram and Kane's "crazy art collection," a detail "much too good to resist," were the only two "pure Hearstian" elements he recognized in *Citizen Kane*.)

In the first draft script, Mankiewicz had written a scene involving the assassination of President McKinley, whose killer, when captured, has a Kane editorial in his pocket. This was Mank's allusion to the fact that McKinley was mercilessly denounced by the Hearst press until his assassination in September 1901, after which the publisher became the target of public rage for having incited the assassination. A provocative poem by the famous Hearst journalist Ambrose Bierce, published months earlier and referring to the assassination of a Kentucky governor in 1900, was widely credited with foreshadowing the shooting of McKinley. Hearst was hanged in effigy, and the circulation of his papers plummeted. "I asked Mr. Mankiewicz, since I was not familiar with any such incident in American history," explained Houseman, "if that had any foundation in fact, and he told me of the Ambrose Bierce quatrain." (Bierce's poem was another bit of writing that Mank easily recalled at the Lundberg trial—well enough to recite it at length from memory.)

Orson expected and welcomed the script's allusions to Hearst, but only up to a point. He wanted Kane to serve as an archetype, not a replication of Hearst. Houseman had failed this part of his task, allowing too many real-life references to Hearst to sneak into the script.

And the Victorville draft failed in another important way: "Outrageously overwritten even for a first draft," in Meryman's words, "American" ran over three hundred pages. "Houseman blandly ignores this fact" in his self-aggrandizing account, as Meryman noted in his book. The first draft was overstuffed with plot, including scenes featuring

Kane roistering in college in Germany, and the first meeting between Kane and Mr. Bernstein in Paris. One scene even featured Kane living decadently abroad, in a palace in Rome, surrounded by art treasures and guests including "pimps, Lesbians, dissipated Army officers, homosexuals, nymphomaniacs and international society tramps." (It is "what we call the Elsa Maxwell scene," Houseman explained drolly to Lundberg's lawyers.)

Also in the first draft, Thatcher's son, Walter Parks Thatcher Jr., hounds Kane about financial matters after his father's demise. The generations multiply: Kane's father, Charles Foster Kane Sr., reappears dramatically, and Kane has a right-wing son who joins a domestic fascist conspiracy and dies in a violent uprising. Susan Alexander meanwhile takes a young lover while sequestered at Xanadu. Under orders from Kane, the sinister butler Raymond has the lover murdered.

Overwriting was not the draft's worst flaw, however. "By far the most serious dramatic problem in 'American,'" according to Robert L. Carringer's astute assessment in his authoritative *The Making of Citizen Kane*, "is its portrait of Kane. Mankiewicz drew a good deal of his material directly from Hearst without really assimilating it to dramatic need. . . . 'American' is by and large a literal reworking of specific incidents and details from Hearst's life." Kane was too Hearstian and not fully realized as a character.

After Welles gave his critique, Houseman and Mankiewicz went back to work on the script, their salaries extended. They would spend several more weeks in Victorville, implementing cuts, additions, and improvements without solving the length problem. The main results of their second pass at the script, according to Carringer, included the elimination of the first Mrs. Charles Foster Kane as a narrative witness, with much of her storytelling reassigned to Jed Leland; the addition of a scene in Madison Square Garden, with Mrs. Kane insisting that she and her husband visit his "love nest" for their fateful encounter with Susan Alexander and Boss Gettys; and a change in Kane's political fortunes, with his stolen gubernatorial victory becoming a wholesale rejection by the electorate.

Still, despite its length and its too-literal Hearstiana, Orson recognized the first draft, in the words of Meryman, as "the blueprint of a masterpiece." And the draft also gave Orson something to show RKO's president George Schaefer as evidence of progress, even as he reassured Schaefer that he would sharpen the drama and rein in the most blatant references to Hearst.

Welles was a master editor. He knew what he could do with Mank's blueprint of a masterpiece. He knew better than anyone else what he could do, as an actor, with Kane, and how to create scenes to show off his strengths. And he knew that the long money was on making Charles Foster Kane an archetype, one that would ensure the greatness of the film for future generations to come for whom the name Hearst would be but a faint echo of a bygone America.

As for Ferdinand Lundberg, he subsequently accepted a $15,000 settlement from RKO, after his lawsuit ended in a hung jury.

John Houseman and Herman Mankiewicz returned to Hollywood to deliver the second draft of "American" to Welles "on or about May 9," according to Robert L. Carringer's book. That "on or about" opens the possibility that it could have been on May 6, Orson's twenty-fifth birthday, the long-awaited day when he would come of age and collect the fortune his father had preserved for him in trust.

"Everything else—the principal as well as all monies earned—is to be administered by the bank in trust for your son, Charles Foster Kane," as Walter Parks Thatcher explains to Mr. and Mrs. Kane in the Kane boardinghouse in the deep backstory of *Citizen Kane*, "until his twenty-fifth birthday, at which time he is to come into complete possession."

The loss of weekly radio income; the Mercury Theatre's considerable debt; the five figures or more that he owed in back taxes; and the increased obligation to his ex-wife, Virginia, and their daughter, Christopher—all this, on top of the lost income from his canceled lectures, made Welles's financial situation desperate. His money blew out the door as fast as it blew in. While the studio was liberal with its overhead allowances, RKO refused to pay out any additional moneys to Welles until principal photography on *Citizen Kane* began.

Throughout March and April, Richard Baer and Arnold Weissberger struggled to pay Orson's bills while conspiring to force him into exigent measures that he continued to resist.

"I have tried to sound as dire as possible," Weissberger wrote to

Baer in early April. "The minute he were to believe that the situation was only bad and not terrible, he would fail to take any cognizance of restrictive measures. For his own protection, therefore, I shall continue to be completely pessimistic in my advices to him."

The small amounts of money that Orson loaned to friends, or payments he authorized for occasional onetime services—payments that looked suspiciously like handouts—Welles refused to itemize or track down for collection. The loans he made to friends he considered gifts, more or less. Meanwhile, the Mercury Theatre was in nearly fathomless arrears. "You have paid over to the Mercury Theatre in the aggregate of $50,000," his lawyer explained to him in a letter. "The cost of *Danton's Death* alone was about $50,000. This will explain to you why Mercury is still so much in debt."

Orson had asked Weissberger to seek an early distribution of his inheritance, which for months leading up to his birthday was believed to be in the neighborhood of $30,000. That was still relatively substantial, if disappointing, and Orson hoped to spend it on overdue bills and sprinkle a little on "American" while pouring the remainder into his future plans. Weissberger warned against dipping into the money—Orson's only money—prematurely.

Finally, in April, Orson dismissed his maid, butler, and gardener. He scouted out a lower-cost house away from Brentwood in the Coldwater Canyon neighborhood of Beverly Hills. He agreed to downsize the Mercury offices in New York, cutting by a third the salaries of both remaining staff members (including Weissberger's long-serving sister, Augusta), and subletting part of the space. And he trimmed the West Coast staff down to Richard Baer and Herbert Drake.

When Weissberger finally reported back on the trust fund, the news was grim. Orson was indeed owed $33,438.18 on his twenty-fifth birthday. But $15,000 of that total was earmarked to repay the several bank loans Orson had negotiated against his inheritance in recent years, and included $2,000 from Columbia Artists that Orson had borrowed as an advance against his various earnings, whose note of guarantee was also held by the bank. Another $12,000 had to be set aside for overdue income taxes, as the federal government was threatening to impose a lien on Welles. Finally, Dr. Maurice Bernstein held a chit for a personal loan to Orson of $1,233.76, which the doctor insisted upon recovering.

That left a mere $5,000 as the residue of the fortune bequeathed to this onetime "rich boy," as Chicago newspaper headlines had called him. Weissberger begged Welles to keep the paltry sum in the bank, where it would earn interest. Orson wanted nothing further to do with the Chicago bank. He gave Weissberger instructions to withdraw the $5,000 and send it his way, where it was quickly sown in the wind. Orson ordered the bank to turn over his father's personal effects— including the grip Dick Welles had carried with him around the world—to Dr. Bernstein.

Virginia was another person keenly attuned to the date of her ex-husband's inheritance. After leaving the hospital and recovering her health, she no longer spoke of returning to New York, nor of acting anymore under the name Anna Stafford. These days she was frequently glimpsed at Hollywood nightspots in the company of writer Charles Lederer. Still contriving to hold on to his mansion, Orson arranged for Virginia and his daughter to live in the lower-cost Beverly Hills house he had rented; in lieu of paying child support he let them use it free.

Like her father, Virginia was by now convinced that Orson stood to gain riches beyond imagining on his twenty-fifth birthday. She had agreed to a temporary reduction in alimony when she thought Orson was engulfed by crisis (and she herself was in the hospital in a vulnerable state). Now she withdrew that concession, submitted a bill for back alimony and other costs, and threatened to hire a lawyer.

Arnold Weissberger had the unpleasant task of sorting out Virginia's financial claims, and an alimony agreement that morphed as often as Orson's RKO contract. This job was further complicated when, a mere ten days after Orson's birthday, Virginia eloped with Lederer; they were married at the home of a justice of the peace in Phoenix, Arizona. The marriage came just four months after her divorce, and her claim to reporters that there was no other romance in her life.

Everyone else saw it coming. Nor was Orson surprised: the couple had privately announced a June ceremony before dashing off to Phoenix. And Welles liked Lederer—a dapper, amusing man in the Hecht-MacArthur circle—as much as everyone else in Hollywood did. But when Virginia moved in with Lederer, she moved out of Orson's rented house—and sublet it to other people at a profit to herself. She then escalated her demands for more alimony, with her unpaid hospital costs a major sticking point. "I consider at this distance from the event that I was ill treated and duped in the whole matter of the divorce settlement," Virginia wrote to Weissberger.

May 6, 1939, was just another unhappy birthday for Orson. His inheritance had proved a mirage. He owed incomprehensible amounts of money to his wife, the banks, the Mercury Theatre's creditors, and the tax collector. The man with a golden contract was very nearly broke.

Show business columnists who had chronicled Orson's life story—the trust fund left to the wunderkind by his wealthy father—chortled publicly over his comeuppance. "Orson Welles received oodles of publicity over the legend that on May 6 he would inherit" a windfall, wrote Walter Winchell, "but taxes, erosions, time and etcetera made him the receiver of the magnificent sum of $28.40."

When, in *Citizen Kane*, Thompson remarks of Charles Foster Kane, "He made an awful lot of money," Mr. Bernstein the business manager offers a piercing rejoinder: "It's no trick to make a lot of money, if all you want is to make a lot of money. You take Mr. Kane—it wasn't money he wanted. Thatcher never did figure him out. Sometimes, even I couldn't."

Although Welles hated parallels between himself and Kane, that was as close as the film came to a declaration of Orson's own principles. It was no trick to have, or to make, a lot of money. Orson, who knew many tricks, often quoted that as one of his favorite lines—the work of Herman Mankiewicz, another pearl dropping from the mouth of Mr. Bernstein.

According to Richard Meryman's biography of Mankiewicz, John Houseman "departed for New York just four days after delivering 'American' to Welles." Although Orson would keep him apprised of successive drafts, asking for his advice and input, Houseman was absent from the substantial rewriting that occurred over the next two and a half months.

Their partnership was still precarious, but around the time the script was delivered, Orson made several public announcements about the future of the Mercury Theatre. Welles told the press that the Mercury was planning a fall Broadway season, to open with his own adaptation of Shakespeare's *King Lear*, presented in two acts on one set. He also announced that he, Houseman, and Mankiewicz would open a West Coast branch of the Mercury to be known as United Productions, with the New York Mercury furnishing two of the five plays to be produced in Los Angeles; the other three would originate locally.

One of the properties Welles set his sights on was a stage version of *Native Son*, Richard Wright's incendiary new novel set in the Negro slums on Chicago's South Side. It was a Book-of-the-Month Club selection, and Orson had read the novel while Houseman and Mankiewicz were in Victorville; he now persuaded Houseman that, with his help and Mankiewicz's, he could turn the acclaimed but difficult-to-dramatize novel into a first-rate stage play. The title role would be perfect for a black actor such as Canada Lee. Houseman agreed to approach Wright quietly, to negotiate the rights.

With Welles, it was always hard to know which of his ideas were real and which were feints. The bicoastal Mercury was a magnificent gesture of confidence in and gratitude to Houseman and Mankiewicz as a script team. Only one United Production would ever come to pass, however, and that was *Native Son*. Early in June, Houseman wrote to say that he'd obtained permission from the author. Miraculously, then, Welles, who conferred with Mankiewicz and worked like a madman after dark, promised by telegraph a "tentative cut-down version [of the *Native Son* script] first two hundred pages tomorrow for your information and suggestions." Although playwright Paul Green eventually earned the credit for the adaptation, Houseman, Mankiewicz, and Welles all contributed to the script; Mank was listed on the eventual stage production credits as associate producer.

The script for "American," meanwhile, was delivered to RKO president George Schaefer. On May 18 Orson mailed another sealed copy—the only copy that circulated outside Hollywood—to Roger Hill in Woodstock, Illinois, asking for his old headmaster's feedback. Although it was merely a working draft, Orson wrote to Skipper, the script was "a source of some gratification."

With Mankiewicz "off to MGM on another assignment," according to Robert L. Carringer, doctoring without credit the Ben Hecht–Charles Lederer script of the anticommunist comedy *Madame X*, Welles had to clear his desk and roll up his sleeves. The 325-page script for

"American" was cluttered and overlong; it had to be reduced by at least half. Even if Mankiewicz had not been otherwise occupied, Orson would have had little choice but to bypass him: Mank was mulishly stubborn when asked to make even the slightest changes to his prose. ("Herman would rather talk for three days than change two innocuous lines of dialogue," Bert Granet, the producer of one Mankiewicz film, told Richard Meryman.)

The drama had to be paced the way Orson lived: like an express train. Orson cut away at the periphery, starting with the flashbacks to Kane as a boy and young man. (One sequence Orson deleted, which showed Kane expelled from a German university for a prank, also echoed too closely an incident in Hearst's life.) He compressed many scenes into "snappy and arresting montages," in Carringer's phrase, including the memorable flash-forward that covered all of Kane's youth. Thatcher is seen bestowing an unwanted sled on Kane as a boy, and trilling, "Well, Charles, Merry Christmas"—with the boy returning his salutation coldly. The screen cuts to Thatcher dictating ". . . a very Happy New Year" to his secretary on Kane's twenty-fifth birthday. (In Mankiewicz and Welles's "shooting script," as published by Pauline Kael, this masterful device is not only missing; it is replaced by Mank's sentimental image of the boy Kane sobbing into a pillow, "Mom! Mom!") Orson's version foreshadowed the sled at the end of the film, fortified the "Rosebud" conceit, and jumped shrewdly past Kane's empty boyhood.

Welles's storytelling strategies, full of tricks he'd gleaned in his years as a stage and radio director, were foreign to Mank. Orson knew how to cut scenes to save screen time and money, often employing sound and visual effects that only he could dream up and pull off. Another striking time lapse in the final film, for example, shows Susan Alexander singing for Kane in her humble apartment; dissolves to her singing within better surroundings set up for her as a kept woman by Kane; then cuts to a group of people applauding Leland as he concludes a speech introducing Kane during his campaign; and finally moves to Kane finishing Leland's sentence from his podium at Madison Square Garden—all done "faster than you could do in radio," as Welles boasted to Peter Bogdanovich.

Often, decisions made during production were crucial contributions—

as in the opening sequence at Xanadu, just as the camera reaches the window of Kane's bedroom, when the room light flicks off and then on again. The published shooting script says nothing about the light going off. Why did Welles choose to do that? asked Peter Bogdanovich. "To interest the audience," Orson explained. "We'd been going on quite a while there with nothing happening. You see a light in the window—you keep coming nearer—and it better go off, or a shadow had better cross, or something better happen. So I turned the light off—that's all. . . .

"Maybe the nurse turned it off because it was getting in [Kane's] eyes. Who knows? Who cares? The other answer is that it symbolized death. Got that? All right.

"He was supposed to die when the light went off, and then you go back a few minutes and see him alive again—if you really want a reason. The other, low-class reason was to keep the audience interested. And they're both valid."

Over and over again, where Mankiewicz simply had jotted "Dissolve out . . . dissolve in," Orson added theatrical effects that made the scene changes memorable. Another example is the abrupt and startling image of a white cockatoo, shrieking in close-up, as Raymond the butler starts describing Kane's tantrum after his second wife leaves him.

"Why did you use the shrieking cockatoo?" asked Bogdanovich.

"Wake 'em up," answered Welles.

"Literally?" said Bogdanovich.

"Yeah. Getting late in the evening, you know," Orson replied. "Time to brighten up anybody who might be nodding off."

"It has no other purpose . . . ?"

"Theatrical shock effect," answered Welles; "if you want to be grand about it—you can say it's placed at a certain musical moment when I felt the need for something short and exclamatory. So it has a sort of purpose, but no meaning. What's fascinating, though, is that, because of some accident in the trick department, you can see through the bird's eye into the scenery behind."

"I always thought that was intentional," said Bogdanovich.

"We don't know why that happened," said Welles. "Some accident."

These were small touches. Far more important was Orson's work in dropping big chunks of the adult Kane's story from the script. Mank argued fiercely to preserve a series of scenes referencing the McKinley assassination, which would have set up an argument between Kane and Leland demonstrating the widening gulf in their friendship. But Orson knew what he wanted and what would work. "I was the one who was making the picture, after all—who made the decisions," Welles recalled. "I used what I wanted of Mank's and, rightly or wrongly, kept what I liked of my own." Although the McKinley scenes were a perfect example of what Meryman called Mank's "banked-up political-historical expertise," they took the script too far away from the main story, while also adding to the cost and length of the production. Besides, the McKinley assassination was dicey territory—a clear swipe at Hearst and his newspaper empire, which Orson recognized, even if Houseman had not. The assassination scenes went into the circular file.

Mank also fought to retain the idea that Kane had Susan's lover murdered—an obvious allusion to Hearst and his possible connection to the death of Thomas Ince aboard Hearst's yacht in 1924. Ince's death was officially attributed to a heart attack, but according to the Hollywood rumor mill Hearst shot Ince by accident, mistaking him for Charles Chaplin, after discovering Chaplin in a romantic clinch with Hearst's mistress, Marion Davies. Mank advanced an interesting argument for keeping the allusions to Ince in the script: doing so, he claimed, would dissuade Hearst from attacking the picture with a lawsuit, because such a suit would entail airing the gossip about Chaplin and Davies in public. Welles and Mank often argued like boys on a seesaw; if one rode up, the other plunged down. In this case, perhaps Mankiewicz should have been left on top. "I cut it out because I thought it hurt the film, and wasn't in keeping with Kane's character," Welles mused years later. "If I'd kept it in, I would have had no trouble with Hearst. He wouldn't have dared admit it was him [being referenced]."*

In late April, even before Houseman and Mankiewicz finished the second draft of "American," Orson had started testing actors for the

---

* Peter Bogdanovich's film *The Cat's Meow*, starring Eddie Izzard as Chaplin, Cary Elwes as Ince, Kirsten Dunst as Marion Davies, and Edward Herrmann as Hearst, would cover this same territory entertainingly on Orson's behalf in 2001.

important roles that he knew would survive the script process. Much of the rewriting revolved around refining the key characters offering their remembrances of Kane, tailoring them expressly for Orson's Mercury players, whom he—as head of that troupe, and as a fellow actor—knew best.

The Mercury players functioned as "a close family," Welles told Peter Bogdanovich, but it was "an Anglo-Saxon type of family where the members leave each other pretty much alone. We had our fun together during working hours—and it was fun, you know. The atmosphere was like a sort of house party. To give you an idea, we always kept a good jazz-piano man on the set. Between jobs, though, we tended to go our separate ways."

Joseph Cotten had been on tour in *The Philadelphia Story* with Katharine Hepburn. With the tour scheduled for a summer break, Orson arranged the production calendar in order to squeeze Cotten's major scenes in before he had to return to the road in the fall. A former newspaperman himself, Cotten was always helpful about the characters he played, and Orson brought him to Mank's house so the two could relax and get to know each other by the swimming pool. Cotten was encouraged to make little changes in his dialogue during the filming.

The scene "Mankiewicz was proudest of in the picture," according to Houseman, was the one when Leland confronts Kane after he has lost the gubernatorial election because of the "love nest" scandal. ("You talk about the people as though you own them . . . as though they belong to you.") But the difference between the discursive version of the published shooting script and that of the film's is striking. Welles and Cotten both worked on the crucial scene, with Welles pruning it to make it more concise, but also rewriting the dialogue for force and clarity.

The last climactic encounter between Kane and Leland occurs in the scene when Kane finds the newspaperman slumped over his typewriter, his devastating pan of Susan Alexander Kane's opera debut unfinished. It was Welles who insisted that Kane then would sit down and complete Leland's damning review. "Mank fought me terribly about that scene: 'Why should he finish the notice? He wouldn't! He just wouldn't print it.' Which would have been true of Hearst." Orson talked the scene out, and Mank was obliged to write it; the final version is close to the published version of the script. As Carringer noted, though, Orson's addition was "an inspired touch," transforming it from Leland's scene to Kane's. "The big moment is when [Kane] types the bad notice," Welles reflected. "That's when he's faithful to himself."

As the actors were lined up, their scenes were reworked. George Coulouris—the only Mercury player who already had appeared in a Hollywood film—was still in Hollywood and eager to play Thatcher. Agnes Moorehead and Everett Sloane, who had always been radio players—not part of the Mercury stage ensemble—were paying their bills with broadcast work; but they were patient and ready and waiting whenever Orson summoned them. Another radio stalwart who now would be blended into the Mercury film contingent was actor-director Paul Stewart. Orson phoned Stewart in New York, and asked him to come out to Hollywood and "do a part for me in my picture." "Yes . . . but what's the part?" Stewart asked. "Never mind. Just come out," Welles said. "Well," Stewart recalled, "when Orson said he had a part for you, you went."

The part in question was Raymond, the butler. ("Knows where all the bodies are buried," says Susan Alexander Kane—one of the final script's few allusions to the Ince affair.) Years later, Stewart recalled that his very first shot in *Citizen Kane* was "a close-up in which Orson wanted a special smoke effect from my cigarette, but somehow the contraption wouldn't exude smoke." Orson cried out: "I want long cigarettes—the Russian kind!" Everything halted while the prop man went in search of Russian cigarettes.

"Just before the scene, Orson Welles warned me: 'Your head is going to fill up the screen at the Radio City Music Hall,'" Stewart continued. (The film's premiere would be held at Radio City.) "Then he said in his gruff manner: 'Turn 'em,'" meaning the cameras.

"Just before I started, he added quietly in his warm voice, 'Good luck.'

"I blew the first take," Stewart recalled, freezing at the prospect of seeing his face on the big screen at Radio City Music Hall. But he blew it in style, saying, "Goldberg? I'll tell you about Goldberg . . ." Orson and everyone else roared with laughter.

"It was thirty-forty takes before I completed a shot that Orson liked," Stewart remembered, "and I only had one line. That was almost thirty years ago, but even today I have people repeat it to me, including young students. The line was:

"'Rosebud? I'll tell you about Rosebud . . .'"

Gus Schilling, Erskine Sanford, and Ray Collins said yes. Schilling would play the headwaiter at El Rancho, where Susan Alexander Kane is found drowning her sorrows. Sanford would portray the addle-pated veteran editor Carter ("an elderly, stout gent"), whom Kane quickly displaces at the *Inquirer.* Orson needed someone with gravitas for Boss Gettys. (In Mank's published script, the character had the bland name Boss Roberts; Orson replaced "Roberts" with Hortense Hill's maiden name.) He tapped Collins, his rock in radio.

The film reaches a turning point in the scene when Kane meets the oily power broker Gettys—big and heavyset, like Collins, as the script describes him—who is wounded by the fact that his wife and children have seen the *Inquirer* caricature of him drawn "in a convict suit with stripes." Gettys uses Kane's wife Emily to lure him to the "love nest" apartment where he threatens to expose Kane's affair with Susan. The scene had to be written as perfectly as possible, and the first draft was crafted "exclusively by my colleague, Mr. Mankiewicz," as Welles said in the Lundberg case. But Orson also consulted Collins. "We also closed the picture for a day in order to rewrite this scene," Orson said. "This rewriting was done by myself and the cast of actors involved."

> KANE
>
> There's only one person in the world to decide what I'm gonna do and that's me.

> EMILY
>
> You decided what you were going to do, Charles, some time ago.

> GETTYS
>
> You're making a bigger fool of yourself than I thought you would, Mr. Kane.

> KANE
>
> I've got nothing to talk to you about.

GETTYS

You're licked. Why don't you . . .

KANE

Get out! If you wanna see me, have the warden write me a
letter.

GETTYS

With anybody else, I'd say what's gonna happen to you
would be a lesson to you. Only you're gonna need more
than one lesson. And you're gonna get more than one
lesson.

KANE

Don't worry about me, Gettys. Don't worry about me! I'm
Charles Foster Kane! I'm no cheap crooked politician,
trying to save himself from the consequences of his
crimes! Gettys! I'm gonna send you to Sing-Sing! Sing-
Sing, Gettys!

The film called for dozens of lesser speaking parts, and Welles
plugged holes with many performers who were not Mercury veterans.
One small but important role was that of Kane's father. In the first
"American" drafts, Kane later encountered his long-lost father with a
"young tart" one night at a stage show. Orson cut that reappearance
from the script, against Mank's protests, but the role was still pivotal,
and when Harry Shannon appeared at a casting call, Orson remembered the comic vaudeville dancer from his boyhood days and gave
him the part.

With so many roles to fill, the casting would go on throughout the
filming. Orson collected people wherever he encountered them. After
seeing the left-wing musical *Meet the People* in Los Angeles, he went backstage to pluck new players from among the singers and dancers. He
found parts for his secretaries; cameos for Herman Mankiewicz and
cameraman Gregg Toland; and roles for everyone in the Mercury retinue, including Richard Wilson and William (no longer "Vakhtangov")
Alland, who had long been penciled in as Thompson, the colorless

reporter. Alland also imitated the stentorian broadcaster Westbrook Pegler for the *News on the March* footage.* "Great imitation," Orson told Bogdanovich, even if Pegler was "pretty easy to imitate." (Welles then proceeded, from memory, to boom out his own imitation of the imitation: "This week, as it must to all men, death came to Charles Foster Kane. . . .")

One bit of casting that had personal meaning for Orson was the uncredited cameo he set aside for sixty-three-year-old actor Landers Stevens, who is glimpsed as an investigator in the Senate hearing that is part of *News on the March*. His casting meant nothing, except to Landers himself; his brother, Ashton Stevens; and his son, George Stevens. After ailing for months, actor Landers Stevens would die in December 1940 from complications during surgery. *Citizen Kane* was his last job.

Not everyone jumped on the bandwagon. Orson cast his net deep into his past, reaching out to William Vance, who had acted in his summer theater; had shot his first short film, *The Hearts of Age*; and had adapted *Everybody's Shakespeare* into half-hour radio shows produced for WTAD in Quincy, Illinois. Orson had stayed in touch with Vance, and now phoned him to invite him to audition for *Citizen Kane*; but Vance's wife was seriously ill, and he had decided he didn't want to be an actor anyway.

Welles also contacted William Mowry Jr., the former Todd School footballer and Mercury Theatre regular. But Mowry had married and moved back to Chicago, and had grown ambivalent about a theatrical career. When Mowry demurred, Welles wired to say no hard feelings: LOVE, ORSON.

---

* Alland also voiced the narration years later for the mock newsreel about Hearst in Welles's *F For Fake*.

CHAPTER 20

June 1940

The Big Brass Ring

As was customary for him, and not uncommon in Hollywood, Welles had to plan ahead, coordinating his ideas for staging and cinematography with the RKO departments even as he was still working on the script. With president George Schaefer's backing, he had the vast studio machinery at his beck and call. In particular, he needed a team of technicians with whom he could commune artistically. Luck served him in that regard—if luck also involves long waiting and studying, and a sharp instinct for reaching and scratching an itch.

Most books say that Van Nest Polglase, the head of RKO's production design department, assigned art director Perry Ferguson to Orson's still-undisclosed project. "There are *Citizen Kane* alumni who maintain to this day that assignment to the Welles unit at RKO was a sure mark of studio disfavor," wrote Robert L. Carringer in *The Making of Citizen Kane.* "Ferguson's case demonstrates the contrary. At the time, he was the RKO art department's rising star."

In at least one published interview, however, Welles said he asked for Ferguson. Born in Texas, long a draftsman before rising to unit art director at RKO in 1935, Ferguson had distinguished himself working with top director Howard Hawks on the screwball comedy *Bringing Up Baby* in 1938 ("one of the costliest pictures made by the studio up to its time," according to Carringer) and on a number of George Stevens productions, culminating in 1939 with *Gunga Din.* Stevens gave the unassuming Texan high marks for ingenuity and cost-efficiency.

Ferguson listened as Orson outlined his unusual ideas for creative camerawork. Welles envisioned using miniatures to conjure the towering Xanadu, for instance, and matte backgrounds to fake crowd scenes. Illustrating his thoughts with quick pencil drawings, Orson explained that he wanted to shoot certain scenes from extremely low angles, and wanted the camera to show the ceilings of rooms. "I suppose I had more low angles in *Kane* just because I became fascinated with the way it looked," Welles said decades later, "and I do it less now because it's become less surprising." His ideas would require unusual adjustments: soundstage floors would have to be dug up for the camera crew, and the sound and light would have to pass through false ceilings.

Ferguson met every idea halfway, suggesting that they could try crafting the ceilings from dyed muslin—a material that was both flexible and, crucially, inexpensive. The script had not yet been evaluated for costs, but Orson and everyone else worried about limiting expenses as much as possible. "It became necessary to cheat many of the settings, particularly those at Xanadu," Simon Callow wrote. Ferguson knew how to design only what the camera would show, with Orson's extreme low angle shots leading the eye into darkness, where the unconstructed borders could be shrouded in velvet drapes, recalling the "black art" of magicians.

Ferguson listened amiably, nodding. He was already preparing preliminary storyboards by the time another man strolled into Orson's studio office in early June. God had sent Orson a gift in the form of cinematographer Gregg Toland—God, or perhaps the veteran director John Ford, one of the unlikely patron saints of *Citizen Kane*. Toland had just shot Ford's films *The Grapes of Wrath* and *The Long Voyage Home*, both released in 1940. Did Ford encourage Toland to visit Orson and volunteer his services? Ford knew that Welles had been studying his pictures, screening them repeatedly, and the veteran director visited the set of *Citizen Kane* on one of the first days of shooting to say a brisk hello. (He also warned Welles that Eddie Donahoe, his assistant director, was a front-office snitch: "Old Snake-in-the-Grass Eddie," Ford muttered.)

Toland was about ten years older than Welles but they had much in common. Both were from Illinois, both were the children of divorced parents. Toland's hometown—Charleston, Illinois, about two hundred miles southeast of Chicago—was not far from Orson's mother's hometown, Springfield, yet it was so far south it was almost Kentucky.

(During the Civil War, half the Tolands joined the antiwar "copper-heads.") When Toland was about ten, his parents had separated bitterly, his father moving to Chicago, his mother taking Gregg to California.

As a young man Toland showed an aptitude for electrical engineering, and at fifteen he dropped out of school to work at the Fox studios, first as an office boy, then joining George Barnes's camera crew, becoming an assistant cameraman in 1920. Since his first cinematography co-credit in the mid-1920s, Toland had established himself as one of the outstanding practitioners of his craft, and in the last five years he had earned five Academy Award nominations, winning for *Wuthering Heights* in 1940, a short time before he reported to work on *Citizen Kane.*

A mustachioed, diminutive figure in thick, buggy glasses, Toland was a man of "extreme reserve," according to one newspaper profile. Although soft-spoken and easygoing, he was highly disciplined at work, with a regular crew that followed his every slight gesture or whispered instruction. (By contrast, Welles told Bogdanovich, Toland was "quite a swinger off the set.") Toland had studied acting, makeup, and costuming to understand the challenges they posed for cinematographers, and he kept up with the theater scene in New York. (One of his Oscar nominations was for the faithful Hollywood adaptation of the Broadway hit *Dead End.*) Toland had been impressed by Welles's Voodoo *Macbeth*, the Nuremberg lighting of his *Julius Caesar*, and the striking scene and lighting designs of several of his other plays. When he met Welles, the cameraman stuck out his hand. "My name is Toland," he said: "I want you to use me on your picture."

Orson, of course, knew Toland's name. When the cameraman asked about the spectacular lighting of Welles's New York productions, he raised an eyebrow at the reply: Orson said that he always designed his own lighting, and that it was common practice for the finest stage directors. Later, during the filming of *Citizen Kane*, Orson initially tried to supervise the lighting himself, with Toland "behind me, of course," in his words, "balancing the lights and telling everybody to shut their faces." Toland wanted to make Welles's ideas work without deflating him, and was infuriated when a subordinate told Welles that the lighting was Toland's job. After that, however, Orson deferred to his cinematographer.

Orson told Toland that the film he was preparing would involve many interior shots with both sharp foregrounds and pristine backgrounds, as well as hung ceilings to strike "the desired note of reality," Toland recalled. The challenge lay in lighting from the floor as much as possible, and obtaining what was then called a "universal focus," bringing clarity to both foreground and background. Toland called it "pan-focus," a technique that kept everything in focus even when the camera was panning (moving from side to side). And the camera, much like Welles himself, would be moving often, almost continuously.

Orson said he wanted to avoid the standard master shots; to limit the use of close-ups; and as often as possible to combine the elements of a conventional two-shot setup into "a single, non-dollying shot," in Toland's words. One example that Toland later cited was the "big-head close-up of a player reading the inscription on a loving-cup" in the scene where Kane displays the photograph of celebrated reporters from a rival newsroom—a shot in which the inscription on the loving cup and the faces of Bernstein and Leland are closest to the viewer. "Beyond this foreground," framing the loving cup, "a group of men from twelve to eighteen feet focal distance" is revealed with equal crispness—as is, finally, a young man in a doorway at the back of the room, far from the camera, shouting, "Here he comes!"

Always the innovator, Welles was eager to test the limits and break the rules of standard camera practices. And Toland was tired of the limits and rules followed by even the very best Hollywood directors—with their studio overseers often forcing their hands. "I want to work with somebody who has never made a movie," Toland explained. Welles, who never forgot Toland's generous gesture, frequently repeated those words to interviewers later in life.

Toland and Ferguson had never collaborated before, and together with Welles they developed a creative team spirit. Like Welles, Toland and Ferguson were fast and flexible. When Orson told them his idea for the fake newsreel *News on the March*, Toland started planning techniques to replicate the scratchy image of a real newsreel. (When *Citizen Kane* was shown in Italy, Welles later told Peter Bogdanovich, audiences "stood up and hissed and booed" during the *News on the March* sequence because the footage appeared "so bad." He added: "You know the total run in Rome in the entire life of *Citizen Kane* is three days—since it was made!") Ferguson made lists of stock set pieces and props the filmmaking team could poach during the filming: train platforms, high balconies, painted backdrops. "There was a big back lot," Welles remembered, "and as we were moving from one place to another, we'd say, 'Well, let's get on the back of the train and make [a shot of Kane] with Teddy Roosevelt, or whoever it was. It was all kind of half improvised—all the newsreel stuff. It was tremendous fun doing it."

They had the same fun on a shoestring with the home movie–type trailer Orson concocted during the filming *about* the filming. It's probably the greatest trailer ever made, four minutes long, voiced by Welles, unseen, who wittily introduces the other leads as they don their makeup or bump into microphones backstage. (Here's Agnes Moorehead—"one of the best actresses in the world"—and Joseph Cotten: "Hey, give Jo a little light. Now smile for the folks, Jo!")

Orson completed his production team with a sensible young editor who later would sit patiently alongside him for months, shuffling through the footage, looking for the perfect combination of shots. Robert Wise, a midwesterner the same age as Welles, had worked genially with Garson Kanin on small comedies and he also had edited *The Hunchback of Notre Dame.* With so many shots that required images to be composited, or overlapped with another image ("One informed estimate is that fifty percent of the film's total footage involves special effects of one kind or another," Robert L. Carringer wrote), Welles also relied heavily on RKO special effects chief Vernon L. Walker and Linwood G. Dunn, the optical illusion master on *King Kong* who had helped with the *Heart of Darkness* tests.

Although Ferguson was entirely responsible for *Citizen Kane's* art direction, studio tradition mandated that his department head, Van Nest Polglase, be given the onscreen credit, with Ferguson listed only as "Associate Art Director." Mindful of this slight, Orson often took care to lavish praise on Ferguson in later interviews. When it came to Toland, however, Orson honored him with an onscreen credit that was almost unique: Welles placed his own credit, "Orson Welles, Direction-Production," on the same card as "Gregg Toland, A.S.C., Photography."

When Welles boasted about the gesture in one of their later interviews, Peter Bogdanovich pointed out that John Ford had given Toland the same special credit on *The Last Voyage Home.*

Welles didn't blink. "Gregg deserved it, didn't he?" he rejoined.

On May 28, RKO issued a program announcement listing fifty-three feature films the studio planned to produce in 1940–1941. Among them was "John Citizen, U.S.A.," the title it was still using for the project. The cameras were scheduled to roll on Orson Welles's first production on June 10. According to the announcement, Welles would star as a "crusading publisher," aging from twenty-two to seventy-five in the course of the story. "Maybe he'll even have the chance to wear a beard again," Edwin Schallert speculated in the *Los Angeles Times*.

Orson went to New York for a studio sales convention at the Waldorf-Astoria, where he joined RKO stars Anna Neagle, Lee Tracy, and Jean Hersholt and director-producer Herbert Wilcox for a luncheon with exhibitors and distributors in the grand ballroom. Afterward, Welles met privately with the studio president George Schaefer. Neither man was enamored of the title "John Citizen, U.S.A.," or the alternative, "American," and it was at this meeting that Schaefer proposed a keeper: "Citizen Kane." Orson leaped at the suggestion. "The head of the studio, imagine that!" Orson recalled to Peter Bogdanovich. "It's a great title." By the time Welles returned to Hollywood, the new title was in place. "One of the quickest title changes on record," noted Thomas M. Pryor in his Hollywood column in the *New York Times*.

Except for the brief flap over his supposed contempt for Hollywood, expressed in his speech in Kansas City, the press had been unusually quiet about Orson since February. The studio had stopped issuing progress reports on *The Smiler with the Knife*. Now the news of the imminent filming of *Citizen Kane* flew across the wires and stirred anticipation in the screen trade.

But June 10 was overly optimistic, Orson told Schaefer in New York. Welles renewed his pledge to start photography before the one-year anniversary of his RKO contract, but first he had to finish work on the script—and to finish it properly he had to get away from the studio and Hollywood. After a night at Ciro's with Dolores Del Rio, who became more conspicuous in his life as the start of filming neared, Orson left town—not for Victorville, more likely for Palm Springs.

"Am just now polishing up a script that needs it very badly," Welles reported in a June 8 telegram to Ashton Stevens in Chicago, "and during the past week have been mostly and literally in the desert pursuing a strict, even fanatical isolationist policy."

Orson's periods of isolation always fueled his creativity. Here, in the California desert, he would finalize the script, although the rewriting and refining would continue throughout the filming. ("I saw scenes written during production," said Orson's secretary, Kathryn Trosper. "Even while he was being made up, he'd be dictating dialogue.")

The character of Charles Foster Kane was a chief focus of the desert getaway. Mankiewicz's characterization of Kane was still too rigidly tied to the real-life Hearst. And just as Orson waited until the last moment to master his own performance in a stage play, he waited until now to surrender his attention to Kane, transforming the character "from Mankiewicz's cardboard portrait," in Robert L. Carringer's words, "to the complex and enigmatic figure we see in the film."

Mankiewicz had written the character as an "egomaniac monster," Welles told biographer Richard Meryman. "I don't think a portrait of a man was ever present in any of Mank's scripts. Everybody assumes that because Mank was an old newspaperman, and because he wrote about Hearst, and because he was a serious reader on politics, then that is the whole explanation of what he had to do with *Kane*. I felt his knowledge was very journalistic, not very close, the point of view of a newspaperman writing about a newspaper boss he despised. . . .

"I don't say that Mank didn't see Kane with clarity," Welles continued. "He saw everything with clarity. No matter how odd or how right or how marvelous his point of view was, it was always diamond white. Nothing muzzy. But the truths of the character, Kane, were not what interested him."

Orson reworked nearly every scene. By slashing away at the sentimental touches (the little boy Kane crying for his lost mother) and easy laughs, he toughened the central portrait and the tone of the drama. Mank, despite his attraction to some of the scandalous elements of Hearst's story, had a certain rueful fondness for the man, whom he'd known at close range. "Personally," Mankiewicz testified in the Lundberg case, "[Hearst] was and is one of the most charming men I have ever known." In the script, and later through his acting, Orson made Kane's charm self-serving and self-satisfied. "[Hearst] was, and is, a horse's ass, no more or less, who had been wrong without exception on everything he's touched," Welles told Mankiewicz during one of their many arguments about Hearst.

Orson wanted to make Kane more sympathetic without sentimentalizing him. He humanized Kane by humanizing his relationships with the other characters. Reworking the script in the desert, he sharpened Kane's relationship with his first wife, Emily Monroe Norton, and drew out his chance meeting with Susan Alexander that follows in the film, the ear-wiggling and shadow-play that evince the buried heart of Kane and the secret childlike side of Orson.

He also injected humor and gaiety into the scene in the newsroom after Kane has purloined the famous reporters of a rival newspaper. "Kane puts two fingers to his mouth and whistles," the published script says. "A band strikes up and enters in advance of a regiment of very magnificent maidens." Orson knew he could stage the "magnificent maidens" brilliantly, with Kane protesting, "I don't know how to dance," as he's pulled into the line of leggy dancers.

The published shooting script does not include the lyrics of the toe-tapping ditty "Charlie Kane," which were jobbed out to songwriter Herman Ruby; and Mankiewicz, testifying in the Lundberg case, was dismissive of the song (by "some Tin Pan Alley lyricist," he scoffed). But Orson liked to sing and dance a little, and the lyrics recall the foolishments at the Todd School:

LEAD SINGER

What is his name?

BERNSTEIN

(*echoing*)

What is his name?

DANCERS

(*singing*)

It's Charlie Kane!

EVERYONE

(*singing*)

> It's Mister Kane!
> He doesn't like the Mister!
> He likes good old Char-lie Kane!

Orson would spend several days filming that scene, using the camera to add layers of richness to the musical number. ("This [scene] was really," sniffed Houseman in his testimony in the Lundberg case, "one of those personal things about Orson, who always fancied himself a ladies' man, and to prance around with a large number of beautiful young ladies would be his idea of heaven.") The scene took time to create, relying on tricky composite photography and layers of sound, but the pretty chorus girls also had to appeal to Orson as much as to Kane. "I threw all the [first] girls out and waited till we got prettier ones," Welles recalled, "and they were marvelous girls, finally."

In every draft of the script, the newsroom party scene was followed by the scene where Kane, Leland, and Bernstein adjourn to the high-class bordello "Georgie's Place," which recalled Chicago's turn-of-the-century Everleigh Club. (Welles imagined that his own father may have cavorted at the Everleigh.) The scene was not at all sexualized, although "it was quite evident the kind of young ladies they were," Houseman explained in his testimony. In early drafts of the scene at Georgie's, Kane urged Leland to write a column "saying exactly what you think" while Kane vacations in Europe, promising him that no one will edit his copy in Kane's absence. ("Leland keeps looking at him with loving perplexity," the published script says, "knowing he will never solve the riddle of that face.") Honing that scene in the desert, Orson shifted some of the Kane-Leland dialogue back to the earlier party sequence. The bordello scene was eventually filmed—it was roughly two minutes long, Welles estimated—but Orson deleted it in its entirety during postproduction. He no longer needed the exposition, and he foresaw that it would be a target for the censors. "It wasn't that good," Welles told Bogdanovich with a shrug.

More than once Orson returned to the Kane-Leland scenes, trying to capture the friendship that perplexes Leland. During filming, he worked with Cotten to touch up Leland's narration, his wheelchair scenes, and the final clash between Kane and Leland after Kane finishes Leland's damning review of Susan's opera debut. "Hello, Charlie," Leland says. "I didn't know we were speaking." Kane: "Sure, we're speaking, Jedediah. You're fired."

Orson revised Kane's early "declaration of principles," and his address at the big rally of his gubernatorial campaign, to accord with his own idea of Kane's politics. Again, his script revisions dictated the way he would eventually stage, direct, and perform the sequence. The rally scene—with its indelible image of Kane onstage in a vast hall, gesturing broadly in front of a gigantic blowup of his face—would be photographed on a bare soundstage, with no crowd. In his performance, Orson adopted "the manner of speaking in a reverberant room waiting for the echoes to die," as sound man James G. Stewart recalled. The illusion of a packed hall, with the speaker glimpsed from afar by Mrs. Kane and Junior in box seats, was created in postproduction through meticulous editing and sound and visual effects.

As Stewart recalled, Orson gave him the raw recording of the scene, made on the empty soundstage, and told him to make it "sound like Madison Square Garden." Anxious to please the director, Stewart reprinted "eight or ten dialogue tracks on film to get the right sound." He proudly played the result for Welles. "You're a bigger ham than I am!" Orson barked with a laugh. "Who's going to look at me with that sound coming at them? It's great, but give me half as much." Recalled Stewart ruefully: "He was right. . . . I toned it down."

Welles took special care with the culminating scenes at Xanadu, when Kane is a heavy, aging, dethroned despot. "Kane was a spoiled child," Welles stated precisely in his deposition in the Lundberg case. "Xanadu was his last toy and it was intended as a monstrous place of refuge from a world which had to a large extent rejected him and his words."

Kane by this time would be seventy-five years old, according to the screenplay, and the scenes were a *Schauspieler*'s dream. From the earliest story sessions, Orson had known that these scenes would add both risk and potential greatness to his performance. His makeup would be crucial, and at RKO he stumbled on another ace to assist in his metamorphosis. Maurice Seiderman had been a junior makeup artist on three recent RKO pictures that interested Welles: *The Hunchback of Notre Dame*, *Gunga Din*, and *Abe Lincoln in Illinois*. (Orson had attended the February premiere of the last-named film with mixed emotions, coveting Lincoln as a subject as much as he despised Raymond Massey as an actor.)

Seiderman, a Russian immigrant, had yet to be granted a single screen credit; he didn't even belong to the makeup artists' union. Seiderman was actually sweeping up hair on a soundstage floor when Orson first encountered him. Yet he proved an eager collaborator for Orson, who had loved enhancing his parts with makeup since boyhood. For the early scenes at the *Inquirer* offices, when Welles was about the same age as the character he was playing, Seiderman sharpened his youth, lacing him into painful corsets to thin him down. But it was the aging Kane that would demand the most of the makeup artist.

For inspiration, Welles gave Seiderman photographs of the real-life Samuel Insull and William Randolph Hearst. "From Insull," wrote Frank Brady, "Seiderman took his brush mustache, his baldness and the general contours of his head; from Hearst, he took his aquiline nose, the receding hairline, and many facial contours." Seiderman thinned Orson's hair, padded his bulk, and applied plastic sculptured pieces over his nose, chin, and eye sockets. For the final scenes, he added a fearsome bald skullcap. "During Orson's first sitting, which took hours," Brady wrote, "Seiderman had William Alland read aloud *The Kingdom of Evil: A Continuation of the Journal of Fantazius Mallare* by Ben Hecht," because Seiderman thought it would help Orson relate to the desired image of old-man Kane: a "gigantic man with a large head" and expressionless face, much like the mad, reclusive artist of Hecht's novel. "Orson loved and accepted the mimesis."

Finishing the image with a sheen of liquid greasepaint applied to the plastic masking, Seiderman fitted Welles with false teeth and special contact lenses to dim Kane's eyes as the character aged onscreen. The contacts "drove you mad with pain," Orson recalled. Some days during filming, the actor arrived for his makeup at 3:30 A.M., sitting for hours as he was fussed over by Seiderman.

Seiderman registered many of his makeup inventions, beloved by Welles, for broader use, including a patent on soft contact lenses. Orson would call on Seiderman to handle his makeup in numerous later films, including *Journey into Fear*, *Jane Eyre*, *Macbeth*, and *Touch of Evil*.

(For the last-named film, another masterpiece of metamorphosis, Sei-derman pasted plastic bags under Orson's eyes, replanted his hairline, stuck a big ugly nose on him, and stuffed him with wadding "to make the fat man even fatter," in Barbara Leaming's words.)

Citizen Kane would open and close at Xanadu, and in the desert Orson painstakingly reexamined the last act of the script, the dissolves from 1930 to 1932 showing Kane dwarfed by the Great Hall, Susan bored with her jigsaw puzzles, and the "twenty cars full of picnickers" heading for Everglades Camp, where Kane and Susan share a well-appointed tent overnight.

Earlier in the month, Orson had gone to see Nat "King" Cole, a jazz musician he'd heard about in Chicago before moving to Los Angeles. Cole and his trio were playing at the Radio Room, the club across the street from NBC in Hollywood. Orson went away humming Cole's version of "This Can't Be Love," a Charlie Barnet–Haven Johnson tune, and when he revisited the scene described in the published shoot-ing script as simply "Long shot—a number of classy tents," he devel-oped it into something else entirely: an extended interlude of carousing picnickers, serenaded by Cee Pee Johnson's ensemble performing a louche-sounding pastiche of Cole's song. Sensing that the moment needed a "beat," something musical, "I kind of based the whole scene around that song," Welles recalled.

The sequence ends in the Kanes' tent, with the sullen Susan provok-ing a bitter argument. Orson condensed and rewrote it:

SINGERS
It can't be love. He said, It can't be love. He said . . .

KANE

(*quietly*)

Whatever I do, I do because I love you.

SUSAN
You don't love me! You want me to love you—sure—"I'm Charles Foster Kane. Whatever you want—just name it and it's yours. But you've gotta love me!"

Without a word, KANE slaps her across the face. He
continues to look at her.

Don't tell me you're sorry.

KANE

I'm not sorry.

Dissolve.

The dissolve takes us back to Xanadu, where Raymond the butler
enters Kane's room to tell him that Susan is packing her bags. Welles
asked Houseman and Mankiewicz for more than one scene baring
Kane's violent temper, but the moment of his second wife's desertion
was climactic. Without irony, testifying in the Lundberg case, Houseman recounted the "night of the flaming Sternos" and insisted that
"this was the incident which gave us our model for that scene."

Of course, the scene as filmed bears little resemblance to the tri-
fling incident at Chasen's the previous Christmas. In the film, "KANE,
in a truly terrible and absolutely silent rage, is literally breaking up
the room," according to the published script, "yanking pictures, hooks
and all off the wall, smashing them to bits—ugly, gaudy pictures—
Susie's pictures in Susie's bad taste. Off tabletops, off of dressing tables,
occasional tables, bureaus, he sweeps Susie's whorish accumulation of
bric-a-brac.

"Raymond stands in the doorway watching him."

Orson had had his eye on this scene from the beginning, reframing
it at each stage. All of the whorish "bad taste" of Susan's decor that
Mankiewicz envisioned was sublimated to the action and performance.
It was like one of the radio scenes in "War of the Worlds," a moment
only Welles would dare to stretch out to an impossible length onscreen.

By chance the room-wrecking scene was one of the last that Orson
shot for *Citizen Kane*, five months down the road in late October. With
four cameras filming the action, Welles recalled, he captured it in
"one take," lunging around spasmodically and smashing up the set
in a splendidly protracted explosion that stretches for almost three
minutes. "Five hours of makeup, and then get on and break it all

up," Welles recalled to Peter Bogdanovich. "Tore my wrists and hands apart. I was bleeding like a pig when I was done with all that glass and everything."

As he did on and off throughout the filming, Welles invited Dr. Maurice Bernstein to visit the RKO studio on that day, knowing he might need his former guardian's medical attention. Bernstein had long since obtained his certificate to practice medicine in California, and by the end of the summer of 1940 he and his wife, Hazel, were living in Beverly Hills, in time to watch Orson as he directed his first film. "Orson cut his fingers and wrists and I had to bandage and plaster the cuts," Dr. Bernstein wrote to Ashton Stevens the day after the room-wrecking performance. "The scene was so realistic, the electrician who was on a scaffold came down to find out if Orson often lost his temper. It was the most intense scene."

In their interview sessions, Bogdanovich asked Welles about an anecdote often told by William Alland, and repeated in many books: that Orson was "exhilarated" after he completed the scene, "and said it was the first time he'd ever felt the emotion while acting a scene."

"Naw," Welles replied. "I'm sure that's one of those memories after the event that are more creative than accurate." He conceded that the room-wrecking scene was "very rough," but added that "the set was wonderfully done by Perry Ferguson. Marvelously dressed—made it very easy to play. My God, it was a wonderful set. I can see it now. [Ferguson] was just brilliant."

At the end of the destructive rampage came the payoff. "[Kane's] eye lights on a hanging whatnot in a corner which had escaped his notice," according to the published version of the script. "Prominent on its center shelf is the little glass ball with the snowstorm in it. He yanks it down. Something made of china breaks, but not the glass ball. It bounces on the carpet and rolls to his feet, the snow in a flurry." Clutching the glass ball, within which swirls a snowstorm, Kane "slowly walks down the corridor, the servants giving way to let him pass, and watching him as he goes. The mirrors which line the hall reflect his image as he moves." Then the published shooting script adds—oddly, since it's really not the point of the scene—"He is an old, old man!"

Then, "KANE turns into a second corridor—sees himself reflected in the mirror—stops. His image is reflected again in the mirror behind

him—multiplied again and again and again in long perspectives—
KANE looks. We see a thousand KANES.

"Dissolve."

Such moments, now immortal, were worked and reworked in the
script for months, then prepared meticulously by art director Perry
Ferguson and cinematographer Gregg Toland. Although he would
make countless emendations in the weeks and months ahead, it was
during his time alone in the desert, furiously cutting and revising, that
Welles completed the final script of *Citizen Kane* for presentation to the
Production Code Office and RKO.

Returning confidently from the desert, Orson focused on his two most
important open slots in the cast: Emily Monroe Norton and Susan
Alexander.

He had cast many of the principal speaking parts by the end of
May, but the two wives of Charles Foster Kane were more problematic
characters. After years of staging all-boy shows at the Todd School,
Orson had far more experience casting men than women; even in New
York, his productions were often dominated by male figures (especially
when he played the lead). He told people he wanted both of these
actresses to be Hollywood newcomers, but he couldn't think of any
Mercury actress who was right for either part. Meanwhile, as the script
work continued, Susan Alexander's role grew in importance—while
Emily Monroe Norton's diminished, especially after Orson ditched
the subplot involving President McKinley's assassination. Emily would
be glimpsed in *News on the March* and in front of the *Inquirer* building in
1898, riding off with Kane to get married. But in the final script she
figured in only two major dialogue scenes.

As a way to compress the drama, Welles came up with the idea of
the breakfast room sequence, using a series of dissolves to show the
deterioration of Kane's first marriage. The script says: "The following
scenes cover a period of nine years—are played in the same set with
only changes in lighting, special effects outside the window, and wardrobe."

The first vignette takes place three years after their marriage. Seated
at the breakfast table, Kane, dressed "in white tie and tails," lovingly

pours a morning glass of milk for Emily, who is similarly "formally attired." "As he finishes, he leans over and playfully nips the back of her neck." Bantering flirtatiously, Kane says he will call Bernstein and put off all appointments till noon. "What time is it?" Kane asks. "I don't know—it's late," replies Emily. "It's early," says Kane; the scene dissolves with the implication that the happily married pair are retiring to bed.

The next exchange was briefer, less sweet. It follows the first immediately, but is one year later, according to the script—1902—with "different clothes—different food." This time Emily is seen blandly complaining that her husband left her dinner party in the lurch the night before, rushing off mysteriously to the *Inquirer*. "What do you do on a newspaper in the middle of the night?" Emily asks. "My dear, your only co-respondent is the *Inquirer*," Kane responds mildly.

Two years later, the third vignette reveals the couple, seated farther apart, with a "change of costume and food." Emily is unhappy that Kane's newspaper has been "attacking the President." Kane corrects her: "You mean Uncle John,"* he says, a "fathead" who is "letting a pack of high-pressure crooks run his administration. This whole oil scandal—" Emily interrupts: "He happens to be the President, Charles—not you." Kane rejoins: "That's a mistake that will be corrected one of these days." Another dissolve.

As further subtle changes advance the marriage to 1905, 1906, and 1908, the couple separate both emotionally and physically, their breakfast table growing longer as they grow apart. Emily grouses about Mr. Bernstein visiting the nursery with "the most incredible atrocity" as a gift for Junior, letting the audience know in passing that the Kanes now have a son. Reacting to this hint of distaste (and anti-Semitism) from his aristocratic wife, Kane tells Emily curtly, "Mr. Bernstein is apt to pay a visit to the nursery now and then." Emily: "Does he have to?" Kane (shortly): "Yes."

The last installment occurs in 1909, with the couple breakfasting

---

* Since McKinley's first name was William, "Uncle John" further distances the script from the real-life assassination while making a separate and distinct allusion to the Harding administration and the Teapot Dome scandal.

in silent tension. As Kane reads his *Inquirer*, Emily flaunts its rival, the *Chronicle*.

"I did the breakfast scene thinking I'd invented it," Welles recalled. "It wasn't in the script originally. And when I was almost finished with it, I suddenly realized that I'd unconsciously stolen it from Thornton [Wilder]." Like many of the details of *Citizen Kane*, it was something he borrowed from his boyhood—in this case, from Wilder's 1931 one-act play *The Long Christmas Dinner*, which he saw as a youth. Orson phoned Wilder to confess the appropriation, and they laughed about it together.

The woman playing Emily Monroe Norton had to be a patrician beauty, someone Orson himself found attractive. After testing a number of Hollywood actresses, Welles remembered a young singer whose path he'd crossed in New York. Her name: Ruth Warrick. "She looked the part of Emily," Welles told Henry Jaglom. "And I'm one of those fellows who thinks, if they look it, then you can make them act it. Particularly a small part."

Warrick was a fellow midwesterner, twenty-three years old, a University of Kansas graduate with only stock theater, commercial advertising, and broadcasting on her résumé. Orson had his staff track her down, then flew to New York to meet with her at the Waldorf-Astoria. Orson told Warrick he was looking for "a lady of breeding" to play his character's first wife in his new film, but after the usual casting calls he'd come to the conclusion that "there *are* no ladies in Hollywood." Would she be willing to come to Hollywood for a screen test?

Warrick felt tension emanating from Orson when she arrived at RKO for her camera audition—as she later recalled in her autobiography, *The Confessions of Phoebe Tyler*—in part because her test was being monitored by "New York brass" visiting the studio lot that day. But Warrick demonstrated the same poise Emily Monroe Norton might have shown in the situation. Instinctively, she reached out to Orson, putting him at his ease. "I chatted, laughed, asked questions, made suggestions, and all the while moved close to him and touched his arm. Little by little I felt the tension begin to drain away."

She won the part, and also his trust. Emily appealed both to Kane and to Orson. "Ruth was a wonderful girl," Welles told Henry Jaglom. "And when she was young, she was quite sexy." In fact, "one night" years later in Hollywood (Warrick is vague on the chronology but suggests it was after Welles's separation from his second wife, Rita Hayworth), Orson phoned Warrick and "begged" her to pay him a surreptitious visit. "He had no one to talk to, he said, and he repeated the line he had used when we first met: There were no ladies in Hollywood, no one with the depth and compassion to understand him," Warrick wrote in her autobiography.

Orson dispatched his limousine to fetch Warrick. She arrived to find him "lolling in great mounds of pillows, looking pale and sallow, as if playing a scene from *Mayerling*," she wrote. Orson spoke morosely about the crass "money men" ruling Hollywood. "Any man whose ability is simply to make money should get down on his knees and beg a man with creative talent to make something of value with that money," he fumed to Warrick. "But they don't seem to know that their money has absolutely no value in itself."

"I, too, in my own life was beginning to have some need of comfort," Warrick's account continued, "and we soothed and held each other through a long evening. And yet, returning to my home later, I knew that somehow I, too, had been used by Orson, that I was a handy balm for a momentary hurt. It was not a role I felt good about." The actress resolved to avoid Orson in the future—until 1980, when Welles made amends by agreeing to appear on *Good Morning America* to help promote her book. Host David Hartman interviewed him by satellite, along with Warrick and Paul Stewart in the studio. ("God save me from my friends," Welles complained to Jaglom the following day. "[Stewart] telling Hartman how much the picture [*Citizen Kane*] cost. He's got it wrong, of course. And sounding as though he were associate producer . . .")

Warrick praised *Citizen Kane* on the TV show; Orson didn't mind the praise, but he insisted to Jaglom that her otherwise flattering memoir couldn't be trusted. "What is interesting about her book is that the reader is likely to think that we had a love affair. She's practically saying it." But Welles himself was elusive on the subject. When Barbara Leaming teased him out about his putative dalliance with Warrick, Welles first strenuously denied an "amorous encounter" (Leaming's careful wording) with the actress. Later, however, he admitted, "It's true."

Why, then, had he denied it? his biographer asked him.

"You don't tell on those kinds of things," Welles explained to Leaming. "I think stout denial—at all times."

After the series of breakfast room vignettes, Emily Kane would have only one big scene—a doozy, the film's emotional watershed. On the night of Kane's triumphant speech at Madison Square Garden, Emily receives an anonymous note. She sends Junior home in a limousine, then lures Kane into a taxi bound for an apartment house on West Seventy-Fourth Street. When they arrive, they find Susan Alexander waiting with Jim Gettys, the corrupt political boss, who threatens to reveal the "love nest" to the rival press unless Kane withdraws from the race for governor.

On occasion, as in the bedroom-wrecking scene at Xanadu, Orson filmed and completed a major scene in one miraculous take. More often, the scenes were written, rewritten, staged, rehearsed, and restaged many times, in a process that could take days or weeks. This was partly because Orson eschewed the traditional studio approach of filming master shots and "coverage" (alternative angles) for each scene, instead building his scenes around the complicated moving shots that became the film's visual signature. "I was constantly encouraged by Toland," Welles recalled, "who said, under the influence of [John] Ford, 'Carry everything in one shot—don't do anything else.' In other words, play scenes through with cutting and don't do alternative versions. That was Toland in my ear."

As a money-saving tactic, Welles rehearsed the actors over and over, then shot multiple takes but printed as few as possible. (Printing was a major expense, as he had learned on *Too Much Johnson*.) It was not uncommon for Orson to shoot fifty or more takes of a scene while making *Kane*, the actor Paul Stewart recalled. "One day he shot a hundred takes and exposed 10,000 feet," Stewart claimed, "without a single print!"

The curious thing about this method was that the multiple takes usually had little to do with camera placement. Often the camera stayed just where Orson initially decided it would go. The retakes were more likely to fine-tune the performances, and the pacing and tone of the scene.

The camera's positioning is "the only thing I'm certain of," Welles told Bogdanovich. "I'm never certain of a performance—my own or the other actors'—or the script or anything. I'm ready to change, move anything. But to me it seems there's only one place in the world the camera can be, and the decision usually comes immediately. If it doesn't come immediately, it's because I have no idea about the scene, or I'm wrong about the scene to begin with."

The "love nest" scene brought together four important characters: Kane, Emily, Susan, and Boss Gettys. It was Warwick's last scene in the film, and the only substantial one for Ray Collins, who is merely glimpsed at Madison Square Garden during Kane's speech. But the scene marked a rare instance when the correct camera decision eluded Orson. The first time he tried staging the scene, Welles recalled, he had to halt the filming abruptly and "just quit for the day—and went home," he confessed to Bogdanovich. "Made a big scandal. I just had no idea what to do. Came back the next day . . . it seemed to me so boring."

"When you came back, it worked?" asked Bogdanovich.

"Yeah," said Welles. "And I didn't figure it out on paper." Even so, Orson claimed to be dissatisfied with the end result, calling the "love nest" confrontation scene "overstated." He told Bogdanovich that the scene showed "some kind of insecurity, I think, visually."

He did not mention what happened during the filming: as Kane hurtled down the steps of the apartment building, shouting at Gettys, the actor playing him stumbled forward, injuring himself badly enough that Orson was whisked off to Good Samaritan Hospital, where tests revealed broken chips in his ankles. For the next two weeks he directed from a wheelchair, acting some scenes with metal braces supporting him.

If the scene is at all "insecure," with stiff groupings and studied angles, it is also one of the film's acting highpoints. For the first time, Kane reveals the fundamental violence and solipsism of his character. Susan Alexander, plaintively crying, "What about me?" foreshadows her later victimhood. Collins, as the corrupt but not unsympathetic Boss Gettys, achieves an almost noble poignancy, while Emily, arguing for her marriage and their son, loses with dignity.

The plot of *Citizen Kane* was stacked against Emily, and Warrick had to keep her likability and poise under the most trying conditions. "You decided what you were going to do, Charles, some time ago,"

Emily says with calm strength—her last words in the film. In Warrick, Welles had found the purposeful lady of the script, a woman he could imagine as his wife.

Another claim that Orson hated in Ruth Warrick's autobiography was her comment that he had isolated Dorothy Comingore, the actress who played Susan Alexander, from the rest of the cast, treating her "with a discourteous contempt that was often painful to watch, while making an obvious display of elaborate courtliness in his dealing with me."

But he "hardly knew" Warrick at the time, Orson protested to Henry Jaglom, while "Comingore and I were great friends." He dismissed Warrick's observations as those of "one actress in a movie talking about another."

Susan Alexander was the true leading lady of *Citizen Kane*, a role that could determine the success or failure of the picture. And Comingore was a virtual unknown in Hollywood. Two years older than Welles and now, at twenty-seven, past her ingenue prime, Comingore had been noticed by Charles Chaplin in a revival of *The Cradle Song* at Carmel's Little Theater. Warner Brothers signed her to a weekly contract, giving her the screen name Linda Winters, but then shuffled her over to Columbia, which released her in turn to freelance for the studios of Poverty Row. As Linda Winters, the actress starred in cheap programmers like *Prison Train* while decorating the background of A pictures on the order of *Mr. Smith Goes to Washington*, where she has a line or two greeting Jimmy Stewart at the train station. Her career was languishing when Orson first met her in the summer of 1939.

Herbert Drake had arranged a publicity date for them, following Orson's arrival in Hollywood. They were photographed at Chasen's, and when the photo was published they were misidentified as "Mr. and Mrs. Welles." Comingore "sat and listened" to Orson all night, a reporter later wrote, "quite content to be entertained." But she was taken aback when the younger man left her on her doorstep with, "God bless you, my child."

Orson told Peter Bogdanovich that he tested "a lot of people" for the part of Susan Alexander, including "a lot of strippers, about ten, none of whom were any good." "You wanted that kind of cheapness?"

asked Bogdanovich. "Yeah," replied Welles. When Herbert Drake reminded him of his publicity date with Linda Winters, Orson brought her in for a meeting and a series of auditions. The actress had just finished emoting in a Three Stooges two-reeler, and she and Orson shared a good laugh about it. Welles was instantly reminded of how sweet and vulnerable she was, and her test showed that she could laugh on cue, with that infectious laughter Orson remembered from the arranged date. She had the look he wanted for the character: the look of a waif Charles Foster Kane might adopt as a cause.

"Was she an intelligent actress?" Bogdanovich asked.

"Yes," Welles replied without hesitation. "Of course, her old-age scenes were tremendously tricked-up. We blew dangerous drugs in her eyes and sprayed her throat so she couldn't talk and everything else. But she was still great." (At this point in the interview with Bogdanovich, Welles recited from memory one of Susan's last lines in the film: "Well, what do you know—it's morning already," adding his own reflection, "That's another favorite moment."*)

By now, it was nearly July 1. Orson brought Herman Mankiewicz in to weigh some of the remaining casting decisions, inviting him to hear Comingore read in Orson's office. "She looks precisely like the image of a kitten we have been looking for," Mank told Welles. Orson told Comingore the job was hers. But not as Linda Winters: Orson disliked such Hollywood tomfoolery—and, besides, as Linda Winters she wouldn't be a "fresh face." Orson wanted her in the film, but as Dorothy Comingore.

That's when Comingore made a confession to Welles: she was pregnant. (She had married screenwriter Richard Collins in 1939.)

"What?" Orson howled.

"A baby," Comingore said timidly.

"When?"

"About seven months."

"It's all the better!" Orson reportedly crowed. "You're hired. If you

---

* Susan says one thing more after "It's morning already . . . ," adding a final grace note to her character before leaving Citizen Kane. "Come around," she tells Thompson the reporter, "and tell me the story of *your* life sometime."

start in the part, it'll really prove to those bums that I'm going to finish the picture on time."

Comingore had to be a courageous as well as an intelligent actress. Her scenes were among the most painful and darkest in *Citizen Kane.* Her character was central to one of the film's bravura sequences: Susan Alexander Kane's opera debut, among Orson's most magnificent concoctions. "INSERT," reads the published shooting script, "FRONT PAGE CHICAGO 'INQUIRER' with photograph proclaiming that Susan Alexander opens at new Chicago Opera House in *Thais* . . . On sound track during above we hear the big expectant murmur of an opening night audience and the noodling of the orchestra."

In the first half of *Kane,* Susan's debut is glimpsed briefly from the point of view of drama critic Jed Leland, who distracts himself from the tedium by cutting his program to ribbons. Later, the humiliating debut is seen again from Susan's point of view and from Kane's. As the performance ends, the camera moves out into the audience with the "ghastly sound of three thousand people applauding as little as possible," pushing in close on Kane, embarrassed but defiant, standing alone and "applauding, very, very hard," according to the script.

The backstage portion concludes with a memorable shot in which the camera rises into the rafters to reveal "two typical stagehands . . . looking down on the stage below. They look at each other. One of them puts his hand to his nose." Welles took script ideas from anyone who crossed his path, and that closing gesture—the stagehand holding his nose—was suggested by a property man working on *Citizen Kane.* "His name was Red," Welles recalled. "We were just going to go up to them looking disgusted or something. Anyway, it was a big contribution."

Comingore had a cracked voice, which added authenticity to her persona. But she wasn't enough of a singer to handle the arias in the script—even as badly as Susan Alexander would. That was no problem for an opera fan like Welles, who found a voice double: the Pasadena-born opera singer Jean Forward, who was appearing in the cast of *Meet the People.*

The meticulous dubbing of Comingore's singing took place entirely in postproduction. Comingore never met Forward until the San Francisco premiere of *Citizen Kane.* Complicating matters, the classically trained Forward had to sing her arias in a voice that was "really pathetic," in the words of the script. "The reason Susan is struggling so hard is *not* that she cannot sing," composer Bernard Herrmann explained later, "but rather that the demands of the part are purposely greater than she can ever meet." The dubbing was "big work," Welles recalled proudly, "very well done by the girl [Forward]. Worked a long time on that."

If not for the ingenious opera pastiche, the sequence would not have been as effective. Orson drew on his many nights at the opera to dictate the feel of the music, detailing his thoughts in long phone conversations and exhaustive telegrams to Herrmann, who did the initial scoring from New York. The Promethean composer was Orson's musical ace in the hole. "If Herrmann was a neophyte to film," as his biographer Steven C. Smith wrote, "it was in practice only. No snob about the cinema, he was familiar not only with American films and film composers but also with their European counterparts." Herrmann had been poised for the go-ahead as the script was being finalized; he and Welles were both comfortable with urgent deadlines.

The film's brooding, neo-Romantic main theme was destined to become a composition against which all other screen music is still compared. The main theme was "a simple four-note figure in the brass," according to Herrmann, that was heard at the opening and reprised at the end of the film. It is the motif of "Kane's power." The second important musical motif is "that of Rosebud," in Herrmann's words. "Heard as a solo on the vibraphone, it first appears during the death scene at the very beginning of the picture. It is heard again and again throughout the film under various guises, and if followed closely, is a clue to the ultimate identity of Rosebud itself."

Herrmann also wrote memorable bridges and transitions. Letting music convey the passage of time was a standard radio technique. For example, the subtly complex underscoring of the breakfast table vignettes integrated "the old classic form of theme and variations," Herrmann recalled. The first vignette referenced a waltz in the style of French dance composer Émile Waldteufel ("a Welles favorite," as Steven C. Smith noted). Then, in the later vignettes, "variations begin. Each scene is a separate variation. Finally, the waltz theme is heard bleakly in the high registers of the violins."

For Herrmann's opera pastiche—"*Kane's* supreme musical sequence," in Smith's words—Welles knew exactly what he wanted. Susan's character "sings as [the] curtain goes up in the first act," he wrote to Herrmann, "and I believe there is no opera of importance where soprano leads with chin like this. Therefore suggest it be original . . . by you—parody on typical Mary Garden vehicle." He suggested that Herrmann model his pastiche on Mussorgsky's nineteenth-century opera *Salammbô*,* "which gives us phony production scene of ancient Rome and Carthage, and Susie can dress like grand opera neoclassic courtesan. . . . Here is a chance for you to do something witty and amusing—and now is the time for you to do it. . . .

"I love you dearly," Orson closed gratefully.

Almost all the music would be composed and recorded before the filming, then deployed as "an enormous playback," in Herrmann's words. The entire "score, like the film, works like a jigsaw," Herrmann said, with all the pieces whirling around in Orson's head.

Despite RKO's roster of exceptional actresses, production head George Schaefer approved Orson's choices of Ruth Warrick and Dorothy Comingore, two leading ladies whose names would mean nothing to the American public. Despite the studio's own small army of composers and musicians, Schaefer also said yes to Herrmann, as long as his salary came out of the picture's budget. When it came to Orson's creative choices, the studio president almost always said yes.

"Schaefer was a hero, an absolute hero," Welles told Bogdanovich.

On June 14, the studio issued a preliminary budget estimate showing "a total picture cost of $1,081,798," according to Robert L. Carringer— above the dangerous million mark. (As one budget department memo noted, the studio had already paid Mercury $55,000 for *Citizen Kane*, and had spent "about $100,000" on *Heart of Darkness* and *The Smiler with the Knife*—both figures in addition to the million-dollar cost projection.) The estimate plunged Welles and Herman Mankiewicz, now back on salary, into a final frenzy of pruning and polishing.

Whenever Orson made a significant change to the script, he and

---

* Herrmann gave the title of the film's pastiche a variant spelling: *Salambo*.

Mank had to rethink the jigsaw one more time to make the pieces fit, sorting out "what each narrator could report based on what only he or she could have known firsthand," in Carringer's words. "The time element is extremely difficult in a picture of this kind," as Houseman later told Lundberg's lawyers. "This is the hardest kind of picture to write." *

Two heads were better than one, and Orson relied on Mankiewicz right up to the start of filming. "Revised pages were passed back and forth between the two," wrote Richard Meryman, "Welles changing Herman, who changed Welles—'often much better than mine,' says Welles."

"Without Mank it would have been a totally different picture," Welles told Meryman. "It suits my self-esteem to think it might have been almost as good, but I could never have arrived at *Kane* as it was without Herman. . . .

"There is a quality in the film—much more than a vague perfume— that was Mank and that I treasured. It gave a kind of character to the movie, which I could never have thought of. It was a kind of controlled, cheerful virulence; we're finally telling the truth about a great WASP institution. I personally liked Kane, but I went with that. And that probably gave the picture a certain tension, the fact that one of the authors hated Kane and one loved him. . . .

"My *Citizen Kane* would have been more concerned with the interior corruption of Kane. The script is most like me when the central figure on the screen is Kane. And it is most like Mankiewicz when he's being talked about. And I'm not at all sure that the best part isn't when they're talking about Kane. Don't misunderstand me! I'm not saying I

---

* Mank tried the "whirling pagoda" approach only one other time in his career aside from the Dillinger project, a few years after *Citizen Kane* with none other than John Houseman as his producer. It was another project for RKO, "Tasker Martin," an adaptation of a Diana Gaines novel of the same title, the story of a ruthless industrialist with more enemies than friends. Developed by Houseman and Mankiewicz in 1950, "Tasker Martin" involved the industrialist's retinue gathering with conflicted emotions to discuss his life after his mysterious disappearance. The script was completed just before Houseman's testimony, though never filmed. Houseman does not mention the failed project in his memoir.

wrote all of one and Mank wrote the other. Mank wrote Kane stuff and I wrote . . . who knows . . .

"I don't suppose that authors ever agree on how much they did when they finish. In their secret selves they all think they wrote what they didn't. I'm sure of that. I'm sure I do."

Once the filming began, however, it was a different story. Mankiewicz found himself on the outside, and his natural paranoia and bile kicked in. Although Orson brought the actors over to his house to meet the writer, Mank was never a full-fledged or wholehearted member of the Mercury family—a role that would have required deferring to Orson as the patriarch of the clan.

Mank visited the set on a few occasions, and for a while he continued to do spot work on the script. As filming continued, he also watched the dailies of important scenes, but his memorandums quickly became unconstructive. He worried about Comingore's pregnancy, criticizing the way she looked. After watching a scene between Bernstein, played by Everett Sloane ("an unsympathetic looking man," Mank wrote), and Thompson the reporter (William Alland), Mank warned Orson against framing "two Jews" in the same shot. "There are not enough standard movie conventions being observed," he told Herbert Drake (who passed on the comments to Welles), "including too few close-ups and very little evidence of action. It is too much like a play."

Mank carried the chip of an underachiever on his shoulder like an epaulet. When Louella Parsons visited the set in late August, she quoted Welles as saying that "I wrote *Citizen Kane*" because the expectations and costs for his first film had grown out of proportion, sabotaging his chances to make *Heart of Darkness* and *The Smiler with the Knife*.

After Parsons's column appeared, Mankiewicz threatened privately to "come down" hard on Welles "because you are a juvenile delinquent credit stealer beginning with the Mars broadcast"—a remark that suggested Houseman had been whispering in his ear. (The two men stayed in touch.) Speaking through Herbert Drake, the aggrieved Mank threatened to take out a full-page advertisement in the trade papers asserting his credit, and to give interviews to the wire services saying the same. ("Said story is prepared," Drake reported, "sez he!!") And he would "permit" Ben Hecht to write a story for the *Saturday Evening Post*, exposing Welles's credit stealing on *Citizen Kane*.

"When Mank turned into a real writer," Welles told Meryman with a sigh, "it was immediately understood between us that he would get first billing since he was a distinguished screenwriter. And I've always said that his credit was immensely deserved.

"But then Mankiewicz persuaded himself that he was the sole and only writer. He wanted his name to be the only name. He wanted mine off. I didn't want mine off.

"And I tried to persuade Houseman to put his name on, since he'd been working all this time. But Houseman was more interested in mischief than glory. And there wasn't any way of discussing it with Mank. I felt that some kind of awful magic mirror had been placed between us."

According to Meryman, Mankiewicz made "angry phone calls to influential friends" and "lodged a protest" with the Screen Writers Guild. Welles's lawyer, Arnold Weissberger, advised Orson that contractually he was entitled to sole credit. But the Guild never became involved: Mank "withdrew his arbitration request," according to Roy Alexander Fowler, whose slender 1946 volume *Orson Welles* was the first book devoted to Welles's life and career, because the screenwriter feared eventual legal retribution from Hearst. Mankiewicz, of course, had fought the very notion of the Guild tooth and nail, alongside the worst reactionaries in Hollywood, so he may have realized he could hardly be assured of a sympathetic hearing. (The Guild, known today as the Writers Guild of America, has no record of any filing by him.)

As late as his testimony in the Lundberg case in 1950, Mankiewicz clung to his grudge. When asked what Orson Welles contributed to the writing of *Citizen Kane*, he replied, "It is a kind of Hollywood definition of writing, I am afraid. . . . He contributed substantially, but in the form of editing and typing. In other words, he was not part of the original dictation."

Though he mocked the writer gently as "Herman J. Mangel-Wurz" in private communications with Drake, Welles did not let the friction warp his moral compass. When RKO began the process of apportioning credit for the film, in 1941, the studio sent Welles a sheet for approval that listed his name first as the screenwriter, and Mankiewicz's second. He circled Mankiewicz "with a pencil," according to production manager Richard Wilson, "and drew an arrow putting him in first place."

One crucial piece of the jigsaw that belonged indisputably to Herman J. Mankiewicz was "Rosebud," the brand name of young Kane's sled, which gives the film its most potent through-line as Kane's mysterious final word.

Never mind the ice skates Orson's mother gave him as his last birthday gift before her death, or the sleds supposedly manufactured for seniors in the Todd School machine shop. For that matter, never mind the claim Richard Meryman makes in his biography of Mankiewicz: that "Rosebud" alluded to a prized Christmas gift, a bicycle (a "vehicle intrinsic to childhood freedom") that was stolen from where it was parked in front of the Wilkes-Barre public library when Mank was ten years old.

In the Lundberg case, Mankiewicz himself stated plainly that he took the word from a famous racehorse of which he was "unjustifiably fond." Old Rosebud was the horse that won the Kentucky Derby in 1914. In his first year at Columbia, Mank had bet on Rosebud, won, and celebrated.

Mankiewicz had been scarred by his childhood, and as an adult he became convinced that long-brewing neuroses had driven him to drink and gamble. In 1937, he started seeing Hollywood psychiatrist Dr. Ernst Simmel, an "eminent German refugee who had been a close friend of Freud's," according to Meryman. His sessions with Dr. Simmel lasted two years before they "ultimately failed," but Simmel helped Mank trace his personal problems back to his domineering father and his boyhood. Old Rosebud symbolized his lost youth, and the break with his family. "I had undergone psycho-analysis," Mankiewicz testified, "and Rosebud, under circumstances slightly resembling the circumstances in [Citizen Kane], played a prominent part."

As the son of a man who lent his name to a famous racehorse—a horse that sired another Kentucky Derby winner, Wintergreen, in 1909—Welles had no problem with the name itself. The cleverness of the conceit was that anyone who saw Citizen Kane could relate to a childhood Rosebud—be it a racehorse, a bicycle, a pair of ice skates, a sled, a favorite summer vacation, or the death of one's parents. But perversely, Orson often dismissed the storytelling device as a cheap gimmick. Shakespeare needed no lost sled, after all, to explain Falstaff or Lear.

"It was the only way we could find to 'get off' [the stage], as they used to say in vaudeville," Welles told Peter Bogdanovich. "It manages to work, but I'm still not too keen about it, and I don't think that [Mankiewicz] was, either."

Early in the script process, Orson proposed an alternative to Rosebud: "a long quote from Coleridge," wrote Meryman. Coleridge's poem "Kubla Khan" is referenced elsewhere in the script, and inspires the name Xanadu. "There was a scene in a mausoleum that I wrote—it was a quotation from a poem or something, I can't remember," Welles said, "and Mankiewicz made terrible fun of it. So I believed him and just said, 'All right. It's no good.' It *might* have been good—I don't remember it, because I was so ashamed from Mankiewicz's violent attack on it."

Orson and Mank not only hotly debated Rosebud but also fought over how often the device should recur during the film. In the Lundberg case, Mankiewicz told the courtroom that he wanted to add scenes "every now and then" in which Kane picked up a paperweight like the one the writer had on his nightstand, shaking it and staring with fascination at the swirling snow. "[Kane] had no idea what this means, what this really meant to him," Mankiewicz said, "and what I would like to have brought out in the picture much better than I had was the identification in his mind of the moment when he was torn from the only true, relaxed, complete, unquestioning happiness he ever had."

Welles too wanted Rosebud planted more firmly in the viewer's mind, but through different means. ("If I were to see Orson today," Mankiewicz mused in the Lundberg courtroom, "we would argue about it some more.") According to Mankiewicz, Welles wanted to include a close shot of the sled as the snow begins to blanket it at the beginning of the film—so close a shot that the audience could read the name Rosebud. Then, "for the rest of the picture," in Mank's words, "while Kane would, to his dying day, not know what his subconscious motivation was, the audience would have [known], and the picture would have thereby gained in clarity, gained in understanding."

Welles ultimately decided against revealing "Rosebud" in the early scene. He did accept Mank's paperweight, but deployed it more subtly. The glass globe can be glimpsed on a table as Mrs. Kane signs away her son; and later another globe appears on Susan Alexander's makeup table on the night she meets Kane, subliminally drawing a connection between Susan and Kane's mother. The sled is left forlornly behind in the snow early in the film, its inscription buried under fresh flurries. Midway through the picture we learn that Kane's dead mother's belongings are stored in a warehouse, where Kane is headed before he meets Susan. The sled then returns in the film's magisterial final moments, lying forgotten next to a picture of Kane and his mother in the treasure- and junk-cluttered basement of Xanadu.

After Kane's death, newspapermen, a photographer, and their assistants gather at Xanadu, pawing over Kane's possessions in a last-ditch effort to find their news angle. They spot a Donatello ("Cost: 45,000 lire"), a fourth-century Venus ("Cost: $23,000"), pieces of a Scottish castle and a Burmese temple, along with "one desk from the estate of Mary Kane, Little Salem, Colorado ("Value: $6.00"), and boxes upon boxes of jigsaw puzzles, according to the shooting script.

The reporter, Thompson, is searching the vast basement with a group of other newsmen, photographers, and assistants. Sharp-eyed movie fans may spot a hatted, pipe-smoking Alan Ladd, making his first screen appearance as one of the newsreel minions. ("We're supposed to get everything," he remarks, "the junk as well as the art.") Talent agent Sue Carol fought to get a part for the diminutive, soft-spoken Ladd, whom she would later marry—any part—in *Citizen Kane*. "He read for me, and I thought he was very good," Welles remembered. "His first movie part, and there he is, wearing his hat the way he wore it for thirty pictures afterwards."

Welles mused about meaning of Rosebud in his deposition in the Lundberg case. "I have some vague recollection of the conversations concerning the possibility of some character in the story being able to finally lead Thompson in the right direction," Welles said, but "since Rosebud itself is both somewhat inconsequential and in no wise a total explanation of the character of Kane, it was better to present such explanation as the sled itself offered in as random and unnoticed a method as possible."

"I wonder," says one of the newsmen in the basement at Xanadu; "you put all this stuff together, the palaces, paintings, toys, and everything. What would it spell?"

"Charles Foster Kane . . . ?" Thompson replies.

"Or Rosebud? How about it, Jerry?" asks the newsman played by Alan Ladd, finally, in the last reel giving audiences Thompson's first name.

"What's Rosebud?" asks someone else.

"Did you ever find out what it means?" the newsman persists.

"THOMPSON has turned around. He is facing the camera for the first time," reads the published version of the script.

THOMPSON

Charles Foster Kane was a man who got everything he
wanted and then lost it. Maybe Rosebud was something
he couldn't get or something he lost, but it wouldn't have
explained anything. I don't think any word explains a
man's life. No—I guess Rosebud is just a piece in a jigsaw
puzzle.

"I guess you might call that a disclaimer," Welles shrugged, talking to Bogdanovich about the scene. "A bit corny too. More than a bit. And it's [my writing,] I'm afraid."

As Thompson and his team leave Xanadu dispiritedly, laborers with shovels move in to clean the place up, throwing useless and discarded possessions into a huge roaring furnace. The butler hovers behind them. "Throw that junk in too," Raymond says.

The camera moves dreamlike toward the junk pile Raymond has indicated, "mostly bits of broken packing cases, excelsior, etc.," according to the published shooting script. (In the script, the sled is lying "on top of the pile"; in the finished film, it is one detail in an ocean of forgotten belongings.) "As camera comes close, it shows the faded rosebud and, though the letters are faded, unmistakably the word 'Rosebud' across it. The laborer drops his shovel, takes the sled in his hands and throws it into the furnace. The flames start to devour it."

Orson's deposition in the Lundberg case shows that, regardless of his later misgivings, he had reflected seriously on the ramifications of Rosebud when writing the script. "Just as it had been stamped on the sled it was stamped on the consciousness of the little boy who was robbed of his childhood," Welles said, "and who, when he grew up, unthinkingly associated the word Rosebud with the loss of his mother and of his childhood. . . . He was a man cheated of mother love, childhood and normalcy."

The scene then closes with an epiphany, framed by Perry Ferguson's meticulous art direction, which created "the very dust heap of a man's life," in Welles's words. The camera does not quit at Rosebud's funeral pyre. Bernard Herrman's glorious music begins to swell. Gregg Toland's camera inches and glides, moving restlessly; and the scene dissolves outside, where there is only moonlight:

> Smoke is coming from a chimney. Camera reverses the
> path it took at the beginning of the picture, perhaps
> omitting some of the stages. It moves finally through
> the gates, which close behind it. As camera pauses for a
> moment, the letter "K" is prominent in the moonlight.

> Just before we fade out, there comes again into the picture
> the pattern of a barbed wire and cyclone fencing. On the
> fence is a sign which reads:

> PRIVATE—NO TRESPASSING
> *Fade Out.*

On June 21, 1940, Arnold Weissberger wrote to Richard Baer to report that Mercury's combined East Coast and West Coast holdings had fallen to $500. Baer wrote back on June 22, explaining that he was typing his memo himself, having let his secretary go for the day to save money. "I have exactly $2.03 on the coast," Baer said. "Orson has made enormous demands. . . . If I don't get a hundred bucks, our credit will really be shot here."

Orson's ex-wife, Virginia, was sending almost daily letters threatening to retain a lawyer to obtain back alimony and other claims against Welles. Her new husband, Charles Lederer, had joined in the pressure with his own letters to Weissberger on Virginia's behalf, mustering all the biting humor of his craft.

Word of Orson's imminent financial collapse reached Hollywood columnists. The *Hollywood Reporter* said that Welles was retrenching economically and might soon take "one room at a hotel." Jimmie Fidler reported that Welles was moving into the Hollywood YMCA. Orson saved a little money on food, dieting for his scenes as the younger Kane, even as columnists renewed their gibes about his pale and "plump" appearance. He put out the unlikely word that he was taking boxing lessons to lose weight. He drank coffee all day, popped Benzedrine into the night.

On Monday, July 1, after Welles had made severe cuts in all categories of physical production, the RKO budgeting department issued a revised estimate of $737,740 for *Citizen Kane*. That pleased everyone, including studio president George Schaefer. The next week, Orson cleaned up the budgeted draft, which became known as the "Second Revised Final" (although Robert L. Carringer identifies it as the sixth draft in sequence), and sent it to the Hays Office for the censors' approval.

With RKO firmly behind him, Orson prepared for the first day of filming.

As broke then as he ever was, or ever would be, Orson was rich in spirit that summer in his all-but-deserted Hollywood home, staying up late, working alone on the script and sketches. He had slept little but had no nightmares. The work was best when it was fun, and the Niagara roar could be heard like an approaching train.

Twenty-five was not extreme youth for a film director. Charles Chaplin had directed his first films by the age of 25. So had Buster Keaton, another clown genius. John Ford was just twenty-three when he directed *The Tornado*, a two-reeler, in 1917. (By contrast, the French filmmaker Jean Renoir, whom Welles admired as much as any English-language director, had waited till he was thirty, in 1924, before directing his own scripts.)

In July, Orson kept his promise to studio head George Schaefer, calling the first take on *Citizen Kane* within one year of his highly publicized arrival in Hollywood. It was Monday, July 15, or maybe Wednesday, July 17—the precise date is lost to history.

Masters such as Chaplin, Keaton, Ford, and Renoir set a high bar artistically for filmmakers, and during his first year in Hollywood, Welles was privileged to watch and study many of their great films as well as films by other superior directors. His predecessors had established rules he had learned and would honor, as well as rules he would ignore and break.

Unlike these other filmmakers, who had all served apprenticeships of various kinds in the profession, Welles was granted the luxury of a full year to prepare his first masterpiece. He often attributed his success to extraordinary good luck in his career, especially when he was young—followed, he liked to say, by equally extraordinary bad luck later in his life. That was a modest pose; it was never just luck, and the good and bad luck often intermingled. Still, an odd kind of good luck had steered Orson's way in Hollywood, forcing him to postpone *Heart of Darkness*, obliging him to abort *The Smiler with the Knife*. It had taken all that torturous length of time for *Citizen Kane* to germinate as the natural fruit of his imagination and experiences.

He had used the time well, forging a relationship with the prickly scenarist Herman Mankiewicz, and bringing together the creative team of editor Robert Wise, art director Perry Ferguson, cinematographer Gregg Toland, and composer Bernard Herrmann.

With a few marked exceptions, Welles had preserved his Mercury Theatre family, casting most of the film from its ranks while adding new faces to its membership. The family now blended the stage and radio Mercury into a new film family. They gathered at Mankiewicz's house for the first full read-through of the script, and they would carry on together through many rehearsals before they were done. Such rehearsal was highly unusual in Hollywood, as were the recordings of the rehearsals Orson made so he and the cast could listen to the scenes, refining their tone and tempo.

His lead actors and actresses were largely unknown in the film industry, but most were well known to Welles—some dating back to his boyhood, others from the Mercury company's radio and stage productions. They could be counted on to work long hours, overnight if need be, having their Scotch and sodas on a silver tray outside the soundstage afterward in the dazzling morning sunlight. Their difficult leader made impossible demands on their patience, goodwill, and talents. Yet many of the players would stay with him through to his final productions—among them Joseph Cotten, Paul Stewart, William Alland, and Richard Wilson, who reunited for *F for Fake*, arguably Welles's last completed masterpiece, in 1973.

John Ford prided himself on his regular stock company and the many loyal technicians who bolstered his films behind the scenes. Yet directors like Ford existed and thrived totally within the comfortable studio system—no small feat, but Welles faced a greater hurdle, keeping his family together largely by dint of willpower and the occasional work he promised.

The date of the first day of filming is uncertain because the press was not alerted. According to many accounts, even RKO was kept in the dark, although that may be too good to be true. The filming began with a bit of fakery, with Orson and the crew pretending to shoot test scenes—Perry Ferguson's idea, Welles always said in later interviews, though it wasn't the first time a director did this to avoid unwanted press scrutiny and studio oversight. But the "tests" Welles photographed on July 15 or 17 were real, and some of the surreptitious footage would make it into the final *Citizen Kane*.

The family of actors arrived early for makeup and costumes, and then waited around for a long time for Welles and Gregg Toland to finish tinkering with the lights. Perhaps the small combo was already on the job, playing jazz. When at last the lights were ready, the family members gathered together, as they often had in the theater, or for radio shows, with Orson talking to them as a group, informally at first, reminiscing or telling an anecdote or joke to set the mood.

Exactly what scene did he direct on the first day? That, too, remains elusive. Welles gave differing accounts over the years, telling Peter Bogdanovich at one point, "The first scene I shot in the movie" was the one that takes place in the projection room, after *News on the March* has finished its cavalcade of clips. *Citizen Kane* then cuts abruptly to a projection room, "a fairly large one," according to the published script, "with a long throw to the screen. It is dark. Present are the editors of a news digest short and of the Rawlston magazines.

"RAWLSTON himself is also present. During this scene, nobody's face is really seen. Sections of their bodies are picked out by a table light, a silhouette is thrown on the screen, and their faces and bodies are themselves thrown into silhouette against the brilliant slanting rays of light from the projection booth."

The scene in the projection room was photographed in shadowy darkness, with only the "strong single light" (Orson's words) shining on the far wall. "We didn't dare turn on the [other] lights," Welles told Bogdanovich, because "I was supposed to be testing, so in case it was good I wanted to save it." To save money, and as a kind of in-joke, the shadowy figures in that early scene were the same actors playing the film's leads—even Joseph Cotten, who mutters "Rosebud!" in a scornful tone. "I used the whole Mercury cast, heavily disguised by darkness," Welles recalled. "There they all are. If you look carefully, you can see them. Everybody in the movie is in it." The sole exception was the man playing Rawlston, the newsreel editor—a Dutch-born stage actor named Philip Van Zandt, whose early work as an assistant to the Great Thurston might have caught Orson's eye.

"Not you too?" Bogdanovich asked Welles.

"Yes, I'm there."

That may have been the first scene filmed, but then again Welles also told Bogdanovich that his cherished idea of presenting "only new faces" in *Citizen Kane* was "ruined by the first day of shooting" when the director asked RKO to supply an actor for the small part of a waiter for the El Rancho Cabaret scene. He told RKO that he wanted the actor just for tests for the scene, which immediately follows the projection room sequence in the film. The casting department sent him someone on the studio payroll: "a tubby little round-faced Italian," Gino Corrado, who had been playing waiters and other small ethnic parts in Hollywood as far back as D. W. Griffith's *Intolerance*. "I couldn't possibly send him away," Welles explained, "on the basis that he was too well-known a face because I was claiming to be testing. So there he is—spoiling the whole master plan in one of the first shots I made!"

One thing is certain: on that first day, Orson was ready. He had spent twenty-five years preparing himself to make *Citizen Kane.* He must have thought proudly of his mother and father that day, though lingering sentimentally was never his nature. His older brother was not far away; perhaps Orson even found Richard some day work as a carpenter on the set, as he did later on *The Magnificent Ambersons.* And Roger Hill and Ashton Stevens and Dr. Maurice Bernstein were all in the know, even when the press and RKO were not. The air of expectancy surrounding the boy genius was always electric, and never more so than today.

Orson gathered everyone around, putting people at ease. Everyone waited for the signal.

"Action!" he called.

The most important word of his life.

V

AFTER THE END

CHAPTER 21

October 10, 1985

Joy and Regrets

The president of the United States on October 9, 1985, was the former Hollywood actor and former governor of California Ronald Reagan. The top movie in America was *Commando*, starring the future governor of California Arnold Schwarzenegger. Although the forecast for the day in Los Angeles was cloudy and breezy, with a chance of showers, the sun would shine and the temperature would hover between sixty and seventy degrees.

Hope rose with the sun, as always for Orson Welles, who woke in his colonnaded home at 1717 North Stanley Avenue in the Hollywood hills with a full day ahead of him. Today, he was going to a television studio for an appearance in which he would perform a card trick that harked back to one he had taught himself in boyhood out of his first Gilbert Mysto Magic Kit. Welles often performed sleight of hand on variety shows, along with sketching caricatures or reciting Shakespeare. He had stopped the show performing Shylock and Falstaff on *The Dean Martin Show*, and intoned Hamlet's advice to the players ("Speak the speech . . .") on Johnny Carson's *Tonight Show*. Today it was *The Merv Griffin Show*, where he was a favorite guest (Griffin estimated he had appeared "close to fifty" times over the past ten years). Sometimes, on these shows—as in his first appearance for Griffin—Welles was happy just to talk "about everything under the sun," as Griffin recalled, "politics, current events, art, cinema (other than his own work), literature, travel."

Welles had planned and rehearsed the card trick over the past several days with Jim Steinmeyer, a young designer of illusions and effects who was part of magician Doug Henning's team. Orson liked Steinmeyer, who was only about a year or two older than he himself had been when he directed *Citizen Kane*. They bonded initially over Steinmeyer's book *Jarrett*, a revised version of the magic manual by the turn-of-the-century illusionist Guy Jarrett, who had designed magic feats for the Great Thurston. Steinmeyer could talk knowledgeably about the history of magic or Broadway, but he came from Oak Park, Illinois, and could also hold his own in a conversation about Kenosha. A fan of Orson's long before they met, he even owned a copy of *Everybody's Shakespeare*.

The magicians who helped Welles with his television appearances, or with constructing the illusions for "The Magic Show," one of his long-gestating, never-completed projects, knew better than to grill him about his famous films. While it was not quite true that Orson never enjoyed reminiscing, he claimed not to have watched *Citizen Kane* since approving its final cut in 1941. (Though he conceded that he did watch it at least partially once more, for his interview sessions with Peter Bog-danovich.) The older Welles could be rude, even belligerent, to anyone who approached him with a fan's fervor and questions, whether it was a television executive, a prospective film producer, or a college student.

Barbara Leaming called this the "Crazy Welles": the temperamen-tal, menacing mask Orson always carried in reserve, yanking it out like a blunt weapon when he felt cornered. Frederick Muller, the editor of *The Trial* and *Chimes at Midnight*, grew tired of the mask, and one day asked him why he treated people so badly.

"Well," Orson replied, "I grew up in very unhappy family circum-stances and this is my defense. I want people to be scared of me."

"But you're not a nasty man," said Muller, "so why do you want to give the impression that you're nasty?"

"It's my defense," insisted Orson, refusing to discuss it any further.

The magicians were not exempt from this reluctance to reminisce; they knew that about Welles and respected it. They were there to serve a different part of his life, to distract him with innocent pleasures from his difficult career struggles and his filmmaking concerns.

He asked the magicians to his house, to perform feats he had read or heard about or seen performed somewhere, perhaps long ago in his boyhood. Wearing his big kaftan, the supreme audience of one would sit in his massive chair in the living room, with his tiny black poodle Kiki barking on his lap, and become a rapt little boy all over again as the magicians demonstrated the trick he intended to learn. As they repeated the trick, articulated its steps, he began to make suggestions, bubbling with ideas as he began to take the trick over himself. He approached a magic trick the way he approached everything, always trying to improve it, seeking the maximum effect—even when that meant overthinking the illusion. Orson knew other magicians would watch him on TV, and he wanted them to be amazed too.

"The thing I like about magic," Welles told Peter Bogdanovich, "is that it's connected with circus, and with a kind of corny velvet-and-gold-braid sort of world that's gone. . . . I never saw anything in the theatre that entranced me so much as magic—and not the wonder of it: it's the kind of slightly seedy, slightly carnival side of it. I'm a terrible pushover for all forms of small-time show business anyway. Small theatres, small circuses, magic, and all that."

The young magicians were like his stand-ins for these informal rehearsals. Grossly overweight by the last decade of his life, unable to keep on his feet for very long, Welles directed the young magicians from his chair while watching their moves carefully and taking mental notes. Like his "slaves" of old, the young magicians gathered his props for him, advised him on handling the props, and offered suggestions and tips for his patter and misdirection.

Steinmeyer had been part of Orson's life for about four years now. The circle of young magicians and illusion designers in Los Angeles passed Welles down like an heirloom, one that carried a curse. Working with him was always thrilling and rewarding, but it could also be a horror show. Sometimes Welles wanted to rehearse at odd hours—after midnight, for example. He could be hard to please, and the rehearsals could be nerve-wracking. Young magicians who were sucked into Orson's vortex suddenly found themselves at his beck and call. If they took their phones off the hook, a messenger arrived: "Your phone is off the hook. Call me. Orson."

Steinmeyer, however, never experienced a single twinge of displeasure. Orson was always gracious and kind to him, phoning Steinmeyer to see how he was doing today, asking what *he* was working on, offering advice. Welles always paid him a little money out of pocket each time

Steinmeyer helped him out with a magic trick. Several times Welles took him to lunch at the West Hollywood bistro, Ma Maison, but occasionally Orson and his companion, Oja Kodar, threw a pasta dinner for Steinmeyer in their home kitchen, which was more wonderful.

Steinmeyer always remembered one night at dinner when Welles had suffered a bad day in the film world—one of many bad days in the last year of his life. Orson's dream of a filmed *King Lear*, financed by French admirers; his hope to convince someone in Hollywood to let him chronicle the saga of *The Cradle Will Rock* on the big screen; his plans to direct an independent film called *The Big Brass Ring*, based on his script about a presidential candidate compromised by a homosexual mentor: all these projects had collapsed earlier in the year. Still, Welles rarely whined or complained. "Everybody wants to give me an award," one of the magicians recalls him saying—memorably, because it was out of character—"but nobody wants to hire me to make a film."

That night, with Steinmeyer, Welles seemed glum over dinner, in a daze. Fumbling for conversation, Steinmeyer mentioned that he'd just read and loved Preston Sturges's play *Strictly Dishonorable*. He knew that Welles, since his youth in Chicago, had followed Sturges and that the two were friends until Sturges's death in 1959. Welles raised an eyebrow in annoyance, perhaps because Pauline Kael had raised the specter of Sturges's *The Power and the Glory* as an influence on *Citizen Kane* in her widely read essay "Raising *Kane*." As if to cut off the conversation, Welles muttered that he'd seen the original Broadway production of *Strictly Dishonorable*. Steinmeyer looked doubtful.

Orson fixed the younger man with a hard stare of one-upmanship. "Tullio Carminati was the Latin Lover in it," Welles drawled. "I would have liked to see Antoinette Perry on the stage, but by this time she was only directing. Later, you know, Cesar Romero did Carminati's part on the road, launching him as a star." Caught up in the subject, Welles went on to deliver a knowing exegesis on the various incarnations of *Strictly Dishonorable*, and the play's strengths and weaknesses. As Orson held forth, his mood lifted, the day's disappointments forgotten. "I walked away from that dinner," Steinmeyer remembered, "realizing how Orson's dismissive manner often earned the reputation for him of being a fabulist, but he had actually been there, seen things, processed them, even if he didn't care to explain in a casual conversation."

Today's trick for *The Merv Griffin Show* involved a pristine deck of cards that would be divided and shuffled by two complete strangers. Handed the decks, Orson would miraculously turn up four aces, two from each separate pile of cards. Like the Great Thurston, who had started out onstage performing with just a deck of cards, these days Orson was a one-man show.

Except not really: Like most magicians, Orson used helpers, such as Steinmeyer—and often, as tonight, a "stooge," or plant, in the studio audience. When it came to stooges, magicians had different schools of thought: certain purists avoided them; others used them without compunctions. Orson liked stooges, Steinmeyer felt, because he was always anxious about performing his magic in public, and a stooge gave him an extra measure of security. He also liked the idea of being propped up by an invisible army of helpers and collaborators. Orson did not wish to meet the stooge beforehand, so he could say honestly that he and the audience member he chose were crossing paths for the first time. He didn't want Merv Griffin to know about the stooge, either.

With swollen, arthritic fingers, Welles no longer had much genuine sleight of hand, but the young magicians learned not to underestimate him, lest he sense their skepticism, grab the deck of cards, and whip off a superb one-hand top-palm. His lifelong reliance on stand-in rehearsals and stooges made for occasional disasters, however: once, on *Merv Griffin*, Orson knocked over the fishbowl he was using, splattering water and glass everywhere—a shattering fishbowl was one contingency no one had anticipated—then asked if anyone in the audience was named Albert, the designated name of the stooge. Another Albert, the wrong one, stood up.

Whether he got his comeuppance in his living room, or onstage in front of a national audience, Orson was generally delighted by the mishaps. He laughed uproariously at his gaffes—laughed so hard, sometimes, that the magicians worried he might keel over and die.

The night before, Orson had stayed up late, going over the new trick in his mind and working on various projects, including his first lesson plans as a professor. On the Thursday morning after the taping of *Merv Griffin*, he was scheduled to meet with officials at UCLA, including Professor Howard Suber, who after a year of courting had finally persuaded Welles to teach a seminar on filmmaking. Orson had resisted such overtures for years, but Suber, an expert on Welles (he had taught an entire course devoted to *Citizen Kane*), finally prevailed after a long lunch at Ma Maison, where Orson characteristically picked up the check. As part of the deal, Orson would also gain access to UCLA soundstages and equipment, with a group of students as his crew. But that Thursday morning meeting threatened to be a bit of a showdown, as word had spread that Orson, with his longtime cameraman Gary Graver, had already taken over a campus soundstage and they were shooting scenes for unspecified purposes. Was Welles serious about teaching at UCLA, or was this another instance of misdirection—trading his name for access? Tomorrow would tell.

Welles called Graver—they spoke nearly every day—reminding the cameraman to pick up equipment at a rental house in Hollywood for a scene he thought he might shoot at UCLA, as long as he was going to be on campus tomorrow. It might be a recitation from the one-man *Julius Caesar* that Orson was planning, or a scene from a loose-knit adaptation of *King Lear* he and Graver had been compiling, or a bit of prestidigitation for "The Magic Show." The cameraman and crew sometimes didn't know exactly what Orson was going to film until he arrived.

Welles checked in with Steinmeyer. The young magician had found a dependable stooge for him, a dancer from magician Harry Blackstone Jr.'s show. At a prearranged signal, she would volunteer to take the decks of cards from Orson onstage and prepare them for handling by the audience members. Her job was to shuffle the cards (awkwardly and tentatively), while keeping the top stock of four aces in place. When the camera was off her, she would quickly cut and rearrange the cards to make sure Orson would find the aces. The stooge would sit up front. Steinmeyer, too, would sit nervously in the audience, an emergency backup.

Orson said he would meet Steinmeyer backstage at the taping but wanted him to get to the studio early, bringing the two decks of cards to Griffin's dressing room. The cards were sealed in cellophane, but—unbeknownst to Griffin—the cellophane had been slit open and the cards reordered before it was sealed again. It was important to Orson that he impress Griffin with his magicianship. Yet magic meant little to Griffin, unlike Johnny Carson, a onetime magician himself. Griffin loved Orson's personality and admired his films; the magic was just an excuse to have him on the show.

At that late-afternoon taping, Orson had a surprise planned for his old friend Merv.

Orson spent the morning alone on the ground floor of his two-story faux-antebellum mansion, with its swimming pool and guesthouse. The expansive grounds with views of the surrounding Hollywood hills were dotted with fruit and palm trees. These days, his immense weight and weak legs made it almost impossible for Welles to climb to the second floor and its master bedroom without a good deal of incentive and assistance. Instead he usually worked on the first floor, where he had a second bedroom and bath, with his typewriter and stacks of scripts, correspondence, and notes spread out across his worktable and the spacious living room.

His companion, the artist and actress Oja Kodar, was away in Europe, as she was periodically. Orson missed her terribly. She had been Welles's "companion, confidant, cohort in . . . conspiracy, closest accomplice, muse," in Peter Bogdanovich's words, for nearly twenty-five years, collaborating with him on numerous projects, and playing a lead in *F for Fake* (1973). Born in Zagreb the year *Citizen Kane* was released, the exotic Kodar had her own busy life and interests, including an art gallery she ran in Yugoslavia. Her nephew Aleksandar stayed in attic space in the house, helping to keep an eye on Welles.

Welles had lived in Hollywood since the late 1970s, but his legal residence was in Las Vegas—as was his legal wife, the Italian countess Paola di Girifalco. Paola—who under her professional name, Paola Mori, played the female lead in *Mr. Arkadin*—had followed Virginia Nicolson and Rita Hayworth to become the third Mrs. Orson Welles in 1955. But Mori had stayed behind in Las Vegas with their grown daughter, Beatrice, when Welles moved to Los Angeles to share a house with Kodar. How estranged Orson and Paola were, how well they got along, no one knew for sure. Orson talked about his love life with less eagerness than he reminisced about *Citizen Kane*.

The magicians and Welles's Hollywood friends all adored Kodar. She was smart, funny, gorgeous, and an equal partner in all of Orson's schemes. After years of relatively chaste filmmaking, Welles had even shot some nude scenes of Kodar, as he had rarely done before with any actress. Kodar rolled her eyes when the young magicians arrived to confer with Orson, the way Welles's mother, Beatrice, had rolled her eyes at his father Dick Welles's enthusiasm for magic, but whatever made Orson happy made Kodar happy, too.

Orson's second wife, Rita Hayworth, was still alive in 1985, although she was reclusive and rumored to be suffering from Alzheimer's disease. Welles had been married to the beautiful Hayworth for five years, from 1943 to 1948, and they had one child, Rebecca, born in 1944. Orson had brought Rebecca into a series of Jim Beam whiskey advertisements he made in the 1970s, but their relationship, never healthy, had since deteriorated, and they were rarely in touch.

Christopher, Orson's firstborn, had by 1985 dropped her boyish first name; today she was Chris Welles Feder, the surname that of her second husband. She had spent some time as an adolescent at the Todd School, with Roger and Hortense Hill in effect foster-parenting her during the long intervals when her actual parents were unavailable. When Orson and Virginia feuded over his financial obligations in the early 1950s, Hortense Hill took Virginia's side, occasioning a rare rupture in his friendship with the headmaster.

Orson's oldest daughter worked hard to effect a reconciliation with her famous father over the decades, efforts she chronicled poignantly in her 2009 memoir *In My Father's Shadow*. She once met up with Welles in Hong Kong, only to lose touch with him for the next eight years. Chris told author Charles Higham—who was working on his biography of Welles in the early 1980s, at the same time as Barbara Leaming—that she had had little or no contact with her father in recent years. The three half sisters had grown up as virtual strangers to one another.

"Only Beatrice," wrote Higham, "a tall and Junoesque beauty with fair hair and a voluptuous figure, has been close to Welles in recent years."

Virginia Nicolson was still alive, too, in England after spending years in Johannesburg, South Africa, with her third husband, Jackie Pringle. Her marriage to the witty and dapper scenarist Charles Lederer had lasted nine years. After she quit acting, Virginia Lederer had written a roman à clef about Hollywood called *Married at Leisure*, in which Orson was not even remotely referenced—perhaps because she was still suing him for alimony and child support. A court eventually found in her favor, but even so Orson managed to wriggle out of paying it all.

Virginia and Orson's daughter preferred Lederer to Pringle as a stepfather, and so did Welles. Orson stayed close to Lederer, one of those ill-starred talents he was fond of. Orson always claimed that he wrote two thirds of Howard Hawks's *I Was a Male War Bride*, a script credited to Lederer, after his friend, hooked on alcohol and various drugs, took one of his periodic dives into dysfunction.

After moving to Johannesburg in 1949, Virginia came under the influence of her new husband, a Briton in every respect except his birthplace: Chicago. A World War II military hero for England, Pringle was also "an accomplished horseman, a crack polo player, and a gifted linguist," in Chris Welles Feder's words. But Pringle had no aptitude for fatherhood, and he had urged Virginia to ship Chris off to finishing schools in Switzerland and the United States. Her mother, meanwhile, had been transformed almost overnight from the bright, openhearted debutante Orson had fallen in love with back in the summer of 1934 to Virginia Nicolson Pringle, a "puff-faced, dowdy British matron," in her daughter's words, with an attitude toward native South Africans as hard and bigoted as her spouse's.

In the mid-afternoon, Freddie Gillette, the last of Welles's long-suffering chauffeurs, arrived to drive him to the Talent Celebrity Theater at Sunset and Vine, less than two miles away.

Perhaps because he always had been driven around as a boy—by his father or Dr. Maurice Bernstein—Orson stubbornly never learned to drive and enjoyed the indulgence of a chauffeur. Gillette was more of a hired hand than the diminutive George "Shorty" Chirello, whom Orson had launched onscreen as his magic assistant in *Follow the Boys* in 1944, later giving him bit parts in *The Lady from Shanghai* and *Macbeth*. Chirello picked up a few acting jobs after Orson went abroad for years and paid him back with friendship, one time flying to Paris and offering his life's savings as a loan to get Welles out of deep hock. (Orson declined.)

Gillette, whom Welles referred to as "a tall Shorty," was a kind, attentive man who answered whenever Orson bellowed his name and fussed obsequiously over his employer's comfort. The two had developed a repertoire of little rituals: When Gillette saw that someone unpleasant had lingered too long at Orson's table at Ma Maison, he would hurry in with an urgent note for Orson—always blank.

Arriving at the theater, Welles found Jim Steinmeyer and asked about the stooge and whether Merv Griffin had received the decks of cards. Then he ambled to the door leading to Griffin's dressing room—which was up a flight of stairs he couldn't manage—and rapped on it with his cane. Griffin came downstairs to greet him. Griffin, who hadn't seen Orson since before his seventieth birthday in May, was taken aback by his "haggard appearance."

Since his birthday, Orson had been shedding weight on his doctor's orders. "He told me my heart wasn't functioning properly, my liver was a mess, and that my blood pressure was off the chart," Welles explained to Roger Hill. "He said, 'Either you lose weight or you will die.'" Orson suffered from diabetes, chronic phlebitis, and atrial fibrillation. At his peak, he carried close to four hundred pounds on his frame (slightly taller than six foot two). Anyone who hadn't witnessed his Falstaffian appetite, in his prime, could be forgiven for doubting the apocryphal tales it inspired. Could he really have eaten an entire turkey one day at lunch? Or seventeen hot dogs at Pink's?

Over time, some comedians and film critics conflated his weight problems with notions of his fabled self-indulgence as a filmmaker. Welles was sensitive about his weight and dismayed by jokes about it. Even Merv Griffin told a version of the episode at Pink's in his 2003 autobiography *Merv: Making the Good Life Last*, claiming that one day, after lunching with Welles at Ma Maison (where Orson dined on his daily "little piece of grilled sole"), he had spotted his friend's car parked at the landmark hot-dog stand at the corner of La Brea and Melrose. Heading for the car with "a tray piled high with at least a dozen hot dogs" was Freddie Gillette, Welles's chauffeur. "People loved to gloat over his weight," Peter Bogdanovich told *Los Angeles* magazine in 2012, "because they felt it would diminish his genius in some strange way."

After his alarming seventieth-birthday physical, Orson finally changed the gluttonous eating and drinking habits that had transformed him, over four decades, from the handsome, baby-faced young mastermind of *Citizen Kane* into an unseemly and unsteady behemoth of a man. "If you'll pardon the pun," Orson told Roger Hill, "I've gone cold turkey, eating little and what little I eat is dispiritingly unappetizing." He no longer smoked, although he often fingered a cigar. He avoided coffee and drank Perrier, not vodka. His diet was fruit, vegetables, and grains.

With iron willpower, Orson had dropped something like one hundred pounds since his birthday in May. He felt only worse. "I've lost a good deal of energy, and I hope to God it comes back because there's so much that needs my attention," he told Hill. "In addition to the intrinsic joy of eating well, dining provides an ideal opportunity for spirited social discourse. Even when I'm dining with others [now], I feel alone and removed."

Some friends thought the shrinkage dangerously precipitous, but people who saw him on a regular basis were used to the waning and waxing of Welles's appearance.

Now, greeting Orson at the bottom of his staircase, Griffin concealed his apprehension.

"Tonight, I feel like talking," Orson told him. Griffin parried with a joke—it was a talk show, after all—but Welles was serious. "Merv, I mean it," he insisted. "I feel expansive tonight. You know all those silly gossipy little questions you've been trying to ask me for years about Rita and Marlene? Well, go ahead and ask them. Ask me anything you want."

Griffin was astonished. "Anything I want? Even about the making of *Citizen Kane*?"

Welles was in a buoyant mood. After his magic trick, he would be joined on the show by Barbara Leaming, whose new biography of Orson was shooting up the best-seller lists. Leaming was going to talk about Welles's life and career with Griffin, and Orson would sit beside her on camera. He had enjoyed working with Leaming on her book, and he wanted to please her.

"Ask me," said Welles, turning and ambling toward the green room.

When he turned seventy in May, Welles became the longest-lived member of his family.

His mother had passed away at age forty-two, his father at fifty-eight. His older brother, Richard, had died after a bout with pneumonia, one month shy of his seventieth birthday, on September 8, 1975. Richard's death certificate listed heart disease as a contributing factor.

Fated to be a footnote in his famous brother's life story, Richard had hung around southern California for much of the 1940s. Orson forgave Richard everything—even his claim, on one occasion, to have written the "panic broadcast" of "War of the Worlds."

His older brother had made an unfortunate splash in the news in 1941, on returning to Los Angeles after marrying Mildred Alice Bill in Reno. "The bulky, blushing brother of Orson, the boogieman," in the words of the *Los Angeles Times* account, lashed out at photographers at the airport, trying to grab their photographic plates away from them. Orson said in interviews that his brother had met his wife, a native Angeleno fifteen years his junior, at a soup kitchen in downtown Los Angeles; Richard had a habit of attaching himself to churches and charities while making ends meet with intermittent jobs.

Occasionally, Richard found outlets for his artistic impulses, which ran deep in the Welles family. In May 1942, for example, he served as "technical director" of the Victory Week celebration staged by the Junior Chamber of Commerce of Sierra Madre, a small city in Los Angeles County, nestled in the foothills of the San Gabriel Mountains. According to wire service accounts, Richard arranged "the public address system" and staged "the parade of victory girl entries" for the event, which culminated in the crowning of a local beauty queen along with the burning of effigies of Hitler and Hirohito. But he never lived in the same place for very long, and after about a year in Sierra Madre he vanished from the city directory.

Richard's marriage lasted five years, before a protracted separation and divorce, with Mildred Welles attesting to his mental cruelty and his failure to support her. The only property he claimed in the divorce were his favorite books, his musical recordings, and a box of family photographs. At the time of the final decree in 1947, Richard was living in a Culver City hotel, working as a salesman for a stove company. Court papers noted his speech impediment.

The divorce, and perhaps Orson's departure for Europe in late 1947, sent Richard back to northern California, where he bobbed between small cities and short-lived jobs and stints with Episcopalian church groups. In 1952 he found a temporary position at the St. Francis Home for Boys in Salina, Kansas, teaching arts and crafts therapy to orphan and delinquent boys, but after two months he returned to northern California's Napa Valley. In mid-1953 he turned up as an attendant at the Grafton State School in North Dakota, teaching recreational activities to people with mental disabilities, but again he lasted only two months before leaving for a new home in Santa Rosa, California.

In early 1954, Richard had his best opportunity at St. Mary's Episcopal School for Indian Girls in Springfield, South Dakota—on the border of Indian lands known as, of all things, the Rosebud Reservation. Flaunting his famous brother's name as much as his own experience in church social work, Richard was hired as recreational director of the small school, promising to stage puppet shows and theatrical productions with the thirty girls, while guiding them in learning to make plastic religious Christmas ornaments to provide "commercial value to the school," in the words of a parish newsletter, and "allow proper expression of Indian art." Installed at St. Mary's by Palm Sunday, Richard hosted services for a congregation of several dozen Episcopalians. The *Yankton Press and Dakotan* covered his arrival at the school; the article was complete with a photograph of the "quiet little man," with glasses and curved-stem pipe, studying a Gilbert and Sullivan script he intended to adapt for the Indian girls.

The article repeated Richard's boast that he had written the script for "War of the Worlds" and had been "associated with his brother" as a writer on other *Campbell Playhouse* broadcasts and Mercury Theatre productions before quitting radio and theater because of "the advent of television." He had returned to the Northwest, Richard said, recalling it fondly after his youthful travels there as a member of a boys' quartet in vaudeville.

Richard had big plans for the future of St. Mary's: introducing a weaving loom to the school, making ceramics from a gas-fired kiln, holding basketry and bead classes. Richard even planned a show with a concept that sounds like a variant of Welles's *Five Kings*, weaving together "portions of four Gilbert and Sullivan operettas," to be pre-recorded by the girls and played under a puppet show performance.

That newspaper interview, surviving correspondence in Richard's hand, and extensive church records support the impression that Richard tended to struggle with positions that made demands on his abilities and coping mechanisms. Richard was well liked at St. Mary's, and he was wholehearted about arts and crafts, but after just a month he started sending the bishopric letters outlining impractical goals and demanding extra compensation for his efforts.

At a meeting of the Sioux Falls church board in late May, Richard proposed an adult extension outreach program at the school, modeled after the Chautauqua circuit. He himself would offer enlightening lectures on art, music, civics, humanities, or travel, accompanied by slides or documentary films. This ambitious new curriculum would include a play-reading group, which Richard would coach through "a standard play such as *Our Town.*" The program would bring in extra revenue for the school, Richard assured the board—in turn facilitating a hike in his salary. His proposal was met with polite remarks, but the reservation school was already in a constant struggle to survive, and its constituency could not be counted on to absorb unusual costs. The bishop admired Richard's ideas for so many "interesting undertakings," but this was no time for grandiose schemes.

Leaning on his rapport with the bishop, Richard started sending him increasingly insistent letters complaining of his sacrifices and asking for additional compensation during the summer. He had "diabetic medical needs," Richard wrote—another echo of his brother, Orson—and was still suffering from a past "fracture of my left leg." He had signed a contract permitting "outside engagements," expecting to promote himself locally "as an entertainer in magic," but these plans had resulted in only one local gig, paying a pitiful $25. He needed a car to expand his territory for better bookings. The bishop wrote back sympathetically but noncommittally.

Finally, Richard escalated his demands for "remunerative work somewhere," asking the diocese to guarantee that his needs be met by July I. This was "not an ultimatum, but only a statement of human necessity." When the board met again in late June, Richard was dismissed from his post—ostensibly because of funding problems, but really because he had become difficult and obstreperous. Richard wrote one last angry letter to the bishop, demanding a good reference letter, which he received. (His *Five Kings*–style Gilbert and Sullivan puppet show was staged by the girls as scheduled at the end of the school year, and from sparse accounts it appears to have been a success.)

Retreating once more to northern California, Richard seems to have withdrawn into his shell. He maintained his interest in arts and crafts and frequented local gem and mineral shows. By the early 1970s, he was "self-employed" as a property manager for buildings, finally landing on Noe Street in San Francisco "in a depressing apartment in the worst part of town," according to Charles Higham's always imaginative account. When Richard died, his estate came to "$470.65 in cash, $504.50 in coins, and $355 in Social Security," Higham detailed, later "attached by the public administrator to pay the costs of his funeral." But Richard was cremated, and there was no funeral.

Orson paid out small sums of money through the years to assist his brother, but he had gradually fallen out of touch with the lost soul, who was as peripatetic in his way as Orson himself. F. X. Feeney, writing in the *Los Angeles Review of Books* in 2011, mused that Richard's tragedy "haunted the Maestro into old age" and was evoked in "the troubled, double-crossing partnerships throughout his body of work." But Charles Foster Kane was an only child, and the brother figure in *Citizen Kane* is his close friend Jed Leland, whom Kane initially admires and adores. It is Kane who betrays Leland, by betraying their ideals, as Orson more than once explained patiently to interviewers. Orson's films often revolved around betrayals, but the characters he played rarely had brothers.

Curiously, Barbara Leaming made no mention of Richard I. Welles's death in her book. But she dwelled on that of Dr. Maurice Bernstein, twenty-one years before, in July 1964.

The doctor and his wife, Hazel, had come to live in Hollywood by the end of the summer of 1940, in time to witness much of the filming of *Citizen Kane*. Bernstein treated Orson when he injured his foot on the set in late August, and again later after the room-wrecking scene in Xanadu. During the last days of filming in December, when Orson was bedridden with a bad cold for several days, the doctor "descended from my bone and joint pedestal and took care of him—shot him full of Vit. B."

The enterprising Bernstein established an office on Camden Drive in Beverly Hills and bought a two-story Mediterranean-style residence with a swimming pool on Schuyler Road near Greystone Park. Orson arranged for his former guardian to enjoy one of the first previews of *Citizen Kane* outside the studio, bringing a print to Bernstein's home to screen the week before the film was officially released to theaters, in late April 1941. It was a thoughtful early present for Bernstein, whose fifty-eighth birthday fell on May 10, four days after Orson's. The two enjoyed extending birthday wishes to each other over the years, even if only by phone.

Among the guests for the early screening at Dr. Bernstein's home were the Russian-born American ballet-master Adolph Bolm, who had danced and choreographed in Chicago in the 1920s before moving to Los Angeles; and the pianist and composer Igor Stravinsky. "The Herrmann music is grand," Hazel Bernstein wrote to Ashton Stevens. "I am very happy that he has made a good film," Dr. Bernstein also wrote to Stevens. "You know how they felt about him here. Bets were being made that Orson would never produce a picture. He has vindicated [RKO president George] Schaefer who stuck by him."

Although Stevens was forbidden to mention *Citizen Kane* or Orson's name in the Hearst newspaper where his column still appeared, he never wavered in his support for Welles—nor, for that matter, in his respect and fondness for his own longtime boss William Randolph Hearst. Stevens managed to separate the two in his mind.

Many of the Bernsteins' old Chicago friends had relocated to Los Angeles, and with the help of the Mario Chamlees, Maurice and Hazel were soon reestablished as fixtures in the city's music and arts community. Dr. Bernstein became a patron of the Long Beach and Los Angeles symphony orchestras, and hobnobbed with classical artists such as Stravinsky and Lotte Lehmann. The doctor saw Stravinsky, a neighbor in Beverly Hills, as often as he could, one time intrepidly arranging to play for the maestro his own cello composition, which he titled "Song Without Words." "How do you find the time?" Stravinsky was said to have commented, politely.

The Bernsteins blended into the film community too. With referrals from Welles and their Chicago connections, the doctor built a thriving practice, counting Errol Flynn, director John Huston, Joseph Cotten, and Rita Hayworth among his first patients. Another client was the Chicago-born silent screen actress Dagmar Godowsky. ("Her father was the famous Leopold Godowsky," Bernstein reminded Ashton Stevens in a letter—Godowsky the prodigy and Chicago teacher who had taught piano technique to Orson's mother.) Hollywood was a small world, and on one occasion Bernstein was even summoned to treat the sacroiliitis of William Randolph Hearst. "He looks very well," Bernstein wrote to Stevens afterward. "I am afraid that when he learns I am related to Orson I shall lose a good patient."

Dr. Bernstein still saw himself as the protector of Orson's reputation and interests. When Orson was in Brazil from February to June 1942, working on his documentary *It's All True*, Bernstein made a point of visiting Dolores Del Rio at RKO, where *The Magnificent Ambersons* was in its editing crisis, and where the final scenes of Welles's Mercury production *Journey into Fear* were being shot, with Del Rio in the cast and Norman Foster directing with Welles's guidance. "I took lunch with Dolores at the studio and watched them shoot the scene in the café ... dancing and so forth," Bernstein wrote to Orson in Brazil. "Dolores looked like a large cute attractive cat in her make-up."

One day the doctor enjoyed "a long visit" with Charles Chaplin at the Godowsky residence. It was shortly after the first press previews of *The Magnificent Ambersons* in May 1942. Bernstein's unfettered account of his talk with Chaplin caused the first real chill in his relationship with Welles. "[Chaplin] thinks that you are a great artist, though still young in your conception of human emotion," Bernstein wrote to his onetime ward, who was still in Brazil. "He has much to say about *Kane*, which he was crazy about, with only the above reservation of emotional value." Welles admired Chaplin and considered him a friend, and later, without credit, he would write an early draft of Chaplin's *Monsieur Verdoux*. But Orson did not care to have his work graded on "human emotion," especially by a master like Chaplin.

Bernstein's relationship to Welles in these years was increasingly intrusive and meddlesome. Scorning the current Mercury business manager, Jack Moss, as an unimaginative yes-man, he suggested instead that Orson partner up with a man like Chaplin, "an unusual man," for whom "Hollywood has not blotted out his appreciation of the fine things in art." Orson once had such an unusual man, Bernstein wrote:

John Houseman, a partner who wasn't afraid to give Orson "an honest opinion" rather than "flatter" him with approval. "[Houseman] is the one person I am sorry you broke with," Bernstein wrote.

"I wish too that you could have a little confidence in me," Bernstein continued in his letter to Orson. "I guided you in a way which I have never regretted. And you still need a guardian! The proof of this is that you have little to show after all your tremendous success. You are now a man, and I am talking to you man to man. I am alarmed when I think of the mercenary people who surround you—Moss—his lawyer, and others who have sucked you dry."

Nor was Bernstein's wife one to censor herself on the subject of Welles. "Have you seen *Mrs. Miniver* yet?" Hazel wrote to Ashton Stevens. "It's quite a picture, with all the human-ness and heart that our precocious Orson's opus (i) lack." The Bernsteins were irrepressible, inexhaustible, uncontrollable. The following year, when Welles married Rita Hayworth, they proved themselves as devoted to his new wife as they had been to Del Rio or Virginia Nicolson. The Bernsteins visited Orson and Rita often at their new "gaudy Hollywood modern mansion," Hazel wrote to Ashton Stevens irreverently, with "a pool of pools, a lake, huge melon shaped, with an island in the middle, and tremendous pavilion and bath house, barbecues, ping pong etc. On a huge scale like Mr. Welles himself. Ah well, what's life without an Orson?"

Bernstein proved indispensable as a medical consultant to Orson's second wife, who was plagued by health concerns, real and imagined. After Rebecca was born in 1944, the doctor became an eager babysitting "grandfather." Orson was away in New York for most of the first half of 1944, preparing for the filming of *The Stranger* in the fall, writing his crusading newspaper column, engaging in war-related activities, and making public appearances. (An entire book could be written about that single year, with much left out.)

"As hard as I try not to write or think of you it is no go," the doctor wrote to Orson poignantly from his Beverly Hills office one day. "I am like a person who tries to see how long he can hold his breath. I hear you every Sunday [on the radio] and hear about you from those New Yorkers who see you regularly in church"—this last a sample of Bernstein's humor.

Orson's marriage to Hayworth collapsed in stages, ending with their separation in 1947. Two years later, she married Prince Aly Khan and moved overseas; thereafter, Bernstein could no longer please Orson by fussing over Rebecca, who was henceforth removed from both of their worlds. Welles himself left America in November 1947, after *The Stranger*, *The Lady from Shanghai* (with Hayworth excelling opposite her estranged husband in an exceptional film noir), and *Macbeth*. Beset by personal and professional financial crises, he saw Hollywood as an increasingly inhospitable place—not least because of the onset of the anticommunist blacklist.

The blacklist cut like a scythe through Orson's circle. Howard Koch, subpoenaed as one of the "Hollywood Nineteen," had to write under pseudonyms until the 1960s. Dorothy Comingore, the Susan Alexander of *Citizen Kane*, saw her career destroyed when her husband, screenwriter Richard Collins, became a cooperative witness for the House Committee on Un-American Activities (HUAC). Orson's "slaves" William Alland and Betty Wilson (Richard Wilson's wife), both onetime communists, also "named names" to HUAC. Georgia Backus, the Radio Guild activist who had a small but unforgettable role in *Citizen Kane* as Miss Anderson, the guardian of the Thatcher Memorial Library, never worked in show business again. John Berry, who stayed with the Mercury Theatre through the tour of *Native Son* before becoming a director in Hollywood, fled to France. Canada Lee, the African American actor who played Banquo in the Voodoo *Macbeth* and Bigger Thomas in *Native Son* on stage for the Mercury, and many, many other friends of Orson's were affected.

In the fall of 1947, Orson was lured overseas by two enticements: an acting job abroad, and a crush on a European actress. Dr. Bernstein saw him off at the airport. "The cutter for *Macbeth* even went to the plane with him to cut to the bitter end," reported Hazel Bernstein. "The baggage was loaded with untold dollars' worth of I. Magnins finery for his latest Italian actress lady-love.* . . . He announces that he

---

* Actually Orson's crush was a French actress, Barbara Laage, later in François Truffaut's film *Bed and Board*. Orson had tried in vain to talk Harry Cohn into letting Laage star in *The Lady from Shanghai*.

is a thoroughly domesticated and changed man, who no longer rages or rants. Hmmmmm!"

For the next six or seven years, Bernstein did not so much as lay eyes on Orson—this was the longest time they had ever been separated. Welles usually phoned Bernstein on New Year's Eve, and around the date of their birthdays, but in between the communication dwindled. "I have not heard from Orson in months," the doctor complained to Ashton Stevens.

Stevens died in 1951, not long after receiving an effusive New Year's cable from Welles. "Orson is such a great-hearted person," Stevens's wife, FloFlo, wrote to the Bernsteins. "Why is everyone surprised when he does something nice?"

Dr. Bernstein kept a hand in the film business while Welles was away. One of his patients was Ida Lupino, and she gave him a bit part in the extended obstetrical sequence in her 1949 film *Not Wanted*. (He later served as a technical consultant for another Lupino film.) Friendly with Hedda Hopper, the doctor turned up regularly in her column, usually touting Orson's latest project; he was often identified by the columnist as Orson's "foster father," which he never was. Bernstein ran little errands in Hollywood for Welles, liaising with makeup artist Maurice Seiderman, for example, and arranging to send dozens of false noses overseas to Orson.

Orson was back in Hollywood by the summer of 1956, lured by a good paycheck into playing a cattle baron for a low-budget Universal Western, *Man in the Shadow*. This led to his guest appearance on *I Love Lucy*, his Desilu TV pilot *The Fountain of Youth*, and making *Touch of Evil* for Universal the following year. Dr. Bernstein was ready with his medical kit when Orson slipped one day on the bank of a canal in Venice—Venice, California—while directing a scene for the film noir. Welles suffered "a severe sprain of the left ankle and knee, facial cuts and a possible break of his left wrist," according to wire service accounts, but the semiretired Dr. Bernstein fixed him up as of yore, and Orson went right back to work.

Welles left again for Europe shortly after the end of filming on *Touch of Evil*, and he was in Italy seven years later when, on the weekend of July Fourth, the eighty-one-year-old doctor fell from a ladder while pruning a tree in his yard, and died.

According to Barbara Leaming, when Welles learned the news he reacted with "mixed feelings." Mingled with "profound regret" and warm memories was his conviction, which had gradually hardened into a certainty by the time Leaming interviewed him, that Bernstein had plundered his trust fund. "Much as he genuinely loved Dadda," Leaming wrote, "Orson also resented him for having kept much of the money Dick Welles had left Orson in his will (a fact of which Skipper did not hesitate to remind Orson)."

Not only had Bernstein lived out his days at a comfortable Beverly Hills address—which Welles believed was paid for by his trust fund—but the premises were sprinkled with Welles family treasures, including his mother's piano and his father's Oriental prayer rug ("of museum quality," according to Welles). His father had loved that prayer rug, Welles told Leaming, and Dick Welles took it on all his travels, yet the doctor had purloined it while his father was still alive. "I do not think that Dadda Bernstein had any notion that he was actually stealing from me," Welles told Leaming. "It was all for my own good. I don't think he could have had a moment of conscience. It was all justified in his mind."

While Dr. Bernstein may have skimmed money, it seems unlikely that he stole the bulk of the fabled trust fund. Bernstein did not live luxuriously in the 1930s, nor did he die a very wealthy man. In his will, as it happened, he bequeathed a half share of his estate to Welles, if his wife predeceased him or died before the will was effected (the other half went to his sole surviving sister). Searching for language in the will to describe his relationship with Welles, the doctor characterized his former ward, for the first time in print, as his "friend."

Hazel Bernstein would live for another six years. During that time, Welles complained later, she dispersed his family treasures among her acquaintances in Beverly Hills, and he had no idea where the piano or prayer rug had landed. She did ship off to Orson in Europe a trunkful of his boyhood letters, journals, and youthful writing projects, which the doctor had kept for the biography of Welles he had hoped to write. In 2014, Orson's youngest daughter, Beatrice, announced that she intended to edit and publish these youthful writings, which may shed light on some of the more persistent mysteries of Orson's boyhood—

from the pulp fiction he may or may not have penned, to his rumored fling with bullfighting in Seville, to the enigma of Dr. Bernstein.

What thoughts went through Welles's mind as he stepped onstage in public for the last time?

"Orson is here—wow!" Merv Griffin announced to his audience on October 9, 1985. "The one and only Orson Welles."

Welles tottered on his legs and supported himself with his favorite cane. His bearded face looked sallow and drawn, pocked with age. A handsome blue greatcoat draped his heavy frame, and a polka-dotted ascot evoked the one he'd worn as a ten-year-old schoolboy for his first press photograph and interview in a Madison, Wisconsin, newspaper in the winter of 1926.

In his introductory patter, he forgot to tell the stooge to remove the jokers from the decks. Nervously, she told him she had removed them, and then she admitted she hadn't. Orson, a little flustered, told her to take them out now. An experienced card handler wouldn't have been fazed by the mistake, and fortunately the stooge was a performer, so she made a show of acting rattled while taking her time getting the jokers out of the deck; and she adjusted the breaks in the cards so that the aces were on top.

Orson told the audience they themselves would guide his magic trick with their mysterious "whamming" powers. He misdirected the audience with his patter, speaking of the good old days of slow crossings on ocean liners where he encountered many famous card-playing con men, fleecing the rich passengers. He chose two audience members to approach the apron. Looming over them, Welles guided the two through dealing the cards, so that he himself did not have to handle them, insisting that the outcome depended on one of them being "a genius of a whammy."

As the aces were finally revealed, the audience erupted in seemingly genuine applause. Welles beamed with delight. In watching the episode today, it's still striking to see how pleased Orson was with his own performance, and how much the audience fed off his enjoyment.

Orson was then led to a chair near Griffin's desk for their first segment of conversation. The two men had a warm and genial relationship dating back to Orson's first extended appearance on Griffin's show, back in 1976, when Griffin told him backstage that he considered *Citizen Kane* the greatest motion picture of all time. "That just shows you have good taste," Welles responded. He had startled Griffin, then, by saying he didn't want to talk about *Citizen Kane* or anything else in his past career. Welles was Griffin's sole guest that night, and the host had to throw out all his notes for the ninety-minute program. But the conversation was natural and wide-ranging, and the two shared a long lunch afterward. ("I thought you'd be bland," Orson told Griffin over lunch. "After all, I'm used to hanging out with Marlene Dietrich. But you're not. You're actually a good listener. For some reason, I think I can confide in you.")

Griffin was an extremely good listener, and he was Welles's staunch supporter through the years, during times when the talk show appearances meant a lot to Orson. The two men privately gossiped about subjects Orson would never air in public, with Orson sometimes adopting his protective coloration (Griffin was a discreet homosexual) and freely speculating about who was gay or closeted in Hollywood. Orson teased Griffin by telling him that Joseph Cotten would never go on his show, because Cotten was homophobic.

Griffin was not bland. He could be daring, as when he reunited Welles and John Houseman in February 1979. The Mercury Theatre partners had not seen nor spoken to each other since a chance meeting in a London restaurant two decades before, which had degenerated into an ugly shouting match. The two men were kept separated backstage until they were introduced. "Both men walked out at the same time from opposite sides of the stage," recalled Griffin. "Meeting in the middle, they embraced each other warmly and the show took off from there."

Although the subsequent on-air discussion touched only mildly "on their estrangement," and "the significance of their rapprochement" was lost on the majority of the TV audience, Griffin knew Orson well enough to realize that "he was truly enjoying himself" that day. The rapprochement lasted only as long as the cameras were on, however; the two former partners never met again and later resumed sniping at each other. (Nothing irritated Welles more than Houseman's Best Supporting Actor Oscar for *The Paper Chase* in 1973. "He's enjoying his senior citizenship as a grand old actor," Welles scoffed when lunching with Henry Jaglom. "He is dreadful. As an actor he can't read a line.")

Griffin could be thoughtful and probing in his interviews, as his final show with Welles attested. The host began by telling Orson how good he looked, complimenting him on his dramatic loss of weight, although in his autobiography Griffin says that Orson's appearance concerned him. "You celebrated a big birthday" since his last appearance, Griffin asked, "didn't you?"

Orson admitted his birthday was "right up there in the double numbers." But, he continued, he hated birthdays, "because you always think, wouldn't it be nice if there were a lot less candles on the cake? As it is now, when they bring out a cake with my right number of candles it looks like the Chicago fire." When Griffin commented that George Bernard Shaw had once made an amusing remark on the subject of old age, Welles countered with a hard truth attributed to French statesman Charles de Gaulle: "Old age is a shipwreck."

Griffin eased into a discussion of Leaming's biography. "It really surprised me" to hear that Orson had cooperated on the book, Griffin ventured, "because I know you well, and you've never wanted trips down memory lane." Orson explained that Leaming had worked long and hard for years without his encouragement, and that after meeting her he became "very fond" of the author and agreed to cooperate.

"Are there certain parts of your life that were really joyous?" Griffin asked.

"Oh yes," Orson replied quite readily, "there are certain parts of almost every day that are joyous. I'm not essentially a happy person, but I have all kinds of joy. And there's a difference, you know, because joy is a great, big electrical experience. . . ."

"What about painful times?"

"Enough of those to do. I'm saving those for my own book."

"Are they usually more associated with your work?" prodded Griffin.

"All kinds of pain," Orson replied, pausing and repeating, "All kinds of pain . . . Bad conscience pain too, you know. That's the worst. Regrets of the things, the times . . . you didn't behave as well as you ought to. That's the real pain."

(Peter Bogdanovich also asked once if he had regrets. "Millions," replied Welles promptly. "But, you know, I like the people who are *ready* and *willing* to make fools of themselves—being, as I am, a full member of the fraternity.")

What about the women in your life? asked Griffin. Will you write about them in your book? Welles scoffed—"If you think I'm going to write a succession of boasts or lies about conquests in that nature, you're mistaken"—but Griffin coaxed him into reminiscing about two women he rarely impugned: his second wife, Rita Hayworth ("one of the dearest and sweetest women that ever lived"); and his longtime pal Marlene Dietrich (one of the "all-time glamour people" and "the most loyal friend").

Griffin mentioned the glory days of the Mercury Theatre. "You were quite young, weren't you?" he asked. "All that success at that age—hard to handle, or easy to handle?"

"Anybody who has trouble being successful doesn't get any sympathy from me," Welles replied quickly and firmly, after reminding Griffin that he'd found stardom in Dublin several years before hitting it big in New York. "I was just awful busy and awful lucky," he added. "I had a tremendous streak of luck, and I was very grateful for that. Because I'm not being fake-modest talking about luck . . . I do really think that it has everything to do with anybody's life."

After the break, Orson moved over to give Barbara Leaming the seat closest to Merv Griffin.

In the conversation that followed, Welles deferred to Leaming as she ran through some of the highlights of her research. When Leaming described how the sixteen-year-old Orson was deflated to be treated like a nobody at the Shubert Office in New York, after playing leads for the Gate Theatre in Dublin, Orson flared his nostrils. "It's an invention!" he barked.

Her source was none other than his former Todd School headmaster Roger "Skipper" Hill, Leaming insisted. But Hill was in his nineties, Welles replied, adding warmly, "We talk on the phone every two or three days."

Orson had recently been helping Joseph Cotten with a memoir of his own, combing through his old friend's work in progress, editing sections, and fact-checking his anecdotes about the Mercury Theatre.

Orson had also struggled to shape his own memories into the script about *The Cradle Will Rock*. And he toyed constantly with his own auto-biography, for which he had already been paid (and returned) at least one advance. Honest recollection and wise reflection were very much on his mind.

What had surprised Leaming most in her research? Griffin asked.

Orson's sense of humor, she replied, which was abundant and often directed at himself. She also mentioned his tireless political campaign-ing on behalf of President Franklin Delano Roosevelt and Welles's left-liberal and social justice crusades in the 1940s. Hearing this gave Orson obvious pleasure. "I was very busy in that arena for a while," Welles said.

Leaming and Griffin giggled over Welles's many reputed love affairs and romantic conquests, but this seemed to disturb Orson, who re-fused to be drawn into their chatter. When Leaming told Griffin that many of the stories of Welles's love life had come from his devoted chauffeur, George "Shorty" Chirello, who boasted prodigiously on his behalf, Orson barked, "It's all a tissue of lies from a lot of people that have safely gone to their reward."

Briefly recapping Welles's career, Griffin introduced a series of film stills, inviting Orson to comment on them for the audience. The first was a shot from *Citizen Kane*, showing Kane alongside Ruth Warrick, whose putative love affair with Welles was explored in Leaming's book.

What about *Citizen Kane*, Griffin asked: "A great boon to your career or a detriment?"

"It was a great piece of luck, because people liked it," Orson replied mildly. "If they hadn't liked it, it would have been bad, it's as simple as that." He was still uncomfortable discussing *Citizen Kane*, squirming over it even with Peter Bogdanovich, who returned to the subject re-lentlessly over the course of their many interviews. Welles resented the fact that some regarded it as his one real success in film, and he did not care to sing his own greatness.

"Which movie are you proudest of, the best one?" asked David Frost during his own televised interview with Welles.

"Oh, let's change the subject," Orson replied. "I don't want to clam up and spoil the show. I'll answer anything you want but don't ask me 'proudest' or anything like that."

Not that he was a perfectionist. Indeed, he enjoyed drawing attention to the imperfections. There was the scene after Kane is splashed
by a passing wagon, when he and Susan Alexander "meet cute" for the
first time. ("The close-up when I had the mud on my face. That's a real
phony movie moment.") There was the scene when Kane rushes into
Susan's room after she has overdosed on pills. ("You see this ID bracelet I had on by accident because I had a girlfriend who made me wear
it. Every time I think of that scene, I think of my reaching down and
you see this awful love charm—nothing at all to do with Kane.") Then
there was Rosebud itself, which he usually dismissed as "corny," and
the "unjustified visual strain at times" in his overall camera direction,
"which just came from the exuberance of discovering the medium."

The success of *Citizen Kane* was a result of good luck, he always said
with undue modesty—the good luck of having an RKO contract with
George Schaefer at the helm of the studio; the good luck of working
with people like Herman Mankiewicz, Bernard Herrmann, and Gregg
Toland; the good luck of having the Mercury Theatre family of actors,
all of them with one thing in common: trust in his creative spark. His
luck had turned bad only later, after *Citizen Kane* was finished. Louella
Parsons crashed an early screening. Offended by the picture's allusions
to William Randolph Hearst, the columnist rallied the Hearst press
and radio organization against *Citizen Kane*; as a result, the film was
banished from the Hearst newspapers' pages and airwaves. Reacting
to a veiled blackmail threat from Hearst officials, Hollywood studio
chiefs, led by Louis B. Mayer, tried to buy the negative and destroy
it. Under enormous pressure, Schaefer was forced to skip the bigger
chains, releasing *Citizen Kane* to only a small number of theaters.

Orson would never forget the film's dismal Chicago premiere,
scheduled to coincide with his twenty-sixth birthday. He had hoped to
impress Dolores Del Rio with a glorious homecoming, and dignitaries from Kenosha and the Todd School were invited, along with local
newspaper people. But the public attendance was sparse, and Ashton
Stevens was not allowed to write about the film, or even mention it.
Instead, Stevens covered the touring *Twelfth Night* with Welles's favorite
actress, Helen Hayes, and, of all people, Maurice Evans as Malvolio.

The discerning local reviews could not cheer him up, even though
C. J. Bulliet in the *Chicago Daily News* compared Orson's film to the

work of Shakespeare, and wrote presciently that "a century from now *Citizen Kane* will be stored away in the archives of New York's Museum of Modern Art. There will be Orson Welles scholars in those days."

Nor could Welles forget the Oscar ceremonies nine months later, when he hoped for vindication. *Citizen Kane* was nominated for nine Academy Awards, surely a record for a first-time director. Orson himself was nominated for Best Screenplay, as cowriter with Herman Mankiewicz, and also for Best Actor, Best Director, and (as its producer) Best Picture. But *Citizen Kane* took only one trophy that night, for Best Screenplay. Orson often recalled people booing whenever his name or the film's title was mentioned from the stage—surely the exaggeration of an unhappy memory, as Welles was not in attendance that night; he was off filming in Brazil.*

"Hearst?" asked Griffin on the talk show. "Did he hurt your career, Orson?"

"Sure," he replied quickly, "but I didn't do him any good either."

That is what Orson usually said, to his credit. Operatives paid by the Hearst organization dogged Welles on his travels throughout 1941, hoping to trap him in hotel rooms with underage women. One night, while attending the San Francisco premiere of *Citizen Kane*, Orson wound up in a Fairmont Hotel elevator with one other person: William Randolph Hearst. "He and my father had been chums," Welles remembered, "so I introduced myself and asked him if he'd like to come to the opening of the picture. He didn't answer. And as he was getting off at his floor, I said, 'Charles Foster Kane would have *accepted.*' No reply."

Welles always insisted that Hearst himself had little or nothing to

---

* One footnote to the Oscar ceremony is that *Citizen Kane* lost in the category of Best Scoring of a Dramatic Picture, which Bernard Herrmann won for *All That Money Can Buy*, a less distinguished RKO picture, directed by William Dieterle, that had followed *Citizen Kane* in Herrmann's Hollywood career.

Herman Mankiewicz was also absent from the Academy Awards ceremony. Mank stayed home, believing that Hollywood lived in dread of Hearst and that he would be humiliated by a loss, according to Richard Meryman. The film's hero, RKO studio president George Schaefer, took the stage to collect the golden statuette and had it delivered to Mank's home with "congratulations and best wishes from a high-priced office boy."

do with the fight to suppress *Citizen Kane.* There is scant proof that the publisher ever watched the picture. In a memoir cobbled together and published fifteen years after her death in 1975, Marion Davies said that neither Hearst nor she had seen it.

Davies was Hearst's paramour for two decades, until his death in 1951. None other than Welles himself wrote a glowing introduction to her posthumous memoir. Orson said more than once that the one thing he felt guilty about was that anyone conflated Susan Alexander with the charming and talented Davies, who was exactly the kind of free-spirited comedienne he liked onscreen. Welles felt he'd let Mankiewicz allude too closely to Davies in the character of Susan Alexander, giving her Davies's penchant for jigsaw puzzles—a hobby that was unknown to Welles.

On the record, Welles never once responded to the provocative rumor that "Rosebud" had a secret meaning—that it was Hearst's private nickname for Davies's genitalia. This assertion first gained prominence with the publication of the second edition of Kenneth Anger's gossipy screen history, *Hollywood Babylon*, in 1975. (It was not mentioned in the first edition in 1965.) Gore Vidal later picked up this factoid and proclaimed it valid, claiming that either Mankiewicz or Charles Lederer, Davies's nephew—who was supposedly whispering in the ear of Mank or Orson or both during the writing of *Citizen Kane*—knew of the nickname, and suggested including it in the film to humiliate or intimidate Hearst.

Welles may have disputed this privately, but it would have horrified him to make even the slightest public reference to this most preposterous explanation for Rosebud. In all his recorded conversations and interviews, whether his words were being taped surreptitiously or not, he made few ungentlemanly references to the anatomy of women. Many otherwise intelligent people believe the gossip ("It links genesis with our genitalia," Peter Conrad wrote), but as David Thomson wrote of the notion, "How can fact keep up with such Velcro stories?"

After a few minutes spent reflecting on *Citizen Kane*, though, Welles told Griffin, "Let's change pictures." The host switched to a still from *The Stranger*, then a clip from the "cuckoo clock" scene with Joseph Cotten from *The Third Man*, which elicited a smile and a few proud remarks from Welles. Directed by Carol Reed, *The Third Man* was a fond highlight of his prolific and checkered acting career, independent of directing. The segment ended fittingly with a still from *Chimes at Midnight*, his Shakespearean masterwork, which Leaming praised as *"Citizen Kane* forty times over." Wasn't *Chimes at Midnight* more successful overseas than in the United States? Griffin asked politely. "It was hardly seen in America. It was a huge hit in Europe," Welles pointed out.

After the taping, Jim Steinmeyer shook Orson's hand backstage, congratulating him on his well-performed card trick. Welles invited the young magician to join him for dinner at Ma Maison with Barbara Leaming and Prince Alessandro Tasca di Cuto, a Sicilian aristocrat who for twenty years had assisted Orson with producing his disparate projects. Steinmeyer had to say no, having promised his friend, the stooge, a meal at a humbler eatery.

"He was in a fantastic mood," Steinmeyer recalled of the last time he saw Welles. "He had had the time of his life. He was very happy about the book and the show."

Merv Griffin walked Welles to the door, where chauffeur Freddie Gillette waited.

The talk show host thanked him with unusual gravity. One biography of Griffin claims that Orson, sensing his friend's concern, made this final comment before parting: "I think what gives dignity and tragedy, as well as meaning and beauty, to life is the fact that we all die. It is one of the great gifts of God, if you happen to believe in Him, that we are going to die. It would be terrible if we weren't." Welles did utter similar thoughts in interviews, but this anecdote, like the story of the seventeen hot dogs at Pink's, is too good to be true.

Around 10 P.M., after their celebratory dinner, Orson was chauffeured back to his Hollywood hills home, where he plunged into a round of telephone calls, including a long conversation with Roger Hill. Their friendship stayed strong. The Hills vacationed wherever Orson camped out over the years, visiting all his homes, solicitous to his wives and children. Skipper Hill was persuaded into various film projects, including an unfinished 1970 project of Welles's called "The Deep," based on a novel by Charles Williams, which involved his heavy participation and called on his love of boating. Tape-recording their talks was nothing new: Orson had created a mock talk-show set in his Arizona living room in the early 1970s, and filmed long reminiscing interviews with Roger and Hortense Hill on the pretext that it might be a pilot episode.

Tonight Orson told Skipper he had just returned from dinner at the "company cafeteria," as he called Ma Maison. "It's been a long day and I'm beat," Welles admitted. Hill told Orson he did sound weary. "I am," Orson agreed, "but will admit it to no one but you. My God, Roger, I look as drained as I feel."

His prize pupil was in a wistful mood, Hill later told his grandson Todd Tarbox. This last phone call between the lifelong friends was not tape-recorded, but Tarbox meticulously reconstructed it over the following days, interviewing his grandfather, and later publishing the conversation as part of his 2013 book *Orson Welles and Roger Hill: A Friendship in Three Acts.*

"How young I once was," Welles mused to Hill that night, echoing words he had spoken during his interview segment on *The Merv Griffin Show.* "Today I am feeling disastrously old. The mind boggles at the thought that you have always been twenty years my senior. But then, in the best sense, you will always be younger than I was when I first checked into Clover Hall. But neither of us can deny that we both suffer the curse of excessive years.

"De Gaulle likened old age to a shipwreck. Isn't that wonderful? He's so right. We can, in our declining years, either sink slowly, clutching to hope and fighting like hell to hold on, or we can sink swiftly in panic and despair."

Orson still dreamed of finishing new work, and his boyhood mentor wished the same. "I would like to live long enough to see *The Other Side of the Wind* and *The Magic Show* completed," Hill replied. "I fear I'm too old to ever see your *Lear* and *Cradle.* But I'll have no regrets if I don't live to see any more of your pictures because I've experienced so very much of your work." Hill reminded Orson of the many highlights: the Todd School plays, the Federal Theatre and Mercury productions in New York, the radio shows and films. His only regret, Hill said, was having missed *Around the World in Eighty Days,* the gigantic stage musical—Welles's "personal favorite among all his stage productions, inspired by the films of Georges Méliès," in the words of Jonathan

Rosenbaum—which drew mixed reviews during its 1946 Broadway run and then closed after seventy-five performances, leaving Welles with years of debt.

"I have the [LP] to your show somewhere," Hill said.

"You're one of the few," Welles responded humorously.

"Many of my projects have foundered for the lack of financial resources," Welles went on. "In the mid-fifties, I began financing and shooting [a film of] *Don Quixote.* Coupled with having to scurry for financing, it wasn't long before a gaggle of howling critics began demanding to know when it would be finished. Novelists and biographers aren't asked every other day, 'When are you going to finish your book?' As you know better than anyone, Quixote and Sancho Panza took a grip on my imagination in my youth. Over the years, I kept changing the movie and throwing the pieces away. You remember, I came close to completing the film, with Quixote journeying to the moon, at about the time astronauts actually accomplished the feat. That spoiled the movie and I threw away ten reels."

"What's the focus now?" asked Hill.

"The film now centers on the pollution and corruption of old Spain and hope for a new Spain. It's developed into a very personal essay, which I'm renaming 'When Are You Going to Finish *Don Quixote*'?"

"What a wonderfully comic and bittersweet designation," said Hill.

"I should do a similar renaming of 'The Other Side of the Wind,'" said Welles, referring to his ambitious film about filmmaking that he had shot between 1970 and 1976, but had been unable to complete because of financial and legal complications.

The two men discussed the differences between performing before a live audience and a camera lens, with Welles comparing James Cagney ("a commanding screen presence") with the great Neapolitan actor Eduardo De Filippo, who was spellbinding onstage but made "many films, without distinction." They talked a little about Joseph Cotten's memoir in progress, which Welles had been reading: "gentle, witty, and self-effacing," Orson said, "just like Jo."

At one point Welles quoted from *Two Gentlemen of Verona* ("I'll be as patient as a gentle stream"), and Hill swiftly matched him with a snatch of *Othello* ("What wound did ever heal but by degrees?")—the kind of erudite quotation-trading the friends had been doing for more than fifty years.

"Is work on 'The Magic Show' more encouraging?" Hill asked.

"There is a bright spot on the horizon," replied Welles. "I'm about to wrap it up, actually. A few more camera set-ups and a slight bit more editing, and that's it, except—"

"Except what?"

"Except I'm tempted to add a new close: the teleportation of a human being along a fiber-optic cable from Los Angeles to New York," said Welles.

Hill reminded him that he'd been working on "The Magic Show" for fifteen years.

"The only real troubles have been the perennial ones of finding money and time," Welles sighed. "But it's been more a labor of love than one of necessity. My 'Magic Show' troubles pale when I think of Okito, who was one of the greatest magicians. He invented one of my favorite tricks, the floating ball. He opened his act by plucking a duck from a cloth. Before making its entrance, the duck is secured in a bag between Okito's legs. At a command performance before the Kings and Queens of Denmark and Holland, the duck somehow extricated its head out of the bag, and grabbed, with exceeding force, the very unsuspecting magician under his robe. Over the years, whenever I begin to believe I have troubles, I think of poor Okito. He's been on my mind a great deal in recent years. But today, there's no duck under my djellabas and the horizon is bright."

Welles always spoke optimistically about the future, and he did so tonight. He had a good role in a new picture coming out soon, called *Someone to Love*, which was the second time Orson had acted for his friend the independent filmmaker Henry Jaglom. (He had also played a magician in Jaglom's 1971 film *A Safe Place*.) Oja Kodar also had a role in *Someone to Love*, which doubled his pleasure. Welles had improvised some dialogue for his character, a mentor to Jaglom's character and a philosopher on life and love, and he was proud of his work.

Orson had reason to believe, he said, that his good luck was returning. He'd heard from an East Coast producer who was interested in putting up finishing money for either *King Lear* or "The Dreamers"—

the latter his adaptation of Isak Dinesen's short stories, for which he had shot a few scenes in the late 1970s and early 1980s. He promised to send Hill a "revised script" of "The Dreamers."

"Luck plays such a large part in our life," Hill remarked.

"Everything to do with an artistic career, from the fellow who eats live lizards for a living to Michelangelo, depends on an element of luck," Welles said, as modest in private as he had been in public. "There's nobody who isn't beholden to luck."

As the call wound down, Welles urged Skipper to come and visit him. He had not seen Hill for several years and had been trying to entice him to travel west. "I fear that, if you wait too long, your trip will be to deliver my eulogy," Welles said.

"I think of you as immortal," returned Hill warmly.

"Maybe in your eyes, but not in the eyes of my doctor," stated Welles. "But thank God this shipwreck is too busy to be destroyed, let alone sink." He finished with a passage from *Cymbeline*: "Fortune brings in some boats that are not steered," he said.

"Good night and good luck," said Hill.

"Good night, Roger."

Talk shows like Merv Griffin's treated Orson royally in a way official Hollywood never had. Orson liked to quip that Hollywood had given him only "half an Oscar," for cowriting *Citizen Kane*. But that wasn't quite true: the Academy of Motion Picture Arts and Sciences board of governors also voted Orson an honorary Oscar in 1971 for "superlative artistry and versatility in the creation of motion pictures." But Welles sent a friend, director John Huston, who was currently acting for him in "The Other Side of the Wind," to appear instead, accepting the award on his behalf. A maverick filmmaker himself, Huston praised Welles's career eloquently in his introduction, ending with the ringing assertion that Orson "is truly that most difficult, unforgivable, and invaluable of God's creations: a man of genius."

Since Orson was busy "filming abroad," Huston told the Academy (and the global television audience), he would accept the Oscar in a special two-minute film clip, the medium he loved most. In fact, Welles was living then in a bungalow in the nearby Beverly Hills Hotel, and he watched the "live" telecast with Oja Kodar, Peter Bogdanovich, and Bogdanovich's girlfriend, actress Cybill Shepherd. Huston said he promised to bring the Oscar to Welles in Spain. Orson yelled good-naturedly at the TV set, "Yeah, bring it right over, John!"

Orson was more inclined to accept the American Film Institute (AFI) Life Achievement Award on February 9, 1975, because the event was produced by George Stevens Jr., the institute's founder. The AFI was dedicated to film education and preservation, a cause Welles believed in, and Stevens's father was George Stevens Sr., Ashton Stevens's nephew, who had welcomed Welles so warmly to RKO in 1939.

As the hour grew late, Welles turned to his typewriter, working fitfully on several projects. Oja Kodar's nephew, Aleksandar, was asleep in the attic. Professor Howard Suber of UCLA was later told that Orson spent the night drafting his first college syllabi and lectures; other people say he was toiling on the script for "The Magic Show," developing his plans for a cross-country fiber-optic teleportation sequence. Knowing Welles, he probably spent time on both, and other projects too. He moved restlessly from one piece of work to the next, keeping to his small downstairs back bedroom, wearing "one of his enormous hooded bathrobes," in the words of Bart Whaley in his self-published *Orson Welles: The Man Who Was Magic*, "as ever living in the present and planning the future."

Sometime after midnight, Welles "left his battered mechanical typewriter and went to the adjoining bathroom," wrote Whaley, who for his account interviewed Freddie Gillette in 1992. "Returning to his high hospital-type bed, he evidently found it too difficult to climb up into. Managing to clutch a pillow, he lay on the floor, and tucked the pillow under his head."

Orson's "wonderful booming voice," in the independent filmmaker Henry Jaglom's words, was discovered by Jaglom on his answering machine when he came home in the early morning. Jaglom had told Welles his mother was undergoing a delicate operation in a hospital. "This is your friend," the wonderful booming voice said on the recording. "Don't forget to call your mother first thing in the morning, find out what the results of her operation are, then call and tell me."

His last known words, expressing concern about someone else's mother, were like a faint echo of Rosebud. When the chauffeur arrived at Welles's house at 10 A.M. on Thursday, October 10, he found Orson slumped and dead on the floor. One of the first people arriving at Welles's address, after hearing the news on the radio and television, was Orson's longtime friend Paul Stewart, the actor who played Raymond, the character who discovers Kane's body in *Citizen Kane*.

"A man is not from where he is born," Welles said once, "but from where he decides to die." He had lived, it turns out, "seventy years of a man's life," words that reverberate from *Citizen Kane*. That film, among all his works, was mentioned in front-page headlines and television and radio broadcasts around the world. "Orson Welles, Film Genius, Entertainment Boy Wonder," read the *Boston Globe*'s headline reporting his death.

Citizen Kane alone would have ensured his place in cinema history. In 1997, an American Film Institute jury of 1,500 "film artists, critics and historians" ranked the picture as the greatest American film of all time. It achieved the same ranking in the same survey in 2007.

For fifty years, *Kane* also took the top slot in *Sight and Sound*'s decennial worldwide poll of "critics, distributors and selected academics and professions"—until 2012, when Alfred Hitchcock's *Vertigo* finally displaced it. *Vertigo*'s winning margin—191 votes to 147 for *Citizen Kane*—was doubtless bolstered by the magazine's generous expansion of its voting pool that year, from 145 in 2002 to 846 in 2012. (The totals came from the cumulative tally of films cited in top-ten lists of favorite or best works submitted by each of the participants.) It couldn't have helped *Kane* that, the year before, the influential critic David Thomson had wondered in print in *Sight and Sound* whether Welles's first picture deserved to hold the top spot forever. "If *Citizen Kane* wins again in 2012, it would be understandable yet depressing," Thomson wrote.

But it is also true that, by 2012, the greatness of *Citizen Kane* was taken for granted among even some of the elder statesmen among Welles experts. Peter Bogdanovich, for instance, declined to participate in the *Sight and Sound* poll that year. "Of course, I didn't know at the time that *Vertigo* was going to win," Bogdanovich wrote later. "Personally, it has never been my favorite Hitchcock." James Naremore voted in the poll—not for *Vertigo*, but not for *Citizen Kane* either. Naremore chose *Touch of Evil* as his Welles selection for the top ten. "I was annoyed by Thomson's *Sight and Sound* essay and could sense which way the wind was blowing," Naremore explained. Even as dedicated a Wellesian as Joseph McBride split hairs in withholding his vote from *Citizen Kane.* "It pained me not to vote for *Kane*, which was my cinematic textbook and still is my touchstone," said McBride, who has written three books about Welles, "but I voted for *The Magnificent Ambersons* and *Chimes at Midnight*, which I think are even better, as did Welles himself."

Hitchcock directed more than fifty pictures. (*Vertigo* was number nine on the AFI's 2007 ranking.) Welles completed only about a dozen. Yet Welles ranked third in the number of votes attracted by *any* director in the *Sight and Sound* poll—behind only Hitchcock and Jean-Luc Godard—with several of his films drawing votes, and five firmly lodged in the top 250 of all time. *Touch of Evil*, his film noir gem from 1958, ranked fifty-sixth. *The Magnificent Ambersons*, even truncated, ranked eighty-first. *Chimes at Midnight* was number 154. *F for Fake* was 235. Welles was also represented by films in which he "merely" acted, with *The Third Man* part of a three-way tie at seventy-third place.

Sight and Sound also conducted a separate poll in which film directors voted for the greatest and their favorites. Among the 358 filmmakers participating were Bong Joon-Ho from South Korea, Faouzi Bensaidi from Morocco, Jiri Menzel from the Czech Republic, Paul Greengrass from the United Kingdom, Luis Miñarro from Spain, Manuel Ferrari from Argentina, Pema Tseden from Tibet, Shinji Aoyama from Japan, and Martin Scorsese from the United States. All these and other contemporary directors voted for one or more Welles pictures—there were even scattered votes for *Mr. Arkadin*—and in the end Welles placed two films in the directors' top hundred: *Touch of Evil* in a four-way tie at twenty-sixth; and *Citizen Kane* number three, behind *Tokyo Story* and *2001: A Space Odyssey.* (*Vertigo*, the top Hitchcock film, was number seven.)

Welles remains a lodestar for fans, critics, and scholars, as well as filmmakers. And, like Jimi Hendrix, whose recordings continue to emerge decades after his death, Welles keeps delivering. In 1992, Spanish filmmaker Jesus Franco released a compilation of his *Don Quixote* footage, though many Welles purists found it a bastardization. Two cinephiles, Bill Krohn and Myron Meisel, worked with Richard

Wilson to restore Orson's equally quixotic 1942 film *It's All True*, shot in Brazil, for a 1993 documentary. In 1999 George Hickenlooper made *The Big Brass Ring*, drawing on Welles and Oja Kodar's script, as rewritten by F. X. Feeney and Hickenlooper. In 2013, his long-lost *Too Much Johnson* footage was unearthed in Italy; the 1938 slapstick comedy footage toured film festivals after a crisp restoration, stunning audiences with its beauty and vitality. ("Deep focus, daring forms of blocking," said James Naremore. "It pretty much knocked my socks off.") The Munich Film Museum has compiled footage from several uncompleted Welles films, including *The Dreamers*, *The Magic Show*, and his one-man *Moby Dick*.

And even "The Other Side of the Wind" may yet find its way through its legal and financial welter. In October 2014, the *New York Times* reported on the front page that a deal had been reached to hand over to a Los Angeles production company the 1,083 reels of negatives sitting in a warehouse in a Paris suburb. Peter Bogdanovich and Hollywood producer Frank Marshall, who has worked often with Steven Spielberg and who began his career as a line producer on "The Other Side of the Wind," would oversee the editing of the film, based on Welles's surviving notes. The main character in the story echoes Hemingway, and the inspiration for the script can be traced to Welles's tussle with Hemingway in 1937; the film is also said to mark one of the most overt explorations of homosexuality in Welles's oeuvre. The cast includes Bogdanovich, John Huston, Susan Strasberg, Lilli Palmer, and Dennis Hopper. "Cinema buffs consider it the most famous movie never released," wrote the *Times*, "an epic work by one of the great filmmakers."

"No one had ever engaged in a dull conversation with Orson Welles," his longtime friend, actor Joseph Cotten, said in a message read to a packed Directors Guild Memorial held one month after Welles died in 1985. "Exasperating, yes; sometimes eruptive, unreasonable, ferocious and convulsive . . . yet eloquent, penetrating, exciting, and always, never failingly always—even at the sacrifice of accuracy and his own vanity—witty and never, never, *never* dull."

Among the friends and colleagues who spoke at the event was

former Todd School headmaster Roger Hill, who finally made his trip to California, as Welles had predicted, to deliver his prize pupil's eulogy. Also on hand was Oja Kodar, who angrily recounted the many discouragements Welles had suffered late in life, denouncing those "whose fingers are still sticky from plucking at his wings."

"I promise you it didn't make him bitter," she told the crowd to Niagara-like ovations.

Sometime after his death, his thirty-year-old daughter Beatrice brought his ashes to Spain, the country of many of Welles's youthful enthusiasms. At his request, his remains were buried in an ancient well covered by flowers on the property of an old friend, bullfighter Antonio Ordoñez, in the mountaintop village of Ronda. Ronda is only a short distance from Seville, where, as a young man, Orson had indulged in the sport of bullfighting, and where, for a brief time, he had felt "untroubled by the itch of ambition," in his words. The mountaintop "well" beckoned to him, Orson jokingly told Ordoñez, as a kindred "Welles."

The private estate bars visitors, although people stream to the place nearly every day, many of them coming from far away. The only way to catch a glimpse of Welles's grave is from the road. There is no lengthy inscription on the marker: no mention of *Citizen Kane*, the Mercury Theatre, "War of the Worlds," or any other work by the outstanding whirling pagoda of the cinema.

"He was some kind of man," Tanya (Marlene Dietrich) says of Hank Quinlan (Welles) at the end of *Touch of Evil*. "What does it matter what you say about people?"

Welles himself always scoffed at posterity. "I'm against posterity in principle," he said often. "I think it's almost as vulgar as success." And such is his legacy that the plaque on his gravestone bears only his dates and his immortal name:

GEORGE ORSON
WELLES
1915–1985

Sources and Acknowledgments

"Two prevailing and diametrically opposed attitudes seem to dictate the way most people currently think about Orson Welles," the critic Jonathan Rosenbaum wrote, when reviewing three books about Welles for *Cinéaste* in 1996. "One attitude, predominantly American, sees his life and career chiefly in terms of failure and regards the key question to be why he never lived up to his promise—'his promise' almost invariably being tied up with the achievement of *Citizen Kane*. Broadly speaking, this position can be compared to that of the investigative reporter Thompson's editor in *Citizen Kane*, bent on finding a single formula for explaining a man's life.

"The other attitude—less monolithic and less tied to any particular nationality, or to the expectations aroused by any single work—views his life more sympathetically as well as inquisitively; this position corresponds more closely to Thompson's near the end of *Kane* when he says, 'I don't think any word can explain a man's life.'"

When I launched my research four years ago, I was acutely aware of the many Thompsons who preceded me on the subject of Orson Welles. I find something worthwhile in even the least of the many books—and many more articles—about Welles. My goal was to collate and fact-check them, to explore fresh research, and to arrive at a different, more balanced, and, yes, more sympathetic account of Welles's life in the years leading up to *Citizen Kane*. The backstory of his life and early career would help explain the genesis and ideas behind the famous film.

Previous books have suffered from both gaping holes and negative assumptions, all of which have contributed to the accepted mythology about Welles, feeding widespread theories about his egomania and self-destructiveness. I hoped to create a chronological narrative that would fill in gaps and blind spots and counter some of this negative mythology.

The job of writing film biographies has certainly changed since the first one I wrote, which I began as an undergraduate in college. Since *Young Orson* was intended to end, except for a final chapter, in 1940, and anyone who was Orson's contemporary in 1940 would be in his or her mid-nineties today, I did fewer actual interviews for *Young Orson* than for any of my other books. Besides, I think it čan be unfair to rely heavily on the fuzzy memories of nonegenarians—unfair to them and to the subject. I burrowed into libraries, archives, courthouses. I read endless microfilm, oral histories, letters, and unpublished memoirs. I pored over electronic records and newspaper and periodical indexes on the Internet. I read everything I could about Welles, including many hundreds of articles and books.

At the end of the long road of every book I write, however, I look back with similar fond memories. I could not tell you how many Oscars *Citizen Kane* was nominated for without looking up the number in my own pages. But I remember the interesting and helpful people I met along the road. I am grateful to those who answered the telephone, welcomed me to their institutions or homes, walked me around the places where young Orson lived, responded to my e-mail queries and persistent requests for information or documents. Behind each name or organization on this list is someone who inched this book toward the finish line.

Advice and assistance: Charles Barr, John Charles Bennett, Matthew Bernstein, Richard Bleiler, Alan Brostoff, Mark Burman, Russell Campbell, Stuart Campbell, Lorenzo Codelli, William G. Contento, Paul Cronin, William Cross, Michael Dawson, Anne Edwards, Scott Eyman, Burt Fields, Touria El Glaoui, Diane Giles, Sidney Gottlieb, Kevin Greenlee, John Gurda, Ron Halberg, Reynold Humphries, Robert James, Josh Karp, Ray Kelly, Marian Wilson Kimber, Daniel Kremer, James Landers, Daniel and Caryl Lemanski, Tom Matthews, Lee Matthias, Patrick McGavin, Russell Merritt, Elliott Miller, Kathryn Morice, Gary Morris, Will Murray, Frank Noack, Holly Gent Palmo, James Robert Parish, Brian Reddin, Jonathan Rosenbaum, Santiago Rubin de Celis, Randy Rutsky, Karl Schadow, Beth Schroeder, Michael Schumacher, Roberta Smoodin, Jim Steinmeyer, Howard

Suber, Peter Tonguette, Mary Troath, Jim Van Hise, Chris Feder Welles, Barry B. Witham, Leigh Woods, Jim Zimmerman.

Cynthia Richardson dug into Chicago court and government records for me. Vanda Krefft gave generously of her time, dipping into files at the Margaret Herrick Library of the Academy of Motion Picture Arts and Sciences. Sky McGilligan conducted research at the Margaret Herrick Library and in the Special Collections of the University of Southern California. Clancy McGilligan read hours of microfilm at the Kenosha Public Library.

For interviews and supplementary material I am especially grateful to the children of persons who figure in Welles's early life story. These include Mrs. Thallis Drake, the daughter of Phyllis Fergus; Bill Mowry, the son of William Mowry Jr.; Ryan O'Neal, the son of actor Charles O'Neal; Cynthia Bulens, the daughter of William Vance; and Mike Woldenberg, the son of Haskell and Edna Woldenberg, the last proprietors of Camp Indianola.

Screenings: Joseph McBride dug into his personal vaults for his tape recording of Welles's last appearance on *The Merv Griffin Show*; Brian Reddin, from Dublin, arranged for a viewing of his documentary *Orson Welles and the Gate Theatre*; Alberto Rojas Maza, from Seville, sent his documentary *El Americano*; Michael Tapper, from Sweden, mailed a copy of *The Well (Brünnen)*.

Photographs: Marie Kroeger, Ryerson Archives, Art Institute of Chicago; Christine Cheng, Federal Theatre Project Collection, Special Collections, George Mason University (Fairfax, Virginia); Dollie Banner, Jerry Ohlinger's Movie Material Store (New York); Cathy Schenck, Librarian, Keeneland (Lexington, Kentucky); Meredith Jumisko, Public Relations, Kenosha Area Convention and Visitors Bureau; Tom Schleif, Executive Director, Kenosha History Center; Ann Tatum, Kentucky Derby Photo Archives, Kinetic (Louisville, Kentucky); Joseph McBride; Heather Winter, Milwaukee Institute of Art Archives, Milwaukee Art Museum; Dudley Crafts Watson Papers, Special Collections Research Center, Syracuse University Libraries; Todd Tarbox, Carol Nishijima, Charles E. Young Research Library, University of California at Los Angeles; Lilly Library, University of Indiana (Bloomington); Special Collections Library, University of Michigan (Ann Arbor); Sandra Garcia-Myers, Charles Higham Collection, Archives of the Cinematic Arts, University of Southern California; Woodstock Public Library (Woodstock, Illinois).

Special thanks to Francy Paquette and Andy Sharlein of Allied Digital Photo in Germantown, Wisconsin, for reproduction services.

Archives and organizations: Gregg Tubbs, Director of Corporate Communications, American Lung Association; Marie Kroeger, Ryerson Archives, Art Institute of Chicago; Elizabeth Thrond, Center for Western Studies, Augustana College (Sioux Falls, South Dakota); Jean L. Green, Head of Special Collections, and Beth T. Kilmarx and Mary E. Tuttle, Tilly Losch Collection, Binghamton University Libraries (Binghamton, New York); Robert T. Muth, Director, Bozeman Fish Technology Center, Bozeman, Montana, and Carlos R. Martinez, Director, Fish Hatchery and Archives (Spearfish, South Dakota); Michele Westberg, Clerk, Bozeman Municipal Court (Montana); CA/RK, Buffalo and Erie County Public Library (New York); Catherine Williamson, Butterfields (Los Angeles, California); Stephanie Buck, Librarian/Archivist, Cape Ann Museum (Gloucester, Massachusetts); Ashlee Wright, Carmel Public Library (Carmel, California); Tina Eger and Danelle Orange, Archivists, Carthage College (Kenosha, Wisconsin); Cedar Rapids Public Library (Iowa); Jeanne Hamilton, Director, and Barbara Krehbiel, Charleston Carnegie Public Library (Charleston, Illinois); Lish Thompson, South Carolina History Room, Charleston County Public Library; Chicago History Museum Research Center; Deborah Hastings and Elizabeth Cline, Reference, Public Library of Cincinnati and Hamilton County (Ohio); Teresa Yoder, Special Collections, Chicago Public Library; Cleveland Public Library (Ohio); Charis Emily Shafer, Brianne LaCamera, Brandi Kalicki, and Kristen La Follette, Mercury Theatre and Theatre Union Collections, Columbia University Center for Oral History, Butler Library, Columbia University (New York); Karen Meier, Dane County Court (Madison, Wisconsin); Sarah Hartwell, Reference, Baker-Berry Library, Dartmouth University (Hanover, New Hampshire); Cully Sommers, Music, Arts, and Literature Department, Detroit Public Library (Michigan); Julie Levang, Reference, Duluth Public Library (Minnesota); Michelle Franklin and Ashley Todd-Diaz, Curator of Special Collections and Archives, Emporia State University (Emporia, Kansas); Cheryl Bronkema, Freeport Public Library (Freeport, Illinois); Nancy Shlaes,

Ann Birk Kuper Papers, Special Collections, Governors State University (Chicago, Illinois); Hope Schneider, Nahman-Watson Library, Greenfield Community College (Greenfield, Massachusetts); Carl White, Greenwich Public Library (Connecticut); Susan Halpert, Vera Zorina Collection, Houghton Library, Harvard University (Cambridge, Massachusetts); Chris Applin, Local History, Hoyt Public Library (Saginaw, Michigan); Ralph A. Pugh, Archivist, Paul V. Galvin Library, Illinois Institute of Technology (Chicago); Taran T. Ley, John Reinhardt, and Sandra Fritz, Reference Librarians, Illinois State Library and Archives (Springfield); Kate Choplin, Public Services, Indianapolis Public Library (Indiana); Dr. John A. Horner, Missouri Valley Room, Kansas City Public Library (Missouri); Peter Shaw Johnson, President and Manager, Historic Green Ridge Cemetery, Kenosha (Wisconsin); Julia Johnas, Highland Park Public Library (Illinois); Kankakee Public Library (Illinois); Cynthia Nelson, Curator/Archivist, Kenosha County Historical Society (Wisconsin); Teresa Sutter, Research and Alumni Coordinator, Latin School (Chicago, Illinois); Ellie Jordan, Lake Geneva Public Library (Wisconsin); Lewis Wyman, George Middleton Papers, Manuscript Division, and Jan Grenci, Prints and Photographs Division, Library of Congress (Washington, D.C.); Romeo Dais, Madison Public Library (Wisconsin); Ken Syke and Carolyn Lowrey, Madison Public Schools Administration (Wisconsin); Nancy Fike, Museum Administrator, McHenry County Historical Society (Illinois); Heather L. Winter, Librarian/Archivist, Milwaukee Art Museum; Missouri State Archives; Jared Brennan, Special Collections, Nashville Public Library (Tennessee); Bonnie Marie Sauer, Archivist, National Archives and Records Administration (New York); Tom Ankner, Charles F. Cummings, New Jersey Information Center, Newark Public Library; Hope Dunbar, Ashton and Florence Stevens Papers, Newberry Library (Chicago, Illinois); John Calhoun, Billy Rose Theatre Division, New York Public Library; Diane Anderson, HR Coordinator, North Dakota Developmental Center (Grafton); Susan Sacharski, Archivist, Northwestern Memorial Hospital, Chicago; Janet C. Olson, Assistant University Archivist, and Nicholas D. Munagian, Gate Theatre Papers, Special Collections, Northwestern University Library (Evanston, Illinois); Edward L. De Sanctis, Oneida County Historical Society (New York); Alice Gerard,

Town Historian, Palisades (New York); Linda White, Perrot Memorial Library (Greenwich, Connecticut); Marilyn Holt, Pennsylvania Department, Carnegie Library of Pittsburgh; Gabriel Swift, Rare Books and Special Collections, Princeton University Library; Curt Phillips, Pulp Mags@yahoogroups.com; Elizabeth Wilkinson, Archivist, George Ade Papers, and Shauna Borger, Digital Collections, Purdue University Libraries (Indiana); Rachel Carter, Archivist, Everett Library, Queens University of Charlotte (South Carolina); Quincy Public Library (Illinois); Racine Public Library (Wisconsin); Linda Balk, Librarian, Renville Genealogical Society (Oliva, Minnesota); Mark Colly (press office) and Freek Heijbroek (author), Rijksmuseum (Amsterdam); Laura Haule, St. Charles Public Library (Illinois); Shirley Andria, Administrat Services Coordinator, Saint Francis Community Services (Salina, Kansas); Peg Koller, Librarian, St. John's Northwestern Military Academy (Delafield, Wisconsin); Judy Oski, Sawyer Free Library (Gloucester, Massachusetts); Sandy Day, Local Historian, Schiappa Library (Steubenville, Ohio); Mahina Oshie, Seattle Public Library (Washington); Debbie R. Henderson, Archival Collection, Sierra Madre Public Library (California); Judith Munns, Skagway Museum (Alaska); Laurie Winship, Museum Director, Skaneateles Historical Society (New York); Erin Kinhart and Elizabeth Botten, Archives of American Art, Smithsonian Institution (Washington, D.C.); Katharine J. Rinehart, Sonoma County Library (Santa Rosa, California); Pamalla Anderson, Ronald Davis Oral History Collection, DeGolyer Library, Southern Methodist University; Tessa Brawley, Dudley Watson Crafts Collection, Special Collections, Syracuse University Library; David Kessler, Bancroft Library, University of California–Berkeley; Christine Colburn and Rena Schergen, Special Collections Research Center, University of Chicago Library; Kelly M. Grogg and Haley Lott, Charles O'Neal Papers, Special Collections and University Archives, University of Iowa Libraries (Iowa City); Andrew Horbal, Hornbake Library, University of Maryland (College Park); Edward (Ned) Comstock, Archives and Special Collections, University of Southern California; David Null, Director, Archives and Records Management, University of Wisconsin–Madison; Troy Reeves, Head, Oral History Program, Steenbock Library, University of Wisconsin–Madison Archives; Dan Hauck, University of Wisconsin–

Milwaukee Area Research Center Reading Room; Melissa Olson, University of Wisconsin–Parkside Archives and Area Research Center (Kenosha); Ginny L. Kilander, American Heritage Center, University of Wyoming–Laramie; Lori B. Bessler, Reference, and Matt Tischer, Scott F. Roller, Richard L. Pifer, Harry L. Miller, and Mary K. Huelsbeck, Archives and Special Collections, Wisconsin State Historical Society (Madison); Neal Kenney, Special Collections, West Chester University Library (West Chester, Pennsylvania); Wheaton Public Library (Illinois); Jane Bouley, Local Historian (Branford, Connecticut), and Alice Pentz, Library Director, Willoughby Wallace Memorial Library (Stony Creek, Connecticut); Lesley Mackey McCambridge, Senior Director of Credits and Creative Rights, Writers Guild of America, West; Andrea Vernola, Martha Hansen, and Julie Fee of the Woodstock Public Library (Illinois); Doris Bannister, Historian, Town of Middlebury and County of Wyoming (New York); Laurie Klein, Thornton Wilder Papers, Beinecke Rare Book and Manuscript Library, Yale University (New Haven, Connecticut).

Special thanks to the numerous librarians and reference specialists, many of them anonymous, who answered my queries, but especially to Patty Bajabir, Suzanne Hildebrandt, Laura Kastelic, Steve M. Hutchens, and the staff of Kenosha Public Library; Curtis Mann, manager of the Sangamon Valley Collection of the Springfield Public Library (Illinois); Craig Simpson, Isabel Planton, and the staff of the Lilly Library, Indiana University at Bloomington; Peggy Daub, Phillip Hallman, and Kate Hutchens in the Special Collections Library of the University of Michigan at Ann Arbor; the staff of the Milwaukee Public Library; and the staff of the Woodstock Public Library.

I am especially grateful to the reference desk and interlibrary loan department of the Raynor Memorial Libraries of Marquette University. The Marquette librarians answered countless queries and repeatedly hunted down source material from other libraries.

In Ireland I was blessed with assistance from Eithne Massey and Ms. Phil Comerford of the Dublin and Irish Local Studies Collections, Dublin City Library and Archive; Mary Qualter, Clerical Officer, Galway County Libraries; the staff and electronic indexes of the National Library (Dublin); and Aisling Lockhart, Manuscripts and Archives, Old Library, Trinity College, Dublin. Eileen Leahy helped with a little eleventh-hour research. Anthony Tracy and Ruth Barton invited me to their colleges to talk, helping me to pay the way for research and travel. Gwenda Young brought me to University College–Cork on a Fulbright, teaching at UCC, furthering my work in Ireland.

In Seville, María Gisèle Royo and Antón Calderon Ferre squired me around. Alberto Rojas Maza shared his knowledge of Welles's bullfighting stint. Francesco Zippel made Rome hospitable. In Paris, Alain Kerzoncuf and Bertrand Tavernier welcomed me, and Marie-Dominique Montel and John Baxter also opened their doors wide. Over the years, Baxter has been a great friend of my books and a human encyclopedia for my questions.

Kathleen Sapltro and John Daab welcomed me to Woodstock with lunch, a screening, and many leads and suggestions.

Ruth Barton read the Irish chapter and made sharp recommendations for revisions. Bonnie Hendrickson, Town Historian at the Oregon Public Library (Illinois); and Duane Paulsen, local historian of Grand Detour, read the Grand Detour sections and made suggestions. Dr. John Hanson of Milwaukee advised me on the medical speculations and diagnoses. Wisconsin historian John Buenker read the Kenosha portion of the book and offered pointers. Jim Steinmeyer consulted on magic and magicians and critiqued the final chapter revolving around the last day of Welles's life. Welles expert James Naremore, also knowledgeable about magic and magicians, read a draft of the manuscript, giving me the benefit of his wide-ranging expertise. Todd Tarbox and his wife, Shirley, read every chapter involving Roger Hill and the Todd School, and went further than just correcting mistakes; they performed line-by-line editing of a draft for syntax and grammar. None of the above people can be blamed, however, for any mistakes of fact or judgment that have persisted into the final form of this book.

For me, every book takes a village of friends and supporters to help me write it. Roger Hill's grandson Todd Tarbox engaged in almost daily communications with me for several years, offering items from his seemingly bottomless trove of Todd School memorabilia, along with advice and good fellowship and the wisdom of his own lifelong experience. Juan Cobos in Spain started me off with long constructive e-mails, sharing his pioneering interviews with Welles, his research, and his thoughts.

Above all, Joseph McBride has run the marathon with me. McBride has written three notable books about Orson Welles, and he could have regarded me as a rival or Johnny-come-lately. But he sent me literally hundreds of e-mails expounding on this or that aspect of Welles's career. He forwarded many pieces by other Welles experts. He mailed recordings, videos, and DVDs and dug up photographs for reference or use. He read the next-to-last and final drafts of the book, editing for style and language as well as for content. He made countless spot-on criticisms and corrections, and tolerated my disagreement on occasion. Although only a few years separate us in age, there is no question as to who is the elder statesman and the last word in Wellesiana. Thank you, Joe.

My agent, Gloria Loomis, and her associate Julia Masnick treat me so nicely it is almost as though I lead the Watkins/Loomis agency in royalties (I don't). For twenty-five years I have been fortunate to have the same agent and also the same editor. I often say, only half-jokingly, that my editor deserves a co-byline. Calvert Morgan Jr. burrowed into Welles and *Citizen Kane*, and became every bit the expert, adding nuances and correcting details—finding a mistake in the very first sentence of the submission draft!—supporting his suggestions with references to the likes of musician Jack White. My job is never done, thankfully, until Cal has added his thoughtful touches and (substantive) line editing.

And my family—my wife, Tina; and sons Clancy, Bowie, and Sky—always live and breathe the subject for as long as I do.

Notes

These books, among the many, many consulted, were my indispensable sources: Michael Anderegg, *Orson Welles, Shakespeare and Popular Culture* (Columbia University Press, 1999); Peter Biskind, *My Lunches with Orson: Conversations Between Henry Jaglom and Orson Welles* (Metropolitan, 2013); Frank Brady, *Citizen Welles: A Biography of Orson Welles* (Scribner, 1989); Simon Callow, *Orson Welles: The Road to Xanadu* (Viking, 1995); Robert L. Carringer, *The Making of Citizen Kane*, revised and updated (University of California Press, 1985); Peter Conrad, *Orson Welles: The Stories of His Life* (Faber and Faber, 2003); Mark W. Estrin, ed., *Orson Welles Interviews* (University Press of Mississippi, 2002); Chris Welles Feder, *In My Father's Shadow: A Daughter Remembers Orson Welles* (Algonquin, 2009); Richard France, *The Theatre of Orson Welles* (Bucknell University Press, 1977); Ronald Gottesman, *Focus on Citizen Kane* (Prentice-Hall, 1971); Charles Higham, *Orson Welles: The Rise and Fall of an American Genius* (St. Martin's, 1985); Roger Hill, *One Man's Time and Chance: A Memoir of Eighty Years, 1895–1975* (Roger Hill, 1977); John Houseman, *Run-Through: A Memoir* (Simon and Schuster, 1972); Barbara Leaming, *Orson Welles: A Biography* (Viking, 1985); Michael Lindsay-Hogg, *Luck and Circumstance: A Coming of Age in Hollywood, New York, and Points Beyond* (Knopf, 2011); Micheál MacLíammóir, *All for Hecuba: An Irish Theatrical Biography* (Methuen, 1946); Joseph McBride, *What Ever Happened to Orson Welles? A Portrait of an Independent Career* (University Press of Kentucky, 2006); Richard Meryman, *Mank: The Wit, World, and Life of Herman Mankiewicz* (William Morrow, 1978); James Naremore, *The Magic World of Orson Welles* (Oxford University Press, 1978); James Naremore, ed., *Orson Welles's Citizen Kane: A Casebook* (Oxford University Press, 2004); Peter Noble, *The Fabulous Orson Welles* (Hutchinson, 1956); Todd Tarbox, *Orson Welles and Roger Hill: A Friendship in Three Acts* (BearManor Media, 2013); Jonathan Rosenbaum, *Discovering Orson Welles* (University of California Press, 2007); David Thomson, *Rosebud: The Story of Orson Welles* (Knopf, 1996); Peter Tonguette, *Orson Welles Remembered: Interviews with His Actors, Editors, Cinematographers and Magicians* (McFarland, 2007); Orson Welles and Peter Bogdanovich *This Is Orson Welles* (HarperCollins, 1972); Orson Welles and Herman Mankiewicz, with "Raising *Kane*" by Pauline Kael, *Citizen Kane: The Complete Screenplay* (Bantam Books, 1971).

A Note on Sources: My research depended heavily on innumerable small press items obtained through examination of microfilm, local clip files, and electronically indexed newspapers and periodicals. I consulted all available government and court documents—birth, death, marriage, divorce, probate, draft, medical, immigration, travel, and so on. Dates and sources are often made clear in the context of the narrative. Only key sources not listed at the beginning of this chapter are specified.

Chapter 1: THE BACKSTORY TO 1905

All quotes from the *Citizen Kane* screenplay, unless otherwise noted, are from the "shooting script," originally published in *The Citizen Kane Book* along with the essay "Raising *Kane*" by Pauline Kael (Little, Brown, 1971). The reporter, Thompson, reads Walter P. Thatcher's "journal" recounting his first meeting with Kane as a boy in 1870, according to the script; but he reads from Thatcher's "unpublished memoirs" (not his "journal") in the film, and the dissolve from the manuscript to Mrs. Kane's boardinghouse clearly shows the date as 1871—one of a thousand ways the film differs from the published script. All citations from Peter Bogdanovich's interview sessions with Welles from Bogdanovich, *This Is Orson Welles*.

"I am almost belligerently Midwestern . . ." from Orson Welles (OW), letter of December 21, 1937, to Wisconsin congressman Thomas R. Amlie, trying to back-pedal from a short profile of him in the *New Yorker*, December 11, 1937, in which the journalist A. J. Liebling quotes OW describing Kenosha as "a nasty little Midwestern City." (The quote about Kenosha was "flagrantly and libelously in error," Welles wrote to Congressman Amlie. "I said 'little,' but never, never, 'nasty.' I have been to Kenosha in recent years and have found it . . . charming and vital.") "The sounds of factory whistles . . ." and other Dr. Maurice A. Bernstein (MAB) quotes about the Welles family from the handwritten "Memoir of Orson Welles's Early Years" in the Richard Wilson–Orson Welles Papers in Special Collections, University of Michigan Library (UM). "Spoke his first words . . ." from a letter of November 20, 1939, from MAB to Mercury Theatre publicist Herbert Drake (UM). "To counteract the local whisky . . ." from James Watson, *Avoid Boring People: Lessons from a Life in Science* (Vintage, 2010). "A quiet tick-tock, tick-tock . . ." from Carl Sandburg, *Abraham Lincoln: The Prairie Years* (Harcourt, Brace, 1926). "Elected on the Republican ticket . . ." from *History of Sangamon County, Illinois* (Inter-State Publishing, 1881). The military pension papers of Richard Jones Wells/Welles courtesy of the National Archives and Records Administration (NARA). All the inventions of Richard Jones Wells/Welles and his son Richard Head Welles can be located with the aid of the Google Patents search engine. "Hundreds of friends" from *St. Joseph* (Missouri) *Gazette*, July 22, 1876. "A desirable ally and . . ." from Head's obituary, *Kenosha Telegraph*, February 25, 1875. "Impetuous and talented" from Victoria Price, *Vincent Price: A Daughter's Biography* (St. Martin's, 1999). John F. Kreidl's unpublished essay on Dick Welles and the Badger Brass company is among Joseph McBride's papers at the Wisconsin State Historical Society. "A little, small-boned man" from the full transcript of the Orson Welles–Roger Hill telephone conversations (UM). The provenance of "Dick Welles" the race horse is traced in Charles Collin's column, "A Line o' Type or Two," *Chicago Tribune*, June 8, 1944. "First in violence, deepest in dirt . . ." from Lincoln Steffens, *The Shame of the Cities* (McClure, Phillips, 1904). "[Caruso] used to be in the house . . ." from Tarbox, *Orson Welles and Roger Hill*.

Chapter 2: 1905–1915

Kenosha Evening News for the following: "illustrating the most dramatic points," December 5, 1906; "fanatics," October 20, 1907; "by machines and girls" December 6, 1907; "one of the quietest holidays ever known," December 25, 1907; "practically gone out of business," February 3, 1908; Dick Welles's involvement in the "kidnapping" of militant Louis Kekst is covered in a series of *News* articles including November 21 and December 23, 1907; "the greatest interest of the evening," April 30, 1909; "There will be no consideration," July 23, 1908. The *Chicago Tribune* reported the anarchist plot to destroy Badger Brass, June 21 and 22, 1908. Beacon Press published Marion Murdoch's *The Hermit Thrush and Other Verses* in 1924. I have also consulted Mary Davison Bradford, *Memoirs of Mary D. Bradford: Autobiographical and Historical Reminiscences of Education in Wisconsin* (Antes, 1932).

"Piece of sponge" and "Battle of the Train Depot" *Chicago Tribune,* July 22, 1911. *Kenosha Evening News* for the following: "while playing in the door yard," August 2, 1911; Beatrice Welles (BW) and the charge of "the insurgents," May 5, 1911; "deplorable social conditions" and "Those departments of city government," Jane Addams, March 29, 1912; "He drove the jitney men," September 14, 1916; Kenosha Woman's Club schism, February 9, 1914 (also *Chicago Tribune,* February 9, 1914): "This is the first opportunity," May 22, 1914; "from many walks of life" and the founding of the Kenosha City Club, June 27, 1914; Charles Witmer's exhibition flights and filmmaking in Kenosha, July 13, 1914; BW expounds on the community Christmas tree and "the real Santa Claus," December 7, 1914; "Men who counted their wealth," December 10, 1914; BW's front-page plea for open-air and special needs schools, November 15, 1914.

Chapter 3: 1915–1921

Kenosha Evening News: meeting of BW, Kenosha suffragists, and President Woodrow Wilson, January 29, 1916; BW's involvement in the campaign to establish a Kenosha board of review to censor "sordid moving pictures," November 28, 1916 (also *Racine Journal,* October 12, 1916); BW's support for "sex hygiene" courses in public schools, October 1, 1915; her "Mother and Child" "storiette," from a series of articles including January 26, January 28, and February 29, 1916; "artistic marching costumes" and the Kenosha suffragists' trip to Chicago for the national assembly and parade to the Republican convention, June 7, 1916; "superbly" from Dudley Crafts Watson (DCW), guest review, November 6, 1916; "Badger Brass Sold Today," January 20, 1917; Mina Elman is described as chic and beautiful in a review of May Robson's play *Mrs. Matt,* January 12, 1917; "a size or two smaller," January 23, 1917; "marked by great delicacy," January 24, 1917; hospital stay of Richard I. Welles (RIW) in Chicago, March 13, 1917; "Suffrage Edition" of the *Kenosha Evening News,* with contributions by BW and Dick Welles, February 27, 1917; "a woman of rare personal charm," from Lucy Ives's obituary, August 10, 1917.

Sarah Bernhardt in *Les Cathédrales, Chicago Tribune,* May 19, 1918. "Touched the hand of . . ." and "a sort of imitation musical Wunderkind" from Bogdanovich,

This Is Orson Welles. "The most fashionable apartment . . . ," DCW quotes here and elsewhere, unless otherwise noted, are from Noble, *The Fabulous Orson Welles.* Marian Wilson Kimber's book *Feminine Entertainments: Women, Music, and the Spoken Word* is forthcoming from the University of Illinois Press. "She had to kill my act . . ." from Chris Welles Feder, *In My Father's Shadow.* I am indebted to Peter Tonguette and his book *Orson Welles Remembered,* and to James Naremore and Jim Steinmeyer for bolstering my knowledge of magic tricks and history. Additionally I drew from several of Steinmeyer's books and from Maurice Zolotow, "Unforgettable Orson Welles," *Reader's Digest,* December 1986. "I idolized him" from Jim Steinmeyer, *The Last Greatest Magician in the World: Howard Thurston* (Tarcher, 2011). The Louis K. Anspacher dinner is reported in *Chicago Tribune,* April 13, 1922. "While I prayed . . ." from Tarbox, *Orson Welles and Roger Hill.* Michael Atkinson first propounded the theory that Charles Foster Kane's real father was "the unseen deadbeat boarder" named "Fred Graves" in the published script of *Citizen Kane:* see Atkinson, "Revisiting Rosebud: The Mystery of Mrs. Kane" (movingimagesource.us, 2013). "He [Bernstein] left Kenosha . . . ," is from Leaming, *Orson Welles.* "The word genius was whispered . . ." from Leaming, *Orson Welles.* "Even when some are cut . . ." from Edward Moore, *Chicago Tribune,* August 13, 1922, roundup of the Ravinia season. Bill Doll, "Ashton Stevens," *Theatre Arts,* July 1951, helped with biographical background.

Chapter 4: 1922–1926

Details of BW's appearances in Milwaukee come from *Art Bulletin* (a Milwaukee Art Institute publication) and scrapbooks in the Milwaukee Art Museum archives. "Very modern compositions . . ." and "Her interest at the present time . . ." from publicity in *Milwaukee Evening Sentinel,* January 28, 1923. "I try to be a Christian . . ." from Eric David's article on Welles and religion, *Christianity Today,* May 19, 2009. The account of BW's "interpretative concert" from *Milwaukee Journal,* November 16, 1923, "Of the most delicate and colorful imagination . . ." from Catherine Pannill Mead's obituary for BW, *Milwaukee Evening Sentinel,* May 12, 1924. OW talked about his mother's penchant for practical jokes and mischief-making on the *David Frost Show,* May 12, 1970: its transcript has been posted by www.wellesnet.com. OW's faux memoir, *Paris Vogue,* December 1983, was made available in English as "A Brief Career as a Musical Prodigy," www.wellesnet.com.

"'The Shadow' was born . . . ," "something of a masterpiece . . . ," and "discoursed intelligently . . ." from Noble, *The Fabulous Orson Welles.* "Emily Watson introduced me . . . ," "He drew a circle on a blackboard . . . ," "We've known each other . . . ," and "I persistently pretended . . . ," from Tarbox, *Orson Welles and Roger Hill.* "I *was* my mother . . ." from Leaming, *Orson Welles.* "Shock of black hair . . ." from Charles Higham's interview with Agnes Moorehead, *Film Digest* no. 21 (Australia), curiously left out of his biography of Welles. OW told slightly varying versions of his several encounters with Houdini; I have favored Jim Steinmeyer's books, which quote Welles from the author's conversations with him. Frederick J. Garner is cited from Noble, *The Fabulous Orson Welles.* Lowell Frautschi is from "Camp

Indianola and Orson Welles, Boy Genius: A Memoir," *Wisconsin Academy Review*, Winter 1994–1995, and from "The Profile" (of Frautschi), *Wisconsin State Journal*, June 27, 1943. OW's summer camp poem (*"From out of the dark and dreary night . . ."*) is extracted from the 1939 special edition of *Campers' Trail* among Marjorie Kantor's papers at the Wisconsin State Historical Society in Madison. "Wonderful city" from Joseph McBride's interview with OW, *Wisconsin State Journal*, September 14, 1970, referenced in McBride, *What Ever Happened to Orson Welles?* Stanley Custer's papers are at the Wisconsin Historical Society along with those of journalist Frank Custer, who wrote about his brother's boyhood friendship with OW and Welles's time in Madison on several occasions in the *Capital Times*, recapping those articles on the occasion of OW's death on October 25, 1985. "From my earliest childhood . . ." from Leaming, *Orson Welles*. "A squat little man . . ." from Steinmeyer, *Hiding the Elephant: How Magicians Invented the Impossible and Learned to Disappear* (Carroll and Graf, 2003).

"Quite a large and discerning . . ." from Noble, *The Fabulous Orson Welles*. "Eastern oysters and Western trout" from OW's piece in *Paris Vogue*, 1983. "I chased him into the hotel . . ." from Higham's *Orson Welles*. Henry C. Warner is quoted from Noble, *The Fabulous Orson Welles*. Annetta Collins's reminiscences are from her tape recording among Todd School oral histories in the McHenry County Historical Society. Notes of Roger Hill (RH) on young OW's "genius" score on the Binet-Simon test were supplied to the author by Todd Tarbox, who described them as "typed and taped by my grandfather on the outside of one of his 'Orson' files." OW mused on "genius" in Michel Mok, "Orson Welles, Who Puts Shakespeare's Romans in Fancy Duds, Discusses Ruffians, Past and Present," *New York Post*, November 24, 1937.

Chapter 5: 1926–1929

"A paradise for boys" from Feder, *In My Father's Shadow*. "I hear we've got another . . ." from Leaming, *Orson Welles*. Unless otherwise noted, John Dexter is quoted from *Reunion 2005 Stories*, a Camp Tosebo Clubhouse CD recording supplied to the author by Daniel and Caryl Lemanski. "Rather too much hair . . . ," "A terrific show," and "No doubt my fascination . . ." from Tarbox, *Orson Welles and Roger Hill*. "When he finished with me . . ." from Callow, *Orson Welles*. "Was always trying to get some money . . ." is from the transcript of Leaming's interview with RH, February 19, 1983, supplied to the author by Todd Tarbox. Issues of *The Red & White* courtesy of Tarbox. "My great pal . . ." from the full OW-RH telephone transcripts. "In many a school . . ." from the Leaming-RH transcript.

"One of those lost worlds . . . ," and "a childhood in the last century . . ." from Bogdanovich, *This Is Orson Welles*. "How easily words flowed . . ." is from Hill, *One Man's Time and Chance*. "One of the sexiest pictures . . ." from the OW-RH phone transcripts. "Our sunshine . . ." from OW's eulogy for Hortense Hill, cited in Feder, *In My Father's Shadow*. "Try to build a mountain . . ." from the OW-RH transcripts. The local newspaper reports I consulted for coverage of the Sheffield fire include

"Sheffield Hotel at Grand Detour Burned Today," *Dixon Evening Telegraph*, May 14, 1928; "Historic Inn at Grand Detour Burned," *Freeport Journal-Standard*, May 14, 1928; and "Grand Detour Hotel Destroyed by Fire," *Ogle County Republican*, May 17, 1928.

"Thirteen-year-old dramatic critic..." from *Highland Park News*, July 6, 1928. "Hitting the High Notes," young OW's column, is quoted from *Highland Park News*, July 6, July 13, July 20, July 27, and August 3, 1928. "I have so many happy memories..." from OW's undated 1970s letter to Ruth Miller (UM). For history and context of the Goodman Theatre I drew on James S. Newell's authoritative PhD thesis, "A Critical Analysis of the Kenneth Sawyer Goodman Memorial Theatre and School of Drama, Chicago, Illinois, 1925–1971" (Wayne State University, 1973). "As Cassius, I killed Caesar..." from *New York Post*, November 24, 1937. "For God's sake, Roger..." from Tarbox, *Orson Welles and Roger Hill*. MAB's letter to young OW, May 21, 1930, is in the Lily Library collection. "Third rate, almost bumming" from OW's first "travel talk," reported in *Woodstock Daily Sentinel*, March 25, 1930. "I was, however, not a wunderkind..." from Leaming, *Orson Welles*. "I was just becoming interested..." from the "Revisiting Vienna" episode of the British television series *Around the World with Orson Welles*, 1955.

Chapter 6: 1929–1931

Young OW's "running fight" with Coach Roskie, his wariness of homosexual classmates, his flirtations with town girls ("Barking and yelling"), his attempted escapes from "the main part of the prison," RH's defense of him before the faculty, and the headmaster's children's resentment of OW: all from the OW-RH phone transcripts. "Was a good kid..." from Callow, *Orson Welles*. "Constant play going of this sort..." from *Woodstock Evening Sentinel*, February 24, 1930. The MAB–Edith Mason "rift" precipitated by young OW from *Chicago Tribune*, January 4, 1930. Details of the divorce proceedings, including Mason's complaint that MAB often boasted of "his feminine conquests," were reported on the front page of the *Chicago Herald and Examiner*, May 5, 1931. "Inklings" ran in the *Highland Park News*, June 20, July 4, August 1, and September 5, 1930. "Find a drink that wouldn't..." and "I'll never forget..." from Feder, *In My Father's Shadow*. "That was the last..." from Leaming, *Orson Welles*. "A funny little fellow..." from the OW-RH phone transcripts. "If you had a lead..." (Hascy Tarbox) and "Keep it moving!..." (John Dexter), both quoted in Callow, *Orson Welles*. "His father would come..." from the Leaming-RH transcript. "Usually pretty heavily cocked..." from Leaming, *Orson Welles*. Ashton Stevens (AS), "A Column or Less," his first piece about young OW, *Chicago Herald and Examiner*, November 11, 1930. "I admire him for that..." from the OW-RH phone transcripts. "Old-timers in the industry..." from *Automobile Topics*, March 7, 1931. "Dr. Bernstein Made Guardian of Rich Boy" from *Chicago Herald and Examiner*, January 3, 1931. "Enormously likable and attractive...," from Kenneth Tynan's interview with Welles, *Playboy*, March 1967, included in Estrin, *Orson Welles Interviews*. "Momentarily, false gods" from Leaming, *Orson Welles*. "I couldn't let them down . . ." from Feder, *In My Father's Shadow*. "China and Japan," OW's talk, is in *Woodstock Evening Sentinel*, January 20, 1931.

"A falling-to-pieces one-volume . . ." from France, *The Theatre of Orson Welles*. "The most outstanding affair . . ." from *Woodstock Daily Sentinel*, June 10, 1931. OW's 1930–31 report card is in the Lilly Library. "At Todd, the guy was really . . ." from the Camp Tosebo reunion recording. "It was only at Todd . . ." from Feder, *In My Father's Shadow*. "I remember we sat down . . ." is from the Leaming-RH transcript. RH's letter of September 6, 1931, to Clyde Tull at Cornell College is posted at www.lettersofnote.com. Young OW's initial *Billboard* advertisement from Hill, *One Man's Time and Chance*; the second from Callow, *Orson Welles*. "Under his wing . . ." from the RH-Tull letter. Welles's letter of August 1931 to RH, announcing his trip to Ireland, from France, *The Theatre of Orson Welles*.

Chapter 7: 1931–1932

There are many letters from young OW to RH and MAB, and some have been excerpted or published in their entirety—for example in the books by Roger Hill, Richard France, Barbara Leaming, Frank Brady, and Simon Callow. Callow apparently saw several letters (including one describing the post–Aran Islands bicycle trip) that are absent from archives. Others survive in handwritten or retyped form at LL or UM, or both. The Ashton Stevens collection at the Newberry Library (NL) also contains copies circulated by MAB. Most lack specific dating, and I have done my best to straighten out their chronology. OW's contemporaneous letters home, when checked against known facts, seem relatively accurate and truthful.

Orson "Ort" Wells is quoted from a letter of June 3, 1934, to George Ade, among Ade's papers. Christopher Townley, "Galway's Early Association with the Theatre," from the *Galway Reader* (Spring, 1953), and the description of the Taibhdhearc Collection at the National University of Ireland, Galway, helped with the Taibhdhearc background. Mysteries shadow OW's time in Dublin. The Gate Theatre archives at Northwestern University are extensive and helpful but sparse when it comes to OW, and there is almost nothing about the branch operations of the Peacock Repertory Theatre. Extensive searches of surviving periodicals, electronic indexes, and archival collections did not turn up any article with OW's pen name "Knowles Noel Shane." Trinity College in Dublin has no record of any application from OW. *All for Hecuba* is a tremendous source, but MacLíammóir also has been accused of embellishing the facts—even, on occasion, describing incidents at which he was possibly not present. (Christopher Fitz-Simon, *The Boys: A Double Biography*, published by Nick Hern Books in 1994, offers a valuable corrective.) Production records for the Peacock could not be traced; nor did the Irish press extensively cover the auxiliary operation. So it appears that OW made his professional directing as well as acting debut in Dublin—but what exact play he directed, when, and to what effect, remains to be discovered.

"The Stately Homos of Ireland" from Joseph McBride, "The Irish Education of Orson Welles," *Irish America*, July 31, 1999. "A violent cloud of dust" and other MacLíammóir commentary, unless otherwise noted, from MacLíammóir, *All for Hecuba.* "Deep, guttural" and "When Orson calls with a smile in his voice . . ." (quoting Paul Stewart) from Milton Berle, *B.S. I Love You: Sixty Funny Years with the Famous and the Infamous* (McGraw-Hill, 1988). "Forced and defensive . . ." (Tennessee Williams) is quoted by Kenneth Tynan in his profile of OW, *Show*, November 1961. J. J. Hayes wrote about the eighteen-year-old "Orson Wells" with Goodman and Theatre Guild experience in "A Yeats Play and an American Actor in Dublin," *New York Times*, November 8, 1931. OW's reminiscences about his salad days in Ireland from the six-part BBC television series *Orson Welles' Sketch Book*, 1955 (including "It was the only thing I could think of . . ."). "With the gallery and the pit . . ." from OW, letter to Hortense Hill, quoted in Callow, *Orson Welles*. The Longfords and Betty Chancellor, unless otherwise noted, are quoted from Noble, *The Fabulous Orson Welles*. "Went to jail . . ." from Biskind, *My Lunches with Orson.*

Young OW discussed *The Dead Rides Fast* disparagingly with Hugh Curran in the *Chicago Tribune*, November 19, 1931. Joseph Holloway's journals, touching on Gate Theatre productions during this period, were edited by Robert Hogan and Michael J. O'Neill and published as *Joseph Holloway's Irish Theatre: Volume Two 1932–1937* (Proscenium, 1970). All of OW's quotes about the supposed jealousy of MacLíammóir and comparing him with Anew McMaster come from Leaming, *Orson Welles*. "Several pounds of nose-putty . . ." from Noble, *The Fabulous Orson Welles*. "Hilton Edwards played Mogu as he played . . ." and Padraic Column's "I don't recognize . . ." from Georgie Hyde-Lees (Mrs. William Butler Yeats), "Yours Affly, Dobbs: George Yeats to Her Husband," in *Essays for Richard Ellmann: Omnium Gatherum*, ed. Susan Dick (McGill-Queen's Press, 1989). "Youngest and only American . . ." from *Irish Tattler and Sketch*, January 1932. "One of the best [Ghosts] I have ever seen . . ." from Noble, *The Fabulous Orson Welles*. "That's a problem . . ." from OW's filmed conversation with Bernard Braden in a Paris hotel room, known as *Orson Welles: The Paris Interview* (1960). "My debt to them . . ." from OW's footage in the Irish television documentary *Orson Welles and the Gate Theatre* (Darren Chan/Brian Reddin, 2013).

Chapter 8: 1932–1933

All the OW quotes in the first half of this chapter, and later, describing his trip to Africa and Spain, are from contemporaneous letters to RH, except where noted. Most of the letters have been published, partially or in full, some originally in Hill, *One Man's Time and Chance.* I fact-checked all the letters, arriving at the conclusion that, however much it goes against the grain of his mythmaking reputation, these contemporaneous accounts are largely truthful and accurate. Most of the letters, albeit with gaps in time, are on deposit at the UM or LL. They are augmented by letters in the Ashton and Florence Stevens Collections at the NL, which also contains correspondence from Welles, from Dr. Maurice and Hazel (Moore) Bernstein, and from Whitford Kane to the Stevenses. Once again, I have tried to sequence the letters, which are typically undated.

"In the throes of Orson" from Hazel Bernstein (HB), letter of May 29, 1948, to AS, and "an intensely interesting person . . ." from HB, letter of May 5, 1948, to Florence Stevens (NL). "Suitable for entertaining . . ." and the rest of RH's account of the New York expedition from Hill, *One Man's Time and Chance*. "I do hope you won't . . ." from Leaming, *Orson Welles*. The accounts of the possible radio job and audition and of young OW's visit to the Whistler retrospective with AS come from a series of undated 1932 letters from OW and AS to Florence Stevens, including AS's letter of November 19, 1932, to his wife, and her undated reply (NL). "There is splendid stuff . . ." from AS, letter of November 27, 1932, to Florence Stevens (NL). "Some very exciting letters . . ." from an undated 1932 letter from OW to Florence Stevens (NL).

"As you love me, do . . ." from OW, letter of January 1933 to RH (UM). "His opera house and his millions . . ." from Hill, *One Man's Time and Chance*. "Tough days those . . ." from John Clayton, "The Man Behind This," *Los Angeles Times*, November 20, 1938. "Stick with this boy!" from Hill, *One Man's Time and Chance*. Roger Hill did stick with "Marching Song," presenting its world premiere, performed by the Todd Troupers, directed by Hascy Tarbox, at the Woodstock Opera House on June 7, 1950. "Debussy and others . . ." from OW, undated letter to RH, winter of 1932–1933 (UM). "The year is tearing by . . ." and "I have decided not to go to college . . ." from OW, letter of January 1933 to RH. "Shakespeare said everything . . ." from *Everybody's Shakespeare: Three Plays Edited for Reading and Arranged for Staging—Twelfth Night, Julius Caesar, Merchant of Venice* (Todd Press, 1934).

"No one believes me . . ." from Callow, *Orson Welles*. James Van Hise, Nils Hardin, and Sam Moskowitz's investigation into OW's pulp fiction credentials was published as "Orson Welles: Pulp Writer?" in *Rocket's Blast and the Comic Collector*, May 2000. OW's deposition in the Ferdinand Lundberg lawsuit (like Herman Mankiewicz's and John Houseman's testimony, quoted elsewhere in this book) is among the voluminous civil case files held in Record Group 21 of the U.S. District Court in the National Archives and Records Administration, New York City. "The home of song and dancing" from Walter Starkie, *Don Gypsy* (John Murray, 1936). The actual facts of Welles's bullfighting stint have thus far eluded the best detectives. OW wrote the introduction to Conchita Cintrón's *Torera! Memoirs of a Bullfighter* (Holt, Rinehart and Winston, 1968). "Juan, you know how much I love . . ." from my correspondence with Juan Cobos, who interviewed OW extensively and worked with him in Spain and who impressed upon me the importance of Walter Starkie, Seville, Triana, Spain, and bullfighting. "[Don Quixote] is better than any . . ." from Cobos's notes and reminiscences.

Chapter 9: 1933–1934

"He turned out literally . . ." from Hill, *One Man's Time and Chance*. MAB quoted from his notes for a memoir. "Jump of association" and the rest of the account of young OW's first encounter with Thornton Wilder (TW) from Noble, *The Fabulous Orson Welles*, with emendations from other sources. "Rather pudgy-faced . . ." and

"The whole town [of Dublin] was staggered . . ." from TW's letter of August 1933 to Alexander Woollcott, published in its entirety in *The Selected Letters of Thornton Wilder*, ed. Robin G. Wilder and Jackson R. Bryer (HarperCollins, 2008). "At times Wilder's mentor . . ." from Penelope Niven, *Thornton Wilder: A Life* (HarperCollins, 2012). "With no more than a 'wotta-mess-I'm in' . . ." from OW's undated letter of late August 1933 to Hortense Hill. "Never passed so serene a Pullman night . . . ," from OW's undated letter of late August 1933 to RH. The rest of OW's fall 1933 correspondence with RH (including, below, "In the simple acceptance of each other . . .") is undated. "Conversation was the most . . ." from Howard Teichmann, *Smart Aleck: The Wit, World, and Life of Alexander Woollcott* (Morrow, 1976). OW's hand-written, nineteen-page letter of September 11, 1933, to TW is in Wilder's papers in Special Collections, Beinecke Library, Yale University. "Physical vitality, psychic intensity . . ." from Michael A. Morrison, *John Barrymore, Shakespearean Actor* (Cambridge University Press, 1999).

"The ghosts of past magnificence . . ." and the outlook for the "grand tour of the country" from "Miss Cornell Starts Her Tour," *New York Times*, November 26, 1933. Basil Rathbone writes about the tour in *In and Out of Character* (Doubleday, 1962). Brenda Forbes's autobiography, also touching on the Cornell tour, is *Five Minutes, Miss Forbes* (Fairmile, 1994). A couple of tour anecdotes come from MAB's notes for a memoir. I also drew from Guthrie McClintic, *Me and Kit* (Little, Brown, 1955), and cited McClintic from Noble, *The Fabulous Orson Welles*. Katharine Cornell is quoted from her six-part "I Wanted to Be an Actress," as told to Ruth Woodbury Segwick, *Stage* magazine, 1939, which evolved into her autobiography *I Wanted to Be an Actress* (Random House, 1939). (Part Five, *Stage*, January/February 1939, centers on the national repertory tour.) In his papers, Stanley Custer recalled greeting OW backstage at the Madison stop of the tour. There are many versions of the cross-country train trip to Seattle, including Alexander Woollcott, "Miss Kitty Takes to the Road," *Saturday Evening Post*, August 18, 1934. I have fact-checked and collated the versions with Seattle press accounts. "Orson at the time always . . ." from France, *The Theatre of Orson Welles*. "Terribly campy" from Callow, *Orson Welles*. "Do reviews ever wound you?" from Michael Parkinson's interview with Welles on BBC's *Parkinson*, 1974. I have a sheaf of clippings from newspapers in U.S. cities, which helped trace the itinerary and events of the tour. Kenneth Tynan mentioned the palmisty and fortune-telling anecdotes in his collected *Profiles*, ed. Kathleen Tynan (Nick Hern Books, 1990); the long portrait of Welles melds his early *Show* piece with later interviews with OW. "About twice a year . . ." (OW) and, below, "gauche and tiresome . . ." (Forbes) from France, *The Theatre of Orson Welles*.

"That hurt for a while . . . ," "some picturesque black chef" and "I expect you to shine brightly . . ." from Callow, *Orson Welles*. I have quoted from OW's letters of April 12 and May 2, 1934, to Hilton Edwards in the Gate Theatre Collection. "Now he had added to . . ." from MacLíammóir, *All for Hecuba*. AS's column about Welles and the Woodstock Summer Theater, undated, is in his NL papers. "I wanted to go to Europe . . ." from France, *The Theatre of Orson Welles*. "A bevy of

stage-struck high school kids" and other RH memories of the summer theater from
Hill, *One Man's Time and Chance*. "A combination Bayreuth and a strawberry festival"
from *Woodstock News*, June 28, 1934. Details of the launch dinner at the Tavern
Club from an undated clipping, Margot Jr., "Thursday Evening All Roads Lead
to Woodstock Opera," *Chicago Daily News*, in the Woodstock Public Library file.
"Joseph Jefferson made a curtain speech . . ." from Margot Jr., "Woodstock, Ill.,
Never Saw Equal of Last Night's Doings in All Its Mellowing Century," *Chicago
Daily News*, July 13, 1934. "Rather mean" and "He revered them . . ." from Leaming,
Orson Welles. "Vigorous non-homosexual" and the debate about "pansies" are also
from Leaming. After proclaiming young OW's genius in the *Chicago Tribune*, Charles
Collins questioned it in "Planting Chicago's 'Fresh Fields,'" *New York Times*, July 15,
1934. John Clayton again quoted from his profile of OW, *Los Angeles Times*.

My section on *The Hearts of Age* is greatly indebted to Professor Russell Merritt
and Joseph McBride. When I was still in high school, my older sister took me to
one of Professor Merritt's film classes, where I first heard him talk about and then
viewed *Citizen Kane* for the first time at the University of Wisconsin–Madison in
1969. Later, as a student myself, I took every class Merritt taught. Joseph McBride,
who was the first to write about *The Hearts of Age*—in "Welles Before *Kane*," *Film
Quarterly*, Spring 1970—was also an invaluable mentor dating back to those years;
his investigation of Welles's filmmaking from the first to last continues to this day.
Charles O'Neal's son Ryan and William Vance's daughter Cynthia filled in with
their memories. "It was a Sunday afternoon . . ." and "certainly nubile, probably a
virgin . . ." from Brady, *Citizen Welles*. "A new star in the making" from *Woodstock Daily
Sentinel*, August 21, 1934. "On the last regretful night . . ." from MacLíammóir, *All
for Hecuba*. OW would "take a vacation . . ." from "Many Attended Final Showing
of *Tsar Paul*," *Woodstock Sentinel*, August 21, 1934.

Chapter 10: 1934–1935
The half dozen OW-to-RH letters and telegrams from 1934–1935, all at UM,
are undated, and I have sequenced them in context. "They fell under . . ." from
"Moral and Domestic," *Irish Times*, April 4, 1941. The Nicolsons are characterized
from Feder, *In My Father's Shadow*. I relied upon Mona Z. Smith, *Becoming Something:
The Story of Canada Lee* (Faber and Faber, 2004), for background on the relationship
between OW and Lee. "Tybalt seldom gets . . ." from MAB's notes for a memoir.
"Your father was a virgin . . ." from Feder, *In My Father's Shadow*. Marriage rumors
were squelched in Judith Cass's society column, *Chicago Tribune*, November 19, 1934;
the betrothal was announced in "Orson Welles, Actor, to Wed," *New York Times*,
November 18, 1934. "In the manner": Katharine Cornell again quoted from the *Saturday Evening Post*. "Friendly and good-natured" is Brian Aherne quoted from *A Proper
Job: An Autobiography of an Actor's Actor* (Houghton Mifflin, 1969). Wedding details
from the December 24, 1934, *Newark Star-Eagle* and *Newark Evening News*. AS wrote
about *Everybody's Shakespeare* in his column in the *Chicago American*, January 18, 1935.

John Houseman (JH) is always quoted from his memoir *Run-Through*, unless otherwise noted. "His British, rather wonderfully cool . . ." from Virgil Thomson's review of *Run-Through*, *New York Review of Books*, May 4, 1972. Archibald MacLeish's (AM) "Never heard of Orson!" and other remembrances of OW from the transcript of Bernard A. Drabeck and Helen E. Ellis's interview with AM published as *Archibald MacLeish: Reflections* (University of Massachusetts Press, 1986). "Generally trochaic, sometimes dactylic . . ." from AM's prefatory notes to the first published edition of *Panic: A Play in Verse* (Houghton Mifflin, 1935). "A rich blank-verse belly blow . . ." from OW, undated letter to AS, Stevens Collection. "A storm of controversy . . ." from "An Interview with Archibald MacLeish, Author of *Panic*, Play of Wall St. Crash," *Daily Worker*, March 15, 1935. "Does not necessarily imply . . ." from *New Masses*, March 19, 1935. Joseph McBride and François Truffaut on OW playing "negative" characters from McBride, *What Ever Happened to Orson Welles?* Jerome's appraisal of *Panic* is in *New Masses*, April 1, 1935; described as the transcript of his "speech delivered as part of *The New Masses-New Theatre* critical symposium which followed the final performance," it includes his line about "the hiss of the bourgeoisie." "Did not come to like . . ." from AM, letter of March 18, 1935, to JH, included in *The Letters of Archibald MacLeish, 1907 to 1982*, ed. R.H. Winnick (Houghton Mifflin, 1983), and also cited in Scott Donaldson, *Archibald MacLeish: An American Life* (Houghton Mifflin, 1992).

James Naremore is quoted from Naremore, *The Magic World of Orson Welles*. "Bright Lucifer" ultimately had its world premiere in 1997, when the Millennium Theater presented Welles's three-act play in Madison, Wisconsin, using a copy of the script tucked away in the State Historical Society archives. "A face-saving offer . . ." and "the literary product of this period . . ." from RH's notes for *One Man's Time and Chance* on deposit at UM. "General subjects of the stage" from *Woodstock Sentinel*, May 13, 1935. As regards *Man of Aran*, whether or not young OW met Robert Flaherty on the Aran Islands, while the latter was shooting *Aran*, remains a mystery; although my research indicates that OW was long gone from the islands and ensconced in Dublin by the time Flaherty was filming, it is possible he found his way back to Galway and sailed to the islands on a weekend, upon hearing that Flaherty, one of his idols, was on the job. One reliable reference for Welles's radio career is *Orson Welles on the Air: The Radio Years* (Museum of Broadcasting, 1988). Joseph Cotten's autobiography, quoted in this chapter, is *Vanity Will Get You Somewhere* (Mercury House, 1987). I have drawn background from William C. Glaekin's profile of Ray Collins, *Sacramento Bee*, November 16, 1957. "While known, are risky . . ." from "Rialto Notes," *New York Times*, July 22, 1934. "If they borrow . . ." from Whitford Kane, letter of September 10, 1935, to AS and Florence Stevens (NL).

Chapter 11: 1936
Elmer Rice announced OW as director of the Negro Unit *Macbeth* in the *New York Times*, January 5, 1936. "Mythical place . . ." from Bosley Crowther, "Macbeth the Moor: *Macbeth* Transplanted," *New York Times*, April 5, 1936. Steven Watson, *Prepare for Saints: Gertrude Stein, Virgil Thomson, and the Mainstreaming of American Modernism* (Uni-

versity of California Press, 1995), provided good background on the Houseman-Thomson-Welles relationship. I also plumbed Kathleen Hoover and John Cage, *Virgil Thomson: His Life and Music* (Thomas Yoseloff, 1959), and Virgil Thomson, *Virgil Thomson* (Dutton, 1985). Thomson cooperated with JH for Houseman's memoir *Run-Through* and is quoted in it. "Orson Welles knew nothing . . ." from Thomson, *Virgil Thomson.* "Instead of telling you . . ." from Callow, *Orson Welles.* I have quoted Federal Theatre Project historian Wendy Smith from Smith, "The Play That Electrified Harlem," *Civilization,* January/February 1996, and have also drawn from Smith, *Real Life Drama: The Group Theatre and America, 1931–1940* (Grove, 1994), and from Joanne Bentley, *Hallie Flanagan: A Life in the Theatre* (Knopf, 1988). "Fashion plate and man about Harlem" from "Jack Carter on Trial in Murder," *New York Amsterdam News,* May 17, 1933. "Slightly derailed energy" from Leaming, *Orson Welles.* "Anyone who could read lines . . ." from France, *The Theatre of Orson Welles.* "I got fifty bucks . . ." and "Great fun . . ." from Bogdanovich, *This Is Orson Welles.* "He liked me . . ." from Dwight Whitney's interview with Everett Sloane, "Beacon in a Sea of Mediocrity," *TV Guide,* April 1, 1961.

Rosetta LeNoire quoted from Bonnie Nelson Schwartz, *Voices from the Federal Theatre* (Terrace Books, 2003). "Houseman never came to [*Macbeth*] rehearsals . . ." from Leaming, *Orson Welles.* "It was really ridiculous . . ." and "He knew what he wanted . . .": Leonard de Paur as quoted in Mona Z. Smith, *Becoming Something: The Story of Canada Lee* (Faber and Faber, 2004). "I *never* scream at actors . . .": OW told this to RH during their phone calls. A "posture" to win him "the authority . . .": de Paur as quoted in Leaming, *Orson Welles.* The report of "prevalent" views about the "blackface" *Macbeth*: "WPA Players Set to Give *Macbeth* with Tropical Locale to Give Color," *New York Amsterdam News,* March 28, 1936. "Orson was constantly on Feder's back . . ." and "Orson began to get very abusive . . ." (Edna Thomas) are from France, *The Theatre of Orson Welles.* "Orson trusted my opinion . . ." is Virginia Welles (VW) quoted in France, *The Theatre of Orson Welles.* "To drink white wine . . ." (Virgil Thomson) is from Houseman, *Run-Through.* Welles's contemporaneous notes on *Macbeth* to cast and crew are from France, *The Theatre of Orson Welles.* The "geographically irreverent *Macbeth* . . ." from *New York Times,* April 5, 1936. "Just a matter of an appalling lack . . ." from Noble, *The Fabulous Orson Welles.* Carlton Moss is quoted from Douglas Bell's oral history (Academy of Motion Picture Arts and Sciences, 1995).

"Excitement . . . fairly rocked the Lafayette Theatre" from Brooks Atkinson's opening-night review, *New York Times,* April 15, 1936. "A dwarf with gold teeth" and "I realize on reflection . . ." from Noble, *The Fabulous Orson Welles.* Besides contributing to my understanding of *The Cradle Will Rock,* Barry B. Witham provided me with "Percy Hammond and the Fable of the Scottish Play," his dissection of the "myths" surrounding the Voodoo *Macbeth,* including the death of Hammond (supposedly caused by voodoo), *New England Theatre Journal,* 2007. "That was magical . . ." from Smith, *Becoming Something: The Story of Canada Lee.* "The heat" and "Harlem simmered yesterday . . ." from "News of the Stage," *New York Times,* July 17, 1936. "The only time anybody's . . ." and "I would go up . . ." from Leaming, *Orson Welles*. David Thomson and Peter Conrad are quoted from their books *Rosebud* and *Orson Welles*, respectively.

"No sooner would you open . . ." from *New York World-Telegram*, cited in Leaming, *Orson Welles*. "The WPA, in a throwaway leaflet . . ." from "L.N.," review of *Horse Eats Hat*, *New York Times*, September 28, 1936. "I would read a speech . . .": Edwin Denby is quoted here and elsewhere in this chapter from Noble, *The Fabulous Orson Welles*. "Within ten minutes of our meeting . . ." (Paul Bowles) is from Callow, *Orson Welles*. "So I went, 'Whoop!' . . ." (Bil Baird) is from John O'Connor and Lorraine Brown, *Free, Adult, Uncensored: The Living History of the Federal Theatre Project* (New Republic Books, 1978). "A jovial cross between P. T. Barnum . . ." from OW, letter of August 28, 1936, to RH (on Batten, Barton, Durstine & Osborne Inc. stationery), furnished to the author by Todd Tarbox. "Two long pieces of continuity . . ." from Virginia Spencer Carr, *Paul Bowles: A Life* (Scribner, 2004). I also consulted *Conversations with Paul Bowles*, ed. Gena Dagel Caponi (University Press of Mississippi, 1993). The malted milk anecdote and "kind, intelligent, generous . . ." from Arlene Francis's oral history, August 14, 1979, in the Columbia Center for Oral History Collection (CCOHC). I also consulted Francis, *Arlene Francis: A Memoir* (Simon and Schuster, 1978). "Sitting in the barbershop . . ." from Biskind, *My Lunches with Orson*. Everett Dirksen's attack on the "salacious tripe" of the Federal Theatre Project quoted from "By Act of Congress," *TAC Magazine*, Issue 12, 1939. Harrison Grey Fiske wrote that the Federal Theatre Project plays were "full of Communists," attacking the Voodoo *Macbeth* and *Horse Eats Hat* among other productions, in "The Federal Theater Doom-Boggle," *Saturday Evening Post*, August 1, 1936. The Marc Connelly–John Dos Passos anecdote is from Connelly, *Voices Off-Stage: A Book of Memoirs* (Holt, Rinehart and Winston, 1968). "I thought it was the best . . ." (Joseph Losey) is from Michel Ciment, *Conversations with Losey* (Methuen, 1985). Hallie Flanagan ("even sorrier for those who didn't enjoy it") is quoted from Callow, *Orson Welles*. The reminiscences of George Coulouris (January 29, 1981) and L. Arnold Weissberger (August 14. 1979) come from their oral histories in CCOHC.

Chapter 12: 1936–1937

"Rather too unsympathetically . . ." and "We didn't have the time . . ." from Bogdanovich, *This Is Orson Welles*. For background on the radio *Hamlet*, I drew on Bernice W. Kliman, *Hamlet: Film, Television and Audio Performance* (Rutherford, 1988). (Kliman gives September 19, 1936, as the air date for the show, but this must be the script date; contemporaneous news clippings indicate the last installment of the two-part broadcast aired in November.) "Everything originated . . ." (Paula Laurence) is from Callow, *Orson Welles*. "In the icy, strained light . . ." and other passages from OW's letters to VW from a series of undated radiotelegrams and letters, 1937–1939, in the Welles-Feder Collection at UM. "He was pleasant . . ." (Augusta Weissberger) is from Noble, *The Fabulous Orson Welles*. "I was probably the only person . . ." from Brady, *Citizen Welles*. In this chapter and elsewhere I have quoted Bernard Herrmann (BH) from Steven C. Smith, *A Heart at Fire's Center: The Life and Music of Bernard Herrmann* (University of California Press, 1991). Some quotes are culled from Herrmann's "Score for a Film," *New York Times*, May 25, 1941 (it is reprinted in Gottesman, *Focus on Citizen Kane*). I have also drawn from Howard Pollack, *Aaron Copland: The Life and Work of an Uncommon Man* (Henry Holt, 1999). "The music is vigorous . . ." from Virgil Thomson, "In the Theatre," *Modern Music*, no. 15, 1938. Welles's dustup with Ernest Hemingway has many variations; I have gravitated to OW's version of events, which I find plausible, while incorporating details from others. "Pompous and complicated . . ." from OW's basic account as told to Juan Cobos, Miguel Rubio, and J. A. Pruneda in 1964, published in *Cahiers du Cinéma in English*, no. 5, 1966, and reprinted in Estrin, *Orson Welles Interviews*. Peter Viertel tells Hemingway's side of the story in Viertel, *Dangerous Friends: At Large with Huston and Hemingway in the Fifties* (Nan A. Talese, 1992). Jeffrey Meyer, in *Hemingway: A Biography* (Harper and Row, 1985), is among those who have described OW's account as "quite fanciful."

OW's fictional re-creation was published as *The Cradle Will Rock: An Original Screenplay* (Santa Teresa, 1994). I have drawn extensively on Barry B. Witham's impressively researched "Backstage at *The Cradle Will Rock*," *Theatre History Studies*, vol. 12, 1992. Witham kindly supplied his discovered transcript of the Washington, D.C., meeting between OW and Federal Theatre Project officials. "Recitatives, arias, revue patters . . ." from Blitzstein's "Lines on The Cradle," *New York Times*, January 2, 1938. "Figurative prostitution—the sell-out . . ." (Brecht) is as quoted in Houseman, *Run-Through*. "He and Virgil were in a huff . . ." from Leaming, *Orson Welles*. "Crazy" and "terrified about it . . ." from Callow, *Orson Welles*. "Orson and Jack are optimistic . . ." from Blitzstein, letter of March 3, 1937, to his sister Josephine, in the Blitzstein papers at the Wisconsin Center for Film and Theatre Research, Wisconsin State Historical Society. "He never tired . . ." from Lehman Engel, *This Bright Day: An Autobiography* (Macmillan, 1974). "In about four weeks . . ." from "News of the Stage," *New York Times*, May 11, 1937. Lawrence Morris is reported to have described *Cradle* as "magnificent," in Noble, *The Fabulous Orson Welles*. "Amateurs Will Be First to Go," *New York Times*, June 12, 1937. "Irrepressible energy and . . ." from Marc Blitzstein, "Out of the *Cradle*," *Opera News*, February 13, 1960. "Ingenuity, speed and daring" from Jean Rosenthal and Lael Wertenbaker, *The Magic of Light: The Craft and Career of Jean Rosenthal* (Little, Brown, 1972). "You may not appear . . .": OW is quoted by Blitzstein in "Out of the *Cradle*." "Too-long speech" and "the situation, the scenes . . ." (Lehman Engel) are from Engel, *This Bright Day*. "The most beautiful voice . . ." is quoted from Leaming, *Orson Welles*. An invaluable source on Welles's contribution to the political culture of the 1930s and 1940s is Michael Denning, *The Cultural Front: The Laboring of American Culture in the Twentieth Century* (Verso, 1998).

Chapter 13: 1937–1938

"One of the happiest . . ." and "Orson devoted himself . . ." from Feder, *In My Father's Shadow*. "It was easy to detect that Helen Menken . . ." from "Radio's *Twelfth*

Night," *New York Times,* September 5, 1937. "That was part of her great charm . . ." from Leaming, *Orson Welles.* David O. Selznick and OW are quoted from Thomson, *Showman: The Life of David O. Selznick* (Knopf, 1992) and from Thomson, *Rosebud.* Goldwyn a "monster" and Mayer "the worst of them all" from Biskind, *My Lunches with Orson.* "Much of the speed and violence . . ." is from the OW-JH proclamation, *New York Times,* August 29, 1937. "He stared at me . . ." from Feder, *In My Father's Shadow.* OW letters to VW from Crawford Notch are in the Feder papers at UM. "The same kind of hysteria . . ." is cited in Michael Denning, "The Politics of Magic: Orson Welles's Allegories of Anti-Fascism," in Naremore, *Orson Welles's Citizen Kane: A Casebook.* "There was never a production . . ." from *Everybody's Shakespeare* (Todd Press, 1934).

I repeatedly referred to Andrea Janet Nouryeh's painstaking and exhaustive thesis, "The Mercury Theatre: A History" (New York University, 1987), incorporating her sources, information, and observations for my chapters on the Mercury Theatre. "They were Welles's shows . . ." and "Some of the people around him . . ." (JH) are quoted in France, *The Theatre of Orson Welles.* "You were production material . . ." from Jean Rosenthal and Lael Wertenbaker, *The Magic of Light* (Little, Brown, 1972). I have consulted and quoted from Howard Pollack, *Marc Blitzstein: His Life, His Work, His World* (Oxford University Press, 2012). Walter Ash (interviewed in 1979), George Coulouris (January 29, 1981), William Mowry Jr. (October 22, 1980), and Elliott Reid (August 17, 1980) are quoted from their oral histories in CCOHC. Maurice Bessy is quoted from Bessy, *Orson Welles* (Crown, 1971). Holly Gent Palmo, coscenarist of *Me and Orson Welles,* told me that the scene suggesting a girlfriend in the cast of *Julius Caesar* in the film "involves Orson and a character we dubbed 'Ingenue.' Orson refers to her as 'Betty' as he hustles her to her seat when Virginia arrives ('Betty, I believe it was Stanislavsky who said—Ginny! What a surprise!'), but the Ingenue is really an anonymous character meant to represent his various flirtations." Unless otherwise noted, Norman Lloyd is quoted from Lloyd, *Stages: Of Life in Theatre, Film and Television* (Scarecrow Press, 1990). "The hoodlum element you find . . ." is OW quoted in Alan Sinfield, *Faultlines: Cultural Materialism and the Politics of Dissident Reading* (University of California Press, 1992). "King actor" and "the fragility of great authority" from Leslie Megahey, filmed interview with Welles for the BBC's two-part "The Orson Welles Story," *Arena* (1982); an edited transcript is included in Estrin, *Orson Welles Interviews.* "At the box-office as well . . ." and "The plan is to open it . . ." from "News of the Stage," *New York Times,* November 15, 1937.

Sidney Slon and Ken Roberts are quoted from Martin Grams Jr., *The Shadow: The History and Mystery of the Radio Program, 1930–1954* (OTR Publishing, 2011). I also consulted Walter B. Gibson, *The Shadow Scrapbook* (Harcourt Brace Jovanovich, 1979). "I remember him arriving" from Elia Kazan, *Elia Kazan: A Life* (Knopf, 1988). "Major design concept," the anecdote about *Shoemaker's Holiday* and Lehman Engel's "Often he tapped out rhythms . . ." are from Nouryeh, "The Mercury Theatre." "Firk was promoted . . ." (Hiram Sherman) is from France, *The Theatre of Orson Welles.*

"From the ordinary marts . . ." from "The Play: Mercury Theatre Adds Dekker's *The Shoemaker's Holiday* to Its Repertory," *New York Times*, January 3, 1938. "He loved you to bite the cue . . .": Arthur Anderson is quoted in France, *The Theatre of Orson Welles*. "On the precise machine-like interplay . . ." from Lehman Engel, *This Bright Day* (Macmillan, 1974). Orson's apron speech preceding the *Shoemaker's Holiday* preview from Lloyd, *Stages*. "Boy genius" and all other Geraldine Fitzgerald quotes, unless otherwise noted, are from her son Michael Lindsay-Hogg's *Luck and Circumstance*. Fitzgerald's "absolutely bowled over . . ." from a footnote quoting the actress in Houseman, *Run-Through*. VW's discovery of OW's apparent infidelity from Feder, *In My Father's Shadow*. The OW-Losch correspondence is in Tilly Losch's papers in Binghamton University Libraries Special Collections.

Chapter 14: JANUARY–AUGUST 1938

The Sardi's dinner anecdote from Virgil Thomson, *Virgil Thomson* (Dutton, 1985). Mrs. Patrick Campbell quoted from *Cecil Beaton's Diaries, 1922–1939: The Wandering Years* (Little, Brown, 1961). Arthur Anderson's helpful memoir is *An Actor's Odyssey: Orson Welles to Lucky the Leprechaun* (BearManor Media, 2010). "An English cavalcade . . ." from "Gossip of the Rialto," *New York Times*, February 27, 1938. "If possible . . ." and "progress report" from "News of the Stage," *New York Times*, March 7, 1938, OW's candidacy on the "liberal slate" for Equity leadership reported in the *New York Times*, March 19, 1938. OW discusses Vincent Price's discomfort with *Heartbreak House* in Tarbox, *Orson Welles and Roger Hill*. Brenda Forbes's recollections of *Heartbreak* from *Five Minutes, Miss Forbes*. The OW–Vera Zorina romance is pieced together from several sources: her papers, including correspondence with OW in the Harvard Theatre Collection at Houghton Library; her memoir, *Zorina* (Farrar, Straus and Giroux, 1986); Leaming, *Orson Welles*; and the OW-RH phone transcripts. "Steaming up various hired cars . . ." from Leaming, *Orson Welles*. The Balanchine anecdotes from the OW-RH transcripts. "The entire Mercury Theatre company . . ." from "Welles to Direct Plays," *New York Times*, June 12, 1938. "The less a radio drama resembles . . ." from *Radio Annual 1939*. "The Summing Up" is also in the *New York Times*, June 12, 1938. Besides Victoria Price, *Vincent Price: A Daughter's Biography* (St. Martin's, 1999), I also consulted James Robert Parish and Steven Price, *Vincent Price Unmasked* (Drake, 1974). "Some of you may have . . ." (OW) is quoted in Andrea Janet Nouryeh's thesis "The Mercury Theatre" (New York University, 1987). "How could you feel part of a . . . ?" and "Orson never so much as . . .": Hiram Sherman as quoted in France, *The Theatre of Orson Welles*. "A sizeable number of the Mercury . . . ," "insure longer employment," "The Mercury Fuehrer . . . ," and "Coincidental with rumored . . ." from "News of the Stage," *New York Times*, June 29, 1938. "He's above taking . . ." from Whitford Kane, undated letter to AS and Florence Stevens (NL). "The high-livers were killing . . ." (Hiram Sherman) is from Nouryeh, "The Mercury Theatre."

"The most hair-raising . . ." from Bogdanovich, *This Is Orson Welles*. "Almost as a precocious child . . . ," "an instinctive, intuitive understanding . . . ," and "an improviser" (Bernard Herrmann) are from the documentary narrated by Leonard Maltin, which is part of the supplementary material for *Theatre of the Imagination* (1995), a multimedia CD about the Mercury Theatre radio broadcasts. "At the start of every broadcast . . ." from Steven C. Smith, *A Heart at Fire's Center*. Richard Wilson is quoted from *Theatre of the Imagination*. "One of the greatest, simplest . . ." from Brady, *Citizen Welles*. "The greatest gagman . . . ," "almost the greatest movie . . . ," and "the most poetic movie . . ." from Biskind, *My Lunches with Orson*. "A bit of a wild man" from *In Touch: The Letters of Paul Bowles*, ed. Jeffrey Miller (Farrar, Straus and Giroux, 1994). For background about Harry Dunham, I also consulted Christopher Sawyer-Lauçane, *An Invisible Spectator: A Biography of Paul Bowles* (Weidenfeld and Nicolson, 1989); Martin Duberman, *The Worlds of Lincoln Kirstein* (Knopf, 2007); and Russell Drummond Campbell, "Radical Cinema in the United States, 1930–1942: The Work of the Film and Photo League, Nykino, and Frontier Films" (thesis, Northwestern University, 1978). I interviewed John Berry extensively for Patrick McGilligan and Paul Buhle, *Tender Comrades: A Backstory of the Hollywood Blacklist* (St. Martin's, 1997). I also consulted Berry's unpublished autobiography. Details concerning the film half of *Too Much Johnson* come from "Metro-Goldwyn-Mercury," *Stage Magazine*, September 1938, the most extensive of the contemporaneous accounts of the filming. The Equity dispute is covered in *Citizen Welles* and reported contemporaneously in newspapers. William Herz and (below) Ruth Ford are quoted from Steve Taravella, *Mary Wickes: I Know I've Seen That Face Before* (University Press of Mississippi, 2014).

Chapter 15: SEPTEMBER–DECEMBER 1938

Previously cited sources contributing to the first half of this chapter include Vera Zorina's archives and her memoir, *Zorina* (Farrar, Straus and Giroux, 1986); Houseman, *Run-Through*; Howard Pollack, *Marc Blitzstein: His Life, His Work, His World* (Oxford University Press, 2012); my interview with John Berry; and Andrea Janet Nouryeh's thesis. George Coulouris's reaction to the *Danton* casting is from Houseman, *Run-Through*. "He was very beastly . . ." Guy Kingsley, here and elsewhere in the book, is quoted from his oral history, December 17, 1980, part of CCOHC. Helen Ormsbee, "Actors Often 'Live in Theater' . . . ," *New York Herald Tribune*, October 23, 1938. "Be changed or the show dropped . . ." from France, *The Theatre of Orson Welles*. "Because the cast and technical staff . . ." from "News of the Stage," *New York Times*, October 28, 1938.

The "War of the Worlds" broadcast is the subject of numerous articles and books. My account draws from multiple sources, but particularly these: JH's memoir *Run-Through*; his revised account in Houseman, *Unfinished Business: Memoirs, 1902–1988* (Applause Theatre Books, 1989); his earlier magazine piece, Houseman, "The Men from Mars," *Harper's Magazine*, December 1, 1948; Howard Koch, *As Time Goes By: Memoirs of a Writer* (Harcourt Brace Jovanovich, 1979); and John Gosling, *Waging the War of the Worlds: A History of the 1938 Radio Broadcast and Resulting Panic* (McFarland, 2009). "Orson railed at the text . . ." from the unpublished memoirs of Richard Baer, later Barr, cited in Callow, *Orson Welles*. (Baer changed his name to Barr, becoming a noted stage director and producer, and president of the League of American Theatres and Producers from 1967 until his death in 1989.) Pauline Kael is quoted from her essay introducing Welles and Mankiewicz, *Citizen Kane: The Complete Screenplay*. Hadley Cantril's book, the first to chronicle the "War of the Worlds" broadcast, is *The Invasion from Mars: A Study in the Psychology of Panic* (Princeton University Press, 1940). (Cantril's book is treated at greater length in my Chapter Nineteen.) "A wave of mass hysteria," "disrupted households . . . ," "radio frequently had interrupted . . . ," and "emphasizing its fictional . . ." from the front page, *New York Times*, October 31, 1938. "Looking for blood . . ." from Tarbox, *Orson Welles and Roger Hill*. Welles's apology for the "War of the Worlds" broadcast, as filmed by newsreel journalists, can be viewed on YouTube nowadays. "For a few days . . ." from Bogdanovich, *This Is Orson Welles*. "Last Saturday night . . ." (Rabbi Jonah B. Wise) is from "Panic over Broadcast Linked to Fear of Hitler—Other Topics Discussed by Rabbis," *New York Times*, November 6, 1938. Dorothy Thompson's "On the Record" column "Mr. Welles and Mass Delusion," *New York Herald Tribune*, November 2, 1938. Curiously, differing variations of Woollcott's telegram have been published; mine is from Bogdanovich, *This Is Orson Welles*. "On Broadway . . ." I have quoted from Norton Russell, "Astounding Outcome of the 'Martian Scare,'" *Radio Mirror*, February 1938. "Actually, it's not a great play . . .": Martin Gabel as quoted in Leaming, *Orson Welles*. The Max Reinhardt anecdote from Biskind, *My Lunches with Orson*. "That harum scarum production . . ." from Brooks Atkinson, "In Quest of the Mercury," *New York Times*, December 18, 1938.

Chapter 16: DECEMBER 1938–JULY 1939

All Burgess Meredith quotes, unless otherwise noted, are from his memoir, *So Far, So Good* (Little Brown, 1994). Jean Rosenthal is quoted from Rosenthal and Lael Wertenbaker, *The Magic of Light* (Little, Brown, 1972). Howard Pollack is from *Aaron Copland: The Life and Work of an Uncommon Man* (Henry Holt, 1949).

The "towering" and "impressionistic rather than realistic" sets of *Five Kings* from *Boston Globe*, February 28, 1939 (review of the play). "Orson Welles Is an Amazing . . ." from John I. Taylor, profile, *Boston Sunday Globe*, February 19, 1939. The Benzedrine anecdote is from Meredith, *So Far, So Good*. "He is almost entirely . . ." from Leslie Megahey, in Estrin, *Orson Welles Interviews*. "Not Henry Irving, not Beerbohm Tree . . ." (Martin Gabel) is quoted in France, *The Theatre of Orson Welles*. "Materially shortened . . ." from "*Five Kings* Now Materially Shortened," *Boston Globe*, March 2, 1939. "At least a year" from "Gossip of the Rialto," *New York Times*, March 12, 1939. "Guild officials have been burning . . ." from Houseman, *Run-Through*. "Certain members of the *Five Kings* . . ." from *Washington Daily News*, March 24, 1939. "It's [Welles's] optimism I remember . . ." (Marc Connelly) is quoted in France, *The Theatre of Orson Welles*. OW's telegram to Walter Ash also from France, *The Theatre of Orson Welles*.

Details of the Charleston trip from "Orson Welles Here to Rest, Goes to Church,

Five Parties," *Charleston News and Courier*, April 11, 1939. "Looks better than I've ever seen her . . . ," OW's undated letter to his wife VW on Villa Margherita stationery is in the Feder papers at UM. "Welles has indicated . . ." from "Screen News Here and in Hollywood," *New York Times*, March 30, 1939. The telephone call from Hollywood to OW, while he was meeting with bankers in Chicago, was reported in June Provines's column "Front Views and Profiles," *Chicago Tribune*, April 28, 1939. Foster Hirsch, *Otto Preminger: The Man Who Would Be King* (Knopf, 2007), helped with background of *My Dear Children*, starring John Barrymore (Preminger was the director). Unless otherwise noted, all of OW's quoted comments about the Barrymore lineage, the crises with *My Dear Children*, and John Barrymore's legacy are from Tarbox, *Orson Welles and Roger Hill*. "New developments regarding Welles . . ." from Leaming, *Orson Welles*. "The tour will probably continue . . ." from "The *Hot Mikado* Closes Tonight," *New York Times*, June 3, 1939. Rita Myers Gagnon's letter to the editor is from the *Los Angeles Times*, October 21, 1985. "That's where they brought . . ." from Houseman, *Run-Through*. "Everything—but everything! . . ." from "Welles, Who 'Scared the World,' Gets a Dose of It from the IATSE in Pitt," *Variety*, June 21, 1939. "At the first show he was Charles Laughton . . ." from "Tarkington Fete May Get New Play," *New York Times*, June 23, 1939. "Who for two years spurned . . ." from "American Way Resumes Tonight," *New York Times*, July 17, 1939. "When you don't really want to go . . ." from Huw Wheldon's televised BBC *Monitor* show, 1960, transcribed in Estrin, *Orson Welles Interviews*. "An almost unbearable bit . . . ," from OW's first letter to VW from California, July 22, 1939, one of the rare dated letters among their correspondence in the Feder papers at UM.

Chapter 17: JULY–DECEMBER 1939

OW letters of July–August 1939 to VW are undated, but I have done my best to sequence them. "Need Fresh Pix Directors," *Variety*, July 26, 1939. OW was cornered at the Helen Hayes party in "Hedda Hopper's Hollywood," *Los Angeles Times*, July 29, 1939. (He was photographed sitting between Norma Shearer and Helen Hayes at a table at the Trocadero party, *Los Angeles Times*, August 6, 1939.) Louella Parsons put quotes around the word "genius" in her first column about Welles, "Welles' Contract Shatters Records," *Los Angeles Examiner*, July 30, 1939. (Later, for her syndicated column, datelined August 24, 1940, Parsons visited the set of *Citizen Kane*, where she shared memories of Dixon, Illinois, with Welles and revised her opinion, removing the skeptical quotes and calling him "indeed a brilliant youth.") Edwin Schallert's first interview with Welles was "Welles Sees Television Boon to Dramatic Arts," *Los Angeles Times*, August 6, 1939. "The only way I was able . . ." and "This is what was said . . .": George Schaefer is quoted in Brady, *Citizen Welles*. "A kind of parable of fascism" from Bogdanovich, *This Is Orson Welles*. The Huxley tea-picnic is recounted in David King Dunaway, *Huxley in Hollywood* (HarperCollins, 1989). The Dolores Del Rio–Jack Warner birthday party is reported in Maxine Bartlett's column "Screen Society," *Los Angeles Times*, August 6, 1939. "That's when I fell in love . . ." and "that sightless, beautiful . . ." from Leaming, *Orson Welles*. I have drawn from Linda B. Hall, *Dolores Del Rio: Beauty in Light and Shade* (Stanford University Press, 2013). I relied heavily on Richard Meryman's excellent biography of Herman Mankiewicz (HM) for material including details in this chapter of Mank's pre–*Citizen Kane* career. "A heavy cast from under . . ." and "A certain man can be . . ." are from HM's testimony in the Ferdinand Lundberg case.

"Became a different man . . ." from HB, undated letter to OW (LL). MAB's noticing William Alland's "pale lemon yellow" complexion, and the subsequent surgery, from *Long Beach Independent*, August 31, 1939. "Most wonderful vacation . . ." from HB, letter to OW, September 20, 1939, (LL). OW and Lucille Ball were photographed at the *Stanley and Livingstone* premiere, *Los Angeles Times*, August 9, 1939. Schaefer's telegram ("RKO WOULD HAVE LOST MONEY . . .") and OW's reply ("YOU HAVE MY WORD . . .") from Brady, *Citizen Welles*. A version of the "Actors and garbage!" anecdote, carried in many show business columns in late 1939, is told in Decla Dunning, "Energy Machine" (profile of OW), *Los Angeles Times Sunday Magazine*, December 24, 1939. Jack Sher's syndicated profile, "The Legendary Orson Welles," was an installment of his column, "Fantasy on 58th Street," *Port Arthur* (Texas) *News*, November 19, 1939. "He sings a siren song . . ." from an undated memo, Diana Bourbon to Ernest Chappell (LL). "Overproduced" and "We're not in the business . . ." from Brady, *Citizen Welles*. "Any 'siren song' I've sung . . ." from Welles's eight-page reply to Bourbon, October 12, 1939, (LL). "The further development of the . . ." from Edwin Schallert, interview with OW, *Los Angeles Times*, August 6, 1939. F. Scott Fitzgerald, "Pat Hobby and Orson Welles," *Esquire*, May 1940. W. R. Wilkerson decried RKO's "gamble" on Welles in his column "Trade Views," *Hollywood Reporter*, September 26, 1939. Sheilah Graham's syndicated column recording OW's candid views on Hollywood stars, "The Sun Is Bright, Too: Orson Welles Not One to Hide His 'Genius,'" *Kansas City Star*, December 5, 1939. "Good friends pulled us apart . . ." from Bogdanovich, *This Is Orson Welles*. The Ward Bond anecdote concerning *The Last Hurrah* (footnote) from Scott Eyman, *John Wayne: The Life and Legend* (Simon and Schuster, 2014). "Orson Welles's popularity . . ." from Jimmie Fidler's column, *Los Angeles Times*, September 12, 1939. "Logically, they should have . . ." and "I think that's a wonderful . . ." from Leaming, *Orson Welles*. "They weren't all of them . . ." from Bogdanovich, *This Is Orson Welles*. The anecdote about Stevens on the set from Joseph McBride, "Some Thoughts on George Stevens," sidebar to McBride and Patrick McGilligan, "George Stevens: A Piece of the Rock," *Bright Lights*, no. 8, 1979. "What a sense [Ford] always has . . ." from Bogdanovich, *This Is Orson Welles*. "As many as forty times" from Brady, *Citizen Welles*. "After dinner every night . . ." from Bogdanovich, *This Is Orson Welles*. The *Playboy* interview of March 1967, is included in Estrin, *Orson Welles Interviews*.

"Supplementing this was a discussion . . ." from Herbert Drake, letter to Leonard Lyons, September 29, 1939, (LL). "When Kurtz begins to talk . . ." (George Schaefer), "HONESTLY AGREE . . ." (OW), and "very black skin" (OW) from Brady, *Citizen Welles*. "Really just seeing what would happen . . ." from Bogdanovich, *This Is Orson Welles*. "Had my first night . . ." from OW, memo of October 18, 1939, to Herbert Drake (LL). "The demands on Orson's time . . ." from Drake, letter of November 24, 1939, to MAB (LL). "I decided I was a little obvious . . ." from Bogdanovich, *This Is Orson Welles.* "A newsreel sequence based on . . ." from Brady, *Citizen Welles.* "Schaefer was enthusiastic . . ." from Arnold Weissberger, letter of November 21, 1939, to OW (LL).

Chapter 18: NOVEMBER–DECEMBER 1939

"I asked Mr. Welles . . ." from Louella O. Parsons's syndicated column, October 11, 1939. "Anna Stafford" was photographed returning from Ireland in the company of Geraldine Fitzgerald: "Notables Arrive on the Manhattan," *New York Times,* October 23, 1939. The Helen Hayes–Molnár anecdote from *Orson Welles on the Air: The Radio Years.* "I urge you now to give Time . . ." from Tarbox, *Orson Welles and Roger Hill.* Sidney Skolsky's column "Tintypes" ("There is no truth to it . . ."), *Hollywood Citizen-News,* December 7, 1939. I have sequenced and quoted from a half dozen mostly undated (a few are marked simply November 1939) pieces of correspondence from MAB to OW (LL). "Solely on money earned . . ." from Richard Baer, letter of November 29, 1939, to Arnold Weissberger (LL). "Exclusive of rent" and "The essential problem is Orson's psychology . . ." from Weissberger, letter of December 18, 1939, to Baer (LL). "I lost my battle . . ." from Leaming, *Orson Welles.* I have telescoped the barbs from *Hollywood Reporter,* Jimmie Fidler, Ed Sullivan, and Hedda Hopper. The *Hollywood Reporter's* prediction that the deal would fall through without Welles's "ever doing a picture" is quoted from the PBS documentary *The Battle over Citizen Kane.* Fidler ("Ha! They're saying Orson Welles . . .") is from McBride, *What Ever Happened to Orson Welles?* "Chic in a silver fox beard . . ." (Ed Sullivan) from a column of June 1940. "Looks like the only hair-raising . . ." from "Hedda Hopper's Hollywood," January 13, 1940. "Working practically day and night . . ." from Edwin Schallert's column "Drama," *Los Angeles Times,* December 28, 1939. "This is no new story . . ." (VW) is from "Reno Bound," *Chicago Tribune,* December 20, 1939. Decla Dunning and OW are quoted from Dunning, "Energy Machine," *Los Angeles Times Sunday Magazine,* December 24, 1939. The Screen Actors Guild holiday party is covered as part of a photo spread in the *Los Angeles Times,* December 25, 1939. Orson named the director he admired "most of all" in *Cahiers du Cinéma in English,* 1966: the article is reprinted in Estrin, *Orson Welles Interviews.* "We stared at each other . . ." from Brady, *Citizen Welles.* "A couple more payments . . ." from Baer, letter of February 5, 1940, to Weissberger (LL). "The greatest female clown around . . ." from Bogdanovich, *This Is Orson Welles.* OW's lunch with Hedda Hopper is reported in her column of January 22, 1940. "The Creation of *Kane,*" Welles's judicious and witty rejoinder to Kael's "Raising *Kane,*" appeared in the (London) *Times,* November 17, 1971. "The man to seem a very different person . . ." from Bogdanovich, *This Is Orson Welles.* In this chapter JH is quoted from his testimony in the Lundberg case, unless otherwise noted. "There were and are Americans . . ." from OW's deposition in the Lundberg case. Whitford Kane takes credit for the last name of Charles Foster Kane in Milton Bracker, "Sir Paddy Cullen Kane" (a profile of the veteran actor), *New York Times*, April 6, 1941. "Only praise for her husband . . ." from the Associated Press account of the divorce, *Rhinelander* (Wisconsin) *Daily News*, February 2, 1938; and "Wife Divorces Orson Welles," *Los Angeles Times*, February 2, 1940. "Assigned all claims . . ." from Carringer, *The Making of Citizen Kane*. "A patient, efficient, nice-looking English girl" is from Houseman, *Run-Through*. "A mammoth, 300-page version" is from Meryman, *Mank*. "The great adventure of the day . . ." from Houseman, *Run-Through*. Rita Alexander is quoted from Meryman, *Mank*.

Chapter 19: FEBRUARY–MAY 1940

The principal sources for my re-creation of the writing of *Kane* should be clear in context. I have woven together strands of Meryman, *Mank*; transcripts of the Lundberg case; Carringer, *The Making of Citizen Kane*; and OW's conversations with Peter Bogdanovich. In this chapter, I am always quoting JH from his testimony in the Lundberg case unless otherwise noted. "I sketched out the character . . ." and "As author of the film . . ." from Bogdanovich, *This Is Orson Welles*. "Welles and his Hollywood love . . ." from "Walter Winchell on Broadway," the last (undated) column of January 1940. "She apparently didn't consider . . ." from Fay Wray, *On the Other Hand: A Life Story* (St. Martin's, 1989). "Absolute sockeroo" and "This may seem a foolish point . . ." from OW, undated memo to his radio show overseers (LL). The footnote about Joan Fontaine is from Fontaine, *No Bed of Roses* (William Morrow, 1978). "Lecture is informal . . ." from Herbert Drake, undated telegram to Sam Zolotow at the *New York Times* (LL). "The business of the actor . . ." and details of the Pasadena speech from "Orson Welles Says 'Actor Is Theater,'" *Pasadena Post*, April 4, 1940. "Of the movies, I will speak . . ." from United Press, "Hollywood! Orson Welles Does Not Approve of You!" *Los Angeles Herald*, April 12, 1940. OW's half-page advertisement ("A movie today is a better bargain . . ."), *Hollywood Reporter*, April 13, 1940. Comments by Ann Sheridan and Pat O'Brien from United Press, "Orson Welles Strictures Draw Wrath of Hollywood," *Eugene* (Oregon) *Register-Guard*, April 13, 1939. "Every time I open . . ." from Frederick C. Othman, "Orson Talks to Replenish Empty Purse," *Hollywood Citizen-News*, April 15, 1940. "Nothing in the world . . ." from Hank Grant, "Rambling Reporter," *Hollywood Reporter*, May 18, 1940. "A really scurvy trick . . ." from Herbert Drake, letter of April 29, 1940, addressed to AS at the *Chicago American* (LL).

Hadley Cantril's letters to OW and OW's replies to Cantril are in the Lilly Library (LL) collection. "To the exclusion of myself . . . ," from OW, letter of March 26, 1939, to Cantril. "The testimony of Mr. Houseman . . ." from OW, letter of April 13, 1940, to Cantril. "WAR OF THE WORLDS WAS NOT . . ." from OW, telegram of April 6, 1940, to Cantril. "Extremely constructive . . ." from Meryman, *Mank*. "I have tried to sound . . ." from Arnold Weissberger, letter of April 4, 1940, to Richard Baer (LL). "You have paid over . . ." from Weissberger, letter of April 30, 1940, to OW (LL). "I consider at this distance . . ." from VW, letter of June 21, 1940, to Weissberger (LL). "Orson Welles received oodles . . ." from Walter Winchell's column, *Wisconsin State Journal* (Madison), May 16, 1940. "Tentative, cut-down version . . ." from OW, telegram of June 6, 1940, to JH, signed, "Love, Orson and Mank." "A source of some gratification" from OW, note of May 18, 1940, to RH (LL). "I was the one who was making . . ." and "I cut it out because . . ." from Bogdanovich, *This Is Orson Welles*.

"Mank fought me terribly . . ." from Meryman, *Mank*. "The big moment is . . ." from Bogdanovich, *This Is Orson Welles*. "Do a part for me in my picture . . ." (Paul Stewart) is from *"Citizen Kane* Remembered," *Action* (the magazine of the Directors Guild), May–June 1969. The "Goldberg" anecdote comes from Joseph McBride's recollection of discussing the scene with Stewart. "We also closed the picture . . ." from OW's deposition in the Lundberg case. *Meet the People*, a Popular Front musical, is discussed in my book *Tender Comrades*; most members of the backstage creative team were later blacklisted.

Chapter 20: JUNE 1940

"I suppose I had more low angles . . ." and "behind me, of course . . ." from Bogdanovich, *This Is Orson Welles*. Helpful biographical background on the cameraman of *Citizen Kane* came from "Citizen Gregg: Charleston Born, California Bound: Reflections on the Life of Gregg Toland," biographical research by Kathryn Morice, Joy Prattle, and Dr. Debra Reid for Coles County Historical Society (Charleston, Illinois). Toland is quoted from "Realism for *Citizen Kane*," *American Cinematographer*, February 1941; and "I Broke the Rules in *Citizen Kane*," *Popular Photography*, June 1941. Robert L. Carringer, "Orson Welles and Gregg Toland: Their Collaboration on *Citizen Kane*" in Carringer, *The Making of Citizen Kane*, was an important reference. "There was a big back lot . . ." from Bogdanovich, *This Is Orson Welles*. "Maybe he'll even have the chance . . ." from Edwin Schallert's column (his first mention of "John Citizen, U.S.A."), *Los Angeles Times*, May 28, 1940. "One of the quickest title changes . . ." from Thomas M. Pryor, "Pot Shots at the News," *New York Times*, June 2, 1940. "Am just now polishing . . ." from OW, telegram of June 8, 1940, to AS (NL). "I saw scenes written . . ." (Kathryn Trosper) is quoted in Peter Bogdanovich, "The *Kane* Mutiny" (his rebuttal to Pauline Kael), *Esquire*, October 1972; it is included among the Editor's Notes in *This Is Orson Welles*. "[Hearst] was, and is, a horse's ass . . ." from Meryman, *Mank*. "I threw all the [first] girls out . . ." from Bogdanovich, *This Is Orson Welles*. "The manner of speaking . . ." (James G. Stewart) is from *"Citizen Kane* Remembered." "Drove you mad with pain," "I kind of based the whole scene . . . ," and "one take" from Bogdanovich, *This Is Orson Welles*. "Orson cut his fingers . . ." from MAB, letter of October 30, 1940, to AS (NL).

"I did the breakfast scene . . ." and "I was constantly encouraged . . ." from Bogdanovich, *This Is Orson Welles*. Ruth Warrick is quoted from Warrick, *The Confessions of Phoebe Tyler* (Prentice-Hall, 1980). "One day he shot a hundred takes . . ." (Paul Stewart) is from *"Citizen Kane* Remembered." The Dorothy Comingore anecdotes are from Kyle Crichton, "The Forward Faun," *Collier's*, January 18, 1941. "She looks precisely like . . ." from Meryman, *Mank*. "His name was Red . . ." and "big work . . ." from Bogdanovich, *This Is Orson Welles*. "The reason Susan is struggling . . ." and "the old classic form . . ." from Smith, *A Heart at Fire's Center*. "Sings as [the] curtain goes up . . ." from a July 18, 1940, telegram from OW to "Benny Herman" at Columbia Broadcasting System in New York (LL). "An enormous playback" and "score, like the film, works . . ." from Smith, *A Heart at Fire's Center*.

"Two Jews" and "There are not enough standard movie conventions . . ." from Herbert Drake, memo of August 26, 1940, to OW, recapping his phone conversations with HM, excerpted in Bogdanovich, *This Is Orson Welles*. "I wrote *Citizen Kane*" from Louella O. Parsons's column, August 24, 1940. Mankiewicz's threat to "come down" hard on OW and "because you are a juvenile delinquent . . ." from an addendum to Drake's memo of August 26, 1940, (LL). "With a pencil, and drew an arrow . . ." (Richard Wilson) is quoted in Meryman, *Mank*. "There was a scene in a mausoleum . . ." from Bogdanovich, *This Is Orson Welles*. The Alan Ladd anecdote is also from *This Is Orson Welles*. "The very dust heap . . ." from OW's official RKO press statement, January 15, 1941, explaining the subject matter of *Citizen Kane* and deflecting comparisons between Kane and William Randolph Hearst. "I have exactly $2.03 . . ." from Richard Baer's June 22, 1940, letter to Arnold Weissberger (LL). "Strong single light" from Bogdanovich, *This Is Orson Welles*. I have also consulted Donald W. Rea, "A Critical-Historical Account of the Planning, Production, and Release of *Citizen Kane*" (thesis, USC, 1966), which contains a letter from OW to Rea, responding to questions about *Kane*; the answers regarding the film's genesis and authorship of the script are remarkably consistent with everything Welles ever said on the subject, from the release of the film through to his Lundberg deposition, his rebuttal to Pauline Kael, and his talks with Peter Bogdanovich.

Chapter 21: OCTOBER 10, 1985
"Close to fifty" and "about everything under the sun . . ." from Merv Griffin, *Merv: Making the Good Life Last* (Simon and Schuster, 2003). The Frederick Muller anecdote is from Tonguette, *Orson Welles Remembered*. The conversation about *Strictly Dishonorable* and all the material about Jim Steinmeyer are from my interview with Steinmeyer. Howard Suber kindly supplied background about the UCLA teaching post. Also helping to fill in blanks was Gary Graver, *Making Movies with Orson Welles: A Memoir* (Scarecrow, 2008), posthumously published. Chris Welles Feder is cited here from Feder, *In My Father's Shadow*. "Haggard appearance" and Griffin's views of OW, including comments on Welles and Houseman's reunion and details of OW's last booking on the show, from Griffin, *Merv*, as well as his more expansive *From Where I Sit: Merv Griffin's Book of People* (Arbor House, 1982). "He told me my heart . . ." and all OW-RH dialogue in this chapter from Tarbox, *Orson Welles and Roger Hill*. "People loved to gloat . . ." (Peter Bogdanovich) is from Chris Nichols's column "Ask Chris," *Los Angeles* magazine website, July 1, 2012.

"The bulky, blushing brother . . ." from "Brother of Orson Welles Vexed on Return with Bride," *Los Angeles Times*, April 17, 1941. Details of Richard I. Welles's (RIW) wartime work in Sierra Madre from "Sierra Madre Selects Queen as Climax of Victory Week," *Los Angeles Times*, May 31, 1942; and "Hitler and Hirohito Will Be Court-Martialed as Salvage for Victory Drive Ends," *Sierra Madre News*, May 28, 1942. RIW's time in South Dakota, including correspondence and church reports, is documented from the St. Mary's School files at the Center for Western Studies, Augustana College, in Sioux Falls. The Center for Western Studies also yielded Les Helgeland's interview with RIW, "Writer of 1938 Hair-Raiser Radio Script Now Teaching at Springfield," *Yankton Press and Dakotan*, undated clipping.

"Descended from my bone . . . ," MAB, undated letter of 1940 to AS (NL). "The Herrmann music is grand . . ." from Hazel Bernstein, letter of December 10, 1940, to AS (NL). "I am very happy . . ." from MAB, letter of March 17, 1941, to AS (NL). "Her father was the famous . . ." and the visit with Chaplin from MAB, letter of May 20, 1942, to AS (NL). "He looks very well . . ." from MAB, undated letter to AS (NL). "I took lunch with Dolores . . ." from MAB, letter of February 19, 1942, to OW (LL). MAB hailed John Houseman as "an unusual man . . ." and gave other details of the visit with Chaplin in his letter of May 14, 1942, to OW (LL). "Have you seen *Mrs. Miniver* . . . ?" from Hazel Bernstein, letter of July 26, 1942, to AS (NL). "Gaudy Hollywood modern mansion . . ." from Hazel Bernstein, letter of July 12, 1944, to AS (NL). "As hard as I try not to write . . ." from MAB, undated letter of 1946, to OW (LL). "The cutter for *Macbeth* . . ." from Hazel Bernstein, letter of May 29, 1948, to AS and "Pals" (NL). "I have not heard from Orson . . ." from MAB, letter of December 14, 1948, to AS (NL). "Orson is such a great-hearted person . . ." from Florence Stevens, letter of January 22, 1951, to the Bernsteins (NL). Hedda Hopper wrote about MAB as OW's "foster father" in her syndicated column "Looking at Hollywood," November 24, 1955. "A severe sprain of . . ." from an Associated Press account of the accident, March 11, 1957.

The anecdote about Joseph Cotten's alleged homophobia comes from Darwin Porter, *Merv Griffin: A Life in the Closet* (Blood Moon, 2009). "Both men walked out . . ." from Griffin, *Merv*. "The close-up when I had the mud . . . ," "You see this ID bracelet . . . ," "unjustified visual strain . . . ," and "He and my father . . ." from Bogdanovich, *This Is Orson Welles*. "I think what gives dignity . . ." is from Bart Whaley, *Orson Welles: The Man Who Was Magic: Part I* (Lybrary.com, 2011). Whaley's book, an exhaustive investigation into Welles's lifetime of fascination with magic, also takes many biographical detours, including a careful depiction of the last hours of his life. The anecdote about OW watching the Academy Awards from a hotel room comes from Peter Bogdanovich's interview in the documentary *Orson Welles: What Went Wrong?* (directed by Peter Guenette, 1992). "A man is not from where he is born" and "untroubled by the itch of ambition" from the Spanish bullfighting documentary *El Americano*. "If *Citizen Kane* wins again . . ." from David Thomson, "The Mark of *Kane*," *Sight and Sound*, January 2011. "Of course, I didn't know . . ." from Peter Bogdanovich, commentary on "The *Sight and Sound* Poll" posted at indiewire.com, August 10, 2012. James Naremore is quoted from his correspondence with me. "It pained me not to vote . . ." from my interview with Joseph McBride for my analysis of the *Sight and Sound* poll, "Hang in There, *Kane*," *Wall Street Journal*, August 15, 2012. "Cinema buffs consider it . . ." from Doreen Carvajal,

"Orson Welles's Last Film May Finally Be Released," *New York Times*, October 28, 2014. "I promise you it didn't . . ." Oja Kodar is quoted in Jon Tuska, *Encounters with Filmmakers: Eight Career Studies* (Praeger, 1991). "I'm against posterity in principle . . ." from Bernard Braden, *Orson Welles's The Paris Interview* (CBC, 1960).

Permissions

Peter Bogdanovich and (editor) Jonathan Rosenbaum have graciously permitted extensive citations from *This Is Orson Welles*.

The reminiscences of William Ash, George Coulouris, Arlene Francis, Guy Kingsley, William Mowry Jr., and L. Arnold Weissberger are quoted courtesy of the Columbia Center for Oral History Collection (CCOHC). In all instances Harry Goldman was the interviewer for the Mercury Theatre/Theater Union Oral History Project.

Index

About the Author

Patrick McGilligan is the author of *Alfred Hitchcock: A Life in Darkness and Light*; *Fritz Lang: The Nature of the Beast*; and *George Cukor: A Double Life*; and books on the lives of directors Nicholas Ray, Robert Altman, and Oscar Micheaux, and actors James Cagney, Jack Nicholson, and Clint Eastwood. He also edited the acclaimed five-volume *Backstory* series of interviews with Hollywood screenwriters and (with Paul Buhle) the definitive *Tender Comrades: A Backstory of the Hollywood Blacklist*. He lives in Milwaukee, Wisconsin, not far from Kenosha, where Orson Welles was born.

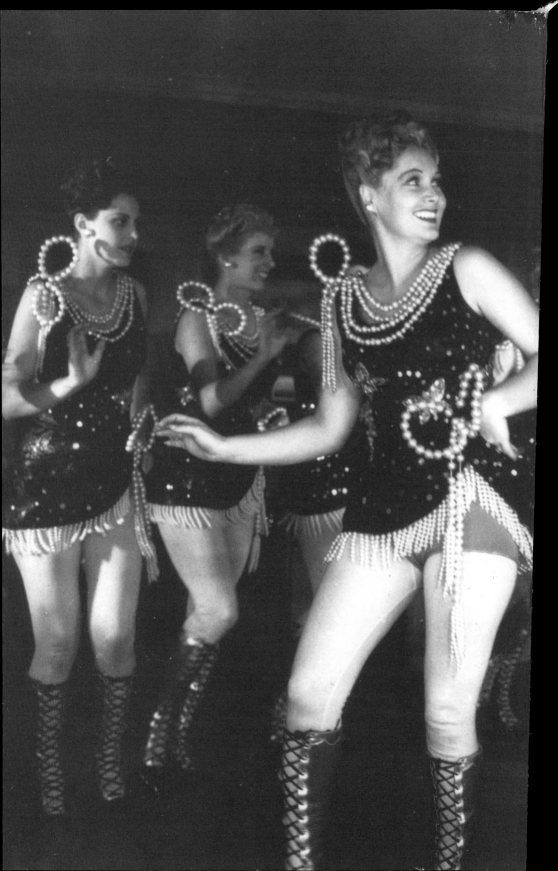